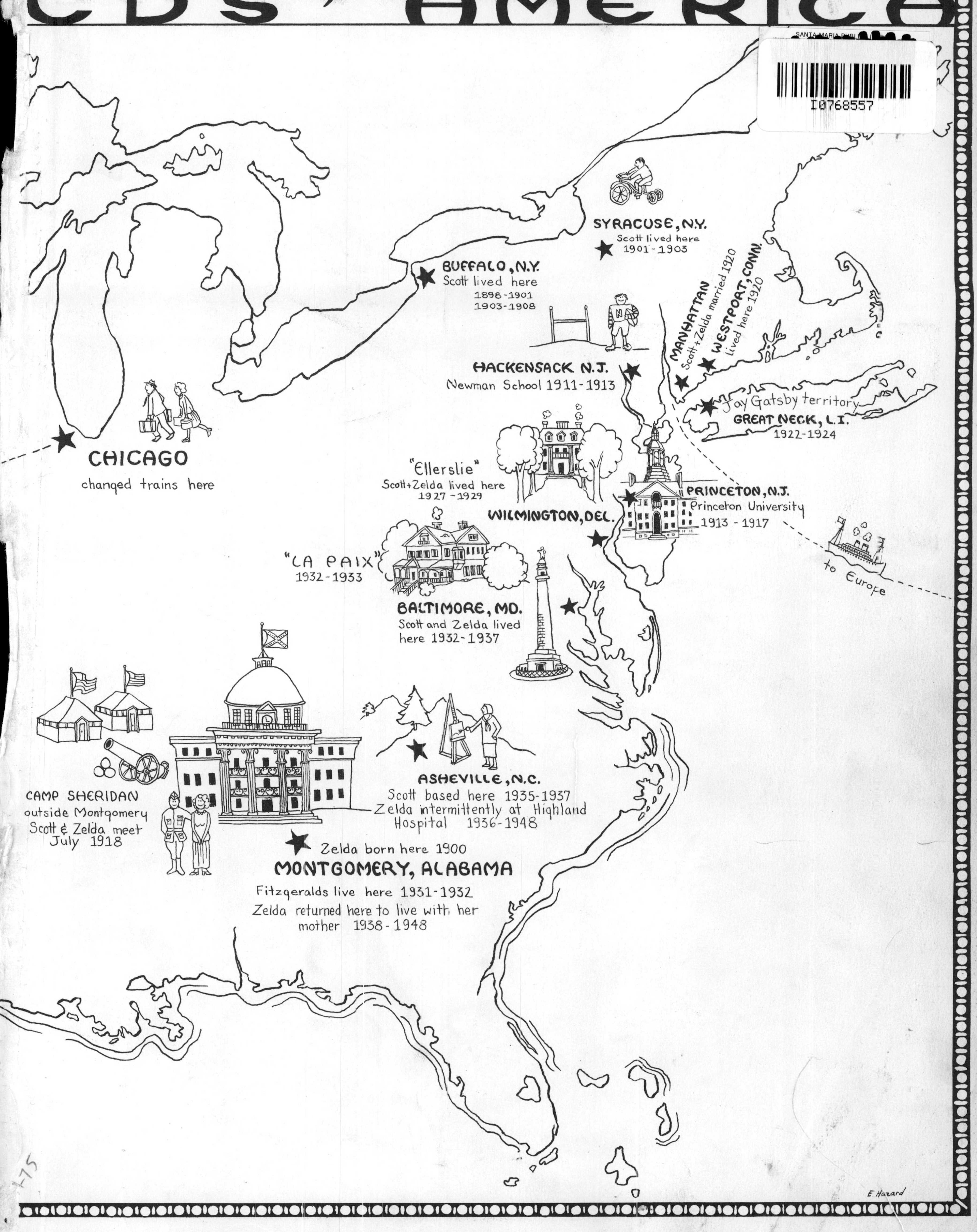
LDS' AMERICA
SYRACUSE, N.Y.
Scott lived here
1901-1903
BUFFALO, N.Y.
Scott lived here
1898-1901
1903-1908
MANHATTAN
Scott+Zelda married 1920
WESTPORT, CONN.
lived here 1920
HACKENSACK N.J.
Newman School 1911-1913
Jay Gatsby territory
GREAT NECK, L.I.
1922-1924
CHICAGO
changed trains here
"Ellerslie"
Scott+Zelda lived here
1927-1929
WILMINGTON, DEL.
PRINCETON, N.J.
Princeton University
1913 - 1917
"LA PAIX"
1932-1933
to Europe
BALTIMORE, MD.
Scott and Zelda lived
here 1932-1937
ASHEVILLE, N.C.
Scott based here 1935-1937
Zelda intermittently at Highland
Hospital 1936-1948
CAMP SHERIDAN
outside Montgomery
Scott & Zelda meet
July 1918
Zelda born here 1900
MONTGOMERY, ALABAMA
Fitzgeralds live here 1931-1932
Zelda returned here to live with her
mother 1938-1948
E Hazard

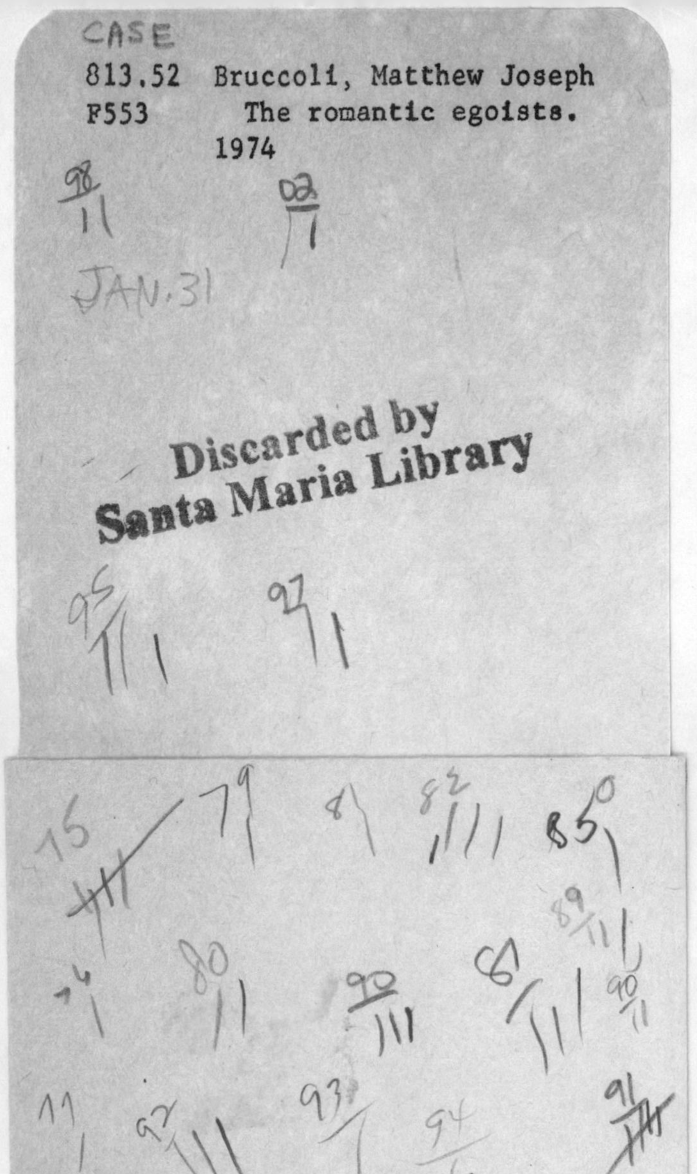

THE ROMANTIC EGOISTS

THE ROMANTIC EGOISTS

EDITED BY

MATTHEW J. BRUCCOLI

SCOTTIE FITZGERALD SMITH

AND

JOAN P. KERR

ART EDITOR

MARGARETA F. LYONS

CHARLES SCRIBNER'S SONS / NEW YORK

1 3 5 7 9 11 13 15 17 19 MD/C 20 18 16 14 12 10 8 6 4 2

PRINTED IN THE UNITED STATES OF AMERICA
Library of Congress Catalog Card Number 74-14012
ISBN 0-684-139235 (Trade)
ISBN 0-684-140861

THIS BOOK IS DEDICATED TO

JOHN BIGGS, JR.

"He left the estate of a pauper and the will of a millionaire,"

Judge Biggs growled when Fitzgerald died

after naming him his Executor.

Then he proceeded for ten years

to administer the virtually non-existent estate,

as a busy Judge on the United States Circuit Court,

selflessly and devotedly—the very incarnation

of the words, "Family Friend."

ACKNOWLEDGMENTS

OUR THANKS TO THE FOLLOWING: most particularly, *Alexander Clark* and *Wanda Randall* of the Princeton University Library, guardians of the Fitzgerald papers and friends to Fitzgerald scholars for many years, and

Peter Shepherd and his colleagues at Harold Ober Associates, who faithfully carry on the distinguished Harold Ober tradition, and

Annabel Fitzgerald Sprague of San Diego, California, Scott's sister, and *Rosalind Sayre Smith* of Montgomery, Alabama, Zelda's sister, two gracious ladies who denuded their walls of pictures and their files of clippings, and

Eugenia McGough Tuttle of Montgomery, who learned to roller-skate from Zelda and combed the memory books of their mutual friends for previously unpublished photographs.

With the most sincere appreciation, our thanks go to those Fitzgerald friends and relatives who lent us pictures, letters, or other memorabilia: Scott's cousin, *Sally Taylor Abeles* of Norfolk, Virginia; *Nathaniel Benchley* of Nantucket, Massachusetts; *Honoria Murphy Donnelly* and *Richard Ober* of Washington, D.C.; *Morrill Cody* of Paris; *Norris Jackson, Sandra Kalman,* and *Sidney Stronge* of St. Paul, Minnesota; *Alice Lee Myers* and *Fanny Myers Brennan* of New York City; *Margaret Finney McPherson* of Durham, North Carolina; *Mrs. Bayard Turnbull, Frances Turnbull Kidder,* and *Dolly Iglehart Purinton* of Baltimore, Maryland; *Katharine Barnes O'Hara* of Princeton, New Jersey; *Ginevra King Pirie* of Lake Forest, Illinois; *Frances Kroll Ring* of Los Angeles, California; *Ruth Sturtevant Smith* of Brooklin, Maine; *Budd Schulberg* of Westhampton Beach, New York; *Addie Sue Young Wimberly* of Rome, Georgia; and, of course, *Sheilah Graham.*

And from Alabama, *Sayre Noble Godwin,* Zelda's great-niece; and friends *Marjorie Morton Baer, Miriam Russell Black, Virginia Browder Breslin, Mary Burton Matthews Hale, Katherine Elsberry Haxton, Elizabeth Thigpen Hill, Myrtle Bowdoin Hutchings, Byrne Wright Jones, Margaret Thorington Kohn, Frances Westcott Lamb, Dr. Taylor Littleton, Grace Gunter Lane, Paul L. McLendon, Franklin Shackleford Mosely, Edward Pattillo,* and *Livye Hart Ridgeway.*

The private collectors who were good enough to provide photos were *C. E. Frazer Clark, Jr., Joseph Corso, Mrs. Ben Hamilton, Harry Sampsonis, R. L. Samsell,* and *Mrs. Alice Wainwright.*

We owe a special debt to the scholars and researchers who assisted us so ably and efficiently: historical researcher *Mary Berwick* in Alabama, *Lillian Gilkes* in North Carolina, *Jeanne Bennett* in California, and the Columbia, South Carolina, team: *Margaret Duggan, Mrs. Linda Berry, Katharine Wade, Ruth B. Lalka,* and *Richard Taylor* (University of South Carolina Information Service). Professor Bruccoli is most appreciative of the research leave arranged for him by *Dr. John Welsh,* Head of the English Department of the University.

We would also like to express our gratitude to *John E. Scott* of the Scott Photographic Services in Montgomery and his patient wife, *June;* to *Milo Howard,* head of the Alabama Department of Archives and History, and his efficient staff members *J. Karen Bevan, Frances W. Clark, Al Craig,* and *Miriam C. Jones;* to *Keith Runyon* of the *Louisville Courier-Journal;* to *Judith Katsung* of the St. Paul Pioneer Press; and to *Dorothy Coover, Edythe Greissman, Gail Roberts,* and *April Ferris* of Charles Scribner's Sons, who helped us through our hours of greatest need while we were piecing together the material.

And, finally, an admiring bow to the members of the staffs of the McKissick Library of the University of South Carolina; the New York Public Library and the Performing Arts Research Center of the New York Public Library at Lincoln Center; the Yale University Libraries; the Minnesota Historical Society; the Princeton University Library; the Museum of Modern Art; the National Portrait Gallery; the *Johns Hopkins Magazine;* and Paramount Pictures . . . all of whom generously provided assistance for this volume.

CONTENTS

F. Scott Fitzgerald
The author of "This Side of Paradise"
The Beautiful and Damned
"The victor belongs to the spoils"
What the critics say:
Best Sellers
SCRIBNER'S
January
Tender is the Night
A Romance
by
F. Scott Fitzgerald
Brentano's Best Sellers
F. SCOTT FITZGERALD
TENDER IS THE NIGHT
TENDER IS THE NIGHT
F. SCOTT FITZGERALD
THE VEGETABLE
BY F. SCOTT FITZGERALD
THE VEGETABLE
By F. Scott Fitzgerald
Tales of the Jazz Age
The Beautiful and Damned
Best Sellers
MY WEDDING

INTRODUCTION

People have often asked me—sometimes almost reproachfully—why I haven't written more about my parents. The answer is very simple: I'd be a big disappointment if I did. The highs and lows of their short, dramatic lives have been examined under so many microscopes (including some pretty inaccurate ones) that I can't distinguish any longer between memories and what I read somewhere. I was much too young to do more than curtsey to Hemingway, Wolfe, Gertrude Stein, and other literary greats my parents came to know in Paris but seldom saw in later years; and, as is altogether too abundantly demonstrated on these pages, my childhood was that of a most pampered and petted doll. I remember being punished only once, for what misdemeanor I don't recall, and being sent to my room for the day without books or toys, a most cataclysmic deprivation! After a few hours my father tiptoed in to see how I was and caught me reading under the covers: a very popular French children's book called *Jean Qui Grogne Et Jean Qui Rit.* Instead of delivering the threatened spanking, he got so intrigued with the book's illustrations that I had to spend the rest of the afternoon reading it aloud to him in English. So much for the sort of reminiscences I would be able to contribute to literary scholarship. . .

The contents of my head must have come to resemble a doll's, too, for when the serious troubles came later, I was so enmeshed in the warm and hospitable cocoon that was pre-World War II Baltimore, a veritable paradise for teenagers, that I'm embarrassed to admit I was largely unaware of them. By the time I finally grew up enough to think of life as something other than a chain of hot fudge sundaes and Fred Astaire-Ginger Rogers movies, Daddy was in Hollywood and our communication was largely epistolary; we have included samples of what I regarded then to be unnecessary parental bombardment. And so for me, collaborating on this book has been a double source of satisfaction: first, I've come to see my parents through my own pair of spectacles rather than through the eyes of others; and second, I've paid a tribute to them which was long overdue. Not that this is any candy-coated version of their lives: we have omitted nothing which rightfully belonged on these pages just because it might paint an unflattering picture.

Another rule we have tried to adhere to faithfully was to include nothing in the text which is not directly autobiographical—even the famous line about the very rich being "different from you and me" had to pass the test, and only did get included because it came back to haunt my father much later. Lovers of *The Great Gatsby,* for example, may be disappointed to find the green light missing, but we could neither illustrate nor integrate it. Similarly, no picture was added which could not have been in the albums at the time they were made; it was a temptation, for instance, to photograph the apartment buildings where we lived in Paris, since they have hardly changed . . . but we resisted it. Ninety percent of the illustrations in this book —and that includes reviews and letters to my father— was taken from the seven scrapbooks and five photograph albums we had to work from. The other ten percent were lent by relatives, friends, or, in a few instances, a library or museum. This is, in short, the real McCoy: their *own* story of their lives, rather than someone else's interpretation of them.

For a man who seems to have been congenitally incapable of balancing a budget, it is extraordinary how meticulous my father was about making and keeping personal records. The first scrapbook takes him from birth into the Army, the second takes my mother from birth through the first few years of marriage, and the remaining five contain reviews, interviews, letters, pictures, and memorabilia of all varieties; we have reproduced several pages exactly as they appear in the original volumes. These scrapbooks stop at 1936, when my father moved to North Carolina from Baltimore and put them temporarily in storage. Although he later sent for his scrapbooks in California, he did not add to them there. The photo albums mostly pertain to Europe and to "Ellerslie," the house they rented near Wilmington, Delaware . . . fortunately, I started one of my own where they left off in 1931, after returning from their last trip abroad. We had also my father's baby book, my baby book, an album decorated with flowers which my mother made for me from the snapshots and postcards she sent home to her mother over the years, and the *Ledger*. This *Ledger* was the most invaluable source of all.

You will find portions of the *Ledger* sprinkled throughout this book, always in my father's handwriting. Nobody is quite sure when he started it, but it may have been as early as 1920. It contains a summary of each year of his life to 1937, with the memorable events of each month, and at the top of each page a capsule comment as to whether the year was fruitful, wasted, sad, happy, etc. It also contains a complete list of everything he wrote, where it was published (or not published), and what became of it: whether it was collected, made into a movie, "stripped" (his word for taking sentences out of a story for a novel), or translated. It also has a list of his earnings year by year, and another one of mother's earnings: a true biographers' delight. Professor Bruccoli believes the *Ledger* proves that my father had intimations of literary immortality; I'm not sure about *that,* but it certainly shows that despite all the moving about and the disorder and confusion, he felt some deep need to keep the record straight.

Speaking of earnings, you'll find a great deal to do about money in this book; it is not out of proportion to the part that money played in my father's life. He worshipped, despised, was awed by, was "crippled by his inability to handle" (as he put it), threw away, slaved for, and had a lifelong love-hate relationship with, money. To have brought it less into this book in favor of more literary aspects of his career would have been to gloss over the fact that money and alcohol were the two great adversaries with which he battled all his life. Fortunately, there was no way to illustrate the latter!

The reader will also find a great many of my father's misspellings on these pages, often in his handwriting. I have a personal theory that one reason Hemingway became so exasperated with him was that Daddy almost never got his name right. He might have felt more tolerant had he seen the scrapbooks, with their headings of "Rivierra" or "Brittish Critisism." We have not gone back and restored the errors in letters which were corrected when they were published in *The Letters of F. Scott Fitzgerald,* but we have kept all the ones in our original sources. Another decision was to save space by not stipulating the date and place of publication with the excerpts in the main body of the book. These are all included in the "Register" in the back, for those who wish to know where they can read a particular story or article.

Our hardest choice was probably what to call this "pictorial autobiography." At first, we toyed with something rather complicated along the lines of "The Tender, Sad, Beautiful, Great, Damned Paradise of the Fitzgeralds," but Burroughs Mitchell, the perspicacious editor of Scribners, who occupies the hallowed office of Maxwell Perkins, managed to temper his enthusiasm with practicality. Then we went to "Scott and Zelda," which is certainly to the point, but that gave us a strong sense of *déja vu . . .* and finally we settled on *The Romantic Egoists*. The main reason was that (without the "s" on the end) it was the first title to my father's first novel, which later became *This Side of Paradise;* since this was the most autobiographical novel he wrote, the descriptive phrase clearly reveals how he thought of himself. We use the word "egoist," of course, in a literary sense and not as a term of disparagement. More than most authors, my father drew on his personal experience, both trivial and tragic, for his fiction and his non-fiction; and my mother's novel, *Save Me the Waltz,* is such thinly disguised autobiography that it caused their most serious quarrel. This interweaving of the inner ego and the outward expression is what we were trying to convey, and we think they would have enjoyed our title. I know they would have enjoyed the maps on the endpapers of the book, which were drawn by their granddaughter, Eleanor Lanahan Hazard. And I *hope* they would have enjoyed the autobiography we've been presumptuous enough to put together for them, on the assumption that if they'd lived longer, it is what they might have done themselves: they were a couple of very honest people.

Scottie Fitzgerald Smith

July 1974

THE ROMANTIC EGOISTS

PART ONE CHRONOLOGY

SCOTT BEFORE MARRIAGE
(1896-1920)

1853
Birth of Edward Fitzgerald on a farm named "Glenmary" near Rockville in Montgomery County, Maryland.

1860
Birth of Mary ("Mollie") McQuillan in St. Paul, Minnesota. She was the daughter of a self-made Irish merchant who was a pillar of the Catholic Church.

February 1890
Marriage of Edward Fitzgerald and Mollie McQuillan in Washington, D.C.

24 September 1896
Birth of F. Scott Fitzgerald at 481 Laurel Avenue, St. Paul.

April 1898
Fitzgerald family moves to Buffalo, N.Y.

January 1901
Fitzgerald family moves to Syracuse, N.Y.

July 1901
Birth of Annabel Fitzgerald.

September 1903
Fitzgerald family moves back to Buffalo.

July 1908
Fitzgerald family returns to St. Paul. FSF enters St. Paul Academy in September.

October 1909
Publication of "The Mystery of the Raymond Mortgage" in *The St. Paul Academy Now & Then*—FSF's first appearance in print.

August 1911
Production of FSF's first play, *The Girl from Lazy J*, in St. Paul.

September 1911
FSF enters Newman School, Hackensack, N.J. Meets Father Sigourney Fay and Shane Leslie.

August 1912
Production of *The Captured Shadow* in St. Paul.

August 1913
Production of *"The Coward"* in St. Paul.

September 1913
FSF enters Princeton University with class of 1917. Rooms at 15 University Place. Meets Edmund Wilson '16, John Peale Bishop '17, and John Biggs Jr. '17, lifelong friends.

August 1914
Production of *Assorted Spirits* in St. Paul.

December 1914
Production of *Fie! Fie! Fi-Fi!*, FSF's first Princeton Triangle Club show.

December 1914
First appearance in *The Princeton Tiger*.

4 January 1915
FSF meets Ginevra King, the model for several of his heroines, in St. Paul at Town and Country Club.

April 1915
"Shadow Laurels," FSF's first appearance in *The Nassau Literary Magazine*.

December 1915
FSF drops out of Princeton for rest of year; though in academic difficulty, he is allowed to leave for health reasons.

December 1915
Production of *The Evil Eye* by the Triangle Club.

December 1916
Production of *Safety First* by the Triangle Club.

September 1917
"The Way of Purgation" accepted—but not published—by *Poet Lore*.

26 October 1917
FSF receives commission as 2nd Lieutenant.

20 November 1917
FSF reports to Fort Leavenworth, Kansas; begins his novel, "The Romantic Egoist," there.

February 1918
FSF reports to Camp Taylor, Louisville, Kentucky.

March 1918
FSF completes first draft of novel while on leave at Princeton and staying in Cottage Club; sends novel to Scribners.

April 1918
FSF transferred to Camp Gordon, Georgia.

June 1918
FSF reports to Camp Sheridan near Montgomery, Alabama.

July 1918
FSF meets Zelda Sayre at a country club dance in Montgomery.

A scrap book Record compiled from many scources of interest to and concerning one

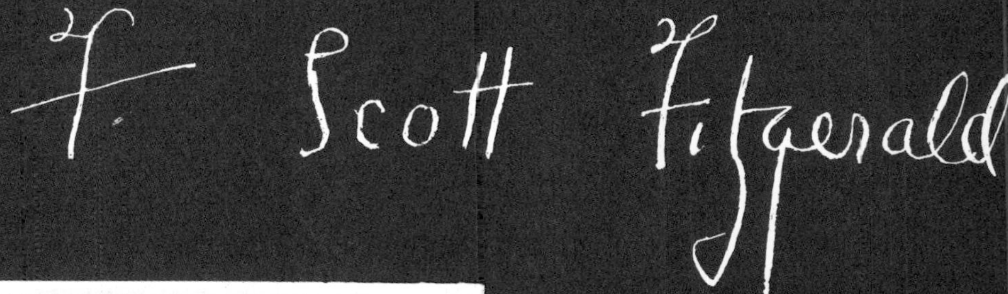

Mary (Mollie) McQuillan before her marriage in 1890.

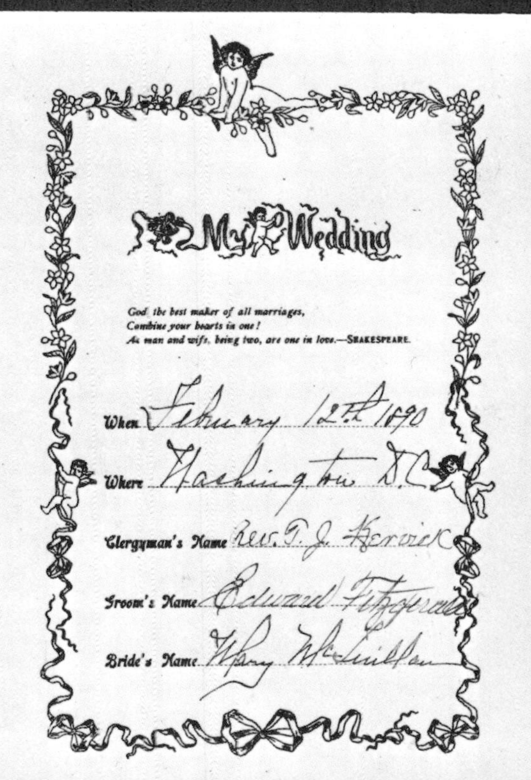

My Wedding

God the best maker of all marriages,
Combine your hearts in one!
As man and wife, being two, are one in love.—SHAKESPEARE.

When February 12th 1890

Where Washington D.C.

Clergyman's Name Rev. T. J. Kervick

Groom's Name Edward Fitzgerald

Bride's Name Mary McQuillan

Mollie McQuillan Fitzgerald's wedding book.

Mollie Fitzgerald with Scott and Annabel, c. 1903.

Edward Fitzgerald with Scott, c. 1899.

Francis Scott Key, for whom Fitzgerald was named.

Scott's paternal grandmother, Cecilia Ashton Scott, of "Glenmary," Rockville, Maryland, was descended from two old Maryland families. Her paternal great-grandfather, Dr. John Scott, "inoculated 500 Continental troops for smallpox at Chestertown and would take no fee." Her maternal grandfather, Philip Barton Key, was a member of the Continental Congress and an uncle of Francis Scott Key. Scott was less proud of another Key relative, Mary Surratt, who was hung for conspiring to assassinate President Lincoln. Michael Fitzgerald, Cecilia's husband, left her a widow when Edward was two years old.

DEATH'S HARVEST.

P. F. McQuillan, Esq., One of the Oldest and Best Known of St. Paul's Citizens and Business Men, Dead.

We have to-day the sorrowful though long anticipated intelligence to announce of the death of P. F. McQuillan, Esq., the senior member of the large wholesale grocery house of McQuillan, Beaupre & Co. The sad event took place at 3 o'clock this morning. Mr. McQuillan has been in failing health for five years past, his decline being very rapid during the last two years. His disease at first was of a pulmonary nature, gradually merging, or rather giving way to the encroachments of Bright's kidney disease, from which he died, his last sickness dating from the 20th of January, since which he has been confined to his house, and most of the time to the bed, being accompanied with great suffering.

Mr. McQuillan was a native of Fermannah county, Ireland. When nine years old, he, with his parents, emigrated to America, the family settling in Galena, Ill. Here he remained until a young man of 23 years, when with a moderate book and fair business education he branched out for himself, choosing St. Paul as his field of operations. This was in 1857. Arriving here he secured a position as bookkeeper with the grocery house of Beaupre & Temple, then the largest house in the city.

Mr. McQuillan retained this position until the fall of 1858, when he retired with the purpose of going into business for himself. The necessary arrangements completed the spring of 1859 finds him established for himself in the general line, in the little one story frame, about 30x50, on the west side of Jackson street below Third, now occupied as a Swede saloon and boarding house. Here he remained until 1862, when the demands of his business requiring larger accommodations, he removed across the street to Prince's new block, occupying the second store room from the corner of Third street. With this move Mr. McQuillan made a new departure in his business—starting in as an exclusively wholesale dealer.

Mr. McQuillan remained at this place eight years, or until 1870, when, again crowded by his increasing business and following the laws of trade, he removed to the large three story brick just below the Merchants, at present occupied by Mayo & Clark.

In 1871, finding the increasing business too much to be borne by one man, the firm of McQuillan & Co., was organized, several of his old and faithful employees being admitted to the partnership.

About the same time he commenced the erection of the four story and basement store now occupied by the firm, corner of Third and Cedar streets. Upon the completion of this building in 1873 it was occupied by the firm, which remained as organized in 1871 until August 1, 1875, when it was again reorganized by the admission of Mr. B. Beaupre.

This is a brief resume of Mr. McQuillan's business career in St. Paul, covering a period of twenty years. He came here a poor boy with but a few dollars in his pocket, depending solely on a clear head, sound judgment, good habits, strict honesty and willing hands, with strict integrity his guiding motive. How these qualities have aided him is shown in the immense business he has built up, the acquisition of large property outside, and the universal respect felt for him by the business men of the country, among whom probably no man was better known or stood higher. His private life is no less bright. Singularly pure in all his instincts, Mr. McQuillan was known but to be loved, and his many quiet deeds of benevolence, the helping hand extended to struggling young men starting out in a business career, kindnesses to those in his own business household, and the many other good deeds springing from his generous nature, which have marked his life in St. Paul, will cause his early death to be most sincerely mourned.

Mr. McQuillan at the time of his death was in his 44th year. He leaves as his immediate family a wife and four children.

Scott's maternal grandfather, Philip McQuillan, came over from Ireland in 1843 at the age of nine. He moved to St. Paul in 1857 and became a prosperous wholesale grocer and pillar of the Catholic Church.

The McQuillan home, St. Paul.

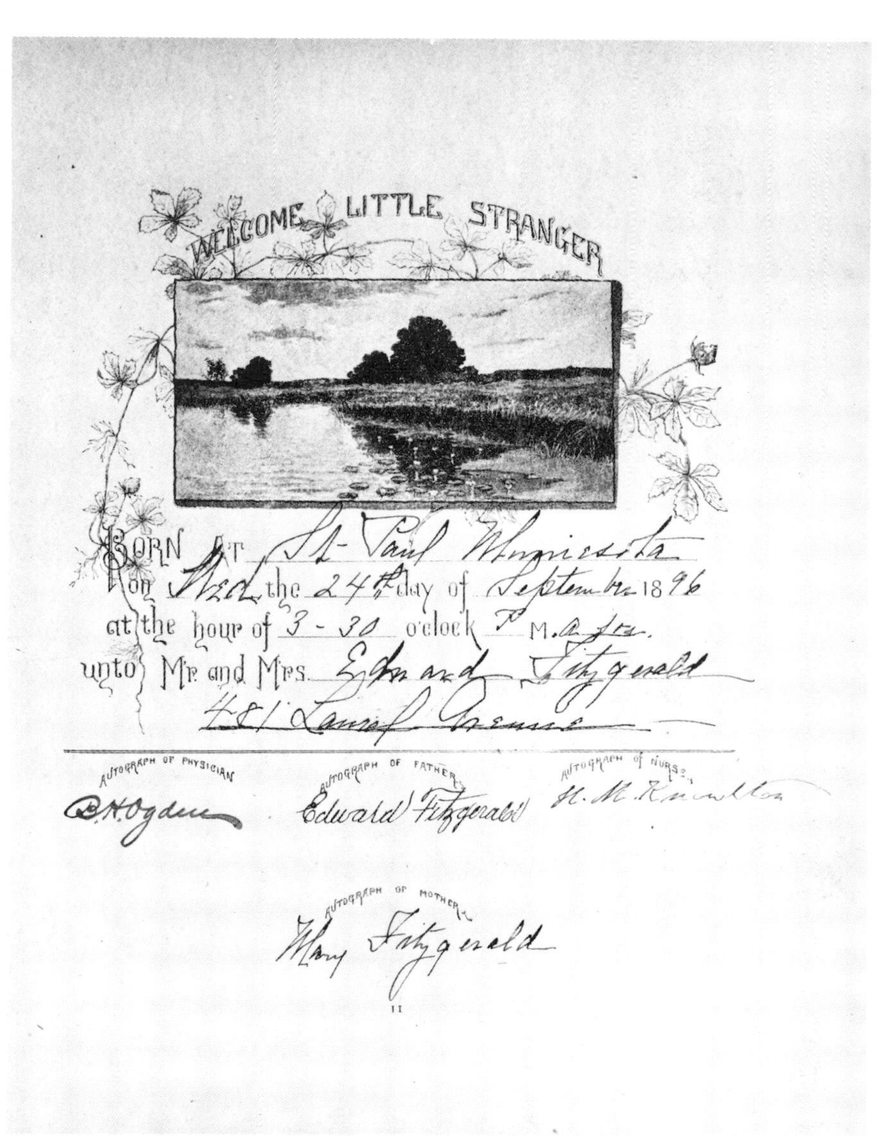
Welcome Little Stranger

Born at St Paul Minnesota
on Wed. the 24th day of September 1896
at the hour of 3-30 o'clock P.M. after.
unto Mr and Mrs. Edward Fitzgerald
481 Laurel Avenue

Autograph of Physician
Autograph of Father Edward Fitzgerald
Autograph of Nurse

Autograph of Mother Mary Fitzgerald

11

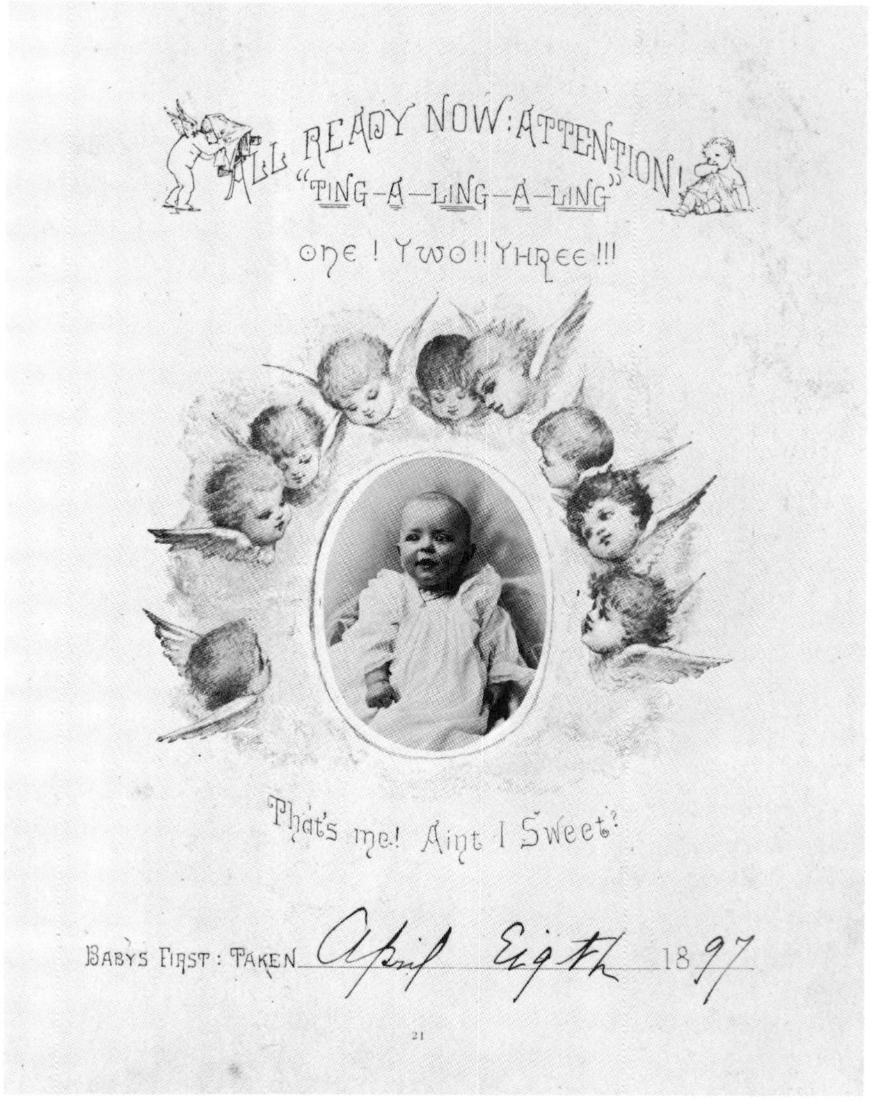
All Ready Now: Attention!
"Ting-a-ling-a-ling"
One! Two!! Three!!!

That's me! Aint I Sweet?

Babys First: Taken April Eigth 1897

21

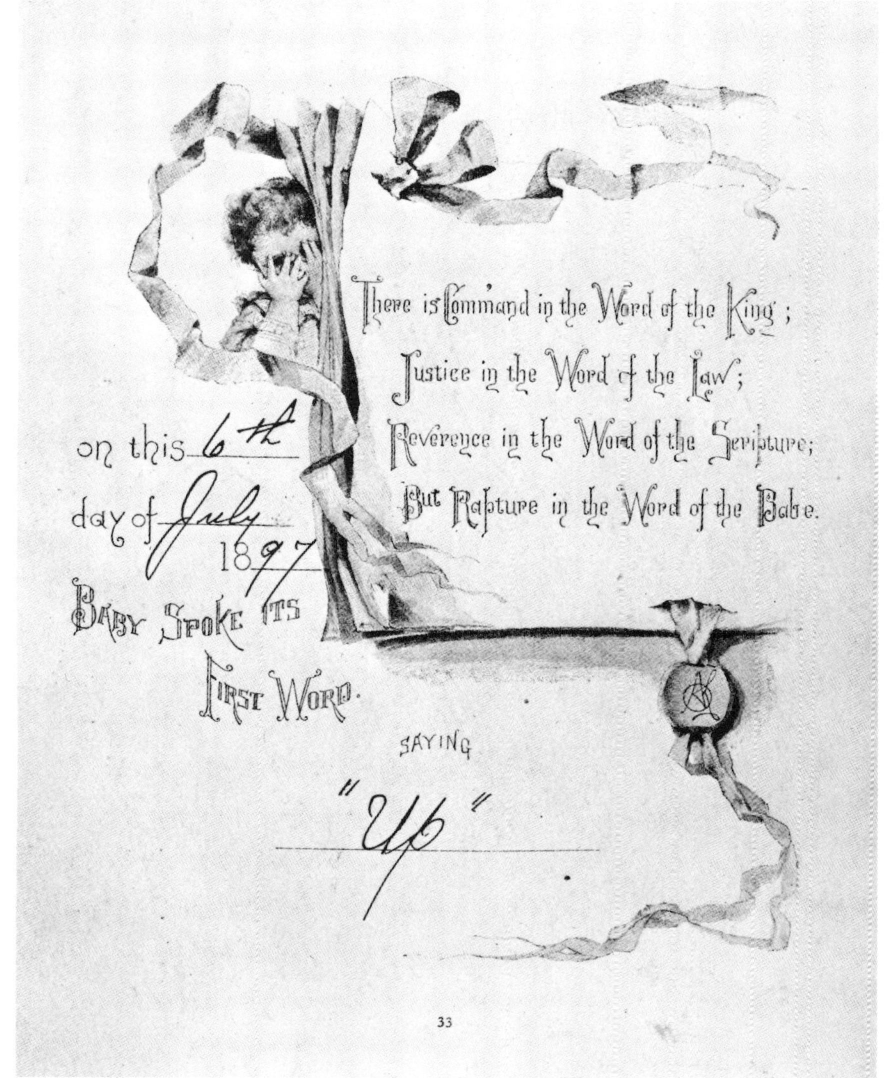
There is Command in the Word of the King;
Justice in the Word of the Law;
Reverence in the Word of the Scripture;
But Rapture in the Word of the Babe.

on this 6th day of July 1897
Baby Spoke its First Word.

Saying
"Up"

33

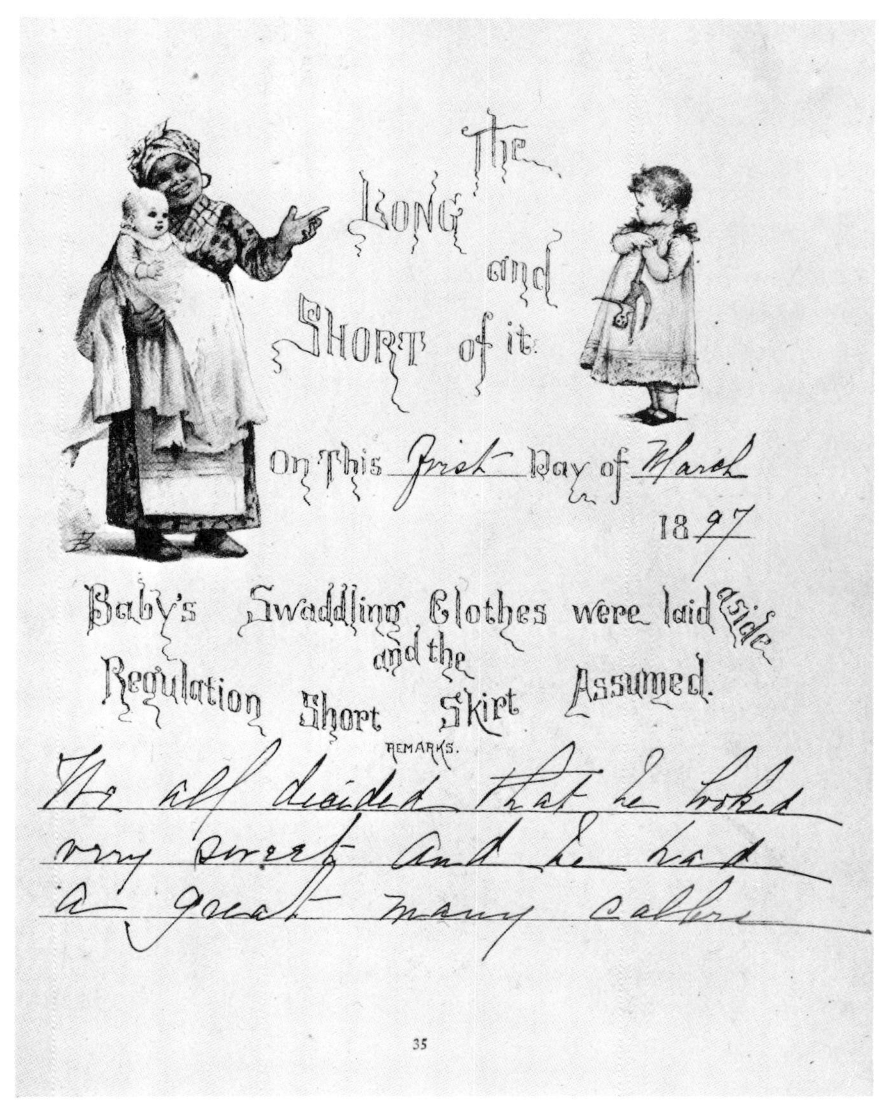
The Long and Short of it.

On This First Day of March 1897

Baby's Swaddling Clothes were laid aside and the Regulation Short Skirt Assumed.

Remarks.
We all decided that he looked very sweet and he had a great many callers

35

F. Scott Fitzgerald's baby book.

The Fitzgerald family moved from St. Paul to Buffalo in April 1898. In 1901 they moved to Syracuse, and then back to Buffalo in 1903.

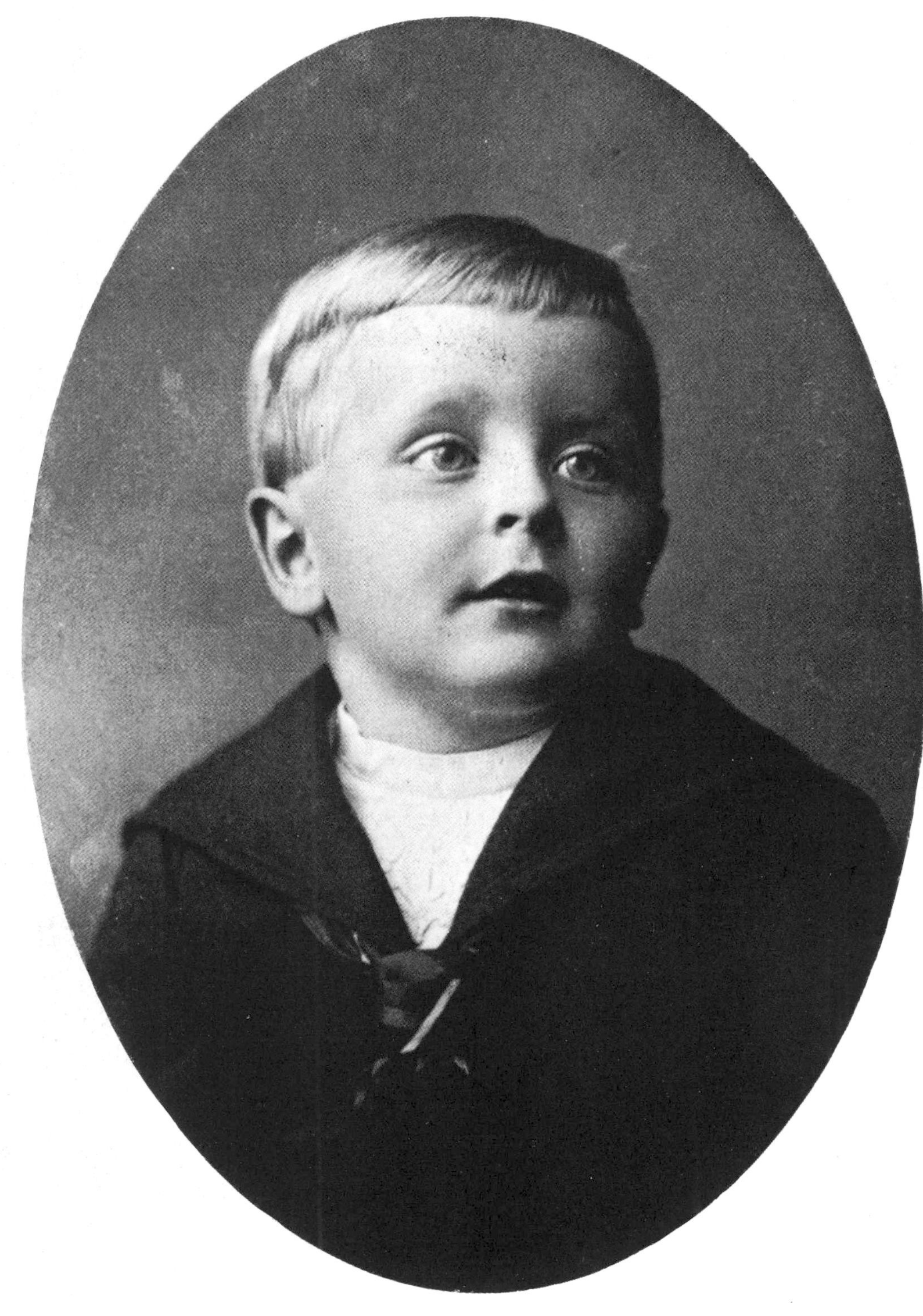

Mother and I never had anything in common except a relentless stubborn quality, but when I saw all this it turned me inside out realizing how unhappy her temperament made her and how she clung, to the end, to all things that would remind her of moments of snatched happiness.

—FSF to Annabel Fitzgerald Sprague, June 1936.

Our hero
Sets out upon
the great voyage—

	Four years Old	155
Sept	He had a party to celebrate his birthday. He wore a sailor suit about this time & told enormous lies to older people about being really the owner of a real yatch.	

Mrs Fitz & [illegible]

Scott in dramatic pose.

Scott and a friend.

—Buffalo—

Fitzgerald at far right in third row.

160 Nine Years Old

Sept For his birthday he received chiefly soldiers. He passed from The Holy Angels Academy to Miss Nardens. Also he moved to Seventy-One Highland Ave in October

Father

As a youngster of nine, my father rowed spies across the river. When he was twelve he felt that life was finished for him. As soon as he could, he went West, as far away from the scenes of the Civil War as possible. He started a wicker furniture factory in St. Paul. A financial panic in the nineties struck him and he failed.

We came back East and my father got a job as a soap salesman in Buffalo. He worked at this for some years. One afternoon—I was ten or eleven—the phone rang and my mother answered it. I didn't understand what she said but I felt that disaster had come to us. My mother, a little while before, had given me a quarter to go swimming. I gave the money back to her. I knew something terrible had happened and I thought she could not spare the money now.

Then I began to pray, "Dear God," I prayed, "please don't let us go to the poorhouse; please don't let us go to the poorhouse." A little later my father came home. I had been right. He had lost his job.

That morning he had gone out a comparatively young man, a man full of strength, full of confidence. He came home that evening, an old man, a completely broken man. He had lost his essential drive, his immaculateness of purpose. He was a failure the rest of his days.

—Interview with Michel Mok

Class at Miss Nardens

Ten Years Old 161

Jan 1907 He went to the charity ball and to the Mack's party at the country club where he wore his juvenile tuxedo and was chased by a cripple named Sears McGraw whom he loathes to this day. Joe Powell took him to a basketball game and he fell madly into admiration for a dark haired boy who played with a melancholy defiance. His mother got the idea he could sing so he performed "Way down in Colon town" and "Don't get married

" any more" for all visitors. He began a history of the U.S. and also a detective story about a necklace that was hidden in a trapdoor under the carpet. Wrote celebrated essay on George Washington & St. Ignatius. Oh-Oh Oscar free.

So thought Terrence R. Tipton, by occupation actor, athlete, scholar, philatelist and collector of cigar bands. He was so exalted that all his life he would remember vividly coming out of the house, the feel of the spring evening, the way that Dolly Bartlett walked to the auto and looked back at him, pert exultant and glowing. What he felt was like fright—appropriately enough for one of the major compulsions had just taken its place in his life. Fool for love was Terrence from now, and not just at a distance but as one who had been summoned and embraced, one who had tasted with a piercing delight and had become an addict within an hour. Two questions were in his mind as he approached his house—how long had this been going on, and when was he liable to encounter it again?

—"That Kind of Party"

Program

Overture . . Selection

1 Two Step Gwendolyn Boardman
2 Two Step Harriet Mack
3 Waltz Isabel Williams
4 Two Step Marie Lauty
5 Waltz Kitty Williams
6 Two Step Gwendolyn Boardman
7 Two Step Margaret Lauty
8 Waltz Honey Chittendon
9 Two Step Dorothy Knox
10 Waltz Edna Steele
11 Two Step Gay Ramsdell
12 Two Step Elizabeth Gould
13 Waltz Harriet Mack
14 Two Step Helen Ingham
15 Two Step Kitty William
16 Waltz Helen Ingham
17 Two Step Esther Nash
18 Waltz Helen Ingham
19 Two Step Kitty Williams
20 GRAND MARCH Marie Lauty

We fall in love

From Kitty

162 Eleven Years Old

Sept He went to Confession about this time and lied by saying in a shocked voice to the priest "Oh no, I never tell a lie." He now had $100.00 in the bank. He played football on a team of which Norbert Sullivan was the star. He weighed sixty-eight lbs.

Oct He asked Kitty to lead the grand march in dancing school the first day. He used to swim with Duky in the Century Club ~~school~~ pool.

we leave home for the 1st time

CAMP CHATHAM
ORILLIA, ONT.
A CAMP FOR BOYS

July 15. 07

Dear Father,

I recieved the St Nickolas today and I am ever so much obliged to you for it.

Your loving son.
Scott Fitzgerald

CAMP CHATHAM
ORILLIA, ONT.
A CAMP FOR BOYS

July 18, 07.

Dear Mother, I recieved your letter this morning and though I would like very much to have you up here I dont think you would like it as you know no one here except Mrs. Upton and she is busy most of the time I dont think you would like the accomadations as it is only a small town and no good hotels. There are some very nice boarding houses but about the only fare is lamb and beef. Please send me a dollar becaus there are a lot of little odds and ends i need. I will spend it carefully. All the other boys have pocket money besides their regular allowence.

Your loving son.
Scott Fitzgerald.

Dear Mother,

I wish you would send me five dollars as all my money is used up. Yesterday I went in a running contest and won a knife for second prize. This is a picture of Tom Penney and I starting on a paper chase

Your loving son
SCOTT FITSGERALD

July | Came out to St. Paul to live with Grandmother. Mother at Fultons. John Fulton, his dirty cousin, the Mitchells, The Fosters, Kath. Tighe, Arthur Foley, Sam Sturgis, the Mudges and Marie. My affair with Violet. Little Ellen Stockton. Met the Hills and played Tennis with them. Playing Indian. The Foley's harmed their eunuch dog. Walking the fence with Betty Mudge. The Complements playing tuth. The quarrels with Violet. Madame O. Keefe and my French Lessons. Adolph Schulte

Twelve's Years Old 163

Sept | The Summit football team. He was Captain. One one game, lost one and tied one. Paul Ballion, Robert Clark and Cecil Read. Broke my rib on St. Paul Academy team. Entered Academy. Mother at Aberdeen. Striker + Ballion the stars.

In July 1908 the Fitzgerald family returned to St. Paul. Scott entered the St. Paul Academy in September, which he attended for three years. Below, Scott is at far right, top row in a school pageant.

June | Wrote the Mystery of the Raymond Mortgage. also "Elavo" (or was that in Buffalo) and a complicated story of some knights. Played base ball. Began to Pitch.

THE MYSTERY OF THE RAYMOND MORTGAGE

BY SCOTT FITZGERALD

1st Appearance in print

July 30, 1909.

Master Scott Fitzgerald,
Frontenac, Minn.

My dear Scott:

Yours of July 29th received. Am glad you are having a good time. Mother and Annabelle are very well and enjoying Duluth. I enclose $1.00. Spend it liberally, generously, carefully, judiciously, sensibly. Get from it pleasure, wisdom, health and experience.

From Father

"What right have you to enter this house?" he demanded.

"The right of the law," replied Syrel.

"I didn't do it" broke out the young man. "It was this way. Agnes Raymond loved me—she did not love Standish—he shot her; and God did not let her murder go unrevenged. It was well Mrs. Raymond killed him, for his blood would have been on my hands. I went back to see Agnes before she was buried. A man came in. I knocked him down. I didn't know until a moment ago that Mrs. Raymond had killed him."

"I forgot Mrs. Raymond" screamed Syrel, "where is she?"

"She is out of your power forever," said the young man.

Syrel brushed past him and, with Smidy and I following, burst open the door of the room at the head of the stairs. We rushed in.

On the floor lay a woman, and as soon as I touched her heart I knew she was beyond the doctor's skill.

"She has taken poison," I said. Syrel looked around, the young man had gone. And we stood there aghast in the presence of death.

—"The Mystery of the Raymond Mortgage"

A year of much activity but dangerous.

Fourteen Years Old

Sept. Third and last year at the S.P.A. Played on the Summits. End and punter.

Beginning in 1910/11, his fourteenth year, he entered a summary or judgment at the head of each year of the Outline Chart in his Ledger.

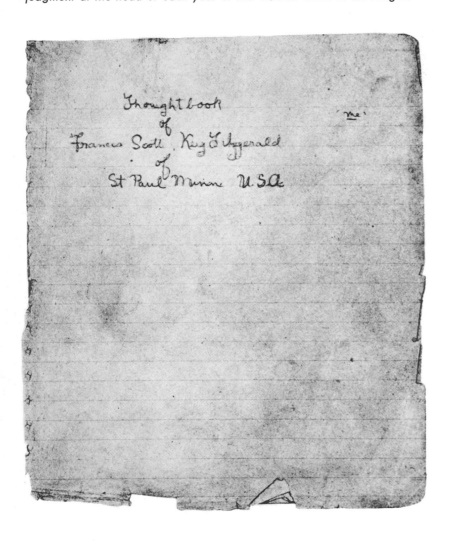

Thoughtbook of Frances Scott Key Fitzgerald of St Paul Minn U.S.A.

me

XI

Indians and Violet Sept 1910

Violet Stockton was a niece of Mrs. Finch and she spent a summer in Saint Paul. She was very pretty with dark brown hair and eyes big and soft. She spoke with a soft southern accent leaving out the r's. She was a year older than I but together with most of the other boys liked her very much. I met her through Jack Mitchell who lived next door to her. He himself was very attached as was Art. Foley and together they sneaked up behind her and cut off her hair. That is a snip of it. We had a game we played called Indians which I made up. One side were the Indians who went off and hid some where. The cowboys then started off to find them and when the indians saw their chance they would jump out and take them by suprise We were all armed with croquet mallets. There were about fifteen of us Kitty Schulze, Betty Mudge, Betty Foster, Elenor Mitchell, Marie Hersey, Dorothy Green, Violet Stockton and Harriet [illegible] [illegible] Adolph Schulze, [illegible]

VIII

My girls August, 1910

My recollections of Nancy are rather dim but one day stands out above the rest. The Gardeners had their home three miles out of town and one day James [illegible], Inky for short, my best friend and I were invited out to spend the day. I was about nine years old Nancy about eight and we were quite infatuated with each other. It was in the middle of the winter so as soon as we got there we began playing on the toboggan. Nancy and I and [illegible] were on our toboggan and Dan (Nancies big brother came along and wanted to get on. He made a leap for the toboggan but I pushed off just in time and [illegible] him on his head. He was awful mad. He said he'd kick me off and that it was my toboggan and that I couldn't play. However Nancy smoothed it over and we went into lunch.

November 1910

One day Marie Hersey wrote me a note which began either "Dear Scott I love you very much, or I like you very much," and ever since then she has been rather shy when she meets me.

Margaret said she liked me best. All the way home I was in the seventh heaven of delight. The next time I saw

I have two new Crushes. To wit, Margaret Armstrong and Marie Hersey. I have not quite decided yet which I like the best. The first is the prettiest the 2nd the best talker. The 1st the most popular with

It was impossible to count the number of times I kissed Kitty that afternoon. At any rate when we

Between August 1910 and February 1911, Scott kept a diary he called his Thoughtbook, which occupied twenty-six pages.

166 A year of real unhappiness excepting the feverish joys of Xmas.

Fifteen Years Old

Sept | 5 ft. 4 in. Moved to 499 Holly Ave. Attended state fair and took chuckmore roller-coaster. Off for Newman School. Dummy Taylor in Penn station. My cigarettes. Alexander's rag-time band Went out to Central with freshmen.

Fitzgerald entered Newman, a Roman Catholic school, in the fall of 1911. There he met Father Sigourney Webster Fay and Shane Leslie, an Anglo-Irish author, who became great influences on him. Father—later Monsignor—Fay, the headmaster, was the model for Monsignor Darcy in This Side of Paradise.

I go to Newman & return for Xmas

ENGAGEMENT BOOK
of
Scott Fitzgerald
for Christmas vacation
1911 – 1912

Friday, December 22d — Arrived, Cec, Bob & Bobby came to see me

Saturday, December 23d — Saw girls at meeting of dramatic club.

Sunday, December 24th — went with Schurmier to call on Winchesters

Monday, December 25th — Christmas day. Schurmier came over

Tuesday, December 26th — Stayed around the house

One-of my most vivid memories is of coming back West from prep school and later from college at Christmas time. Those who went farther than Chicago would gather in the old dim Union Station at six o'clock of a December evening, with a few Chicago friends, already caught up into their own holiday gayeties, to bid them a hasty good-by. I remember the fur coats of the girls returning from Miss This-or-That's and the chatter of frozen breath and the hands waving overhead as we caught sight of old acquaintances, and the matchings of invitations: "Are you going to the Ordways'? the Herseys'? the Schultzes'?" and the long green tickets clasped tight in our gloved hands. And last the murky yellow cars of the Chicago, Milwaukee & St. Paul railroad looking cheerful as Christmas itself on the tracks beside the gate.

When we pulled out into the winter night and the real snow, our snow, began to stretch out beside us and twinkle against the windows, and the dim lights of small Wisconsin stations moved by, a sharp wild brace came suddenly into the air. We drew in deep breaths of it as we walked back from dinner through the cold vestibules, unutterably aware of our identity with this country for one strange hour, before we melted indistinguishably into it again.

That's my Middle West—not the wheat or the prairies or the lost Swede towns, but the thrilling returning trains of my youth, and the street lamps and sleigh bells in the frosty dark and the shadows of holly wreaths thrown by lighted windows on the snow. I am part of that, a little solemn with the feel of those long winters, a little complacent from growing up in the Carraway house in a city where dwellings are still called through decades by a family's name.

—The Great Gatsby

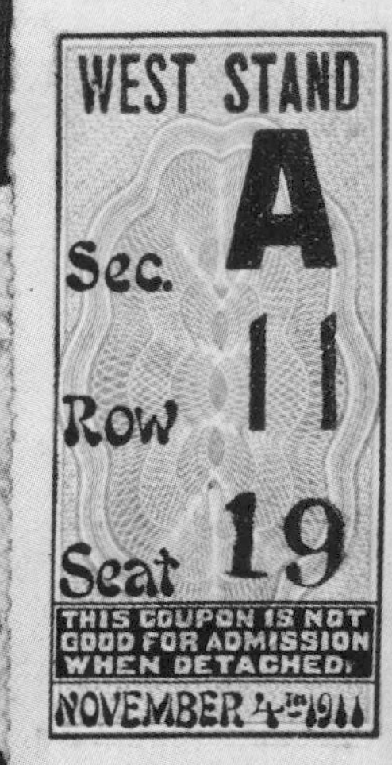

WEST STAND
Sec. A
Row 11
Seat 19
THIS COUPON IS NOT GOOD FOR ADMISSION WHEN DETACHED.
NOVEMBER 4th 1911

Sam White decides me for Princeton

Miserable, confined to bounds, unpopular with both faculty and students—that was Amory's first term. But at Christmas he had returned to Minneapolis, tight-lipped and strangely jubilant.

"Oh, I was sort of fresh at first," he told Frog Parker patronizingly, "but I got along fine—lightest man on the squad. You ought to go away to school, Froggy. It's great stuff."

—*This Side of Paradise*

I was at prep school in New Jersey with Pulitzer Prizeman Herbert Agar and novelists Cyril Hume and Edward Hope Coffey. Hope and I were destined to follow a similar pattern—to write librettos at Princeton, "drool" for the college comic and, later, college novels. But I remember him best when he was center and I was quarterback on the second team at school. We were both fifteen—and awful. There were a couple of one-hundred-eighty-pound tackles (one of them now headmaster for his sins) who liked to practice taking me out, and Hope gave me no protection—no protection at all—and I would have paid well for protection. We were the laziest and lowest-ranking boys in school.

—"My Generation"

NEWMAN—7 KINGSLEY—0

The next game Newman played was with Kingsley School, of Essex Fels, N. J., on Newman Field, October 26. This game was without doubt the most exciting one ever seen on Newman field. It resulted in a seven to nothing victory for Newman. The teams were evenly matched and both played an excellent game. The lone touchdown which won for Newman was made in the last five minutes of play by Quarterback Donohoe. Kingsley had three good chances to score; three times they forced the ball to the two-yard line, and as many times their backs hurled themselves in vain against the stonewall defense of the Black and White. The joy of the victory was a little clouded because of the injury of Captain Graham, who sprained his shoulder.

The stars of the game were Donohoe, Dohan, Fitzgerald and Morrison for Newman; Sperry, both Maxwells and Barrias for Kingsley. The defensive playing of Havens, Newman's fullback, was also remarkable. Fitzgerald's fine running with the ball and Donohoe's splendid generalship were particularly noticeable. In the last quarter Newman received the ball on downs on its eight-yard line. By consistent circling of the ends, Fitzgerald, Dohan and Havens carried the ball to Kingsley's three-yard line. Fitzgerald and Havens each made a yard, and Donohoe finally shot through centre for the winning touchdown. Dohan kicked the goal.

NEWMAN		KINGSLEY
Shanley, Yates	Right End	Barrios
Morrison	Right Tackle	Hurd
Dickey, W. O'Brien	Right Guard	McIntosh
Nelson	Centre	Ford
Hart	Left Guard	Goggin, Marvel
Malarkey	Left Tackle	A. Maxwell (Capt.)
Pallen	Left End	Whitaker
C. Donohoe	Quarterback	Farrand
Dohan, Shanley	Right Halfback	Sperry
Graham (Capt.), Fitzgerald	Left Halfback	Bingham
Webb (Havens)	Fullback	G. Maxwell

Touchdown—Donohoe. Goal from Touchdown—Dohan. Referee—McGall. Umpire—Waring. Head Linesman—Mr. Fleming. Time of Quarters—10 minutes.

From there to the goal line it was easy running, and as Reade laid the pigskin on the ground and rolled happily over beside it he could just hear another slogan echo down the field: "One point—two points—three points—four points—five points. Reade! Reade! Reade!"

—"Reade, Substitute Right Half"

Reward in fall for work of previous summer. A better year but not happy.

Sixteen Years Old

167

I am afraid that I gave you too much assurance of your inevitable safety, and you must remember that I did that through faith in your springs of effort; not in the silly conviction that you will arrive without struggle. Some nuances of character you will have to take for granted in yourself, though you must be careful in confessing them to others. You are unsentimental, almost incapable of affection, astute without being cunning and vain without being proud.

Don't let yourself feel worthless; often through life you will really be at your worst when you seem to think best of yourself; and don't worry about losing your "personality," as you persist in calling it; at fifteen you had the radiance of early morning, at twenty you will begin to have the melancholy brilliance of the moon, and when you are my age you will give out, as I do, the genial golden warmth of 4 P.M.

If you write me letters, please let them be natural ones. Your last, that dissertation on architecture, was perfectly awful—so "highbrow" that I picture you living in an intellectual and emotional vacuum; and beware of trying to classify people too definitely into types; you will find that all through their youth they will persist annoyingly in jumping from class to class, and by pasting a supercilious label on every one you meet you are merely packing a Jack-in-the-box that will spring up and leer at you when you begin to come into really antagonistic contact with the world. An idealization of some such a man as Leonardo da Vinci would be a more valuable beacon to you at present.

You are bound to go up and down, just as I did in my youth, but do keep your clarity of mind, and if fools or sages dare to criticise don't blame yourself too much.

You say that convention is all that really keeps you straight in this "woman proposition"; but it's more than that, Amory; it's the fear that what you begin you can't stop; you would run amuck, and I know whereof I speak; it's that half-miraculous sixth sense by which you detect evil, it's the half-realized fear of God in your heart.

Whatever your metier proves to be—religion, architecture, literature—I'm sure you would be much safer anchored to the Church, but I won't risk my influence by arguing with you even though I am secretly sure that the "black chasm of Romanism" yawns beneath you. Do write me soon.

With affectionate regards,

THAYER DARCY
—This Side of Paradise

Monsignor Fay

Newman News 5

THE TRAIL OF THE DUKE

By SCOTT FITZGERALD.

It was a hot July night. Inside, through screen, window and door fled the bugs and gathered around the lights like so many humans at a carnival, buzzing, thugging, whirring. From out the night into the houses came the sweltering late summer heat, over-powering and enervating, bursting against the walls and enveloping all mankind like a huge smothering blanket. In the drug stores, the clerks, tired and grumbling handed out ice cream to hundreds of thirsty but misled civilians, while in the corners buzzed the electric fans in a whirring mockery of coolness. In the flats that line upper New York, pianos (sweatting ebony perspiration) ground out rag-time tunes of last winter and here and there a wan woman sang the air in a hot soprano. In the tenements, shirt-sleeves gleamed like beacon lights in steady rows along the streets in tiers of from four to eight according to the number of stories of the house. In a word, it was a typical, hot New York summer night.

Monsignor was forty-four then, and bustling—a trifle too stout for symmetry, with hair the color of spun gold, and a brilliant, enveloping personality. When he came into a room clad in his full purple regalia from thatch to toe, he resembled a Turner sunset, and attracted both admiration and attention. He had written two novels: one of them violently anti-Catholic, just before his conversion, and five years later another, in which he had attempted to turn all his clever jibes against Catholics into even cleverer innuendoes against Episcopalians. He was intensely ritualistic, startingly dramatic, loved the idea of God enough to be a celibate, and rather liked his neighbor.

Children adored him because he was like a child; youth revelled in his company because he was still a youth, and couldn't be shocked. In the proper land and century he might have been a Richelieu—at present he was a very moral, very religious (if not particularly pious) clergyman, making a great mystery about pulling rusty wires, and appreciating life to the fullest, if not entirely enjoying it.

He and Amory took to each other at first sight—the jovial, impressive prelate who could dazzle an embassy ball, and the green-eyed, intent youth, in his first long trousers, accepted in their own minds a relation of father and son within a half-hour's conversation.

—This Side of Paradise

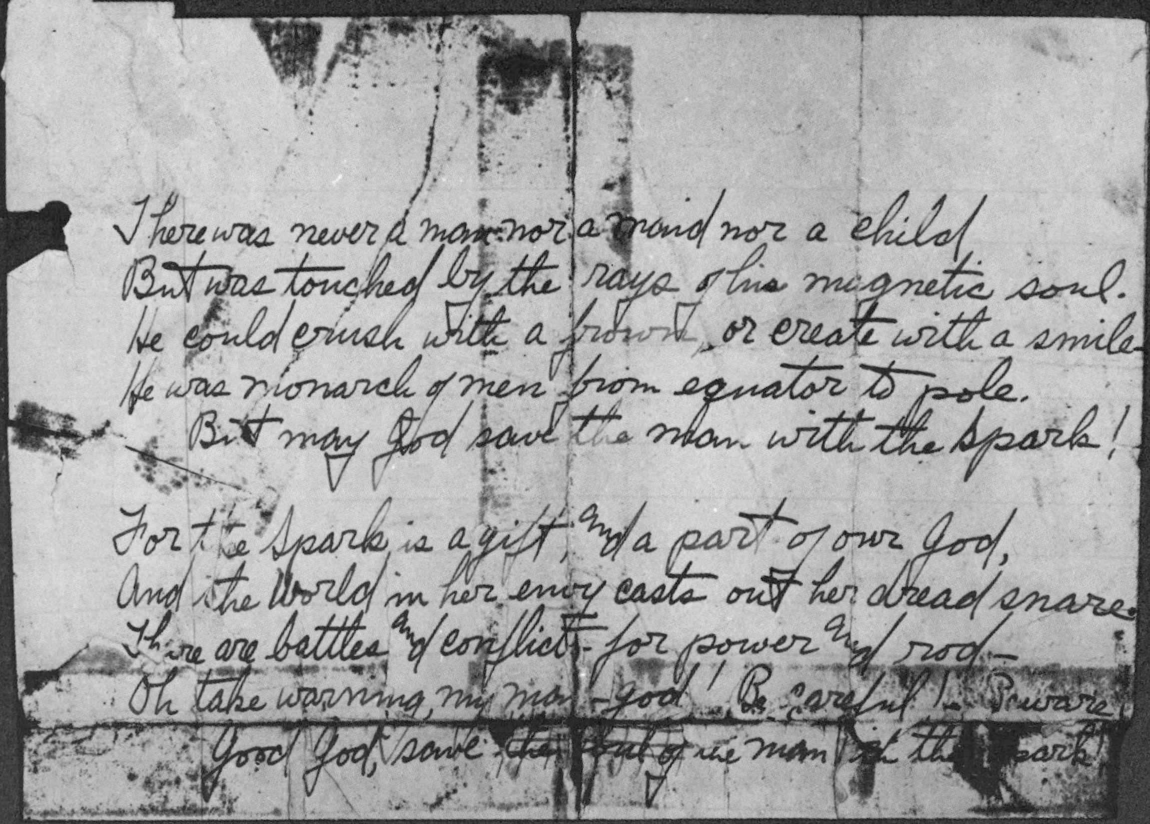
There was never a man nor a maid nor a child
But was touched by the rays of his magnetic soul.
He could crush with a frown, or create with a smile
He was monarch of men from equator to pole.
But may God save the man with the Spark!

For the Spark is a gift, and a part of our God,
And the World in her envy casts out her dread snare.
There are battles and conflict for power and rod—
Oh take warning, my man-god! Be careful! Beware
Good God, save the soul of the man of the Spark!

Miss Magoffin wrote this poem to Scott.

Elizabeth Magoffin

Miss Elizabeth Magoffin sponsored a theatrical group in St. Paul called the Elizabethan Dramatic Club, in her honor. Fitzgerald wrote and acted in four plays: "The Girl from Lazy J" (1911), "The Captured Shadow" (1912), " 'The Coward' " (1913), and "Assorted Spirits" (1914).

"The Coward" to Be Given Tuesday at the Yacht Club.

THE "COWARD," which was presented Friday evening at the Y. W. C. A. by the members of the Elizabethan Dramatic club, was such a decided success that the youthful players have been requested to again give the performance Tuesday evening at the White Bear Yacht club. The actors are children of prominent St. Paul families, and the play Friday evening attracted a large and fashionable audience. Lawrence Boardman played the title role of the "Coward," and Miss Dorothy Greene, daughter of Dr. and Mrs. Charles Greene, was Lindy Douglas, the heroine of the playlet. Scott Fitzgerald, the author, played the part of Lieut. Charles Douglas with great success. Gustave Schurmeier played the humorous role of Lieut. Percy Atwater, a typical Englishman. Miss Julia Dorr, daughter of Mrs. William Dorr, showed marked ability in her part of Angelina Bangs, and the comedy part, played by Miss Elizabeth McDavitt, daughter of Dr. and Mrs. Thomas McDavitt, as Miss Print, drew many smiles from the audience. Miss Kitty Schulze, daughter of Mr. and Mrs. Theodore Schulze, looked very beautiful in the part of Virginia Taylor, and Miss Eleanor Alair's, daughter of Mr. and Mrs. W. E. Alair, portrayal of Cecelia Ashton, was artistic. Miss Alice Lyon, daughter of Mr. and Mrs. N. H. Lyon, as Mrs. Douglas, showed histrionic ability. The part of Judge Douglas was carried by Robert Clark. Rudolf and Lettis Patterson took the juvenile parts. Miss Elizabeth Magoffin trained the cast, and the play was given for the benefit of the Baby Welfare league. The proceeds Tuesday will be used for the same cause. Before the performance Tuesday, Mr. and Mrs. Worell Clarkson, Dellwood, will give a dinner at the White Bear Yacht club in honor of the young and talented actors.

—THE GREAT EVENT—

"COWARD"

A comedy in two acts by Scott Fitzgerald. Presented by the Elizabethan Dramatic Club for the benefit of The Baby Welfare Association.

CAST

James Holworthy	Laurence Boardman
Lieut. Charles Douglass, C. S. A.	Scott Fitzgerald
Lieut. Percy Altwater, C. S. A.	Gustave Schurmeier
Capt. Ormsby, U. S. A.	Robert Barton
Judge Arthur Douglass	Robert Clark
Tommy Douglass	Rudolph Patterson
Jefferson	Theodore Parkhouse
Private Willings, U. S. A.	Gustave Schurmeier
Private Barkis, U. S. A.	Wharton Smith
Private Johnson	Scott Fitzgerald
Mrs. Douglass	Alice Lyon
Lindy Douglass	Dorothy Greene
Clara Douglass	Letitia Magoffin
Cecelia Ashton	Eleanor Alair
Virginia Taylor	Katherine Schulze
Miss Pruit	Elizabeth McDavitt
Angelina Bangs	Julia Dorr

Act I. The Douglass home in Virginia, 1862.
Act II. The same—Three years later.

STAFF

Directress	Miss Elizabeth Magoffin
Stage Manager	Mr. Scott Fitzgerald
Business Manager	Mr. Gustave Schurmeier
Asst. Business Manager / Treasurer	Mr. Robert Clark

Gustave B. Schurmeier
PRESENTS
LAURANCE BOARDMAN
IN
Scott Fitzgerald's Comedy
"THE COWARD"
AT THE
Y. W. C. A.--August 29, 1913
Tickets 25c | ON SALE AT Y. W. C. A. and Y. M. C. A.
Given for the Benefit of the Baby Welfare

BOYS STAGE DRAMA WITH CHILD ACTORS

"Coward," Written by 17-year-old Lad, to Be Played for Chairty.

A drama of war times in the South, written by Scott Fitzgerald, 17 years old, produced by Gustav Schurmeier, a lad of the same age, and presented by a cast composed of children all under 18, whose star is Lawrence Boardman, 17 years old, will be staged next Friday evening in the auditorium of the Y. W. C. A. The proceeds will be donated to the Babies' Welfare league.

Deals With Southerner.

The title of the play is "Coward" and it deals with the life and character of a Southern man who feared to don a uniform and fight for the independence of the South. It is said that the play itself is excellently written and that the acting of the members of the cast, all of whom are members of prominent St. Paul families, is of professional quality.

The cast follows:

Judge Douglas	Robert Clark
Mrs. Douglas	Alice Lyon
Lindy Douglas	Dorothy Greene
Lieutenant Charles Douglas, C. S. A.	Scott Fitzgerald
James Holworthy	Lawrence Boardman
Lieutenant Percy Atwater	Gustav Schurmeier
Cecelia Ashton	Eleanor Alair
Virginia Taylor	Kitty Schultz
Clara Douglas	Letitia Magoffin
Tommy Douglas	Rudolf Patterosn
Jefferson	Theodore Parkhouse
Miss Print	Elizabeth McDavitt
Private Williams	Richard Stryker
Private Barkis	Wharton Smith
Captain Ormsby	Robert Barton
Angelina Bangs	Julia Dorr

All the young people are members of the Elizabethan Dramatic club, under whose auspices the performance will be given. Three annual benefit affairs have preceded it.

Paul Young People to Produce Play Written by Member of Dramatic Club

HE ELIZABETHAN Dramatic club, an organization of children of prominent St. Paul families, will produce "Coward," an original play by one of its members, Scott Fitzgerald, 16 s old, at the Y. W. C. A. auditorium, Friday evening. The production will be for the benefit the Baby Welfare league. The pictures are of two scenes in the play. In the upper one the ors are (left to right)—Lawrence Boardman, Gustav Schurmeier, Scott Fitzgerald, Robert rton and Miss Dorothy Greene. The lower picture is that of Misses Greene, Eleanor Alair, l Alice Lyon, Rudolph Patterson and Misses Elizabeth McDavitt and Laetitia Magoffin, in th der named.

AMATEUR JUVENILES ACCOMPLISHED ON STAG

Performance for Benefit of Baby We fare League Will Be Repeated at Lake.

Juvenile St. Anthony hill took dip into dramatic art Friday nigl and today a dozen boys and girls a wearing laurel wreaths and the Ba. Welfare league is $150 the richer.

"The Coward" was the play presen ed by the juvenile company at th Y. W. C. A. auditorium. It was wr ten by Scott Fitzgerald, who also too one of the leading roles. The tit role was played by Laurence Boar man. Gustave Schurmeier, Whart Smith, Alice Lyon, Dorothy Gree Eleanore Alair, Katherine Schulz Elizabeth McDavitt, Julia Dorr, Le tia Magoffin and Robert Barton we members of the cast. Theodore Par house was the leading comedian.

The play will be repeated ne Tuesday night at the White Be Yacht club, and the Baby Welfa league will again be the beneficiary.

"FIRST NIGHT" IS SOLD OUT

"Coward" Will Be Presented by Amateurs at Y. W. C. A. Auditorium Tonight.

Every ticket has been sold for the first performance of "Coward," an amateur play which will be produced at the Auditorium of the Y. W. C. A. this evening at 8:30, by the Elizabethan Dramatic club, consisting of sons and daughters of prominent families of St. Paul.

In order to accommodate every one, the play will be repeated next week at the White Bear Yacht club at Dellwood, and tickets purchased for this evening's performance will be good at that time.

"Coward" is a two-act drama dealing with life in the South at the time of the Civil war, written by Scott Fitzgerald, son of Mr. and Mrs. Edwar Fitzgerald. The leading part, that of a Southerner who was unwilling don a uniform and fight for the ind pendence of the South, is taken Lawrence Boardman, son of Mr. a Mrs. H. A. Boardman, who distinguished himself in amateur dramatics at Central high school last year. The manager of the production is Gustave Schurmeier, the son of Mrs. Gustave Schurmeier, 644 Summit avenue.

Others in the play are: Robert Clark, Alice Lyon, Dorothy Greene, Eleanor Alair, Kitty Schuutz, Letitia Magoffin, Rudolf Patterson, Theodore P house, Elizabeth McDavitt, R Stryker, Wharton Smith, Rober ton and Julia Dorr.

Miss Elizabe[illegible]

ENTER SUCCESS!

JUVENILE PLAY PLEASES.

"Coward" Is Given at White Bear Yacht Club.

The Elizabethan Dramatic club, composed of children of prominent St. Paul families, scored another decided success last evening in its performance of "The Coward" at the White Bear Yacht club. The crowd of nearly three hundred was even more enthusiastic than that which witnessed the opening performance at the Y. W. C. A. last Friday night.

There was a second and a third act scene that were very similar. In each of them The Shadow, alone on the stage, was interrupted by Miss Saunders. Mayall De Bec, having had but ten days of rehearsal, was inclined to confuse the two, but Basil was totally unprepared for what happened. Upon Connie's entrance Mayall spoke his third-act line and involuntarily Connie answered in kind.

Others coming on the stage were swept up in the nervousness and confusion, and suddenly they were playing the third act in the middle of the second. It happened so quickly that for a moment Basil had only a vague sense that something was wrong. Then he dashed down one stairs and up another and into the wings, crying:

"Let down the curtain! Let down the curtain!"

The boys who stood there aghast sprang to the rope. In a minute Basil, breathless, was facing the audience.

"Ladies and gentlemen," he said, "there's been changes in the cast and what just happened was a mistake. If you'll excuse us we'd like to do that scene over."

He stepped back in the wings to a flutter of laughter and applause.

"All right, Mayall!" he called excitedly. "On the stage alone. Your line is: 'I just want to see that the jewels are all right,' and Connie's is: 'Go ahead, don't mind me.' All right! Curtain up!"

In a moment things righted themselves. Someone brought water for Miss Halliburton, who was in a state of collapse, and as the act ended they all took a curtain call once more. Twenty minutes later it was over. The hero clasped Leilia Van Baker to his breast, confessing that he was The Shadow, "and a captured Shadow at that"; the curtain went up and down, up and down; Miss Halliburton was dragged unwillingly on the stage and the ushers came up the aisles laden with flowers. Then everything became informal and the actors mingled happily with the audience, laughing and important, congratulated from all sides. An old man whom Basil didn't know came up to him and shook his hand, saying, "You're a young man that's going to be heard from some day," and a reporter from the paper asked him if he was really only fifteen. It might all have been very bad and demoralizing for Basil, but it was already behind him. Even as the crowd melted away and the last few people spoke to him and went out, he felt a great vacancy come into his heart. It was over, it was done and gone—all that work, and interest and absorption. It was a hollowness like fear.

—"The Captured Shadow"

168
A year of work and ~~vivid~~ vivid experience

Seventeen Years Old

Sept 138 lbs. 5 ft. 7 in. ~~On Bank St with Mac, Crawford~~. 14 Univ. Place. Hazing. Admitted to Princeton. Sap, Joe, Black, Bob, Paul, Bunny, Wash, Ozzie, Tic. Freshman football. The Rushes, the singing. Electing class officers. Prep school nice fellows begin to drop out—i.e. Slagle & Bunny Shanley.

Oct Fight in Trenton. B. Wilson. Sweet Holley Baker. Being Horsed. ~~Elizabeth Clarkson~~. Van Winkle. The A meeting.

A25 WESTERN UNION TELEGRAM Form 168

THEO. N. VAIL, PRESIDENT

RECEIVED AT Pioneer Bldg., 332 Robert Street, St. Paul, Minn. ALWAYS OPEN

25 NY 11 COLLECT

PRINCETON N J SEP 24 13

MRS EDWARD FITSGERALD

499 HOLLY AVE STPAUL MINN

ADMITTED SEND FOOTBALL PADS AND SHOES IMMEDIATELY PLEASE WAIT TRUNK

SCOTT

907P

[illegible handwritten notations]

Fitzgerald was cut from the Princeton freshman football squad during the first week of practice, thus ending one dream of success.

"Once upon a time" (I tell myself) "they needed a quarterback at Princeton, and they had nobody and were in despair. The head coach noticed me kicking and passing on the side of the field, and he cried: 'Who is *that* man—why haven't we noticed *him* before?' The under coach answered, 'He hasn't been out,' and the response was: 'Bring him to me.'

". . . we go to the day of the Yale game. I weigh only one hundred and thirty-five, so they save me until the third quarter, with the score—"

—But it's no use—I have used that dream of a defeated dream to induce sleep for almost twenty years, but it has worn thin at last. I can no longer count on it—though even now on easier nights it has a certain lull . . .

—"Sleeping and Waking"

Princeton is in the flat midlands of New Jersey, rising, a green Phoenix, out of the ugliest country in the world. Sordid Trenton sweats and festers a few miles south; northward are Elizabeth and the Erie Railroad and the suburban slums of New York; westward the dreary upper purlieus of the Delaware River. But around Princeton, shielding her, is a ring of silence—certified milk dairies, great estates with peacocks and deer parks, pleasant farms and woodlands which we paced off and mapped down in the spring of 1917 in preparation for the war. The busy East has already dropped away when the branch train rattles familiarly from the junction. Two tall spires and then suddenly all around you spreads out the loveliest riot of Gothic architecture in America, battlement linked on to battlement, hall to hall, arch-broken, vine-covered—luxuriant and lovely over two square miles of green grass. Here is no monotony, no feeling that it was all built yesterday at the whim of last week's millionaire; Nassau Hall was already thirty years old when Hessian bullets pierced its sides.

—"Princeton"

Horsing "His First Shave"

"SPIRES AND GARGOYLES"

TIGER OUT TO-MORROW FOR FIRST AIRING OF YEAR

University Humorous Publication to Commence Tickling Undergraduates' Funny Bones—Many Laughs

October 22d is going to be a regular day around here. Not only is the Graduate College to go on a party, but the gloom caused by the faculty's refusal to allow the undergraduates to study on that auspicious occasion is to be permanently dispelled by the first roar of the Tiger, or as the Printers call it, The Fall Number.

Of course, it is unusually humorous, but at the same time strikes a new note among college funny papers—there is only one reference to "September Morn" in it! The cover is by R. H. Gibson 1914, and the center page by I. E. Swart 1915, is of special interest to the Freshmen. Other members of the staff are represented by some of their best work. The debutantes are Fitzgerald 1917 and Chester 1917.

FIRST APPEARANCE

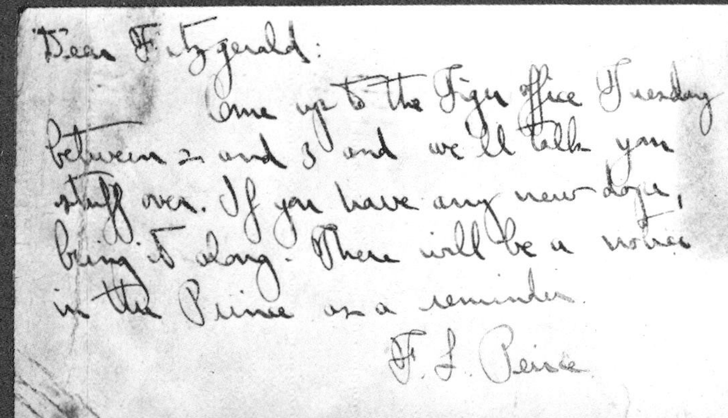

Dear Fitzgerald:
Come up to the Tiger office Tuesday between 2 and 3 and we'll talk your stuff over. If you have any new dope, bring it along. There will be a notice in the Prince as a reminder.
F. L. Peirce

Tiger Elections.

At a meeting of the Tiger yesterday, F. S. Fitzgerald 1917, was elected to the editorial department, and R. L. Bruch 1918, was elected to the art department.

Dec 22nd — Orpheum, Bettie's dance
Dec 23d — Cec, Don & Mac came over
Dec 24th — Christmas Eve at Aunt L's
Dec 25th — Call at Dunns & Hills
Dec 26th — Operation
Dec 27th — Schurmeiers, refused Hill
Dec 28th — Refused Bob's, Toby's pink tea
Dec 29th — Univ. Club dinner, Lane's dance
Dec 30th — Refused Minnie & Orpheum, D.C.D
Dec 31st — Cotillion dance - Ref. Aux. recep.
Jan 1st — Orton's matinee dansant
Jan 2nd — Refused Hill's dinner
Jan 3d — Leave for East

XMAS 1913-14

HOME FROM PRINCTON

OPERATION !!!

Fitzgerald went out for The Princeton Tiger, the humor magazine, and for the Nassau Literary Magazine. His first identifiable Tiger contribution appeared in December 1914; and his first appearance in the Lit was "Shadow Laurels" in April 1915.

A year of tremendous rewards that toward the end overreached itself and ruined me. Ginevra - Triangle year.

Sept. ~~Moved to 593 Summit Ave.~~ Princeton 71 Patton Hall. Play accepted. Ineligable.

Oct Trials. Worry about clubs. Tom Pierson. Also Rip Van Winkle. Elkins Oliphant.

Fie! Fie! Fi-Fi!

A Musical Comedy in Two Acts

Presented by

The Princeton University Triangle Club

Season of 1914-1915

President	WALKER M. ELLIS, 1915
Manager	JAMES F. ADAMS, 1915
Secretary	C. LAMBERT HEYNIGER, 1916
Ass't Manager	WILTON LLOYD-SMITH, 1916
Advertising Manager	G. FREDERIC RIEGEL, 1915

PRODUCTION ARRANGED AND STAGED BY LEWIS HOOPER

~~BOOK~~ Revision BY WALKER M. ELLIS, 1915

Book + LYRICS BY F. SCOTT FITZGERALD, 1917

MUSIC BY D. D. GRIFFIN, 1915; A. L. BOOTH, 1915; P. B. DICKEY, 1917

COMPLETE MUSICAL SCORE ON SALE DURING THE INTERMISSION AND AT THE CONCLUSION OF THE PERFORMANCE

PRICE, $1.00

THE TRIANGLE CLUB

The Characters

LIEUT. ARCHIBALD CHOLMONDELEY, absent on leave	E. M. McIlvain, 1918
BILL TRACY, alias His Excellency Yuan Castile, Prime Minister of Monaco	J. W. Bailey, Jr., 1915
FERNANDO DEL MONTI, former Prime Minister, now a Bandit Chief	C. L. Heyniger, 1916
GUISEPPE, his Lieutenant	W. M. Barr, 1915
DR. BLOSSOM, a smooth article	J. B. Everett, 1918
SIGNOR LENTONA, managing proprietor of the Hotel Della Parma	P. D. Nelson, 1917
POMPINE, Lieutenant of the gendarmes	L. S. Fowler, 1917
A WAITER	R. L. Farrelly, 1918
CELESTE, a dancer (my part - Oh Hell!)	D. D. Griffin, 1915
MRS. BOVINE, of Keokuk, her mother	J. A. Swineford, 1915
CLOVER BLOSSOM, the doctor's superannuated daughter	W. E. Johnson, 1915
DULCETTE, Lentona's niece	W. J. Warburton, 1918
SADY HANKS, alias Fi-Fi! Gormilley, manicurist	Walker M. Ellis, 1915

The Princeton University Triangle Club, which Booth Tarkington had helped found, produced an original musical comedy every year that went on tour during the Christmas vacation. These productions enjoyed national prominence, and election to office in the Triangle Club was one of the roads to undergraduate success at Princeton. Fitzgerald wrote the lyrics for 3 shows: Fie! Fie! Fi-Fi! *(1914),* The Evil Eye *(1915), and* Safety First *(1916).*

Every night for the last week they had rehearsed "Ha-Ha Hortense!" in the Casino, from two in the afternoon until eight in the morning, sustained by dark and powerful coffee, and sleeping in lectures through the interim. A rare scene, the Casino. A big, barnlike auditorium, dotted with boys as girls, boys as pirates, boys as babies; the scenery in course of being violently set up; the spotlight man rehearsing by throwing weird shafts into angry eyes; over all the constant tuning of the orchestra or the cheerful tumpty-tump of a Triangle tune. The boy who writes the lyrics stands in the corner, biting a pencil, with twenty minutes to think of an encore; the business manager argues with the secretary as to how much money can be spent on "those damn milkmaid costumes"; the old graduate, president in ninety-eight, perches on a box and thinks how much simpler it was in his day.

—This Side of Paradise

I spent my entire freshman year writing an operetta for the Triangle Club. I failed in algebra, trigonometry, coordinate geometry and hygiene, but the Triangle Club accepted my show, and by tutoring all through a stuffy August I managed to come back a sophomore and act in it as a chorus girl. A little later I left college to spend the rest of the year recuperating in the West.

—*Interview with Charles C. Baldwin*

PRINCETON UNIVERSITY

PRINCETON, N. J., JUNE, 1914

The following is the Official Report of the standing of

Francis Scott Fitzgerald

of the Freshman Class for the term ending June 16, 1914.

Average for Term 4.78 Average for Year 4.97

General Group for the Year 5

Rank in Each Subject:

The numbers immediately following the subjects indicate the course numbers as found in the University Catalogue; the single numbers thereafter indicate the groups attained.

Latin 104 5
Mathematics 108 absent – repeat
English 102 3
Physics ~~104~~ 102 5
Chemistry 104
French 204 4
German
Phys. Education 102 passed
Hygiene 102 4

Total number of absences incurred during the term 31

A student who for any cause incurs fifty absences in any term or in any two successive terms, must take an extra course the following term.

By order of the Faculty

Registrar.

PRINCETON UNIVERSITY

PRINCETON, N. J., FEBRUARY, 1914

The following is the Official Report of the standing of

Francis Scott Fitzgerald

of the Freshman Class for the term ending February 11, 1914.

Average for Term 5.17 Group for Term 5

Rank in Each Subject:

The numbers immediately following the subjects indicate the course numbers as found in the University Catalogue; the single numbers thereafter indicate the groups attained.

Latin 103 5
Mathematics 101 failed
English 101 4
Physics 101 5
Chemistry 103
French 203 5
German
Hygiene 101 failed
Phys. Education passed
Mathematics 105 failed

Total number of absences incurred during the term 18

A student who for any cause incurs fifty absences in any term or in any two successive terms, must take an extra course the following term.

By order of the Faculty

Registrar.

Princeton grades operated on a 7-point system, with 5 as the lowest passing grade.

Fitzgerald provided the idea for this Tiger cartoon.

In Fitzgerald's time much of the social structure at Princeton revolved around the eating clubs, which undergraduates joined in sophomore year. These clubs occupied imposing structures. Membership was by election, and the clubs had varying degrees of prestige.

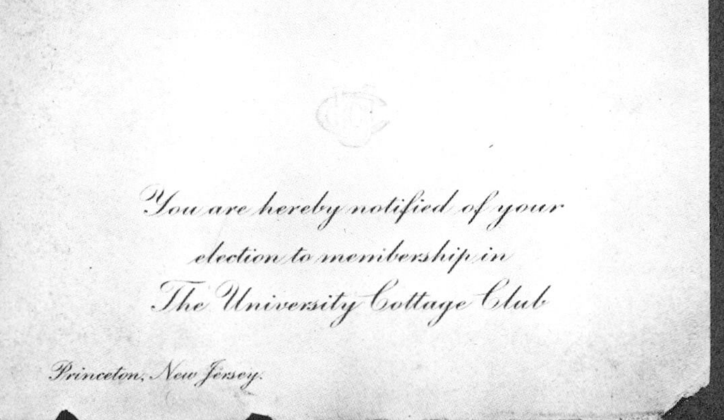

You are hereby notified of your election to membership in The University Cottage Club

Princeton, New Jersey.

The upper-class clubs, concerning which he had pumped a reluctant graduate during the previous summer, excited his curiosity: Ivy, detached and breathlessly aristocratic; Cottage, an impressive melange of brilliant adventurers and well-dressed philanderers; Tiger Inn, broad-shouldered and athletic, vitalized by an honest elaboration of prep-school standards; Cap and Gown, anti-alcoholic, faintly religious and politically powerful; flambuoyant Colonial; literary Quadrangle; and the dozen others, varying in age and position.

—*This Side of Paradise*

170

Nineteen Years Old

A year of terrible disappointments & the end of all college dreams. Everything bad in it was my own fault.

Fitzgerald was not permitted to perform in any of his Triangle shows because of academic problems, but this photo of him as a chorus girl was widely published. He created a mild sensation by appearing in this costume at a University of Minnesota dance.

THE PRINCETON UNIVERSITY TRIANGLE CLUB
PRESENTS
THE EVIL EYE
PRINCETON
Monday, December 20, 1915

F. SCOTT FITZGERALD AS HE IS AND AS HE APPEARS IN "THE EVIL EYE"

THE·DAILY·PRINCETONIAN

VOL. XXXVIII. NO. 294 PRINCETON, N. J. THURSDAY, OCTOBER 28, 1915 PRICE THREE CENTS

TRIANGLE CLUB WILL OFFER 'THE EVIL EYE'

This Year's Book Written by Edmund Wilson, Jr. 1916—Comedy In Two Acts.

TRIP THIS YEAR LONGEST EVER ARRANGED FOR CLUB

List of Bookings Announced Later—Music by Dickey 1917 and Guilbert 1919.

The Triangle Club announces that it will present this year a musical comedy in two acts, entitled "The Evil Eye." The trip to be taken this year is the longest ever arranged for the club. The list of bookings is now being completed and will be announced in a few days.

The book to be used this year was written by Edmund Wilson, Jr. 1916, and is full of clever dialogue. The lyrics have been composed by F. Scott Fitzgerald 1917, who was responsible for many of the catchy lyrics in "Fie! Fie! Fi-Fi!," last year's Triangle Club presentation. The music is by P. B. Dickey 1917 and F. Warburton Guilbert 1919.

Plot of "The Evil Eye."

The scene is laid in the little fishing village of Niaiserie, on the coast of Normandy. At the opening of the first act a shipwreck has just taken place. A girl is the lone survivor. When she recovers it is apparent that she is suffering from aphasia. The shock of the wreck has caused her to lose her memory completely. She has been rescued by Jacques Lonche, who besides being the richest and strongest man in the town, is the possessor of the worst reputation. The peasants believe that he has "the evil eye," for his glance is supposed to bring a curse. He is considered as a sort of superman, who is shunned by all men and who is lonely in his consciousness of superiority.

When the girl whom he has rescued falls in love with him, he believes that at last he is to be blessed with happiness. But this path is blocked by the schemes of the unscrupulous and the superstitions of the vulgar. The Mayor of Niaiserie, whom we may consider the most corrupt official in France, has determined that his daughter, Dulcinea, shall marry Jacques and thus bring into the possession of one family all the local wealth. However, Dulcinea is in love with Claude, an honest villager, who returns her affection. The Mayor then forms a plot with Count La Rochefoucauld Boileau, a disreputable travelling salesman, who peddles perfumery. Boileau agrees to pretend that he is the husband of the shipwrecked girl. At the same time Claude has found some peasants to testify that they have seen Jacques talking to the Devil. The taking of the girl by Boileau and the imprisonment of Jacques as a result of the charge brought against him, bring about a series of complications from which the hero and heroine are extricated only just in time to sing the closing chorus.

Mme. Mirlflore, a mysterious Parisian lady; Mr. Harris, an American detective; Old Margot, the keeper of the Le Poisson D'Or, the village inn; and Francoise, the keeper of the light-house, also have parts in the story.

MASS MEETING TO-NIGHT TO PRACTICE NEW SONG

"A Cheer for Princeton" Will Be Tried for First Time—P-rade Forms at 7.45.

A mass meeting to practice songs and cheers will be held in Alexander Hall to-night at 8 o'clock. A p-rade will form at the Cannon at 7.45. The new song, "A Cheer for Princeton," will be practiced and all men are expected to bring with them copies of this, "Going Back to Nassau Hall," and the list of Princeton songs, now being distributed in the PRINCETONIAN Office.

The words of the new song are:

"Glory, Glory to the Black and Orange,
It's the Tiger's turn to-day.
Glory, glory, it's the same old story
Soon as Princeton starts to play.
Eli, Eli, all your hopes are dead
For the Tiger's growling in his lair.
Don't you hear him?
You'll learn to fear him,
Try to face him if you dare.

CHORUS:
Princeton, cheer for Princeton,
Raise your voices, loud and free
Strong and steady
Ever ready
For defeat or victory.
Princeton, cheer for Princeton,
Always sure to win renown,
So we'll raise our praise to Nassau
To the pride of the Tiger town.

In the fall of 1915, a competition was held at Princeton for a new football song. Fitzgerald's "A Cheer for Princeton" was selected, but it did not catch on.

Marie Hersey had grown up with Fitzgerald on Summit Avenue and was one of the close female friends with whom he conducted an elaborate correspondence.

. . . I no longer regard St. Paul as my home any more than the eastern seaboard or the Riviera. This is said with no disloyalty but simply because after all my father was an easterner and I went East to college and I never did quite adjust myself to those damn Minnesota winters. I was always freezing my cheeks, being a rotten skater, etc.—though many events there will always fill me with a tremendous nostalgia.

—FSF to Marie Hersey Hamm, 4 October 1934.

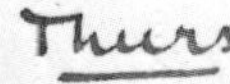

Thurs

My Very Very Dear Marie:
I got your little note
For reasons very queer Marie
You're mad at me I fear Marie,
You made it very clear Marie
You cared not what you wrote

The letter that you sent Marie
Was neither swift nor fair
I hoped that you'd repent Marie
Before the start of Lent Marie
But Lent could not prevent Marie
From being debonaire

So write me what you will Marie
altho' I will it not
My love you can not kill Marie
And tho' you treat me ill Marie
Believe me I am still Marie
Your fond admirer
Scott

(Letter sent to Marie Jan 29, 1915)

Oh Scott – you are a poet – true
theres no denying that!
Your verses were most clever, Scott
I'm sure no would could ever, Scott
There equal quite discover – Scott
On this I'll bet a hat!

But Scott, you quite misunderstood
the note I wrote to you
Why should you think that I was mad?
I'm sure no cause I ever had!
So don't think that – t'would be too bad
Now what I say is true.

Will Give Bob Party And Supper Tonight For Guest

Miss Elizabeth McDavitt to Entertain for Miss Genevera King of Chicago, House Guest of Miss Marie Hersey.

IN HONOR of Miss Genevera King of Chicago, who is the house guest of Miss Marie Hersey, 475 Summit avenue, Miss Elizabeth McDavitt, 596 Grand avenue, will give a bob party this evening followed by a supper at the home of Miss McDavitt. Among the guests will be the Misses Alida Bigelow, Katherine Ordway, Marie Hersey, Mary Johnston, Grace Warner, Betty Mudge, Constance James, Betty Foster, Eleanor Alair, Mary Butler and Joanne Orten; Messrs. Vernon Rinehart, Frank Hurley, Reuben Warner, Jr., Gustave Schurmeier, Lawrence Boardman, William Lindeke, Robert Barton, James Armstrong, Jr., James Porterfield, Robert Dunn, Scott Fitzgerald, Harrison Johnston.

B 32 BLUE
WATERBURY CONN 850 AM NOV 11 1915

SCOTT FITZGERALD
32 LITTLE HALL PRINCETON

WILL YOU COME TO DINNER ON SATURDAY THE THIRTEENTH AT THE ELTON WATERBURY AFTER YALE PRINCETON GAME WITH SAM CONANT TELL HIM THAT C CRAPO IS COMING TOO YOU MUST ARRANGE IT

GENEVRA KING

One Ginevra King comes to Town —

Fitzgerald met Ginevra King, the daughter of a wealthy Lake Forest family, at Christmas 1914 in St. Paul when she was visiting Marie Hersey. Ginevra was his first serious love, and he conducted an impassioned courtship by mail during 1915. They broke off in January 1917 partly because—as Fitzgerald noted in his Ledger—"Poor boys shouldn't think of marrying rich girls." Ginevra King provided the model for Isabelle in This Side of Paradise *and for many of his gilded heroines.*

. . . Oh, it's so hard to write you what I really *feel* when I think about you so much; you've gotten to mean to me a *dream* that I can't put on paper any more. Your last letter came and it was wonderful! I read it over about six times, especially the *last* part, but I do wish, sometimes, you'd be more *frank* and tell me what you really do think of me, yet your last letter was too good to be true, and I can hardly wait until June! Be sure and be able to come to the prom. It'll be fine, I think, and I want to bring *you* just at the end of a wonderful year. I often think over what you said on that night and wonder how much you meant. If it were any one but you—but you see I *thought* you were fickle the first time I saw you and you are so popular and everything that I can't imagine your really liking me *best.*

Oh, Isabelle, dear—it's a wonderful night. Somebody is playing "Love Moon" on a mandolin far across the campus, and the music seems to bring you into the window. Now he's playing "Good-by, Boys, I'm Through," and how well it suits me. For I *am* through with everything. I have decided never to take a cocktail again, and I know I'll never again fall in love—I couldn't—you've been too much a part of my days and nights to ever let me think of another girl. I meet them all the time and they don't interest me. I'm not pretending to be blasé, because it's not that. It's just that I'm in love. Oh, *dearest* Isabelle (somehow I can't call you just Isabelle, and I'm afraid I'll come out with the "dearest" before your family this June), you've *got* to come to the prom, and then I'll come up to your house for a day and everything'll be perfect. . . .

—This Side of Paradise

She can't Come!

On such paper, but with the Princeton seal, I used to write endless letters throughout sophomore and junior years to Ginevra King of Chicago and Westover, who later figured in This Side of Paradise. *Then I didn't see her for twenty-one years, though I telephoned her in 1933 to entertain your mother at the World's Fair, which she did. Yesterday I get a wire that she is in Santa Barbara and will I come down there immediately. She was the first girl I ever loved and I have faithfully avoided seeing her up to this moment to keep that illusion perfect, because she ended up by throwing me over with the most supreme boredom and indifference. I don't know whether I should go or not. It would be very, very strange. These great beauties are often something else at thirty-eight, but Ginevra had a great deal besides beauty.*

—FSF to Scottie, October 1937.

The Triumph of Youth.

What a realization of the supreme power of youth is forced on us by these so-called "war weddings." The old and wise look on with awe at the valorous determination of the young to snatch happiness from the tremendous conflagration which is burning up our outworn failure of a civilization. The flames light up the radiant faces of our boys and girls as, two by two, they join hands and smilingly undertake to cope with the great catastrophe.

In the shadows of the outer circle their elders look on, stretching out detaining but ineffectual hands, in helpless anguish. They are part of a closing chapter. To their sons and daughters belong both the present and the future. Each of these war marriages is a further manifestation of the triumph of youth.

But these are thoughts that only lurk in the outskirts of the mind. Last Wednesday at the marriage of Miss Ginevra King, daughter of Mr. and Mrs. Charles Garfield King, to Ensign William H. Mitchell, son of Mr. and Mrs. John J. Mitchell, the extreme youth of the bridal couple, their gay and gallant air, their uncommon good looks, the distinguished appearance of both sets of parents, the smart frocks and becoming uniforms, all made an impression of something brilliant, charming, and cheerful.

The company snapped its fingers at the weather (which was certainly in an unfriendly mood) and thoroughly enjoyed the beautiful ceremony in St. Chrysostom's Episcopal church.

Ceremony Beautiful and Impressive.

The church, a favorite sanctuary for war weddings, never looked more beautiful than it did that afternoon. Great garlands of fruit, that Lucca della Robbia himself might have designed, outlined the arches. The altar, with its wonderful blue reredos, was adorned with flowers in blue vases set on a piece of filet lace, rich and rare enough for a royal marriage. The bridal couple walked to the altar on a blue velvet carpet that matched reredos and vases.

The carrying of the flag at the head of the wedding procession was a most impressive feature of the ceremony. As it was borne up the aisle every one stood up. Our flag means so inexpressibly much to us nowadays!

A gay reception at the Kings' utterly charming house, 1450 Astor street, followed. Every one said that there never was a more beautiful bride, or more stunning wedding presents. The former is a decided brunette and one of the prettiest, most attractive girls that ever came out of Chicago.

The bridegroom, Ensign Mitchell, U. S. A., is as pronounced a blond as she is a brunette, and a good looking young aviator he makes. He is an instructor in the naval aviation camp at Key West, and there the honeymoon will be spent.

The bride of an aviator must be of heroic stuff to keep smiling these days. But that's what our American girls and women are. The whimperer is rare.

Taking things hard—from Ginevra to Joe Mank. That's the stamp that goes into my books so that people can read it blind like Braille.

—*The Crack-Up*

Mr. and Mrs. Charles Garfield King

request the honour of your presence

at the marriage of their daughter

Ginevra

to

Mr. William Hamilton Mitchell

Ensign, Flying Corps, U.S.N.R.F.

on Wednesday, the fourth of September

at four o'clock in the afternoon

St. Chrysostom's Church

Chicago

THE END OF A ONCE POIGNANT STORY

John Peale Bishop

Henry T. Dunn

Alec McKaig

"Sap" Donahoe

Paul B. Dickey

In college I was luckier. I knew the future president of many banks and oil companies, the Governor of Tennessee, and among the intellectuals encountered John Peale Bishop, warbird Elliott Springs, Judge John Biggs and Hamilton Fish Armstrong. Of course I had no idea who they were, and neither did they, or I could have started an autographed tablecloth.

—"My Generation"

pregnant year of endeavor. Outwardly failure with moments of anger but the foundation of my literary life

Twenty years Old

PRINCETON UNIVERSITY

PRINCETON, N. J., FEBRUARY, 1915

The following is the Official Report of the standing of

Francis Scott Fitzgerald

of the Sophomore Class for the term ending February 10, 1915.

Group for Term

Average for Term 4.50 5

Rank in Each Subject:

The numbers immediately following the subjects indicate the course numbers as found in the University Catalogue; the single numbers thereafter indicate the groups attained.

Logic 201 3
Latin 203 5
Chemistry 201 absent min
English 201 3
French 301A 5

EXTRA COURSE FOR ENTRANCE COND.

Latin (extra) 5

Total number of absences incurred during the term 50

A student who for any cause incurs fifty absences in any term or in any two successive terms, must take an extra course the following term.

By order of the Faculty

Registrar.

Disgraceful—but happy

Fitzgerald spent the summer of 1915 at the Montana ranch of his school friend, "Sap" Donahoe. This experience later provided the setting for "The Diamond as Big as the Ritz."

. . . I left Princeton in junior year with a complaint diagnosed as malaria. It transpired, through an X-ray taken a dozen years later, that it had been tuberculosis—a mild case, and after a few months of rest I went back to college. But I had lost certain offices, the chief one was the presidency of the Triangle Club, a musical comedy idea, and also I dropped back a class. To me college would never be the same. There were to be no badges of pride, no medals, after all. It seemed one March afternoon that I had lost every single thing I wanted—and that night was the first time that I hunted down the spectre of womanhood that, for a little while, makes everything else seem unimportant.

—"Pasting It Together"

PRINCETON UNIVERSITY
PRINCETON, NEW JERSEY

OFFICE OF THE
DEAN OF THE COLLEGE

May 8, 1916.

My dear Mr. Fitzgerald:

This is for your sensitive feelings. I hope you will find it soothing. I hope also that your health is very greatly improved and that you will be able to return to the University next autumn in condition to go on to a very satisfactory completion of your course.

Very cordially yours,

Howard McClenahan

To-
F. Scott Fitzgerald, Esq.,
St. Paul, Minn.

Although Fitzgerald returned in the fall of 1915 to repeat his junior year and dropped back a class, he always regarded himself as a member of the class of 1917.

PRINCETON UNIVERSITY
PRINCETON, NEW JERSEY

OFFICE OF THE
DEAN OF THE COLLEGE

May 8, 1916.

TO WHOM IT MAY CONCERN:

This is to certify that Mr. F. Scott Fitzgerald withdrew from Princeton voluntarily on January third, nineteen hundred and sixteen, because of ill health and that he was fully at liberty, at that time, to go on with his class, if his health had permitted.

Howard McClenahan

Dean of the College.

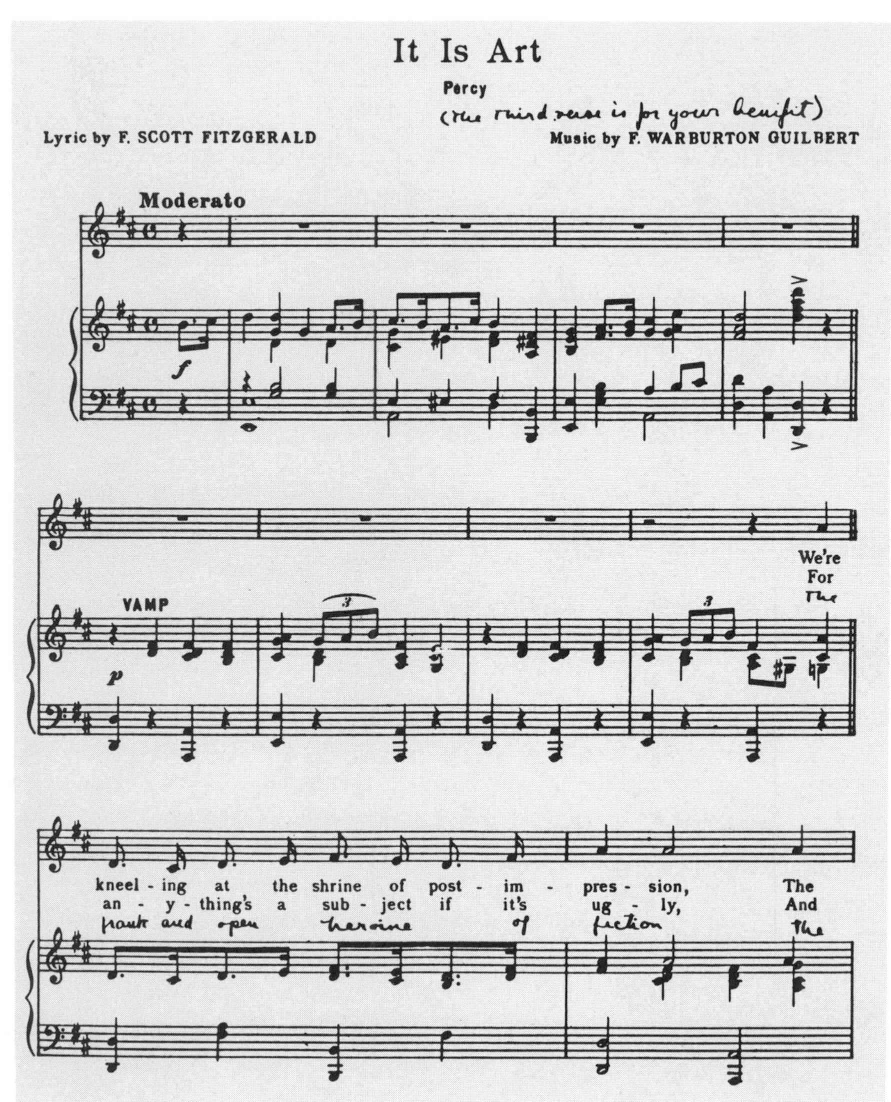

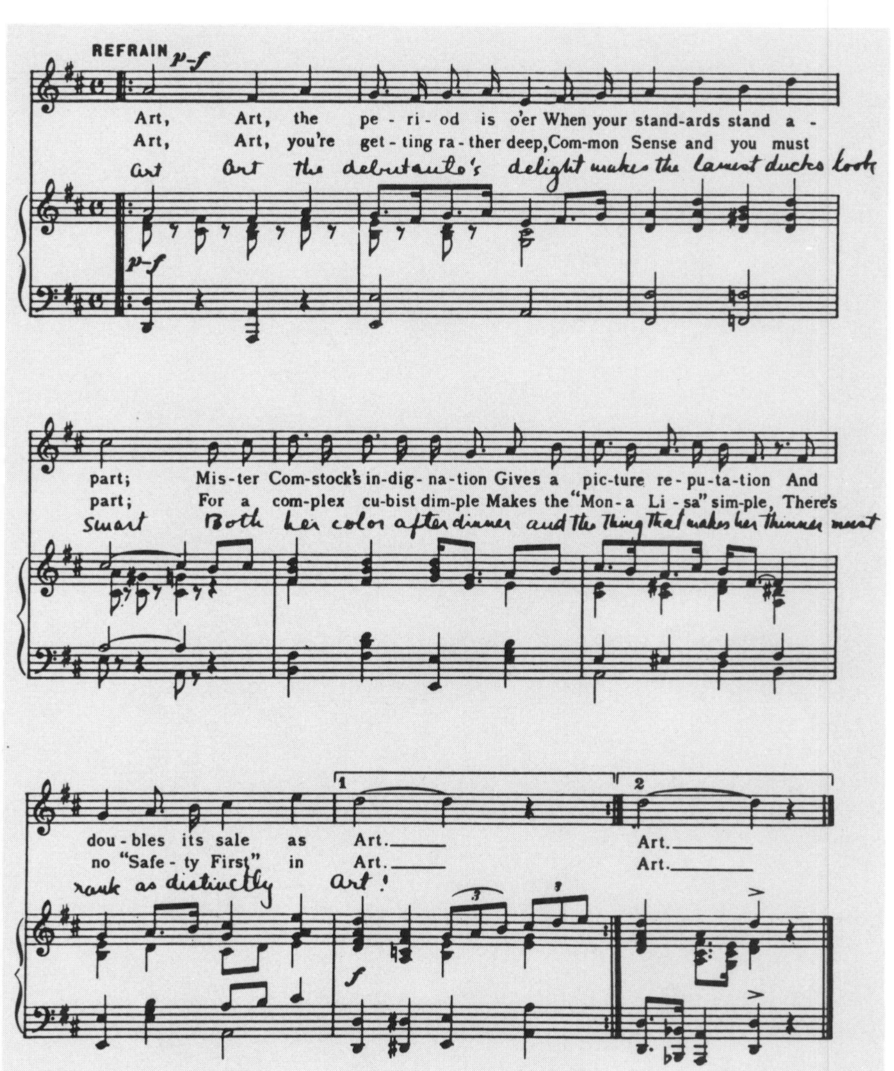

"It is Art" from Safety First (1916), with an additional set of lyrics Fitzgerald wrote for Ruth Sturtevant, a St. Paul friend.

12 **THE PRINCETON TIGER**

CEDRIC THE STOKER.

(The true story of the Battle of the Baltic.)

THE grimy coal-hole of the battleship of the line was hot, and Cedric felt the loss of his parasol keenly. It was his duty to feed the huge furnace that sent the ship rolling over and over in the sea, heated the sailors' bedrooms, and ran the washing machine. Cedric was hard at work. He would fill his hat with a heap of the black coals, carry them to the huge furnace, and throw them in. His hat was now soiled beyond recognition, and try as he might he could not keep his hands clean.

He was interrupted in his work by the jingle of the telephone bell. "Captain wishes to speak to you, Mr. Cedric," said the girl at the exchange. Cedric rushed to the phone.

"How's your mother," asked the Captain.

"Very well, thank you, sir," answered Cedric.

"Is it hot enough for you, down there?" said the Captain.

"Quite," replied Cedric, courteously.

The Captain's voice changed. He would change it every now and then. "Come to my office at once," he said, "we are about to go into action and I wish your advice."

Cedric rushed to th[...]

threw it open. He shrank back, aghast. Bearing down upon them, and only ten miles away, was the huge *Hoboken,* the biggest of all ferry-boats, captured by the enemy from the Erie Railroad in the fall of '92. So close she was that Cedric could read her route sign "Bronx West to Toid Avenoo." The very words struck him numb. On she came, and on, throwing mountains of spray a mile in front of her and several miles to her rear.

"Is she coming fast, boy?" asked the Captain.

"Sir, she's making every bit of a knot an hour," answered Cedric, trembling.

The Captain seized him roughly by the shoulders. "We'll fight to the end," he said; "even though she is faster than we are. Quick! To the cellars, and stoke, stoke, STOKE!!"

Cedric unable to take his
ran backwards down the
elevator shaft, and rushed
carried coal back and fort
nace door, and then back to
of the ship had increased.
in twenty-foot jumps. But
worked more madly, and
he had thrown the last
There [...] nothing [...]

Our American Poets.

I.

Robert Service.

THE red blood throbs
And forms in gobs
On the nose of Hank McPhee.
With a wild "Ha-Ha!" he shoots his pa
Through the frozen artic lea.

II.

Robert Frost.

A rugged young rhymer named Frost,
Once tried to be strong at all cost
The mote in his eye
May be barley or rye,
But his right in that beauty is lost.

Though the meek shall inherit the land,
He prefers a tough bird in the hand,
He puts him in inns,
And feeds him on gins,
And the high brows say, "Isn't he grand?"

F. S. F.

THE STAYING UP ALL NIGHT.

THE warm fire.
The comfortable chairs.
The merry companions.
The stroke of twelve.
The wild suggestion.
The good sports.
The man who hasn't slept for weeks.
The people who have done it before.
The long anecdotes.
The best looking girl yawns.
The forced raillery.
The stroke of one.
The best looking girl goes to bed.
The stroke of two.
The empty pantry.
The lack of firewood.
The second best looking girl goes to bed.
The weather-beaten ones who don't.
The stroke of four.
The dozing off.
The amateur "life of the party."
The burglar scare.
The scornful cat.
The trying to impress the milkman.
The scorn of the milkman.
The lunatic feeling.
The chilly sun.
The stroke of six.
The walk in the garden.
The sneezing.
The early risers.
The volley of wit at you.
The feeble come back.
The tasteless breakfast.
The miserable day.
8 P. M.—Between the sheets.

F. S. F.

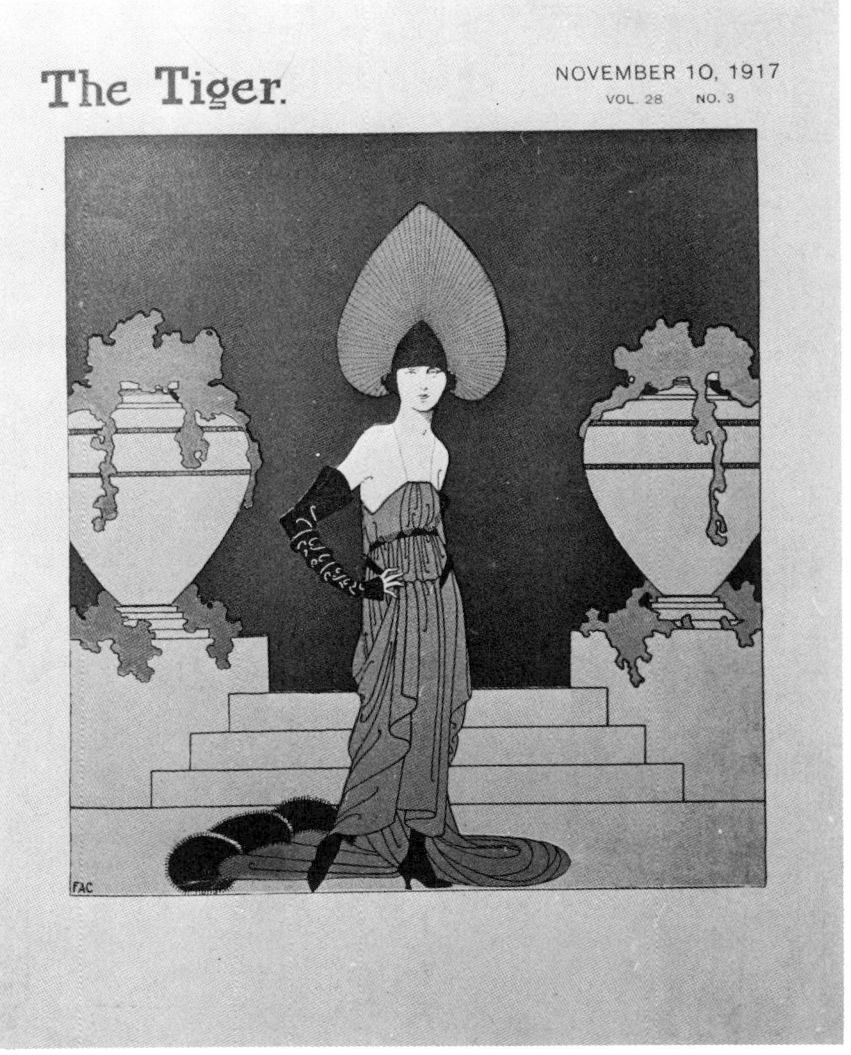

When it was late to press, John Biggs and I used to write whole issues in the interval between darkness and dawn.

—"Princeton"

172 Twenty-one Years Old

A year of enormous importance. Work and Zelda. Last year as a Catholic.

Sept Minnekada Club "Ode to Ginevra". Poet Lore accepts a poem

The Nassau Literary Magazine

VOLUME LXXIII JUNE No. 3

SENTIMENT—AND THE USE OF ROUGE

I.

This story has no moral value. It is about a man who had fought for two years and how he came back to England for two days, and then how he went away again. It is unfortunately one of those stories which must start at the beginning, and the beginning consists merely of a few details. There were two brothers (two

Damned muddle—everything a muddle, everybody offside, and the referee gotten rid of—everybody trying to say that if the referee were there he'd have been on their side. He was going to go and find that old referee—find him—get hold of him, get a good hold—cling to him—cling to him—ask him—.

—F. Scott Fitzgerald.

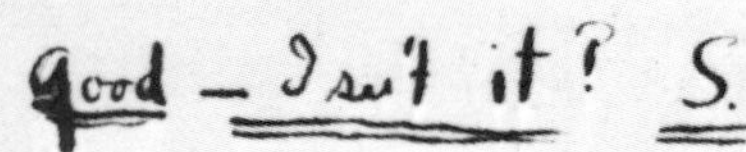

Fitzgerald sent this copy of the Lit to his cousin Cecilia.

Cecilia Delihant Taylor was Fitzgerald's first cousin on the Scott-Key side. She was widowed as a young woman and raised her four daughters in Norfolk, Virginia, where Scott went frequently to visit her and his Aunt Eliza Delihant, his father's sister. He wrote of "Cousin Ceci" as Clara in This Side of Paradise.

She was immemorial. . . . Amory wasn't good enough for Clara, Clara of ripply golden hair, but then no man was. Her goodness was above the prosy morals of the husband-seeker, apart from the dull literature of female virtue.

—*This Side of Paradise*

change Connecting all Departments. Cables

THE POET LORE COMPANY

PUBLISHERS OF BOOKS IN BELLES LETTRES AND

Poet Lore

Title Registered as a Trade Mark

A MAGAZINE OF LETTERS. ESTABLISHED 1889

194 Boylston Street, Boston, U. S. A.

25 September, 1917.

Mr. Scott Fitzgerald,
593 Summit Ave.,
St. Paul, Minn.

My dear Mr. Fitzgerald:

We should be glad to publish THE WAY OF PURGATION in POET LORE, and to furnish you with two copies of the issue containing it.

Trusting that this arrangement may be satisfactory to you, we beg to remain,

Faithfully yours,

RH/MM The Poet Lore Co.

Fitzgerald's first acceptance from a non-school magazine. The poem was never published by Poet Lore.

THE NASSAU HERALD

FRANCIS SCOTT KEY FITZGERALD. "Fitz." He was born in St. Paul, Minn., September 24, 1896, and has lived in St. Paul and in Buffalo, N. Y.

He is the son of Edward Fitzgerald and Mary McQuillan. His father, a graduate of Georgetown, is a broker. He has one sister. Among his relatives is Dr. Samuel C. Chew '56.

Fitzgerald prepared at Saint Paul Academy, St. Paul, Minn., and at the Newman School, Hackensack, N. J. He was on the School Papers and in Dramatics at each.

In Princeton, he has been a member of the Triangle Club, (1) (2) (3), Secretary, (3), editor of the *Tiger* and the *Nassau Literary Magazine*. Whig Hall. Cottage Club. Roman Catholic. Progressive.

Freshman Year he roomed at 15 University Place alone; Sophomore Year in 107 Patton alone; Junior Year in 185 Little, with P. B. Dickey.

Fitzgerald was forced to leave college in December 1915 because of illness. He will pursue graduate work in English at Harvard, then he will engage in newspaper work. His permanent address is 593 Summit Ave., St. Paul, Minn.

The most important year of life. Every emotion and my life work decided. Miserable and ecstatic but a great success.

Sept | Fell in love on the 7th

The President of the United States of America

To all who shall see these presents greeting:

Know Ye, *That reposing special trust and confidence in the patriotism, valor, fidelity, and abilities of* Francis Scott Fitzgerald *I do appoint him* provisionally a second lieutenant of Infantry *in the service of the United States: to rank as such from the* twenty sixth *day of* October, *nineteen hundred and* seventeen. *He is therefore carefully and diligently to discharge the duty of the office to which he is appointed by doing and performing all manner of things thereunto belonging.*

Fitzgerald received his commission as a second lieutenant in the infantry in October 1917 and reported to Fort Leavenworth, Kansas. Although he was ordered overseas, the war ended before he shipped out, producing a life-long sense of disappointment.

About the army, please let's not have either tragedy or Heroics because they are equally distasteful to me. I went into this perfectly cold-bloodedly and don't sympathize with the

"Give my son to country" etc.

etc.

etc.

or

"Hero stuff"

because I just went *and purely for* social reasons. *If you want to pray, pray for my soul and not that I won't get killed—the last doesn't seem to matter particularly and if you are a good Catholic the first ought to.*

To a profound pessimist about life, being in danger is not depressing. I have never been more cheerful. Please be nice and respect my wishes.

—FSF to Mrs. Edward Fitzgerald, 14 November 1917.

Lt. F. Scott Fitzgerald met Zelda Sayre at the Country Club of Montgomery, July 1918.

I am transferred twice and ordered overseas

General Ryan the big goopher

In officers' training camp during 1917 I started to write a novel. I would begin work at it every Saturday afternoon at one and work like mad until midnight. Then I would work at it from six Sunday morning until six Sunday night, when I had to report back to barracks. I was thoroughly enjoying myself.

—"What I Think and Feel at Twenty-five"

CHARLES SCRIBNER'S SONS
PUBLISHERS - IMPORTERS
FIFTH AVENUE AT 48TH STREET
NEW YORK

Aug. 19, 1918.

Lieutenant F. Scott Fitzgerald,
Hq. Co. 67th Infantry,
Camp Sheridan, Ala.

Dear Sir:

We have been reading "The Romantic Egoist" with a very unusual degree of interest;-in fact no ms. novel has come to us for a long time that seemed to display so much originality, and it is therefore hard for us to conclude that we cannot offer to publish it as it stands at present. Of course, in this we are considerably influenced by the prevailing conditions, including a governmental limitation on the number of publications and very severe manufacturing costs which make profitable publication far more difficult than ordinarily; but we are also influenced by certain characteristics of the novel itself. We generally avoid criticism as beyond our function and as likely to be for that reason not unjustly resented by an author but we should like to risk some very general comments this time because, if they seemed to you so far in point that you applied them to a revision of the ms., we should welcome a chance to reconsider its publication.

The chief of these is that the story does not seem to us to work up to a conclusion;-neither the hero's career nor his character are shown to be brought to any stage which justifies an ending. This may be intentional on your part for it is certainly not untrue to life; but it leaves the reader distinctly disappointed and dissatisfied since he has expected him to arrive somewhere either in an actual sense by his response to the war perhaps, or in a psychological one by "finding himself" as for instance Pendennis is brought to do. He does go to the war, but in almost the same spirit that he went to college and school,-because it is simply the thing to do. It seems to us in short that the story does not culminate in anything as it must to justify the reader's interest as he follows it; and that it might be made to do so quite consistently with the characters and with its earlier stages.

It seems to us too that not enough significance is given to some of those salient incidents and scenes, such as the affairs with girls. We do not suggest that you should resort to artificiality by giving a significance inconsistent with that of the life of boys of the age of the hero, but that it would be well if the high points were heightened so far as justifiable; and perhaps this effect could partly be gained by pruning away detail you might find could be spared elsewhere. Quite possibly all that we have said is covered by your own criticism of the ms, as at present a little "crude" and that the revision you contemplate will itself remove the basis of our criticism, and if when you make this you allow us a second reading we shall gladly give it. We do not want anything we have said to make you think we failed to get your idea in the book,-we certainly do not wish you to "conventionalize" it by any means in either form or manner, but only to do those things which it seems to us important to intensify its effect and so satisfy a reader that he will recommend it,-which is the great thing to accomplish toward a success.

We know how busy you are and how absorbed you must be in your present work, and it is rather difficult to think of you as being able to do this revising too; but as you have yourself spoken of it we have less hesitation in making suggestions toward it and in sending back the ms;-we hope we shall see it again and we shall then reread it immediately,-in fact our present delay was due to a misapprehension which led us to think you did not care about an early decision.

Very truly yours,

Charles Scribner's Sons

I can't tell you how I feel about Monsignor Fay's death—He was the best friend I had in the world and last night he seemed so close and so good that I was almost glad—because I think he wanted to die. Deep under it all he had a fear of that blending of the two worlds, that sudden change of values that sometimes happened to him and put a vague unhappiness into the stray corners of his life.

But selfishly I am sorry. Never more "will we drink with the sunlight for lamp Myself and the dead"

—FSF to Shane Leslie, 13 January 1919.

HACKENSACK NJ JAN 11 1919

LT SCOTT K FITZGERALD

17TH BRIGADE HEADQUARTERS CAMPSHERIDAN ALA

MONSIGNEUR FAY DIED AT FIVE PM FRIDAY OF PNEUMONIA FUNERAL TEN OCLOCK TUESDAY MORNING CHURCH OF OUR LADY OF LOURDES NEWYORKCITY COME IF POSSIBLE AND MAKE SCHOOL HEADQUARTERS

C E DILBOS

308AM JAN 12

The end of a story

R 8

FY NEW YORK NY 3PM OCT 25 1918

F SCOTT FITZGERALD

HQRS CO 67 INFY CAMPSHERIDAN ALA

CANNOT DECIDE BEFORE MONDAY HOPE TO WIRE THEN

MAXWELL PERKINS

530PM

The end of a dream

After "The Romantic Egoist" was declined in August by Scribners, Fitzgerald re-wrote it at Camp Sheridan and re-submitted it. Again Scribners declined to publish.

Maxwell E. Perkins, the legendary Scribners editor who became Fitzgerald's lifelong friend and supporter, was just commencing his brilliant career when Fitzgerald submitted his novel.

Shane Leslie, a Scribners author, sent Fitzgerald's novel to Perkins.

PART TWO CHRONOLOGY

ZELDA BEFORE MARRIAGE (1900-1920)

1858
Birth of Anthony D. Sayre in Tuskegee, Alabama.

1860
Birth of Minnie Buckner Machen in Eddyville, Kentucky.

June 1884
Marriage of Anthony Sayre and Minnie Machen at "Mineral Mount," Willis B. Machen's tobacco plantation near Eddyville, Kentucky.

24 July 1900
Birth of Zelda at Sayre home on South Street, Montgomery, Alabama.

1906
Zelda enters grade school but is allowed to withdraw.

1907
Zelda re-enters grade school. The family moves into a house at 6 Pleasant Avenue, her home until her marriage.

1909
Judge Sayre of the City Court is appointed an Associate Justice of the Supreme Court of Alabama.

1914
Zelda enters Sidney Lanier High School.

31 May 1918
Zelda graduates from Sidney Lanier High School.

July 1918
Zelda meets FSF at a country club dance in Montgomery.

August 1918
Scribners returns "The Romantic Egoist." FSF revises it, but by the end of October it is finally rejected.

November 1918
FSF reports to Camp Mills, Long Island, to await departure for overseas. The war ends as his unit is about to ship out.

December 1918
FSF returns to Camp Sheridan and becomes aide-de-camp to the commander, General A. J. Ryan.

February 1919
FSF discharged from army and goes to New York to seek his fortune; finds employment at Barron Collier advertising agency; lives in a room at 200 Claremont Avenue. Informally engaged to Zelda.

Spring 1919
FSF visits Montgomery 3 times as Zelda remains reluctant to commit herself to marriage.

June 1919
Zelda breaks engagement.

Book of Zelda Sayre Fitzgerald

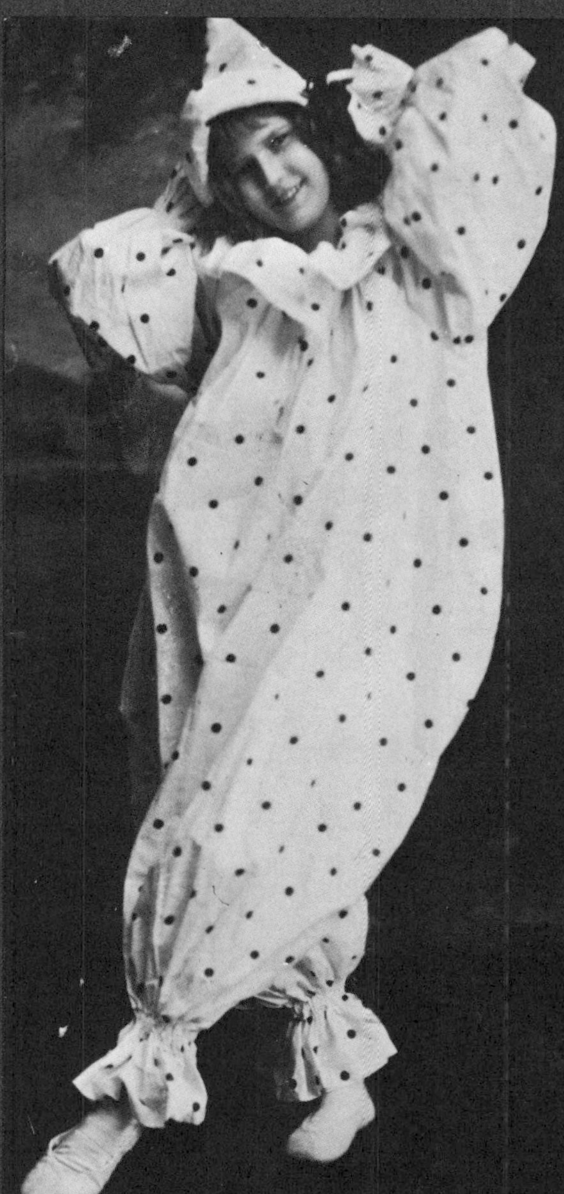

Anthony Dickinson Sayre, c. 1880.

Minnie Machen, c. 1880.

William Sayre arrived in Montgomery in 1819, shortly after Alabama became a state. He brought with him his brother Daniel, aged 11, and raised him in the house which later became the White House of the Confederacy, shown below. He was a merchant and helped found the first Presbyterian church in Montgomery in 1824.

Daniel Sayre, 1808–1888, Zelda's grandfather.

Musidora Morgan Sayre, 1817–1907, Zelda's grandmother.

DEATH OF MR. DANIEL SAYRE.

The Peaceful Close of a Long and Useful Life.

After several weeks of illness, Mr. Daniel Sayre died Saturday night at his home in this city. There was no man better known in Alabama, or who had a wider circle of acquaintances and friends.

He was born in Franklin county, Ohio, January 13th, 1808, and he was therefore in the eighty-first year of his age at the time of his death. He came to Montgomery in 1820, then a boy only twelve years old. He became the editor of the Talladega Watchtower in 1844. He afterwards moved to Tuskegee where he edited and published the Tuskegee Republican, the Whig organ of the staunch old Whig county of Macon. He occupied this position until 1854 when he was elected Grand Secretary of the Grand Lodge of Masons of Alabama, when he moved to this city, where he has ever since resided. Continuously from that time at every meeting of the Grand Lodge he has been chosen to succeed himself as secretary, having ably and satisfactorily filled the position nearly thirty-four years. He had also for many years been the Grand Secretary of the Grand Chapter, and Grand Recorder of the Grand Council and the Grand Commandery of the State. In 1860 Mr. Sayre edited, in connection with Col. J. F. Gaines, with distinguished ability, the Montgomery Post, a paper established by the supporters of Bell and Everett.

Every person in Montgomery knew this beloved and venerable gentleman. He was quiet and unobtrusive, but he had strong views and convictions on all subjects, and never hesitated to express them. It was never a difficult matter to ascertain what he thought on any question of importance. In every sense of the word he was a kind and charitable man, and delighted in doing good for his fellowman. The widow and the orphan found him a sympathizing friend and one ready to help them in times of distress and sorrow.

SISTER OF SENATOR JOHN T. MORGAN GOES TO REWARD.

Was Mother of Judge A. D. Sayre and Had Lived in Capitol City for Seventy-five Years.

At the eventide of life, with the shadows of eternity gathering about her, as a child tired from the stress of a long, long day, Mrs. Musidore Morgan Sayre, only sister of United States Senator John T. Morgan, closed her tired eyes, and, as the first flush of dawn streamed across the horizon yesterday morning, quietly breathed her last and sank to sleep.

For ninety years the presence of this good woman had blessed the world, sowing the seeds of kindness, patience, love and mercy, and to her now has come the time of her reward.

In March, 1817, in the little village of Huntsville, she first saw the light of day, a member of one of the most illustrious of Alabama families.

Fitted by nature to take a first place among the women of the State, she was essentially feminine in her tastes and ambitions. She looked at the world through a pair of bright and discerning eyes and believed in women.

In 1832, with her husband, Colonel Daniel Sayre, she came to Montgomery when the now thriving city was but a village with less than a thousand people. Consequently, she is one of the few of those who have witnessed the growth of Alabama's capitol, through the past seventy-five years, and it was always a pleasure to her friends to hear her talk of the Montgomery of those days compared to the Montgomery of today.

The Daily Post.

DANIEL SAYRE, EDITOR.

MONTGOMERY:

Monday Evening, October 29, 1860.

The Constitution of the Country, the Union of the States, and the Enforcement of the Laws.

The danger of voting for Breckinridge.

The Presidential election is now only one week off, and our *Weekly* that contains this article will be the last one that will reach most of subscribers before they will be called upon to vote upon the great issue now before them. And we should like to say to them a few last words. Perhaps many who read these words will disregard them, but nevertheless, we hope that many will so far consider them as to allow themselvess to be entreated seriously to reflect upon the great matter upon which they have so soon to act.

The issue now before the people of Alabama is not simply whether the State shall be carried by Bell, or Breckinridge, or Douglas; but that other and greater question is before them—Union or disunion; for as the State may go in the present election, so it will be most likely to go when the question of secession shall be presented directly to them, as it will be in case Lincoln should be elected,

The question of breaking up any sort of a government is always a very serious one; and more especially is it a serious one when it refers to such an one as ours, which has existed for upwards of three quarters of a century, the wonder and admiration of the world.—Even supposing it could be done peaceably, and without the firing of a gun, or the shedding of a drop of blood, still it would be the most serious question that can ever be presented to the present generation. Because, if this government is ever dismembered, there is no prospect of its ever again being united. It will probably be dismembered for all time to come, and more likely to be broken again and again, until the fragments will hardly be worth preserving; for when the work of destruction once commences, there is no telling where it will stop. And we commend that thought to the serious consideration of the reader. Even if half a dozen States should agree in forming a confederacy, how long would it last? And supposing that confederacy shouln be again broken, as it is almost certain that it would be, and each of its parts should go off by itself, what sort of government would one of the States make by itself?

U.S. Senator John Tyler Morgan of Alabama, brother of Musidora Morgan Sayre, was a frequent visitor at the Sayre home. It was in part due to his friendship with Senator Machen that Minnie was sent to Montgomery to school, where she met Anthony Sayre.

U.S. Senator Willis B. Machen of Kentucky, 1810–1893, Zelda's maternal grandfather.

Victoria Mims Machen, 1838–1895, third wife of Senator Machen, Zelda's maternal grandmother.

Editorial in the Princeton, Kentucky, Bulletin, April 1861. Colonel Machen was at that time in the State Legislature. After war was declared, he represented Kentucky in the Confederate Congress; in 1872 he was elected to the U.S. Senate by the Legislature.

"The speech delivered by Col. Machen was one worthy of the occasion. It portrayed in true colors, without deviating to the right or left, the issue of the day and the stand Kentucky should take. He maintained that so long as the Star of Hope beamed above the horizon, Kentucky should extend the olive branch of peace to the conflicting sections; heal, if possible, the wounds and perpetuate the Union; then, if every effort had been made, every honorable compromise tendered to the North, she should still cling to the mad fanaticism which now characterizes her, the position, the interests of Kentucky in every respect require her to stake her destiny with the South. Where is the true Kentuckian in whose breast this will not find a hearty 'amen'? None we hope".

Mama says: when she was five yrs old her house on the Cumberland River was shelled. She & her mother, sister & body servants fled to her uncle's house, 8 miles back in the country. When they returned, the house had been demolished so they lived in her father's law office until he sent for them to come to Canada —whither he had fled to escape the persecutions of Lincoln's cabinet, which wanted to hang all confederate senators. When Grant came into office, he pardoned Senator Machen, who then returned to Kentucky & rebuilt his plantation.

—ZF to Scottie, c. 1947.

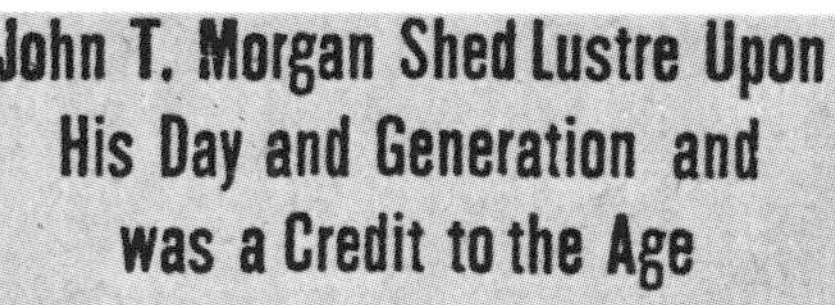

John T. Morgan Shed Lustre Upon His Day and Generation and was a Credit to the Age

BEGAN IN A HUMBLE HOME

From Playmate of Indians in Boyhood He Became a Statesman of the Class of Gladstone, a Lawyer and Legislator of Renown Over the Entire World.

At 11:15 o'clock the knell was rung. Flashing over every wire in the land of America at the same time went the message, short but of momentous import, "Morgan is dead, Alabama's senior senator"—and those hearing the message for a while stopped still. "Morgan is dead, Alabama's senior senator in the United States senate," went the message through the cables that touch a hundred foreign ports, and princes and mighty potentates, who knew of the summons for a moment pondered over the shortness of life, and the fulfillments of its promises.

When the war ended Morgan returned to Selma, where he again entered upon the study of law this time with a large and successful practice, but barely remunerative. Being nominated as a presidential elector at large in 1876, he again canvassed the state and renewed the spell that he had cast over men's minds sixteen years before this time.

Elected to Senate.

Resulting from his splendid canvass, he was elected the ensuing winter a member of the United States senate, defeating the Hon. George S. Houston, who was then Alabama's governor, and since that time had been elected every six years to return to Washington as Alabama's representative.

History will record Morgan as one of the leaders in the movement to build an isthmian canal. By studying judiciously the queston he became the recognized authority on the subject, and to his indefatigable energies in this direction is due, to a great extent, Uncle Sam's determination to begin the great work.

A story of Senator Morgan's career in the senate would take volumes. His figure stands out pre-eminently in every question that the country was confronted with. His speeches were ones to ring all over the United States whenever they were uttered, until at last, when old age came upon him and weakened his voice, the ears of the world's foremost legislative body were bent to hear whatever the silvery-voiced orator had to say.

Died a Poor Man.

Senator Morgan died a poor man. His ideas of wealth were peculiar ones, insomuch that he would not even receive compensation for special articles that he prepared at much expense of time and patience. Beyond his salary as Alabama's representative he had no income, and even prided himself on the fact.

Senator Morgan was a man of the strictest honesty and integrity. He had a power of argument that was fairly amazing. "If he had any weakness," said an esteemed friend of his, talking of him, "it was the readiness with which he poured out the wealth of his ideas on all the leading subjects mooted in the senate."

Early in his life Senator Morgan married Miss Willis, a daughter of a leading merchant in Madison county. Judge A. D. Sayre, of this city, was a nephew of the deceased.

Minnie Machen (right) with her mother and younger sister, c. 1865.

The Montgomery Advertiser.

VOLUME LXXXII. MONTGOMERY, ALABAMA, SUNDAY, MARCH 26, 1911 NUMBER 85

CHILDREN OF THE ALABAMA JUDICIARY

By MARIE BANKHEAD OWEN

ZELDA SAYRE.

One of the rules given to a cub reporter by teh city editor is "When you are interviewing a man don't, if possible, make your notes in his presence".

That is the way Miss Zelda Sayre was interviewed for this story. She had been running with her little playmates and was entirely out of breath. It was an easy matter to catch her therefore and being a friendly and direct little girl in her manner of speech and of thought, she was found to be a fine subject, although unconscious of the purpose of the questions fired at her.

Of course she may resort to a repudiation of the foregoing interview, in which case these columns are open to her gifted pen. It is taken for granted that her pen is gifted because her mother in such a clever writer. Some time ago when Montgomery authors were featured in a local story the name of this brilliant woman, a native of Kentucky, but for many years a loyal Albamian, ranked high up in the list.

One of her short stories called, "The Beasts That Bore Me" was undoubtedly the forerunner and inspiration of a celebrated novel that, appeared a few years ago, the work of a Kentucky girl who was about Zelda Sayre's age when the first story was given to the public.

"What do you like best of every thing?" Miss Zelda was asked when interviewed.

"To play," and evidently she was not attempting to deceive the interviewer for her dancing eyes and merry laughter confirmed the declaration as the other children gathered about, unconsciously interrupting the solemn matters in hand by a game of tag.

"And what games do you prefer?" "Robber", "Indian," came promptly back. "I like them best of all because running is such great fun."

"Do you like story books?" was the next serious question.

"I dearly love them. Reading is my favorite study at school, because there are such beautiful tales in the books."

"And your favorite story?" "Water Babies! O, how I wish poor little Tom could have had a happier life!"

Next to stories, including those in her reading lessons, Miss Zelda likes geography, "because it is true and telsl of interesting countries and people." She thinks Indians are the most entertaining people on earth because they are fearless and "such great riders and swimmers;" and then she is sorry for them becuase she thinks they have not always been fairly treated by white men. She likes moving pictures that portray Indian life.

When asked about music she declared that it was alright but that she liked drawing and painting better and was emphtaic in her opinion that when she was a grown woman she was going to give picture recitals instead of musicals.

She also likes chocolate cream! "I dearly love the theatre and my friends."

Rather a fine interview for a little miss of so few summers! If she were a little mister instead of the little lady she is, it would be a safe prediction to forecast that she would emulate her father who ranks as one of Alabama's ablest judges, or her great uncle, General John T. Morgan, who adorned the Senate of the United States for so many years. It was not thought to ask Miss Zelda how she stood on the suffrage question. It may be that as time goes by she will live in a state when women sit in legislative halls. In that case she begins with the unanimous endorsement of the Editor of the Woman's Page of this publication on the justifiable grounds of old friendship.

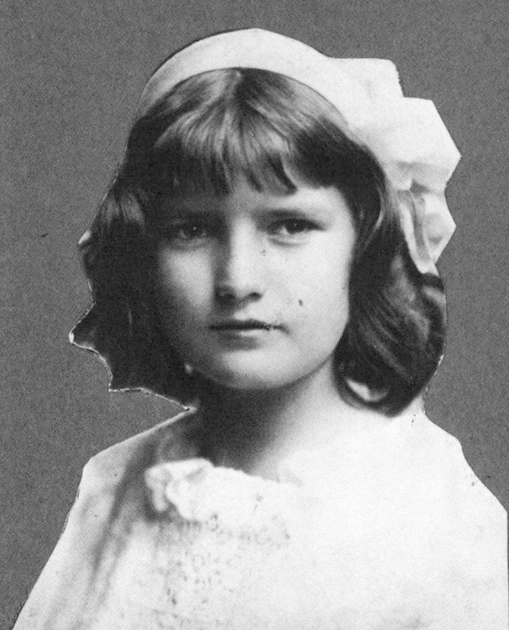

Zelda grew up at 6 Pleasant Avenue in Montgomery. She was born in 1900, the youngest of six children. Her father, a lawyer, had been President of the State Senate and was Judge of the City Court at the time of her birth. From 1909 to 1931 he was an Associate Justice of the Alabama Supreme Court.

Marjorie Sayre, b. 1882.

Rosalind Sayre, b. 1889.
First girl "of good family" in Montgomery to hold a job other than teaching (at the First National Bank).

Clotilde Sayre, b. 1891.
The Beauty, "Joan," in Save Me the Waltz.

"Those girls," people said, "think they can do anything and get away with it."

That was because of the sense of security they felt in their father. He was a living fortress. . . . Judge Beggs entrenched himself in his integrity when he was still a young man; his towers and chapels were builded of intellectual conceptions. So far as any of his intimates knew he left no sloping path near his castle open either to the friendly goatherd or the menacing baron. That inapproachability was the flaw in his brillance which kept him from having become, perhaps, a figure in national politics. The fact that the state looked indulgently upon his superiority absolved his children from the early social efforts necessary in life to construct strongholds for themselves.

* * *

One of Millie Beggs' school friends said that she had never seen a more troublesome brood in her life than those children when they were little. If they cried for something, it was supplied by Millie within her powers or the doctor was called to subjugate the inexorabilities of a world which made, surely, but poor provision for such exceptional babies.

* * *

"If my children are bad," she answered her friend, "I have never seen it."

The sum of her excursions into the irreconcilabilities of the human temperament taught her also a trick of transference that tided her over the birth of the last child. When Austin, roused to a fury by the stagnations of civilization, scattered his disillusions and waning hope for mankind together with his money difficulties about her patient head, she switched her instinctive resentment to the fever in Joan or Dixie's twisted ankle, moving through the sorrows of life with the beatific mournfulness of a Greek chorus. Confronted with the realism of poverty, she steeped her personality in a stoic and unalterable optimism and made herself impervious to the special sorrows pursuing her to the end.

—*Save Me the Waltz* (ZF)

Anthony D. Sayre, Jr., b. 1894, became an Engineer.
An older son, Daniel, died in infancy.

Marjorie's pen-and-ink sketch after a Charles Dana Gibson drawing.
She was considered the "artistic" one.

PAGEANT-MASQUE OF WAR AND PEACE.

On the evening of Friday, March 22, 1918, at eight-thirty the Senior cl[ass] presented a Pageant-Masque of War and Peace, arranged and directed by Miss Rutson Hatchett. The performance was a most excellent and creditable one.

Alice Smith representing Joan of Arc was specially good, while Zelda Sayre as War was excellent. The Faun Dance by Goldye Simon and Sophy Trum was beautiful. Indeed too much praise cannot be accorded the many and lovely characters and their capable teacher, Miss Hatchett.

By many requests it was replayed on Saturday evening, April 13, 1918. The proceeds of the two performances are going to the Alabama boys in France.

WAR PAGEANT
LANIER AUDITORIUM
Cor. Scott and McDonough Streets
Saturday, April 13, 1918
At 8:15 o'clock
ADMISSION 25c
Proceeds to go to the Alabama Boys in France

OVER THE TOP WITH PERSHING

The night was dark, the rain came down,
The boys stepped off with never a frown,
Into the trench all mud and slime,
And thousands of miles from their nat[ive clime.]
They took their places in face of death,
And waited their turn with bated breath
'Till the order came to open fire,
They screwed their courage higher and [higher.]

Then the ready gunner with trigger cock[ed,]
Let go the charge that the cannon rocked
And out of the mist a tongue of flame
Across the darkness wrote his name,
"A red-haired gunner," the message read
"As over the top a volley sped."
And khaki boys on victory bent
Over the top with Pershing went.

Over the top they go to fight
For suffering friends and human right,
Over the top they see their way
To a clearer aim and a freer day,
Over the top, O God of Might
Help our laddies to win the fight..

ZE[LDA]

OVER THE TOP WITH PERSHING.

The night was dark, the rain came
down,
The boys stepped off with never a
frown.
Into the trench all mud and slime,
And thousands of miles from their na-
tive clime.
They took their places in face of
death,
And waited their turn with bated breath
'Till the order came to open fire,
They screwed their courage higher
and higher.

Then the ready gunner with trigger
cocked,
Let go the charge that the cannon
rocked,
And out of the mist a tongue of
flame
Across the darkness wrote his name.
"A red-haired gunner," the message
read
"As over the top a volley sped."
And the khaki boys on victory bent
Over the top with Pershing went.

Over the top they go to fight
For suffering friends and human right,
Over the top they see their way
To a clearer aim and a freer day,
Over the top, O God of Might,
Help our laddies to win the fight.

—Zelda Sayre, '18.

Zelda, top row center.

Zelda, second from right.

Zelda's mother often helped her with her compositions, as evidenced by her quip written on the poem above. A sample of Minnie Sayre's own poetry appears below.

TO CHRISTMAS.

[WRITTEN FOR THE ADVERTISER]

Fair Christian flower with roots in Pagan Earth,
Beloved of Time thy pristine freshness glows,
Upon the breast of ages as at birth,
All Summer tinted 'mid the Winter snows.

Gift of the Sun-God when rude man as child,
Knelt to the great mysterious source of Light,
Warming his heart toward brother man the while
Offering gifts as Nature gave him might.

Caught he the strains with wondering ear, afar,
"Peace on the Earth, on Earth good will to men";
Saw he the faintest glow of Bethlehem's star,
Breathing the dawn of Now from night of Then.

Take up the chant, O world, and sing it free!
Open thy window soul, speeding the Dove!
Over Time's restless waves, Eternity,
Sendeth a living pledge of deathless Love!

—MINNIE MACHEN SAYRE.

JR. PICNIC TO SENIORS 5.(4).18
WHETSTONE'S LAKE
"TUT"
ELEANOR BROWDER
JANE MASSEY
ANNE NELSON
MARGARET TUTTLE
ZELDA SAYRE

PRETTIEST AND HANDSOMEST—To land first place in this race called for marked ability as a campaigner and politician. Zelda Sayre came out in the lead, with Mary Scott again a close second. As handsomest Irby Jones won over Frank Mosley by a small majority.

MOST ATTRACTIVE—Among the girls this race was long, close, and exciting. The votes came in thick and fast for Zelda Sayre, Lurline Pierson and Genie Blue Howard and each of the three had her turn in the lead. The winner was hard to choose, but the final vote brought Zelda Sayre out ahead, with Lurline, then Genie Blue close upon her as seconds. The race was not very close among the boys. Lee Callaway led.

Thirty-Fourth
Annual Commencement
Sidney Lanier High School
Montgomery, Alabama

Grand Theatre
Friday, May 31st, 1918
8:00 P. M.

WHAT WOULD HAPPEN IF—

Eleanor Browder came to school on time?
Zelda Sayre ever said anything serious?
Mary Elmore Persons stopped using big words?
Miss Black ever got angry?
Anne Paul Goldthwaite stopped grinning?
Theodosia Lee ever reported "unprepared"?
Lee Callaway stopped writing "poetry"?
Martha Teague didn't wear a bow of hair-ribbon?
Margaret Hix didn't "stick out her tongue"?
Margaret Dannelly didn't have a "Flivver"?
Wilmer Daniels wasn't a "vamp"?
Birds Terry wasn't popular?

In the afternoon there was a large swimming party at Cobb's Ford. Zelda and Irby proved themselves the champion swimmers of the Senior class. Mr. "Mac" was the best checker player.

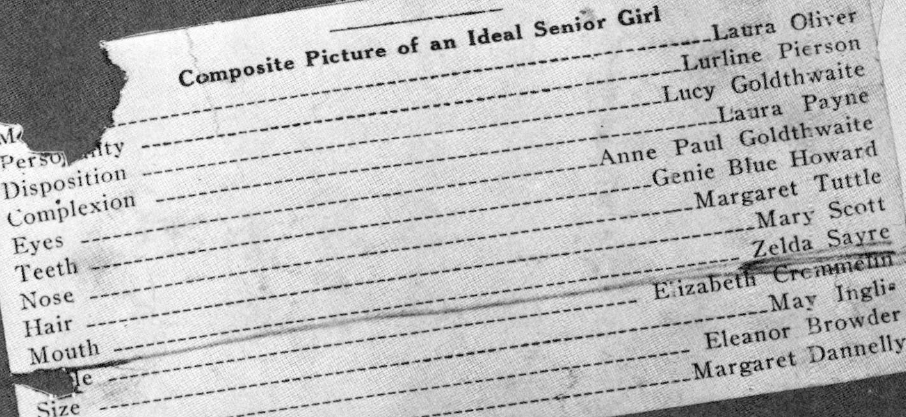

Composite Picture of an Ideal Senior Girl

M...	Laura Oliver
Personality	Lurline Pierson
Disposition	Lucy Goldthwaite
Complexion	Laura Payne
Eyes	Anne Paul Goldthwaite
Teeth	Genie Blue Howard
Nose	Margaret Tuttle
Hair	Mary Scott
Mouth	Zelda Sayre
...le	Elizabeth Cremmelin
Size	May Ingli-
Wit	Eleanor Browder
Athletic Glory	Margaret Dannelly

ZELDA SAYRE
"Why should all life be work, when we all can borrow,
Let's only think of today, and not worry about tomorrow."
Debating Club.
Dramatic Club.

"But oh," laughed Lois, "You never could imagine Elizabeth Adams and Zelda Sayre's occupations. Elizabeth joined the Salvation Army and decided to try and "convert" Zelda. She succeeded so well that now Zelda's stopped dancing at the Follies" and has become matron for an orphan asylum; and wonder of wonders, she hasn't murdered a single orphan—yet!"

Beautiful Ball By Les Mysterieuses.

The ball given Thursday night by Les Mysterieuses at the City Auditorium, was a remarkably brilliant social event.

The auditorium was beautifully decorated and represented fairy land, its plan and adjustment.

A delightful play written by Mrs. A. D. Sayre and staged by her daughter, Mrs. Newman Smith represented "Folly's" Court.

The "Peacock Ball" was recalled by Miss Livye Hart, a picturesque costume and the Red Cross was represented by Miss Myra Whitt and Mr. William Lawrence.

Miss Zelda Sayre, represented "Folly" in a very attractive costume of yellow and black with a staff with a jester's tifully executed "The Folly Dance," with miniature balloons.

The queen wore royal robes of great beauty, and the jester, Miss Goodwyn was attired in a regular yellow smock, adn black with a staff with a jester's head.

An excellent orchestra furnished the music and punch was served during the evening. Boutonieres of yellow ribbons and bells were given at the first dance and serpentine ribbons for the second dance.

"She's the wildest one of the Beggs, but she's a thoroughbred," people said.

Alabama knew everything they said about her—there were so many boys who wanted to "protect" her that she couldn't escape knowing. She leaned back in the swing visualizing herself in her present position.

"Thoroughbred!" she thought, "meaning that I never let them down on the dramatic possibilities of a scene—I give them a damned good show."

—*Save Me the Waltz* (ZF)

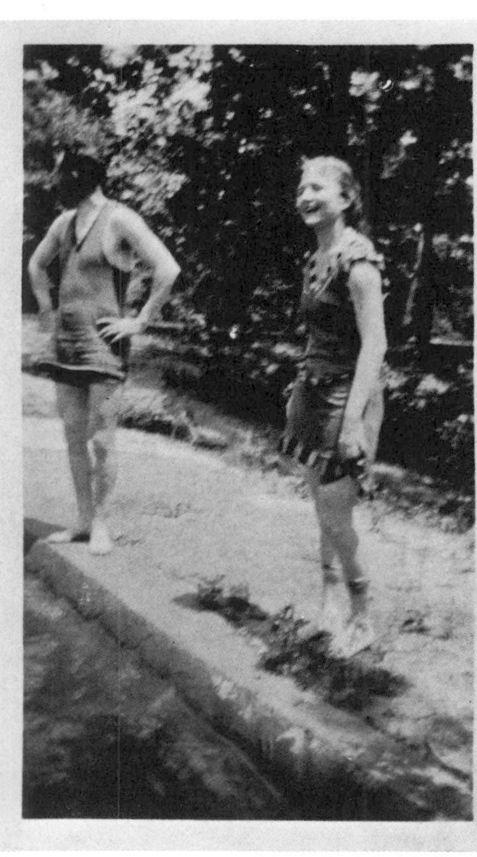

We knew all about each other in Jeffersonville: how each other swam and danced and what time our parents wanted us to be home at night, and what each one of us liked to eat and drink and talk about, so that we all were one against the taller, broader, older youth in uniform which had begun from boredom to invade the ice-cream parlors and the country-club dances, and to change into something serious the casualness of an intimate social world founded on the fact that people like filling the same hours with the same things. We swam at five o'clock because the glare of the sun on the water was too hot to permit swimming before that, but with the advent of a colder-climate-organization that five o'clock swim and the six o'clock soda became self-conscious rituals that moved along more robustly than the long legged, affable young men of Jeffersonville could follow with ease.

There weren't enough girls to go around. Girls too tall or too prim for the taste of Jeffersonville were dragged from their spinsterly pusuits to dance with the soldiers and make them feel less lonely through the summer nights. You can imagine how the popular ones fared! Harriet's sagging veranda was almost completely in uniform. It looked like a recruiting station.

—"Southern Girl" (ZF)

Key-Ice Club

Friday, January 25th, 1918

R. J. Staggers...Leader

Floor Committee

W. A. Leland, Jr. Brewer Dixon

R. J. Staggers

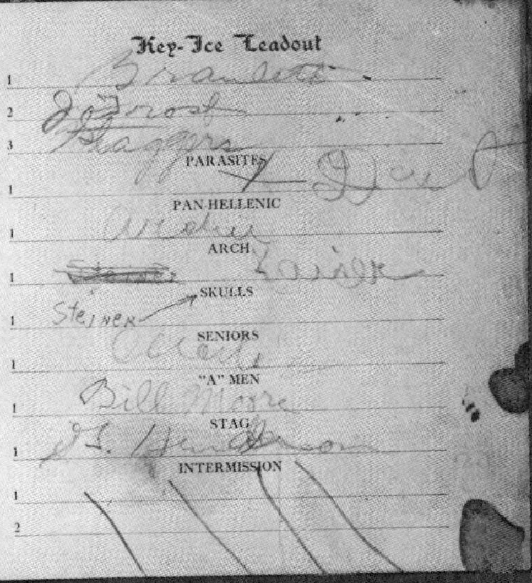
Key-Ice Leadout

1 Brandon
2 J. Frost
3 Staggers
PARASITES
1
PAN-HELLENIC
1
ARCH
1
SKULLS
1 Steiner
SENIORS
1
"A" MEN
1 Bill Moore
STAG
1
INTERMISSION
1
1
2

ANNUAL BANQUET
OF
PHI DELTA THETAS

University of Alabama

KEY ICE

KEY-ICE

Allied Nations Speak to Rotarians Through Lips of Montgomery Maids

Local Rotary Club Stages Remarkably Interesting Patriotic Meeting Last Night

With dozens of visitors as guests, the Montgomery Rotary Club held the largest and most enthusiastic patriotic meeting in its history on Wednesday night at the Exchange Hotel. The management of the hotel tendered the club the use of its main dining room for the event and it was filled with Rotarians and those they brought as their guests.

The Allies There.

America, Roumania, Serbia, Italy, Belgium, England and France spoke to the throng with the lips of charming Montgomery girls, each gowned to represent the country she spoke for. The costumes of the Allied countries were planned by Mrs. C. A. Thigpen, who has always taken keen interest in the work of the Rotary Club.

The young ladies and the countries they represented were:

Miss Janice Weil, Roumania; Miss Theodosia Lee, Serbia; Miss Mary Rushton, Italy; Miss Jean MacDonald, Belgium; Miss Zelda Sayre, England; Miss Elizabeth Thigpen, France; Miss Ruby Page Ferguson, America.

England's Declaration.

England (Miss Zelda Sayre), after summing up her efforts for civilization, asked America for assistance in these staunch words:

"Interrupted in these benevolent pursuits, for over three years I have been engaged in bloody warfare and the end is not yet. O, America, young republic of the West, blood of my blood and faith of my faith, for humanity's sake together we fight! The Stars and Stripes on the battle lines of glorious France have strengthened my hand and filled my heart with cheer. You have been the hope and the inspiration of oppressed peoples and the generous friend of starving nations. In this hour of great peril, the young manhood of your great republic is needed in all of its strength. Prussian militarism must be crushed to earth. To this task I have dedicated my life, confident that the God of nations is on the side of truth and righteousness."

The Cry of France.

France (Miss Elizabeth Thigpen) after telling of the atrocities inflicted upon her by the Huns, made this appeal to her sister republic:

"May we remind you, friend and comrade, O, sister republic that we gave our blood and treasure on your soil that you might attain your birth of freedom. We, after 140 years, are engaged in a bloody struggle to save our life and our liberty. Your cities and farms are not laid waste, mine are despoiled and desolate. Your loved ones are rich and prosperous, my people in large numbers are starving and driven insane with agony. Come on, America, O great democracy—won't you heed our call, won't you hear our appeal? The Maid of Orleans from her hallowed shrine rises with outstretched arms to beckon you on. Lafayette, of cherished memory and beloved of your people, calls to you in the hour of his country's peril to come now.

Girls' Patriotic League

On Wednesday evening from 8 to 10:30 the original unit of the Girl's Patriotic League entertained at a frolic at the Girl's Club in honor of the soldiers and the new units. The club was beautifully decorated in southern smilax, moss and yellow chrysanthemums.

Delicious punch was served from a prettily appointed table by Mrs. Cecil Todd and Misses Marcelle Sabel and Irma Wollner.

In spite of the inclement weather about 125 guests were present. One of the most enjoyable features of the evening was a patriotic dance given by Miss Annie Mary Powers. Miss Lucile Smith was the musician for the evening. A grand march was directed by Miss Edith Kimball, the gymnasium teacher. Sergeant Jerger from the 84th Field Artillery was quite an addition to the party. His sleight of hand tricks created much interest.

The success of the evening was largely due to the following young women who were chairmen of committees: Miss Jeanetta Haas decorating; Mrs. Cecil Todd, refreshments; Misses Isabel Levystein and Zelda Sayre entertainment.

REGIMENTAL ADJUTANT

Alpha Aau Omega Fraternity Entertains—

Montgomery will be very gay socially this Christmas and during the week a number of delightful social functions will be given. The program of activities was opened Monday evening, when the Alpha Tau Omega Fraternity entertained at a brilliant dance at the Country Club. The club was beautiful in its decorations, breathing the very spirit of Christmas-tide, with decorations of smilax, mistletoe, bambo, and holly berries with their scarlet gleam everywhere. The lights were festooned with holly and fraternity colors, sky blue and gold, while at one end of the ball room was the fraternity pin, a Maltese cross, in sky blue and gold electric lights. The excellent Jazz Band of the 46th infantry rendered music and dancing was enjoyed until a late hour, with special lead outs, for the Phi Delta Theta, Sigma Alpha Epsilon, and other fraternities and the Delta Sigma Phi sorority. A feature of the evening was the exquisite solo dance, given by Miss Zelda Sayre, a pretty and popular member of the younger set. Miss Sayre wore a costume of blue and gold tarleton, and gave the dance in a spot light. During the evening, several no break waltzes were given, when all of the lights were extinguished, except that in the fraternity pin.

The clubhouse sprouted inquisitively under the oaks like a squat clump of bulbs piercing the leaves in spring. The car drew up the gravel drive, poking its nose in a round bed of cannas. The ground around the place was as worn and used as the plot before a children's playhouse. The sagging wire about the tennis court, the peeling drab-green paint of the summer house on the first tee, the trickling hydrant, the veranda thick in dust all flavored of the pleasant atmosphere of a natural growth. It is too bad that a bottle of corn liquor exploded in one of the lockers just after the war and burned the place to the ground. So much of the theoretical youth—not just transitory early years, but of the projections and escapes of inadequate people in dramatic times—had wedged itself beneath the low-hung rafters, that the fire destroying this shrine of wartime nostalgias may have been a case of combustion from emotional saturation. No officer could have visited it three times without falling in love, engaging himself to marry and to populate the countryside with little country clubs exactly like it.

—*Save Me the Waltz* (ZF)

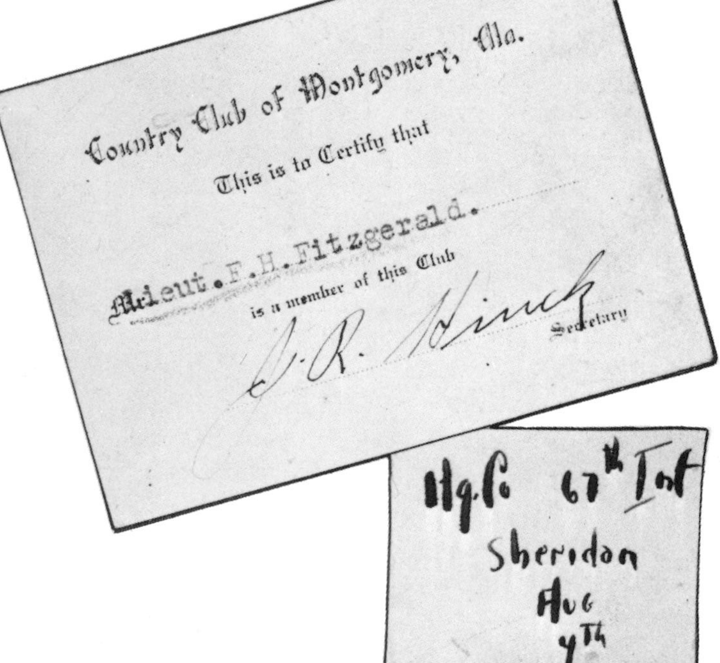

Country Club of Montgomery, Ala.

This is to Certify that

Lieut. F.H. Fitzgerald.

is a member of this Club

Secretary

Hq. Co 67th Inf
Sheridan
Aug
9th

Lt. F. Scott Fitzgerald met Zelda Sayre at the Country Club of Montgomery, July 1918.

A blond lieutenant with one missing insignia mounted the Beggs' steps. He had not bought himself a substitute because he liked imagining the one he had lost in the battle of Alabama to be irreplaceable. There seemed to be some heavenly support beneath his shoulder blades that lifted his feet from the ground in ecstatic suspension, as if he secretly enjoyed the ability to fly but was walking as a compromise to convention. Green gold under the moon, his hair lay in Cellinian frescos and fashionable porticoes over his dented brow. Two hollows over his eyes like the ends of mysterious bolts of fantasy held those expanses of electric blue to the inspiration of his face. The pressure of masculine beauty equilibrated for twenty-two years had made his movements conscious and economized as the steps of a savage transporting a heavy load of rocks on his head.

—*Save Me the Waltz* (ZF)

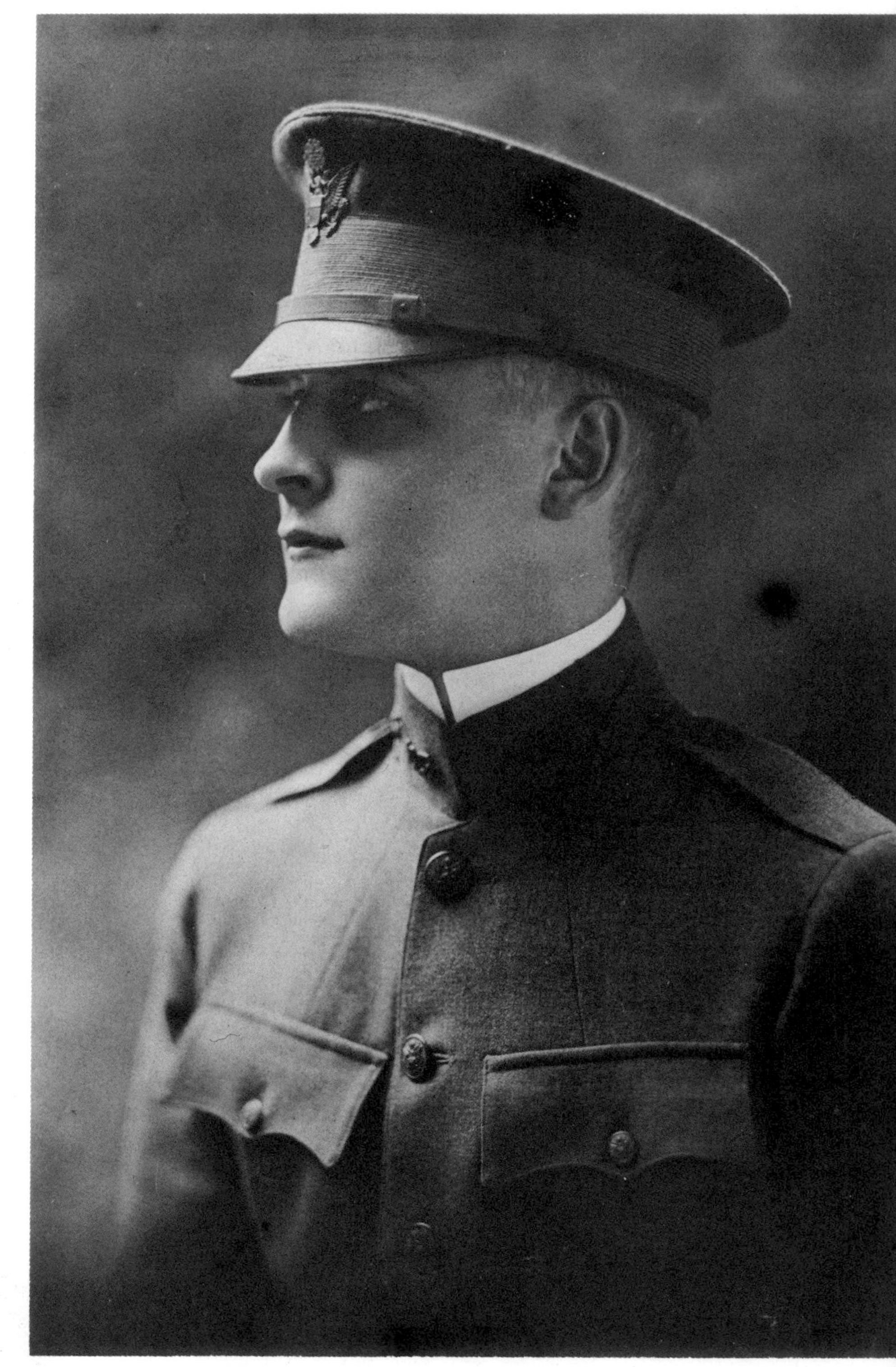

879 Aero Squadron Dance

Election Day

Tuesday, August Thirteenth,
Nineteen Hundred Eighteen
City Auditorium
Montgomery, Alabama

The post library at Camp Sheridan, where Fitzgerald revised "The Romantic Egoist."

4th
O T S
Camp Sheridan
Ala.

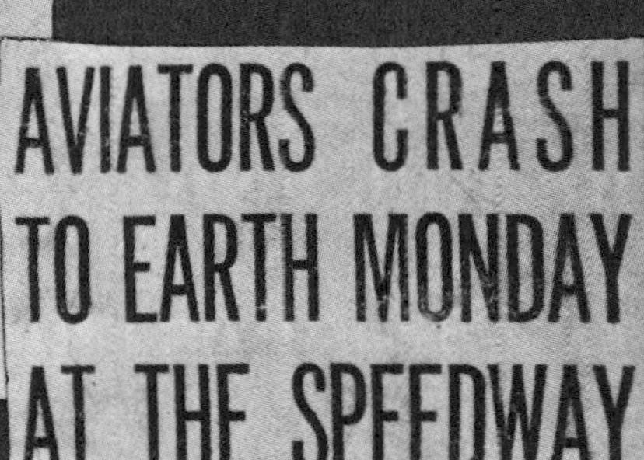

AVIATORS CRASH TO EARTH MONDAY AT THE SPEEDWAY

Henry Watson, of Douglasville, Ga., and Lincoln Weaver, of Wilkinsburg, Pa., Are Badly Injured While Attempting Tailspin.

"War! There's going to be a war!" she thought.

Excitement stretched her heart and lifted her feet so high that she floated over the steps to the waiting automobile.

"There's gonna be a war," she said.

"Then the dance ought to be good tonight," her escort answered.

All night long Alabama thought about the war. Things would disintegrate to new excitements. With adolescent Nietzscheanism, she already planned to escape on the world's reversals from the sense of suffocation that seemed to her to be eclipsing her family, her sisters, and mother. She, she told herself, would move brightly along high places and stop to trespass and admire, and if the fine was a heavy one—well, there was no good in saving up beforehand to pay it. Full of these presumptuous resolves, she promised herself that if, in the future, her soul should come starving and crying for bread it should eat the stone she might have to offer without complaint or remorse. Relentlessly she convinced herself that the only thing of any significance was to take what she wanted when she could. She did her best.

—*Save Me the Waltz* (ZF)

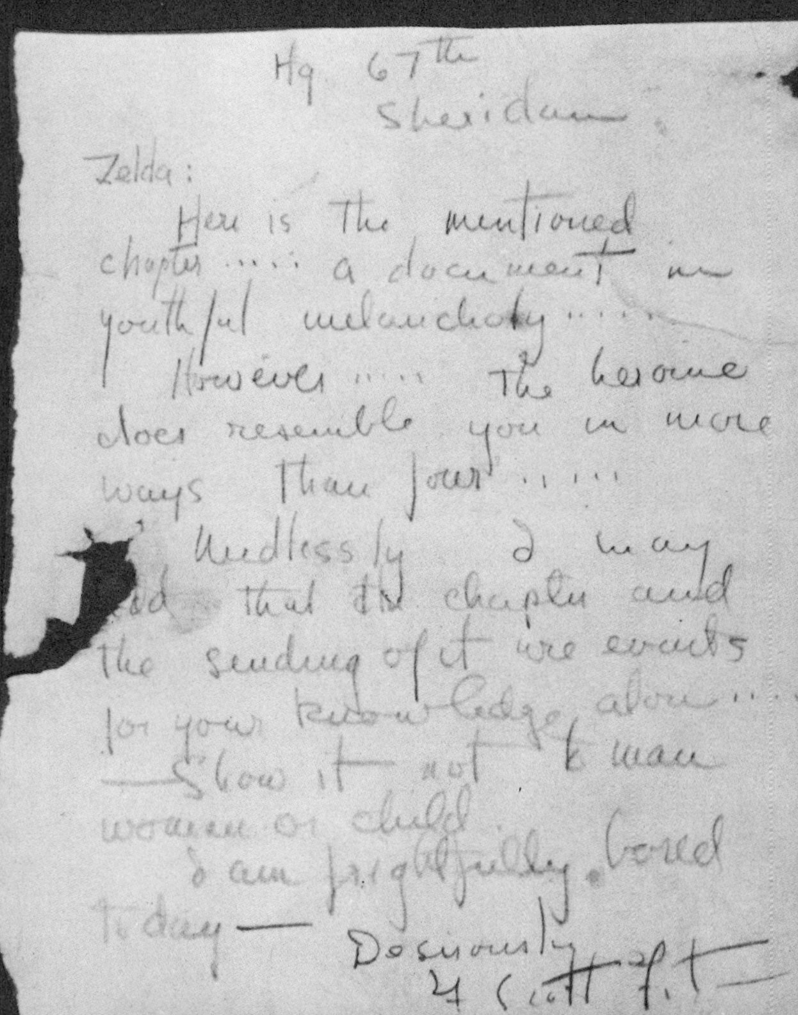

Hq 67th
Sheridan

Zelda:

Here is the mentioned chapter.... a document in youthful melancholy.....

However.... the heroine does resemble you in more ways than four.....

Needlessly I may add that the chapter and the sending of it are events for your knowledge alone....
—Show it not to man woman or child.

I am frightfully bored today—

Deviously
F Scott Fit—

CHARLOTTE N C 122AM FEBY 21ST 1919

MISS TELDA FAYRE

CARE FRANCES STUBBS

AUBURN ALA

YOU KNOW I DO NOT YOU DARLING

SCOTT
1103AM

Stubbs

You are cordially invited to attend the
Social Entertainments
at Auburn
during the week of February twenty-second

Social Committee

Have a date with you Saturday P.M. Sah and Stubbs
F.B.

Miss Zelda Sayre and Miss Livve Hart, two Montgomery belles who have for several years been loyal supporters of Auburn, have been picked as Auburn sponsors and maid.

ALABAMA POLYTECHNIC INSTITUTE
Auburn, Alabama

Mid-W
February

"Pete" Bonner—Picked on Every All-Southern Team—A Genuine Tiger.

MISS SELDA SAYRE

6 PLEASANT AVE MON ALA

329

DARLING HEART AMBITION ENTHUSIASM AND CONFIDENCE I DECLARE EVERYTHING GLORIOUS THIS WORLD IS A GAME AND WHITE I FEEL SURE OF YOU LOVE EVERYTHING IS POSSIBLE I AM IN THE LAND OF AMBITION AND SUCCESS AND MY ONLY HOPE AND FAITH IS THAT MY DARLING HEART WILL BE WITH ME SOON.

HT NEWYORK NY MAR 22 1919

MISS LILDA SAYRE

501

6 PLEASANT AVE MONTGOMERY ALA

DARLING I SENT YOU A LITTLE PRESENT FRIDAY THE RING ARRIVED TONIGHT AND I AM SENDING IT MONDAY I LOVE YOU AND I THOUGHT I WOULD TELL YOU HOW MUCH ON THIS SATURDAY NIGHT WHEN WE OUGHT TO BE TOGETHER DONT LET YOUR FAMILY BE SHOCKED AT MY PRESENT

SCOTT

Montgomery, Ala., Nov. 27.
Pete Bonner:
Care Auburn football team, Piedwont Hotel, Atlanta, Ala.,
Shooting a seven, aren't we awfully proud of the boys, give them my love—knew we could.
ZELDER SAYRE.

Miss Lelda Sayre

Six Pleasant Ave Montgy-Ala.

Sweetheart I have been frightfully busy but you know I have thought of you every minute will write at length tomorrow got your letter and loved it everything looks fine you seem with me always hope and pray to be together soon good night darling.

MISS TELDA SAYRE 620

SIX PLEASANT AVE MONTGOMERY ALA

TELDA FOUND KNOCKOUT LITTLE APARTMENT REASONABLE RATES I HAVE TAKEN IT FROM TWENTY SIXTH SHE MOVES INTO SAME BUILDING EARLY IN MAY BETTER GIVE LETTER TO YOUR FATHER IM SORRY YOURE NERVUS DONT WRITE UNLESS YOU WANT TO I LOVE YOU DEAR EVERYTHING WILL BE MIGHTY FINE ALL MY LOVE

SI NEWYORK NY 250PM APRIL 14 1919

MISS TILDA SAYRE 346

6 PLEASANT AVE MONTGOMERY ALA

AM TAKING APARTMENT IMMEDIATELY RIGHT UNDER TILDES NEW APARTMENT LOVE

SCOTT

I FIND THAT I CANNOT GET A BERTH SOUTH UNTIL FRIDAY OR POSSIBLY SATURDAY NIGHT WHICH MEANS I WONT ARRIVE UNTIL THE ELEVENTH OR TWELFTH PERIOD AS SOON AS I KNOW I WILL WIRE YOU THE SATURDAY EVENING POST HAS JUST TAKEN TWO MORE STORIES PERIOD ALL MY LOVE

Zelda, third from left, with cast of Junior League vaudeville show "for the benefit of Devastated France."

When David left for the port of embarkation, he wrote Alabama letters about New York. Maybe, after all, she would go to New York and marry.

"City of glittering hypotheses," wrote David ecstatically, "chaff from a fairy mill, suspended in penetrating blue! Humanity clings to the streets like flies upon a treacle stream. The tops of the buildings shine like crowns of gold-leaf kings in conference—and oh, my dear, you are my princess and I'd like to keep you shut forever in an ivory tower for my private delectation."

The third time he wrote that about the princess, Alabama asked him not to mention the tower again.

—*Save Me the Waltz* (ZF)

Ordnance Detachment
P. S. & T. Division

DINNER-DANCE

Wednesday, January 23, 1919
Exchange Hotel

ADMIT ONE
TO
SENIOR HOP
GEORGIA TECH.
EAST LAKE COUNTRY CLUB
MON., JUNE 16. '19

When Fitzgerald was discharged from the army in February 1919, he went to New York to seek his fortune in order to marry Zelda, and in his absence bombarded her with telegrams. Unable to find a newspaper job, he went to work for an advertising agency. Meanwhile, Zelda continued to play the role of "Southern Belle" at proms and parties. Scott visited Montgomery three times that spring as Zelda became increasingly restless. When she broke their engagement in June, he quit his job and went home to St. Paul to rewrite his novel.

PART THREE CHRONOLOGY

EARLY SUCCESS & MARRIAGE (1920-1924)

July–August 1919
FSF quits New York job, returns to St. Paul and rewrites novel at 599 Summit Avenue.

September 1919
"Babes in the Woods" published in *The Smart Set,* FSF's first commercial magazine appearance.

16 September 1919
Maxwell Perkins of Scribners accepts *This Side of Paradise.*

November 1919
First sale to *The Saturday Evening Post:* "Head and Shoulders," published February 1920. FSF becomes client of Harold Ober at the Reynolds agency.

November 1919
FSF visits Zelda in Montgomery; engagement resumed.

November 1919–February 1920
The Smart Set publishes "The Debutante," "Porcelain and Pink," "Benediction," and "Dalyrimple Goes Wrong."

Mid-January 1920
FSF lives in a boarding house at 2900 Prytania Street in New Orleans, where he stays less than a month.

March–May 1920
The Saturday Evening Post publishes "Myra Meets His Family," "The Camel's Back," "Bernice Bobs Her Hair," "The Ice Palace," and "The Offshore Pirate."

26 March 1920
Publication of *This Side of Paradise.*

3 April 1920
Marriage at rectory of St. Patrick's Cathedral in New York. Honeymoon at the Biltmore and later at Commodore Hotel.

May–September 1920
Fitzgeralds rent house at Westport, Connecticut.

July 1920
"May Day" in *The Smart Set.*

Summer 1920
FSF and ZF drive their unreliable second-hand Marmon to Montgomery; this trip becomes the basis for "The Cruise of the Rolling Junk." By mid-August they return to Westport.

10 September 1920
Publication of *Flappers and Philosophers,* FSF's first short story collection.

1920
The Chorus Girl's Romance ("Head and Shoulders"), first movie made from FSF work.

October 1920–April 1921
Apartment at 38 West 59th Street, New York City.

May–July 1921
First trip to Europe. Sail to England on the *Aquitania,* then visit France and Italy. Return home on the *Celtic* and visit Montgomery.

Mid-August 1921–September 1922
Fitzgeralds travel to St. Paul; rent a house at Dellwood, White Bear Lake; after birth of their daughter take a house at 646 Goodrich Avenue; in June 1922 move to White Bear Yacht Club for the summer.

September 1921–March 1922
The Beautiful and Damned is serialized in *Metropolitan Magazine.*

26 October 1921
Birth of Scottie.

4 March 1922
Publication of *The Beautiful and Damned.*

June 1922
"The Diamond as Big as the Ritz" in *The Smart Set.*

1922
The Beautiful and Damned made into movie by Warner Bros.

22 September 1922
Publication of *Tales of the Jazz Age,* second collection of short stories.

Mid-October 1922–April 1924
Fitzgeralds rent a house at 6 Gateway Drive in Great Neck, Long Island; Gatsby conceived.

December 1922
"Winter Dreams" in *Metropolitan Magazine.*

27 April 1923
Publication of *The Vegetable.*

November 1923
The Vegetable fails at its tryout in Atlantic City, N.J.

Mid-April 1924
Fitzgeralds sail for France on the *Minnewaska.*

Seventeen years ago this month I quit work or, if you prefer, I retired from business. I was through—let the Street Railway Advertising Company carry along under its own power. I retired, not on my profits, but on my liabilities, which included debts, despair, and a broken engagement and crept home to St. Paul to "finish a novel."

That novel, begun in a training camp late in the war, was my ace in the hole. I had put it aside when I got a job in New York, but I was as constantly aware of it as of the shoe with cardboard in the sole, during all one desolate spring. It was like the fox and goose and the bag of beans. If I stopped working to finish the novel, I lost the girl.

So I struggled on in a business I detested and all the confidence I had garnered at Princeton and in a haughty career as the army's worst aide-de-camp melted gradually away. Lost and forgotten, I walked quickly from certain places—from the pawn shop where one left the field glasses, from prosperous friends whom one met when wearing the suit from before the war—from restaurants after tipping with the last nickel, from busy cheerful offices that were saving the jobs for their own boys from the war.

Even having a first story accepted had not proved very exciting. Dutch Mount and I sat across from each other in a car-card slogan advertising office, and the same mail brought each of us an acceptance from the same magazine—the old *Smart Set*.

"My check was thirty—how much was yours?"

"Thirty-five."

The real blight, however, was that my story had been written in college two years before, and a dozen new ones hadn't even drawn a personal letter. The implication was that I was on the down-grade at twenty-two. I spent the thirty dollars on a magenta feather fan for a girl in Alabama.

—"Early Success"

When I got back to New York in 1919 I was so entangled in life that a period of mellow monasticism in Washington Square was not to be dreamed of. The thing was to make enough money in the advertising business to rent a stuffy apartment for two in the Bronx. The girl concerned had never seen New York but she was wise enough to be rather reluctant. And in a haze of anxiety and unhappiness I passed the four most impressionable months of my life.

New York had all the iridescence of the beginning of the world. The returning troops marched up Fifth Avenue and girls were instinctively drawn East and North toward them—this was the greatest nation and there was gala in the air. As I hovered ghost-like in the Plaza Red Room of a Saturday afternoon, or went to lush and liquid garden parties in the East Sixties or tippled with Princetonians in the Biltmore Bar I was haunted always by my other life—my drab room in the Bronx, my square foot of the subway, my fixation upon the day's letter from Alabama—would it come and what would it say?—my shabby suits, my poverty, and love. While my friends were launching decently into life I had muscled my inadequate bark into midstream. The gilded youth circling around young Constance Bennett in the Club de Vingt, the classmates in the Yale-Princeton Club whooping up our first after-the-war reunion, the atmosphere of the millionaires' houses that I sometimes frequented—these things were empty for me, though I recognized them as impressive scenery and regretted that I was committed to other romance. The most hilarious luncheon table or the most moony cabaret—it was all the same; from them I returned eagerly to my home on Claremont Avenue—home because there might be a letter waiting outside the door. One by one my great dreams of New York became tainted. The remembered charm of Bunny's apartment faded with the rest when I interviewed a blowsy landlady in Greenwich Village. She told me I could bring girls to the room, and the idea filled me with dismay—why should I want to bring girls to my room?—I had a girl. I wandered through the town of 127th Street, resenting its vibrant life; or else I bought cheap theatre seats at Gray's drugstore and tried to lose myself for a few hours in my old passion for Broadway. I was a failure—mediocre at advertising work and unable to get started as a writer. Hating the city, I got roaring, weeping drunk on my last penny and went home. . . .

—"My Lost City"

599 Summit Ave., St. Paul, where Fitzgerald wrote This Side of Paradise.

My friends who were not in love or who had waiting arrangements with "sensible" girls, braced themselves patiently for a long pull. Not I—I was in love with a whirlwind and I must spin a net big enough to catch it out of my head, a head full of trickling nickels and sliding dimes, the incessant music box of the poor. It couldn't be done like that, so when the girl threw me over I went home and finished my novel.

—"Early Success"

Fitzgerald with St. Paul friends (from left) Helen Sloan, Sydney Stronge, Grace Warner, and Lucius P. Ordway, Jr., putting on a mock wedding at a photographer's studio.

13.

Chapter One

Amory, son of Beatrice

Amory Blaine inherited from his mother every trait except the stray inexpressible few that made him worth while. His father, an ineffectual, inarticulate man with a taste for Byron and a habit of drowsing over the Encyclopedia Brittanica, grew wealthy at thirty through the deaths of two elder brothers, successful Chicago brokers, and in the first flush of feeling that the world was his went to Bar Harbor and met Beatrice O'Hara. In consequence Stephen Blaine

The first page of the manuscript of This Side of Paradise. It appears that this chapter was originally to have come later in the book.

Construction of an elaborate "Ice Palace" was a St. Paul institution which so captured Fitzgerald's imagination that he wrote a story about it soon after finishing This Side of Paradise.

It was one of those tragic loves doomed for lack of money, and one day the girl closed it out on the basis of common sense. During a long summer of despair I wrote a novel instead of letters, so it came out all right, but it came out all right for a different person. The man with the jingle of money in his pocket who married the girl a year later would always cherish an abiding distrust, an animosity, toward the leisure class—not the conviction of a revolutionist but the smouldering hatred of a peasant. In the years since then I have never been able to stop wondering where my friends' money came from, nor to stop thinking that at one time a sort of *droit de seigneur* might have been exercised to give one of them my girl.

—"Pasting It Together"

174 Twenty-Three years Old

Revelry and Marriage. The rewards of the year before. The happiest year since I was 18.

Sept Novel accepted Mac Well Seymour. First story sent out. on

CHARLES SCRIBNER'S SONS
PUBLISHERS
FIFTH AVENUE AT 48TH STREET

NEW YORK Sept. 16, 1919.

Dear Mr. Fitzgerald:

I am very glad, personally to be able to write to you that we are all for publishing your book, "This Side of Paradise". Viewing it as the same book that was here before, which in a sense it is, though translated into somewhat different terms and extended further, I think that you have improved it enormously. As the first manuscript did, it abounds in energy and life and it seems to me to be in much better proportion. I was afraid that, when we declined the first manuscript you might be done with us as hopeless conservatives. I am glad you are not. The book is so different that it is hard to prophesy how it will sell, but we are all for taking a chance and supporting it with vigor. As for terms, we shall be glad to pay a royalty of 10% on the first five thousand copies and of 15% thereafter,- which by the way, means more than it used to, as the retail prices upon which the percentage is calculated, have so much advanced.

Hoping to hear from you, we are,

Sincerely yours,
Maxwell E. Perkins

To Mr. F. Scott Fitzgerald
599 Summit Avenue
St. Paul, Minnesota

P.S. Our expectation would be to publish your book in the early Spring. Now, if you are ready to have us do this and have the time, we should be glad to have you get together any publicity matter you could for us, including a photograph. You have been in the advertising game long enough to know the sort of things.

And then, suddenly, everything changed, and this article is about that first wild wind of success and the delicious mist it brings with it. It is a short and precious time—for when the mist rises in a few weeks, or a few months, one finds that the very best is over.

It began to happen in the autumn of 1919 when I was an empty bucket, so mentally blunted with the summer's writing that I'd taken a job repairing car roofs at the Northern Pacific shops. Then the postman rang, and that day I quit work and ran along the streets, stopping automobiles to tell friends and acquaintances about it—my novel *This Side of Paradise* was accepted for publication. That week the postman rang and rang, and I paid off my terrible small debts, bought a suit, and woke up every morning with a world of ineffable toploftiness and promise.

—"Early Success"

Of course I was delighted to get your letter and I've been in a sort of trance all day; not that I doubted you'd take it but at last I have something to show people. It has enough advertisement in St. Paul already to sell several thousand copies & I think Princeton will buy it (I've been a periodical, local Great-Expect[at]*ions for some time in both places.)*

Terms ect I leave to you but one thing I can't relinquish without at least a slight struggle. Would it be utterly impossible for you to publish the book Xmas—or say by February? I have so many things dependent on its success—including of course a girl—not that I expect it to make me a fortune but it will have a psychological effect on me and all my surroundings and besides open up new fields. I'm in that stage where every month counts frantically and seems a cudgel in a fight for happiness against time. Will you let me know more exactly how that difference in time of publication influences the sale & what you mean by "early Spring"?

Excuse this ghastly handwriting but I'm a bit nervous today. I'm beginning (last month) a very ambitious novel called "The Demon Lover" which will probably take a year also I'm writing short stories. I find that what I enjoy writing is always my best—Every young author ought to read Samuel Butler's Note Books.

I'm writing quite a marvellous after-the-war story. Does Mr. Bridges think that they're a little passé or do you think he'd like to see it?

I'll fix up data for advertising and have a photo taken next week with the most gigantic enjoyment (I'm trying H.G. Well's use of vast garagantuan words)

Well thank you for a very happy day and numerous other favors and let me know if I've any possible chance for earlier publication and give my thanks or whatever is in order to Mr. Scribner or whoever else was on the deciding committee.

Probably be East next month or Nov.

P.S. Who picks out the cover? I'd like something that could be a set—look cheerful and important like a Shaw Book. I notice Shaw, Galesworthy & Barrie do that. But Wells doesn't—I wonder why. No need of illustrations is there? I knew a fellow at College who'd have been a wonder for books like mine—a mixture of Aubrey Beardsly, Hogarth & James Montgomery Flagg. But he got killed in the war.

Excuse this immoderately long and rambling letter but I think you'll have to allow me several days for recuperation.

—FSF to Maxwell Perkins, 18 September 1919.

After *This Side of Paradise* had been accepted, Fitzgerald visited Zelda in November 1919 and January 1920, and they became re-engaged.

Property of

F Scott Fitzgerald

2 Record of Published Fiction — Novels, Plays, Stories

Name	Date written	Magazine	Date	English Magazine	Date	Book Published by	Date	English Publisher	Date
The Debutante Play in One Act (Should be second)	April 1919	Smart Set	Nov 1919			Scribner	Mar. 26th '20	Collins	May '21
Babes in the Woods Short Story (First Thing Published)	Jan. 1917	Smart Set	Sept 1919			Scribner	Mar 26 '20	Collins	May '20
Porcelain and Pink Play in One Act	Oct 1919	Smart Set	Jan 1920			Scribner	Oct 1922	Collins	Mar 23
Dalyrimple Goes Wrong Short Story	Sept 1919	Smart Set	Feb 1920			Scribner	Aug 1920	Collins	March 22
Benediction Short Story	Oct 1919	Smart Set	Feb 1920			Scribner	Aug 1920	Collins	March 22
Head and Shoulders Short Story	Nov 1919	Sat. Eve. Post	Feb 21, 1920	Yellow Mag. "Topsy Turvy"	March 1922	Scribner	Aug 1920	Collins	mar '22
Mr. Icky One Act Play	Nov. 1919	Smart Set	Mar. 1920			Scribner	Oct 1922	Collins	mar 23
Myra Meets his Family Short Story	Dec 1919	Sat. Eve. Post	Mar 14, '20	The Sovereign (or Strand?)	July 1921				
This Side of Paradise Novel	Nov '17–Mar '18 July '19–Sept '19	[illegible] S.S. Syndicated				Scribner Hodder + Staughton Australia Capp, Clark + Co. Canada	Mar 26, '20	Collins	May '21
The Camel's Back Short Story	Jan 1920	Sat Eve. Post	April 24, '20	Pearsons	[illegible] 1921	Scribner.	Oct 1922		
						O. Henry Memorial Collection	Dec 1920	Collins	mar '23
The Cut Glass Bowl Short Story	Oct 1919	Scribners	May 1920			Scribner	Aug 1920	Collins	mar '22
Bernice Bobs her Hair Short Story	Jan. 1920	Sat Eve Post	May 3, 1920	Pan(?) or 20 story(?)	[illegible] 1921	Scribner	Aug 1920	Collins	mar '22
The Ice Palace Short Story	Dec. 1919	Sat Eve. Post	May 20, 1920			Scribner	Aug 1920	Collins	mar '22
The Off-Shore Pirate Short Story	Feb 1920	Sat Eve Post	May 29, 1920	The Sovereign	Feb 1922	Scribner	Aug 1920	Collins	mar '22
The Four Fists Short Story	May 1919	Scribners	June 1920			Scribner	Aug 1920	Collins	mar '22
The Smilers Short Story	Sept 1919	Smart Set	June 1920						
May Day Short Story [Very Long]	March 1920	Smart Set	July 1920			Scribner	Oct 1922	Collins	mar '23

The beginning of Fitzgerald's career as a professional author.

1

Contents

3

Produced by	Date	Movie Made by	Sources	Remarks	Disposition
Dramatic Club Univ. Ala. Feb 1921		See T. S. of P.	Play in Nassau Litt Mag January 1917		Included in This Side of Paradise
		See T. S. of P.	Published in Nassau Litt.		Included in This Side of Paradise
Players League april 16th, 1923 Δ March, 1924				2nd Serial "College Stories"	In Tales of the Jazz Age
					In Flappers and Philosophers
			Story in Nassau Litt Mag. June 1915		In Flappers and Philosophers
Bayard Veiller offer turned down		Metro (Dana) "The Chorus Girl's Romance"			In Flappers and Philosophers
			The Usual Thing Nassau Litt. Dec. 1916.		In Tales of the Jazz Age
		Fox (Percy) "The Husband Hunter"	Sitah Meets his Family april 1919	Stripped and —	Permanently Buried
See Debutante		Famous Players	The Romantic Egotist Nov 1917 – Mar 1918 And destroyed stories 1919	Cheap editions, Burt & Collins. Popular Seven 2nd serial Daily News etc	This Side of Paradise
		Still [illegible] Bros "Conductor 1492"			In Tales of the Jazz Age
				O'Brien, two stars	In Flappers and Philosophers
					In Flappers and Philosophers
				Anthology "Trumps"	In Flappers and Philosophers
		Metro (Dana)			In Flappers and Philosophers
				O'Brien, two stars	In Flappers and Philosophers
			Smile Smile, Smile June 1919	Stripped and —	Permanently Buried
					In Tales of the Jazz Age

First pages of the Ledger Fitzgerald kept until 1937, listing everything he wrote and what became of it.

PAUL R. REYNOLDS
70 Fifth Avenue
New York

PAUL R. REYNOLDS
HAROLD OBER

TELEPHONE
CHELSEA 6450

REPRESENTATIVE OF
WM. HEINEMANN
CONSTABLE & CO., LTD.
OF LONDON

CABLE ADDRESS
CARBONATO NEW YORK

November 22,1919.

F. Scott Fitzgerald,
599 Summit Avenue,
St. Paul, Minn.

My Dear Mr. Fitzgerald;

We have sold your story HEAD AND SHOULDERS to the Saturday Evening Post for four hundred dollars ($400.00), provided you are willing to let them omit two or three paragraphs on page 16, referring to the heroine's past. Mr. Lorimer says these seem to him necessary to the working out of the story.

If you can send us other stories as good as this one, I am sure we can do very well with your work. Please let me know if The Post can omit the paragraphs on page 16.

Very truly yours,

Paul R. Reynolds

F. Scott Fitzgerald, Esq.
2900 Prytania Street
New Orleans, La.

Dear Mr. Fitzgerald:

We have sold "The Camel's Back for five hundred dollars. We shall probably get the check next Tuesday and I shall send it on to you at once.

Yours sincerely

Harold Ober

On the strength of the acceptance of This Side of Paradise, *Fitzgerald became a client of the Paul R. Reynolds literary agency, where he was assigned to Harold Ober, commencing a close 20-year association.*

Then there was a pair of white flannels bought with the first money ever earned by writing—thirty dollars from Mencken's and Nathan's old *Smart Set*. The moths had also dined upon a blue feather fan paid for out of a first *Saturday Evening Post* story; it was an engagement present—that together with a southern girl's first corsage of orchids.

—"Auction—Model 1934" (ZF)

Then dinner was over, and he and Jonquil were alone in the room which had seen the beginning of their love affair and the end. It seemed to him long ago and inexpressibly sad. On that sofa he had felt agony and grief such as he would never feel again. He would never be so weak or so tired and miserable and poor. Yet he knew that that boy of fifteen months before had had something, a trust, a warmth that was gone forever. The sensible thing—they had done the sensible thing. He had traded his first youth for strength and carved success out of despair. But with his youth, life had carried away the freshness of his love.

"You won't marry me, will you?" he said quietly.

Jonquil shook her dark head.

* * *

He told her of a despairing two weeks in New York which had terminated with an attractive if not very profitable job in a construction plant in Jersey City. When the Peru business had first presented itself it had not seemed an extraordinary opportunity. He was to be third assistant engineer on the expedition, but only ten of the American party, including eight rodmen and surveyors, had ever reached Cuzco. Ten days later the chief of the expedition was dead of yellow fever. That had been his chance, a chance for anybody but a fool, a marvellous chance—

"A chance for anybody but a fool?" she interrupted innocently.

"Even for a fool," he continued. "It was wonderful. Well, I wired New York——"

"And so," she interrupted again, "they wired that you ought to take a chance?"

"Ought to!" he exclaimed, still leaning back. "That I *had* to. There was no time to lose——"

"Not a minute?"

"Not a minute."

"Not even time for—" she paused.

"For what?"

"Look."

F. Scott Fitzgerald, Esq.
599 Summit Avenue
St. Paul, Minn.

Dear Mr. Fitzgerald:

I have just received a letter this morning from the Saturday Evening Post saying that they will be will glad to keep "The Ice Palace". They will pay four hundred dollars for it.

Yours sincerely

Harold Ober

He bent his head forward suddenly, and she drew herself to him in the same moment, her lips half open like a flower.

"Yes," he whispered into her lips. "There's all the time in the world. . . ."

All the time in the world—his life and hers. But for an instant as he kissed her he knew that though he search through eternity he could never recapture those lost April hours. He might press her close now till the muscles knotted on his arms—she was something desirable and rare that he had fought for and made his own—but never again an intangible whisper in the dusk, or on the breeze of night. . . .

Well, let it pass, he thought; April is over, April is over. There are all kinds of love in the world, but never the same love twice.

—" 'The Sensible Thing' "

Mr. Icky

The Quintessence of Quaintness in One Act

By F.

The Scene is the Exterior ... Cottage in the east part of ... Suffolkshire on a quiet after... in August. Mr. Icky, very qu... dressed in the costume of an ...

BABES IN THE WOODS

By F. Scott Fitzgerald

SHE paused at the top of the staircase. The emotions of divers on spring-boards, leading ladies on opening nights, and ...

coming tonight. He's heard *so* much about you—"

It had pleased her to know this. It put them on more equal terms, although she was accustomed to stage her own romances with or without a send-off.

But following her ...

Porcelain and Pink

(A One-Act Play)

By F. Scott Fitzgerald

A room in the downstairs of a summer cottage ... an art frieze of a fisherman with a pile of nets at ...

Tarquin of Cheapside

By F. Scott Fitzgerald

I

RUNNING footsteps—light, soft-soled shoes made of curious ...

of Flowery Boots leaves a black trail of spots until he binds himself clumsily as he runs, with fine lace caught from his throat.

It was no affair for the watch: Satan was out tonight and Satan seemed to ... appeared dimly in front, heel

The Smilers

By F. Scott Fitzgerald

I

WE all have that exasperated moment!

There are times when you almost tell the harmless old lady next door what you really think of her ...

is the plot. He ... it one story ... He makes ... and end.

The late ... ing pleasant ...

The Diamond as Big as the Ritz

[A Complete Novelette]

By F. Scott Fitzgerald

(Author of "This Side of Paradise," "The Beautiful and Damned," etc.)

CHAPTER I

JOHN T. UNGER came from a family that had been ...

departure. Mrs. Unger, with maternal fatuity, packed his trunks full of linen suits and ...

JUNE, 1922 35 Cents

The SMART SET

Edited by George Jean Nathan and H.L. Mencken.

"The Diamond as Big as the Ritz"

By F. Scott Fitzgerald

A Complete Novelette by the Author of "The Beautiful and Damned"

After the acceptance of his novel, Fitzgerald returned to New York. His short stories were accepted by magazines, and he began to appear regularly in The Smart Set. Although H. L. Mencken and George Jean Nathan welcomed his contributions to their magazine, they did not pay well, and he turned his attention to writing stories for The Saturday Evening Post.

2900 Prytania St.
New Orleans

I certainly touched the depths of depression tonight. The action on that book Madeline, *has knocked hell out of my new novel* "Darling Heart" *which turned completely on the seduction of the girl in the second chapter. I was afraid all along because of Susan Lennox, and the agitation against Drieser but this is the final blow. I don't know what I'll do now—what in hell is the use of trying to write decent fiction if a bunch of old women refuse to let anyone hear the truth!*

I've fallen lately under the influence of an author who's quite changed my point of view. He's a chesnut to you, no doubt, but I've just discovered him—Frank Norris. I think McTeage & Vandover *are both excellent. I told you last November that I'd read* Salt *by his brother Charles and was quite enthusiastic about it. Odd! There are things in "Paradise" that might have been written by Norris—those drunken scenes for instance—in fact all the realism. I wish I'd stuck to it throughout! Another of my discoveries is H.L. Menken who is certainly a factor in present day literature. In fact I'm not so cocksure about things as I was last summer—this fellow Conrad seems to be pretty good after all.*

I've decided I'd rather not use Nathan's name at all in connection with my book and in fact that whole forward strikes me as being rather weak. Couldn't one of your advertising men write it?

I'm glad you're fixing it up about those sub-titles. I'm anxiously awaiting the cover.

Those stories I sold the Post *will start to appear Feb. 21st. I have* Dalyrimple & Bendiction *in the current* Smart Set *& I had a one act play in the January number which got several vaudeville offers. Read it if you can. It was called* Porcelain & Pink *and its excellent.* Smart Set, Scribners & Post *are the only three magazines.*

I'm going to break up the start of my novel & sell it as three little character stories to Smart Set. *I'll only get $40 apiece but no one else would take them, I don't think—and besides I want to have Menken & Nathan hot on my side when my book comes out. As soon as I've done that I'm going to do two or three stories for Mr. Bridges. If I give up the idea of* "Darling Heart" *which I've practically decided to do, at least as a serial and plan not to start my fall novel until June & finish it in August, my idea will be to do 3 stories a month, one for* Smart Set, *one for* Scribners, *and one for the* Post. *The latter are now paying me $600.00 which is a frightful inducement since I'm almost sure I'll get married as soon as my book is out.*

Have you any idea of the date yet? And when my short stories will begin to appear?

P.S. Please forward any mail that may come there for me. I expect to be in New York about the 24th—leave here the 20th.

—FSF to Maxwell Perkins, 3 February 1920.

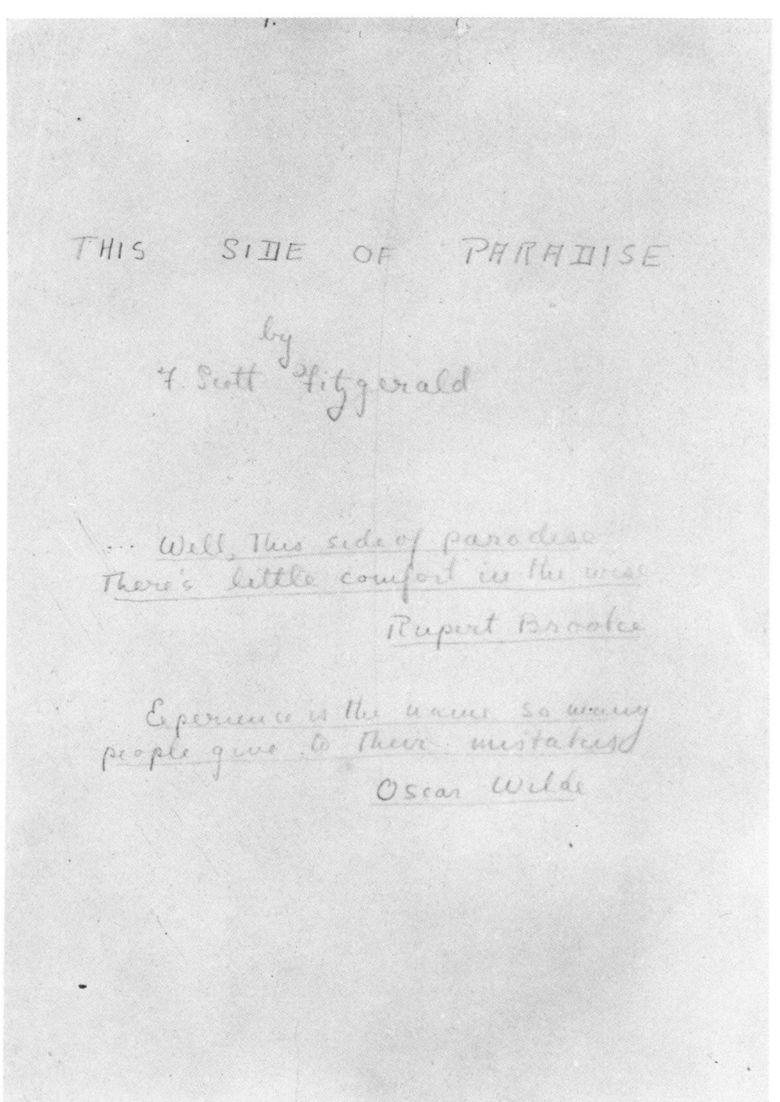

THIS SIDE OF PARADISE

by

F. Scott Fitzgerald

... Well, This side of paradise

There's little comfort in the wise.

Rupert Brooke

Experience is the name so many people give to their mistakes

Oscar Wilde

This Side of Paradise was published on 26 March 1920—a week before Scott and Zelda were married. The novel went through 9 printings in 1920 for a total of 41,000 copies.

THIS SIDE OF PARADISE

By

F. SCOTT FITZGERALD

. . . Well this side of Paradise! . . .
There's little comfort in the wise.
—Rupert Brooke.

Experience is the name so many people give to their mistakes.
—Oscar Wilde.

NEW·YORK
CHARLES SCRIBNER'S SONS
1920

TO
SIGOURNEY FAY

ROSALIND: I can't, Amory. I can't be shut away from the trees and flowers, cooped up in a little flat, waiting for you. You'd hate me in a narrow atmosphere. I'd make you hate me.

(*Again she is blinded by sudden uncontrolled tears.*)

AMORY: Rosalind—

ROSALIND: Oh, darling, go— Don't make it harder! I can't stand it—

AMORY: (*His face drawn, his voice strained*) Do you know what you're saying? Do you mean forever?

(*There is a difference somehow in the quality of their suffering.*)

ROSALIND: Can't you see—

AMORY: I'm afraid I can't if you love me. You're afraid of taking two years' knocks with me.

ROSALIND: I wouldn't be the Rosalind you love.

AMORY: (*A little hysterically*) I can't give you up! I can't, that's all! I've got to have you!

ROSALIND: (*A hard note in her voice*) You're being a baby now.

AMORY: (*Wildly*) I don't care! You're spoiling our lives!

ROSALIND: I'm doing the wise thing, the only thing.

AMORY: Are you going to marry Dawson Ryder?

ROSALIND: Oh, don't ask me. You know I'm old in some ways—in others—well, I'm just a little girl. I like sunshine and pretty things and cheerfulness—and I dread responsibility. I don't want to think about pots and kitchens and brooms. I want to worry whether my legs will get slick and brown when I swim in the summer.

AMORY: And you love me.

ROSALIND: That's just why it has to end. Drifting hurts too much. We can't have any more scenes like this.

—This Side of Paradise

N.Y. Tribune

Books
By Heywood Broun

The enthusiasm in many quarters about F. Scott Fitzgerald's "This Side of Paradise" leaves us not only cold but puzzled. Although the style of the book makes no appeal whatsoever to us, we have not sufficient faith in our ear to be surprised when many other critics say that it is monstrously well written. We are puzzled chiefly because such a number of reviewers find this novel of Princeton life by a young graduate—he is twenty-three, we understand—sensational. For instance, John V. A. Weaver, in "The Chicago Daily News," quotes with apparent wonderment and awe:

"On the Triangle trip, Amory had come into constant contact with that great current American phenomenon, the 'petting-party.' None of the Victorian mothers—and most of them were Victorian—had any idea how casually their daughters were accustomed to be kissed. . . . He never realized how widespread it was until he saw the cities between New York and Chicago as one vast juvenile intrigue. . . . Amory found it rather fascinating to feel that any popular girl he met before 8 he might possibly kiss before 12."

As Bunker Bean remarked, "I can imagine nothing of less consequence."

Even so it is, perhaps, interesting to consider the protest of a Princeton undergraduate who writes: "As a member of the Triangle Club who took the Christmas trip last year, I would like to protest against Fitzgerald's description of 'petting' as a national institution. Although there was a great deal of liquor and much talk of wild women, or, perhaps more accurately, much wild talk of women, I think I can testify to the gentlemanly conduct of a few dozen members, and, of those whose shoulders bore the imprint of blond hair and powdered faces, none, I believe, was later troubled by Mephistophelian visitations."

We are rather afraid that not a few undergraduates are given to the sin of not kissing and then telling anyway. It seems to us that we knew one or two such back in 1910. Still, Amory may have cut just as wide a swath from New York to Chicago as he has led his author to believe. It is, we fancy, a trait of the very young to keep careful statistics of the "rose red dots over the 'i' in 'loving.'" To our mind, Mr. Fitzgerald is a little too old to be another Daisy Ashford, and yet still too immature to qualify as an interesting and faithful observer of life. We do not mean for an instant to imply that the mental reactions of eighteen to twenty-five are not valuable literary material, but we do maintain that the man of that age usually understands himself so imperfectly that he is seldom qualified to describe himself. The self-consciousness of Fitzgerald is a barrier which we are never able to pierce. He sees himself constantly not as a human being, but as a man in a novel or in a play. Every move is a picture and there is a camera man behind each tree.

"I am surprised," our correspondent continues, "that you never mentioned such nauseating love scenes as that which contains the line: 'His lips moved lazily over her face. "How good you taste," he sighed.'"

It is a bit thick, to be sure, and yet we are rather more amused than nauseated. We fancy a demoniac smile flitted across the face of Fitzgerald as he wrote that, and he murmured, "I'll show these mid-Victorians what life in the raw really is."

Perhaps it is this raw! raw! raw! quality which chiefly disturbs our attention and drowns our interest in "This Side of Paradise."

One factor which makes the novel difficult for us is the alien slang which it employs. Thus, when we find that somebody has been awarded "the iron pansy" it takes several seconds for us to realize that he means "the brown derby."

"Our complete characterizer," continues our Princeton correspondent, "has divided the book, like Gaul, into [illegible] parts:
[Im]itation of Booth Tarkington.
[Im]itation of Oscar Wilde.
[Im]itation of H[. G.] Wells."

Chicago Tribune

A Youth in the Saddle; Notes

BY BURTON RASCOE.

If you have not already done so, make a note of the name, F. Scott Fitzgerald. It is borne by a 23 year old novelist who will, unless I am much mistaken, be much heard of hereafter. His first novel, "THIS SIDE OF PARADISE" [Scribner's] gives him, I think, a fair claim to membership in that small squad of contemporary American fictionists who are producing literature. It is sincere, it is honest, it is intelligent, it is handled in an individual manner, it bears the impress, it seems to me, of genius. It is the only adequate study that we have had of the contemporary American in adolescence and young manhood.

F. SCOTT FITZGERALD
PHOTO © WHITE

Beside it Tarkington's "Seventeen," Johnston's "Stover at Yale," and Samuel Merwin's yarns are amusing and superficial sketches. Here are not the obviously ridiculous episodes of youth, the maturely callow reflections upon callow sentiments; but the truth about prep school boys and American collegians by a young man who has just emerged from their experiences.

Ten years from now, it seems safe to say, Mr. Fitzgerald could not have written this book. He may—I think he will—write better books; but, ten years from now, he could not, probably, give us so sincere a record of the activities, the reactions, the reflections, and the problems of the adolescent and immature. At 35 the episodes herein related would have taken on a more romantic cast; nostalgia would have empurpled the grayest fact; the skepticism of age would have discounted the relevance of important points; and caution would have killed its charming frankness.

As a picture of contemporary life, and as an indication of codes of conduct obtaining among the American young, the novel is revelatory and valuable. It is a comment upon the times. It shows definitely that, whatever the teachings of our elders, the Victorian checks, taboos, and reticences are no longer in force among the flappers, the debutantes, and collegians of the present generation. The handsome youth in the novel assures us that his prospects of kissing before midnight a girl he has met at 8 are fairly well assured; and that unchaperoned "petting" on sink-down sofas is an established diversion among the younger set in enlightened communities between New York and San Francisco. The young women are shrewd, sophisticated, slightly cynical, capable of taking care of themselves—that is to say, of planning their lives to their own advantage.

The love affairs in this book, rapid and numerous as they are, are delightful; they, too, are chivalric and romantic (while they last), showing the inevitable power of illusion in youth. They are productive also of exalted emotions and depth of feeling, for all the young author's shrewd analysis of them. Yes, this is a sardonic yet splendid and fascinating book.

TABLOID BOOK REVIEW
By Fannie Butcher

Best sellers for the past week at Brentano's:

"THIS SIDE OF PARADISE," by F. Scott Fitzgerald. (Scribners). A story of the very youthful young told by one who knows the ropes.

"BLACKSHEEP! BLACKSHEEP!" by Meredith Nicholson. (Scribners). Respectable clubman finds himself member-in-good-standing of biggest crook gang in country.

"WOMAN TRIUMPHANT," by Blasco Ibanez. (Dutton). Great artist, after years of earnest endeavor to find his ideal of beauty, finds it in his wife.

"THE EYE OF ZEITOON," by Talbott Mundy. (Bobbs-Merrill). Story of the African jungle.

"SUNNY DUCROW," by Henry St. John Cooper. (Putnam). Red-haired cockney actress proves her motto: "Nothing is impossible so long as you hold up your head."

"SARAH AND HER DAUGHTER," by Bertha Pearl. (Scott & Seltzer). Life on the East Side of New York around Essex and Hester streets. Cleverely done.

"PETER JAMESON," by Gilbert Franklin. (Knoff). Modern English romance.

Public Library (Fifth avenue and Forty-second street) has had more demands for the following seven books of popular fiction within the last week:

"THIS SIDE OF PARADISE," by F. Scott Fitzgerald.

"TATTERDEMALION," by John Galsworthy. Post-bellum state of mind and war episodes.

"BLACKSHEEP! BLACKSHEEP!" by Meredith Nicholson.

"PORTEGEE," by Joseph Lincoln. Modern story of Cape Cod folk.

"MAN OF THE FOREST," by Zane Grey. Story of a United States western forester.

"WOMAN TRIUMPHANT," by Ibanez.

"HARVEST," by Mrs. Humphry Ward. Forests in England; farmerettes and war.

On Second Thought

By JAY E. HOUSE

The exact measure of Mr. F. Scott Fitzgerald's talent as a writing man remains in controversy. Upon that point we have no opinion worth expressing, but we bow in admiration of the realism of his presentations. He is, we believe, the only writing man relying entirely on sex contact for his motif, who boldly permits the hero to kiss the heroine before he becomes engaged to her.

* * *

Mr. Fitzgerald is ridiculously young—only twenty-three, to be exact. But his stories indicate that in so far as he has experimented with life, he has lived it.

* * *

The Catholic *intelligentsia* often show curious imbecilities, perhaps because the American clergy, on the æsthetic side, share the general backwardness of the country. I hear from the Jesuits that they are now furiously against F. Scott Fitzgerald, the finest artist that the faith has thrown off in 20 years. These same critics, two or three years ago, were trying to set up Joyce Kilmer as a great poet.

Balt. Sun

BRITTISH CRITISISM

THIS SIDE OF PARADISE.

THIS SIDE OF PARADISE, by F. SCOTT FITZGERALD (Collins, 7s. 6d. net) will interest readers less for its own sake than as evidence of the intellectual and moral reaction that has set in among the more advanced American circles. As a novel, it is rather tiresome; its values are less human than literary, and its characters, men and women alike, with hardly an exception, a set of exasperating *poseurs*, whose conversation, devoted largely to minute self-analysis, is artificial beyond belief. Consider, for example, the following fragment of a conversation that is supposed to take place between a boy of fifteen and his mother:—

London Times

"Are you quite well now, Beatrice?"
"Quite well—as well as I will ever be. I am not understood, Amory. I know that can't express it to you, Amory, but—I am not understood."
Amory was quite moved. He put his arm round his mother, rubbing his head gently against her shoulder.
"Poor Beatrice—poor Beatrice."
"Tell me about *you*, Amory. Did you have two horrible years?"
Amory considered lying, and then decided against it.
"No, Beatrice. I enjoyed it. I adapted myself to the bourgeoisie. I became conventional."

Is such a dialogue credible, even in America, where black cats are doubtless blacker and egoists more fantastically self-absorbed than in our less precocious European countries?

YOUNG AMERICA?

THIS SIDE OF PARADISE. By F. Scott Fitzgerald. London: W. Collins, Sons, and Co. Pp. 292. 7s. 6d. net.

Mr. Fitzgerald's book is not negligible, and it raises many moral issues. There is some queer, poor, semi-occult stuff about the devil being after the hero, which we may take as middling nightmare, and altogether it is long odds on hell against heaven. The world is not as bad as that, and, indeed, the world is not like that. The women in the book, with one uninteresting exception, are horrid, and if they are the fine flower of civilisation it is time to try Bolshevism. Thrown over by one hussy, the hero takes to drink and is pulled up by Prohibition. He achieves sacrifice, but the impulse is analysed to the point of negation. His poverty and bitter disillusion are well done, and the story winds up with a good revolutionary lecture; very cleverly Mr. Fitzgerald lets us see that this is experimental, opinion in the making. The man has gained self-knowledge, and that is all. Perhaps it is enough. But what people! What a set! They are well lost. A. N. M.

Manchester Guardian

NOVELS.

THIS SIDE OF PARADISE. By F. Scott Fitzgerald. London: Collins. 7/6.

This, it appears, is a first novel by a young American which has already sold 30,000 copies in America and is still in demand. For ourselves, we are more blasé in the matter of "clever first novels" than American readers: we get too many of them to review, and, unfortunately for our appreciation of them, they almost invariably identify themselves with an obsession of the sex problem. The book is clever, eager, keenly impressionistic, yet neurotic, scarcely healthy. While pretending to represent a section of the young intellectual American with money and brains, it concerns itself mainly with almost intolerable juvenile intrigue, and "ragging" at college. Despite his wealth and position, the hero starts with such a handicap that it is a wonder he does not come off more badly than the ending would show—it, by the way, faintly excites one with the hope that a sequel is to follow.

A DEPRESSING WORLD.

London Daily news

"This Side of Paradise." By F. Scott Fitzgerald. Collins. 7s. 6d. net.

If Mr. Fitzgerald had a little more passion he might be a good satirist. This novel of American life suffers from the weakness which is liable to attack all thesis fiction; it is amusing as an essay on the girls and boys of to-day; but the author is so preoccupied with his account of manners that he has taken insufficient pains to vitalise his characters. Amory, his hero, after a boyhood of vivid eccentricity, goes to school and college and lingers over the photograph of a college football captain—a sad declension into normality. He has nervous vigour, and rags, flirts, drinks, and philosophises with the scattered energy of undirected leisure. He goes to the war, and his time there is only sketched for us in a few letters: in one of them Amory sums up his generation's attitude in the epigram, "I think four men have discovered Paris to one that discovered God."

BOOKS AND OTHER THINGS.

By ROBERT C. BENCHLEY.

Copyright, 1920, by the Press Publishing Co. (The New York World).

One of the troubles with writing book reviews is that one has so little time for reading. I never seem to be able to catch up with the new books. For weeks and weeks people have been writing and talking about young Mr. F. Scott Fitzgerald's "This Side of Paradise" (Scribners), and I have been intending to read it, so that the young man might not have to wait too long before finding out what I thought about his first book. I really owed it to Mr. Fitzgerald, it seemed to me. So I read it and liked it.

As an account of the career of a boy through preparatory school, Princeton, love and life, "This Side of Paradise" may not be a great book. Frankly, I don't know a great book when I see one. I have to wait and find out what other people think about it. But in spite of its immaturity, its ingenuousness and its many false notes, it is something *new*, and for this alone Mr. Fitzgerald deserves a crown of something very expensive.

He tells a story in a new way, without regard to rules or convention, and it is an interesting story. In these days when any one can (and does) turn out a book which has been done hundreds of times before and bids fair to be done hundreds of times again, simply by following Stevenson's advice and playing "the sedulous ape" to successful predecessors, I should be inclined to hail as a genius any twenty-three-year-old author who can think up something new and say it in a new way so that it will be interesting to a great many people.

Mr. Fitzgerald's characters are very clever most of the time. Especially when they are making love. I may have been particularly gauche about my own love-making, but as I remember it (and I am corroborated in this by the only other witness) the affair did not go off anywhere near so smoothly or cleverly as that of Mr. Fitzgerald's Amory (aged twenty-three) and Rosalind (aged nineteen). It was Mr. Fitzgerald's whim to write this scene in the manner of a play.

"He—You and I are somewhat alike—except that I'm years older in experience.
"She—How old are you?
"He—Almost twenty-three. You?
"She—Nineteen—just.
"He—I suppose you're the product of a fashionable school.
"She—No, I'm fairly raw material. I was expelled from Spence—I've forgotten why.
"He—What's your general trend?
"She—Oh, I'm bright, quite selfish, emotional when aroused, fond of admiration——
"He (suddenly)—I don't want to fall in love with you——
"She (raising her eyebrows)—Nobody asked you to.
"He (continuing coldly)—But I probably will. I love your mouth.
"She—Hush! Please don't fall in love with my mouth—hair, eyes, shoulders, slippers—but not my mouth. Everybody falls in love with my mouth.
"He—It's quite beautiful.
"She—It's too small.
"He—No, it isn't—let's see.
(He kisses her again with the same thoroughness.)
"She (rather moved)—Say something sweet.
"He (frightened)—Lord help me!
"She (drawing away)—Well, don't, if it's so hard.
"He—Shall we pretend? So soon?
"She—We haven't the same standards of time as other people.
"He—Already it's—other people.
"She—Let's pretend.
"He—No, I can't; it's sentiment.
"She—You're not sentimental?
"He—No, I'm romantic—a sentimental person thinks things will last—a romantic person hopes against hope that they won't. Sentiment is emotional."

Either Mr. Fitzgerald got tired or Amory and Rosalind had just a little good stuff worked up in advance and used it all at their first meeting. Two weeks is a short time for a couple of high-class conversationalists to go bad in. Maybe they were really in love.

A Batch of Novels.—F. Scott Fitzgerald's "This Side of Paradise" (Scribner's, $1.75), a clever young writer's first story, reads like a biography. The career of Amory Blaine, who calls his mother by her first name, is followed from his pampered childhood in a Western town, up through Princeton and then to New York where he yields to all the city's allurements. The novel's central figure is an egotistic, unprincipled philandering youth, who seems to be a fair example of our non-Catholic college's output. Amory's friend and counselor, Monsignor Darcy, mildly regretted that the boy had not been brought up a Catholic and felt "sure he would be much safer anchored to the Church," but Amory thought that "There was a certain intrinsic lack in those to whom orthodox religion was necessary," so he ends as a Socialist. If the parties to Amory's various love-affairs are faithful portraits of the modern American girl, the country is going to the dogs rapidly.—

BOOKS OF THE HOUR IN ENGLAND

N.Y. Eve. By SHANE LESLIE Post

American books launched on the English market are being sampled and sipped rather than read. "Main Street" may be true to Middle Western life, but the English reader can only judge it by a literary standard. Scott Fitzgerald's "This Side of Paradise" has received a start through the publication in a review of the real names of characters in the book, such as Henry Adams and Monsignor Fay. The English reader knows where he is in a "roman à clef." Fitzgerald's Monsignor D'Arcy is thought the best of that ilk since Disraeli sketched Monsignor Capel as Catesby in "Lothair."

Proposed exhibit of Fitzgeraldiania for Chas. Scribner's Sons

(Borrowed from J. P. B.)

Original copy of Rupert Brooke's poems from which title was taken

Old writing desk of the Fitzgerald family found in the attic of the family mansion at St. Paul

Three double malted milks from Joe's

The Original Petting Shirt worn by Amory Blaine

Overseas cap never worn over seas

Copy of Sinister Street (borrowed from E. W.) used as inspiration for T. S. of P.

Genevra King's letters and photographs

Map of Montgomery, Alabama, with X, marking spot where the murder was committed

Three stones from Patton Hall

1 bottle of Oleaqua

Original cocktail shaker used by Amory Blaine

Bound copy of the Mann Act

Entire Fitzgerald library consisting of seven books, one of them a notebook and two made up of press clippings

Original MS of first printed work of Fitzgerald's - Shadow Laurels -

Photograph of Newman foot-ball team with Fitzgerald as half-back (with certificate signed by the Headmaster and vouching for the genuineness of the photograph)

First Brooks suit worn by Fitzgerald

Automobile given away by Fitzgerald in Cincinnati, - purchased and restored by the Government

First yellow silk shirt worn by Fitzgerald at the beginning of his great success

Mirror

P.B. Ew.

THE BOOKMAN'S MONTHLY SCORE 373

FICTION IN DEMAND AT PUBLIC LIBRARIES

COMPILED BY FRANK PARKER STOCKBRIDGE IN COOPERATION WITH THE AMERICAN LIBRARY ASSOCIATION

The following lists of books in demand in October in the public libraries of the United States have been compiled from reports made by two hundred representative libraries, in every section of the country and in cities of all sizes down to ten thousand population. The order of choice is as stated by the librarians.

NEW YORK AND NEW ENGLAND STATES

1. The Portygee	*Joseph C. Lincoln*	APPLETON
2. Kindred of the Dust	*Peter B. Kyne*	COSMOPOLITAN
3. Harriet and the Piper	*Kathleen Norris*	DOUBLEDAY
4. The Top of the World	*Ethel M. Dell*	PUTNAM
5. The Great Impersonation	*E. Phillips Oppenheim*	LITTLE, BROWN
6. Mary Marie	*Eleanor H. Porter*	HOUGHTON

SOUTH ATLANTIC STATES

1. The Top of the World	*Ethel M. Dell*	PUTNAM
2. The Book of Susan	*Lee Wilson Dodd*	DUTTON
3. Kindred of the Dust	*Peter B. Kyne*	COSMOPOLITAN
4. Harriet and the Piper	*Kathleen Norris*	DOUBLEDAY
5. A Poor Wise Man	*Mary Roberts Rinehart*	DORAN
6. This Side of Paradise	*F. Scott Fitzgerald*	SCRIBNER

NORTH CENTRAL STATES

1. This Side of Paradise	*F. Scott Fitzgerald*	SCRIBNER
2. Harriet and the Piper	*Kathleen Norris*	DOUBLEDAY
3. A Man for the Ages	*Irving Bacheller*	BOBBS-MERRILL
4. The Top of the World	*Ethel M. Dell*	PUTNAM
5. The Valley of Silent Men	*James Oliver Curwood*	COSMOPOLITAN
6. Woman Triumphant	*Vicente Blasco Ibáñez*	DUTTON

SOUTH CENTRAL STATES

1. This Side of Paradise	*F. Scott Fitzgerald*	SCRIBNER
2. Kindred of the Dust	*Peter B. Kyne*	COSMOPOLITAN
3. The Valley of Silent Men	*James Oliver Curwood*	COSMOPOLITAN
4. The Great Impersonation	*E. Phillips Oppenheim*	LITTLE, BROWN
5. The Man of the Forest	*Zane Grey*	HARPER
6. The Great Desire	*Alexander Black*	HARPER

WESTERN STATES

1. Kindred of the Dust	*Peter B. Kyne*	COSMOPOLITAN
2. The Foolish Lovers	*St. John Ervine*	MACMILLAN
3. The Moon and Sixpence	*W. Somerset Maugham*	DORAN
4. The Man of the Forest	*Zane Grey*	HARPER
5. The Valley of Silent Men	*James Oliver Curwood*	COSMOPOLITAN
6. This Side of Paradise	*F. Scott Fitzgerald*	SCRIBNER

FOR THE WHOLE UNITED STATES

1. This Side of Paradise	*F. Scott Fitzgerald*	SCRIBNER
2. Kindred of the Dust	*Peter B. Kyne*	COSMOPOLITAN
3. Harriet and the Piper	*Kathleen Norris*	DOUBLEDAY
4. The Top of the World	*Ethel M. Dell*	PUTN M
5. The Portygee	*Joseph C. Lincoln*	APPL
6. The Valley of Silent Men	*James Oliver Curwood*	COSMOPO

With its publication I had reached a stage of manic depressive insanity. Rage and bliss alternated hour by hour. A lot of people thought it was a fake, and perhaps it was, and a lot of others thought it was a lie, which it was not. In a daze I gave out an interview—I told what a great writer I was and how I'd achieved the heights. Heywood Broun, who was on my trail, simply quoted it with the comment that I seemed to be a very self-satisfied young man, and for some days I was notably poor company. I invited him to lunch and in a kindly way told him that it was too bad he had let his life slide away without accomplishing anything. He had just turned thirty and it was about then that I wrote a line which certain people will not let me forget: "She was a faded but still lovely woman of twenty-seven."

In a daze I told the Scribner Company that I didn't expect my novel to sell more than twenty thousand copies and when the laughter died away I was told that a sale of five thousand was excellent for a first novel. I think it was a week after publication that it passed the twenty thousand mark, but I took myself so seriously that I didn't even think it was funny.

—"Early Success"

Fitzgerald's college friends, John Peale Bishop and Edmund Wilson, compiled this list for a proposed exhibit in Scribners' bookstore window as a playful comment on Fitzgerald's sudden fame.

FALSE STANDARDS OF LIFE

Beatrice Fairfax Urges Girls to Believe in the Higher Ideals.

By Beatrice Fairfax.

Who Occupies a Unique Position in the Writing World as an Authority on the Problems of Girls.

THE heroine of the story was young and beautiful and rich and possessed of whatever is current to-day for the "good breeding, once supposed to be a requisite for heroines of impeccable social position. And the most important content of her vocabulary was "Shut up."

"Shut up!"

That was almost inevitably her rejoinder to any suggestion made by the poor gentleman who happened to be her guardian and her uncle. When any situation arose to threaten her own selfish certainty that whatever she wished ought to be hers and whatever anyone else wished for her ought to be flung overboard, she disposed of it by a casual "Shut up."

The author who created the "shut up" girl is young, too. He knows to-day. He writes of it uncritically, perhaps with a certain youthful enjoyment in its daring. He doesn't doubt that his heroine is alluring and charming and the sort of young thing whom men desire. He accepts her—"shut up," stockingless feet, selfishness and all such charming qualities. And the reason he accepts her is because he's part of to-day and to-day has lost its way and is groping blindly without realizing that it is blind.

The older generation, however, remembering a less jazz-full, clothesless day stands off sorrowfully and mourns for the decadence of modern life.

"PETTING"

On the Triangle trip Amory had come into constant contact with that great current American phenomenon, the "petting party."

None of the Victorian mothers—and most of the mothers were Victorian—had any idea how casually their daughters were accustomed to be kissed. "*Servant*-girls are that way," says Mrs. Huston-Carmelite to her popular daughter. "They are kissed first and proposed to afterward."

But the Popular Daughter becomes engaged every six months between sixteen and twenty-two, when she arranges a match with young Hambell, of Cambell & Hambell, who fatuously considers himself her first love, and between engagements the P. D. (she is selected by the cut-in system at dances, which favors the survival of the fittest) has other sentimental last kisses in the moonlight, or the firelight, or the outer darkness.

Amory saw girls doing things that even in his memory would have been impossible: eating three-o'clock, after-dance suppers in impossible cafés, talking of every side of life with an air half of earnestness, half of mockery, yet with a furtive excitement that Amory considered stood for a real moral let-down. But he never realized how widespread it was until he saw the cities between New York and Chicago as one vast juvenile intrigue.

* * *

The "belle" had become the "flirt," the "flirt" had become the "baby vamp." The "belle" had five or six callers every afternoon. If the P.D., by some strange accident, has two, it is made pretty uncomfortable for the one who hasn't a date with her. The "belle" was surrounded by a dozen men in the intermissions between dances. Try to find the P. D. between dances, just *try* to find her.

The same girl . . . deep in an atmosphere of jungle music and the questioning of moral codes. Amory found it rather fascinating to feel that any popular girl he met before eight he might quite possibly kiss before twelve.

—This Side of Paradise

The Conning Tower

To our notion Mr. F. Scott Fitzgerald's "This Side of Paradise" is sloppy and cocky; impudent instead of confident; and verbose. It is doubtful whether the Scribner proofreading is at fault for the numerous errors; and if they are the author's, they indicate a sloppy carelessness that it will pay Mr. Fitzgerald to overcome.

He speaks, for example, of "Frank on the Mississippi." The book is "Frank on the Lower Mississippi," as any slippered pantaloon who used to read Harry Castlemon will recall. Other instances of Mr. Fitzgerald's disregard for accuracy follow:

Ashville
Collar and Daniel's "First-Year Latin"
Mary Roberts Rhinehart
cut a swathe
[Swinburne's] "Poems and Ballades"
"Jenny Gerhardt"
[Compton] McKenzie
Fanny Hurst
Lorelie
"Ghunga Dhin"
flambuoyant
"Come Into the Garden, Maude"
flare [for *flair*]
[Arnold] Bennet
Gouveneer Morris

"My, How That Boy

THIS SIDE OF PARADISE

BY F. SCOTT FITZGERALD

Have You Read It? A Novel About Princeton

READ WHAT THEY SAY

THE NEW YORK TIMES SAYS:
"The glorious spirit of abounding youth glows throughout this fascinating tale. As a picture of the daily existence of what we call loosely 'college men', this book is as nearly perfect as such a work could be. It could have been written only by an artist who knows how to balance his values, plus a delightful literary style."

WILLIAM LYON PHELPS SAYS IN THE YALE ALUMNI WEEKLY:
"One of the best stories of college life in America I have ever read. The author will go far, and I shall read everything he publishes in book form."

E. W. OSBORN, LITERARY EDITOR OF THE NEW YORK WORLD, PROCLAIMS it "one of the season's brilliancies and bewilderingly interesting."

JOHN BLACK, OF THE BROOKLYN EAGLE, SAYS: "The most independent, daring and challenging adventure in American fiction since Dreisler's early days."

THE NEW YORK EVENING POST SAYS: "A very enlivening book, indeed, a book really brilliant and glamorous, making as agreeable reading as could be asked."

HARRY E. DOUNCE, LITERARY EDITOR OF THE NEW YORK SUN, calls it the most promising first novel by an American novelist which has ever come to him in his work as reviewer.

BURTON RASCOE OF THE CHICAGO TRIBUNE, SAYS: "It bears the impress, it seems to me, of genius. It is the only adequate study that we have had of the contemporary American in adolescence and young manhood."

At Bookstores Everywhere $1.75

CHARLES SCRIBNER'S SONS, Publishers

More than a best-seller—a national tonic

FOR THE WHOLE UNITED STATES

1.	This Side of Paradise	*F. Scott Fitzgerald*	SCRIBNER
2.	Kindred of the Dust	*Peter B. Kyne*	COSMOPOLITAN
3.	Harriet and the Piper	*Kathleen Norris*	DOUBLEDAY
4.	The Top of the World	*Ethel M. Dell*	PUTNAM
5.	The Portygee	*Joseph C. Lincoln*	APPLETON
6.	The Valley of Silent Men	*James Oliver Curwood*	COSMOPOLITAN

(From Frank Parker Stockbridge's October score of fiction in demand at public libraries, compiled for the Bookman in cooperation with the American Library Association: see December Bookman.)

"Make it a Fitzgerald Christmas" My God!

Charles Scribner's  **Sons, Publishers**

FIFTH AVENUE AT 48th STREET, NEW YORK

Fitzgerald Can Write!"

—Harry Hansen, Literary Editor, Chicago News.

THIS SIDE OF PARADISE

BY F. SCOTT FITZGERALD

Written by a Princeton Man

THE HARVARD CRIMSON SAYS: "The story is a little slice carved out of real life, running over with youth and jazz and sentiment and romance and virile American humor —everything in short that is dear to a Princeton man (Mr. Fitzgerald himself) or a Yale man, or a Harvard man, or just any kind of a man."

THE DAILY DARTMOUTH SAYS: "'This Side of Paradise' should be read by every Dartmouth undergraduate, if for no other reason than the tremendous insight it gives him into life at another, and somewhat differe nt college."

THE LITERARY CRITIC OF THE CHICAGO DAILY NEWS WRITES:

Advertising Manager,
Charles Scribner's Sons,,
New York City.

Dear ———

My, how that boy Fitzgerald can write! I have just had a wonderful evening with "This Side of Paradise." It is probably one of the few really American novels extant. Most writers feel that if they want to portray American life they have got to go down to the steel mills or into a mining town. Can you imagine any college man passing up this book? I don't know what the book will do but I know I will back it up to the last ditch as real writing.

Cordially yours,
(Signed) HARRY HANSEN.

F. SCOTT FITZGERALD

Fifth Avenue at 48th Street, New York

Life

Rhymed Reviews

This Side of Paradise

(By F. Scott Fitzgerald. Chas. Scribner's Sons)

OF Amory let others boast
  As brilliant, handsome, great or greater;
I celebrate him as a most
  Extraordinary osculator.

On meeting any kindly maid,
  To introduce himself, he'd kiss her;
But, fie! how soon the fickle blade
  Would condescendingly dismiss her!

He let his noble presence give
  To Princeton's halls an august blessing.
His fellow students let him live.
  (How Princeton must be retrogressing!)

He wrote some poems, rather thin,
  Like most young springals—Heaven speed them!
But was it fair to put them in
  A book like this to make you read them?

He won the war; then played a part
  In further billing, likewise cooing;
But Rosalind she broke his heart,
  A thing that really needed doing.

And now at twenty-three or four,
  So old, so wise, so proud about it,
So sadly brave, if slightly sore,
  He cries, "I know myself!"—I doubt it.

He knows that Pride may have a fall;
  That Life hath stings as well as honey;
But can he know himself at all
  Who never dreams that he is funny?

Precocious children, hold! enough!
  But will they stop it? Never, never.
They know they write such clever stuff,
  But not that it is stuff, though clever.

Arthur Guiterman.

Alec Waugh, 17-Year-Old Author, the Missing Link Between Daisy Ashford and C. Scott Fitzgerald

adv

"Young Mr. Waugh is amazing," says a New York *Post* review of Alec Waugh's book, "The Loom of Youth" (Doran), written when the author was seventeen years old. "He is the missing link between Daisy Ashford at nine and F. Scott Fitzgerald at twenty-three. If the successful fiction of the future is to be written by audacious children what are our deans of literature to do? Sit at their feet and relearn the art?"

"And, Amory, we're beautiful, I know. I'm sure God loves us—"

"He loves you. You're his most precious possession."

"I'm not his, I'm yours. Amory, I belong to you. For the first time I regret all the other kisses; now I know how much a kiss can mean."

—This Side of Paradise

MISS ZELDA SAYRE
SIX PLEASANT AVE MONTGOMERY ALA

DEAR YOUR LETTER JUST CAME I HAD COUNTED ON YOUR LEAVING MONTGOMERY ON THE THIRTIETH OF THIS MONTH BUT IF YOU ARE READY TO COME EARLIER SAY ON THE TWENTIETH WIRE ME TODAY YOU KNOW I WANT YOU ALL THE TIME DEAREST GIRL YOUR PICTURE HAS NOT COME AM WRITING

NCETON NJ 1117AM MAR 23 1920
MISS ZELDA SAYRE
6 PLEASANT AVE MONTGOMERY ALA

GOOD MORNING ZELDA DEAR YOU KNOW I DO
SCOTT

NJ NEWYORK NY MAR 30 1920
MISS TILLA SAYRE
6 PLEASANT AVE MONTGOMERY ALA

TALKED WITH JOHN PALMER AND ROSALIND AND WE THINK BEST TO GET MARRIED SATURDAY NOON WE WILL BE AWFULLY NERVOUS UNTIL IT IS OVER AND WOULD GET NO REST BY WAITING UNTIL MONDAY FIRST EDITION OF THE BOOK IS SOLD OUT ADDRESS COTTAGE UNTIL THURSDAY AND SCRIBNERS AFTER THAT
LOVE
SCOTT

Darling Heart, our fairy tale is almost ended, and we're going to marry and live happily ever afterward just like the princess in her tower who worried you so much — and made me so very cross by her constant recurrence — I'm so sorry for all the times I've been mean and hateful — for all the miserable minutes I've caused you when we could have been so happy. You deserve so much — so very much —

I think our life together will be like these last four days — and I do want to marry you — even if you do think I "dread it" — I wish you hadn't said that — I'm not afraid of anything — To be afraid a person has either to be a coward or very great and big. I am neither. Besides, I know you can take much better care of me than I can, and I'll always be very, very happy with you — except sometimes when we engage in our weekly debates — and even then I rather enjoy myself. I like being very calm and masterful, while you become emotional and sulky. I don't care whether you think so or not — I do.

Here are 3 more pictures I unearthed from a heap of clothes under my bed — [illegible]

Our honored mother had disposed of 'em for reasons of her own, but personally I like the attitude of my emaciated limbs, so I solicit your approval. [illegible] waxed artistic and ruined one —

Sweetheart — I miss you so — I love you so — and next time I'm going back with you — I'm absolutely nothing without you — just the doll that I should have been born — You're a necessity and a luxury and a darling, precious lover — and you're going to be a husband to your wife —

Zelda's love letter to Scott, written shortly before their marriage.

Next time you're in New York I want you to meet Zelda because she's very beautiful and very wise and very brave as you can imagine—but she's a perfect baby and a more irresponsible pair than we'll be will be hard to imagine.

—FSF to Ruth Sturtevant, 26 March 1920.

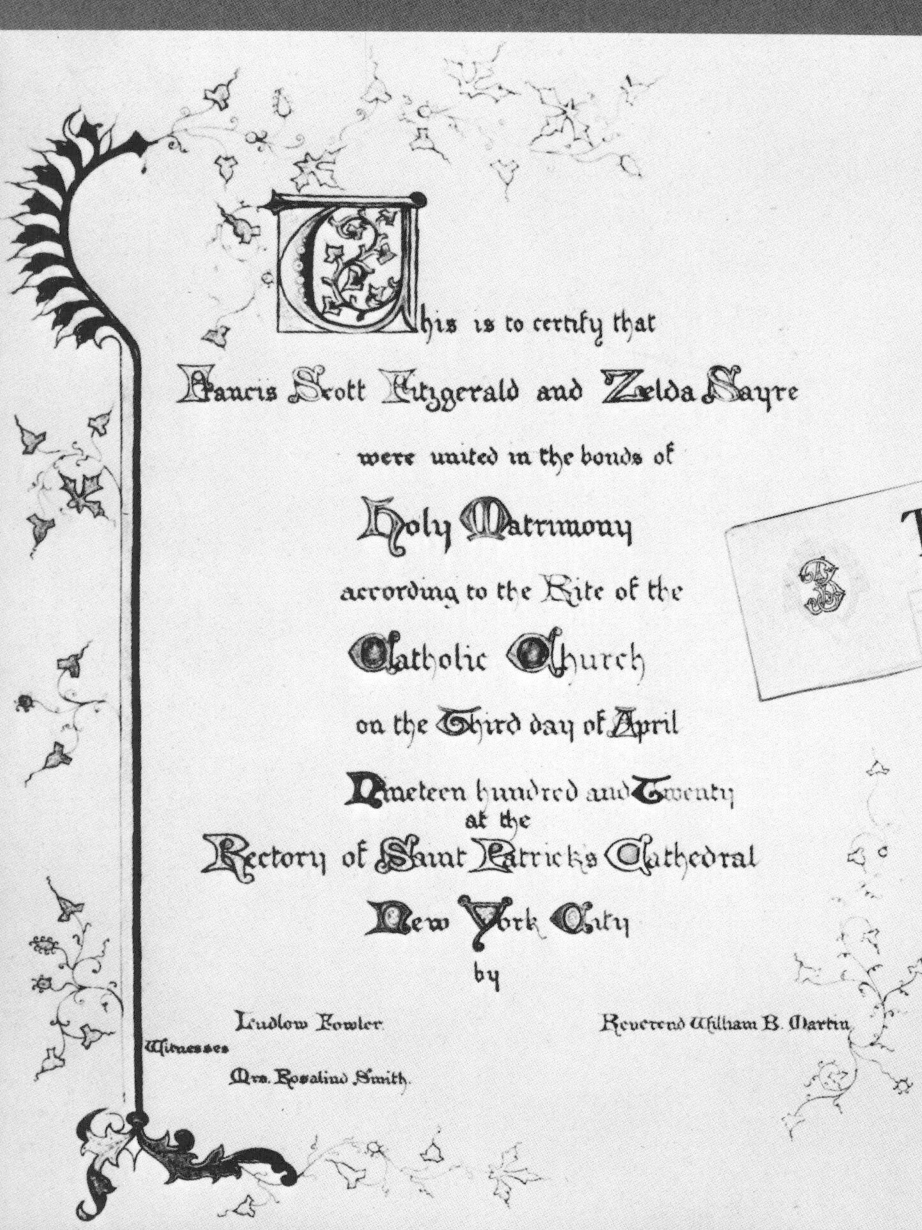
This is to certify that
Francis Scott Fitzgerald and Zelda Sayre
were united in the bonds of
Holy Matrimony
according to the Rite of the
Catholic Church
on the Third day of April
Nineteen hundred and Twenty
at the
Rectory of Saint Patrick's Cathedral
New York City
by
Reverend William B. Martin

Witnesses
Ludlow Fowler
Mrs. Rosalind Smith

With best wishes:
Charles Scribner jr.
Maxwell E. Perkins
John W. Rogers
Whitney Darrow
Robert Bridges
Roger Burlingame

THE BILTMORE
TABLE NO. 69 COVERS 4 ROOM NO. 2109

Miss Zelda Sayre Weds Scott Fitzgerald—

Miss Zelda Sayre, the lovely and attractive daughter of Judge and Mrs. A. D. Sayre, of Montgomery, was married Saturday at high noon in New York City to Francis Scott Fitzgerald, son of Mr. and Mrs. Edward Fitzgerald, of Minnesota, at the Rectory of St. Patrick's Cathedral. The marriage was the culmination of a romance that was begun when Lieutenant Fitzgerald was stationed at Camp Sheridan with the ninth division.

Miss Sayre was graduated in 1918 and was a social favorite in the city and throughout the South and was always a popular member of the social circles.

Mr. Fitzgerald finished at Princeton in 1918 and enlisted at once for overseas service, receiving a commission and later being made aid de camp to General Ryan. He was distinguished at Princeton for his literary ability, and has since made an enviable reputation as a writer of short stories for the Saturday Evening Post and other current magazines. On March 26 Scribner issued his first novel, "This Side of Paradise," which has attracted much favorable notice and already gone into the second edition.

Mr. and Mrs. Fitzgerald are at the Biltmore in New York for the month of April, after which they will go to Rye on the Coast for the summer.

As soon as David could make the arrangements, he sent for her. The Judge gave her the trip north for a wedding present; she quarrelled with her mother about her wedding clothes.

"I don't want it that way. I want it to drop off the shoulders."

"Alabama, it's as near as I can get it. How can it stay up with nothing to hold it?"

"Aw, Mamma, you can fix it."

Millie laughed, a pleased sad laugh, and indulgent.

"My children think I can accomplish the impossible," she said, complacently.

Alabama left her mother a note in her bureau drawer the day she went away:

> *My dearest Mamma:*
> I have not been as you would have wanted me but I love you with all my heart and I will think of you every day. I hate leaving you alone with all your children gone. Don't forget me.
> *Alabama.*

The Judge put her on the train.

"Good-bye, daughter."

He seemed very handsome and abstract to Alabama. She was afraid to cry; her father was so proud. Joan had been afraid, too, to cry.

"Good-bye, Daddy."

"Good-bye, Baby."

The train pulled Alabama out of the shadow-drenched land of her youth.

* * *

Alabama lay thinking in room number twenty-one-o-nine of the Biltmore Hotel that her life would be different with her parents so far away. David David Knight Knight Knight, for instance, couldn't possibly make her put out her light till she got good and ready. No power on earth could make her do anything, she thought frightened, any more, except herself.

—*Save Me the Waltz* (ZF)

For just a moment, before it was demonstrated that I was unable to play the role, I, who knew less of New York than any reporter of six months standing and less of its society than any hall-room boy in a Ritz stag line, was pushed into the position not only of spokesman for the time but of the typical product of that same moment. I, or rather it was "we" now, did not know exactly what New York expected of us and found it rather confusing. Within a few months after our embarkation on the Metropolitan venture we scarcely knew any more who we were and we hadn't a notion what we were. A dive into a civic fountain, a casual brush with the law, was enough to get us into the gossip columns, and we were quoted on a variety of subjects we knew nothing about. Actually our "contacts" included half a dozen unmarried college friends and a few new literary acquaintances —I remember a lonesome Christmas when we had not one friend in the city, nor one house we could go to. Finding no nucleus to which we could cling, we became a small nucleus ourselves and gradually we fitted our disruptive personalities into the contemporary scene of New York. Or rather New York forgot us and let us stay.

. . . From the confusion of the year 1920 I remember riding on top of a taxi-cab along deserted Fifth Avenue on a hot Sunday night, and a luncheon in the cool Japanese gardens at the Ritz with the wistful Kay Laurel and George Jean Nathan, and writing all night again and again, and paying too much for minute apartments, and buying magnificent but broken-down cars. The first speakeasies had arrived, the toddle was *passé,* the Montmartre was the smart place to dance and Lillian Tashman's fair hair weaved around the floor among the enliquored college boys. The plays were *Declassé* and *Sacred and Profane Love,* and at the Midnight Frolic you danced elbow to elbow with Marion Davies and perhaps picked out the vivacious Mary Hay in the pony chorus. We thought we were apart from all that; perhaps everyone thinks they are apart from their milieu. We felt like small children in a great bright unexplored barn. Summoned out to Griffith's studio on Long Island, we trembled in the presence of the familiar faces of the *Birth of a Nation;* later I realized that behind much of the entertainment that the city poured forth into the nation there were only a lot of rather lost and lonely people. The world of the picture actors was like our own in that it was in New York and not of it. It had little sense of itself and no center: when I first met Dorothy Gish I had the feeling that we were both standing on the North Pole and it was snowing. Since then they have found a home but it was not destined to be New York.

* * *

And lastly from that period I remember riding in a taxi one afternoon between very tall buildings under a mauve and rosy sky; I began to bawl because I had everything I wanted and knew I would never be so happy again.

—"My Lost City"

My wife and I were married in New York in the spring of 1920, when prices were higher than they had been within the memory of man. In the light of after events it seems fitting that our career should have started at that precise point in time. I had just received a large check from the movies and I felt a little patronizing toward the millionaires riding down Fifth Avenue in their limousines—because my income had a way of doubling every month. This was actually the case. It had done so for several months—I had made only thirty-five dollars the previous August, while here in April I was making three thousand—and it seemed as if it was going to do so forever. At the end of the year it must reach half a million. Of course with such a state of affairs, economy seemed a waste of time. So we went to live at the most expensive hotel in New York, intending to wait there until enough money accumulated for a trip abroad.

—"How to Live on $36,000 a Year"

Twilights were wonderful just after the war. They hung above New York like indigo wash, forming themselves from asphalt dust and sooty shadows under the cornices and limp gusts of air exhaled from closing windows, to hang above the streets with all the mystery of white fog rising off a swamp. The far-away lights from buildings high in the sky burned hazily through the blue, like golden objects lost in deep grass, and the noise of hurrying streets took on that hushed quality of many footfalls in a huge stone square. Through the gloom people went to tea. On all the corners around the Plaza Hotel, girls in short squirrel coats and long flowing skirts and hats like babies' velvet bathtubs waited for the changing traffic to be suctioned up by the revolving doors of the fashionable grill. Under the scalloped portico of the Ritz, girls in short ermine coats and fluffy, swirling dresses and hats the size of manholes passed from the nickel glitter of traffic to the crystal glitter of the lobby.

—"A Millionaire's Girl" (ZF)

I was talking to Mrs. Flandrau last night and her saying that she'd gotten offers for movie rights to her Post *story reminded me of something I wanted to ask you. Is there money in writing movies? Do you sell scenarios?*

The day I called you were out & I talked to Mr. Reynolds. I asked him not to offer my stuff to Smart Set. *You see they only pay $40.00 so they'd know you'd tried everybody else first and as I'm on rather good terms with Mr. Nathan and intend to send him half a dozen little one act plays a year, I want to keep on terms with them.*

* * *

Go ahead & have the soiled manuscripts retyped. I'll fix up "Barbara Bobs her Hair"—and I'm also writing a lot more.

One more question—Is there any market at all for the cynical or pessimistic story except Smart Set *or does realism bar a story from any well-paying magazine no matter how cleverly its done?*

I gave your address to a very clever young writer who was in my class at Princeton. His name is Biggs & I think perhaps you can get him better luck than he's having by himself.

—FSF to Harold Ober, 1920.

While I waited for the novel to appear, the metamorphosis of amateur into professional began to take place—a sort of stitching together of your whole life into a pattern of work, so that the end of one job is automatically the beginning of another. I had been an amateur before; in October, when I strolled with a girl among the stones of a southern graveyard, I was a professional and my enchantment with certain things that she felt and said was already paced by an anxiety to set them down in a story—it was called *The Ice Palace* and it was published later. Similarly, during Christmas week in St. Paul, there was a night when I had stayed home from two dances to work on a story. Three friends called up during the evening to tell me I had missed some rare doings: a well-known man-about-town had disguised himself as a camel and, with a taxi-driver as the rear half, managed to attend the wrong party. Aghast with myself for not being there, I spent the next day trying to collect the fragments of the story.

"Well, all I can say is it was funny when it happened." "No, I don't know where he got the taxi-man." "You'd have to know him well to understand how funny it was."

In despair I said:

"Well, I can't seem to find out exactly what happened but I'm going to write about it as if it was ten times funnier than anything you've said." So I wrote it, in twenty-two consecutive hours, and wrote it "funny," simply because I was so emphatically told it was funny. *The Camel's Back* was published and still crops up in the humorous anthologies.

—"Early Success"

The Howard Tates are, as every one who lives in Toledo knows, the most formidable people in town. Mrs. Howard Tate was a Chicago Todd before she became a Toledo Tate, and the family generally affect that conscious simplicity which has begun to be the earmark of American aristocracy. The Tates have reached the stage where they talk about pigs and farms and look at you icy-eyed if you are not amused. They have begun to prefer retainers rather than friends as dinner guests, spend a lot of money in a quiet way, and, having lost all sense of competition, are in process of growing quite dull.

The dance this evening was for little Millicent Tate, and though all ages were represented, the dancers were mostly from school and college—the younger married crowd was at the Townsends' circus ball up at the Tallyho Club. Mrs. Tate was standing just inside the ballroom, following Millicent round with her eyes, and beaming whenever she caught her eye. Beside her were two middle-aged sycophants, who were saying what a perfectly exquisite child Millicent was. It was at this moment that Mrs. Tate was grasped firmly by the skirt and her youngest daughter, Emily, aged eleven, hurled herself with an "Oof!" into her mother's arms.

"Why, Emily, what's the trouble?"

"Mamma," said Emily, wild-eyed but voluble, "there's something out on the stairs."

"What?"

"There's a thing out on the stairs, mamma. I think it's a big dog, mamma, but it doesn't look like a dog."

"What do you mean, Emily?"

The sycophants waved their heads sympathetically.

"Mamma, it looks like a—like a camel."

Mrs. Tate laughed.

"You saw a mean old shadow, dear, that's all."

"No, I didn't. No, it was some kind of thing, mamma—big. I was going down-stairs to see if there were any more people, and this dog or something, he was coming up-stairs. Kinda funny, mamma, like he was lame. And then he saw me and gave a sort of growl, and then he slipped at the top of the landing, and I ran."

Mrs. Tate's laugh faded.

"The child must have seen something," she said.

—"The Camel's Back"

16 THE SATURDAY EVENING POST February 21, 1920

HEAD AND SHOULDERS

By F. Scott Fitzgerald

ILLUSTRATED BY CHARLES D. MITCHELL

IN 1915 Horace Tarbox was thirteen years old. In that year he took the examinations for entrance to Princeton University and received the Grade A—excellent—in Cæsar, Cicero, Vergil, Xenophon, Homer, Algebra, Plane Geometry, Solid Geometry and Chemistry.

Two years later, while George M. Cohan was composing Over There, Horace was leading the sophomore class by several lengths and digging out theses on The Syllogism as an Obsolete Scholastic Form, and during the Battle of Château-Thierry he was sitting at his desk deciding whether or not to wait until his seventeenth birthday before beginning his series of essays on The Pragmatic Bias of the New Realists.

After a while some newsboy told him that the war was over, and he was glad, because it meant that Peat Brothers, publishers, would get out their new edition of Spinoza's Improvement of the Understanding. Wars were all very well in their way, made young men self-reliant or something, but Horace felt that he could never forgive the President for allowing a brass band to play under his window on the night of the false Armistice, causing him to leave three important sentences out of his thesis on German Idealism.

The next year he went up to Yale to take his degree as Master of Arts.

He was seventeen then, tall and slender, with near-sighted gray eyes and an air of keeping himself utterly detached from the mere words he let drop.

"I never feel as though I'm talking to him," expostulated Professor Dillinger to a sympathetic colleague. "He makes me feel as though I were talking to his representative. I always expect him to say, 'Well, I'll ask myself and find out.'"

And then, just as nonchalantly as though Horace Tarbox had been Mr. Beef the butcher or Mr. Hat the haberdasher, life reached in, seized him, handled him, stretched him and unrolled him like a piece of Irish lace on a Saturday-afternoon bargain counter.

To move in the literary fashion I should say that this was all because when way back in colonial days the hardy pioneers had come to a bald place in Connecticut and asked of each other, "Now what shall we build here?" the hardiest one among 'em had answered, "Let's build a town where theatrical managers can try out musical comedies!" How afterward they founded Yale College there, to try the musical comedies on, is a story everyone knows. At any rate one December, Home James opened at the Shubert and all the students encored Marcia Meadow, who sang a song about the Blundering Blimp in the first act and did a shaky, shivery, celebrated dance in the last.

Marcia was nineteen. She didn't have wings, but audiences agreed generally that she didn't need them. She was a blonde by natural pigment and she wore no paint on the streets at high noon. Outside of that she was no better than most women.

It was Charlie Moon who promised her five thousand cigarettes if she would pay a call on Horace Tarbox, prodigy extraordinary. Charlie was a senior in Sheffield and he and Horace were first cousins. They liked and pitied each other.

Horace had been particularly busy that night. The failure of the Frenchman, Laurier, to synchronize the sources of the new realists was preying on his mind. In fact, his only reaction to a low, clear-cut rap at his study was to make him speculate as to whether any rap would have actual existence without an ear there to hear it. He fancied he was verging more and more toward pragmatism. But at that moment, though he did not know it, he was verging with astounding rapidity toward something quite different.

The rap sounded—three seconds leaked by—the rap sounded.

"Come in," muttered Horace automatically.

He heard the door open and then close, but, bent over his book in the big armchair before the fire, he did not look up.

"Leave it on the bed in the other room," he said absently.

"Leave what on the bed in the other room?"

Marcia Meadow had to talk her songs, but her speaking voice was like byplay on a harp.

"The laundry."

"I can't."

Horace stirred impatiently in his chair.

"Why can't you?"

"Why, because I haven't got it."

"H'm!" he replied testily. "Suppose you go back and get it."

Across the fire from Horace was another easy chair. He was accustomed to change to it in the course of an evening by way of exercise and variety. One chair he called Berkeley, the other he called Hume. He suddenly heard a sound as of a rustling, diaphanous form sinking into Hume. He glanced up.

"Well," said Marcia with the sweet smile she used in Act Two—"Oh, so the Duke liked my dancing!"—"Well, Omar Khayyam, here I am beside you singing in the wilderness."

Horace stared at her dazedly. The momentary suspicion came to him that she existed there only as a phantom of his imagination. Women didn't come into men's rooms and sink into men's Humes. Women brought laundry and took your seat in the street car and married you later on when you were old enough to know fetters.

This woman had clearly materialized out of Hume. Why, the very froth of her brown gauzy dress was an emanation from Hume's leather arm there! If he looked long enough he would see Hume right through her and then he would be alone again in the room. He passed his fist across his eyes. He really must take up those trapeze exercises again.

"For Pete's sake don't look so critical!" objected the emanation pleasantly. "I feel as if you were going to wish me away with that patent dome of yours. And then there wouldn't be anything left of me except my shadow in your eyes."

Horace coughed. Coughing was one of his two gestures. When he talked you forgot he had a body at all. It was like hearing a phonograph record by a singer who had been dead a long time.

"What do you want?" he asked.

"I want them letters," whined Marcia melodramatically—"them letters of mine you bought from my grandsire in 1881."

Horace considered.

"I haven't got your letters," he said evenly. "I am only seventeen years old. My father was not born until March 3, 1879. You evidently have me confused with someone else."

"You're only seventeen?" repeated Marcia suspiciously.

"Only seventeen."

"I knew a girl," said Marcia reminiscently, "who went on the ten-twenty-thirty when she was sixteen. She was so stuck on herself that she could never say 'sixteen' without putting the 'only' before it. We got to calling her 'Only Jessie.' And she's just where she was when she started—only worse. 'Only' is a bad habit, Omar—it sounds like an alibi."

"My name is not Omar."

"I know," agreed Marcia, nodding—"your name's Horace. I just call you Omar because you remind me of a smoked cigarette."

"And I haven't your letters. I doubt if I've ever met your grandfather. In fact, I think it very improbable that you yourself were alive in 1881."

Marcia stared at him in wonder.

"Me—1881? Why sure! I was second-line stuff when the Florodora Sextette was still in the convent. I was the original nurse to Mrs. Sol Smith's Juliette. Why, Omar, I was a canteen singer during the War of 1812."

Horace's mind made a sudden successful leap and he smiled.

"Did Charlie Moon put you up to this?"

Marcia regarded him inscrutably.

"Who's Charlie Moon?"

"Small—wide nostrils—big ears."

She grew several inches and sniffed.

"I'm not in the habit of noticing my friends' nostrils."

"Then it was Charlie?"

Marcia bit her lip—and then yawned.

"Oh, let's change the subject, Omar. I'll pull a snooze in this chair in a minute."

"Yes," replied Horace gravely, "Hume has often been considered soporific."

"Who's your friend—and will he die?"

Then of a sudden Horace Tarbox rose slenderly and began to pace the room with his hands in his pockets. This was his other gesture.

"I don't care for this," he said as if he were talking to himself—"at all. Not that I mind your being here—I don't. You're quite a pretty little thing, but I don't like Charlie Moon's sending you up here. Am I a laboratory experiment on which the janitors as well as the chemists can make experiments? Is my intellectual development humorous in any way? Do I look like the pictures of the little Boston boy in the comic magazines? Has that callow ass, Moon, with his eternal tales about his week in Paris, any right to ——"

"No!" interrupted Marcia emphatically. "And you're a sweet boy. Come here and kiss me."

Horace stopped quickly in front of her.

"Why do you want me to kiss you?" he asked intently. "Do you just go round kissing people?"

"I Hope I Haven't Given You the Impression That I Consider Kissing Intrinsically Irrational"

In 1920 The Saturday Evening Post *published six of Fitzgerald's stories about young love, but his more pessimistic stories were sold to* Scribner's Magazine *and* The Smart Set, *which paid small prices.*

16 THE SATURDAY EVENING POST April 24, 1920

THE CAMEL'S BACK

By F. Scott Fitzgerald

ILLUSTRATED BY ARTHUR WILLIAM BROWN

THE restless, wearied eye of the tired magazine reader resting for a critical second on the above title will judge it to be merely metaphorical. Stories about the cup and the lip and the bad penny and the new broom rarely have anything to do with cups and lips and pennies and brooms. This story is the great exception. It has to do with an actual ...

The room upstairs was full of those innocent hotel pictures of little girls eating apples and sitting in swings and talking to dogs. The other decorations were neckties and a pink man reading a pink paper devoted to ladies in pink tights.

"When you have to go into the ...

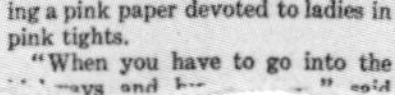

"You 'Fraid of Me?" Said Betty. "Don't Be. You See I'm a Snake Charmer, But I'm Pretty Good at Camels Too"

18 THE SATURDAY EVENING POST May 22, 1920

THE ICE PALACE

By F. Scott Fitzgerald

ILLUSTRATED BY JAMES H. CRANK

THE sunlight dripped over the house like golden paint over an art jar and the freckling shadows here and there only intensified the rigor of the bath of light. The Butterworth and Larkin houses flanking were intrenched behind great stodgy trees; only the Happer house took the full sun and all day long faced the dusty road-street with a tolerant kindly patience. This was the city of Tarleton in southernmost Georgia—September

Up in her bedroom window Sal

Hanging round he found not at all difficult; a crowd of little girls had grown up beautifully, the amazing Sally Carrol foremost among them; and they enjoyed being swum with and with and made love to in the flower- —and

"Girl told me you were engaged to a Yankee you met up in Asheville last summah."

Sally Carrol sighed.

"Never saw such an old town faw rumors."

"Don't marry a Yankee, Sally Carrol. We need you round here."

Sally Carrol was silent a moment.

"Clark," she demanded

I marry?"

They Passed Through the Gateway and Followed a Path That Led Through a Wavy Valley of Graves

"Those are the Confederate dead," said Sally Carrol simply.

They walked along and read the inscriptions, always only a name and a date, sometimes quite indecipherable.

"The last row is the saddest—see, 'way over there. Every cross has just a date on it, and the word 'Unknown.' "

She looked at him and her eyes brimmed with tears.

"I can't tell you how real it is to me, darling—if you don't know."

"How you feel about it is beautiful to me."

"No, no, it's not me, it's them—that old time that I've tried to have live in me. These were just men, unimportant evidently or they wouldn't have been 'unknown'; but they died for the most beautiful thing in the world—the dead South. You see," she continued, her voice still husky, her eyes glistening with tears, "people have these dreams they fasten onto things, and I've always grown up with that dream. It was so easy because it was all dead and there weren't any disillusions comin' to me. I've tried in a way to live up to those past standards of noblesse oblige—there's just the last remnants of it, you know, like the roses of an old garden dying all round us—streaks of strange courtliness and chivalry in some of these boys an' stories I used to hear from a Confederate soldier who lived next door, and a few old darkies. Oh, Harry, there was something, there was something! I couldn't ever make you understand, but it was there."

"I understand," he assured her again quietly.

—"The Ice Palace"

10 THE SATURDAY EVENING POST May 29, 1920

THE OFFSHORE PIRATE

By F. Scott Fitzgerald

ILLUSTRATED BY LESLIE L. BENSON

THIS unlikely story begins on a sea that was a blue dream, as colorful as blue silk stockings, and beneath a sky as blue as the irises of children's eyes. From the western half of the sky the sun was shying little golden disks at the sea—if you gazed intently enough you could see them skip from wave tip to wave tip until they joined a broad collar of golden coin that was collecting half a mile out and would eventually be a dazzling sunset. About halfway between the Florida shore and the golden collar a white steam yacht, very young and graceful, was riding at anchor and under a blue-and-white awning aft a yellow-haired girl reclined in a wicker settee reading The Revolt of the Angels, by Anatole France.

She was about nineteen, slender and supple, with a spoiled, alluring mouth and quick gray eyes full of a radiant curiosity. Her feet, stockingless, and adorned rather than clad in blue satin slippers which swung nonchalantly from her toes, were perched on the arm of a settee adjoining the one she occupied. And as she read she intermittently regaled herself by a faint application to her tongue of a half lemon that she held in her hand. The other half, sucked dry, lay on the deck at her feet and rocked very gently to and fro at the almost imperceptible motion of the tide.

The second half lemon was well-nigh pulpless and the golden collar had grown astonishing in width when suddenly the drowsy silence which enveloped the yacht was sound of heavy footsteps and an elderly man

"No. It's too low. It's run along the bottom. Five min——"

"Well, I'll be darned! Gosh! Science is golden or something—isn't it?"

"Will you let me say what I started to?"

"Shoot!"

"Well, it seems—well, I am up here——" He paused and swallowed several times distractedly. "Oh, yes. Young woman, Colonel Moreland has called up again to ask me to be sure to bring you in to dinner. His son Toby has come all the way from New York to meet you and he's invited several other young people. For the last time, will you——"

"No," said Ardita shortly, "I won't. I came along on this darn cruise with the one idea of going to Palm Beach, and you knew it, and I absolutely refuse to meet any darn old colonel or any darn young Toby or any

"Is it a Proposal of Marriage? Extra! Ardita Farnam Becomes Pirate's Bride. Society Girl Kidnaped by Ragtime Bank Robber"

I am enclosing under a separate cover "The Lees of Happiness" an excellent if somewhat somber story of The Chicago Tribune. They won't get it, I imagine for several weeks & probably couldn't print it until mid-August but I want to ask them for personal reasons not to print it until September first.

In my contract with the Metro people I notice that they have sixty days in which to choose the ones they want from my stories already published. The contract was dated May 27th which gives them less than two weeks to decide for or against.

The Camel's Back / *Bernice Bobs Her Hair* }	*Sat. Eve. Post*
and	
The Four Fists	*Scribners*

Now there is at least one of these—The Camel's Back for which you said you had had several feelers at the time of publication but am I to understand that in case they have not notified you by July 26th I should try to sell them elsewhere.

I want to do what you think best. You remember that there was one story for which you got no offers. It was called Myra Meets His Family. So after waiting six weeks you told me to go ahead and see if I could get rid of it. So I took it to a Miss Webster, a movie agent of no particular standing, and she managed to get me $1000 for it from The Fox Film Co. My only instinct on the subject is not to waste any of them. That is—I'd rather get $1000 or $1500 than nothing. Will you please let me know at the expiration of that time what I'd better do. I feel perfectly sure that both "The Four Fists" and "The Camel's Back" would make excellent movies and that I could get a good price for them.

If "The I. O. U." comes back from the Post I wish you'd return it to me as I think I can change it so there'll be no trouble Selling it.

I am starting on that novel for the Metropolitan Magazine. It will probably be done about October 1st so there will probably be no more short stories this summer.

—FSF to Harold Ober, 17 July 1920.

Copyright by White

The Author's Apology

I don't want to talk about myself because I'll admit I did that somewhat in this book. In fact, to write it took three months; to conceive it—three minutes; to collect the data in it—all my life. The idea of writing it came on the first of last July: it was a substitute form of dissipation.

My whole theory of writing I can sum up in one sentence: An author ought to write for the youth of his own generation, the critics of the next, and the schoolmasters of ever afterward.

So, gentlemen, consider all the cocktails mentioned in this book drunk by me as a toast to the American Booksellers Association.

May, 1920

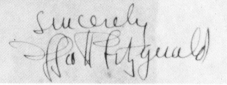

Sincerely
F Scott Fitzgerald

In the spring of 1920 Scribners prepared copies of This Side of Paradise *with a special note by Fitzgerald for the American Booksellers Association meeting.*

PRINCETON UNIVERSITY
PRINCETON, N. J.

PRESIDENT'S ROOM

May 27th,1920.

My dear Mr. Fitzgerald:-

It has been in my mind for some time to write to you. Last evening I read your story in the current number of "Scribners" magazine, entitled "The Four Fists." It is so admirably written and I finished it with a feeling of such deep satisfaction, that the long delayed purpose of writing you takes shape again today.

Now I hope that you will allow me to add a word also in reference to your Princeton book, "This Side of Paradise. It is because I appreciate so much all that is in you of artistic skill and certain elemental power that I am taking the liberty of telling you very frankly that your characterization of Princeton has grieved me. I cannot bear to think that our young men are merely living for four years in a country club and spending their lives wholly in a spirit of calculation and snobbishness.

* * *

I have written these words not in any spirit of carping criticism, but to let you know my full mind concerning you,and my pride in your power,already demonstrated in the world of letters and promise of a still richer fulfillment. I should like to learn from your own lips, in what you feel the Princeton of the present fails.

With warm regards,

Faithfully yours,

John Grier Hibben

Mr. F. Scott Fitzgerald,
C/o Messrs Charles Scribner Sons,
48th and Fifth Avenue,
New York City.

I want to thank you very much for your letter and to confess that the honor of a letter from you outweighed my real regret that my book gave you concern. It was a book written with the bitterness of my discovery that I had spent several years trying to fit in with a curriculum that is after all made for the average student. After the curriculum had tied me up, taken away the honors I'd wanted, bent my nose over a chemistry book and said "No fun, no activities, no offices, no Triangle trips—no, not even a diploma if you can't do chemistry" —after that I retired. It is easy for the successful man in college, the man who has gotten what he wanted to say.

"It's all fine. It makes men. It made me, see"—

—but it seems to me it's like the captain of a company when he has his men lined up at attention for inspection. He sees only the tightly buttoned coat and the shaved faces. He doesn't know that perhaps a private in the rear rank is half crazy because a pin is sticking in his back and he can't move, or another private is thinking that his wife is dying and he can't get leave because too many men in the company are gone already.

I don't mean at all that Princeton is not the happiest time in most boys' lives. It is, of course—I simply say it wasn't the happiest time in mine. I love it now better than any place on earth. The men—the undergraduates of Yale and Princeton are cleaner, healthier, better-looking, better dressed, wealthier and more attractive than any undergraduate body in the country. I have no fault to find with Princeton that I can't find with Oxford and Cambridge. I simply wrote out of my own impressions, wrote as honestly as I could a picture of its beauty. That the picture is cynical is the fault of my temperament.

My view of life, President Hibben, is the view of the Theodore Dreisers and Joseph Conrads—that life is too strong and remorseless for the sons of men. My idealism flickered out with Henry Strater's anticlub movement at Princeton. "The Four Fists," latest of my stories to be published, was the first to be written. I wrote it in desperation one evening because I had a three-inch pile of rejection slips and it was financially necessary for me to give the magazine what they wanted. The appreciation it has received has amazed me.

I must admit however that This Side of Paradise *does overaccentuate the gayety and country club atmosphere of Princeton. For the sake of the reader's interest that part was much overstressed, and of course the hero, not being average, reacted rather unhealthily I suppose to many perfectly normal phenomena. To that extent the book is inaccurate. It is the Princeton of Saturday night in May. Too many intelligent classmates of mine have failed to agree with it for me to consider it really photographic any more, as of course I did when I wrote it.*

Next time I am in Princeton I will take the privilege of coming to see you.

I am, sir,

Very respectfully yours,

—FSF to President Hibben of Princeton, 3 June 1920.

WHO'S WHO—AND WHY

REG. U. S. PAT. OFF.

Sat. Evening Post

Serious and Frivolous Facts About the Great and the Near Great

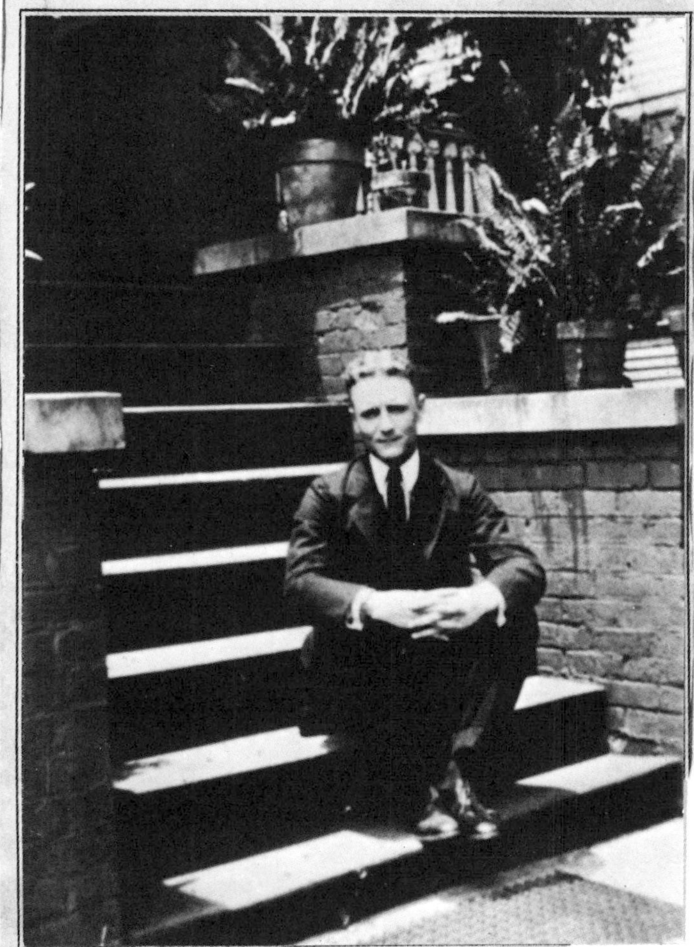

PHOTO. BY ELLIE NEWMAN LIGON, MONTGOMERY, ALA.

In Two Months He Wrote Eight Stories and Sold Nine

F. Scott Fitzgerald

The history of my life is the history of the struggle between an overwhelming urge to write and a combination of circumstances bent on keeping me from it.

When I lived in St. Paul and was about twelve I wrote all through every class in school in the back of my geography book and first year Latin and on the margins of themes and declensions and mathematics problems. Two years later a family congress decided that the only way to force me to study was to send me to boarding school. This was a mistake. It took my mind off my writing. I decided to play football, to smoke, to go to college, to do all sorts of irrelevant things that had nothing to do with the real business of life, which, of course, was the proper mixture of description and dialogue in the short story.

But in school I went off on a new tack. I saw a musical comedy called The Quaker Girl, and from that day forth my desk bulged with Gilbert & Sullivan librettos and dozens of notebooks containing the germs of dozens of musical comedies.

Near the end of my last year at school I came across a new musical-comedy score lying on top of the piano. It was called His Honor the Sultan, and the title furnished the information that it had been presented by the Triangle Club of Princeton University.

That was enough for me. From then on the university question was settled. I was bound for Princeton.

I spent my entire Freshman year writing an operetta for the Triangle Club. To do this I failed in algebra, trigonometry, coördinate geometry and hygiene. But the Triangle Club accepted my show, and by tutoring all through a stuffy August I managed to come back a Sophomore and act in it as a chorus girl. A little after this came a hiatus. My health broke down and I left college one December to spend the rest of the year recuperating in the West. Almost my final memory before I left was of writing a last lyric on that year's Triangle production while in bed in the infirmary with a high fever.

The next year, 1916–17, found me back in college, but by this time I had decided that poetry was the only thing worth while, so with my head ringing with the meters of Swinburne and the matters of Rupert Brooke I spent the spring doing sonnets, ballads and rondels into the small hours. I had read somewhere that every great poet had written great poetry before he was twenty-one. I had only a year and, besides, war was impending. I must publish a book of startling verse before I was engulfed.

By autumn I was in an infantry officers' training camp at Fort Leavenworth, with poetry in the discard and a brand-new ambition—I was writing an immortal novel. Every evening, concealing my pad behind Small Problems for Infantry, I wrote paragraph after paragraph on a somewhat edited history of me and my imagination. The outline of twenty-two chapters, four of them in verse, was made, two chapters were completed; and then I was detected and the game was up. I could write no more during study period.

This was a distinct complication. I had only three months to live—in those days all infantry officers thought they had only three months to live—and I had left no mark on the world. But such consuming ambition was not to be thwarted by a mere war. Every Saturday at one o'clock when the week's work was over I hurried to the Officers' Club, and there, in a corner of a roomful of smoke, conversation and rattling newspapers, I wrote a one-hundred-and-twenty-thousand-word novel on the consecutive week-ends of three months. There was no revising; there was no time for it. As I finished each chapter I sent it to a typist in Princeton.

Meanwhile I lived in its smeary pencil pages. The drills, marches and Small Problems for Infantry were a shadowy dream. My whole heart was concentrated upon my book.

I went to my regiment happy. I had written a novel. The war could now go on. I forgot paragraphs and pentameters, similies and syllogisms. I got to be a first lieutenant, got my orders overseas—and then the publishers wrote me that though The Romantic Egotist was the most original manuscript they had received for years they couldn't publish it. It was crude and reached no conclusion.

It was six months after this that I arrived in New York and presented my card to the office boys of seven city editors asking to be taken on as a reporter. I had just turned twenty-two, the war was over, and I was going to trail murderers by day and do short stories by night. But the newspapers didn't need me. They sent their office boys out to tell me they didn't need me. They decided definitely and irrevocably by the sound of my name on a calling card that I was absolutely unfitted to be a reporter.

Instead I became an advertising man at ninety dollars a month, writing the slogans that while away the weary hours in rural trolley cars. After hours I wrote stories—from March to June. There were nineteen altogether; the quickest written in an hour and a half, the slowest in three days. No one bought them, no one sent personal letters. I had one hundred and twenty-two rejection slips pinned in a frieze about my room. I wrote movies. I wrote song lyrics. I wrote complicated advertising schemes. I wrote poems. I wrote sketches. I wrote jokes. Near the end of June I sold one story for thirty dollars.

On the Fourth of July, utterly disgusted with myself and all the editors, I went home to St. Paul and informed family and friends that I had given up my position and had come home to write a novel. They nodded politely, changed the subject and spoke of me very gently. But this time I knew what I was doing. I had a novel to write at last, and all through two hot months I wrote and revised and compiled and boiled down. On September fifteenth This Side of Paradise was accepted by special delivery.

In the next two months I wrote eight stories and sold nine. The ninth was accepted by the same magazine that had rejected it four months before. Then, in November, I sold my first story to the editors of THE SATURDAY EVENING POST. By February I had sold them half a dozen. Then my novel came out. Then I got married. Now I spend my time wondering how it all happened.

In the words of the immortal Julius Caesar: "That's all there is; there isn't any more."

—"Who's Who—and Why"

The article in The Saturday Evening Post, *18 September 1920, was part of a regular* Post *series. Fitzgerald made his first appearance in* Who's Who in America *in 1921 (right).*

FITZGERALD, Francis Scott Key, author; *b.* St. Paul, Minn., Sept. 24, 1896; *s.* Edward and Mary (McQuillan) F.; Princeton, 1913-17; left coll. to join army; *m.* Zelda Sayre, of Montgomery, Ala., Apr. 3, 1920. Commd. 2d lt. 45th Inf., Nov. 1917; 1st lt. 67th Inf., July 1918; served as a.-d.-c. to Brig.-Gen. J.A. Ryan, Dec. 1918-Feb. 1919; hon. discharged, Feb. 1919. Socialist. *Clubs:* Cottage (Princeton); University (St. Paul). *Author:* This Side of Paradise, 1920; Flappers and Philosophers, 1920; The Beautiful and Damned, 1921. *Home:* 599 Summit Av., St. Paul, Minn.

In May 1920 the Fitzgeralds rented a house on Compo Road in Westport, Connecticut, where they spent a riotous summer entertaining their New York friends, including George Jean Nathan (right).

It was dark when the real-estate agent of Marietta showed them the gray house. They came upon it just west of the village, where it rested against a sky that was a warm blue cloak buttoned with tiny stars. The gray house had been there when women who kept cats were probably witches, when Paul Revere made false teeth in Boston preparatory to arousing the great commercial people, when our ancestors were gloriously deserting Washington in droves. Since those days the house had been bolstered up in a feeble corner, considerably repartitioned and newly plastered inside, amplified by a kitchen and added to by a side-porch—but, save for where some jovial oaf had roofed the new kitchen with red tin, Colonial it defiantly remained.

—*The Beautiful and Damned*

Westport —
July 1920

ILLUSTRATING HIS OWN TITLE!

F. SCOTT FITZGERALD, *the youthful author of "This Side of Paradise," was—according to St. Paul—born in 1896 and spent his early infancy in that Minnesota metropolis. Growing up in Buffalo, Syracuse, Washington and other local stops, he returned at the age of eleven to St. Paul. "Prep" work took him East again to the Newman School, Hackensack, N. J., and he was graduated from Princeton University in 1917. Then he went to War—and wrote the greater part of his remarkably popular novel while serving as second and later as first lieutenant in the 67th Infantry. And now, within a few months after the publication of that book, this fortunate youngster has won not only an enviable reputation as a writer but also an undeniably charming wife to share with him the joys of "This Side of Paradise."*

George Jean Nathan

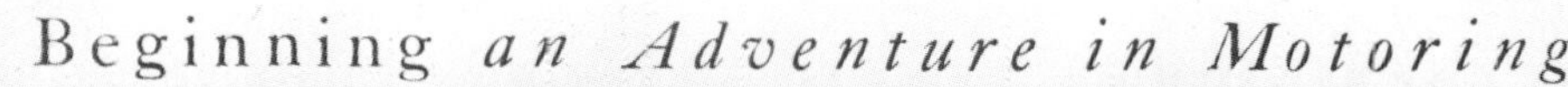
Beginning *an Adventure in Motoring*

In the summer of 1920 the Fitzgeralds drove to Montgomery in their Marmon, which was abandoned there. Fitzgerald wrote a series of articles about this trip, which was published later in Motor magazine with a group of posed photographs.

The Cruise *of the* ROLLING JUNK

By F. Scott Fitzgerald

THE SUN, which had been tapping for an hour at my closed lids, pounded suddenly on my eyes with broad, hot hammers. The room became crowded with light and the fading frivolities on the wall paper mourned the florid triumph of the noon. I awoke into Connecticut and a normal world.

Zelda was up. This was obvious, for in a moment she came into my room singing aloud. Now when Zelda sings soft I like to listen, but when she

But she only stared at me, fascinated, and said, "We can't. The car won't go that far. And besides we oughtn't to."

I perceived that these were mere formalities.

"Biscuits," I said suggestively. "Peaches! Pink and yellow, luscious —"

"Don't! Oh, don't!"

"Warm sunshine. We can surprise your father and mother. We can just

Zelda in a
Triumphant pose.
Do you like our pants?

At the O. Henry in Greenville they thought a man and his wife ought not to be dressed alike in white knickerbockers in nineteen-twenty and we thought the water in the tubs ought not to run red mud.

—" 'Show Mr. and Mrs. F. to Number—' " (ZF)

Work at the beginning but dangerous at the end. A slow year, dominated by Zelda & on the whole happy

Twenty-four Years Old

175

Gareth Hughes is her leading man.
She shook a wicked shoulder and she owned a wicked wink- The Yale "grind" fell for her so hard that he married her: & then she proved to have a wise little head on those naughty little shoulders.
VIOLA DANA
in THE CHORUS GIRL'S ROMANCE
Adapted from "HEAD AND SHOULDERS" by F. SCOTT FITZGERALD
Scenario by PERCY HEATH and direction by WILLIAM C. DOWLAN
METRO

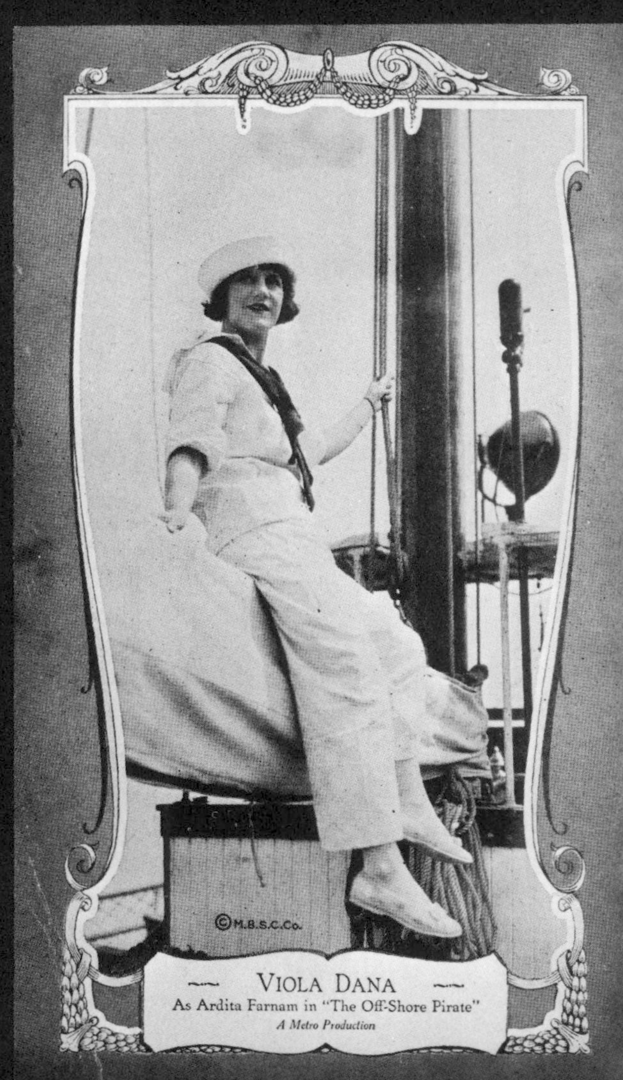

©M.B.S.C.Co.
VIOLA DANA
As Ardita Farnam in "The Off-Shore Pirate"
A Metro Production

In 1920/21 three movies were made from Fitzgerald stories: The Chorus Girl's Romance *("Head and Shoulders"),* The Husband Hunter *("Myra Meets his Family"), and* The Offshore Pirate.

The Husband Hunter

Viola Dana Charms In Highly Amusing Screen Offering

"The Off-Shore Pirate," Creation Of F. Scott Fitzgerald, Abounds In Fun And Excitement.

THE CAST.

Ardita Farnum..........Viola Dana.
Toby Moreland........Jack Mulhall.
Uncle John Farnam.Edward Jobson.
Ivan Nevkova.........Edward Cecil.

By ROBERT GARLAND.

"The Off-Shore Pirate," at the New, proves that lots of things can happen to a chap in six fleeting years.

Back in 1915 a very likable chap named F. Scott Fitzgerald came down from Princeton to do female impersonations in the Triangle Club's production of "The Evil Eye" at the theater now known as the New Lyceum. Today he is the author of that mighty fine novel called "This Side of Paradise," a regular and highly paid contributor to the leading magazines and the adroit scenarist of Viola Dana's latest and most amusing film.

The story of "The Off-Shore Pirate" deals with Anita Farnam, a young, capricious heiress; a wily Russian in search of a rich American wife, and a dashing young fellow who turns pirate to save Ardita. This young lady's life has just been "one darn proposal after another" (to use her own words). She is bored until the Russian comes and wins her with what the press agent calls "continental suavity." While on a short cruise she is accosted by a pirate with a gang of cut-throats—and then the fun and excitement begin.

Mr. Fitzgerald has told his story with skill, with considerable delightful "kidding" on the side. So adroitly is this tongue-in-cheek-ness laid on, that if you take the movies as seriously as the directors would like you to, you'll not notice that the youthful author is laughing up his literary sleeve. The plot is novel and sufficiently entertaining, and, despite slip-shod directing, it gets across effectively.

Viola Dana is charming as the heiress in the case. Her role is almost actionless, and, therefore, difficult to project wordlessly, but she manages it with considerable histrionic skill. Jack Mulhall is handsome enough as the "pirate;" his "six black buddies" do their piratical parts with humor and ease. The others in the story haven't much to do, which is a good thing for all concerned. And for once the ocean remains unagitated when a camera man is around.

There are two good reasons for going to see "The Off-Shore Pirate." One is F. Scott Fitzgerald. The other Viola Dana.

FLAPPERS
AND PHILOSOPHERS

BY
F. SCOTT FITZGERALD
AUTHOR OF "THIS SIDE OF PARADISE"

NEW YORK
CHARLES SCRIBNER'S SONS
1920

TO ZELDA

Flappers and Philosophers, *Fitzgerald's first story collection, was published in September 1920. It required 6 printings, totalling 15,300 copies.*

CONTENTS

14 THE SATURDAY EVENING POST May 1, 1920

BERNICE BOBS HER HAIR

By F. Scott Fitzgerald

ILLUSTRATED BY MAY WILSON PRESTON

After dark on Saturday night one could stand on the first tee of the golf course and see the country club windows as a yellow expanse over a very black and wavy ocean.

Every Saturday night he danced a long arduous duty dance with her to please Marjorie, but he had never been anything but bored in her company.

The idea for "Bernice Bobs Her Hair" came from the instructions on how to be popular that Fitzgerald prepared for his younger sister, Annabel.

You are as you know, not a good conversationalist and you might very naturally ask 'What do boys like to talk about?' Boys like to talk about themselves—much more than girls. Here are some leading questions for a girl to use. . . . (a) You dance so much better than you did last year. (b) How about giving me that sporty necktie when you're thru with it? (c) You've got the longest eyelashes! (This will embarrass him, but he likes it.) (d) I hear you've got a 'line'! (e) Well who's your latest crush? Avoid *(a) When do you go back to school? (b) How long have you been home? (c) It's warm or the orchestra's good or the floor's good. . . .*

* * *

With such splendid eyebrows as yours you should brush them or wet them and train them every morning and night as I advised you to do long ago. They oughtn't to have a hair out of place. . . .

—FSF to Annabel.

"All right—I'll just give you a few examples now. First, you have no ease of manner. Why? Because you're never sure about your personal appearance. When a girl feels that she's perfectly groomed and dressed she can forget that part of her. That's charm. The more parts of yourself you can afford to forget the more charm you have."

"Don't I look all right?"

"No; for instance, you never take care of your eyebrows. They're black and lustrous, but by leaving them straggly they're a blemish. They'd be beautiful if you'd take care of them in one-tenth the time you take doing nothing. You're going to brush them so that they'll grow straight."

Bernice raised the brows in question.

"Do you mean to say that men notice eyebrows?"

"Yes—subconsciously.

—"Bernice Bobs Her Hair"

Did Mother Cross Her Knees, Say "D—mn" Occasionally Or Flirt a Wee Bit?

F. Scott Fitzgerald, 23-Year-Old Author, Depicts the Present-Day Heroes and Heroines as Unconventional—Mature Critics Deny Such Conduct Characterized Their Boy and Girlhood Days.

By Roger Batchelder.

When father was a little boy,
All little boys were good
And did just what their nurses
And their parents said they should:
So now, when I am naughty,
He takes me on his knee,
And tells, when he was little,
How good he used to be.

That verse, incorrectly quoted perhaps, but one which rings in the ears of more than one grown-up boy and girl of to-day, is an excellent abstract, and reflects naively, but none the less satirically, on the past behaviour of what youth of to-day terms lightly, "The other generation." We of to-day have the fixed idea that father and mother in their childhood and early youths acted differently, thought differently than we did ten years ago. We have the fixed idea; whether we regard it as Gospel is another matter. We have the fixed idea, just the same.

And so, again comes up the old question, which is passed down from generation to generation, "Are we like our fathers?" Was their youth as dissimilar to ours as the halo of age has made it appear in retrospect?

Did mother cross her knees, say "Damn" occasionally, or flirt?

Did father stay out late, smoke, or take an occasional drink?

These questions are almost unanswerable, for we can't exactly ask mother and father and expect to get an accurate answer. Perhaps they have forgotten. At any rate, we have often wondered.

And now comes a youth by the name of F. Scott Fitzgerald, who, at the age of twenty-three wrote a book called "This Side of Paradise." and followed it closely by "Flappers and Philosophers" (Scribners).

Critics hail him as a genius, though they hint that his genius is precocious. His first novel was the "startler" of the year, simply because he took the youths of the present generation and depicted them as he knew them, as he saw them. That same youth snickered en masse, and said "Well?" And though the critics beamed, and again hinted that the young man would grow older, the fathers and mothers of to-day drew themselves up haughtily and said: "Ridiculous; our children don't act that way at all—at least, if they do, we know nothing of it. And certainly we never acted that way when we were young."

Now therein lies the point of this article.

Books of a period are supposed to be accurate reflections of the life of the period, and if we may gauge correctly the youth of our parents by the books which appeared at that time, we may well believe the truth of the little song. Moreover, on reading of Mr. Fitzgerald's heroes and heroines, we may wonder about ourselves, of those who are now tagging on at the end of 'this generation' and perhaps we may wonder whether he is right or whether the parents of the youth whom he depicts are arranted in their denunciations of his pen-pictures.

Read these extracts from "Travelling Companions," a story by Henry James, written a generation ago. They may be said to reflect the customs and manners of the period.

"The young lady rose slowly, drawing on a glove. Her age I fancied to be twenty-two. The was of middle stature, with a charming slender figure. She was largely characterized by that physical delicacy and that personal elegance which seldom fail to betray Americans in Europe.

"There are long periods when she cordially loathes her entire family. She is quite unprincipled; her philosophy is carpe diem for herself, and laissez faire for others. She loves shocking stories; she has that coarse streak that usually goes with natures that are both fine and big. She wants people to like her, but if they do not, it never worries her or changes her."

Five minutes later Rosalind "kisses definitely and thoroughly" a man whom she has never seen before. Her unconventionality startles the reader, but nevertheless he cannot but envy the hero of the moment.

So there we are. Fifty years ago, true to the rhyme, men and women were differently depicted. The men bowed, made love only after long acquaintance, and then, in discreet woodland nooks. The women stopped before a picture and wanted to photograph it because of its beauty.

To-day Rosalind, fiery, passionate, spoiled, yet wholly lovable, kisses almost on sight, loathes her family at times, likes naughty stories, and, if necessary, would be perfectly willing to admit these things.

Are Rosalind and the other characters of to-day's fiction true to type and true to life? Is the fact that they are the reason why the "other generation" denies the charges? Or are they unreal, as was possibly, the fictional character of fifty years ago, who wanted to photograph a beautiful picture, the exception, rather than the rule?

"Flappers and Philosophers" is a far more melancholy spectacle than "The Book of Susan." We were among the first to welcome the richness, the verve, the promise of Mr. Fitzgerald's "This Side of Paradise." We were not blind to his essential immaturity of outlook and, therefore, were a little astonished at Professor Phelps's certainty that he would "go far." Alas, he has gone far. He has gone from the polished literary dexterity of his first book to the manner of writing that makes "lay" an intransitive verb and zestfully employs that indescribable particle "onto." No, this is not pedantry. An illiterate genius can afford such luxuries. In him they argue no insensitiveness or ugly haste or careless drifting with the crowd. Mr. Fitzgerald is a university-bred man and seemed to be a poet. The substance of the eight stories in his volume is in harmony with his new manner. They have a rather ghastly rattle of movement that apes energy and a hectic straining after emotion that apes intensity. The surface is unnaturally taut; the substance beneath is slack and withered as by a premature old age. The Offshore Pirate is on the level of a musical comedy "book"; The Ice Palace and Benediction are falsely effective bits of sentimentality; Head and Shoulders is sheer trickery—a prestidigitator's "stunt" in writing. The Cut Glass Bowl and Bernice Bobs Her Hair touch human nature and the course of life more closely. But both share the ugly hardness of the book's title. This hardness is the hardness of neither austerity nor disillusion; it is neither ascetic nor cynical. It is merely harsh and flippant.

What has happened to Mr. Fitzgerald? His first book has had a well-merited success. Did he retire, after a very proper interval of gaiety, to his study in order to write a deeper, richer, riper book? Unhappily we are in an environment where only failure can save the soul of youth. In "This Side of Paradise" there was both gold and dross. Instead of wringing his art, in Mr. Hergesheimer's fine expression, free of all dross, Mr. Fitzgerald proceeded to cultivate it and to sell it to the *Saturday Evening Post*. Why write good books? You have to sell something like five thousand copies to earn the price of one story. *Sic transit gloria artis.* The Nation

For my point of vantage was the dividing line between the two generations, and there I sat—somewhat self-consciously. When my first big mail came in—hundreds and hundreds of letters on a story about a girl who bobbed her hair—it seemed rather absurd that they should come to me about it. On the other hand, for a shy man it was nice to be somebody except oneself again: to be "the Author" as one had been "the Lieutenant." Of course one wasn't really an author any more than one had been an army officer, but nobody seemed to guess behind the false face.

—"Early Success"

Throughout the previous winter one small matter had been a subtle and omnipresent irritant—the question of Gloria's gray fur coat. At that time women enveloped in long squirrel wraps could be seen every few yards along Fifth Avenue. The women were converted to the shape of tops. They seemed porcine and obscene; they resembled kept women in the concealing richness, the feminine animality of the garment. Yet—Gloria wanted a gray squirrel coat.

—The Beautiful and Damned

PHOTOGRAPH BY GORDON BRYANT

The wife of F. Scott Fitzgerald, who put her in two brilliant novels, "This Side of Paradise" and "The Beautiful and Damned," does not need to join the Lucy Stone League in order to identify herself as a personality. Everything Zelda Fitzgerald says and does stands out

Eulogy on the Flapper

By Zelda Sayre Fitzgerald

THE Flapper is deceased. Her outer accoutrements have been bequeathed to several hundred girls' schools throughout the country, to several thousand big-town shop-girls, always imitative of the several hundred girls' schools, and to several million small-town belles always imitative of the big-town shop-girls via the "novelty stores" of their respective small towns. It is a great bereavement to me, thinking as I do that there will never be another product of circumstance to take the place of the dear departed.

I am assuming that the Flapper will live by her accomplishments and not by her Flapping. How can a girl say again, "I do not want to be respectable because respectable girls are not attractive," and how can she again so wisely arrive at the knowledge that "boys *do* dance most with the girls they kiss most," and that "men *will* marry the girls they could kiss before they had asked papa?" Perceiving these things, the Flapper awoke from her lethargy of sub-deb-ism, bobbed her hair, put on her choicest pair of earrings and a great deal of audacity and rouge and went into the battle. She flirted because it was fun to flirt and wore a one-piece bathing suit because she had a good figure, she covered her face with powder and paint because she didn't need it and she refused to be bored chiefly because she wasn't boring. She was conscious that the things she did were the things she had always wanted to do. Mothers disapproved of their sons taking the Flapper to dances, to teas, to swim and most of all to heart. She had mostly masculine friends, but youth does not need friends—it needs only crowds, and the more masculine the crowds the more crowded for the Flapper. Of these things the Flapper was well aware!

Now audacity and earrings and one-piece bathing suits have become fashionable and the first Flappers are so secure in their positions that their attitude toward themselves is scarcely distinguishable from that of their débutante sisters of ten years ago toward *themselves*. They have won their case. They are blasé. And the new Flappers galumping along in unfastened galoshes are striving not to do what is pleasant and what they please, but simply to outdo the founders of the Honorable Order of Flappers; to outdo *everything*. Flapperdom has become a game; it is no longer a philosophy.

I came across an amazing editorial a short time ago. It fixed the blame for all divorces, crime waves, high prices, unjust taxes, violations of the Volstead Act and crimes in Hollywood upon the head of the Flapper. The paper wanted back the dear old fireside of long ago, wanted to resuscitate "Hearts and Flowers" and have it instituted as the sole tune played at dances from now on and forever, wanted prayers before breakfast on Sunday morning—and to bring things back to this superb state it advocated restraining the Flapper. All neurotic "women of thirty" and all divorce cases, according to the paper, could be traced to the Flapper. As a matter of fact, she hasn't yet been given a chance. I know of no divorcées or neurotic women of thirty who were ever Flappers. Do you? And I should think that fully airing the desire for unadulterated gaiety, for romances that she knows will not last, and for dramatizing herself would make her more inclined to favor the "back to the fireside" movement than if she were repressed until age gives her those rights that only youth has the right to give.

I refer to the right to experiment with herself as a transient, poignant figure who will be dead tomorrow. Women, despite the fact that nine out of ten of them go through life with a death-bed air either of snatching-the-last-moment or with martyr-resignation, do not die tomorrow—or the next day. They have to live on to any one of many bitter ends, and I should think the sooner they learned that things weren't going to be over until they were too tired to care, the quicker the divorce court's popularity would decline.

"Out with inhibitions," gleefully shouts the Flapper, and elopes with the Arrow-collar boy that she had been thinking, for a week or two, might make a charming breakfast companion. The marriage is annulled by the proverbial irate parent and the Flapper comes home, none the worse for wear, to marry, years later, and live happily ever afterwards.

I see no logical reasons for keeping the young illusioned. Certainly disillusionment comes easier at twenty than at forty—the fundamental and inevitable disillusionments, I mean. Its effects on the Flappers I have known have simply been to crystallize their ambitious desires and give form to their code of living so that they *can* come home and live happily ever afterwards—or go into the movies or become social service "workers" or something. Older people, except a few geniuses, artistic and financial, simply throw up their hands, heave a great many heart-rending sighs and moan to themselves something about what a hard thing life is—and then, of course, turn to their children and wonder why they don't believe in Santa Claus and the kindness of their fellow men and in the tale that they will be happy if they are good and obedient. And yet the strongest cry against Flapperdom is that it is making the youth of the country cynical. It is making them intelligent and teaching them to capitalize their natural resources and get their money's worth. They are merely applying business methods to being young.

Metropolitan Magazine *(June 1922)*

Fitzgerald, Flappers and Fame

An Interview with F. Scott Fitzgerald

By Frederick James Smith

F. SCOTT FITZGERALD is the recognized spokesman of the younger generation—the dancing, flirting, frivoling, lightly philosophizing young America — since the publication of his now famous flapper tale, "This Side of Paradise." Perhaps our elders were surprised to discover, as Mr. Fitzgerald relates, that the young folk, particularly the so-called gentler sex, were observing religion and morals slightly flippantly, that they had their own views on ethics, that they said damn and gotta and whatta and 'sall, that older viewpoints bored them and that they both smoked cigarets and admitted they were "just full of the devil."

All of which *is* the younger generation as Fitzgerald sees it. Indeed, the blond and youthful Fitzgerald, still in his twenties, is of, and a part of, it. He left Princeton in the class of '17 and, like certain young America, slipped into the world war *via* the training camp and an officership. We suspect he did it, much as the questioning hero of "This Side of Paradise," because "it was the thing to do." He was a lieutenant in the 45th Infantry and later an aide to Brigadier General Ryan. It was in training camp that he first drafted "This Side of Paradise."

F. SCOTT FITZGERALD
Study by Gordon Bryant

"We all knew, of course, we were going to be killed," relates Fitzgerald with a smile, "and I, like everybody else, wanted to leave something for posterity." But the war ended and Fitzgerald tried writing advertising with a New York commercial firm. All the time he was endeavoring to write short stories and sell them, but every effort came back with a rejection slip. Finally, Fitzgerald resolved upon a desperate step. He would go back to his home in St. Paul and live a year with his parents, aiming consistently to "get over."

Then he sold his first story to *Smart Set* in June, 1918, receiving thirty dollars therefrom. He worked for three months rewriting "This Side of Paradise — and sold it to Scribner's. Success came with a bang and now Fitzgerald is contributing to most of the leading magazines. At the present moment he is completing his second novel, to be ready shortly.

"I realize that 'This Side of Paradise' was immature and callow, just as such critics as H. L. Menken and others have said, altho they were kind enough to say I had possibilities. My new novel will, I hope, be more mature. It will be the story of two young married folk and it will show their gradual disintegration—broadly speaking, how they go to the devil. I have one ideal—to write honestly, as I see it.

"Of course, I know the sort of young folks I depict *are* as I paint them. I'm sick of the sexless animals writers have been giving us. I am tired, too, of hearing that the world war broke down the moral barriers of the younger generation. Indeed, except for leaving its touch of destruction here and there, I do not think the war left any real lasting effect. Why, it is almost forgotten right now.

"The younger generation has been changing all thru the last twenty years. The war had little or nothing to do with it. I put the change up to literature. Our skepticism or cynicism, if you wish to call it that, or, if you are older, our callow flippancy, is due to the way H. G. Wells and other intellectual leaders have been thinking and reflecting life. Our generation has grown up upon their work. So college-bred young people, here and in England, have made radical departures from the Victorian era.

"Girls, for instance, have found the accent shifted from chemical purity to breadth of viewpoint, intellectual charm and piquant cleverness. It is natural that they want to be interesting. And there is one fact that the younger generation could not overlook. All, or nearly all, the famous men and women of history—the kind who left a lasting mark—were, let us say, of broad moral views. Our generation has absorbed all this. Thus it is that we find the young woman of 1920 flirting, kissing, viewing life lightly, saying damn without a blush, playing along the danger line in an immature way—a sort of mental baby vamp. It is quite the same with the boys. They want to be like the interesting chaps they read about.

(*Continued on page 75*)

continued

Yes, I put it all up to the intellectuals like Wells.

"Personally, I prefer this sort of girl. Indeed, I married the heroine of my stories. I would not be interested in any other sort of woman."

We asked Fitzgerald about motion pictures. "I used to try scenarios in the old days," he laughed. "Invariably they came back. Now, however, I am being adapted to the screen. I suspect it must be difficult to mold my stuff into the conventional movie form with its creaky mid-Victorian sugar. Personally, when I go to the pictures, I like to see a pleasant flapper like Constance Talmadge or I want to see comedies like those of Chaplin's or Lloyd's. I'm not strong for the uplift stuff. It simply isn't life to me."

Shadowland (*January 1921*)

Money Earned by writing since leaving Army

51

Record for 1919

Stories

Babes in the Woods			$ 30.00
The Debutante (Play)			35.00
The Four Fists			150.00
The Cut Glass Bowl			150.00
Porcelain & Pink (Play)			35.00
Dalyrimple goes Wrong			40.00
Benediction			40.00
Head and Shoulders	400.00	Commission 10%	360.00
A Dirge (Poem)			4.00
Mr. Icky (Play)			35.00
Total Earnings			879.00

Something in his nature never got over things, never accepted his sudden rise to fame, because all the steps weren't there.
—"The Note-Books"

52

Record for 1920

Stories	The Ice Palace	$400.00	Commission	10%	$360.00
*	Myra Meets His Family	400.00	"	"	360.00
	The Camels Back	500.00	"	"	450.00
	Bernice Bobs her Hair	500.00	"	"	450.00
	The Off-Shore Pirate	500.00	"	"	450.00
	The Smilers				35.00
	May Day				200.00
	Tarquin of Cheapside				50.00
	The Jelly bean	900.00	"	"	810.00
	The Russet Witch	900.00	"	"	810.00
	Total				3,975.00
Movies	Head and Shoulders	2500.00	"	"	2,250.00
	Myra Meets His Family	1000.00	"	"	900.00
	The Off Shore Pirate	2250.00	"	"	2,025.00
	Option on my out put	3000.00	"	"	2,700.00
	Total				7,425.00
Other Writings	This is a Magazine				75.00
	Total				75.00
From Books	This Side of Paradise				6,200.00
	Flappers and Philosophers				500.00
	Total				6,700.00
	Total				$18,175.00

* Commission --- The Lees of Happiness $750.00, Com 10% $675.00
Total $18,850.00

Montgomery —
March 1921

MONTGOMERY ALA 1253PM MAR 13 1921
F SCOTT FITZGERALD 38 WEST 59 ST NEWYORK NY
062
I LOVE YOU MY DARLING WILL YOU BRING BOX BILTMORE WHITE POWDER
BLUE FAN AND SCRAP BOOK I MISS YOU SO
ZELDA

In March 1921 Zelda visited her parents in Montgomery; Scott joined her there.

april | Planning our trip on the Aquitania.

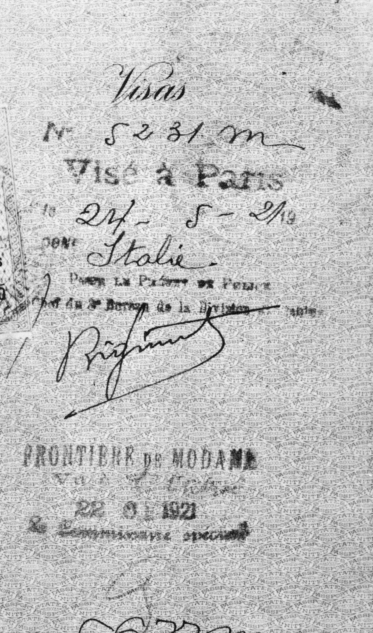

Visas

No 5231 m

Visé à Paris

le 24 - 5 - 21/19

pour Italie

Pour le Préfet de Police

Chef du 3e Bureau de la Division

VISA DE PASSEPORTS 2F & 2/10

FRONTIÈRE DE MODANE

22 05 1921

R.M.S. AQUITANIA

The many Montgomery friends of Mr. and Mrs. F. Scott Fitzgerald, of New York, will be interested to learn that they will sail on Wednesday, May 3, on the Steamship Acquitania, for Europe, where they will remain until the late fall.

ABSTRACT OF LOG OF THE

Cunard R.M.S. "Aquitania" (Quadruple Screw Turbine)

(Captain Sir. James T. W. Charles, K.B.E., C.B., R.D., R.N.R.)

NEW YORK TO CHERBOURG & SOUTHAMPTON.

Date 1921	Dist.	Latitude	Longtitude	Weather, etc.
Tuesday May 3				At 2-58 p.m. N.Y.T. left Company's Pier, New York
" " "		N.	W.	At 4-50 p.m. N.Y.T Ambrose Channel L'tship abeam
Wednesday " 4	423	39·59	64·37	Fresh wind; mod. sea
Thursday " 5	504	39·41	53·41	Strong wind ; rough sea; Heavy rain storms
Friday " 6	503	41·08	43·21	Mod. breeze; mod. sea; clear
Saturday " 7	491	44·49	33·21	Light wind ; slight sea ; clear
Sunday " 8	498	47·34	22·03	Mod. wind and sea ; clear
Monday " 9	505	49·16	9·38	Light Wind; siight sea ; clear
" " "	318	To Cherbourg		

Arrived at Cherbourg Breakwater on Tuesday, May 10th., at 3-0 a.m. (G.M.T.)

Distance—3242 nautical miles. Passage— 6 days, 6 hours, 10 minutes. Average speed—21.6

CUNARD LINE

1840

NEW YORK · CHERBOURG · SOUTHAMPTON
DIRECT

HOTEL CECIL,
STRAND,
LONDON, W.C.

JULY 4. 1921.
SAVOY HOTEL.
BALL ROOM
PASS OUT
ONE

Please come
to tea today
at 5 and
bring Mrs Fitz

This part to be RETAINED.
Keith. Prowse & Co. Ltd.
162, New Bond St., W. Tel. 6000 Regent. 12 lines.
Gaiety Theatre
EVENING.
16 MAY 1921
day Tues
Admit
STALLS B 5. 6
ISSUED AT

May Sailed the 3d. Tullochs, Heywards, Engalicheff. Celebrities. London 10th
Kingsley, Leslie, Galesworthy, Lady Churchill. The Cecil. Oxford. Paris 17
Folies, Kay Laurel, Café de la Paix. Cherbourge. Cabinot. Wapping
Venice 26th The Stuyvesant, Robbins. Pietro. Versailles. Malmaison. Clothes
June Florence 3d Rome 8th Lolia Carter, Americans, Embassy. Paris
the 22nd Quai Dorsay - before the St James London 30th
Claridges, Cavendish, Bob Handley, Tim Douglass, Brown
Baker. Dancing in Savoy. ~~The 4th~~. Venice - man kicked in stomach
because he wasn't a Roman. The women weeping in Vatican. The loot of 20 centuries
July The 4th Cambridge. Clothes in London. The Celtic. The
Duncans & Lord Bruce. The Biltmore New York.
Montgomery on 27th. The obnoxiousness of the australians, cockney
& rural american. The hills near Rome. Cherbourg at dawn.

The Fitzgeralds spent the winter of 1920/21 in New York in an apartment at 38 West 59th Street. They took a trip to Europe from May to July, visiting England, France, and Italy.

TEL. P.O. HAMPSTEAD 3684.

Grove Lodge,
The Grove, Hampstead,
London, N.W.3.

May 13

Dear Mr. Scott Fitzgerald,
Mr. Maxwell Perkins tells me you are just arrived over here. It would be a great pleasure to my wife & myself if Mrs. Fitzgerald and you could come and dine here with us at 8 o'clock. The St. John Ervines are coming, and possibly Lennox Robinson, the Irish playwright.
If you come by 'Tube', take your train at 'Strand' station, to Hampstead station, and we are 4 minutes walk, up Holly Hill into The Grove, and turn to the left towards the tall white Admiral's House. Grove Lodge adjoins it.
Much hoping to see you. Sincerely yours
John Galsworthy
By taxi-cab it's about twenty minutes from the hotel Cecil. J.G.

"The men observe the rules of thought"
Grantchester Brooke

"And is there honey yet for tea?"
Grantchester

. . . We went to London to see a fog and saw Tallulah Bankhead which was, perhaps, about the same effect. Then the fog blew up and we reconstituted Arnold Bennett's Pretty Lady *and the works of Compton McKenzie which Daddy loved so, and we had a curious nocturnal bottle of champagne with members of the British polo team. We dined with Galsworthy and lunched with Lady Randolph Churchill and had tea in the mellow remembrances of Shane Leslie's house, who later took us to see the pickpockets pick in Wopping. They did.*

—ZF to Scottie, c. 1944.

Goofo at Trinity, Col. Cambridge

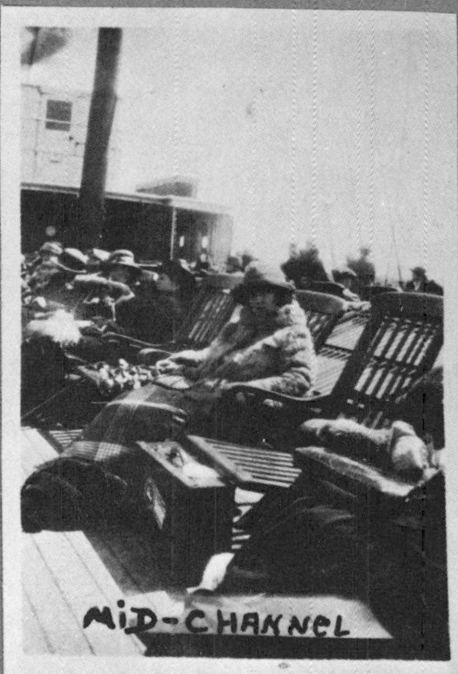
MID-CHANNEL

Confusion in the Cecil

Goofo vamping the Navy (Lt. Robbins, Venice)

Goofo at Fiesole

These wops! (Fiesole)

"Me and Goofo in a Gondola"

New York lay behind them. The forces that produced them lay behind them. That Alabama and David would never sense the beat of any other pulse half so exactly, since we can only recognize in other environments what we have grown familiar with in our own, played no part in their expectations.

"I could cry!" said David, "I want to get the band to play on the deck. It's the most thrilling God-damned thing in the world—all the experiences of man lie there to choose from!"

"Selection," said Alabama, "is the privilege for which we suffer in life."

"It's so magnificent! It's glorious! We can have wine with our lunch!"

"Oh, Continent!" she apostrophized, "send me a dream!"

—*Save Me the Waltz* (ZF)

God damn the continent of Europe. It is of merely antiquarian interest. Rome is only a few years behind Tyre and Babylon.

—FSF to Edmund Wilson, May 1921.

"Doc" on the Celtic

Goofo & dog, homeward bound

BRIDE ON FIRST VISIT TO ST. PAUL

Mrs. F. Scott Fitzgerald, of New York, with Mr. Fitzgerald, arrived here the past week. They have taken a house at Dellwood where they will spend some time. Mrs. Fitzgerald was formerly Miss Zelda Sayre of Montgomery, Ala., and is visiting in St. Paul for the first time since her marriage. Mr. Fitzgerald, who is a well known author, is the son of Mr. and Mrs. Edward Fitzgerald, 599 Summit avenue.

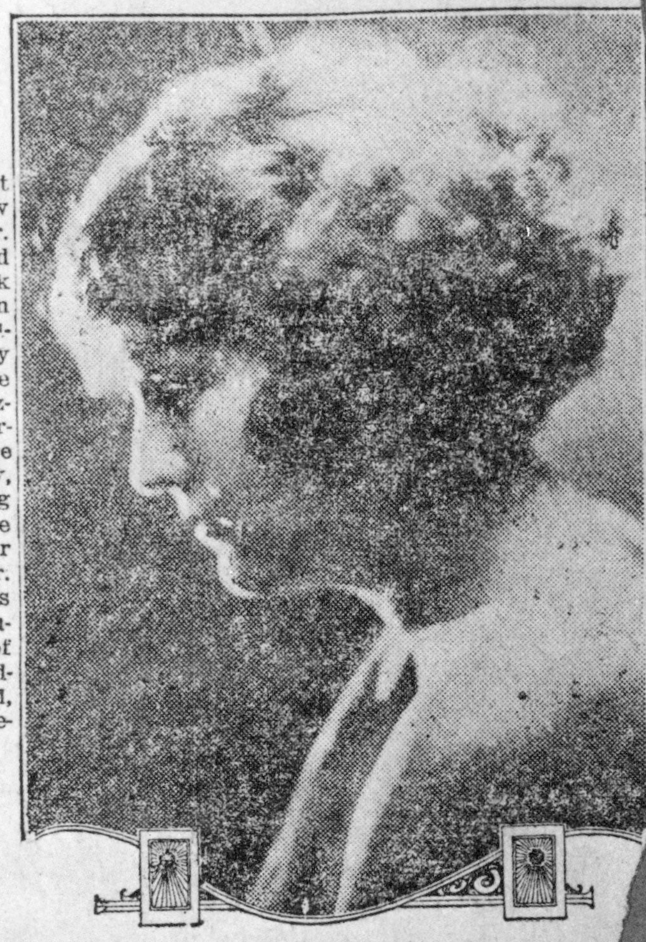

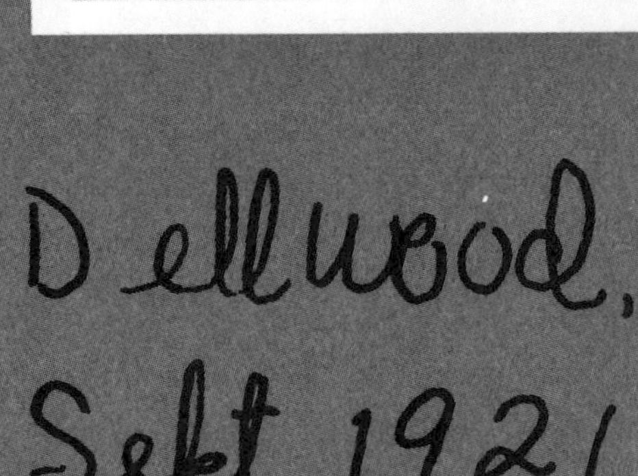

Dellwood. Sept 1921

Upon returning from Europe the Fitzgeralds visited Montgomery. They considered remaining for the birth of their child, but the heat drove them to Minnesota, where they first lived at Dellwood on White Bear Lake.

It was typical of our precarious position in New York that when our child was to be born we played safe and went home to St. Paul—it seemed inappropriate to bring a baby into all that glamour and loneliness.

—"My Lost City"

Her tears dissolved in a twisted smile.

"Well—you shouldn't have said that, then. Let's talk about the b-baby."

Anthony paced the floor and spoke as though rehearsing for a debate.

"To put it briefly, there are two babies we could have, two distinct and logical babies, utterly differentiated. There's the baby that's the combination of the best of both of us. Your body, my eyes, my mind, your intelligence—and then there is the baby which is our worst—my body, your disposition, and my irresolution."

"I like that second baby," she said.

—*The Beautiful and Damned*

NEWYORK NY 26
MRS FRANCIS SCOTT FITZGERALD
485
599 SUMMIT AVE STPAUL MINN
CONGRATULATIONS FEARED TWINS HAVE YOU BOBBED HER HAIR LOVE FROM ALL
TOWNSEND ALEC JOHN AND LUDLOW.
Martin McKaig Peale Bishop Fowler

MONTGOMERY ALA 4
MRS F SCOTT FIRTGERALD
459
599 SUMMIT AVE STPAUL MINN
CONGRATULATIONS ZELDA DEAR KNOW SHES THE SWEETEST LITTLE THING IMAGINABLE
BALLIE.

Scotty Fitzgerald
October twenty-sixth
Nineteen twenty-one

Scotty's Book

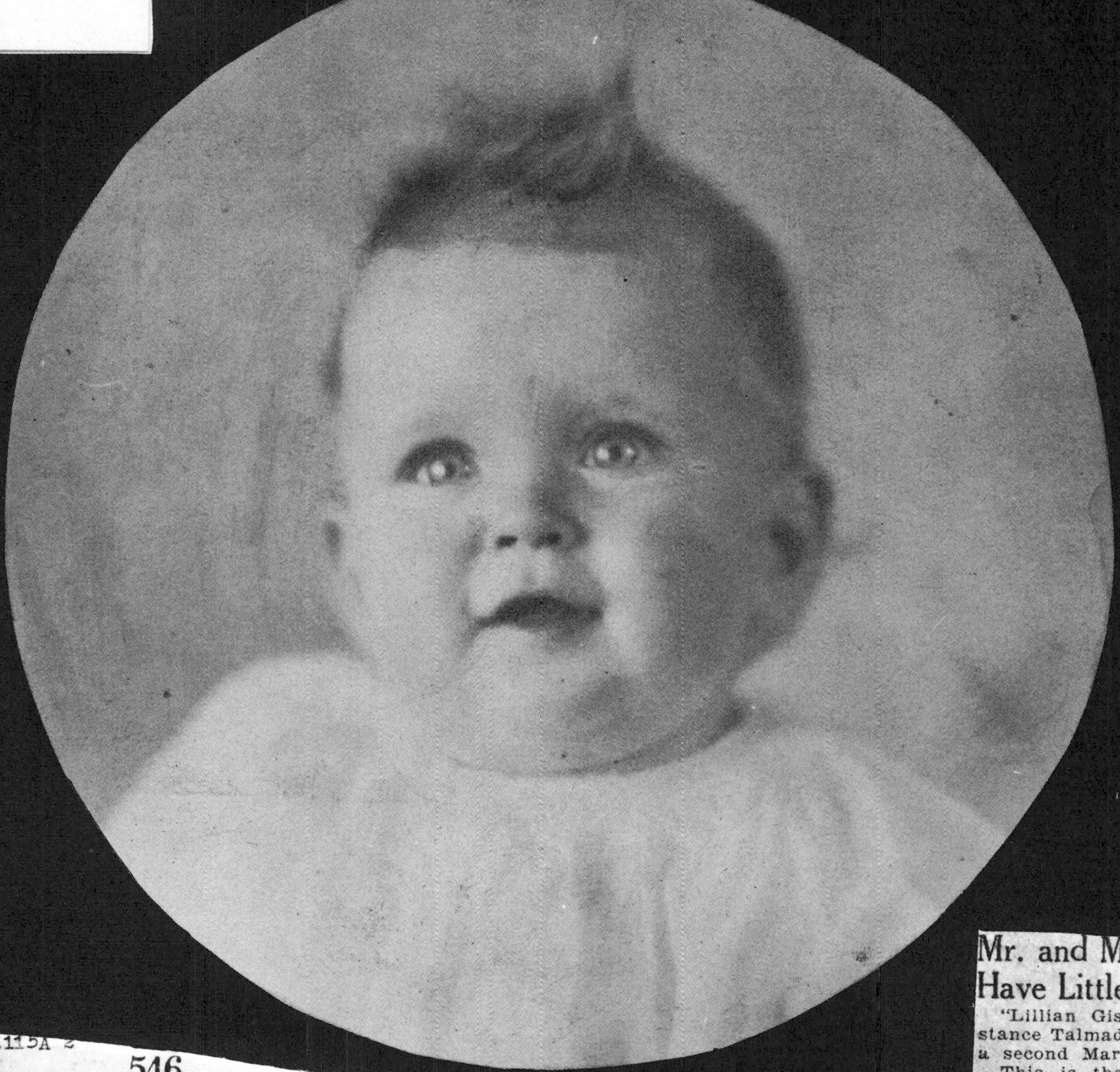

CAMBRIDGE MASS 1115A 2
MR AND MRS F SCOTT FITZGERALD
546
593 SUMMITT AVE STPAUL MINN
SCOTT AND FELDA HEARTIEST CONGRATULATIONS CC AND HAM ENVIOUS FELICITATIONS
JOHN BRIGGS JR.

FY MONTGOMERY ALA 910A 27
MR AND MRS F SCOTT FITZGERALD
545
Commodore Hotel
599 SUMMIT AVE STPAUL MINN
THE NEWS IS GREAT WE ARE PROUD LOVE AND CONGRATULATIONS
MAMA AND PAPA.

Mr. and Mrs. Fitzgerald Have Little Daughter—

"Lillian Gish is in mourning; Constance Talmadge is a back number; and a second Mary Pickford has arrived".

This is the telegram which Judge and Mrs. A. J. Sayre of this city have just received from Mr. and Mrs. F. Scott Fitzgerald, announcing the birth of a little daughter, whom they have named Scottie for her father.

Mrs. Fitzgerald is widely known both in Montgomery, her native home, and in New York where she has resided since her marriage to the noted young novelist, short story writer and critic.

It is with interest and pleasure that this announcement will be read not only in Montgomery but throughout Alabama where both Mr. and Mrs. Fitzgerald are extremely popular.

Many telegrams of congratulations have already reached Mr. and Mrs. Fitzgerald who are visiting relatives in St. Paul, Minn.

F. SCOTT FITZGERALD IS FATHER OF BABY GIRL

Mr. and Mrs. F. Scott Fitzgerald, Commodore hotel, are receiving congratulations on the birth of a daughter, born yesterday.

The baby has been named Scottie Fitzgerald.

Mr. Fitzgerald is the young St. Paul novelist and short story writer.

" 'All right,' I said, 'I'm glad it's a girl. And I hope she'll be a fool—that's the best thing a girl can be in this world, a beautiful little fool.' "
—*The Great Gatsby*

Weather Rotten

THE ST. PAUL DAILY DIRGE

Mortuary Edition

PRICE—A SWEET KISS. ST. PAUL, MINNESOTA, FRIDAY, JANUARY 13, 1922. VOL. I, NO. 1.

COTILLION IS SAD FAILURE

Frightful Orgy at University Club

The benedict's cotillion given Friday, the 13th, was the worst social failure of the year. In a sordid first fight started by Mr. William Motter four noses were broken and one removable bridge was bent out of all recognition.

The fight was said to have started because some remark derogatory to Yale was made before Mr. Motter.

The "Bad Luck Ball," as it was called by the vain, shallow and frivolous society people who were present, was opened by Gov. Preus, who did a tasty clog dance with Mrs. L. P. Ordway, Jr. (the Twin City correspondent for Town Topics). This was followed by a piano, zither and harp number rendered by Mrs. William Motter and Mrs. Samuel Ray, who is visiting here from her home in Jersey City, N. J.

Mr. Homer Sweeney, who with Mr. Clifford Corning was to have led the cotillion, unfortunately arrived in no condition to lead anything. In fact the only leading in which he participated was when he was led from the room by Mr. Eddie Saunders, whose feelings were naturally outraged by this performance.

Mr. Ted White, the well-known Harvard lacrosse player, wore a braided surtout of feathered duveteen and a diamond tiara. Mr. Alvah Warren was splendid in a Worth creation with slashed pockets and a pearl and cocoanut stomacher.

Mrs. C. O. Kalman was there, in rags as usual. Mrs. Samuel Ray wore a dress of pink gingham, a Woolworth creation, and a beautiful imitation diamond.

In fact the whole party was simply obnoxious. Nobody had any luck at all, and when it was over the two leaders were presented with large life-sized lemons in thanks for their wretched services.

It is hoped that these vain, frivolous peacocks who strut through the gorgeous vistas of the exclusive and corrupt St. Paul clubs will learn to conduct themselves in a more normal, wholesome way.

"It is disgusting," said Mr. T. J. Bunk, the well-known old settler. "In my day things were different. When we danced we did not do the toddle or any of the modern lascivious dances. We stuck to the good old lancers and the shimmee. In those days it was the proper thing to have biblical readings during the evening and the festivities always closed with a good rousing prayer. We did not have scotch and rye then or any of these immoral dishes like caviare and anchovy a couple of doughnuts and a pint of moonshine apiece for everybody was all that was needed. We were red-blooded, bulge-chest, two-fisted he men in those days, and don't you forget it."

A SCENE FROM LOUISA ALCOTT'S NEW JAZZ NOVEL — LITTLE WOMEN.

Flax Man Fears Fluke

Mr. Shreve Archer was thrown into a heavy gloom this evening when the news reached St. Paul that flax had fallen to 40 cents. He has sold his Dellwood home to Mr. Otto Finkelbaum, the well-known farrier and will spend next summer at Bald Eagle lake. He has resigned from the White Bear Yacht club and been elected a member of the Phalen links. Flax is expected to go still lower. Mr. Archer says he has ceased to care.

Business Rotten, Says Bootlegger

Mr. Chuck Kennedy, a well known bootlegger of this vicinity, gave out an interview to our reporter in which he says that business is no good.

Mr. Kennedy has just returned from the Canadian border with a truckload of Scotch whisky.

Boost St. Paul! Patronize local bootleggers!

PARIS HAT MODES. POSED BY MRS. HORACE IRVINE AND MRS. JOHN ORDWAY.

NO STILLS IN STILLWATER, SAYS CONVICT

William Skinner, better known as "Hardboiled Billy," for years a notorious safe cracker and gunman, was released from Stillwater last night, after having served an eight-year term. His hair had turned perfectly white and his hand trembled as he kissed the warden goodby.

"The 10 happiest years of my life," he said, as he walked away with our reporter. "Nothing to worry about."

Mr. Skiner will soon publish his book of prison verses "Bread and Water."

SELLS SECOND HAND AND THIRD HA...

...ey ...ed Fizz

Chilie... N...

BIG BUSINESS MAN INTERESTED IN...

Mr. Frederick Ritzinger of this city is said to be interested in designing automobile bodies. Visit his shop some day in the cellar of the Hamm building. He says that since the egg market crashed, business has been a pain. He is reported to have referred to his friends' double chins as "spares."

GROWS EY... OVER N...

Matron Surprises Friends by Her Vivid Orbs.

A NEW STATUE OF JOAN OF ARC JUST ERECTED BY FRENCH GOVERNMENT.

PROMINENT PLUMBER IS PESSIMISTI...

"Things are terrible," said ... G. Ordway, sitting in a luxur... tub in the Crane-Ordway ... shop on Selby ave. ... only thing that will save ... Ordway are on the rocks ... fall before spring."

Mr. Ordway is a well-... uate of the Union Theological seminary.

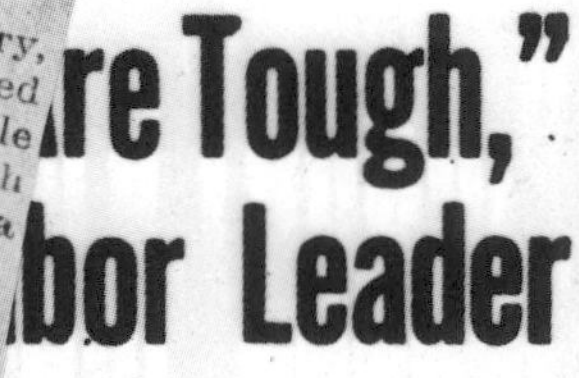

MRS. T. L. WANN, JR. IN DASHING BATHING SUIT.

...are Tough," ...bor Leader

"WHY DIE?" FUR MAN DEMANDS

"I never expect to die," says Mr. Jule Hannaford, formerly editor of the Twin City Reporter, and now in the fur trade. "I shall live forever."

"How?" he was asked.

"Well," he answered, "I survived the Bad Luck Ball given by the benedicts, and so it's certain that nothing can harm me."

With this he struck our reporter a sharp blow on the ear and hurried off.

ENTERTAINS FOR YALE PROFESSOR

Mr. William Motter, the president of the Yale Alumni association of St. Paul and one of the most ardent Yale men in the city, entertained in his office this afternoon for Mr. William Lyon Phelps, the Yale professor. The meeting was concluded by Mr. Motter leading the Yale men in Bright College Years. Mr. Motter has a son entering Yale this fall.

Princeton was represented on this present occasion by Mr. Theodore Driscoll.

LAWYER LANGUISHES IN LOCKUP.

Mr. Samuel Ordway, a young lawyer of the city, was arrested on the corner of Selby and Western aves. for stealing a tube of Pepsodent tooth paste from W. A. Frost, the celebrated druggist. Fortunately Mr. Ordway's theft was observed by Mr. Frost's little assistant, Carl Schumeman, and the youth yelled lustily for the police. Mr. Ordway slept soundly in his cell during the night.

F. Scott Hides Following Bow of "The Dirge"

Society Paper May Cause St. Paul Author to Write "Why the Editor Left Town."

F. Scott Fitzgerald, St. Paul's youngest literary celebrity, is said to have locked the doors of his Goodrich ave. home, barred the windows, drawn the shades, and denied himself to all callers.

He fears mob violence following the appearance of "The Dirge," a newspaper which made its bow to that part of the public which attended the Bad Luck Ball at the University club last night. He is accused of being the editor.

Among the items gleaned from the somewhat spicy columns are these:

Mrs. Horace Irvine and Mrs. John Ordway, society leaders, will open a millinery shop on 7th st. to help support their husbands.

John Upham and Pual Kalman are suspected of selling repainted automobiles for new ones.

William Skinner, alias Hard-boiled Billy, has been released from Stillwater.

Samuel Ordway, prominent lawyer, was arrested for stealing a tube of tooth paste.

The first number of the paper was described as the "Mortuary edition," and the price given as "a sweet kiss."

The paper says that the cotillion was a sad failure, terming it in many respects a "frightful orgy." It sets forth that Homer Sweney and Clifford Corning, who were to have led the cotillion, were "in no condition to lead anything."

"Ted White," says the lead story, "wore a braided surtout of feathered duvetyn and a diamond tiara, while Alvah Warren was splendid in a Worth creation with slashed pockets and a pearl and cocoanut stomacher."

The society notes divulge that Mrs. C. O. Kalman was there "in rags as usual," while Mrs. Samuel Rea wore "a dress of pink gingham, a Woolworth creation, and a beautiful imitation diamond."

Among the advertisements was the following:

Matron Surprises Friends by Her Vivid Orbs.

Mrs. F. Scott Fitzgerald had always wanted eyelashes. She had used every preparation, including stove-polish and blackberry wine with no result. She went into a store and bought a set of **Pigman's Portable Eyelashes** and now she is not ashamed to go anywhere.

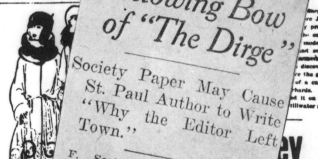

"Pigman's Portable Eyelashes go on easily," she writes, "and a pair of pliers will remove them with sucess."—Advertisement.

The paper was strikingly illustrated.

Mr. Fitzgerald is said to be working on a new story entitled, "Why the Editor Left Town."

St. Paul News

Fitzgerald wrote and published this parody newspaper distributed at a dance in St. Paul, January 1922.

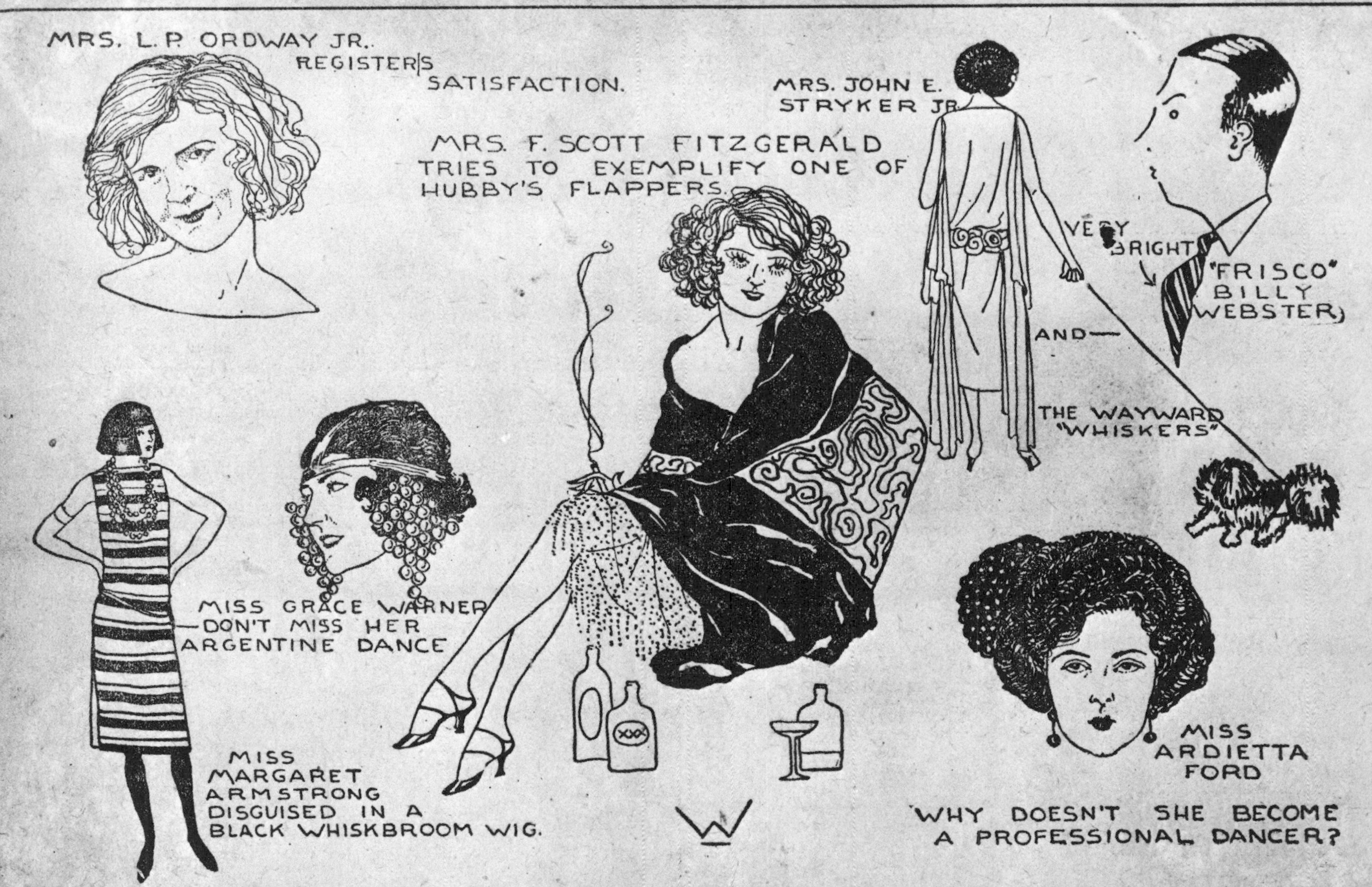
JUNIOR LEAGUE REHEARSAL—By Helen Wallace
MRS. L. P. ORDWAY JR. REGISTERS SATISFACTION.
MRS. F. SCOTT FITZGERALD TRIES TO EXEMPLIFY ONE OF HUBBY'S FLAPPERS.
MRS. JOHN E. STRYKER JR.
VERY BRIGHT "FRISCO" BILLY WEBSTER
AND—
THE WAYWARD "WHISKERS"
MISS GRACE WARNER —DON'T MISS HER ARGENTINE DANCE
MISS MARGARET ARMSTRONG DISGUISED IN A BLACK WHISKBROOM WIG.
MISS ARDIETTA FORD
WHY DOESN'T SHE BECOME A PROFESSIONAL DANCER?

THE DAILY NEWS STAFF ARTIST TAKES A SLANT AT ST. PAUL SOCIETY GIRLS IN THEIR FINAL DRESS REHEARSAL FOR THE JUNIOR LEAGUE ANNUAL FROLIC TOMORROW NIGHT.

F. Scott Fitzgerald's "Midnight Flappers" Headlines Amateur Vaudeville —Noted Screen Star Comes in Vaudeville Playlet—Charles Aldrich, Character Actor of Fame, at New Palace.

FOR another week vaudeville has things to itself in St. Paul, with even more than the regular variety theaters presenting it.

The Junior league's annual vaudeville show will be given at the Auditorium tomorrow night, with "Midnight Flappers," F. Scott Fitzgerald's musical revue, "headlined."

6. "Midnight Flappers" (musical revue by F. Scott Fitzgerald).

Scene—a fashionable cabaret. Time—The present.

CAST.

Maitre d'hotel.......................George Lamb
Abie.......................George Harris
Rachel.......................Alice Warren
A flapper.......................Mrs. F. Scott Fitzgerald
A Yale man.......................Harry G. Allen, Jr.
A roue.......................Cornelius Van Ness
A playmate.......................Mrs. L. P. Ordway, Jr.
Sailor waiter.......................John Eagan
Soldier waiter.......................Howard Johnson
A vamp.......................Grace Warner
A guest.......................Mark Orton
Prohibition agent.......................Fitzhugh Burns
Jazz twins.......................Clifford and Foster Carling
The sheik.......................Howard Hitz, baritone
A mammy.......................Margaret Buckley
Black and white girls..Helen Clarkson, Ardietta Ford
Chanticleer (a side dish).Mrs. Charles Dudley Warner
Spanish dancers......Grace Warner and Mark Orton

ST. PAUL AUDITORIUM
APRIL 17th at 8:15

THE
JUNIOR LEAGUE
FROLIC

176

Twenty-five years Old

A bad year. No work. Slow deteriorating repression with outbreak around the corner

Sept | Zelda Helpless. Dog squeaking.

Oct | St. Paul Hotel. The Commodore. My office. Baby born on 26th. Oh God, goofo I'm drunk. Mark Twain. Isn't she smart—she has the hiccups. I hope its beautiful and a fool—a beautiful little fool.

Nov | Baby baptized. Commodore + 626 Goodrich. University Club.

Dec | Zelda's weight. Cotillion dances + bob rides. Joe Ordway. Mrs. Clark on Mencken. She hoped Grampa Dean wouldn't be too depressed at Elizabeth's marriage

1922 Jan | Joseph Hergesheimer. The Bad luck Ball.

Feb | Both sick. Drinking. The B. + D. published. Father tells me about the ungratefulness of Dan Morgan.

Mar | Trip New York. Constance Bennett. Marrylyn Miller. Virginia Dechaven. Alec, Engalitcheff. O Sullivan. Quarrel with Alec. Selznick studio

April | Coached Junior League Play.

We are both simply mad to get back to New York. This damn place is 18 below zero and I go around thanking God that, anatomically and proverbially speaking, I am safe from the awful fate of the monkey.

—ZF to Ludlow Fowler, December 1921.

SPS

The Committee
Requests
Mr *Fitzgerald's* Presence
Costumed
With A Costumed
Lady
At
The University Club
For
The Post Lenten Cotillion
Friday
The Twenty-eighth Of April
At
Nine Thirty
This Invitation Must Be Presented
At The Door

Zelda made this composite picture of herself and baby for her scrapbook.

Published Weekly
The Curtis Publishing Company
Cyrus H. K. Curtis, President
C. H. Ludington, Vice-President and Treasurer
P. S. Collins, General Business Manager
Walter D. Fuller, Secretary
William Boyd, Advertising Director
Independence Square, Philadelphia
London: 6, Henrietta Street
Covent Garden, W. C.

THE SATURDAY EVENING POST

Founded A^D. 1728 by Benj. Franklin

Copyright, 1922, by The Curtis Publishing Company in the United States and Great Britain
Title Registered in U. S. Patent Office and in Foreign Countries

George Horace Lorimer
EDITOR
Churchill Williams, F. S. Bigelow,
A. W. Neall, Arthur McKeogh,
T. B. Costain, Associate Editors

Entered as Second-Class Matter, November 18, 1879, at the Post Office at Philadelphia, Under the Act of March 3, 1879
Additional Entry as Second-Class Matter at Columbus, Ohio, at Decatur, Illinois, at Chicago, Illinois, and at Indianapolis, Ind.
Entered as Second-Class Matter at the Post-Office Department, Ottawa, Canada

Volume 194 | 5c. THE COPY 10c. in Canada | PHILADELPHIA, PA., FEBRUARY 11, 1922 | $2.00 THE YEAR by Subscription | Number 33

THE POPULAR GIRL

"Who Was the Gentleman With the Invisible Tie?" Scott Asked. "Is His Personality as Diverting as His Haberdashery?"

By F. Scott Fitzgerald

ILLUSTRATED BY CHARLES D. MITCHELL

The Leaders.

Who are the leading American writers? If one studies the magazines and papers one finds that Scott Fitzgerald, Joseph Hergesheimer, Edna Ferber, Fanny Hurst, and Sinclair Lewis are among the best. Of all that batch Joseph Hergesheimer is to me the only one approaching our best men, and that only occasionally.

Scott Fitzgerald has a brilliancy that cannot be denied, the two lady writers are also capable at their job, and Sinclair Lewis needs a bigger canvas, to my mind. All write clever, readable short stories, but great short stories, no.

It was in St. Paul that F. Scott Fitzgerald spent his childhood, rose-white boyhood and radiant young manhood. As a boy and youth Fitzgerald was always ready to give to those that were older than himself the full benefit of his inexperience, and as a grown-up he has not changed his spots, they say. The only difference seems to be that instead of talking gratuitously, he now sells his opinions for many shekels.

HIS CHILDREN'S CHILDREN—Arthur Train—*Scribner.* Just one more great-wealth-and-high-society novel. The Chambers formula, not the Fitzgerald one.

In This Number: F. Scott Fitzgerald—Kenneth L. Roberts—St. John Ervine Louise Dutton—Samuel Merwin—Earl Derr Biggers—Harry Leon Wilson

The Bowling Green

The "reactions" of the critics to Sherwood Anderson's new novel line them up in an unusual assortment. Thus:—

PRO: Henry Seidel Canby and F. Scott Fitzgerald.
CON: N. P. Dawson and Burton Rascoe.

Many Marriages, we can't help saying to ourself makes strange bedfellows.

TOWN AND GOWN *Lynn and Lois Seyster Montross*

A sensation! The first penetrating studies of our co-ed universities. "All the equipment of F. Scott Fitzgerald plus sympathy and humanity."—JOHN V. A. WEAVER, Brooklyn *Eagle*. $2.00

F. Scott Fitzgerald—The Flapper Laureate.

What could be finer than the great Dean Wall in *The Camel's Back*, or Ellicock in *Hamlet?*"

SOCIETY WOMEN COMPETE IN GOLF TOURNAMENT

Left, Mrs. F. Scott Fitzgerald.
Right, Mrs. C. O. Kalman

In April the winter ceased abruptly. The snow ran down into Black Bear Lake scarcely tarrying for the early golfers to brave the season with red and black balls. Without elation, without an interval of moist glory, the cold was gone.

Dexter knew that there was something dismal about this Northern spring, just as he knew there was something gorgeous about the fall. Fall made him clinch his hands and tremble and repeat idiotic sentences to himself, and make brisk abrupt gestures of command to imaginary audiences and armies. October filled him with hope which November raised to a sort of ecstatic triumph, and in this mood the fleeting brilliant impressions of the summer at Sherry Island were ready grist to his mill.

—"Winter Dreams"

FY NEWYORK NY 320P 20
F SCOTT FITZGERALD
626 GOODRICH AVE STPAUL WINN
BEAUTIFUL WARNER BROS OFFER TWENTY FIVE HUNDRED CASH SAY SUCCESS
PROBLEMATICAL THIS A LOW OFFER BUT BEST WE CAN GET WIRE
DECISION
HAROLD OBER.

When summer came, all the people who liked summer time moved out to the huge, clear lake not far from town, and lived there in long, flat cottages surrounded with dank shrubbery and pine trees, and so covered by screened verandas that they made you think of small pieces of cheese under large meat-safes. All the people came who liked to play golf or sail on the lake, or who had children to shelter from the heat. All the young people came whose parents had given them for wedding presents white bungalows hid in the green—and all the old people who liked the flapping sound of the water at the end of their hollyhock walks. All the bachelors who liked living over the cheerful clatter of plates and clinking locker doors in the Yacht Club basement came, and a great many handsome, sun-dried women of forty or fifty with big families and smart crisp linen costumes that stuck to the seats of their roadsters when they went to meet their husbands escaping from town in the five o'clock heat.

—"The Girl the Prince Liked" (ZF)

Photo by William B

Mrs. F. Scott Fitzgerald
Mrs Ralph McFaul

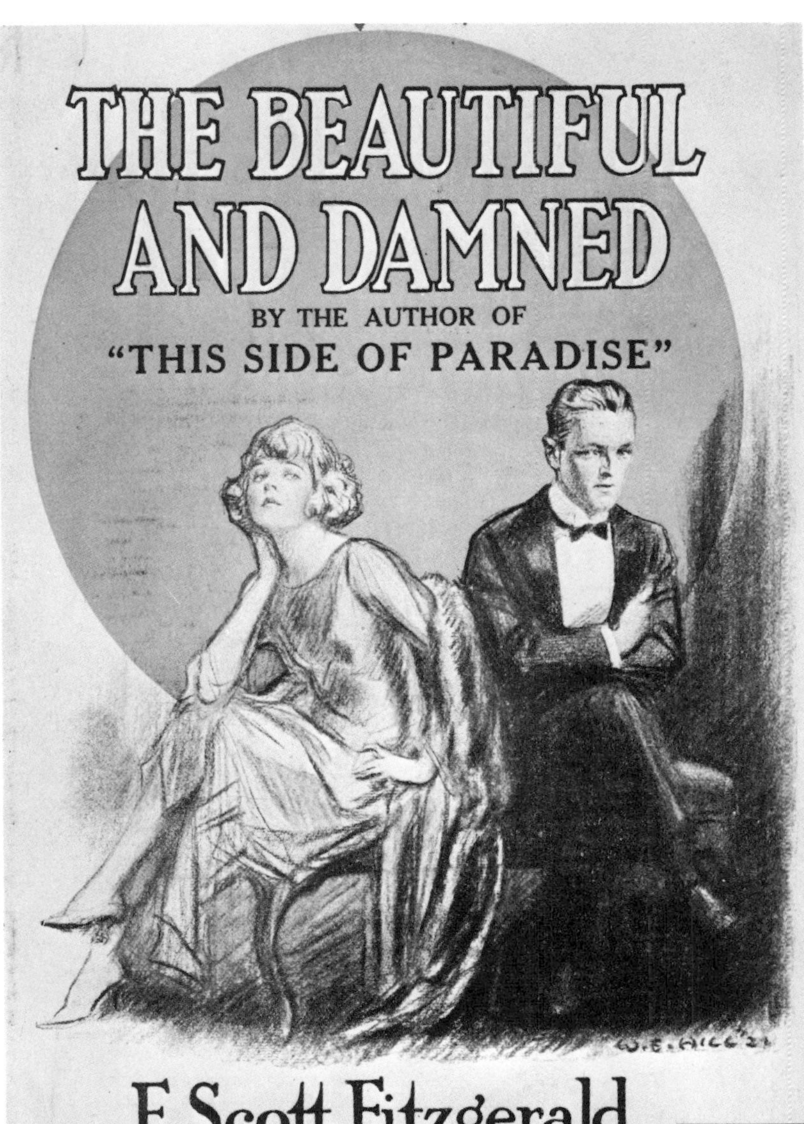

THE BEAUTIFUL AND DAMNED

BY F. SCOTT FITZGERALD

The appearance of "This Side of Paradise" infused a new vitality into American fiction. It opened that striking literary movement which, whatever its crudities, was marked by an intense sincerity and courage that make the novel a vital factor in life. It became a chief topic of discussion and a "best seller."

"The Beautiful and Damned" will certainly not cause less of a stir. In relating the story of the love and marriage of Anthony Patch and the vivid beauty, Gloria, it reveals with devastating satire a section of American society which has never before been recognized as an entity—that wealthy, floating population which throngs the restaurants, cabarets, theatres, and hotels of our great cities—people adrift on a sea of luxury, without the anchors of homes and the rudders of responsibilities—people without roots or backgrounds.

Fitzgerald shows in particular these two young people—Anthony and Gloria—of natural charm and beauty, cast upon this shining sea and floating toward that awful whirlpool that may do worse than kill: it may destroy the soul and leave only the body. This he does with such brilliance of dialogue and withering comment, with so effective a succession of scenes and incidents, that this floating society, in all its glitter and color, is brought before the very eyes of the reader. Through the medium of a fascinating story he reveals a significant phase of modern life hitherto unrealized.

CHARLES SCRIBNER'S SONS

THE BEAUTIFUL AND DAMNED

—

Fitzgerald

Fitzgerald repairing Fitzgerald for his writings

SCRIBNERS

TO

SHANE LESLIE, GEORGE JEAN NATHAN AND MAXWELL PERKINS

IN APPRECIATION OF MUCH LITERARY HELP AND ENCOURAGEMENT

THE BEAUTIFUL AND DAMNED

By

F. SCOTT FITZGERALD

The victor belongs to the spoils.
—Anthony Patch.

NEW YORK
CHARLES SCRIBNER'S SONS
1922

The Beautiful and Damned *was serialized in* Metropolitan, *September 1921–March 1922. The book was published in March 1922, and sold 50,000 copies.*

Your second letter came and I want to apologize to you for mine. I might have known you did not mean what in haste I imagined you did. The thing was *flippant—I mean it was the sort of worst of George Jean Nathan. I have changed it now—changed "godalmighty" to "deity," cut out "bawdy," and changed several other words, so I think it is all right.*

Why, really, my letter was so silly, with all those absurd citations of Twain, Anatole France, Howells, etc., was because I was in a painic because I was afraid I might have to cut it out and, as you say, it does round out the scene.

I hope you'll accept my apology.

Is the girl beautiful *in the W. E. Hill picture? Are you going to have a light blue background on the jacket as I suggested—I mean like you had for your Lulu Ragdale book two years ago? And did you catch that last correction I sent you before it was too late?*

I have put a new ending on the book—that is, on the last paragraph, instead of the repetition of the Paradise scene of which I was never particularly fond. I think that now the finish will leave the "taste" of the whole book in the reader's mouth as it didn't before—if you know what I mean.

I can't tell you how sorry I am about that silly letter. I took that "Oh Christ" out as you suggested. As you say, "Oh, God" won't fill the gap but "Oh my God" does it pretty well.

With my changing of the extreme last and fixing up the symposium I am almost, but not quite, satisfied with the book. I prophesy that it will go about 60,000 copies the first year—that is, assuming that Paradise *went about 40,000 the first year. Thank God I'm thru with it.*

—FSF to Maxwell Perkins, c. 16 December, 1921.

The Quill Drivers

The week's best sellers in representative Detroit book stores, listed in order of their popularity, were:

FICTION. June 25th

"Men of Affairs," Roland Pertwee; "Gentle Julia," Booth Tarkington; "Secret Places of the Heart," H. G. Wells; "Cytherea," Joseph Hergesheimer; "Abbe Pierre," Jay W. Hudson; "The Beautiful and Damned," F. Scott Fitzgerald.

The best circulators in the Detroit Public Library were, in order of calls for them:

FICTION.

"Brass," Charles Norris; "Three Soldiers," John Dos Passos; "Maria Chapdelaine," Louis Hemon; "Cytherea," Joseph Hergesheimer; "The Beautiful and Damned," F. Scott Fitzgerald

The best circulators in the Detroit Public Library were, in order of calls for them:

July 16th

FICTION.

"Memoirs of a Midget," Walter de la Mare; "The Beautiful and Damned," F. Scott Fitzgerald;

The week's best sellers in representative Detroit book stores, listed in order of their popularity, were:

FICTION.

"Gentle Julia," Booth Tarkington; "The Vehement Flame," by Margaret Deland; "The Beautiful and Damned," F. Scott Fitzgerald;

The best circulators in the Detroit Public Library were, in order of calls for them:

July 2nd

FICTION.

"Brass," Charles Norris; "The Beautiful and Damned," F. Scott Fitzgerald;

The best circulators in the Detroit Public Library were, in order of calls for them:

FICTION. July 23

"The Beautiful and Damned," F. Scott Fitzgerald;

The week's best sellers in representative Detroit book stores, listed in order of their popularity, were:

FICTION.

"Gentle Julia," Booth Tarkington; "The Vehement Flame," Margaret Deland; "The Beautiful and Damned," F. Scott Fitzgerald

The best circulators in the Detroit Public Library were, in order of calls for them:

July 30th

FICTION.

"Memoirs of a Midget," Walter de la Mare; "The Beautiful and Damned," F. Scott Fitzgerald

The week's best sellers in representative Detroit book stores, listed in order of their popularity, were:

FICTION.

"Gentle Julia," Booth Tarkington; "The Beautiful and Damned," F. Scott Fitzgerald

FICTION.

"Memoirs of a Midget," Walter de la Mare; "The Beautiful and Damned," F. Scott Fitzgerald; "Secret Places of the Heart," H. G. Wells; "The Vehement Flame," Margaret Deland; "Cytherea," Joseph Hergesheimer; "Gentle Julia," Booth Tarkington. Aug 6th

AT THE PUBLIC LIBRARY.

Six books most in demand at the Chicago public library last week were: "The Beautiful and Damned," by F. Scott Fitzgerald. June 18th

AT THE PUBLIC LIBRARY.

The six books most in demand at the Chicago public library last week were identical with the preceding week's, as follows:

"The Beautiful and Damned," by F. Scott Fitzgerald.

AT THE PUBLIC LIBRARY.

Six books most in demand at the Chicago public library last week were: "The Beautiful and Damned," by F. Scott Fitzgerald. July 22

The Ten Best Sellers

The best sellers at Brentano's during the last week were:

Trib FICTION July 23

"The Vehement Flame," by Margaret Deland (Harper). The romance of a middle-aged bride and youthful husband destroyed by jealousy.

"The Secret Places of the Heart," by H. G. Wells (Macmillan). The erotic difficulties of a middle-aged man.

"The Beautiful and Damned," by F. Scott Fitzgerald (Scribner). An arraignment of the present generation.

A part of F. Scott Fitzgerald's novel "The Beautiful and Damned" is placed in Westport, Conn. The "little gray house" in the Connecticut village is where the young couple had their "radiant hour," and where, "close together on the porch, they would wait for the moon to stream across the silver acres of farmland, jump a thick wood, and tumble waves of radiance at their feet." It was in the "little gray house," also, alas! that some truly rosy hours are said to have been passed, so amazingly described in the story.

Last month three books had the greatest sale in Washington shops: Zane Grey's "To the Last Man," Scott Fitzgerald's "Beautiful and Damned," and "Helen of the Old House," by Harold Bell Wright.

After Marriage, What?

If you have been married a week, A THOUSAND WAYS TO PLEASE A HUSBAND.
If you have been married a year, THE BEAUTIFUL AND DAMMED.
If you have been married fifteen years, tackle CYTHEREA.
If your husband has committed poverty, MR PROHACK.

The trouble is, in part, that the prematurely and self-electedly elderly gentlemen who have been attacking their immediate juniors have in their minds a composite photograph of Amory Blaine, Three Soldiers, and John V. A. Weaver. There is no such creature.

July Tabloid Book Review

NY News **By FANNY BUTCHER.**

Last week's best sellers in a leading New York bookstore were:

FICTION.

"Dancers in the Dark," by Dorothy Speare.
"The Beautiful and Damned," by F. Scott Fitzgerald.

Of those writers whose nationalities are readily recognizable, fifteen Americans are advertised in England only—including James Oliver Curwood, Mrs. Rinehart, F. Scott Fitzgerald, and Edith Wharton.

F. SCOTT FITZGERALD
HACK WRITER AND PLAGIARIST
SAINT PAUL MINNESOTA

No one could possibly be so young as Scott Fitzgerald seems in "This Side of Paradise" and "The Beautiful and Damned"—the flippancy carries no thought of disparagement, but is meant in genuine appreciation of Mr. Fitzgerald's high talent—and Fitzgerald was Princeton vintage of 1917.

The vogue of the younger generation, as vogue, is due largely to Mr. F. Scott Fitzgerald, and to him not because he wrote a good book or a bad one, but because he wrote one which sold. He did something less than Byron and it was natural that many other young men and women should try to do as much; but they did not succeed—not even in being praised by Mr. Canby.

Even a flapper's "petting" has qualities that deserve admiration! Those world-famous "petting parties" have come into vogue only through F. Scott Fitzgerald, and whether or not it was his full intention, he has shown her in her glory.

There is one striking difference between a story by Edith Wharton and one by F. Scott Fitzgerald; Mrs. Wharton plays true to the great American puritanic tradition. In depicting a sophisti- ed society she and Mr. Fitzgerald seek the same theme, but Mrs. Wharton's hero and heroine turn against the easy-going morals of her philistines.

Why should she, of all persons, behave as if she had said, "Go to, I will prove that I can out-Fitzgerald Scott Fitzgerald himself"?

BIOGRAPHY OF F. S. FITZGERALD.

To the Friend of the People:

Will you please give me the biography of F. Scott Fitgerald author of "The Beautiful and Damned."

MISS M. M. M.

Francis Scott Key Fitzgerald was born in St. Paul, Minn., on September 24, 1896; attended Princeton 1913-17; left college to join the army; married Zelda Sayre of Montgomery, Ala., April 3, 1920; Second Lieut. 45th Infantry, November, 1917; First Lieut., 67th Infantry, July, 1918; served as D. C. to Brig. Gen. J. A. Ryan, Dec., 1918 until Feb., 1919; honorably discharged, Feb., 1919. He is a Socialist. Member Cottage Club (Princeton); University Club of St. Paul, Minn. Author: "This Side of Paradise," "Flappers and Philosophers" and "The Beautiful and Damned." His present address is: 599 Summit avenue, St. Paul, Minn.

"Mr. F. Scott Fitzgerald"—and a slim youth with light hair rushed nervously and unsteadily in.

Week's Best Sellers

Balt News FICTION July 1st

"The Vehement Flame"—Deland.
"The Beautiful and Damned"—Fitzgerald.

Week's Best Sellers

Balt FICTION July 22

"The Vehement Flame," Deland.
"The Vanishing Point," Dawson.
"The Moon Out of Reach," Pedler.
"The Beautiful and Damned," Fitzgerald.

BROWNIE—"The Beautiful and Damned" by F. Scott Fitzgerald; published by Scribners'. The smart novel of modern youth by one of the brightest of them, that everybody's reading.

Even in America, some still more juvenile Scott Fitzgerald, issuing from Harvard more concerned with sacraments than with flappers, will give us an intimate and popular picture of the soul of a Cowley Father.

Week's Best Sellers

FICTION.

"The Moon Out of Reach," Pedler.
"The Head of the House of Coombe," Burnett.
"If Winter Comes," Hutchinson.
"The Vehement Flame," Deland.
"Gentle Julia," Tarkington.
"The Beautiful and Damned," Fitzgerald. Balt News

It was almost as definitely dated as the novels of Scott FitzGerald and other young contemporaries whose fame will hardly outlive their decade.

MARRIAGE has been credited, by Scott Fitzgerald, D. H. Lawrence, or Jan-Ibn-Jan, the Solomon of Solomons, with making strange bedfellows.

Olga Printzlau, the scenarist, is adapting F. Scott Fitzgerald's novel, "The Beautiful and Damned," for the screen. The cast is being selected by S. L. Warner at the Warner Bros. coast studios. "Brass" is now being translated into screen terms by Monte Katterjohn, while Harry Rapf, the producer, is signing up a star roster for this special.

Heaven knows that Scott Fitzgerald's characters are as piffling and worthless as any Mrs. Glyn has striven to portray; but his people are living and real to the uttermost core, coherent in their very incoherence, steadfast and honest in their vacillation and immorality, true human beings, born of the creative gift. He knows them, inside and outside, and he makes his reader as conscious of them as though he had laid hands upon them.

On Second Thought

By JAY E. HOUSE

We have not yet read Mr. F. Scott Fitzgerald's presumably frank confession in the current American. But we plan to do so. We want to know whether Mr. Fitzgerald, following precedent, blames it on his mother.

F. Scott Fitzgerald

the author of

"This Side of Paradise"

has done it again. His new novel, "The Beautiful and Damned,"

has met the grilling test that awaits the second book by every writer of a brilliant first novel. The critics are skeptical of second novels, and they sharpened their pencils particularly for Fitzgerald. "This Side of Paradise" was the fiction sensation of 1920; it showed Fitzgerald so audacious, so provocative in his startling originality and impatience with literary shackles that the most cold-blooded analysis was inevitably in store for his next venture.

And again he has stirred the literary world to enthusiasm. "The Beautiful and Damned" is being hailed as a huge forward stride in the career of an indubitable artist. "Better than 'This Side of Paradise'," is the general verdict. He has gained in power without sacrificing his freshness and sparkle.

The Beautiful and Damned

"The victor belongs to the spoils"

What the critics say:

Henry Seidel Canby— *in The Literary Review, New York Evening Post* *"Growing artistic power"*

"This book proves that he has the artist's conscience . . . Evidences of a great and growing artistic power . . . No finer study of the relations between boy husband and girl wife has been given us in American fiction. Gloria is an original creation, frightening in her truth . . . And how this novelist can write."

James Branch Cabell— *"Gratifying"*

"Gratifyingly solid, moving, human, brilliant at times, and always nicely ironic. The ending could hardly be happier."

N. P. Dawson— *in the New York Globe* *"Greatest natural talent"*

"Confirms the impression made by his first novel, that of the younger American novelists he has the greatest natural talent. He has romance and imagination and a gayety unknown to most of the young moderns . . . Great facility in writing . . . Beauty and felicity of expression . . . But, above all, he is able to tell a story."

E. W. Osborn— *in the New York World* *"True"*

"A true story, and he tells it exceedingly, exceptionally well . . . Deep in interest."

John V. A. Weaver— *in the Brooklyn Eagle* *"Irrepressible vitality"*

"Better than 'This Side of Paradise' . . . A huge stride forward . . . Even when he is most disillusioned he cannot keep enthusiasm out; even when he is most 'cynical' there is an irrepressible glow of vitality; even when he is most sophisticated there is an undimmed naivete underneath . . . A novel to read which is a duty and privilege that you owe to yourself."

Sidney Williams— *in the Philadelphia North American* *"Vivid and true"*

". . . The freshness of close observation . . . It is vivid writing and true social history."

R. S. Lynd— *in the Book Review* *"Exhilarating"*

"Mr. Fitzgerald continues to be one of the most original of our American novelists, and reading him is an exhilarating experience, like zooming along in an airplane."

John Peale Bishop— *in the New York Herald* *"Magnificently alive"*

"An advance on 'This Side of Paradise' . . . Magnificently alive."

Sidney Howard *"Brilliant"*

"Brilliant, and it cuts horribly deep. Now we know that 'This Side of Paradise' wasn't all. There's no stopping him; he will make them all look up this time."

"The Beautiful and Damned" is on sale at all bookstores and news stands, $2.00

CHARLES SCRIBNER'S SONS — FIFTH AVENUE, NEW YORK

F. Scott Fitzgerald Tells How He Discovered The Flapper In "The Beautiful And Damned"

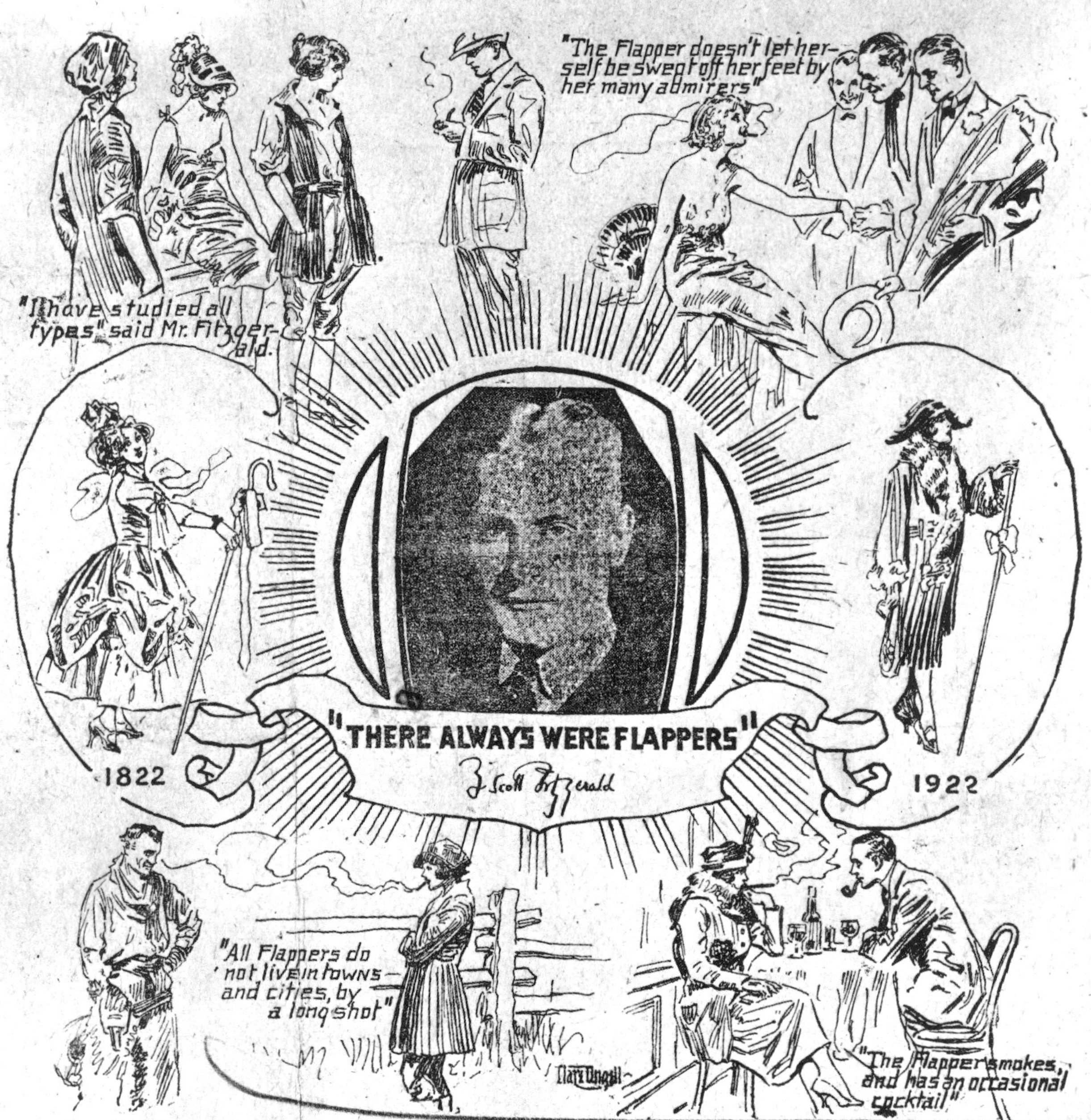
"The Flapper doesn't let herself be swept off her feet by her many admirers"
"I have studied all types," said Mr. Fitzgerald.
"THERE ALWAYS WERE FLAPPERS"
F. Scott Fitzgerald
1822
1922
"All Flappers do not live in towns and cities, by a long shot"
"The Flapper smokes, and has an occasional cocktail"

FITZGERALD'S LATEST NOT FOR ALL PALATES

"The Beautiful and Damned" a Story of Deterioration, Brilliantly Written

THE BEAUTIFUL AND DAMNED
by F. Scott Fitzgerald, Charles Scribner's Sons, New York, $2.00.

In this part of the country, we are not familiar with the idle rich, Consequently it is rather hard for a local reviewer to estimate the truth, or falsity of F. Scott Fitzgerald's characterizations and settings in his recent best-seller, The Beautiful and Damned, which is a story of that class. Anthony and Gloria, who are respectively the damned and the beautiful, are like no one that we would be apt to meet, even in Durham. In reading of their surprising lives, we glimpse a social stratum with which the average Tar Heel is wholly unacquainted.

The Beautiful and Damned is a disagreeable, but always interesting story of the steady deterioration of personality of both the main characters. Nothing, not even the War, halts their unrelieved decline. To begin with, Anthony is a graceful dilettante, and Gloria is a beautiful coquette. On the final page Anthony is a drunken wreck and Gloria hasn't even looks enough to break into the movies. Fitzgerald marries Gloria and Anthony off early in the book and proceeds to dissect their subsequent relations. In the aimlessness of both characters, there appears to be only one purpose, which is to make ducks and drakes of the millions of Anthony's grandfather as soon as he dies. Whereupon, the unobliging old relative, who is an ardent Prohibitionist, breaks in upon one of their particularly wet revels, and cuts them off without a cent.

Liquor flows through the pages of The Beautiful and Damned in a steady stream. It wouldn't be easy to find two harder drinkers than Anthony and Gloria. The reader wonders what they might be like if they would occasionally sober up,—say, just for a week or two. They are the world's champion stagers of liquor parties, in which their friends join with enthusiasm. If you have a suppressed desire to participate vicariously in such orgies, then you should read The Beautiful and Damned by all means and get all the lurid details for only two dollars.

NEW FLAPPER SLANG IN VOGUE SAYS MARIE PREVOST

A brand new line of slang known as "flapper slang" has crept into existence, according to Marie Prevost, the featured player in the Warner Brothers production, "The Beautiful and Damned," which will be shown at the Olympic theatre, beginning Monday. The picture was adapted from the novel by F. Scott Fitzgerald.

Preparing for Princeton

"Who wrote 'Paradise Lost'?" asked a teacher at the Horace Mann School

"F. Scott Fitzgerald," came the answer from the star scholar whose hand the pedagogue had recognized.

—New York Morning Telegraph.

Author of "Main Street" Praises F. Scott Fitzgerald.

The praise accorded F. Scott Fitzgerald, author of "This Side of Paradise," by Sinclair Lewis, author of "Main Street," in his recent lecture at town hall, New York, focusses attention once more upon this brilliant young novelist. "Fitzgerald," said Mr. Lewis, "is going to be a writer the equal of any young European." Mr. Fitzgerald, who recently turned 24, is also the author of "Flappers and Philosophers," a volume of short stories. His books are published by Charles Scribner's Sons.

Alas, we are in the midst of a time when it is smart to be bad; considered clever to sneer at decent standards, and spell God with a small 'g;' to ridicule a girl who wears her skirt below her knees and doesn't smoke or stay out all night. How it would help if somebody like you, who has a chance and good publicity, would say what you really think and not praise a book like that beautiful and damned thing just because a smart and undesirable lot of young nobodies call it literature. It is a pitiful thing to see a young man like Fitzgerald, with a wonderful talent, going as he has, but it is not too late for him, and here is hoping that he will do the great thing which he can and write a book which people would not fear to read aloud to their mothers and other decent folk. You know, old man, there are a few left yet. —NELLIE BLY.

EVENING WORL

F. Scott Fitzgerald, Novelist,

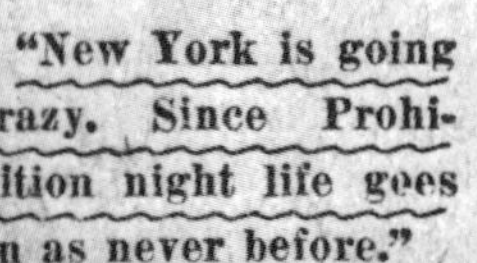

"New York is going crazy. Since Prohibition night life goes on as never before."

"Everybody is drinking harder. Possessing liquor is a proof of respectability."

"The attitude of the young is: 'This is ALL. What does it matter? Let's GO!'"

Middle West Girl More at Home in Kitchen Than in Ballroom, Says F. Scott Fitzgerald

F. Scott Fitzgerald classifies American flappers according to their locality

"Haven't you ever kissed any one like you've kissed me?"

"No," she answered simply. "As I've told you, men have tried—oh, lots of things. Any pretty girl has that experience. . . . You see," she resumed, "it doesn't matter to me how many women you've stayed with in the past, so long as it was merely a physical satisfaction, but I don't believe I could endure the idea of your ever having lived with another woman for a protracted period or even having wanted to marry some possible girl. It's different somehow. There'd be all the little intimacies remembered—and they'd dull that freshness that after all is the most precious part of love."

Rapturously he pulled her down beside him on the pillow.

—The Beautiful and Damned

NOVELIST SAYS SOUTHERN TYPE OF FLAPPER BEST

Most Attractive, Says Writer, Who Wedded One; Midwest Girls Have Only Health.

LACKING IN SOCIAL GRACE

New York, April 14.—"And as for the girl of the middle west—"

F. Scott Fitzgerald inhaled deeply and paused before he released a cloud of cigarette smoke and a shower of burning adjectives.

"She is unattractive, selfish, snobbish, egotistical, utterly graceless, talks with an ugly accent and in her heart knows that she would feel more at home in a kitchen than in a ballroom."

Fitzgerald.

The author who has been hailed as the interpreter of American youth halted for a moment. Fitzgerald, frankly good-looking, the hero of half a hundred proms, the realistic reporter of parlor fights and petting parties, plunged ahead into his analysis of the great American flapper.

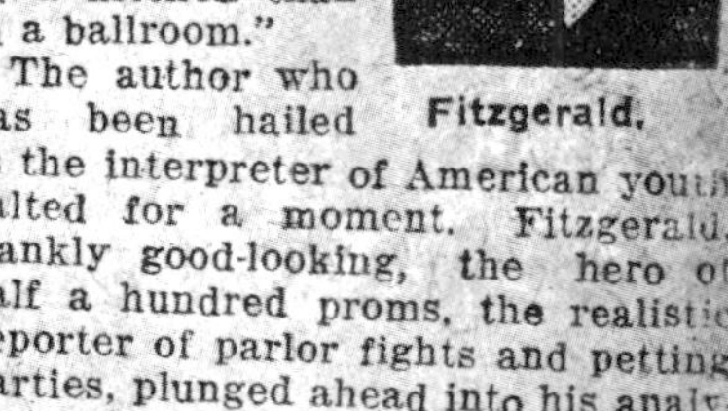

Making Ears Burn!

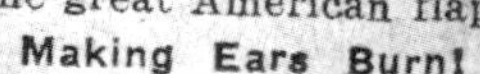

"There is much of the uncouthness of the pioneer left in the middle western flapper," continued Fitzgerald. "She lacks the social grace of entertaining men. Her idea is to get everything and give nothing.

"There is in her a respect for the primitive feminine talents; she would really make a good cook but her family has made money in the last generation and there is no excuse for her to go into the kitchen. She doesn't know what she wants to do."

Fitzgerald should know. He was born in St. Paul. Furthermore, his judgment carries authority. For critics agree the author of "This Side of Paradise" and "The Beautiful and Dammed" understands women—flappers, at least.

Lauds Southerners.

"The southern girl is easily the most attractive type in America," continued Fitzgerald, with a wave of his cigarette. "Next the girl from the east. At the bottom of the list the middle-western flapper."

"Hasn't she any good points?" I asked rather hopefully.

"Yes. She has her health," he admitted.

"Now for the southern girl." Here "First of all, remember that I married a southern girl. A characteristic is that she retains and develops her ability to entertain men. The middle-western girl lacks this utterly. With the sophisticated eastern girl it is a give-and-take proposition.

"No matter how poor a southern girl may be, and many of them are very poor, she keeps up her social activities."

D TEN-SECOND NEWS MOVIES

Shocked by "Younger Marrieds" and Prohibition

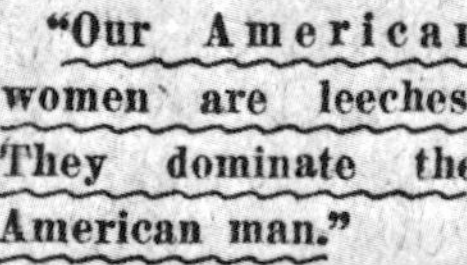

"Our American women are leeches. They dominate the American man."

"They are a useless fourth generation, trading on pioneer great-grandmothers."

"A woman's entitled to all she can get—when she marries she gets the whole thing."

"Work is salvation for all, even if we work to forget there's nothing to work for."

"Just being in love, really in love—doing it well—is work enough for a woman."

An Ironic Story of a "Flapper"

A Man and a Maid Tread The Maze of Modern Life

F. Scott Fitzgerald, in His Latest Novel, "The Beautiful and Damned," Satirizes Modernity

By Samuel Abbott

THE BEAUTIFUL AND DAMNED. By F. Scott Fitzgerald. Published by Charles Scribner's Sons. $2.

One of these wreckers of routine is F. Scott Fitzgerald's "The Beautiful and Damned," a novel that surprised, amused and vexed us. It is as vagrant as a young thistledown caught by pirate breezes and tossed to and fro in a conflict of contending whims. It derides old conventions in writing, it flouts modern ideals of balance and yet it gets beneath the hide of a reader's complacent assurance and pricks him to a confession that, in spots, it is egregiously and effectively shrewd, brilliant and rapier-like.

N.Y. Tribune

Les Enfants Terribles—By Gene Markey

GM

N.Y. Tribune

(John Dos Passos and F. Scott Fitzgerald)

F. Scott Fitzgerald, the debonair young author of last season's great novel of the parlor snake, "This Side of Paradise," sailed last week for Europe to rest up after the completion of his new novel. We were informed by John Peale Bishop, who has read it, that Fitzgerald has written this book to be true to himself, not to please the public. There is not, Bishop says, one line of popular or truckling stuff in it. Fitzgerald does not care whether it sells or not. It is called "The Beautiful and Damned," and concerns the disintegration of a young man who becomes disillusioned at 26. It is full of savage humor and of powerful characterization. Whether the Metropolitan will use it for serialization is a large question. But Fitz has put the brakes on himself, and he will probably yet be one of America's greatest, instead of (as he threatened to become) one of America's most sensational writers.

Bklyn Eagle

From the gentleman who has read Scott Fitzgerald's latest novel, the following communication:

"I think you've gone too far in saying that Fitzgerald does not care whether 'The Beautiful and Damned' sells. I cannot imagine his being quite so indifferent to money. And the book may be, for all I know, a best seller. Its acidulous humor, its burnishing of American stupidities, may quite suit the public mood. Scott has not yet freed himself of his immaturities, but I think the book is quite sincere to his present temper. There is at least no deliberate truckling to popular vanities. It is far better constructed and more cautiously written than 'This Side of Paradise.' It is always as readable as his more popular stuff, and full of alcoholics. So it may well displace 'Main Street' among the best sellers. JOHN PEALE BISHOP."

Brooklyn Eagle

The dream had been early realized and the realization carried with it a certain bonus and a certain burden. Premature success gives one an almost mystical conception of destiny as opposed to will power—at its worst the Napoleonic delusion. The man who arrives young believes that he exercises his will because his star is shining. The man who only asserts himself at thirty has a balanced idea of what will power and fate have each contributed, the one who gets there at forty is liable to put the emphasis on will alone. This comes out when the storms strike your craft.

—"Early Success"

The first movie version of a Fitzgerald novel was The Beautiful and Damned *(Warner Brothers, 1922). The movies also bought—but did not produce—*This Side of Paradise.

N.Y. Globe

It is doubtful if this new class of fiction is important enough to be given a special caption. Its significance would be the better understood were it made a sub-head under "Alcohol in Literature." As such it would show, even better than the triumph of the Anti-Saloon League, that the dusk of intoxicants was falling. There is a certain atmosphere of unfinality about the drinking bouts that make so wet, and for some so glamorous, the pages of Messrs. Scott and Hergesheimer. Alcohol for the characters of these authors seems but a halfway house on the road to something infinitely stronger. One can fancy their coming to say "mere booze" in the tone that critics use in speaking of "mere literature." Gone, at any rate, is all sparkle or conviviality. It is late afternoon for alcohol as it figures in the written word; it has come a long and sad way since the Psalmist wrote amiably of "wine that maketh glad the heart of man."

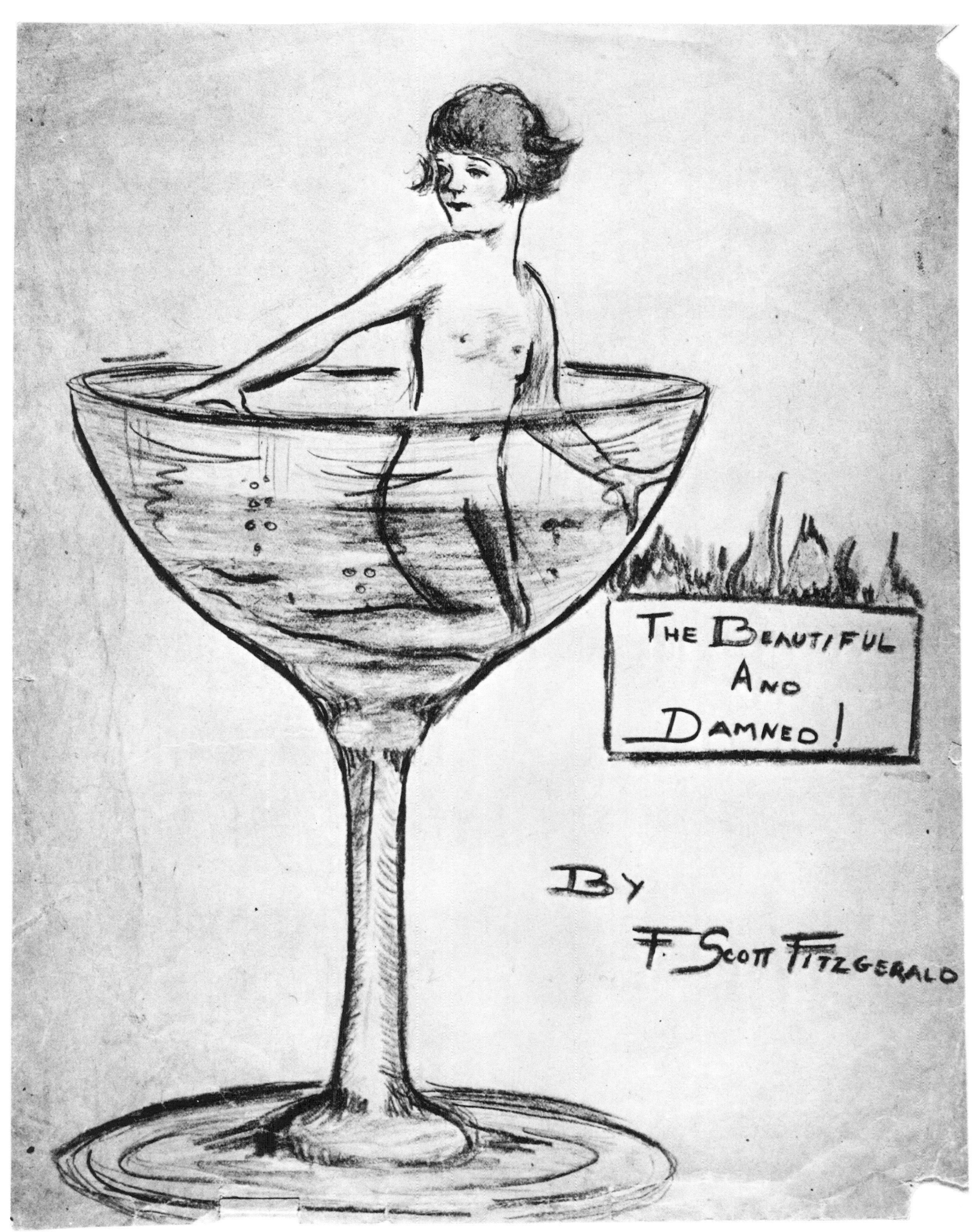

Zelda's proposal for the dust-jacket.

Mrs. F. Scott Fitzgerald Reviews "The Beautiful and Damned"

Friend Husband's Latest

By Zelda Sayre (Mrs. F. Scott Fitzgerald)

I NOTE on the table beside my bed this morning a new book with an orange jacket entitled "The Beautiful and Damned." It is a strange book, which has for me an uncanny fascination. It has been lying on that table for two years. I have been asked to analyze it carefully in the light of my brilliant critical insight, my tremendous erudition and my vast impressive partiality. Here I go!

To begin with, every one must buy this book for the following æsthetic reasons: First, because I know where there is the cutest cloth of gold dress for only $300 in a store on Forty-second Street, and also if enough people buy it where there is a platinum ring with a complete circlet, and also if loads of people buy it my husband needs a new winter overcoat, although the one he has has done well enough for the last three years.

Now, as to the other advantages of the book—its value as a manual of etiquette is incalculable. Where could you get a better example of how not to behave than from the adventures of Gloria? And as a handy cocktail mixer nothing better has been said or written since John Roach Straton's last sermon.

It is a wonderful book to have around in case of emergency. No one should ever set out in pursuit of unholy excitement without a special vest pocket edition dangling from a string around his neck.

For this book tells exactly, and with compelling lucidity, just what to do when cast off by a grandfather or when sitting around a station platform at 4 a. m., or when spilling champagne in a fashionable restaurant, or when told that one is too old for the movies. Any of these things might come into any one's life at any minute.

Just turn the pages of the book slowly at any of the above-mentioned trying times until your own case strikes your eye and proceed according to directions. Then for the ladies of the family there are such helpful lines as: "I like gray because then you have to wear a lot of paint." Also what to do with your husband's old shoes—Gloria takes Anthony's shoes to bed with her and finds it a very satisfactor way of disposing of them. The dietary suggestion, "tomato sandwiches and lemonade for breakfast" will be found an excellent cure for obesity.

Now, let us turn to the interior decorating department of the book. Therein can be observed complete directions for remodeling your bathroom along modern and more interesting lines, with plans for a bookrack by the tub, and a detailed description of what pictures have been found suitable for bathroom walls after years of careful research by Mr. Fitzgerald.

It seems to me that on one page I recognized a portion of an old diary of mine which mysteriously disappeared shortly after my marriage, and also scraps of letters which, though considerably edited, sound to me vaguely familiar. In fact, Mr. Fitzgerald—I believe that is how he spells his name—seems to believe that plagiarism begins at home.

I find myself completely fascinated by the character of the heroine. She is a girl approximately ten years older than I am, for she seems to have been born about 1890—though I regret to remark that on finishing the book I feel no confidence as to her age, since her birthday is in one place given as occurring in February and in another place May and in the third place in September. But there is a certain inconsistency in this quite in accord with the lady's character.

What I was about to remark is that I would like to meet the lady. There seems to have been a certain rouge she used which had a quite remarkable effect. And the strange variations in the color of her hair from cover to cover range entirely through the spectrum—I find myself doubting that all the changes were of human origin; also the name of the unguent used in the last chapter is not given. I find these æsthetic deficiencies very trying. But don't let that deter you from buying the book. In every other way the book is absolutely perfect.

* * *

THE other things that I didn't like in the book—I mean the unimportant things—were the literary references and the attempt to convey a profound air of erudition. It reminds me in its more soggy moments of the essays I used to get up in school at the last minute by looking up strange names in the Encyclopædia Britannica.

I think the heroine is most amusing. I have an intense distaste for the melancholy aroused in the masculine mind by such characters as Jenny Gerhardt, Antonia and Tess (of the D'Urbervilles). Their tragedies, redolent of the soil, leave me unmoved. If they were capable of dramatizing themselves they would no longer be symbolic, and if they weren't—and they aren't—they would be dull, stupid and boring, as they inevitably are in life.

The book ends on a tragic note; in fact a note which will fill any woman with horror, or, for that matter, will fill any furrier with horror, for Gloria, with thirty million to spend, buys a sable coat instead of a kolinsky coat. This is a tragedy unequaled in the entire work of Hardy. Thus the book closes on a note of tremendous depression and Mr. Fitzgerald's subtle manner of having Gloria's deterioration turn on her taste in coats has scarcely been equaled by Henry James.

Mrs. F. Scott Fitzgerald

April 24th.—I want to marry Anthony, because husbands are so often "husbands" and I must marry a lover.

There are four general types of husbands.

(1) The husband who always wants to stay in in the evening, has no vices and works for a salary. Totally undesirable!

(2) The atavistic master whose mistress one is, to wait on his pleasure. This sort always considers every pretty woman "shallow," a sort of peacock with arrested development.

(3) Next comes the worshipper, the idolater of his wife and all that is his, to the utter oblivion of everything else. This sort demands an emotional actress for a wife. God! it must be an exertion to be thought righteous.

(4) And Anthony—a temporarily passionate lover with wisdom enough to realize when it has flown and that it must fly. And I want to get married to Anthony.

What grubworms women are to crawl on their bellies through colorless marriages! Marriage was created not to be a background but to need one. Mine is going to be outstanding. It can't, shan't be the setting—it's going to be the performance, the live, lovely, glamourous performance, and the world shall be the scenery. I refuse to dedicate my life to posterity. Surely one owes as much to the current generation as to one's unwanted children. What a fate—to grow rotund and unseemly, to lose my self-love, to think in terms of milk, oatmeal, nurse, diapers. . . . Dear dream children, how much more beautiful you are, dazzling little creatures who flutter (all dream children must flutter) on golden, golden wings—

Such children, however, poor dear babies, have little in common with the wedded state.

—The Beautiful and Damned

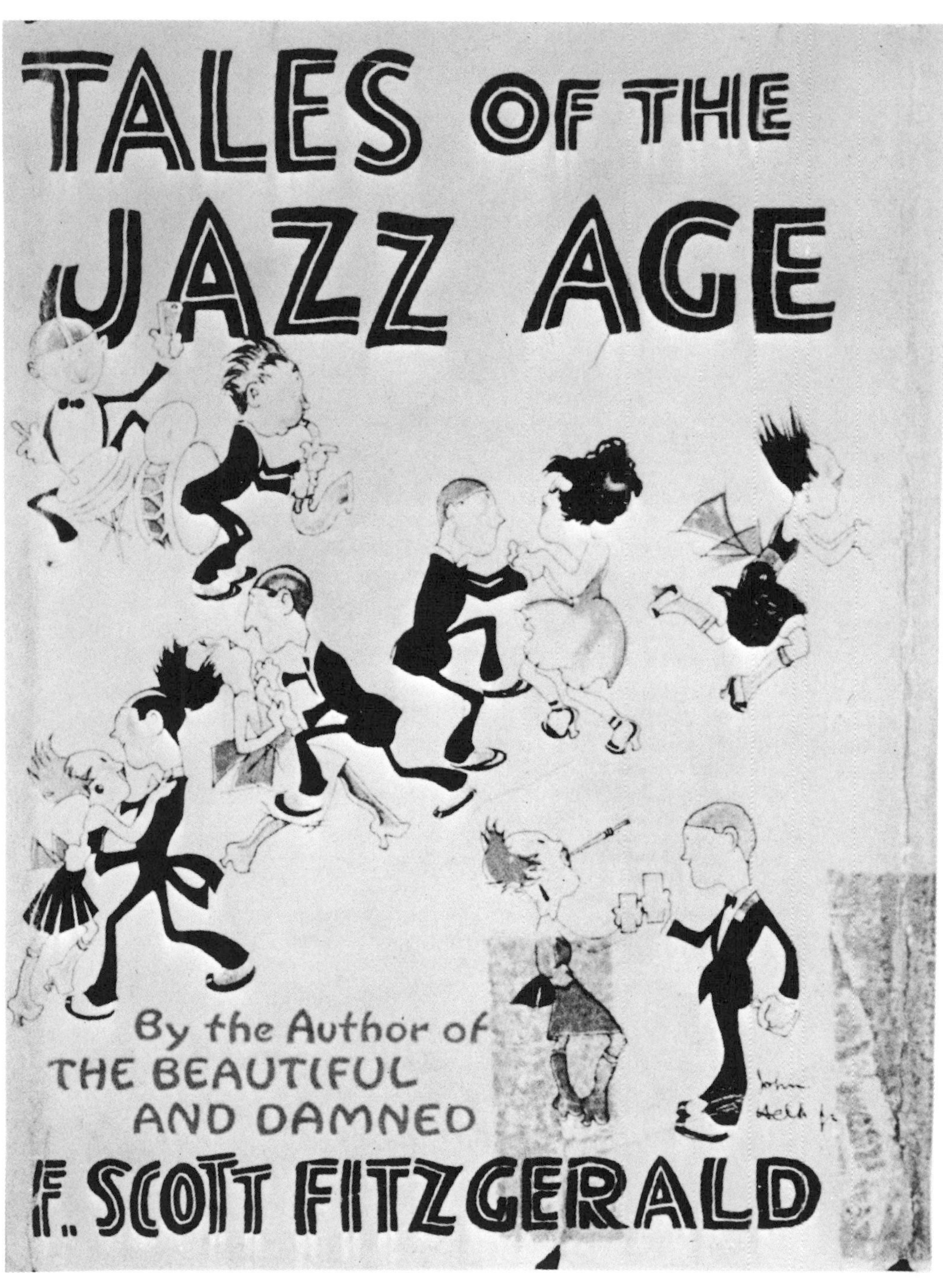

TALES OF THE
JAZZ AGE

BY

F. SCOTT FITZGERALD

NEW YORK
CHARLES SCRIBNER'S SONS
1922

QUITE INAPPROPRIATELY

TO MY MOTHER

Tales of the Jazz Age, Fitzgerald's second story collection, was published in September 1922. The dust jacket was by John Held, Jr., the most popular cartoonist of the jazz age.

A TABLE OF CONTENTS

MY LAST FLAPPERS

This is a Southern story, with the scene laid in the small city of Tarleton, Georgia. I have a profound affection for Tarleton, but somehow whenever I write a story about it I receive letters from all over the South denouncing me in no uncertain terms. "The Jelly-Bean," published in "The Metropolitan," drew its full share of these admonitory notes.

It was written under strange circumstances shortly after my first novel was published, and, moreover, it was the first story in which I had a collaborator. For, finding that I was unable to manage the crap-shooting episode, I turned it over to my wife, who, as a Southern girl, was presumably an expert on the technique and terminology of that great sectional pastime.

I suppose that of all the stories I have ever written this one cost me the least travail and perhaps gave me the most amusement. As to the labor involved, it was written during one day in the city of New Orleans, with the express purpose of buying a platinum and diamond wrist watch which cost six hundred dollars. I began it at seven in the morning and finished it at two o'clock the same night. It was published in the "Saturday Evening Post" in 1920, and later included in the O. Henry Memorial Collection for the same year. I like it least of all the stories in this volume.

My amusement was derived from the fact that the camel part of the story is literally true; in fact, I have a standing engagement with the gentleman involved to attend the next fancy-dress party to which we are mutually invited, attired as the latter part of the camel—this as a sort of atonement for being his historian.

vii

viii A TABLE OF CONTENTS

This somewhat unpleasant tale, published as a novelette in the "Smart Set" in July, 1920, relates a series of events which took place in the spring of the previous year. Each of the three events made a great impression upon me. In life they were unrelated, except by the general hysteria of that spring which inaugurated the Age of Jazz, but in my story I have tried, unsuccessfully I fear, to weave them into a pattern—a pattern which would give the effect of those months in New York as they appeared to at least one member of what was then the younger generation.

"And do you write for any other magazines?" inquired the young lady.

"Oh, yes," I assured her. "I've had some stories and plays in the 'Smart Set,' for instance——"

The young lady shivered.

"The 'Smart Set'!" she exclaimed. "How can you? Why, they publish stuff about girls in blue bathtubs, and silly things like that!"

And I had the magnificent joy of telling her that she was referring to "Porcelain and Pink," which had appeared there several months before.

FANTASIES

These next stories are written in what, were I of imposing stature, I should call my "second manner." "The Diamond as Big as the Ritz," which appeared last summer in the "Smart Set," was designed utterly for my own amusement. I was in that familiar mood characterized by a perfect craving for luxury, and the story began as an attempt to feed that craving on imginary foods.

One well-known critic has been pleased to like this extravaganza better than anything I have written. Personally I prefer "The Off Shore Pirate." But, to tamper slightly with Lincoln: If you like this sort of thing, this, possibly, is the sort of thing you'll like.

THE CURIOUS CASE OF BENJAMIN BUTTON . . . . Page 192

This story was inspired by a remark of Mark Twain's to the effect that it was a pity that the best part of life came at the beginning and the worst part at the end. By trying the experiment upon only one man in a perfectly normal world I have scarcely given his idea a fair trial. Several weeks after completing it, I discovered an almost identical plot in Samuel Butler's "Note-books."

The story was published in "Collier's" last summer and provoked this startling letter from an anonymous admirer in Cincinnati:

"Sir—

I have read the story Benjamin Button in Colliers and I wish to say that as a short story writer you would make a good lunatic I have seen many peices of cheese in my life but of all the peices of cheese I have ever seen you are the biggest peice. I hate to waste a peice of stationary on you but I will."

TARQUIN OF CHEAPSIDE . . . . . Page 225

Written almost six years ago, this story is a product of undergraduate days at Princeton. Considerably revised, it was published in the "Smart Set" in 1921. At the time of its conception I had but one idea—to be a poet—and the fact that I was interested in the ring of every phrase, that I dreaded the obvious in prose if not in plot, shows throughout. Probably the peculiar affection I feel for it depends more upon its age than upon any intrinsic merit.

O RUSSET WITCH! . . . . Page 234

When this was written I had just completed the first draft of my second novel, and a natural reaction made me revel in a story wherein none of the characters need be taken seriously. And I'm afraid that I was somewhat carried away by the feeling that there was no ordered scheme to which I must conform. After due consideration, however, I have decided to let it stand as it is, although the reader may find himself somewhat puzzled at the time element. I had best say that however the years may have dealt with Merlin Grainger, I myself was thinking always in the present.

It was published in the "Metropolitan."

UNCLASSIFIED MASTERPIECES

THE LEES OF HAPPINESS . . . . . Page 275

Of this story I can say that it came to me in an irresistible form, crying to be written. It will be accused perhaps of being a mere piece of sentimentality, but, as I saw it, it was a great deal more. If, therefore, it lacks the ring of sincerity, or even of tragedy, the fault rests not with the theme but with my handling of it.

It appeared in the "Chicago Tribune," and later obtained, I believe, the quadruple gold laurel leaf or some such encomium from one of the anthologists who at present swarm among us. The gentleman I refer to runs as a rule to stark melodramas with a volcano or the ghost of John Paul Jones in the rôle of Nemesis, melodramas carefully disguised by early paragraphs in Jamesian manner which hint dark and subtle complexities to follow. On this order:

"The case of Shaw McPhee, curiously enough, had no bearing on the almost incredible attitude of Martin Sulo. This is parenthetical and, to at least three observers, whose names for the present I must conceal, it seems improbable, etc., etc., etc.," until the poor rat of fiction is at last forced out into the open and the melodrama begins.

MR. ICKY . . . . Page 302

This has the distinction of being the only magazine piece ever written in a New York hotel. The business was done in a bedroom in the Knickerbocker, and shortly afterward that memorable hostelry closed its doors forever.

When a fitting period of mourning had elapsed it was published in the "Smart Set."

JEMINA . . . . Page 311

Written, like "Tarquin of Cheapside," while I was at Princeton, this sketch was published years later in "Vanity Fair." For its technique I must apologize to Mr. Stephen Leacock.

I have laughed over it a great deal, especially when I first wrote it, but I can laugh over it no longer. Still, as other people tell me it is amusing, I include it here. It seems to me worth preserving a few years—at least until the ennui of changing fashions suppresses me, my books, and it together.

With due apologies for this impossible Table of Contents, I tender these tales of the Jazz Age into the hands of those who read as they run and run as they read.

TALES OF THE JAZZ AGE. By F. Scott Fitzgerald. New York: Charles Scribner's Sons. N.Y. Times

We all know delightful hosts who, introducing you to a group at a country house party, will give you, in a sentence or two, some bit of illuminating information with each name. A preface to a book is supposed to perform something of the same office; but Scott Fitzgerald has gone the preface one better, and has added to each title in the table of contents to his new book, "Tales of the Jazz Age," a telling bit of explanation or exposition, as the case may be, a snatch of anecdote or history, a word that makes you feel at home with the story and predisposed in its favor.

It is an excellent idea and it is done as well as Fitzgerald does anything that has to do with writing, which is very well indeed. Indeed, if ever a writer was born with a gold pen in his mouth, surely Fitzgerald is that man. The more you read him, the more he convinces you that here is the destined artist. Here is the kind of writing that all the short or long story schools and books will never teach to a single student. You may not like what he writes about, you may deplore the fact that most of his characters are rotters or weaklings, base or mean. That has nothing to do with the fact that he is a writer whom it is a joy to read; and if he chooses to write, for the moment anyhow, of the life and the persons with which and whom he is most intimate, if he prefers to paint with startling vividness and virility the jazz aspect of the American scene, why not? It exists. It is quite as real as Main Street, and a deal more amusing in some of its manifestations. More than that, it is astonishingly sincere and unself-conscious. Fitzgerald is interested in it at present, he knows it, and he is portraying it with talent. Some day he may—but let us wait and see.

FITZGERALD "COLLECTS."

Chi. News BY JOHN GUNTHER.

TALES OF A JAZZ AGE. By F. Scott Fitzgerald. Scribner's.

I AM one of those half-dozen people in the world who still think that "This Side of Paradise" had greatness in it, and therefore I approached Mr. Fitzgerald's new book, "Tales of a Jazz Age," with hope and charity in my bosom. But I was disillusioned.

There is nothing in this new collection to match the first dazzling section of "This Side of Paradise," or the story "Benediction" in "Flappers and Philosophers," or the drunken party scene in "The Beautiful and Damned." Nothing in the book except a play to be mentioned anon has the spirited brilliance and easy vivid dash of much of Fitzgerald's earlier work. Some of the stories in the book are good stories, true enough, but a collection containing only a few mere good stories is hardly enough from a man with the promise of Fitzgerald. And some of the stuff in the volume is absolute rot.

Another thing—the table of contents will give you pleasure. In it the author elaborately and successfully explains and apologizes for each effort. And the dedication is amusing—"Quite Inappropriately, to My Mother."

Well, it appears that Fitzgerald is marking time. "Tales of a Jazz Age" is a poorly assembled mixture of bad, fair and good—but not best. He intimates that he is not going to write about flappers any more. Let us hold our thumbs and hope!

Wilson in Vanity Fair

The Jazz King Again

SCOTT Fitzgerald's new book of short stories—*Tales of the Jazz Age* (Scribner's) is very much better than his first. In it he lets his fancy, his humor and his taste for nonsense run wild; it is the Fitzgerald harlequinade with a minimum of magazine hokum. Though he still suffers from the weakness of not focusing his material sufficiently—so that what we see is likely to be a confused cloud of gaiety and color rather than a sharply realized situation, in *The Diamond as Big as the Ritz*, at least, he has done a sustained and full-rounded fantasy—the work of a more brilliant Frank Stockton—and in such spontaneous nonsense as *Mr. Icky* no one cares about situations, anyway.

In the latter part of the book, however, among the most delightful burlesques, is a story called *The Lees of Happiness*. I read it with ever increasing admiration at Fitzgerald's mastery of the nuances of the ridiculous. I had never before realized that he was capable of such restrained and ingenious satire. It was the bitter short story of Mrs. Wharton and of fiction since Maupassant generally made exquisitely absurd yet maintaining always the inexorable technique of grimness. One of the passages that amused me most was that in which, after the heroine's husband has been stricken with paralysis and she is obliged day after day for a period of eight years to tend a speechless, living corpse, the author culminates with the following detail: "She acquired a character in the village—a group of little stories were told of her: how when the country was frozen over one winter so that no wagons nor automobiles could travel, she taught herself to skate so that she could make quick time to the grocer and druggist, and not leave Jeffrey alone for long."

This is in his best Gilbertian manner! I thought. It reminds me of the scene he invented for a college play years ago—in which the faithful old lighthouse keeper, when his light has suddenly gone out, first lights a candle as a *pis aller* and then when the candle has expired, still indomitably sticks to his post with a lighted cigarette. What was my astonishment when I had finished the story to discover that it was intended to be serious.—Yes, Fitzgerald is the most incalculable of our novelists; you never can tell what he is going to do next. He always has some surprise: just when you think the joke is going to be on you, it may turn out to be on him.—Nonetheless, in *Tales of the Jazz Age*, he has staged the most charming of ballets—something like the Greenwich Villiage Follies with overtones of unearthly music.

"THE BEAUTIFUL AND DAMNED" DOES NOT LOOK ALL OF THAT

F. Scott Fitzgerald, his wife and their 2-year-old daughter, "Scotty," at their summer home on Long Island. Mrs. Fitzgerald is the heroine of her husband's successful novel, "The Beautiful and Damned."

—Fotograma.

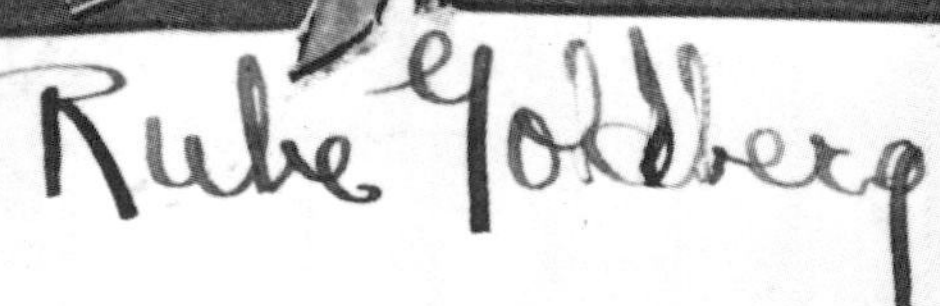

THE BEAUTIFUL BUT NOT THE DAMNED. Mrs. Scott Fitzgerald, whose husband is the youthful recorder of the Age of the Flapper, poses for an attractive photograph with Fritz, her prize-winning police dog, himself a beauty of no small attainments.

Fotograms.

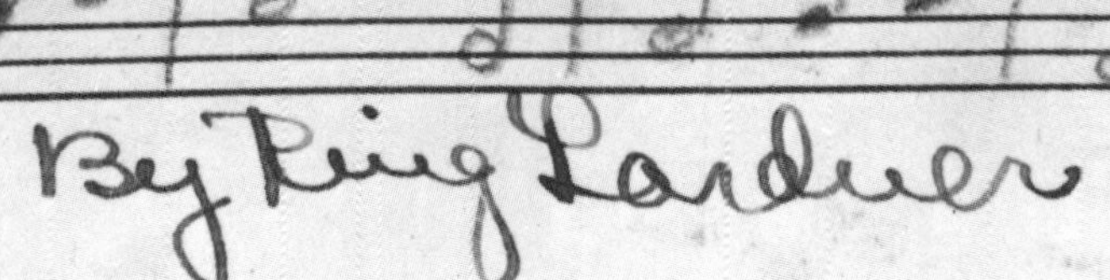

In October 1922 the Fitzgeralds rented a house at 6 Gateway Drive in Great Neck, Long Island. One of their neighbors was Ring Lardner, with whom Fitzgerald developed a close friendship. The Fitzgeralds remained at Great Neck until May 1924, when they went to France.

The repression breaks out
A comfortable but dangerous
and deteriorating year at
Great Neck. No ground under our feet.

Twenty six years old

Proud, shy, solemn, shrewd, polite, brave, kind, merciful, honorable—with the affection these qualities aroused he created in addition a certain awe in people. His intentions, his will, once in motion, were formidable factors in dealing with him—he always did every single thing he said he would do. Frequently he was the melancholy Jacques, and sad company indeed, but under any conditions a noble dignity flowed from him, so that time in his presence always seemed well spent.

—"Ring"

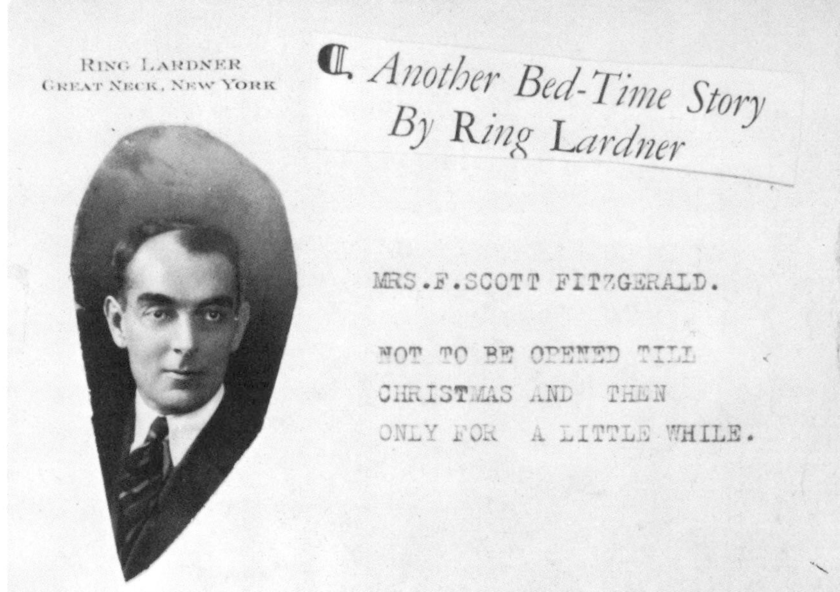

RING LARDNER
GREAT NECK, NEW YORK

Another Bed-Time Story
By Ring Lardner

MRS. F. SCOTT FITZGERALD.

NOT TO BE OPENED TILL
CHRISTMAS AND THEN
ONLY FOR A LITTLE WHILE.

A CHRISTMAS WISH—AND WHAT CAME OF IT.

Of all the girls for whom I care,
And there are quite a number,
None can compare with Zelda Sayre,
Now wedded to a plumber.

I knew her when she was a waif
In southern Alabama.
Her old granddaddy cracked a safe
And found therein her grandma.

A Glee Club man walked up New York
For forty city blocks,
Nor did he meet a girl as sweet
As Mrs. Farmer Fox.

I read the World, I read the Sun,
The Tribune and the Herald,
But of all the papers, there is none
Like Mrs. Scott Fitzgerald.

God rest thee, merry gentleman!
God shrew thee, greasy maiden!
God love that pure American
Who married Mr. Braden.

If it is dark when home I go
And safety is imperilled,
There's no policeman that I know
Like Zelda Sayre Fitzgerald.

I met her at the football game;
'Twas in the Harvard stadium.
A megaphone announced her name:
"It's Mrs. James S. Braden!"

So here's my Christmas wish for you:
I worship Leon Errol,
But the funniest girl I ever knew
Is Mrs. Scott Fitzgerald.

From Ring Lardner.

HEARST'S INTERNATIONAL

MAY, 1923

Photographed by Alfred Cheney Johnston

SCOTT AND ZELDA FITZGERALD

Mrs. F. Scott Fitzgerald *started the flapper movement in this country. So says her husband, the best-loved author of the younger generation. His first book,* This Side of Paradise, *was finished when he was twenty-two. He began it at Princeton and wrote portions of it at military camps during the war.* Mr. Fitzgerald *says he wrote it because he was certain that all the young people were going to be killed in the war and he wanted to put on paper a record of the strange life they had led in their time. The novel made an* immediate success. *Since then he has written,* The Beautiful and Damned *and two collections of short stories which are to the* young people *of* this generation *what O. Henry was to the last. All of F. Scott Fitzgerald's new fiction will appear in* HEARST'S INTERNATIONAL.

55

Record for 1923

	$		$
Option from Hearsts	1500.00	Com. 10%	1350.00
"Dice, Brassknuckles and Guitar"	1500.00	"	1350.00
Hot and Cold Blood	1500.00	"	1350.00
"Diamond Dick"	1500.00	"	1350.00
"Our Own Movie Queen" (half Zelda)	1000.00	"	900.00
Gretchen's Forty Winks	1200.00	"	1080.00
Winter Dreams (English Rights)	125.00	"	112.50
Total			7,442.50
This Side of Paradise			10,000.00
The Camel's Back			1,000.00
Grit			2,000.00
Titles for Glimpses of the Moon			500.00
Total			13,500.00
	500.00	Com. 10%	450.00
Imagination and a few Mothers	1000.	Com 10%	900.00
The Cruise of the Rolling Junk	300.	"	270.00
Making Monogamy Work	300.	"	270.00
Our Irresponsible Rich	350.	"	315.00
The Most Disgraceful Thing I ever did			20.00
Review of 'Being Respectable'			15.00
" " Many Marriages			5.00
" " Through the Wheat			5.00
Total			1,800.00
Syndicate Returns	74.75	Com 10%	67.28
This Side of Paradise			880.00
Flappers and Philosophers			98.00
The Beautiful and Damned			292.00
Tales of the Jazz Age			270.43
Total (figures estimated)			1,510.00
Advance on new Novel (The Great Gatsby)			3939.00
Total			5,450.00
Total			$ 28,759.78

Over our garage is a large bare room whither I now retired with pencil, paper and the oil stove, emerging the next afternoon at five o'clock with a 7,000-word story. That was something; it would pay the rent and last month's overdue bills. It took twelve hours a day for five weeks to rise from abject poverty back into the middle class, but within that time we had paid our debts, and the cause for immediate worry was over.

But I was far from satisfied with the whole affair. A young man can work at excessive speed with no ill effects, but youth is unfortunately not a permanent condition of life.

I wanted to find out where the $36,000 had gone. Thirty-six thousand is not very wealthy—not yacht-and-Palm-Beach wealthy—but it sounds to me as though it should buy a roomy house full of furniture, a trip to Europe once a year, and a bond or two besides. But our $36,000 had bought nothing at all.

So I dug up my miscellaneous account books, and my wife dug up her complete household record for the year 1923, and we made out the monthly average. Here it is:

Household Expenses

	Apportioned per Month
Income tax	$ 198.00
Food	202.00
Rent	300.00
Coal, wood, ice, gas, light, phone and water	114.50
Servants	295.00
Golf clubs	105.50
Clothes—three people	158.00
Doctor and dentist	42.50
Drugs and cigarettes	32.50
Automobile	25.00
Books	14.50
All other household expenses	112.50
Total	$1,600.00

"Well, that's not bad," we thought when we had got thus far. "Some of the items are pretty high, especially food and servants. But there's about everything accounted for, and it's only a little more than half our income."

—"How to Live on $36,00 a Year"

In 1923 the Fitzgeralds spent $36,000 at Great Neck while he earned $28,759.78.

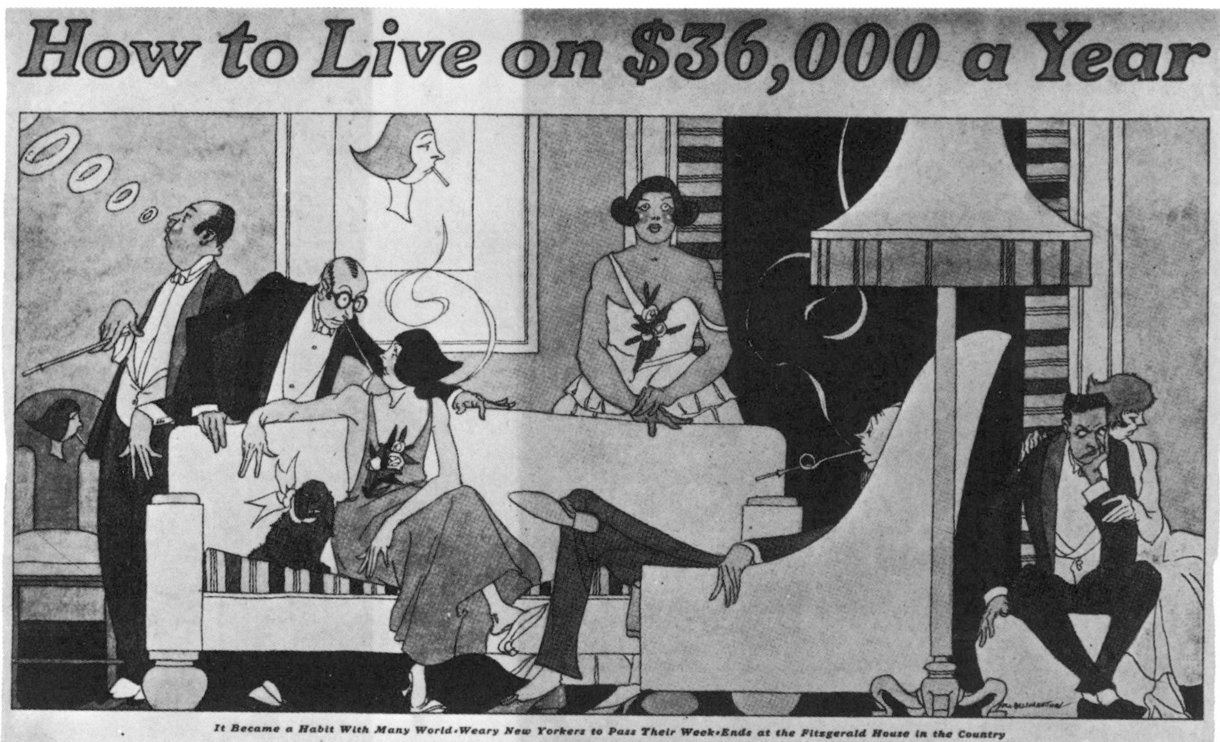

How to Live on $36,000 a Year
It Became a Habit With Many World-Weary New Yorkers to Pass Their Week-Ends at the Fitzgerald House in the Country
By F. Scott Fitzgerald
ILLUSTRATED BY M. L. BLUMENTHAL

BREAKFAST

Mrs. F. Scott Fitzgerald

Wife of author of *The Beautiful and Damned, The Jazz Age,* etc.

See if there is any bacon, and if there is ask the cook which pan to fry it in. Then ask if there are any eggs, and if so try and persuade the cook to poach two of them. It is better not to attempt toast, as it burns very easily. Also in the case of bacon do not turn the fire too high, or you will have to get out of the house for a week.

Serve preferably on china plates, though gold or wood will do if handy.

A party at the Great Neck house ("me" in upper left hand corner is ZF). Below, the only photograph of the house in Zelda's album, which she sometimes decorated with paste-on flowers.

Then we worked out the average monthly expenditures that could be included under pleasure.

Hotel bills—this meant spending the night or charging meals in New York	$ 51.00
Trips—only two, but apportioned per month	43.00
Theater tickets	55.00
Barber and hairdresser	25.00
Charity and loans	15.00
Taxis	15.00
Gambling—this dark heading covers bridge, craps and football bets	33.00
Restaurant parties	70.00
Entertaining	70.00
Miscellaneous	23.00
Total	$400.00

Some of these items were pretty high. They will seem higher to a Westerner than to a New Yorker. Fifty-five dollars for theater tickets means between three and five shows a month, depending on the type of show and how long it's been running. Football games are also included in this, as well as ringside seats to the Dempsey-Firpo fight. As for the amount marked "restaurant parties"—$70 would perhaps take three couples to a popular after-theater cabaret—but it would be a close shave.

We added the items marked "pleasure" to the items marked "household expenses," and obtained a monthly total.

"Fine," I said. "Just $3,000. Now at least we'll know where to cut down, because we know where it goes."

She frowned; then a puzzled, awed expression passed over her face.

"What's the matter?" I demanded. "Isn't it all right? Are some of the items wrong?"

"It isn't the items," she said staggeringly; it's the total. This only adds up to $2,000 a month."

—"How to Live on $36,00 a Year"

Drawing by John Held, Jr.: Copr. 1927, 1955. *The New Yorker Magazine, Inc.*

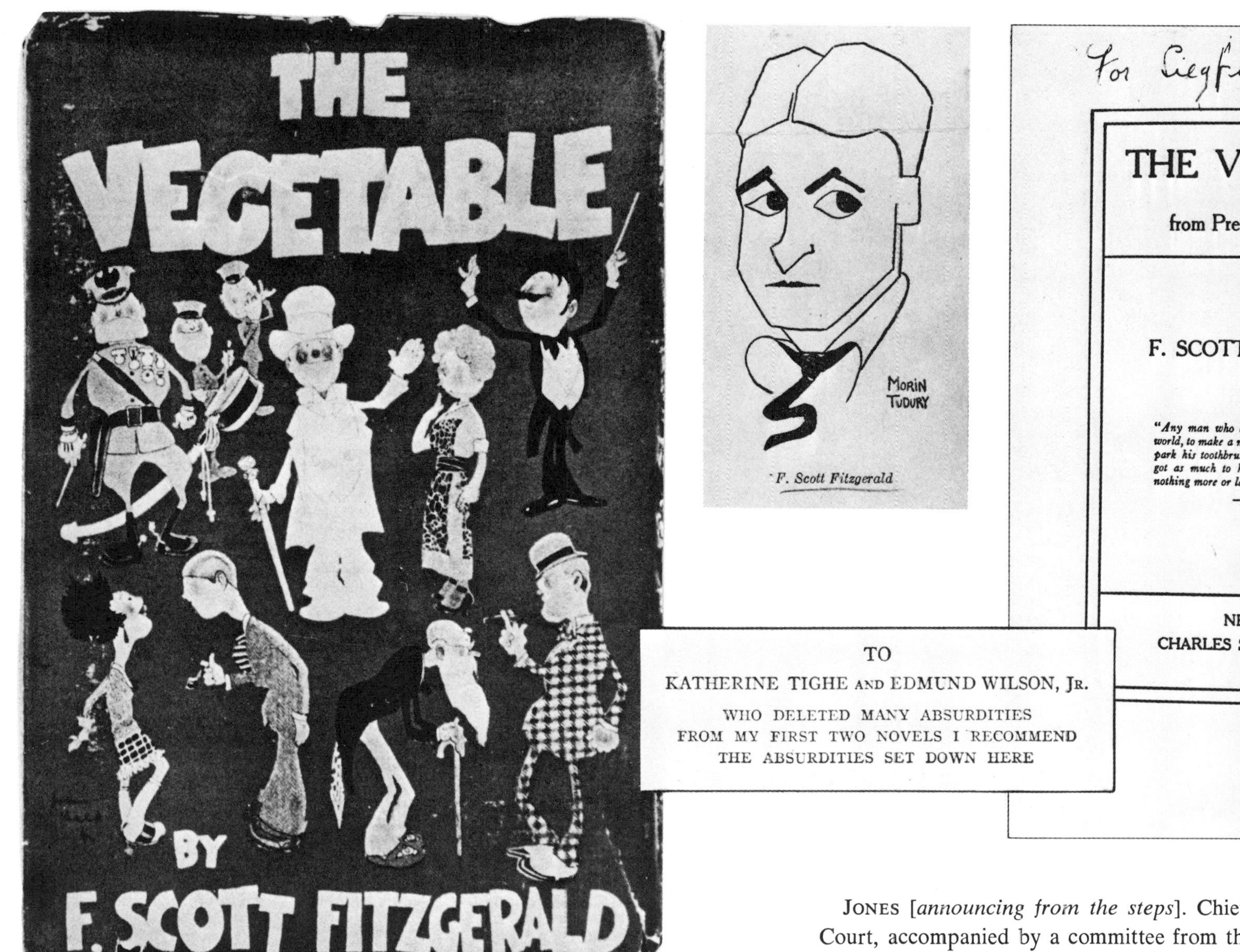

For Siegfried Wiesberger
from the author
F Scott Fitzgerald

THE VEGETABLE

or

from President to postman

By

F. SCOTT FITZGERALD

"Any man who doesn't want to get on in the world, to make a million dollars, and maybe even park his toothbrush in the White House, hasn't got as much to him as a good dog has—he's nothing more or less than a vegetable."

—From a Current Magazine.

NEW YORK
CHARLES SCRIBNER'S SONS
1923

TO
KATHERINE TIGHE AND EDMUND WILSON, JR.
WHO DELETED MANY ABSURDITIES
FROM MY FIRST TWO NOVELS I RECOMMEND
THE ABSURDITIES SET DOWN HERE

In need of money, Fitzgerald published The Vegetable *in April 1923, begore the play was produced.*

626 Goodrich Ave
St. Paul, Minn.

DEC 27

Dear Mr. Ober:

My play won't be finished until about the 10th of January & I'm getting sort of low again. Does Harry still owe about $500 on that last short story? If he's still paying slow let me know and I'll put my play aside for a week & tear off another Post story.

My play is the funniest ever written & will make a fortune. I'd suggest offering it to Miller (of Frohmans) first, as they heard of it in a round about way & wrote me. Harris was also interested about a year ago—do you remember

As Ever
F Scott Fitzgerald

JONES [*announcing from the steps*]. Chief Justice Fossile of the Supreme Court, accompanied by a committee from the Senate!

CHARLOTTE [*to Jerry*]. Speak right up to them. Show them you're not just a vegetable.

Here they come! Chief Justice Fossile, in a portentous white wig, is walking ponderously at the head of the procession. Five of the six Senators who follow him are large, grave gentlemen whose cutaway coats press in their swollen stomachs. Beside them Senator Fish seems frail and ineffectual.

The delegation comes to a halt before Jerry, who regards it defiantly, but with some uneasiness.

JUDGE FOSSILE. To the President of the United States—greetings.

JERRY [*nervously*]. Greetings yourself.

Mr. Jones has provided chairs, and the Senators seat themselves in a row, with Judge Fossile in front. Fish looks miserably at Doris. The Honorable Snooks lurks in the shadow of the Special Tree.

JUDGE FOSSILE. Mr. President, on the motion of the gentleman from Idaho—[*He points to Fish, who tries unsuccessfully to shrink out of sight.*] we have come to analyze you, with a view to impeachment.

JERRY [*sarcastically*]. Oh, is that so? [*He looks for encouragment at Charlotte. Charlotte grunts.*]

JUDGE FOSSILE. I believe that is the case, Senator Fish?

FISH [*nervously*]. Yes, but personally I like him.

CHARLOTTE. Oh, you do, do you? [*She nudges Jerry.*] Speak right up to them like that.

JERRY. Oh, you do, do you?

JUDGE FOSSILE. Remove that woman!

No one pays any attention to his request.

JUDGE FOSSILE. Now, Mr. President, do you absolutely refuse to resign on the request of the Senator from Idaho?

JERRY. You're darn right I refuse!

JUDGE FOSSILE. Well, then, I——

At this point Mr. Stutz-Mozart's Orang-Outang Band outside of the wall launches into a jovial jazz rendition of "Way Down upon the Swanee River." Suspecting it to be the national anthem, the Senators glance at each other uneasily, and then, removing their silk hats, get to their feet, one by one. Even Judge Fossile stands at respectful attention until the number dies away.

—The Vegetable

Boston Herald

THE VEGETABLE

A Scott Fitzgerald Comedy of Many Sparkling Absurdities

The Vegetable, by F. Scott Fitzgerald; Charles Scribner's Sons.

You may recall that young Mr. Fitzgerald in "This Side of Paradise," by which he climbed to sudden fame, cast whole pages of his novel into the form of a play. There was verse, too, and various other literary experiments in that sparkling piece of fiction which reflected so pitilessly the young life of the time. Now he gives us a book that is the conventional comedy form—that is, as nearly conventional as Mr. Fitzgerald will allow himself to become. He confesses—or perhaps it is a boast—that "The Vegetable" has been rejected by several New York producers and managers. Perhaps it wouldn't have "staged" well. It read so well, however, that we congratulated the far larger audience which it will reach in its present form. You may get the impression that it is a sheaf of absurdities from beginning to end, but under all its hilarity there is some of the most exquisite satire that it was ever our privilege to read.

It is the story of Jerry Frost, designed by a kindly nature to be a wholly successful postman, but having visions, especially after he had been "analyzed" and also filled with "sympathetic" gin, of becoming president. The first act is in the New York flat where Jerry and his wife Charlotte have what is called by courtesy a home. Oh, yes, Jerry's deaf and doddering father, aged 88, lives there, too, one of the most delightful characters in the whole cast. The second act finds Jerry filling the office of president. His father is secretary of the treasury.

Perhaps it is all a dream, but it is staged realistically enough. Not the least of Jerry's achievements in this act is to solve the Borah problem—though it isn't phrased that way—by swaping Idaho for the Buzzard islands. The trade is made with the new Irish-Polish republic in central Europe, of which Jerry's old bootlegger friend is now the ambassador. The transaction gives the army clique its much desired excuse for war.

The third act finds us back in the Frost home again with Charlotte and her sister, Doris, whose engagement complications provide no little enjoyment for the reader, trying to solve the mystery of Jerry's disappearance after his solitary hootch party. Everything ends happily. Then you want to turn back to the beginning and read the book right through a second time. Don't miss "The Vegetable." If you can't borrow a copy, then buy one.

F. SCOTT FITZGERALD

His New Book, "The Vegetable" (Charles Scribner's Sons) is a Satire of the Times in Dramatic Form

THE VEGETABLE

OR FROM PRESIDENT TO POSTMAN

By F. Scott Fitzgerald -17

A Play in Three Acts

Farce, burlesque, comedy—or disquisition on "boobery"—this is one of the most amusing books ever published. God meant Jerry to be a "good egg" and a postman; but, having been created in a democratic age, free and equal, he thought he *ought* to rise in the world—he thought he ought to want to become President, *and he does.* THE VEGETABLE is brilliant satire.

$1.50

DADA

DORIS JOSEPH FISH

CHARLOTTE

JERRY FROST

MAJOR-GENERAL PUSHING

THE BOOTLEGGER

CHARLES SCRIBNER'S SONS FIFTH AVENUE, NEW YORK

Springfield Repub.

FITZGERALD WRITES A PLAY

Creator of the Flapper Tries to Satirize Democracy

The fact that the varying opinions of two "severe and celebrated" dramatic critics led three metropolitan managers to refuse to stage F. Scott Fitzgerald's new play, "The Vegetable" (Charles Scribner's Sons, $1.50), is enough to whet the curiosity of the young writer's admirers. But even the flapper, whose popularity has been very largely due to this apostle of the "younger generation" cannot fail to be disappointed at Mr Fitzgerald's attempt at dramatic writing.

"The Vegetable" is a satire on the current form of democracy where all men, because they are created free and equal, seek to push ahead, and, if possible, to become president, instead of holding down the jobs they are really fitted for. Jerry Frost was such a man. He was a "good egg" and had it in him to be a good postman, an excellent servant of the public in a humble capacity. But he was made president and conducted the affairs of the nation with the intelligence that God had allotted him to use as a postman.

The humor, which is often amusing in the author's short stories and novels, is in this case the humor of a "tacky party," where comedy is made as obvious and as unattractive as possible. The satire directed toward the White House, politicians and government officials is of the cheapest sort of burlesque. The heartiest laughs are afforded by "Mr Snooks," the bootlegger, who is intimately portrayed. Even "Dumbell Doris," the flapper, is a disappointment. She is an inferior copy of the author's original brand of astounding young girls. Her dialogue, which once might have been acclaimed as "a good line," now sounds stale and out of date.

Just what the two celebrated dramatic critics said about the play is unknown. But they might easily have declared it a shame to produce so thin a play under the name of a popular young author who has shown himself capable of better work.

NEW COMEDY AT SHORE

Scott Fitzgerald's "The Vegetable" Produced at Atlantic City

Atlantic City, N. J., Nov. 20.—F. Scott Fitzgerald made his debut as a playwright at the Apollo Theatre here last evening with "The Vegetable," a comedy based on his book of that name. The apostle of the flappers has abandoned his theme of the deadly young female species and turned his satirical realism to X-ray-ing the great American home of a humble white collar worker, with little gray matter above the white.

In the first act, with the artful aid of Ernest Truex at his best and funniest, he skilfully shows, or rather, shows up, the more or less happy, more or less turbulent, home of Jerry Frost, railroad clerk, and his nagging wife, Charlotte. Nothing much happens, except that Jerry, after a deal of verbal buffeting from his spouse and her sister, is visited by his tough but genial bootlegger, and on the wings of synthetic gin soars far above the cares of family life.

The second act, supposed to show Jerry's gin-fizzled dream of himself in the White House as President, does little else than demonstrate that Mr. Fitzgerald would better stick to his modernist realism and leave fantasy to those of lighter touch and whim.

The third act comes back to that horror of amateur interior, decorating which to Jerry is home, and his sitting room. It develops that Jerry, after his bad dreams of realizing his boyhood ambition to become President, has fled from his home to bring to actual realization his later ambition, always stifled by his wife, to be a postman. He comes back after two weeks to a wife reduced to tearful contrition for her past nagging, and a happy ending is achieved but not until Mr. Fitzgerald has revealed that he is as little at home with tender and old-fashioned sentiment as he is with fantasy.

However the comedy has many bright moments of keen mockery of our foibles and inanities. Minna Gombel, as the wife; Ruth Hammond, as Doris, the one lone Fitzgeraldized flapper of the piece, and Malcolm Williams, as Snooks, the irresistible bootlegger, all do their best to emphasize Mr. Fitzgerald's strong points, though they can't quite lift that second act out of the bog.

Scene in front of Scribner's window: Fanny Hurst, with a copy of "The Vegetable" under her arm, and F. Scott Fitzgerald, looking at the collection of Conrad manuscripts

F. SCOTT FITZGERALD WRITES PLAY ABOUT VEGETABLE FAMILY AND IT IS HILARIOUS READING

Buffalo Express

Satirical comedy, refused by theatrical producers, is put out in book form—Maxwell has new work called A Day's Journey—Other recent publications.

F. Scott Fitzgerald has gone and done it again, this time turning out a satirical comedy entitled The Vegetable, or from President to Postman. He has taken his theme from the following quotation from a recent magazine; "Any man who does not want to get on in the world, to make a million dollars, and maybe even park his toothbrush in the White House, hasn't got as much to him as a good dog has—he's nothing more nor less than a vegetable."

And a real vegetable family has been chosen for this comedy satire, Jerry and his nagging wife, a bootlegger, dada, aged 80 odd, and Charlotte's would-be flapper sister, Doris, also her young man, a dreary creature. The funniest part of the satire is the descriptive matter and the business inserted by the author in his play. According to the publishers, Charles Scribner's Sons of New York, the comedy, in slightly different form, has been refused by three leading metropoliton managers, but, because the publishers think it has the particularly individual flavor of the previous works by the author, they are putting it out in book form. Whether it will make playable material may be a matter of doubt, especially to those who do not pretend to qualify as dramatic critics, but there can be little doubt that Vegetable makes uncommonly hilarious reading.

Nixon's Apollo Theatre

Telephone—Marine 3146

The Nixon Apollo Theatre Company	Lessees
FRED G. NIXON-NIRDLINGER	Pres. & Gen'l Mgr.
Guy S. Burley	Business Manager
Harold Manypenny, Clarence D. Stewart	Treasurers
Walter Raymond	Stage Manager
Charles G. Miller	Electrician
James J. Brown	Advertising Agent
C. B. Riley	Properties

One Week Commencing Monday, November 19, 1923

Mats. Wednesday and Saturday

SAM H. HARRIS Presents

Ernest Truex

in

F. SCOTT FITZGERALD'S Comedy

The Vegetable

(From President to Postman)

Staged by Sam Forrest

The characters concerned in the disclosure are:

Jerry Frost
(The Vegetable himself)..........Ernest Truex

Charlit
(His wife, who means practically no good) Minna Gombel

Dada
(Jerry's father and a great thinker. He will never see eighty-eight again)..David Higgins

Doris
(Charlotte's sister, who learned about life from the silver screen)..........Ruth Hammond

Mr. Snookes (or Snukes)
(An astounding product of our constitution) Malcolm Williams

Joseph Fish
(An Idaho sheik, beloved of Doris) Donald MacDonald

Major General Pushing, U. S. A.
(You will hear more of him later)..Walter Walker

Chief Justice Fossile
(Of the Supreme Court. He needs no introduction)..........Harry Hammill

Mr. Jones
(Highly recommended by the King of England)..........Harold de Becker

Mr. Stutz-Mozart
(The venerable Jazz King)..........Luis Alberni

A Chauffeur
(Who is also a herald)..........H. H. Gibson

A Newsboy
(He will speak for himself)..........Barney Warren

A Postman
(Just a common postman)..William H. Pendergast

Mr. McSullivan
(The well-known politician)....William H. Malone

Also a Drummer and a Fifer
Their real names are..Walter Millar, Leslie Millar

And finally there are some Senators
In private life they are known as
Robert Mack, Harry Ford, Frank Bronson, John Paul, Horace Grey, Miller Cushman

THE FIRST ACT
is the living room in the Frosts' house. It was not designed by Elsie de Wolf. It just happened.
But when you come to

THE SECOND ACT
you will be glad to learn that we're now on the lawn of the White House—yes, the Executive Mansion itself, at Washington, D. C.
However, the pace is pretty fast there, so in

THE THIRD ACT
(Which occurs two weeks after the first) we return to the dear little love nest of the Frost family.

But we were no longer important. The flapper, upon whose activities the popularity of my first books was based, had become *passé* by 1923—anyhow in the East. I decided to crash Broadway with a play, but Broadway sent its scouts to Atlantic City and quashed the idea in advance, so I felt that, for the moment, the city and I had little to offer each other. I would take the Long Island atmosphere that I had familiarly breathed and materialize it beneath unfamiliar skies.

—"My Lost City"

Mrs. Lardner and Zelda at Atlantic City.

THE COURIER-JOURNAL, LOUISVILLE, SUNDAY MORNING, SEPTEMBER 30, 1923

What a "Flapper Novelist" Thinks of His Wife

Scott Fitzgerald, Creator of Modern Girl Types in Current Fiction, Interviews His Own Bride in the Intimacy of Their Happy Long Island Home

Is She His Model?

IS Zelda Sayre Fitzgerald, wife of Scott Fitzgerald, author of flapper fiction stories, the heroine of her husband's books? That's what a lot of "best seller" patrons have been wondering.

If so, is she the living prototype of that species of femininity known as the American flapper? If so, what is a flapper like in real life? Here is a tabloid picture of Zelda Fitzgerald:

Flappers. She likes them reckless and unconventional, because of their quest in search of self-expression.

Sports. Golf and swimming.

Jazz music, "because it is artistic," and dancing for its sheer abandon. Not ambitious to be a "joiner"—just enjoy life to the full. Large families "so children have a chance to be what they want to be." Wants her own daughter to be "rich, happy and artistic."

If she had to earn her own living would go in for the ballet or the movies. Failing in that, she would try writing.

Home is the place to do what you like to do—not to live by the clock in a conventional way.

"I like girls like Rosalind in 'This Side of Paradise,'" says Zelda Sayre Fitzgerald, wife of the American novelist, "for their courage and recklessness. Three or four years ago girls of her type were pioneers. They did what they wanted to for self-expression. Now they do it because it's the thing to do—every one does"

"So this is to be all about me?" asked Mrs. Scott Fitzgerald vivaciously. "I've never been interviewed before!"

She leaned far back into the plastic depths of an overstuffed chair, querying expectantly, "Now what do we do? Is it going to be very formal? Scott, please come into the living room and help me be interviewed."

Obediently Scott Fitzgerald left his study—scene of the creation of those brilliant tales to which American flappers thrill en masse. Tall, blond, broadshouldered, he towers above his petite wife, whose blue eyes and yellow hair match his own.

"My stories?" Mrs. Fitzgerald said, "Oh, yes, I've written three. I mean, I'm writing them now. Heretofore, I've done several magazine articles. I like to write. Do you know, I thought my husband should write a perfectly good ending to one of the tales, and he wouldn't! He called them 'lop-sided,' too! Said that they began at the end."

She waved a gayly protesting white hand at her husband's efforts to explain that they were "good."

"Writing has its advantages," she continued. "Just think: I buy ever so many of Scott's presents that way. And buy ever so many other things on the theoretical proceeds of stories I'm going to write some day.

"Spending money is fun, isn't it?—Oh, yes, I wrote them in long hand. Typewriters are an unknown institution here at Great Neck."

Thus is necessitated the explanation that the abode of this charming and brilliant young couple among the newer lights of the modern literary world is a charming country house at Great Neck, Long Island.

Speaking "in domestic vein," which isn't the usual thing for her, Mrs. Fitzgerald remarked upon the absence of the butler. "He must be taking his saxophone lessons. Yes, today is the day. My great disappointment is that I've never heard him play; just infrequent tootings from afar.

"Yes. I love Scott's books and heroines. I like the ones that are like me! That's why I love Rosalind in 'This Side of Paradise.' You see, I always read everything he writes. It spoils the fun, the surprise, I mean, a bit. Sometimes I act as official critic.

"But Rosalind! I like girls like that," she continued, shaking a curly crop of honey-yellow bobbed hair. "I like their courage, their recklessness and spendthriftness. Rosalind was the original American flapper.

"Three or four years ago girls of her type were pioneers. They did what they wanted to, were unconventional, perhaps, just be-

cause they wanted to for self-expression. Now they do it because it's the thing every one does."

* * *

Asked to use his much-lauded gift for description in composing a word picture of his wife, he replied laconically and readily. "She is the most charming person in the world."

"Thank you, dear," was the gracious response.

Asked to continue the description thus commenced so auspiciously, he said: "That's all. I refuse to amplify. Excepting—she's perfect."

This last was given with an ardor worthy of one of his best heroes—Amory Blaine, for instance.

"But you don't think that," came the protest from the overstuffed arm chair. "You think I'm a lazy woman."

"No," judicially, "I like it. I think you're perfect. You're always ready to listen to my manuscripts at any hour of the day or night. You're charming—beautiful. You do, I believe, clean the ice box once a week."

* * *

"Oh, yes, I can draw. Scott says I don't know much about it, but that I draw well. And I play golf.

"I've a hearty liking for jazz music, especially Irving Berlin's," she continued. "It's most artistic. One of the first principles of dancing is abandon, and this is a quality that jazz music possesses. It's complex. It will, I believe, occupy a great place in American art."

* * *

At this juncture her husband decided to take a hand in the matter of interviewing. He propounded a series of questions with startling rapidity.

"Whom do you consider the most interesting character in fiction?"

After a considerable discussion no less a person than Becky Sharpe was decided upon.

"Only, I do wish she'd been pretty," the interviewee remarked wistfully.

"What would your ideal day constitute?"

"Peaches for breakfast," was the prompt response. "There, that's a good start, isn't it? Let me see. Then golf. Then a swim. Then just being lazy. Not eating or reading, but being quiet and hearing pleasant sounds—rather a total vacuity. The evening? A large, brilliant, gathering, I believe."

"Am I ambitious?" she echoed the next question. "Not especially, but I've plenty of hope. I don't want to belong to clubs. No committees. I'm not a 'joiner.' Just be myself and enjoy living."

"Do you like to study?"

This question asked, her husband eyed her merrily, as though expecting an outburst.

It was forthcoming.

"You know I don't. Never did. But my ancestors made up for any lack of brilliance of mine in that line."

* * *

"Do you like large or small families?"

"Large ones. Yes, quite large. The reason is that then children have a chance to be what they want to be—not oppressed by too much 'looking after,' nor influenced by ordinary life in any way.

"Children shouldn't bother their parents, nor parents their children. If possible to establish friendly relations, mutual understanding, between them, it's an excellent thing, but if this isn't possible, it seems worse to bring them together too much. Let children work cut their own ideas as to duty to their parents, immortality and choosing a career."

"What do you want your daughter to do, Mrs. Fitzgerald, when she grows up?" Scott Fitzgerald inquired in his best reportorial manner, "not that you'll try to make her, of course, but—"

"Not great and serious and melancholy and inhospitable, but rich and happy and artistic. I don't mean that money means happiness, necessarily. But having things, just things, objects makes a woman happy. The right kind of perfume, the smart pair of shoes. They are great comforts to the feminine soul."

* * *

"What would you do if you had to earn your own living?" the catechism was continued.

"I've studied ballet. I'd try to get a place in the Follies. Or the movies. If I wasn't successful, I'd try to write."

Speaking of home life in general, and that of the Scott Fitzgeralds in particular, she declared that "Home is the place to do the things you want to do. Here, we eat just when we want to. Breakfast and luncheon are extremely movable feasts. It's terrible to allow conventional habits to gain a hold on a whole household; to eat, sleep and live by clock ticks."

Her favorite among her husband's writings are the episodes of Rosalind in "This Side of Paradise," the last half of "The Beautiful and the Damned," the short story, "The Off Shore Pirate" and the play, "The Vegetable."

* * *

All of which leads to the conclusion that Zelda Sayre Fitzgerald, though by her own declaration "not ambitious," is responsible in no small degree for the remarkable success of her distinguished author-husband.

—Interview, "What a 'Flapper Novelist' Thinks of His Wife"

Making Monogamy Work

Utilizing Jealousy As "the Greatest Prop to Love"—Most Potent Factor in Matrimony

By F. SCOTT FITZGERALD

The Mooted Effects of the "Petting Party"—Racial Experience With the Mating Instinct—The Baffling Formula of "Intellectual Compatibility"—Essentials to Successful Matches—The Roving Tendency.

EDITOR'S NOTE: Whether in dissent from, or in agreement with, the wisdom of experience as voiced by other notable contributors to this great forum on LOVE, MARRIAGE AND THE MODERN WOMAN, certain it is that the younger generation should have its hearing. For whatever the conclusions that may be formulated from this important discussion, it will be upon the shoulders of the younger generation to work them out.

Of this generation, few, if any, have made a more conspicuous literary mark than F. Scott Fitzgerald. It is of more than usual interest, therefore, to have revealed the problem of marriage as it appears through such keen, and particularly modern, eyes.

was over, Harry and Georgianna were to be free to ramble. They were exceptionally well-mated, exceptionally congenial, and the fascination endured well into the fourth year of their marriage.

Then they made two discoveries—that they were still in love with each other, and that they were no longer completely unaware of the other men and women in the world. Just as they made these discoveries circumstances threw them suddenly into gayest New York. Harry, through the nature of his occupation, came into almost daily contact with dozens of charming and foot-loose young women, and Georgianna began to receive the attentions of half a dozen charming and foot-loose young men.

ONE COUPLE AND A QUICK SOLUTION

"If ever a marriage seemed bound for the rocks this one did. We gave them six months—a year at the outside. It was too bad, we felt, because fundamentally they loved each other, but circumstances had undoubtedly doomed them—as a matter of fact they are now in process of living happily together forever after.

"Did they decide that the best way to hold each other was to let faithfulness be entirely voluntary? They did not. Did they come to an arrangement by which neither was to pry into the other's life? They did not. On the contrary they tortured each other into a state of wild, unreasoning jealousy—and this solved the problem neatly in less than a week."

This article was syndicated under various titles in February 1923.

There never was a good biography of a good novelist. There couldn't be. He is too many people, if he's any good.

—"The Note-Books"

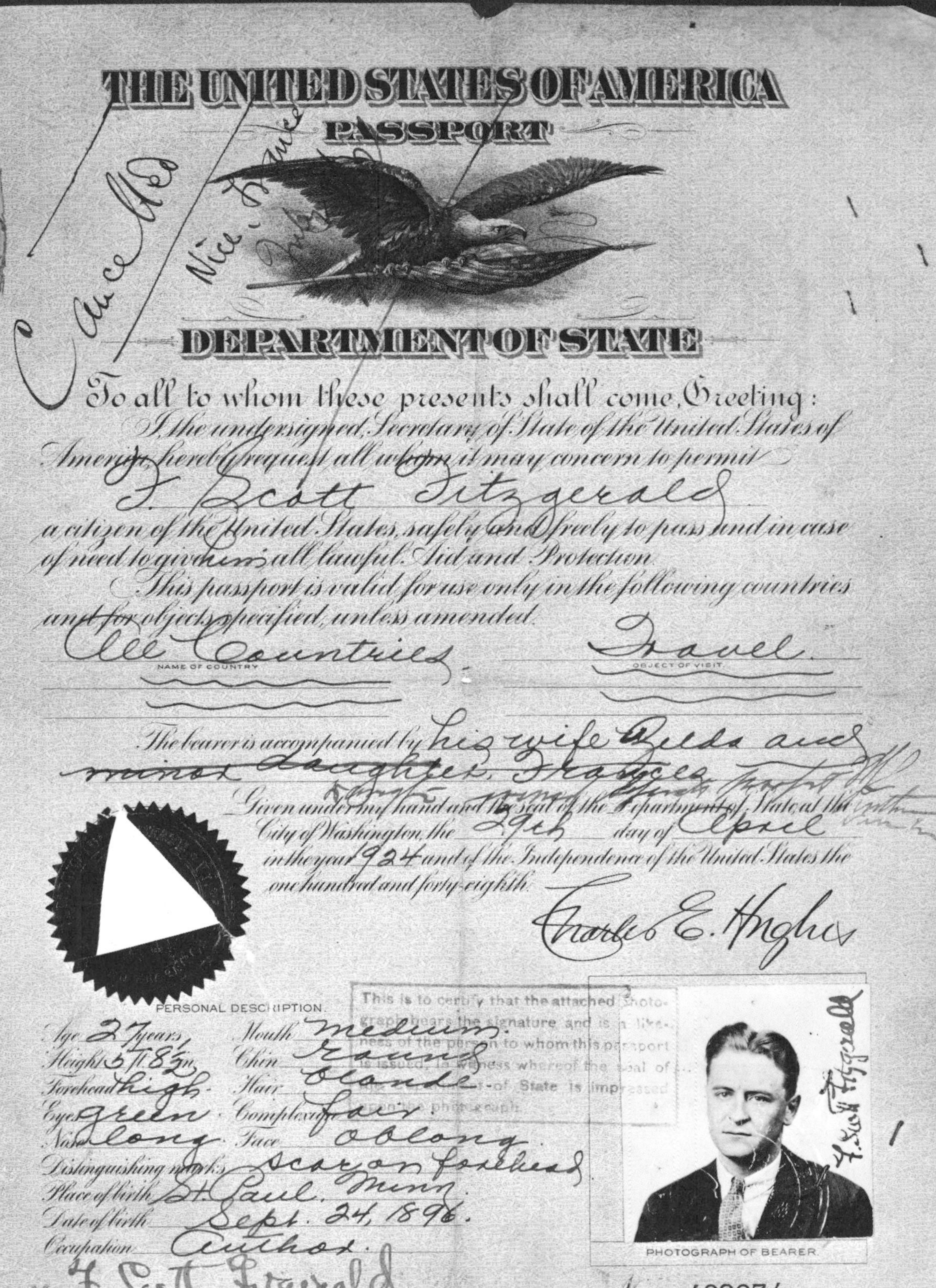

THE UNITED STATES OF AMERICA
PASSPORT

Cancelled
Nice

DEPARTMENT OF STATE

To all to whom these presents shall come, Greeting:
I, the undersigned, Secretary of State of the United States of America, hereby request all whom it may concern to permit F. Scott Fitzgerald a citizen of the United States, safely and freely to pass, and in case of need to give him all lawful Aid and Protection.
This passport is valid for use only in the following countries and for objects specified, unless amended.

All Countries — Travel
NAME OF COUNTRY — OBJECT OF VISIT

The bearer is accompanied by his wife Zelda and minor daughter Frances

Given under my hand and the seal of the Department of State, at the City of Washington, the 29th day of April in the year 1924 and of the Independence of the United States the one hundred and forty-eighth.

Charles E. Hughes

PERSONAL DESCRIPTION.
Age 27 years — Mouth medium
Height 5 ft. 8½ in. — Chin round
Forehead high — Hair blonde
Eyes green — Complexion fair
Nose long — Face oblong
Distinguishing marks: scar on forehead
Place of birth: St. Paul, Minn.
Date of birth: Sept. 24, 1896.
Occupation: Author.
F. Scott Fitzgerald
SIGNATURE OF BEARER

This is to certify that the attached photograph bears the signature and is a likeness of the person to whom this passport is issued, in witness whereof the seal of the Department of State is impressed on the photograph.

PHOTOGRAPH OF BEARER

No 402634

In May 1924 the Fitzgeralds sailed to France in the hope of living economically while he wrote The Great Gatsby.

To Z.S.F.

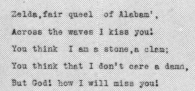

Zelda, fair queel of Alabam',
Across the waves I kiss you!
You think I am a stone, a clam;
You think that I don't care a damn,
But God! how I will miss you!

For months and months you've meant to me
What Mario meant to Tosca.
You've gone, and I am all at sea
Just like the Minnewaska.

I once respected him you call
Your spouse, and that is why, dear,
I held my tongue—And then, last Fall,
He bared a flippancy and gall
Of which I'd had no idear.

When I with pulmonary pain
Was seized, he had the gumption
To send me lives of Wilde and Crane,
Two brother craftsmen who in vain
Had battled with consumption.

We wreak our vengeance as we can,
And I have no objection
To getting even with this "man"
By stealing your affection.

So, dearie, when your tender heart
Of all his coarseness tires,
Just cable me and I will start
Immediately for Hyeres.

To hell with Scott Fitzgerald then!
To hell with Scott, his daughter!
It's you and I back home again,
To Great Neck, where the men are men
And booze is ½ water.

My heart goes with you as you sail.
God grant you won't be seasick!
The thought of you abaft the rail,
Diffusing meat and ginger ale,
Makes both my wife and me sick.

Ring W. Lardner

AMENDMENTS AND EXTENSIONS.

THIS PASSPORT IS VALID FOR A PERIOD OF TWELVE MONTHS AND EXPIRES APR 29 1925. IT IS SUBJECT TO ONE OR MORE EXTENSIONS, PROVIDED THE FINAL DATE OF EXPIRATION IS NOT LATER THAN TWO YEARS AFTER THE DATE OF ITS ISSUANCE.

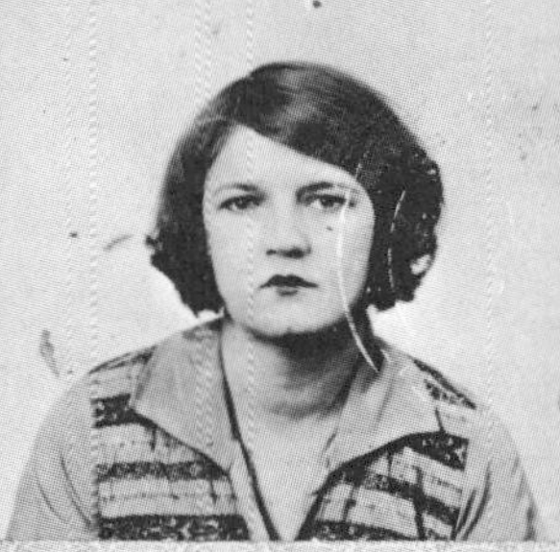

4783 June 26. 1925
twelve
Apr. 29. 1925 Apr. 29. 1926

VISAS.

AMERICAN CONSULATE GENERAL
PASSPORT DEPARTMENT
PARIS, FRANCE
THE PASSPORT IS HEREBY AMENDED TO reinclude the name of the bearer's minor daughter Frances
DATE July 24, 1924
AMERICAN VICE CONSUL

It costs more to ride on the tops of taxis than on the inside; Joseph Urban skies are expensive when they're real. Sunshine comes high to darn the thoroughfares with silver needles—a thread of glamor, a Rolls-Royce thread, a thread of O. Henry. Tired moons ask higher wages. Lustily splashing their dreams in the dark pool of gratification, their fifty thousand dollars bought a cardboard baby-nurse for Bonnie, a second hand Marmon, a Picasso etching, a white satin dress to house a beaded parrot, a yellow chiffon dress to snare a field of ragged-robins, a dress as green as fresh wet paint, two white knickerbocker suits exactly alike, a broker's suit, an English suit like the burnt fields of August, and two first class tickets for Europe.

—*Save Me the Waltz* (ZF)

PART FOUR CHRONOLOGY

TRIUMPH & DETERIORATION

(1924-1930)

May 1924
Stay in Paris for several days, then leave for Riviera. Stop at Grimm's Park Hotel in Hyères and settle in June at Villa Marie, Valescure, St. Raphaël. FSF writes *The Great Gatsby* during summer-fall 1924.

June 1924
"Absolution" in *The American Mercury.*

July 1924
" 'The Sensible Thing' " in *Liberty.*

Winter 1924–25
Rome, at Hôtel des Princes near the Piazza di Spagna, where FSF revises *The Great Gatsby.*

February 1925
Fitzgeralds travel to Capri, stay at Hotel Tiberio.

10 April 1925
Publication of *The Great Gatsby.*

Late April 1925
Trip to Paris by car through the south of France; stop over at Lyon and continue to Paris by train.

May–December 1925
Apartment at 14 rue de Tilsitt in Paris near the Etoile.

May 1925
FSF meets Ernest Hemingway in the Dingo Bar.

August 1925
Leave Paris for a month at Antibes.

January 1926
Fitzgeralds take "cure" at Salies-de-Beárn.

January and February 1926
"The Rich Boy" in *Red Book Magazine.*

February 1926
Play version of *The Great Gatsby,* by Owen Davis, produced on Broadway.

26 February 1926
Publication of *All the Sad Young Men,* third short story collection.

Early March 1926
Return to Riviera and rent Villa Paquita, Juan-les-Pins.

May 1926
Hemingways join Murphys and Fitzgeralds on Riviera. The Fitzgeralds turn their villa over to the Hemingways and move to the Villa St. Louis, Juan-les-Pins, where they remain until the end of 1926.

December 1926
Return to America on the *Conte Biancamano.*

1926
First movie version of *The Great Gatsby.*

January 1927
First trip to Hollywood to work on "Lipstick" (unproduced) for United Artists. At Ambassador Hotel.

March 1927–March 1928
The Fitzgeralds rent "Ellerslie," near Wilmington, Delaware.

April 1928
Return to Europe on the *Paris.*

April–August 1928
Apartment at 58 rue Vaugirard, Paris.

April 1928
Publication of the first Basil Duke Lee story, "The Scandal Detectives," in *The Saturday Evening Post.* This eight-story series about FSF's youth appears in the *Post* from April 1928 to April 1929.

Mid-summer 1928
ZF commences dancing lessons with Lubov Egorova in Paris.

September 1928
Fitzgeralds return to America on the *Carmania.*

September 1928–March 1929
At "Ellerslie."

Winter 1928–1929
ZF begins writing the series of short stories dealing with the lives of six young women for *College Humor.*

March 1929
"The Last of the Belles" in *The Saturday Evening Post.*

March 1929
Return to France on the *Conte Biancamano,* traveling from Genoa along the Riviera and then to Paris.

June 1929
Fitzgeralds leave Paris for Riviera, renting the Villa Fleur des Bois, Cannes.

October 1929
Fitzgeralds return by car to Paris by way of Provence; take apartment at 10 rue Pergolèse.

February 1930
FSF and ZF travel to North Africa.

To the French Riviera May 1924

Photoes 1924 -1929
Hyeres, France
St. Raphael, France
Rome, Italy
Paris, France
Salies-de-Bearn, France
Juan les Pins France
Brandywine Hundred, Delaware
Battlefields France
La Baule France

The Fitzgeralds arrived in France in May 1924. After staying at a hotel in Hyères, they rented the Villa Marie in St. Raphaël, where Fitzgerald wrote The Great Gatsby. The Fitzgeralds' meeting with Gerald and Sara Murphy and the crisis over Zelda's involvement with Edouard Jozan, a French aviator, occurred this summer.

Within an hour we had seen our home, a clean cool villa set in a large garden on a hill above town. It was what we had been looking for all along. There was a summerhouse and a sand pile and two bathrooms and roses for breakfast and a gardener who called me milord. When we had paid the rent, only thirty-five hundred dollars, half our original capital, remained. But we felt that at last we could begin to live on practically nothing a year.

—"How to Live on Practically Nothing a Year"

The Riviera

By RING LARDNER

On the following morning we went by train to St. Raphael where who was at the station to meet us but Mr. and Mrs. F. Scott Fitzgerald. Mr. Fitzgerald is a novelist and Mrs. Fitzgerald is a novelty. They left the United States last May because New Yorkers kept mistaking their Long Island home for a road house.

We was going to order a taxi to take us to our hotel, but Mr. Fitzgerald insisted on taking us in his car which is one of the kind that seats three comfortably. They was four of us.

St. Raphael is right on the Mediterranean, a kind of sea that runs clear from Gibraltar to Turkey. We set on the porch of the hotel all afternoon admiring the sea, and then went out to the Fitzgeralds' for a home-cooked meal. I made Mr. Fitzgerald a present of some rare perfume that said Johnnie Walker on the outside of it which I had picked up at Marseilles. It was coals to Newcastle, so I took it back to the hotel.

Mr. Fitzgerald said we must see Cannes and Nice and Monte Carlo while we was in the vicinity and we set a date to make the trip to those points. Mr. Fitzgerald said he would drive us in his car, but I had often rode with him around Great Neck, Long Island, so I said how could he enjoy the scenery if he had to keep watching the road and let's hire a car and a driver.

I made Mr. Fitzgerald a present of some rare perfume that said Johnnie Walker on the outside of it which I had picked up at Marseilles.
RALPH BARTON

The Ring Lardners' visit to the Fitzgeralds at St. Raphaël in September 1924 resulted in this Liberty article.

Villa Marie
Progress of "The Great Gatsby

We are living here in a sort of idyllic state among everything lovely imaginable in the way of Mediterranean delights. Unlike you I have only an occasional lust for the exotic streets of the metropolis—at present I am content to work and become excruciatingly healthy under Byron's and Shelley's and Dickens' sky.

—FSF to Carl Van Vechten, c. June 1924.

We are idyllicly settled here & the novel is going fine—it ought to be done in a month—though I'm not sure as I'm contemplating another 16,000 words which would make it about the length of Paradise—not quite though even then.

—FSF to Maxwell Perkins, 18 June 1924.

Self Portrait

The Fitzgeralds with Miss Maddox, Scottie's "Nanny."

Above: The garden at the Murphys' villa. Below: Gerald Murphy raking the beach at La Garoupe, Antibes.

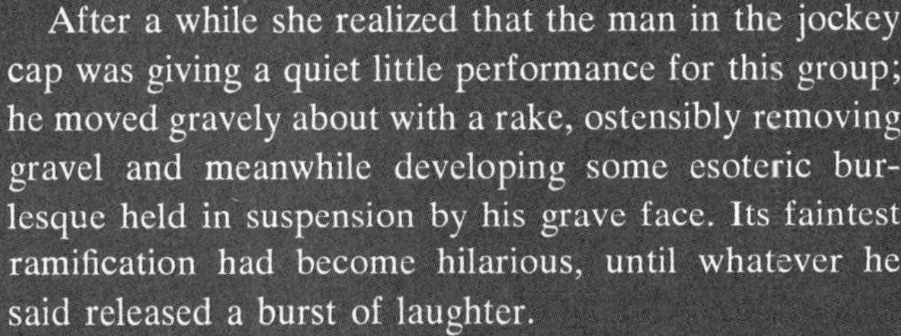

After a while she realized that the man in the jockey cap was giving a quiet little performance for this group; he moved gravely about with a rake, ostensibly removing gravel and meanwhile developing some esoteric burlesque held in suspension by his grave face. Its faintest ramification had become hilarious, until whatever he said released a burst of laughter.

—*Tender Is the Night*

Under separate cover I'm sending you my third novel:

The Great Gatsby

(I think that at last I've done something really my own), but how good "my own" is remains to be seen.

I should suggest the following contract.

15% up to 50,000

20% after 50,000

The book is only a little over fifty thousand words long but I believe, as you know, that Whitney Darrow has the wrong psychology about prices (and about what class constitute the bookbuying public now that the lowbrows go to the movies) and I'm anxious to charge two dollars for it and have it a full size book.

Of course I want the binding to be absolutely uniform with my other books—the stamping too—and the jacket we discussed before. This time I don't want any signed blurbs on the jacket—not Mencken's or Lewis' or Howard's or anyone's. I'm tired of being the author of This Side of Paradise *and I want to start over.*

* * *

I have an alternative title:

Gold-hatted Gatsby

After you've read the book let me know what you think about the title. Naturally I won't get a nights sleep until I hear from you but do tell me the absolute truth, your first impression of the book & *tell me anything that bothers you in it.*

—FSF to Maxwell Perkins, 27 October 1924.

The year of Zelda's sickness and resulting depression. Drink, loafing & the Murphys

Twenty-eight years Old

AMERICAN WRITER FINDS A HOME IN ROME

Mr. Scott Fitzgerald Says He Is There to Keep Wolf from Door.

(*Special Correspondence.*)

ROME, Tuesday.—Mr. Scott Fitzgerald, the American novelist and short story writer, has arrived in Rome where he intends to spend the winter. Mr. Fitzgerald is accompanied by Mrs. Fitzgerald and their little girl, Scottie.

Two years ago, Mr. Fitzgerald published a story dealing with his effort to live in America on $36,000 a year, but times have changed since then. The first visit of the Fitzgerald family in the Eternal City was to the living successor of the legendary wolf of Rome—the life sustainer of Romulus and Remus, the founders of the city—who lives in melancholy confinement on the slope of the Capitoline Hill.

"The main and avowed purpose of our European sojourn being to keep the wolf from the door," explained Mr. Fitzgerald "we thought it advisable to find out her whereabouts as soon as possible. We do not expect her to return the visit, but if she does, we shall not hesitate to slay and eat her.

As an additional precautionary measure the Fitzgeralds will probably take an apartment at the opposite and more fashionable end of the city.

Since their arrival in Europe, the author of "This Side of Paradise," "The Beautiful and Damned" and his family have lived in almost every country of the Continent. Their experience in cosmopolitan house-getting-and-keeping is consequently as wide as their doctrine, and the "Thirty-Six-Thousand-Dollars-a-Year-with-No-Luxury-Margin" articles which Mr. Fitzgerald has recently written, are founded on a series of poignant personal experiences of domestic finance.

"What at first seemed a secluded villa just right for us to live in quietly," said Mrs. Fitzgerald with her brightest smile, "had a habit of developing into a sort of charity institution, owing to the mysterious complaints by which the domestic personnel was stricken down, necessitating the presence of their relatives, sometimes down to the third and fourth generations."

House-hunting in Rome.

The results of house-hunting in Rome so far strike the Fitzgeralds as being in inverse proportion to the elaborateness of the apparatus and the number of competent co-operative forces enlisted in the process.

Both Mr. and Mrs. Fitzgerald are much interested in what they define as the "gorgeous personalities of the vigorous gestures, such as Mussolini and D'Annunzio."

In November 1924 the Fitzgeralds went to Rome where he revised The Great Gatsby. *They lived at the Hôtel des Princes until February, when the cold weather drove them to the island of Capri, Italy.*

I'm a bit (not very—not dangerously) stewed tonight & I'll probably write you a long letter. We're living in a small, unfashionable but most comfortable hotel at $525.00 a month including tips, meals ect. Rome does not *particularly interest me but its a big year here, and early in the spring we're going to Paris. There's no use telling you my plans because they're usually just about as unsuccessful as to work as a religious prognosticaters are as to the End of the World. I've got a new novel to write—title and all, that'll take about a year. Meanwhile, I don't want to start it until this is out & meanwhile I'll do short stories for money (I now get $2000.00 a story but I hate worse than hell to do them) and there's the never dying lure of another play.*

Now! Thanks enormously for making up the $5000.00 I know I don't technically deserve it considering I've had $3000.00 or $4000.00 for as long as I can remember. But since you force it on me (inexecrable [or is it execreble] joke) I will accept it. I hope to Christ you get 10 times it back on Gatsby—and I think perhaps you will.

For:

I can now make it perfect but the proof (I will soon get the immemorial letter with the statement "We now have the book in hand and will soon begin to send you proof" [what is 'in hand'—I have a vague picture of everyone in the office holding the book in the light and reading it]) will be one of the most expensive affairs since Madame Bovary. Please *charge it to my account. If its possible to send a second proof over here I'd love to have it. Count on 12 days each way—four days here on first proof & two on the second. I hope there are other good books in the spring because I think now the public interest in* books *per se rises when there seems to be a group of them as in 1920 (spring & fall), 1921 (fall), 1922 (spring). Ring's & Tom's (first) books, Willa Cathers* Lost Lady *& in an inferior, cheap way Edna Ferber's are the only American fiction in over two years that had a really excellent press (say, since Babbit).*

With the aid you've given me I can make "Gatsby" perfect. The chapter VII (the hotel scene) will never quite be up to mark—I've worried about it too long & I can't quite place Daisy's reaction. But I can improve it a lot. It isn't imaginative energy that's lacking—its because I'm automaticly prevented from thinking it out over again because I must get all those characters to New York *in order to have the catastrophe on the road going back & I must have it pretty much that way. So there's no chance of bringing the freshness to it that a new free conception sometimes gives.*

The rest is easy and I see my way so clear that I even see the mental quirks that queered it before. Strange to say my notion of Gatsby's vagueness was O.K. What you and Louise & Mr. Charles Scribner found wanting was that:

I myself didn't know what Gatsby looked like or was engaged in *& you felt it. If I'd known & kept it from you you'd have been* too impressed with my knowledge to protest. *This is a complicated idea but I'm sure you'll understand. But I know now—and as a penalty for not having known first, in other words to make sure I'm going to tell more.*

It seems of almost mystical significance to me that you thot he was older—the man I had in mind, half unconsciously, was *older (a specific individual) and evidently, without so much as a definate word, I conveyed the fact.—or rather, I must qualify this Shaw-Desmond-trash by saying that I conveyed it without a word that I can at present and for the life of me, trace. (I think Shaw Desmond was one of your bad bets—I was the other)*

Anyhow after careful searching of the files (of a man's mind here) for the Fuller Magee case & after having had Zelda draw pictures until her fingers ache I know Gatsby better than I know my own child. My first instinct after your letter was to let him go & have Tom Buchanan dominate the book (I suppose he's the best character I've ever done—I think he and the brother in "Salt" & Hurstwood in "Sister Carrie" are the three best characters in American fiction in the last twenty years, perhaps and perhaps not) but Gatsby sticks in my heart. I had him for awhile then lost him & now I know I have him again. I'm sorry Myrtle is better than Daisy. Jordan of course was a great idea (perhaps you know its Edith Cummings) but she fades out. Its Chap VII thats the trouble with Daisy & it may hurt the book's popularity that its a man's book.

Anyhow I think (for the first time since The Vegetable failed) that I'm a wonderful writer & its your always wonderful letters that help me to go on believing in myself.

—FSF to Maxwell Perkins, c. 20 December 1924.

Fitzgerald never felt confident about The Great Gatsby as a title. Shortly before publication he tried to change it to "Under the Red, White, and Blue," but by then it was too late.

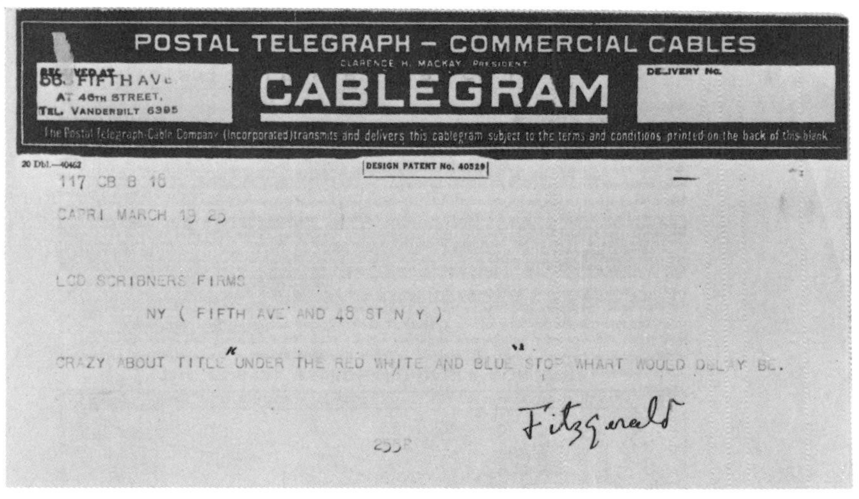

POSTAL TELEGRAPH – COMMERCIAL CABLES

CLARENCE H. MACKAY, PRESIDENT

CABLEGRAM

117 CB 8 16

CAPRI MARCH 19 25

LCD SCRIBNERS FIRMS

NY (FIFTH AVE AND 48 ST N Y)

CRAZY ABOUT TITLE "UNDER THE RED WHITE AND BLUE" STOP WHAT WOULD DELAY BE.

Fitzgerald

Much later, Fitzgerald started an elaborate stamp collection for his daughter, cutting the stamps off nearly all the postcards they had sent back to their parents during their travels.

A southern sun drugged the court of the Quisisana to somnolence. Strange birds protested their sleepiness beneath the overwhelming cypress while Compton Mackenzie told us why he lived in Capri: Englishmen must have an island.

The Tiberio was a high white hotel scalloped about the base by the rounded roofs of Capri, cupped to catch rain which never falls. We climbed to it through devious dark alleys that house the island's Rembrandt butcher shops and bakeries; then we climbed down again to the dark pagan hysteria of Capri's Easter, the resurrection of the spirit of the people.

—" 'Show Mr. and Mrs. F. to Number—' " (ZF)

BEST SELLERS OF THE WEEK

FICTION.

"Soundings," by Hamilton Gibbs.
"Mayfair," by Michael Arlen.
"Barren Ground," by Ellen Glasgow.
"The Painted Veil," by H. Somerset Maugham.
"Cruel Fellowship," by Cyril Hume.
"The Great Gatsby," by F. Scott Fitzgerald.

NONFICTION.

"John Keats," by Amy Lowell.
"Brigham Young," by M. R. Werner.
"Ten Years Later," by Philip Gibbs.

AT THE PUBLIC LIBRARY.

"A Mother's Recompense," by Edith Wharton.
"The Great Gatsby," by F. Scott Fitzgerald.

BEST SELLERS OF THE WEEK

FICTION.

"The Smiths," by Janet Fairbank.
"Drums," by James Boyd.
"Thunderstorm," by G. B. Stern.
"The Great Gatsby," by F. Scott Fitzgerald.
"The Constant Nymph," by Margaret Kennedy.
"The Mother's Recompense," by Edith Wharton.

NONFICTION.

"Brigham Young," by M. R. Werner.
"Anatole France, Himself," by Jean Jacques Brousson.
"Cruise of the Nonah," by Hilaire Belloc.

AT THE PUBLIC LIBRARY.

"The Great Gatsby," by F. Scott Fitzgerald.

Brooklyn's Best Sellers

The appended list is an actual composite scoring list, based on reports of this week's sales from Abraham & Straus, Miss Adams' Book Shop, Frederick Loeser & Co., Rodgers' Book Stores, Ross' Book Store, T. B. Ventres and A. R. Womrath:

Fiction.

"The Mother's Recompense" (26), Edith Wharton; Appleton.
"The Constant Nymph" (21), Kennedy; Doubleday, Page.
"Soundings" (15), A. H. Gibbs; Little, Brown.
"Barren Ground" (9), Glasgow; Doubleday, Page.
"Arrowsmith" (7), Lewis; Harcourt, Brace.
"The Great Gatsby" (5), Fitzgerald; Scribner.

Best Sellers of the Week

FICTION

"A Mother's Recompense" —Edith Wharton
"Barren Ground" —Ellen Glasgow
"The Constant Nymph" —Margaret Kennedy
"The Painted Veil" —Somerset Maugham
"The Great Gatsby" —Scott Fitzgerald

Six Best Sellers

FICTION.

ARROWSMITH, by Sinclair Lewis.
THE CONSTANT NYMPH, by Margaret Kennedy.
THE GREAT GATSBY, by F. Scott Fitzgerald.

This Week's Suggestions

"THE SORY OF WILBUR THE HAT." By Hendrik Van Loon. (Boni & Liveright.)
"THE GREAT GATSBY." By F. Scott Fitzgerald. (Scribner.)

The week's best circulators in the Detroit Public Library are listed below in order of their popularity:

FICTION.

"The Constant Nymph," Margaret Kennedy; "The Glorious Apollo," E. Barrington; "The Great Gatsby," F. Scott Fitzgerald

T[...] Gatsby

Here is a novel, glamorous, ironical, compassionate—a marvellous fusion into unity of the curious incongruities of the life of the period which reveals a hero like no other—one who could live at no other time and in no other place. But he will live as a character, we surmise, as long as the memory of any reader lasts.

"There was something gorgeous about him, some heightened sensitivity to the promises of life. . . . It was an extraordinary gift for hope, a romantic readiness such as I have never found in any other person and which it is not likely I shall ever find again."

It is the story of this Jay Gatsby who came so mysteriously to West Egg, of his sumptuous entertainments, and of his love for Daisy Buchanan—a story that ranges from pure lyrical beauty to sheer brutal realism, and is infused with a sense of the strangeness of human circumstance in a heedless universe.

It is a magical, living book, blended of irony, romance, and mysticism.

CHA[...]ER'S SONS

The week's best circulators in the Detroit Public Library are listed below in order of their popularity:

FICTION.

"The Constant Nymph," Margaret Kennedy; "Arrowsmith," Sinclair Lewis; "The Spring Flight," Lee J. Smits; "Soundings," Arthur Hamilton Gibbs; "The World's Illusion," Jacob Wasserman; "The Great Gatsby," F. Scott Fitzgerald.

Six Best Sellers.

Fiction.

THE MOTHER'S RECOMPENSE, by Edith Wharton.
BARREN GROUND, by Ellen Glasgow.
THE GREAT GATSBY, by F. Scott Fitzgerald.

The week's best circulators in the Detroit Public Library are listed below in order of their popularity:

FICTION.

"Arrowsmith," Sinclair Lewis; "The Green Hat," Michael Arlen; "The Constant Nymph," Margaret Kennedy; "The Great Gatsby," F. Scott Fitzgerald;

The week's best circulators in the Detroit Public Library are listed below in order of their popularity:

FICTION.

"Arrowsmith," Sinclair Lewis; "The Constant Nymph," Margaret Kennedy; "The Green Hat," Michael Arlen; "The Great Gatsby," F. Scott Fitzgerald;

Six Best Sellers

Fiction

"Mother's Recompense" — Edith Wharton.
"The Constant Nymph"—Margaret Kennedy.
"Arrowsmith"—Sinclair Lewis.
"The Painted Veil"—W. Somerst Maugham.
"The George and the Crown"—Shelia Kaye-Smith.
"The Great Gatsby"—F. Scott Fitzgerald.

Six Best Sellers.

Fiction.

THE MOTHER'S RECOMPENSE, by Edith Wharton.
BARREN GROUND, by Ellen Glasgow.
THE GREAT GATSBY, by F. Scott Fitzgerald.

BEST SELLERS OF

FICTION.

"The Smiths," by Janet Fairbank.
"Mayfair," by Michael Arlen.
"The Painted Veil" by W. Somerset Maugham
"The Constant Nymph," by Margaret Kennedy.
"The Great Gatsby," by F. Scott Fitzgerald.
"Thunderstorm," by G. B. Stern.

NONFICTION.

"Brigham Young," by M. R. Werner.
"Anatole France, Himself," by Jean Jacques Brousson.
"So You're Going to Italy," by Clara E. Laughlin.

AT THE PUBLIC LIBRARY.

"The Great Gatsby," by F. Scott Fitzgerald.

The greatest of the new books rated by demand, are announced by publishers to include "The Green Hat," Michael Arlen; "Mayfair," Michael Arlen; "Drums," Thomas Boyd; "So Big," Edna Ferber; "The Great Gatsby," F. Scott Fitzgerald;

BEST SELLERS OF THE WEEK

FICTION.

"The Smiths," by Janet Fairbank.
"Mayfair," by Michael Arlen.
"The Mother's Recompense," by Edith Wharton.
"The Constant Nymph," by Margaret Kennedy.
"The Great Gatsby," by F. Scott Fitzgerald.
"The Crazy Fool," by Donald Ogden Stewart.

NONFICTION.

"Anatole France, Himself," by Jean Jacques Brousson.
"Brigham Young," by M. R. Werner.
"Travel Diary of a Philosopher," by Carl Count Keyserling.

AT THE PUBLIC LIBRARY.

"The Great Gatsby," by F. Scott Fitzgerald.

BEST SELLERS OF THE WEEK

FICTION.

"Mayfair," by Michael Arlen.
"A Mother's Recompense," by Edith Wharton.
"The Great Gatsby," by F. Scott Fitzgerald.
"Arrowsmith," by Sinclair Lewis.
"Barren Ground," by Ellen Glasgow.
"Sea Horses," by Francis Brett Young.

NONFICTION.

"So You're Going to Italy!" by Clara E. Laughlin.
"Troubadour," by Alfred Kreymborg.
"Travel Diary of a Philosopher," by Carl Count Keyserling.

AT THE PUBLIC LIBRARY.

"A Mother's Recompense," by Edith Wharton.
"The Great Gatsby," by F. Scott Fitzgerald.

AT THE PUBLIC LIBRARY.

"The Smiths," by Janet Fairbank.
"The Peasants," by L. Reymont.
"The Great Gatsby," by F. Scott Fitzgerald.

Best Selling Fiction

1. Constant Nymph, by Kennedy. Feb. 13, 1925. $2.00.
2. May Fair, by Arlen. May 22, 1925. $2.50.
3. Arrowsmith, by Lewis. Mar. 5, 1925. $2.00.
4. Mother's Recompense, by Wharton. Apr. 24, 1925. $2.00.
5. Soundings, by A. H. Gibbs, Mar. 7, 1925. $2.00.
6. Barren Ground, by Glasgow, Apr. 15, 1925. $2.50.
7. Destiny, by R. Hughes, May 15, 1925. $2.00.
8. Stolen Idols, by Oppenheim, May 8, 1925, $2.00.
9. Drums, by Boyd. Mar. 27, 1925. $2.50.
10. Great Gatsby, by Fitzgerald. Apr. 10, 1925 $2.00.

(List from Baker & Taylor Co., Wholesale Book Dealers, N. Y. City.)

The GREAT GATSBY
FITZGERALD
SCRIBNERS

The GREAT GATSBY
F·SCOTT·FITZGERALD

Best Selling Books.

MARSHALL FIELD & CO.

"The Painted Veil," by W. Somerset Maugham.
"Soundings," by A. Hamilton Gibbs.
"Love," by Elizabeth.
"The Great Gatsby," by F. Scott Fitzgerald.
"Barren Ground," by Ellen Glasgow.
"John Keats," by Amy Lowell.
"The Lost Oasis," by A. M. Hassameim.
"The Prophet," by Kahlil Gibran.

THE FAIR.

"The Painted Veil," by W. Somerset Maugham.
"Moonlight on the Ranges," by Edison Marshall.
"The Reckless Lady," by Philip Gibbs.
"The Green Hat," by Michael Arlen.
"The Constant Nymph," by Margaret Kennedy.
"The Rocking Moon," by Barrett Willoughby.
"Arrowsmith," by Sinclair Lewis.

THE CHICAGO BOOK STORE.

"The Mother's Recompense," by Edith Wharton
"The Great Gatsby," by F. Scott Fitzgerald.
"Troubadour," by Alfred Kreymborg.
"The Travel Diary of a Philosopher," by Count Herman Keyserling.
"Jones' Grammar of Ornament."

BRENTANO'S.

"The Mother's Recompense," by Edith Wharton.
"The Great Gatsby," by F. Scott Fitzgerald.

On a Week-End The "Dial" Says Read:
"The Great Gatsby," by F. Scott Fitzgerald.

Six Best Sellers

FICTION.

THE MOTHER'S RECOMPENSE, by Edith Wharton.
THE CONSTANT NYMPH, by Margaret Kennedy.
ARROWSMITH, by Sinclair Lewis.
THE PAINTED VEIL, by W. Somerset Maugham.
THE GEORGE AND THE CROWN, by Sheila Kaye-Smith.
THE GREAT GATSBY, by F. Scott Fitzgerald.

BEST SELLERS OF THE WEEK

FICTION.

"The Smiths," by Janet Fairbank.
"Barren Ground," by Ellen Glasgow.
"Thunderstorms," by G. B. Stern.
"The Constant Nymph," by Margaret Kennedy.
"The Great Gatsby," by F. Scott Fitzgerald.

AT THE PUBLIC LIBRARY.

"The Smiths," by Janet Fairbank.
"The Great Gatsby," by F. Scott Fitzgerald.

BEST SELLERS OF THE WEEK

FICTION.

"Mayfair," by Michael Arlen.
"The Smiths," by Janet Fairbank.
"The Painted Veil," by W. Somerset Maugham.
"A Mother's Recompense," by Edith Wharton.
"The Constant Nymph," by Margaret Kennedy.
"The Great Gatsby," by F. Scott Fitzgerald.

BEST SELLERS OF THE WEEK

FICTION.

"The Great Gatsby," by F. Scott Fitzgerald.

BEST SELLERS OF THE WEEK

FICTION.

"The Great Gatsby," by F. Scott Fitzgerald.

H.L.MENCKEN
1524 HOLLINS ST.
BALTIMORE.

(1925)

April 16th

Dear Fitz:-

" The Great Gatsby" fills me with pleasant sentiments. I think it is incomparably the best piece of work you have done. Evidences of careful workmanship are on every page. The thing is well managed, and has a fine surface. My one complaint is that the basic story is somewhat trivial-- that it reduces itself, in the end, to a sort of anecdote. But God will forgive you for that.

I'll probably do a review of it for the Chicago Tribune, which supplies 25 or 30 papers, with a total circulation of 3,000,000. I assume that one reader in every 30,000 will read the review.

You are missing many spiritual immensities by staying away from the Republic. Future generations will look back to the Coolidge era as upon a Golden Age. I wake up every morning with a glow of anticipation, and am roaring with mirth by the time my senile tea and Zwieback come on.

Yours in Xt.,

HLMencken

THE GREAT GATSBY

BY

F. SCOTT FITZGERALD

Then wear the gold hat, if that will move her;
If you can bounce high, bounce for her too,
Till she cry "Lover, gold-hatted, high-bouncing lover,
I must have you!"
—THOMAS PARKE D'INVILLIERS.

NEW YORK
CHARLES SCRIBNER'S SONS
1925

ONCE AGAIN
TO
ZELDA

The Great Gatsby *was published in April 1925. It required only 2 printings for a total of 23,870 copies.*

What little I've accomplished has been by the most laborious and uphill work, and I wish now I'd never *relaxed or looked back—but said at the end of* The Great Gatsby: *"I've found my line—from now on this comes first. This is my immediate duty—without this I am nothing."*

—FSF to Scottie, 12 June 1940.

The First Reader

Great Scott

"The Great Gatsby" is F. Scott Fitzgerald's latest. It is the tale of a curious and shady fellow who conducts a large and lusty country house for a miscellany of random guests in the vicinity of Westhampton, L. I. It is published by Charles Scribner's Sons.

Fitzgerald introduced the gin-and-petting novel of college life, wrote some excellent short stories, tried his hand at another novel—a study of flapper marriage—and topped it with some indifferent work spelled out for the sake of the easy money.

In this new book he is another fellow altogether. "The Great Gatsby" evidences an interest in the color and sweep of prose, in the design and integrity of the novel, in the development of character, like nothing else he has attempted. If you are interested in the American novel this is a book for your list.

• • •

Even the staid fellows who shrugged at Fitzgerald's stuff when he first brutally rang the bell of notoriety in "This Side of Paradise" must have known, and fearsomely too, that the child would some day be father to the novelist.

He was, in writing, something like the prodigals of his fiction: bursting with a gorgeous zest of life, interesting, highly diverting, above all possessed of a streak of talent as broad as it was erratic.

"The Great Gatsby" is no spontaneous burst of erratic divertisement proffered with an insolent grace. It is a novel written with pace and fine attention. Above all, handling the most exaggerated social scheme in the new world, it never once overdoes the thing.

The talent is here aplenty; the erratic streak is curbed, the impudence takes on the civilized urbanity of the man at ease in art. . . . You will not find, in others of Fitzgerald's works, such a paragraph as this one on his married heroine:

For Daisy was young and her artificial world was redolent of orchids and pleasant, cheerful snobbery and orchestras which set the rhythm of the year, summing up the sadness and suggestiveness of life in new tunes. All night the saxophones wailed the hopeless comment of the "Beale Street Blues" while a hundred pairs of golden and silver slippers shuffled the shining dust. At the gray tea hour there were always rooms that throbbed incessantly with this low, sweet fever, while fresh faces drifted here and there like rose petals blown by sad horns around the floor.

Now, the novelist who wrote that is not the Bacchic young man who leered over the minor amorous artifices of our younger fellows.

• • •

Fitzgerald, writing of his hero Gatsby and his unquenchable love for a woman several aeons above him in point of sophistication, writes in the first person and by some unaccountable paradox achieves impersonality in theme and treatment. Gatsby, darkling adventurer with a fortune made in bootlegging, in swindling, by other devious trades and bargains, lives in this fiction. Lives in his palace of country life—an establishment which Lewis Mumford has rightly analyzed as the Utopia of modern escape from the urban canyons—and lives against a background of all Fitzgerald's world.

Gatsby, come to the village of West Egg mysteriously to rear his shining palace on the sand and fill it with any whoever has painted a bad picture, written a bad novel, or made a million dollars, has come for love of the woman Daisy.

"There was something gorgeous about him," says the novelist, "some heightened sensitivity to promises of life." Fitzgerald, making him grow, would be as tender about his bootlegger-magnate as Keats was about Endymion. The man does grow, and through an honest process, for Fitzgerald unburdens all Gatsby's past before his reader, even hewing desperately to the truth of his fall.

• • •

I do not think for one moment in reading this book that "here is a great novel" or, even, that "here is a fine book." The novelist has not brought it off in grand style; has, in fact, supplied little more than a sheaf of notes on a gorgeous plan for a novel on the topside life about us.

But in this, even though it not be God's plenty, there is more worth than in all his other work. One reading it knows that the fair-haired boy of American fiction will not sink gracefully into the sort of middle-aged precocity who once rang the bell. There is a sincerity of feeling for Gatsby, put forward with a delicacy of irony pointed with occasional lapses into brutality, which is distinguished, and worth many better matured novels.

Gatsby himself lingers after the book is done. That is the real criticism of the novel, for his lingering is due to the lack of breadth in the portrait. Miss Cather's "A Lost Lady" was identical in its effect, and from this fault. Only the full maturation of the fiction was in question. The maturity of viewpoint in "The Great Gatsby" no more than in "A Lost Lady" could be questioned.

Also, it is the first authentic book, from the civilized point of view, upon the scene it surveys. The earlier Fitzgerald was barbarous; those who have followed him have aped his barbarity. I think that this book leaves all this far behind. I should like to read a review of it by Thomas Beer, author of "Sandoval," and peer of all our young men.

LAURENCE STALLINGS.

New Fiction

THE GREAT GATSBY, by F. Scott Fitzgerald. New York: *Charles Scribner's Sons.*
BARREN GROUND, by Ellen Glasgow. Garden City: *Doubleday, Page & Company.*
THE CONSTANT NYMPH, by Margaret Kennedy. Garden City: *Doubleday, Page & Company.*
SEA HORSES, by Francis Brett Young. New York: *Alfred A. Knopf.*

MENCKEN

OF THESE novels, the one that has given me most pleasure is Fitzgerald's, if only because it shows the author to be capable of professional advancement. He is still young and he has had a great success: it is a combination that is fatal to nine beginning novelists out of ten. They conclude at once that the trick is easy—that it is not worth while to sweat and suffer. The result is a steady and melancholy decline; presently the best-selling *eminentissimo* of yesterday vanishes and is heard of no more. I could adorn this page with a list of names, but refrain out of respect for the dead. Most of the novelists who are obviously on solid ground today had heavy struggles at the start: Dreiser, Cabell, Hergesheimer, Miss Cather. Fitzgerald, though he had no such struggle, now tries to make it for himself. "The Great Gatsby" is full of evidences of hard, sober toil. All the author's old slipshod facility is gone; he has set himself rigorously to the job of learning how to write. And he shows quick and excellent progress. "The Great Gatsby" is not merely better written than "This Side of Paradise"; it is written in a new way. Fitzgerald has learned economy of words and devices; he has begun to give thought to structure; his whole attitude has changed from that of a brilliant improvisateur to that of a painstaking and conscientious artist. I certainly don't think much of "The Great Gatsby" as a story. It is in part too well-made and in part incredible. But as a piece of writing it is sound and laudable work.

Thanks for your letter about the book. I was awfully happy that you liked it and that you approved of the design. The worst fault in it, I think is a BIG FAULT: I gave no account (and had no feeling about or knowledge of) the emotional relations between Gatsby and Daisy from the time of their reunion to the catastrophe. However, the lack is so astutely concealed by the retrospect of Gatsby's past and by blankets of excellent prose that no one has noticed it—tho everyone has felt the lack and called it by another name. Mencken said (in a most enthusiastic letter received today) that the only fault was that the central story was trivial and a sort of anecdote (that is because he has forgotten his admiration for Conrad and adjusted himself to the sprawling novel) and I felt that what he really missed was the lack of any emotional backbone at the very height of it.

—FSF to Edmund Wilson, Spring 1925.

N.Y. Post

Books on Our Table

F. SCOTT FITZGERALD'S new novel will surprise a great many people who have read his earlier books. It did us. We had not read a half-dozen pages before we were saying: "Why, the man's perfectly at his ease in a serious piece of writing. His style fairly scintillates, and with a genuine brilliance; he writes surely and soundly." The rest of the book confirmed the impression. It does not seem to us a great novel, but as an index of the direction in which one of our young writers is going, it is of prime value. We must confess to the previous belief that Mr. Fitzgerald would be forgotten as soon as the vogue for the cocktail-flapper-jazz novel had vanished, that he might go on writing clever and mildly amusing stories; but that he could turn his hand to a social study as important in its implications as "The Great Iatsby" (Scribner, $2), never once occurred to us. But he's done it. And in addition to demonstrating an admirable mastery of his medium both in style and construction, he has written a story that at its best is very, very good.

"THE GREAT GATSBY" is a tale of present-day life on Long Island. Gatsby is an enormously wealthy unknown, who takes a vast house, stocks the cellar, hires innumerable servants, and gives a sort of continuous party to which people of all kinds flock in droves. Nobody knows anything about his antecedents; nobody cares. The quality of his liquor is excellent, so why worry about anything else? He has had a love affair with a girl in Louisville, Ky., while in an officers' training camp. The girl appears on the scene as the unhappy wife of a famous polo player and society man. Her husband has a mistress, which makes it easy for her to enter into a liaison with Gatsby. From this situation arises a terrific, smashing tragedy, told with a brutal directness that makes the reader shudder—as powerful a piece of writing as we have met for a long time and really the high spot in the novel from an artistic standpoint. Other tragedies follow rapidly until Gatsby is shot to death and buried, with all his fair-weather friends vanished. . . .

THE plot and its developments work out too geometrically and too perfectly for "The Great Gatsby" to be a great novel, but Mr. Fitzgerald manipuates his people and his situations with a master hand, and it is not until the book has been finished and put aside that the sense of the stage director managing his puppets comes to temper one's admiration. In a way the book is as perfectly constructed as a good short story, and even the best short stories have something of the managed and diagrammed about them. But the handling is excellent, and one cannot withhold admiration from the creation of atmosphere which Mr. Fitzgerald does so well, nor from his blending of a cold and aloof irony with a sort of compassion for every one involved in the curious tangle, even for the great Gatsby, who has come up from nothing at all to the position of a famous Long Island host. He is unsparing with his characters, and for the most part they are a pretty rotten lot—true enough to life, though. Too true.

MR FITZGERALD'S prose is distinguished, nothing short of it. It has color, richness, an abundance of imagery, and a fine sense of the picturesque. Perhaps a quotation will serve to illustrate:

> We walked through a high hallway into bright, rosy-colored space, fragilely bound into the house by French windows at either end. The windows were ajar and gleaming white against the fresh grass outside that seemed to grow a little way into the house. A breeze blew through the room, blew curtains in at one end and out at the other like pale flags, twisting them up toward the frosted wedding-cake of the ceiling, and then rippled over the wine-colored rug, making a shadow on it as wind does on the sea. The only completely stationary object in the room was an enormous couch on which two young women were buoyed up as though upon an anchored balloon. They were both in white, and their dresses were rippling and fluttering as if they had just been blown back after a short flight around the house. . . .

WE shall have more to say about "The Great Gatsby" later. With it Mr. Fitzgerald definitely deserts his earlier fiction which brought him a lot of money and a certain kind of renown, and enters into the group of American writers who are producing the best serious fiction. On the basis of this book alone Mr. Fitzgerald gives about as much promise as any young writer we have, and that is a thoughtful opinion.

TO THE reader, who cares less for such technical matters than for the story itself, we may well add that "The Great Gatsby" is fascinating. If you begin it you'll go straight through to the end, and you will be conscious that you have read an excellent piece of writing. Mr. Fitzgerald will bear watching.

H. B.

"Fitzgerald Is a Strange Little Bird"

"F. Scott Fitzgerald is a strange little bird. I can't make head or tail of him. I did not read 'This Side of Paradise' until I had had my head talked off about it, so that it fell a little short of what I had been led to expect, through no fault of Mr. Fitzgerald's. In order to set myself straight about him, I read all his other books the moment they came out and they did seem to me to be terrible. Now I have just read 'The Great Gatsby' . . . with a note on the jacket to the effect that 'it is a magical, living book, blended of irony, romance, and mysticism.' Well, of course, I suppose the Scribner jacket-writer wants to sell as many books as he can, otherwise I swear I would think he had gone completely mad. Find me one chemical trace of magic, life, irony, romance, or mysticism in all of 'The Great Gatsby' and I will bind myself to read one Scott Fitzgerald book a week for all the rest of my life. The boy is simply puttering around. It is all right as a diversion for him, probably. He does, obviously, like to use hifalutin words and hifalutiner notions to concoct these tales. There may be those who like to read him. But why he should be called an author, or why any of us should behave as if he were, has never been explained satisfactorily to me."

—RUTH HALE in the Brooklyn *Daily Eagle.*

DAUGHTER OF FORMER ST. PAULITES WEDS NAVAL MAN

—Photo Copyright by Harris and Ewing.

Lieutenant Clifton A. F. Sprague and Mrs. Sprague were snapped by the photographer immediately after their marriage which took place late Tuesday afternoon at The Highlands, Washington.

Mrs. Sprague was formerly Miss Annabel Fitzgerald, daughter of Mr. and Mrs. Edward Fitzgerald of Washington, formerly of St. Paul.

Lieutenant Sprague is a member of the Naval Air service. Mrs. Sprague wore a gown of powder blue chiffon with a large picture hat to match and carried an arm bouquet of Killarney roses.

In April 1925 Fitzgerald's sister Annabel married Lt. Clifton A. Sprague of the U.S. Navy. Later, as Admiral Sprague he became a hero of the Battle of Leyte Gulf in World War II.

Fitful, shameful useless but the 30,000 rewards of 1924 work. Self disgust. Health gone.

180 Twenty-nine Years Old

H. L. Mencken

Your letter was the first outside word that reached me about my book. I was tremendously moved both by the fact that you liked it and by your kindness in writing me about it. By the next mail came a letter from Edmund Wilson and a clipping from Stallings, both bulging with interest and approval, but as you know I'd rather have you like a book of mine than anyone in America.

There is a tremendous fault in the book—the lack of an emotional presentment of Daisy's attitude toward Gatsby after their reunion (and the consequent lack of logic or importance in her throwing him over). Everyone has felt this but no one has spotted it because it's concealed beneath elaborate and overlapping blankets of prose. . . . At any rate I have learned a lot from writing it, and the influence on it has been the masculine one of The Brothers Karamazov, *a thing of incomparable form, rather than of the feminine one of* The Portrait of a Lady. *If it seems trivial or "anecdotal" (sp) it is because of an aesthetic fault, a failure in one very important episode, and not a frailty in the theme. At least I don't think so. Did you ever know a writer to calmly take a just criticism and shut up?*

—FSF to H. L. Mencken, 4 May 1925.

Edith Wharton (seated above) wrote to thank Fitzgerald for sending her a copy of Gatsby and to invite him to call on her (right). He did—but only after having conspicuously fortified himself, causing several conflicting anecdotes.

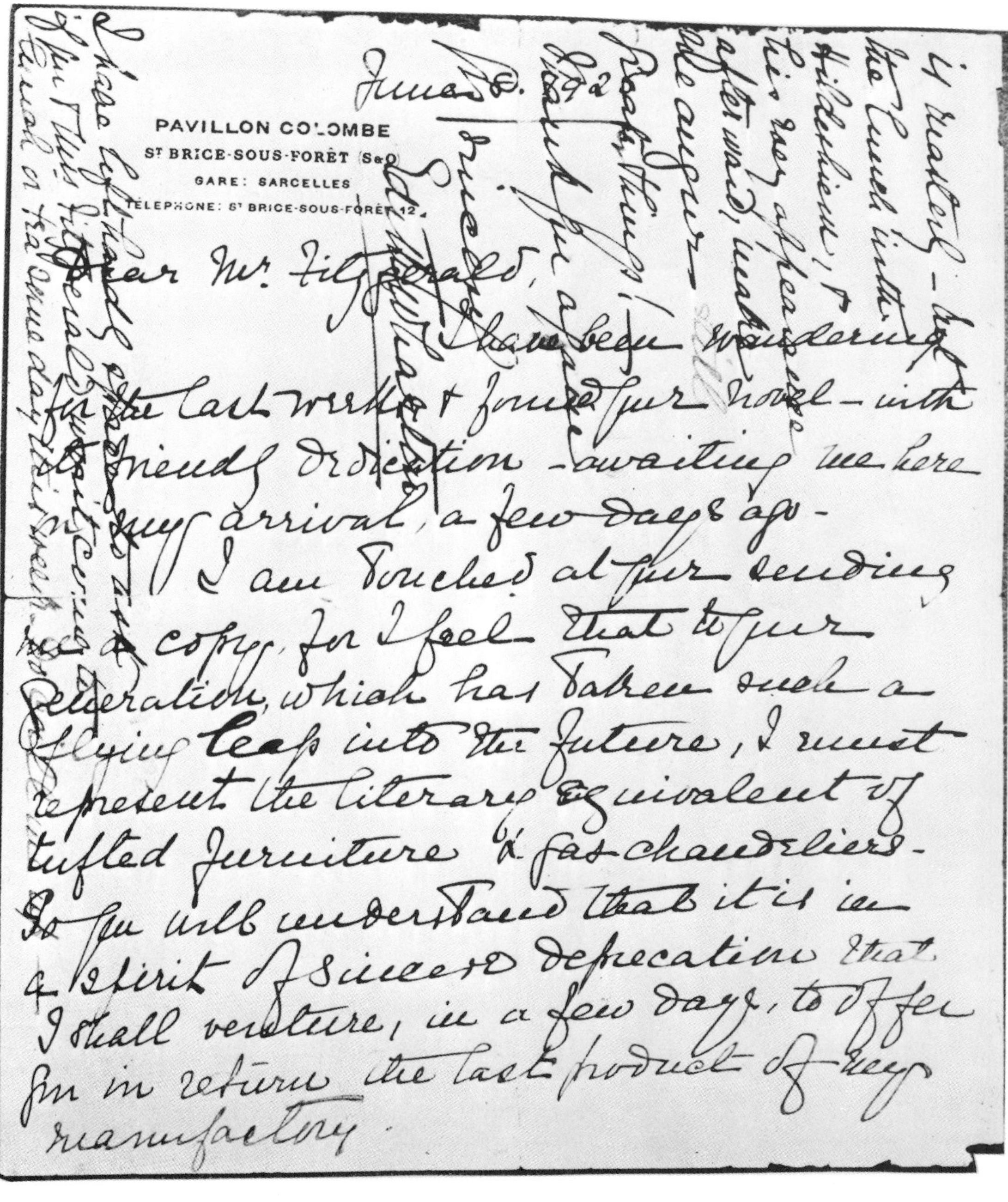
PAVILLON COLOMBE
St BRICE-SOUS-FORÊT (S&O)
GARE: SARCELLES
TELEPHONE: St BRICE-SOUS-FORÊT 12

June 8. 1925

Dear Mr. Fitzgerald,

I have been wandering for the last weeks & found your novel - with its friendly dedication - awaiting me here on my arrival, a few days ago -

I am touched at your sending me a copy, for I feel that to your generation, which has taken such a flying leap into the future, I must represent the literary equivalent of tufted furniture & gas chandeliers - So you will understand that it is in a spirit of sincere deprecation that I shall venture, in a few days, to offer you in return the last product of my manufactory.

The Great Gatsby   I   (1)

In my younger and more vulnerable years my father told me something that I've been turning over in my my mind ever since.

"When you feel like criticizing anyone," he said, "just remember that everyone in this world hasn't had the advantages that you've had."

He didn't say anymore but we've always been unusually communicative in a reserved way and I understood that he meant a great deal more than that. In consequence I'm inclined to reserve all judgements, a habit that has opened up many curious natures to me and also made me the victim of not a few collossal bores. The abnormal mind is quick to detect and attach itself to this quality when it appears in a ~~otherwise~~ normal person, and so it came about that in college I was ~~often~~ unjustly accused of being a politician, because I was privy to the secret griefs of wild, unknown men. Most of the confidences were unsought — frequently I have feigned sleep, ~~—~~ preoccupation or a hostile levity when I realized by some unmistakeable sign that an intimate revelation was quivering on the horizon ~~because~~ — for the intimate revelations of young men or at any rate the terms in which they express them vary no more than the heavenly messages ~~from Paradise~~ which reach us over the psychic radio. Reserving judgements is a matter of infinite hope. I am still a little afraid of missing something if I forget that, as my father snobbishly suggested and I snobbishly repeat, a sense of the fundamental decencies is parcelled out unequally at birth.

And, after boasting this way of my tolerance, I come to the admission that it has a limit. Conduct may be founded on the hard rock or the wet marshes but after a certain point I don't care what it's founded on. When I came back here from the east ~~west~~ last autumn I felt that I wanted the world to be in uniform and at a sort of moral attention forever; I wanted no more riotous excursions with privileged glimpses into the human heart. It was only Gatsby himself that was exempted from my

First page of manuscript of The Great Gatsby.

Zelda's address book.

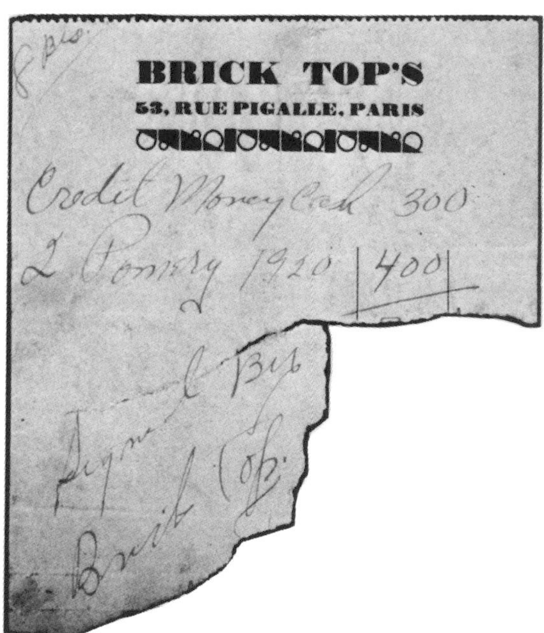
BRICK TOP'S
53, RUE PIGALLE, PARIS

Bricktop, an American Negro woman, presided over a famous Right-Bank nightclub.

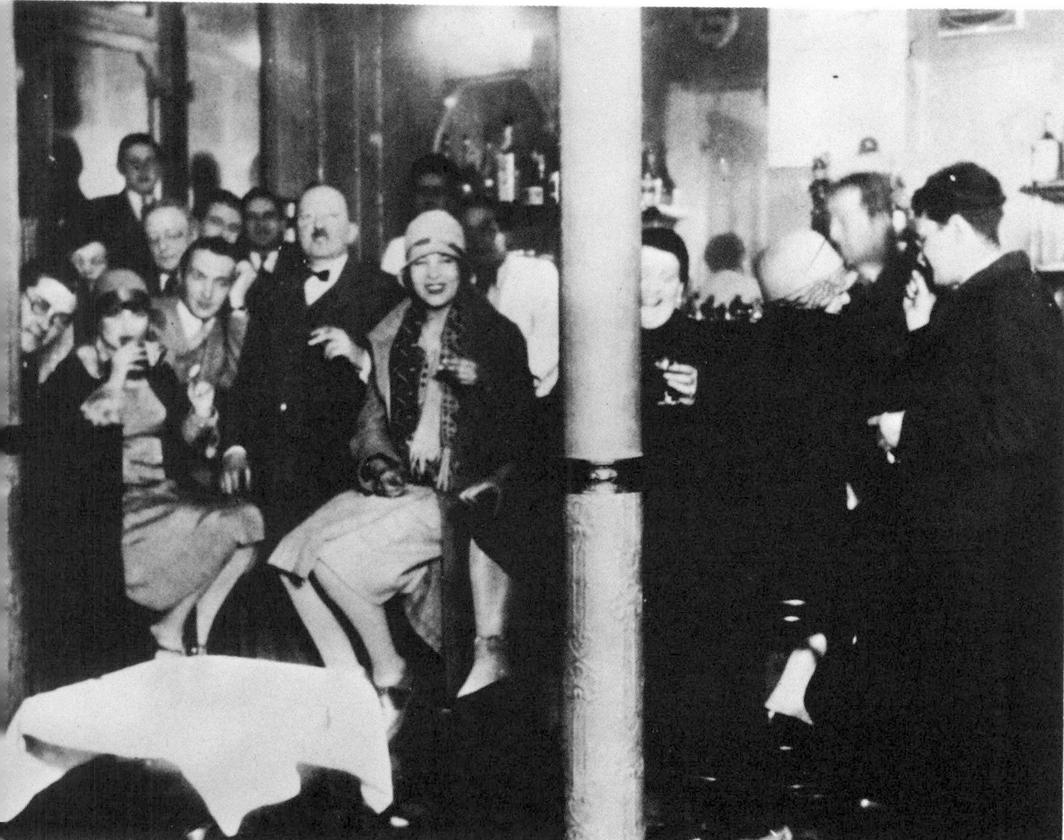

Fitzgerald first met Ernest Hemingway at the Dingo, rue Delambre, on the Left Bank in May 1925. (Neither is in picture above.)

The Americans gave indications of themselves but always only the beginning like some eternal exposition, a clef before a bar of music to be played on the minors of the imagination. They thought all French school boys were orphans because of the black dresses they wore, and those of them who didn't know the meaning of the word "insensible" thought the French thought that they were crazy. All of them drank. Americans with red ribbons in their buttonholes read papers called the *Éclaireur* and drank on the sidewalks, Americans with tips on the races drank down a flight of stairs, Americans with a million dollars and a standing engagement with the hotel masseuses drank in suites at the Meurice and the Crillon. Other Americans drank in Montmartre, "pour le soif" and "contre la chaleur" and "pour la digestion" and "pour se guérir." They were glad the French thought they were crazy.

—*Save Me the Waltz* (ZF)

I've gotten to like France. We've taken a swell apartment until January. I'm filled with disgust for Americans in general after two weeks sight of the ones in Paris—these preposterous, pushing women and girls who assume that you have any personal interest in them, who have all (so they say) read James Joyce and who simply adore Mencken. I suppose we're no worse than anyone, only contact with other races brings out all our worse qualities. If I had anything to do with creating the manners of the contemporary American girl I certainly made a botch of the job.

—FSF to Edmund Wilson, Spring 1925.

THE TORRENTS OF SPRING

A Romantic Novel In Honor of The Passing Of A Great Race.

By ERNEST HEMINGWAY.

To Scott and Zelda with love from Ernest.

And perhaps there is one reason why a comic writer should of all others be the least excused for deviating from nature, since it may not be always so easy for a serious poet to meet with the great and the admirable; but life everywhere furnishes an accurate observer with the ridiculous.

Henry Fielding.

This is to tell you about a young man named Ernest Hemmingway, who lives in Paris, (an American) writes for the transatlantic Review *and has a brilliant future. Ezra Pount published a collection of his short pieces in Paris, at some place like the Egotist Press. I haven't it hear now but it's remarkable & I'd look him up right away. He's the real thing.*

—FSF to Maxwell Perkins, c. 10 October 1924.

Outside Shakespeare & Co.; Sylvia Beach next to Hemingway.

FSF to Maxwell Perkins, 1 June 1925.

DATA ON NEW FITZGERALD BOOK.
Title
ALL THE SAD YOUNG MEN
(9 short stories)

Print list of previous books as before with addition of this title under "Stories". Binding uniform with others.
Jacket plain (,as you suggest,) with text instead of picture
Dedication: To Ring and Ellis Lardner
The Stories (now under revision) will reach you by July 15th. No proofs need be sent over here.

It will be fully up to the other collections and will contain only one of those *Post* stories that people were so snooty about. (You have read only one of the stories *("Absolution")*—all the others were so good that I had difficulty in selling them, except two.

They are, in approximate order to be used in book:

1. The Rich Boy (Just finished. Serious story and very good) — 13,000 wds.
2. Absolution (From *Mercury*) — 6,500 ″
3. Winter Dreams (A sort of 1st draft of the Gatsby idea from *Metropolitan* 1923) — 9,000 ″
4. Rags Martin-Jones and the Pr-nce of Wales (Fantastic Jazz, so good that Lorimer & Long refused it. From *McCalls*) — 5,000 ″
5. The Baby Party (From *Hearsts*. A fine story) — 5,000 ″
6. Dice, Brass Knuckles and Guitar (From *Hearsts*. Exuberant Jazz in my early manner) — 8,000 ″
7. The Sensible Thing (Story about Zelda & me. All true. From *Liberty*) — 5,000 ″
8. Hot & Cold Blood (good story, from *Hearsts*) — 6,000 ″
9. Gretchen's Forty Winks (From Post. Farrar, Christian Gauss and Jesse Williams thought it my best. It isn't.) — 7,000 ″

Total—about 64,500

(And possibly one other short one)

This title is because seven stories deal with young men of my generation in rather unhappy moods. The ones to mention on the outside wrap are the 1st five or the 1st three stories.

* * *

Advertising Notes

Suggested line for jacket: "Show transition from his early exuberant stories of youth which created a new type of American girl and the later and more serious mood which produced *The Great Gatsby* and marked him as one of the half dozen masters of English prose now writing in America. . . . What other writer has shown such unexpected developments, such versatility, changes of pace"

ect—ect—ect—I think that, toned down as you see fit, is the general line. Don't say "Fitzgerald has done it!" & then in the next sentence that I am an artist. People who are interested in artists aren't interested in people who have "done it." Both are O.K. but don't belong in the same ad. This is an author's quibble. All authors have one quibble.

He went back into his house and Nicole saw that one of his most characteristic moods was upon him, the excitement that swept everyone up into it and was inevitably followed by his own form of melancholy, which he never displayed but at which she guessed. This excitement about things reached an intensity out of proportion to their importance, generating a really extraordinary virtuosity with people. Save among a few of the tough-minded and perennially suspicious, he had the power of arousing a fascinated and uncritical love. The reaction came when he realized the waste and extravagance involved. He sometimes looked back with awe at the carnivals of affection he had given, as a general might gaze upon a massacre he had ordered to satisfy an impersonal blood lust.

But to be included in Dick Diver's world for a while was a remarkable experience: people believed he made special reservations about them, recognizing the proud uniqueness of their destinies, buried under the compromises of how many years. He won everyone quickly with an exquisite consideration and a politeness that moved so fast and intuitively that it could be examined only in its effect. Then, without caution, lest the first bloom of the relation wither, he opened the gate to his amusing world. So long as they subscribed to it completely, their happiness was his preoccupation, but at the first flicker of doubt as to its all-inclusiveness he evaporated before their eyes, leaving little communicable memory of what he had said or done.

—*Tender Is the Night*

Today a letter from Gerald, a week old, telling me this and that about the awful organ music around us, made me think of you, and I mean think *of you (of all people in the world you know the distinction). In my theory, utterly opposite to Ernest's, about fiction, i.e., that it takes half a dozen people to make a synthesis strong enough to create a fiction character—in that theory, or rather in despite of it, I used you again and again in* Tender:

"Her face was hard and lovely and pitiful"

and again

"He had been heavy, belly-frightened with love of her for years"

—in those and in a hundred other places I tried to evoke not you *but the effect that you produce on men—the echoes and reverberations—a poor return for what you have given by your living presence, but nevertheless an artist's (what a word!) sincere attempt to preserve a true fragment rather than a "portrait" by Mr. Sargent.*

—FSF to Sara Murphy, 15 August 1935.

. . . a fourth man had come to dictate my relations with other people when these relations were successful: how to do, what to say. How to make people at least momentarily happy (in opposition to Mrs. Post's theories of how to make everyone thoroughly uncomfortable with a sort of systematized vulgarity). This always confused me and made me want to go out and get drunk, but this man had seen the game, analyzed it and beaten it, and his word was good enough for me.

—"Pasting It Together"

Sara's Mister Murphys.

When in Paris we knew Picasso (a dear friend of Gerald Murphy); Pascin, a friend of the Dudleys who brought Josephine Baker to Paris, Léger—whom we met at the Murphys in Austria—and other modern geniuses whom we met at Gertrude Stein's left-bank salon. They were interesting and sympathetic and indeed I have never known a painter whose intuitive responsivity was not acute and immediate & I liked them very *much. We also knew Brancusi & have visited his studio in the rue Monsieur with great wonderment & awe.*

—ZF to Scottie, c. 1944.

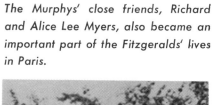

The Murphys' close friends, Richard and Alice Lee Myers, also became an important part of the Fitzgeralds' lives in Paris.

The beach at La Garoupe. Sara Murphy under the umbrella; Gerald Murphy in cap.

Gerald Murphy at his Villa America.

Ellen Barry, Beoth Murphy, Philip Barry, and Gerald Murphy.

La Garoupe Beach

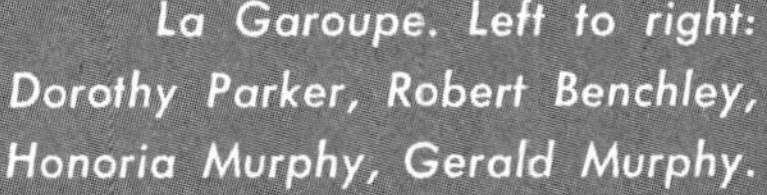

La Garoupe. Left to right: Dorothy Parker, Robert Benchley, Honoria Murphy, Gerald Murphy.

Eden Roc, Antibes

There was no one at Antibes this summer except me, Zelda, the Valentinos, the Murphys, Mistinguet, Rex Ingram, Dos Passos, Alice Terry, the MacLeishes, Charlie Brackett, Maude Kahn, Esther Murphy, Marguerite Namara, E. Phillips Oppenheim, Mannes the violinist, Floyd Dell, Max and Crystal Eastman, ex-Premier Orlando, Etienne de Beaumont—just a real place to rough it, and escape from all the world. But we had a great time. I don't know when we're coming home—

—FSF to John Peale Bishop, c. September 1925.

What Became of Our Flappers and Sheiks?

BY F. SCOTT FITZGERALD *and* ZELDA SAYRE FITZGERALD

ILLUSTRATED BY JOHN HELD, JR.

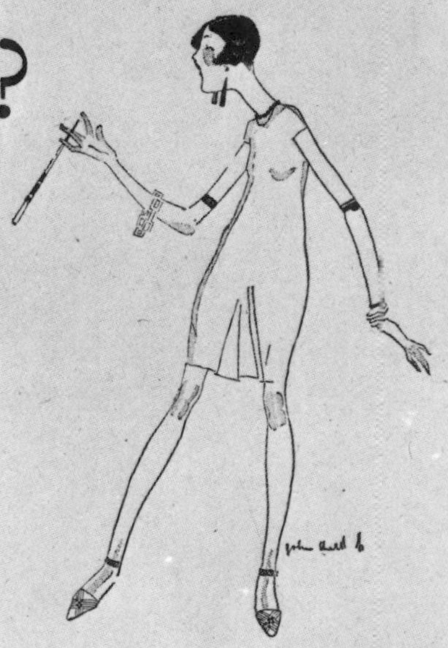

"Where do we go from here?" says the Flapper to her little brother, the Sheik. And that is what all the world wants to know. For every season brings a new crop of Flappers and Flapper-Jacks with ever-changing styles—the girls' bobs grow shorter and shorter and their skirts likewise, while their brothers at Yale or Princeton or Harvard wear their hair longer and longer—to match trousers, which are also fuller and fuller. What will become of this season's flappers, and what will all our sleek-haired young sheiks be doing in 1926? If you have a little sheik or flapper in your home, you will welcome these twin articles by the man who discovered the flapper and the sheik, and by the woman who was the model for the original flapper. F. Scott Fitzgerald, her discoverer, married her after he had described her and himself, in his famous novels, "This Side of Paradise" and "The Beautiful and Damned."

BY F. SCOTT FITZGERALD

A FEW years ago there were so many experts on the younger generation, like for instance, the lady who wrote "Dancing with the Darkies" (which I may say I have never seen done in my own city), and Madame Glynn who said that young ladies always checked their corsets at dances. So every time I went to a dance in those days I always inquired for the corset check-room because I wanted to see a lot of corsets all hung up in a row. I even asked young ladies, while entering a dance, if there was anything they would like to check, but they never handed me anything immoral—even when I shut my eyes and held out my hand in case they should be embarrassed.

Then came the kind of younger generation who were all dressed up in bell-bottom trousers. The excitement was at fever heat. The newspapers in my town were afraid that the bell-bottoms would seize the city hall, raise a pair of trousers on the flag-staff and kill all the he-men.

Personally it made me nervous to have bells or any sort of musical instruments attached to my trousers, but I had no objections to anyone else doing it if he liked.

If you want to read about any of these kinds you had better lay this down right now. This is about the young man who was once saddled with the ghastly name of "male flapper"—a name that is as depressing as "lady wrestler," and was about as popular with the young man as "Liberty Lads" was with the doughboys.

The midland cities have changed. Apartment houses have risen on the vacant lots where football teams composed of wealthy boys once played against football teams composed of "muckers." At fourteen the wealthy boy is no longer anxious to have enormous muscles and be Ted Coy of Yale, but to own a sport car and be Ben Lyons—or even Michael Arlen. The cheap literature of daring, of Nick Carter and Young Wild West, has vanished. It is a conquered world into which the post-war boy grows up; there are no outposts of civilization to grasp his imagination. He gets the impression that everything has been done. Instead of the Henty books he reads the moving picture magazines.

If by the time he is fifteen he hasn't a car of his own, some one else in his crowd is sure to have one—some one a little older or some one whose parents are too careless or too new to their money to think what having a car may mean. With a car one can be downtown, across a city, out of sight in fifteen minutes. So young [*Turn to page 42*]

F. SCOTT FITZGERALD *and* ZELDA SAYRE FITZGERALD

BY ZELDA SAYRE FITZGERALD

FLAPPER wasn't a particularly fortunate cognomen. It is far too reminiscent of open galoshes and covered up ears and all other proverbial flapper paraphernalia, which might have passed unnoticed save for the name. All these things are—or were—amusing externals of a large class of females who in no way deserve the distinction of being called flappers. The flappers that I am writing this article about are a very different and intriguing lot of young people who are perhaps unstable, but who are giving us the first evidence of youth asserting itself out of the cradle. They are not originating new ideas or new customs or new moral standards. They are simply endowing the old ones that we are used to with a vitality that we are not used to. We are not accustomed to having *our* daughters think our ideas for themselves, and it is distasteful to some of us that we are no longer able to fit the younger generation into our conceptions of what the younger generation was going to be like when we watched it in the nursery. I do not think that anything my daughter could possibly do eighteen years from now would surprise me. And yet I will probably be forbidding her in frigid tones to fly more than 3,000 feet high or more than five hundred miles an hour with little Willie Jones, and bidding her never to go near that horrible Mars. I can imagine these things now, but if they should happen twenty years from now, I would certainly wonder what particular dog my child was going to . . . .

The flapper springs full-grown, like Minerva, from the head of her once declassé father, Jazz, upon whom she lavishes affection and reverence, and deepest filial regard. She is not a "condition arisen from war unrest," as I have so often read in the shower of recent praise and protest which she has evoked, and to which I am contributing. She is a direct result of the greater appreciation of beauty, youth, gaiety and grace which is sweeping along in a carmagnole (I saw one in a movie once, and I use this word advisedly) with our young anti-puritans at the head. They have placed such a premium on the flapper creed—to give and get amusement—that even the dumb-bells become Dulcies and convert stupidity into charm. Dulcy is infinitely preferable to the kind of girl who, ten years ago, quoted the Rubaiyat at you and told you how misunderstood she was; or the kind who straightened your tie as evidence that in her lay the spirit of the eternal mother; or the kind who spent long summer evenings telling you that it wasn't the *number* of cigarettes you smoked that she minded but just [*Turn to page 30*]

Accrediting the flapper with invidious ways of life has superceded the unveiling of grotesque statues of poets

The name Flapper is reminiscent of open galoshes

Even the stupid dumb-bells became Dulcies with charm

What Became of Our Flappers and Sheiks?

[*Continued from page 12*]

Tommy gets his car and the fun begins. What could be more harmless than for Tommy to take Marjorie to the movies? Why Marjorie's mother and Tommy's mother have known each other all their lives. Besides, it's done—other children do it. So Tommy and Marjorie are licensed to drift where they will through the summer night.

The probabilities are that Tommy and Marjorie will never so much as kiss. He tells her how he once "picked up a chicken" and took her to ride, and Marjorie is impressed with his temerity. Sometimes there is a faint excitement, a faint glow between them. Usually—not always, but usually—there is nothing more.

Tommy becomes sixteen. He goes out every night now—to the movies, to a dance, to a gathering on a girl's porch. It seems to his parents that there is always something and that the something always sounds harmless and is always what the other boys are doing. In fact, what worries Tommy's parents is what he is *not* doing. He was bright, as a little boy, but now, because he never has time to work at night, his report cards from his local private school are invariably unsatisfactory. There remains a solution of course—the prep-school. Smiles of relief from the parents. The prep-school will do the trick. Nothing easier than passing it off on somebody else. It is discovered, however, that most of the stricter and more thorough prep-schools have an annoying habit of asking for the boy before fifteen—and refusing to take him any older. So he is sent instead to some small prep-school in New York state or New Jersey that is not so particular.

A year passes. The popular Tommy takes his preliminary examinations for college. The examinations are an absurd hodge-podge and as the preparations for them have failed to intrigue Tommy's interest he scratches through, say, one out of five. He is glad to be home for the summer. He has his car again, and with the other boys of his age, is beginning to go to dances at various country clubs. He finds this most amusing—an unbearably pleasant contrast to the childish restraint of his prep-school. In fact, when autumn comes he persuades his father to send him to one of those curious institutions that are springing up all over the east—the tutoring schools.

Now the tutoring school has neither the discipline of a prep-school nor any of the restraining force that lies in the modeled public opinion of a great university. Theoretically the fact that there is no football team gives the boy time to concentrate on cramming. Actually it gives him time to do what he likes. The masters are smarter and better-paid than the masters in the small prep-schools. In fact they are so smart and they explain everything so clearly that they completely cure Tommy of any faculty of working things out for himself. It is notorious that although the tutoring school boys generally get into college they seldom survive the first mid-year examinations.

Meanwhile the lack of athletic activities in the school drives Tommy to express his vitality in other ways. He smokes incessantly and experiments with alcohol. Some of the boys are twenty and twenty-one years old. They are dull and unimaginative or they would long since have passed their examinations, so, for stimulus and amusement they turn to—New York. And Tommy does too. Many of the boys have automobiles because their parents realize how bored they would otherwise be.

We are almost all newly rich in America, and the number of millionaires who have any definite idea of a modern education is so small as to be negligible. They are aware, however, that their sons require an astonishing lot of money to keep up with the "other boys." An Englishman goes through an Eton and Oxford that are not so different from what they were in his father's time. The Harvard graduate of 1870 could keep a pretty good tab on his Harvard son of 1900. But all that Mr. Thomas senior in San Francisco knows about his son's school is that it promises to get Tommy into college.

Tommy is now eighteen. He is handsomely dressed and an excellent dancer, and he knows three chorus girls in the Follies by their first names. He takes this side of life much more seriously than does the college man—he has no senior societies or upper class clubs to hold up a warning finger. His life is one long week-end.

Coming home for another summer Tommy resumes his country-club existence in a somewhat haughty manner. His home town, if it happens to be in the middle west, bores him now. With a rather pathetic wistfulness he still reads the moving-picture magazines and thinks naively that he would like to have a test taken for the screen. He sees in the newspaper that the younger generation has been debauched by the movies and corrupted by jazz music, and in a dim way he supposes that the newspapers are right. He finds that the only things which do not seem to have given his friends a shove downward are the pie-eating contest and the penny arcade. Mingled with such nonsense he finds the statement that the boy of today is a great deal less courteous than his older brother in the preceding generation. And this, despite Tommy's ease of manner and his apparent worldliness, is quite true. It is due in some measure to modern dancing—not, as our local Savonrolas think, to the steps that are danced, but to the "cutting in" system which has cut the ground from under the unattractive girl.

In the age of the program, two or three dances were always devoted to the fat girl or the female Ben Turpin because Tommy's father and her father were friends. It wasn't anything to look forward to, even then, but nowadays if Tommy should ask her to dance he would have to dance with her until the musicians packed up their sandpaper and went home.

Tommy has never learned courtesy. He has no faith in any conventions but his own. If you tell him that his manners or his dance are "common," are borrowed from the lower classes, he will laugh at you and be right. He knows that if he wants to see close dancing forbidden or steps censored he must go to the cheap dance halls, the amusement park pavillions or the cabarets in small cities where the bouncer and the policewoman are on the alert to enforce the proprieties and keep the patrons from being—"common."

He is now nineteen. By this time he has managed to pass off almost enough examinations to get into college. But his ambition to enter college is on the wane—at least it fails to inspire him to successful effort. Perhaps the war occurred when he was at tutoring school and in the attendant disorganization of the universities he came to feel that it was the natural thing to give up going or leave in mid-term or find one's educational status in a sort of bizarre jumble. Besides, he thinks that he has had all the college has to offer—except the curriculum. So he comes home at twenty, perhaps after a hectic half-year at New Haven or Princeton, having now assumed to himself all the privileges of aristocracy without any of its responsibilities. He is a complete parasite, polished without being cultured, and "fast" without being vicious. There is nothing effeminate about him. He is healthy, good looking, a bit vacuous—perfectly useless.

I like Tommy personally. He interests me. He is pleasant company. And if he is useless, he knows it and makes a joke of it, says he is "dumb" and blames himself. He is convinced that he wasn't smart enough to get through college. He prefers married women to flappers, who rather bore him. You couldn't call him a "male flapper" to his face because he would probably knock you down—golf and boxing are liable to be his two accomplishments. He is simply a boy who under different circumstances might have been what is known in the editorials as "a useful member of society." He might have done more than cornered the wheat or manufactured a new potato peeler. If the wilderness is conquered there is a whole world of science, theoretical and applied, calling out for recruits who have money and time to spare.

I must admit that personally I have passed on. I am not even part of the younger generation. I have reached the stage where I ask, "How is the food?" instead of "How is [*Turn to page 69*]

What Became of Our Flappers and Sheiks?

[*Continued from page 42*]

the music?" And I have learned my dance. Once I was always among those two or three couples who stand up at the overture and hesitate and look at other couples to see who will begin—and finally get off that world famous remark: "We don't want to give an exhibition!"

But that was back before the civil war when we used to do the good old lancers and the shimmee. Since then I have learned my dance. It is not much—in fact it is so out of date that I have been asked if it is something new—but I am going to stick to it.

And I can still watch the comedy from the chaperone's bench.

I have no solutions, although I am profoundly interested. Perhaps it is just as well that we cannot produce an aristocracy that is capable of surviving. Perhaps Tommy's ineffectuality is some indirect economic re-assertion of the principle of equality. Who knows? Perhaps he will turn about at thirty and reshape the world upon his own desire. It's little we can guess.

"The old-fashioned girl was pokey. She wouldn't drink with you, perhaps, but she would drive you to drink. The old-fashioned girl bores men nowadays and there is no stimulus to be old-fashioned. Men don't want the clinging vine back—when they go to see a girl they go for a good time."

"They talk rot when they say that the modern girl is selfish because she doesn't want to let herself in for the cares and risks of marriage until she has an everlasting good time out of her youth. The modern girl has a sane argument. Marriage clips your wings, whether you are a man or a girl."

What Became of Our Flappers and Sheiks?

[*Continued from page 12*]

the *principle*, to show off her nobility of character. These are some of the bores of yesterday. Now even bores must be original, so the more unfortunate members of the flapper sect have each culled an individual line from their daily rounds, which amuses or not according to whether you have seen the same plays, heard the same tunes or read reviews of the same books.

The best flapper is reticent emotionally and courageous morally. You always know what she thinks, but she does all her feeling alone. These are two characteristics which will bring social intercourse to a more charming and more sophisticated level. I believe in the flapper as an involuntary and invaluable cupbearer to the arts. I believe in the flapper as an artist in her particular field, the art of being—being young, being lovely, being an object.

For almost the first time we are developing a class of pretty yet respectable young women, whose sole functions are to amuse and to make growing old a more enjoyable process for some men and staying young an easier one for others.

Even parents have ceased to look upon their children as permanent institutions. The fashionable mother no longer keeps her children young so that she will preserve the appearance of a débutante. She helps them to mature so that she will be mistaken for a step-mother. Once her girls are old enough to be out of finishing-school a period of freedom and social activity sets in for her. The daughters are rushed home to make a chaotic début and embark upon a feverish chase for a husband. It is no longer permissible to be single at twenty-five. The flapper makes haste to marry lest she be a left-over and be forced to annex herself to the crowd just younger. She hasn't time to ascertain the degree of com- [*Turn to page* [illegible]]

[*Continued from page 30*]

patibility between herself and her fiance before the wedding, so she ascertains that they will be separated if the compatibility should be mutually rated zero after it.

The flapper! She is growing old. She forgets her flapper creed and is conscious only of her flapper self. She is married 'mid loud acclamation on the part of relatives and friends. She has come to none of the predicted "bad ends," but has gone, at last, where all good flappers go—into the young married set, into boredom and gathering conventions and the pleasure of having children, having lent a while a splendour and courageousness and brightness to life, as all good flappers should.

Christmas 1925, 14 rue de Tilsitt, Paris.

I write to you from the depth of one of my unholy depressions. The book is wonderful—I honestly think that when it's published I shall be the best American novelist (which isn't saying a lot) but the end seems far away. When it's finished I'm coming home for awhile anyhow though the thought revolts me as much as the thought of remaining in France. I wish I were twenty-two again with only my dramatic and feverishly enjoyed miseries. You remember I used to say I wanted to die at thirty—well, I'm now twenty-nine and the prospect is still welcome. My work is the only thing that makes me happy—except to be a little tight—and for those two indulgences I pay a big price in mental and physical hangovers.

—FSF to Maxwell Perkins, 27 December 1925.

I remember the trees we had in Europe: one Christmas we spent drinking under the gold statue of Victor Emmanuel in Rome, lost in time and space & the majestic prettiness of that square before the cavernously echoing Piazza Cologna. The tree was covered with silver bells which rang hauntedly through the night by themselves . . . and we had a tree in Paris covered with mushrooms & with snowy houses which was fun. There were myriad birds of paradise on the tree with spun glass tails. And Nanny kept busily admonishing us about the French customs: how they did not give gifts at Christmas but at New Years . . . then we had a tree on the Avenue McMahon which Nanny & I decorated between sips of champagne until neither we nor the tree could hold any more of fantaisie or decor. We kept our decorations for years in painted toy boxes and when the last of the tails wilted & the last house grew lopsided, it was almost a bereavement.

—ZF to Scottie, c. 1947.

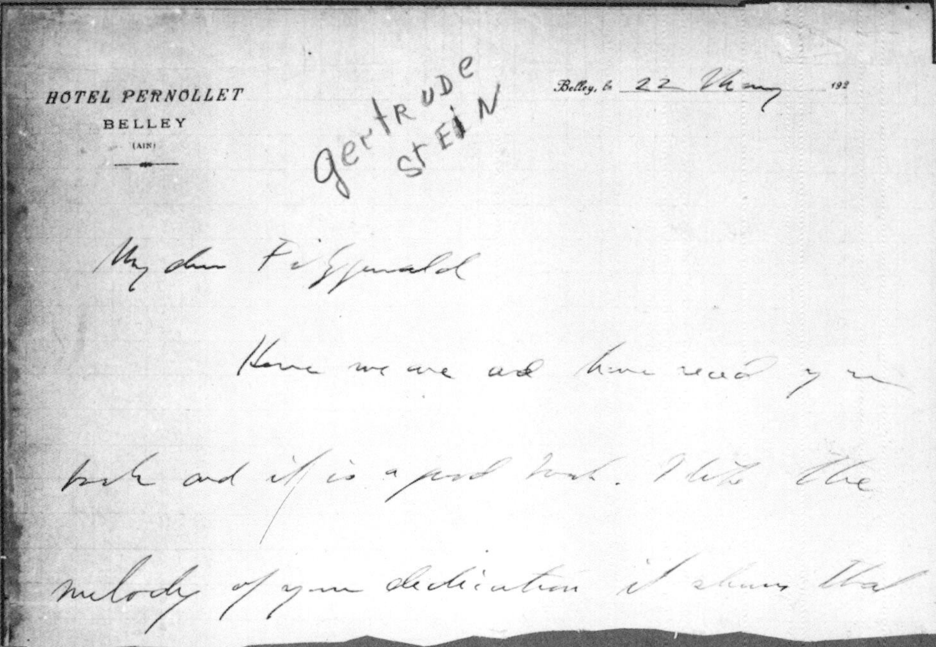

HOTEL PERNOLLET
BELLEY
(AIN)

Belley, le 22 May 192

Gertrude Stein

My dear Fitzgerald

Here we are and have read your book and it is a good book. I like the melody of your dedication it shows that

Here we are and have read your book and it is a good book. I like the melody of your dedication and it shows that you have a background of beauty and tenderness and that is a comfort. The next good thing is that you write naturally in sentences and that too is a comfort. You write naturally in sentences and one can read all of them and that among other things is a comfort. You are creating the contemporary world much as Thackeray did his in Pendennis *and* Vanity Fair *and this isn't a bad compliment. You make a modern world and a modern orgy strangely enough it was never done until you did it in* This Side of Paradise. *My belief in* This Side of Paradise *was alright. This is as good a book and different and older and that is what one does, one does not get better but different and older and that is always a pleasure. Best of good luck to you always, and thanks so much for the very genuine pleasure you have given me. We are looking forward to seeing you and Mrs. Fitzgerald when we get back in the Fall. Do please remember me to her and to you always*

—Gertrude Stein to FSF, 22 May 1925.

Gertrude Stein's letter of congratulation on The Great Gatsby. *Alice B. Toklas and Gertrude Stein photographed by Man Ray at their Paris apartment.*

Thank you. None of your letter was "a bad compliment" and all of it "was a comfort." Thank you very much. My wife and I think you a very handsome, very gallant, very kind lady and thought so as soon as we saw you, and were telling Hemingway so when you passed us searching your car on the street.

—FSF to Gertrude Stein, June 1925.

For T. S. Eliot
Greatest of Living Poets
from his entheusiastic
worshipper
F. Scott Fitzgerald

Paris,
Oct,
1925,

In his capacity as an editor at Faber & Gwyer, T. S. Eliot considered publishing an English edition of The Great Gatsby.

FABER and GWYER Ltd.
PUBLISHERS

TELEPHONE: MUSEUM 9543.

24, Russell Square,
London, W.C.1.

31st December, 1925.

F. Scott Fitzgerald, Esqre.,
C/o Charles Scribners & Sons,
New York City.

Dear Mr Scott Fitzgerald,

"The Great Gatsby" with your charming and overpowering inscription arrived the very morning that I was leaving in some haste for a sea voyage advised by my doctor. I therefore left it behind and only read it on my return a few days ago. I have, however, now read it three times. I am not in the least influenced by your remark about myself when I say that it has interested and excited me more than any new novel I have seen, either English or American, for a number of years.

When I have time I should like to write to you more fully and tell you exactly why it seems to me such a remarkable book. In fact it seems to me to be the first step that American fiction has taken since Henry James.

I have recently become associated in the capacity of a director with the publishing firm whose name you see above. May I ask you, if you have not already committed yourself to publish "The Great Gatsby" with some other publishing house in London, to let us take the matter up with you? I think that if we published the book we could do as well by you as anyone.

By the way, if you ever have any short stories which you think would be suitable for the CRITERION I wish you would let me see them.

With many thanks,

I am,

Yours very truly, T. S. Eliot

P.S. By a coincidence,
Gilbert Seldes in his New York
Chronicle in the CRITERION for January 14th has chosen
your book for particular mention.

THE STAGE

By Alexander Woollcott

Great Scott

"THE GREAT GATSBY," adapted by Owen Davis from F. Scott Fitzgerald's novel. Presented by William A. Brady. Directed by George Cukor. At the Ambassador.

THE CAST

Lieut. Carson	Ralph Sprague
Mrs. Fay	Margherita Sargent
Sally	Virginia Hennings
Jay Gatsby	James Rennie
Tom Buchanan	Elliot Cabot
Nick Carroway	Edward H. Wever
Mrs. Morton	Grace Heyer
Meyer Wolfshiem	Charles Dickson
Ryan	Edward Butler
Wilson	Robert W. Craig
Daisy Buchanan	Florence Eldridge
Jordan Baker	Catherine Willard
Myrtle Wilson	Josephine Evans
Doc Civit	Porter Hall
Milt Gav	William Clifford
Tom Turner	Richard Rawson
Mrs. Rogers	Ellen Mason
Catherine Carey	Carol Goodner
Mrs. Turner	Gladys Feldman
Donovan	Gordon Mullen
Crosby	William Leith

While the younger Brady was loftily sponsoring a revival of "Little Eyolf" yesterday afternoon, the old block was busy putting the finishing touches on his own production for the day—the dramatization of "The Great Gatsby," which was formally presented to a bulging audience last night at the Ambassador.

This is the play which, with a kind of cunning that would also come in handy in working out jig-saw puzzles, Owen Davis has fashioned from the fine, vivid novel by Scott Fitzgerald. He has carried the book over on to the stage with almost the minimum of spilling: the result is a steadily interesting play, with a cast chosen with a good deal of shrewdness and then goaded into giving a vociferous performance.

"The Great Gatsby" is, to my notion, an engrossing book written with fine art. It is notable for its portrait of the shiny bounder, Gatsby, a portrait painted with humor and with compassion. It is notable, too, for its acute sensitiveness to the changing complexion of the times, its almost journalistic report on the post-war manners of Great Neck, which is plausibly credited with having inspired its gaudy West Egg, Long Island.

This novel, wherewith Master Fitzgerald conquered new territory, has now been done into a play that adopts its substance without its sequence, and for its purposes, makes only one small shift in the personnel. For the convenience of a playwright who did not want to pick up his play and go traipsing all over Long Island with it, the obscure fellow with whose wife Buchanan dallies so disastrously is now given a job as chauffeur under Buchanan's own roof and so moves into the play, bag and, as you might say, baggage.

Gatsby, as you ought to know already, old sport, is a young climber out of the unclassified Middle West who, in the freemasonry of the training camps, when all doors were open to personable young officers, caught a glimpse of the kind of interior and the kind of girl he might never even have dreamed of had they really kept us out of war. The play employs a prologue to reveal a moment out of that inciting 1917 prelude to his tragedy. Then, in the post-war scenes it devotes itself to his crude, bold reach for the place in this world and the things of this world he thought would lift him to her level. It is a study of the rise and fall of the great Gatsby, that criminal, child-like, grotesque, pathetic great Gatsby.

James Rennie proved, I think, a felicitous choice for this role—this made-while-you-wait gentleman of Fitzgerald's imagining. Then Elliott Cabot and Edward H. Wever afforded the most nicely graded contrast to bring out Gatsby's weakness and to bring out Gatsby's strength. And there were good bits well managed by Catherine Willard, Charles Dixon and Charles W. Craig.

How much all that unfolded on the Ambassador's stage may have seemed clear and interesting to those who brought no knowledge of the play with them to the theatre, I cannot say. To those of us who had done our home-work it was an interesting evening. At the risk of seeming captious I should like to point out, however, that people from Louisville do not call it Loo-ee-vil. They call it Loo-a-vl.

IN TITLE ROLE in "The Great Gatsby," Adapted From Fitzgerald's Novel

JAMES RENNIE

A shining exception to the impression that good novels rarely make successful plays is the New York production of F. Scott Fitzgerald's novel, "The Great Gatsby," dramatized by Owen Davis, which has found immediate favor both with critics and play-goers.

According to J. Brooks Atkinson in the New York Times: "Of the seevral attempts to portray on the stage these restless moderns, whose cynicisms and infidelities keep the calamity-howlers hoarse, none has been more able or moving than 'The Great Gatsby' * * * The dramatic version retains most of the novel's peculiar glamor * * * provides something more substantial than an evening's entertainment." Alexander Woollcott, in the World, says: "The fine vivid novel * * * is carried over on to the stage with almost the minimum of spilling; the result is a steadily interesting play." Percy Hammond in the Herald-Tribune acclaims "that noble upstart, Mr. Gatsby * * * * capably transferred from the pages of Scott Fitzgerald's most thoroughbred book * * * * *An intelligent and interesting entertainment * * * * A dramatization so able that it managed to emphasize the subtle qualities of Mr. Fitzgerald's study of a golden vagabond * * * * lit it up skilfully and with considerable reverence. Added to Mr. Davis' achievement was the help of several excellent actors." The New York Telegraph calls "The Great Gatsby" "an enthralling drama" and says that "the story is expertly handled and the characters finely sketched."

So liquid is the stage business in "The Great Gatsby," which brought Long Island's guzzling set to the Ambassador last night, that the producer is said to have let long term contracts for the ginger ale, mineral waters and cigarettes consumed in wholesale quantities by the players. In this respect it is considered the most aquatic exhibition outside the Hippodrome tank, and at the present estimate of ninety-two cigarettes a performance it is probable that somebody will have to stand in front of the theatre every night to shoo the fire trucks away. Observing the cost of buying the necessary properties at retail, Mr. Brady is said to have contracted for a supply of everything on an optimistic six months' basis.

THE NEW YORKER 21

THE FINAL POT SHOT AT THE GREAT GATSBY

How Owen Davis makes Drama out of Scott Fitzgerald's romantic vulgarian, the great bootlegger and the near-great lover, at the Ambassador Theatre. Here depicted are James Rennie writhing in the noble agonies of his small catastrophe and Florence Eldridge whooping large whoops in an effort to get away without too much Long Island mud on her reputation.

Drawing by Covarrubias; copr. 1926, 1954 The New Yorker Magazine, Inc.

"Great Scott! What a Play!"

said Frank Vreeland, of the Evening Telegram.

The Great GATSBY

"Magnificent dramatization by Owen Davis of the great novel by F. Scott Fitzgerald. It affords to James Rennie the most complete and promising opportunity that has come to that young actor." *E. W. OSBORNE, EVENING WORLD.*

"Provides recreation for the adult theatregoer. Intelligent and interesting entertainment." *PERCY HAMMOND, HERALD TRIBUNE.*

"'The Great Gatsby' is fine. Another of James Rennie's rough diamonds, romantic, trusting, determined, rough as to voice, crude as to manners, grand as to clothes, true in heart, and fascinating in action." *BURNS MANTLE, DAILY NEWS.*

"Of the several attempts to portray on the stage these restless moderns whose cynicisms and infidelities keep the calamity howlers hoarse, none has been more able or moving than 'The Great Gatsby.'" *J. BROOKS ATKINSON, THE TIMES.*

"A steadily interesting play, shrewdly cast." *ALEXANDER WOOLLCOTT, THE WORLD.*

"Bound to win popular approval by its sincerity and honesty." *ROBERT COLEMAN, MIRROR.*

Ambassador—Now (and for months to come)

NEXT GATSBY MAT. TOM'W (Special Matinee Lincoln's and Washington's B'days.)

F SCOTT FITZGERALD
HOTEL BELLVUE
SALIES DE BEARN

WIMAN

GATSBY GREAT SUCCESS MR BRADY SENDS BEST WISHES, CONGRATULATIONS
(signed) DWIGHT, NEWYORK FULLSTOP FIRST NIGHT MARKED SUCCESS. REVIEWS
EXCELLENT (signed) SCRIBNERS, NEWYORK

SCOTT FITZGERALD
HOTEL BELLEVUE
SALIESDEBEARN BP

GOOD PLAY. SHOULD COIN MONEY
(signed) BRACKETT, NEWYORK

FEB. 4 1926. 3

TO:
SCOTT FITZGERALD
HOTEL BELLEVUE
SALIES DE BEARN BP

AUDIENCE ENTHUSIASTIC OVER GATSBY. PREDICT REAL SUCCESS. PLAY CARRIED GLAMOR OF STORY. EXCELLENTLY CAST AND ACTED. REVIEWS ALL VERY FAVORABLE. WRITING.
(signed) HAROLD OBER, NEWYORK

Ambassador Theatre

49th Street, Between Broadway and Eighth Avenue
SHUBERT THEATRE CORPORATION, Lessee
Direction of LEE and J. J. SHUBERT

FIRE NOTICE: Look around NOW and choose the nearest Exit to your seat. In case of fire, walk (not run) to THAT Exit. Do not try to beat your neighbor to the street.
THOMAS J. DRENNAN, Fire Commissioner.

"Once before we mentioned the fact, when you hear of a musical show's being notable for its good singing and superior score you are likely to find that it is presented by the Messrs. Shubert. While the present season offers several productions which are musically remarkable, the fact still remains that "The Student Prince" and "The Love Song" are in the first rank of shows to which you would not be ashamed to take a real musician, and they fly the Shubert banner." *ROBERT BENCHLEY, in "LIFE."*

BEGINNING TUESDAY EVENING, FEBRUARY 2, 1926
Matinees Wednesday and Saturday

WILLIAM A. BRADY
Presents
A New Drama by
OWEN DAVIS

The Great Gatsby

From the Novel by F. Scott Fitzgerald
—with—
JAMES RENNIE
Staged by George Cukor

The Cast
PROLOGUE

Lieut. Carson .... Ralph Sprague
Mrs. Fay .... Margherita Sargent
Daisy Fay .... Florence Eldridge
Sally .... Virginia Hennings
Jay Gatsby .... James Rennie
Tom Buchanan .... Elliot Cabot

THE PLAY

Nick Carraway .... Edward H. Wever
Mrs. Morton .... Grace Heyer
Jay Gatsby .... James Rennie
Meyer Wolfshiem .... Charles Dickson
Ryan .... Edward Butler

PROGRAM CONTINUED ON SECOND PAGE FOLLOWING

While the Fitzgeralds were still abroad, a dramatization of The Great Gatsby by Owen Davis was successfully produced on Broadway in 1926.

Newyork 3131 16 V. PQ =

Gastsby picture possible offer forty five thousand advise acceptance

cable quinck = Ober =.

THE GREAT GATSBY

. . . has been a successful character. He was a best seller when he made his first public appearance between the covers of the F. Scott Fitzgerald novel. Then he made his stage début and there was a continual line at the Broadway box-office. And now he is to try his fortune on the screen. Warner Baxter, judging from this photograph, will do well by Gatsby.

"THE GREAT GATSBY"

Produced by Paramount.
Directed by Herbert Brenon.
Presented at the Oriental theater.

THE CAST:

J. Gatsby	Warner Baxter
Daisy Buchanan	Lois Wilson
Nick Carraway	Neil Hamilton
Myrtle Wilson	Georgia Hale
George Wilson	William Powell
Tom Buchanan	Hale Hamilton
Charles Wolf	George Nash
Bert	"Gunboat" Smith

Mae Tinée.

Good Morning!
Good picture!

If you liked the book, "The Great Gatsby," by F. Scott Fitzgerald, you will like the picture better. If you liked the play—you'll like the picture better. If you didn't care for either the book or the play—you WILL care for the picture.

THAT, if you ask me, is praise!

It's a picture that grips every step of the way. (Sounds like a shoe ad.) Its people are real and their actions and reactions wholly comprehensible. And the story of Gatsby, a man who clings to a promise and a dream, laying at last his life on the altar he has raised to them, is beautifully presented. So beautifully, so poignantly, that you become oblivious even of the continuous, vacuous titters of the few tiresome morons who persist in their endeavors to ruin the Oriental shows for the majority.

Mr. Baxter's impersonation of Gatsby is a true and touching performance. You're so sorry for him that you ache. Lois Wilson as the girl who didn't wait and married another man has a rôle much different from her usual ones, but one that she plays exactly as well as she has the good little girl parts that fall to her lot as a rule. It was not so long ago that she threatened to leave Paramount if they didn't, so to speak, stop putting starched petticoats on her, and I guess the warning fell on fallow ground.

Hale Hamilton is great as the man she married. Neil Hamilton—open season for the Hamiltons, evidently—gives a splendid performance of the cousin. William Powell has some memorable entranes as the garage owner, and Georgia Hale as his wife, whom Daisy's husband prefers, is also somebody to bear in mind. The entire cast, for that matter, is irreproachable.

So, I should say, is the entire picture. And my advice to you is to see it.

"Great Gatsby" a Hit at Rialto

"THE GREAT GATSBY," with F. Scott Fitzgerald written all over it, is this week's attraction at the Rialto, and it is a mighty good one.

The picturization has changed the novel a bit, but not enough to hurt, and it leaves plenty of the Fitzgerald touch.

The story, without any unnecessary moralizing, is that of a poor youth who rises to affluence thru unscrupulous assistance. This does not come in time, however, for him to win the girl of his choice, a rather feather-brained creature, it seems.

Gatsby, even after making his fortune, continues to pine for this girl, who in the meantime has married another. The author brings about an unusual ending after Gatsby meets the young wife, dazzles her with his wealth and success, and then is confounded at the husband's charges that he has done things he shouldn't have done with the young wife.

Warner Baxter and Lois Wilson have the lead roles, with the latter doing much the better work. Others in a good cast are Georgia Hale, Neil Hamilton and William Powell.

'The Great Gatsby' Enters the Cinema Mill—'The Flaming Forest,' a Capitol Success.

By JOHN S. COHEN, Jr.

With Herbert Brenon productions holding forth at the Criterion and the new Paramount Theater, another, namely, "The Great Gatsby," entered the lists of Broadway over the week end. This film recounting of the Scott Fitzgerald novel is ensconsed in the Rivoli, soon to be a drydock for "Old Ironsides," and truth to tell, it is the least of Mr. Brenon's current works. Except for some minor changes and a slight missing of the point of Mr. Fitzgerald's book, the plot-outline remains the same as before. But the production is so commonplace that the photoplay, despite its good story, remains only an ordinary program picture.

Gatsby's romantic yearnings were admirably projected by Mr. Fitzgerald's book, as was a sardonic sense of their futility. Nor did Owen Davis's play miss them by any wide margin. But Mr. Brenon has permitted his actors to be so cold and prosaic, so wooden (except in a few isolated cases) that the only sense of romantic yearning projected through the photoplay at the Rivoli is, ostensibly, a romantic yearning on the part of the players and director to be through with "The Great Gatsby" as soon as possible.

Here, on the screen of the Rivoli, one of the very best stories in modern American fiction is offered. Yet the picture is half way dull, half way cold and uninteresting. Why? Because producers in filmdom don't realize as yet that pictures are pictures and unless the pictorial section of a photoplay is good, the result is bound to be futile. The purchasing of all the good plays and novels in Christendom will in no whit aid movies unless they are filtered through the mind of a director who knows the meaning of cinema.

Practically all of the atmosphere and most of the story at the Rivoli are put across by the subtitular sections of the film. That the story happens to be a good one is the only reason by which the film will pass. Here as usual, Gatsby, ill born, falls in love with Daisy of Louisville. Here as usual, he retains her unattainable image before him as he builds, from bootlegging profits, Long Island castles in order to be near her. Here, he is again shot down before the end, and here (and this is decidedly not usual) there comes a slightly moronic title explaining that some people (meaning that magnificent he-man Gatsby) live and die, but for the happiness of others. The picture illustrating this subtitle shows Daisy and her husband Tom and their tot draped beautifully on the porch of their happy home. . . .

True, the title writer somehow resisted injecting, "Came the dawn of a new day . . . !" But he should have put it in. It would have fitted perfectly the generally bad English, inappropriate wording, length, and cheap fictional rubber stamping contained in the rest of the titles. In one respect, "The Great Gatsby" is unique. It boasts of the longest bit of reading matter in the history of the cinema. This is a title which comes along somewhere in the middle of the film, and it stretches from the top of the screen to the bottom. Of course, with such wordy interruptions, &c., the picture has no visual flow whatsoever. It is about as smooth pictorially as sandpaper, and the individual composition were unquestionably conceived by the office boy.

Lois Wilson makes a desperate effort to be a madcap Southern belle and succeeds rather well. As *Gatsby*, Warner Baxter isn't half bad, but unfortunately his face seemed far more aristocratic than those about him. Georgia Hale was first rate in a minor role and Neil Hamilton and Hale Hamilton were adequate. William Powell nearly stole the picture. I wish that I could generally commend Mr. Brenon's direction, but I can't. There is no feeling whatsoever in "The Great Gatsby"—except, possibly in the very last reel!

Three in Cast Dominate 'Great Gatsby' on Screen

RIVOLI THEATRE—"The Great Gatsby," a Paramount picture, directed by Herbert Brenon; adapted by Elizabeth Meehan; screen play by Becky Gardiner from the novel by F. V. Scott Fitzgerald and play by Owen Davix.

THE CAST:

Jay Gatsby . . . . Warner Baxter
Daisy Buchanan . . . . Lois Wilson
Nick Carraway . . . . Neil Hamilton
Mrytle Wilson . . . . Georgia Hale
George Wilson . . . . William Powell
Tom Buchanan . . . . Hae Hamitonl

By EILEEN CREELMAN.

UUOFFICIALLY, quite unofficially, this appears to be Herbert Brenon week in the Publex theatres. While "Beau Geste" continues blithely on at the Criterion, the director's two latest pictures opened within twelve hours of each other at the Paramount and Rivoli.

"The Great Gatsby," perhaps the least important of the Brenon trio, need not feel abashed beside the others. It may not prove a smashing box office success, but for several reasons it is worth seeing. And the first of these reasons embraces three individual performances.

Warner Baxter plays the "Great Gatsby" with understanding and courage. This eager, tragic figure is the same Gatsby that stood out from the pages of Scott Fitzgerald's book. His childish pride in that overwhelming house, in his dozens and dozens of monogrammed shirts, his confident devotion to Daizy and his loneliness needed real acting, and got it.

Yet it is Lois Wilson who caused a sensation in the Rivoli audience. Miss Wilson, the demure heroine of some scores of placid screen romances, has suddenly thrown old care to the wind and turned flapper. There she is, smoking and drinking in the well known Longuyland set—apologies to Alan Dale—and enjoying it all. One scene, with a bobbed-haired Lois quite hopelessly drunk in a bathtub, must be seen to be believed. Poor photography did much to mar Lois' work. Not only she, but the rest of the cast, have a good-sized bone—should they care to pick it—with the inventor of these lighting effects.

Neither lights nor photography bothered William Powell, intent on a brand new charactrization. A fin actor, this Powell, whether as a Western cattle thief or a bewildered and vengeful husband.

Not all the cast was so happily chosen. Nor is the continuity always clear. Surely, a younger Tom Buchanan would have made that attempted happy end[illegible] plausible. Hale Hamilton could never forget that his part was heavy. He was far more menacacing than Powell himself.

As for that happy ending, it was inevitable—and so impossible that no one need object. "The Great Gatsby" follows its originals almost too closely at times. The continuity was somewhat inflexible, while the procession of subtiles describing each character was both unnecessary and annoying. Warner Baxter, Dois Wilson and William Powell needed no explanations.

The Rivoli has also a Paul Oscard revue, "In a Music Shop."

You've been a peach, Max, about writing and wiring news about the play. Here we are in the Pyrenees with the following events taking place in the great world.

(1.) Gatsby *on the stage.*
(2) Gatsby *in England.*
(3.) Gatsby *translation being placed with publisher in Paris.*
(4.) *All the Sad Young Men* in New York.

So, in spite of a side trip once a week to Biarritz or Pau or Lourdes or St. Sebastian, we feel a bit out of date. We expect to leave for Nice on March 1st or thereabouts. The letter to Hemminway must have crossed him. By now you've seen him in New York. Your letter was your usual responsive yet tactful self. I hope you get his novel.

—FSF to Maxwell Perkins, c. 13 February 1926.

SALIES-DES BEARN
PYRENEES

NEAR SALIES

PORTRAIT OF THE ARTIST WITH PORTRAIT OF THE ARTIST

TO

RING AND ELLIS LARDNER

ALL THE SAD YOUNG MEN

By

F. SCOTT FITZGERALD

NEW YORK
CHARLES SCRIBNER'S SONS
1926

All the Sad Young Men, Fitzgerald's third story collection, was published in February 1926. It required 3 printings, totalling 16,200 copies.

CONTENTS

Let me tell you about the very rich. They are different from you and me. They possess and enjoy early, and it does something to them, makes them soft where we are hard, and cynical where we are trustful, in a way that, unless you were born rich, it is very difficult to understand. They think, deep in their hearts, that they are better than we are because we had to discover the compensations and refuges of life for ourselves. Even when they enter deep into our world or sink below us, they still think that they are better than we are. They are different.

—"The Rich Boy"

THE BOY GROWS OLDER.

BY HARRY HANSEN.

ALL THE SAD YOUNG MEN. By F. Scott Fitzgerald. Scribner.

SIX years ago F. Scott Fitzgerald blazed across the literary horizon with "This Side of Paradise," and captured the startled attention of all the sad young men and all the glad young women. His seniors immediately predicted his quick demise. For several years F. Scott hovered between brisk fun, irony and tragedy, and then came "The Great Gatsby," which proved him a competent painter of the American scene. And now he presents "All the Sad Young Men," a collection of short stories published within the last year in various colored magazines, green, blue, red and yellow, and giving excellent proof of his ability to write well in half a dozen manners. It is a joy to read these tales. They lack sameness; they are ironical, and sad, and jolly good fun by turns; they scintillate. Moreover, they show F. Scott Fitzgerald keeping step with his generation. He is of our own time and we are glad that he is.

All the Sad Young Men, by F. Scott Fitzgerald (Scribner's).

Mr. Fitzgerald, like his characters, is growing up. He writes no longer of the bright lights which are dazzling his young eyes nor of the cocktails consumed by debutantes, but has plunged instead into the everlasting havoc that these things bring about. His subject is no longer cause, but effect.

In this collection of short stories he takes a very considerable step upwards and onwards. By following a group of young men on pleasure bent to the end of their days he sees them turned into sad effigies of their former selves, with a backward glance at what might have been. If it is a depressing sight, it is none the less a mature one. And because he writes smartly and well the growing pains do not seem to have affected his gay spirit in this wiser outlook on life.

F. Scott Fitzgerald is a master at selecting arresting and felicitous titles, and to this rule his new collection of short stories, "All the Sad Young Men," (Charles Scribner's Sons) is no exception. There are nine of these stories, abounding in fine perception, delicate satire, originality, realism and fantasy. Of all the tales two, "Winter Dreams" and "Absolution," strike the deepest truest note. Most of the stories are interesting, some humorous, some irritating—each different from the rest. The two already designated are outstanding—equal, perhaps superior, to anything this promising young author has yet produced.

Scott Fitzgerald's
ALL THE SAD YOUNG MEN

ANSON HUNTER

"The very rich are different from you and me — they're soft where we are hard and cynical where we are trustful."

CHARLES HEMPLE

He was on his wife's nerves—he kept rubbing his face with his hand, at the table, at the theatre, even in bed.

JAMES MATHER

"The trouble with you," said his wife, "is that you've got the ideas of a college freshman — you're a professional nice fellow."

"Stories of fine insight and finished craft. . . . Mellow, mature, ironic, entertaining stories, and one of them, at least, challenges the best of our contemporary output."
—New York Times.

"A delicious literary compote. . . . Originality, freshness, intriguing plot, natural yet unexpected surprise, and an easy manner of writing."
—Boston Evening Transcript.

"The story 'Absolution' we believe to be as fine an achievement in the field of the brief tale as any by a living American."
—New York Evening Post.

"Entertainment for nine evenings."*—New York World.*

"It is a joy to read these tales. . . . They are ironical, and sad, and jolly good fun by turns; they scintillate. . . . Nobody else can do these glad young women and these sad young men so well as F. Scott Fitzgerald."
—Chicago Daily News.

$2.00 *at all bookstores*

GEORGE O'KELLY

"All kinds of love in the world, but never the same love twice."

DEXTER GREEN

"Lots of women fade just like that—you must have seen it happen."

JOHN ANDROS

He went to "The Baby Party" to call for his wife and child.

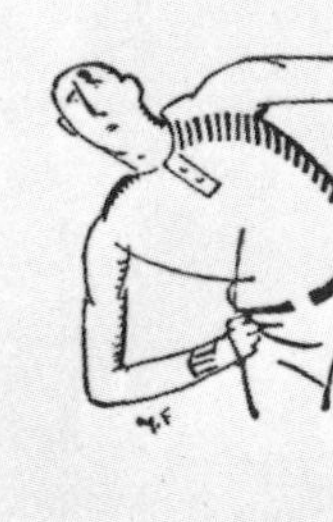

GEORGE TOMPKINS

He worked too hard at leading a balanced life.

CHARLES SCRIBNER'S SONS · FIFTH AVENUE · NEW YORK

GENIUS AND PAINS
By Thomas Boyd

F. Scott Fitzgerald: All the Sad Young Men. New York: Charles Scribner's Sons.
Walter Noble Burns: The Saga of Billy the Kid. New York: Doubleday, Page & Co.

ONE of the gayest talkers, one of the most amusing persons, perhaps the most talented writer, showing now and again the licking flame of genius, F. Scott Fitzgerald, once of Summit avenue, in St. Paul, stands out in the English speaking world as a charming cavalier of letters. This is not a nonsensical statement; it is a fact.

Thomas Boyd

So far as Fitzgerald's conversation goes, Ernest Boyd has truly remarked that Scott's house was about the only place in New York where bright, stimulating talk could be heard. The young author who made so many misquotations in his first novel, "This Side of Paradise," is always discussing the latest trends in literature, organizing a phalanx of arguments for or against Gertrude Stein, James Joyce, Ernest Hemingway, Virginia Woolf and T. S. Eliot; gaily charging that Glenway Westcott is a fake and that Hemingway is tremendously worth watching. Ideas pass, are challenged and inspected; the listener is given the opinion that somewhere in America authors talk of something besides royalties, serialization and motion picture rights.

Yet Fitzgerald is no more of a philosopher than Peter Piper. He has a superb respect for wealth and will seek to convince you that the possession of riches gives the possessor a charm that is as valuable, and authentic as if it were singular beauty or great intellect. He says that he was once a socialist (in "Who's Who" for 1922 he mentioned socialism as his politics), but that he has long since passed through that stage. In religious he is a skeptic, haunted forever by the mysteries of his church. But he is always smiling, always naive, brilliantly enthusiastic over life and ideas; what he has to say always seems worth listening to.

* * *

FITZGERALD'S books, from "This Side of Paradise" to his latest collection of stories, "All the Sad Young Men," show his riotous fancy, that quality which enabled him to write such weird and enchantingly absurd tales as "The Diamond as Big as the Ritz," "The Curious Case of Benjamin Button," and "The Vegetable." But there is much more to Fitzgerald than unusual conceits. In his latest novel, "The Great Gatsby," which, by the way, is now a success in New York as a play, he gave evidence of his perfect control over words and materials. In this bok there is scarcely a word out of place, not a single detail that does not advance the story to its overwhelming climax and its puzzling implications.

* * *

BENT on such affairs as these, Fitzgerald will spend month after month laboring over a manuscript, keeping up the mood of the novel, maintaining the proper rhythm, feeling for the form. His much condemned and more misunderstood "Beautiful and Damned" showed how much documentary evidence he could get into a book; it created a buldgeoning picture of the awful strength of the weak, of the degenerating effect of a given kind of life upon a given kind of individual, and there was much in it which most married people realized as the inevitable lot of the first few nuptial years.

The "Beautiful and Damned" was successful because, largely, of its force of documentation. But "The Great Gatsby" was spare and cut to the bone. Economy was practiced as scarcely ever before. Fitzgerald, the giddy youth who dashes off stories for the magazines and has been paid 75 cents a word for an article, spent months and months rewriting "The Great Gatsby."

* * *

IT is out of such hard work as this that stories like his "Absolution" (in the latest collection, "All the Sad Young Men") are made. There is perfection of mood, of form and implication for the reader who cares enough to know about those things. No matter whether all the stories in "All the Sad Young Men" are equal to "Absolution," there is this to be said: everything that Scott Fitzgerald writes contains something that is worth reading.

The position of this much discussed young man in literature can be left for hands of a later generation to decide. It is enough that he is always engaging and often astoundingly good in his writing, that he is a delightful person to know, one who is not fooled by the things which he writes for ready markets, nor mistaken in the books which he flings up towards the moon.

Art's Bread and Butter

ALL THE SAD YOUNG MEN. By F. Scott Fitzgerald. New York: Charles Scribner's Sons. 1926. $2.

Reviewed by WILLIAM ROSE BENÉT

WITH "The Great Gatsby," it is generally agreed, Mr. Fitzgerald came into his full maturity as a novelist. His natural gifts were displayed therein in abundance, but their exercise was controlled and chastened. He had learned form and the value of reticence. He had come to closer grips with life. The vorpal blade of youth, dulled by slashings, had been ground to a new cutting edge.

A young writer who is earning his living at literature must work fast and put his books close together. Mr. Fitzgerald has elected so to live. His ingenuity at evolving marketable ideas is extraordinary. But one naturally feels, behind most of the writing in this book, the pressure of living conditions rather than the demand of the spirit. As a writer of short stories the author more displays his astonishing facility than the compulsions of his true nature. He is keeping his hand in and paying the rent. And the performance is energetic with a certain gallantry. But now that he has written "The Great Gatsby" we are, perhaps, exorbitant in our demands.

Scott Fitzgerald's
New Book
ALL THE SAD YOUNG MEN

The Sad Young Men Are To Be Found in—

THE RICH BOY—WINTER DREAMS—THE BABY PARTY—ABSOLUTION—RAGS MARTIN-JONES AND THE PR-NCE OF W-LES—THE ADJUSTER—HOT AND COLD BLOOD—"THE SENSIBLE THING"—GRETCHEN'S FORTY WINKS.

$2.00

Both books at all bookstores.

Mr. Fitzgerald's THE GREAT GATSBY, as dramatized by Owen Davis, is the shining success of the New York stage—generally acclaimed as a fine rendering of a superb novel. $2.00

CHARLES SCRIBNER'S SONS, FIFTH AVENUE, NEW YORK

"All the Sad Young Men" Who Did Not Marry Sylvia

Philbert—now adept at the "Mabel" game (see any Yale man).

Sylvester—registering first impression of Folies Bergeres.

Elmer—back to the little girl in South Bend, Ark.

SOME of them took to the Charleston and some of them took to books, some of them sailed for Paris and some of them started searching their little black tomes for telephone numbers.

But each had the good taste and the sportsmanship to travel to Ovington's and select, as he dallied among so many lovely gifts, one which told the lady that he thought worlds of her taste in things, even if he thought nothing of her judgment of men!

OVINGTON'S

"The Gift Shop of Fifth Avenue, Inc."

Fifth Avenue at 39th Street

Bertie—lately gone native in Larchmont.

Wilfred—ready for anything, anywhere (f. o. b. McDougal Street).

Paul—viewing set of Carlyle's Complete Works (just purchased).

("ALL THE SAD YOUNG MEN." By F. Scott Fitzgerald. Chas. Scribner's Sons, New York, $2.)

With the publication of "Great Gatsby,' Mr. Fitzgerald definitely emerged from the "promising" class into the established ranks. "The Great Gatsby," according to those supposed to know, was a novel of sustained brilliance.

Not all Mr. Fitzgerald's "Sad Young Men" are of the same calibre but this is hardly to be expected in a volume of short stories. His publishers' contention, however, that the book shows a marked advance over his earlier collections, "Flappers and Philosophers" and "Tales of the Jazz Age," is partly justified. If some of these later stories are no better than the average run of their predecessors, others have a distinction and significance which shows Mr. Fitzgerald at the height of his powers. There is in them less of the hard-boiled cynicism, characteristics of those earlier studies of modern youth, and a mature insight and sympathy that give them a deeper poignancy.

"Winter Dreams," for instance, is certainly something more than just another clever piece of satire. Underneath the sparkle and the irony, Mr. Fitzgerald reveals the eternal tragedy of youth, the tragedy of lost illusion. Very subtly he does it. There is no emotional overflow. But the story remains with one.

It is the story of Dexter Green who loves a girl who marries another man. And the tragedy is not that she marries the other man, not that he loses her herself; but that he loses his dream of her.

"He wanted to care and he could not care. For he had gone away and he could never go back any more. The gates were closed, the sun was gone down, and there was no beauty but the gray beauty of steel that withstands all time. Even the grief he could have borne was left behind in the country of illusion, of youth, of the richness of life, where his winter dreams had flourished."

Or take that apparently light and superficial tale, "The Adjuster," of the ultra-sophisticated young Mrs. Charles Hemple who hates keeping house and whose baby bores her. Herein is concealed a moral that many a less sophisticated young wife would do well to take to heart.

The stories number nine and range from "Absolution," the finest bit of literary workmanship in the collection and one to be taken seriously, to such humorous trifles as "The Baby Party" and "Rags Martin Jones and the Prince of Wales" which are in the author's earlier style.

NEW YORK BEST-SELLER LIST.

Reported by Brentano's.

FICTION.

"The Private Life of Helen of Troy," by John Erskine (Bobbs-Merrill). $3.

"Gentlemen Prefer Blondes," by Anita Loos (Boni & Liveright). $2.

"All the Sad Young Men," by F. Scott Fitzgerald (Scribner). $2.

"All the Sad Young Men" is a collection of short stories. Some of these are "The Rich Boy," "The Baby Party," "Rags Martin-Jones and the Pr-nce of W-les," "Hot and Cold Blood" and "The Sensible Thing." The themes cover a wide range and give Mr. Fitzgerald a chance to be wise and witty, deliberately superficial and delicately poignant. But why the book's name? one queries, since no one of the stories bears it as a title. Is it used for its provocative quality of an atmosphere that it creates of weary and sophisticated civilization? One supposes so. At any rate, it is intensely modern and Manhattanese. It would hardly have been coined twenty years ago, nor would it be used today by an author from the Western prairies. It is redolent of a particular place and time of all the young men (sad indeed!) who occupy apartments or hall bedrooms who ride in taxis with their sweethearts or walk alone in this our year and on this our island. Mr. Fitzgerald, you have chosen well. But the ability to pick telling titles has always been one of your strongest evidences of genius. "This Side of Paradise," "The Beautiful and Damned," "The Great Gatsby." They are good. But "All the Sad Young Men" is a masterpiece. It has nuance, subtlety, aroma. One hopes the stories will not fall too far short of the hope this title raises. They will be reviewed at length in an early issue of The Literary Review.

"Mr. Scott Fitzgerald, questioned as to what is making all the sad young men so sad, explains that they are all growing up and settling down," says Keith Preston in the Chicago Daily News.

Interesting in themselves, F. Scott Fitzgerald's tales are made still more interesting by the fact that their author is he who wrote "This Side of Paradise." For in them there is a definite sounding of the note of personal responsibility, a note most clearly heard in that one of the nine tales which is called "The Adjuster." This is the story of Luella Hemple, who wanted "the light and glitter" of the world, believing them not merely the best, but "all there is in life"; who wanted to sit in the audience "without helping to make the play," but who learned at last that, being grown-up, she must accept the grown-up's obligation of looking after other people:

> You've got to give security to young people and peace to your husband, and a sort of charity to the old. . . . You've got to cover up a few more troubles than you show, and be a little more patient than the average person, and do a little more instead of a little less than your share. . . . Happy things may come to you in life, but you must never go seeking them any more. It is your turn to make the fire.

Luella had always taken, never given. She and her husband belonged to "that enormous American class who wander over Europe every summer, sneering rather pathetically and wistfully at the customs and traditions and pastimes of other countries, because they have no traditions or pastimes of their own," or, in other words, to that class which has no roots. And because she was very pretty, she had been able to indulge her selfishness with impunity, since "it is one of the many flaws in the scheme of human relationships that selfishness in women has an irresistible appeal to many men."

The longest story in the book, and the one which has been given the place of honor, is "The Rich Boy," the tale of a "conscious superiority" divorced from obligations, while an acceptance of them has much to do with "The Baby Party." The desire for beauty, the wistfulness of lost dreams, sounds through many of the stories like an exquisite threnody. It was the loss of the dream more than the loss of the woman that hurt Dexter Green of "Winter Dreams"; the two who did "The Sensible Thing" won material benefits, but they lost something lovely, something intangible, which, once gone, was gone for all time. "All the Sad Young Men" are sad for the loss of beauty and of dreams.

Like every collection of short stories, this one is uneven. Through the best of the tales runs a stream of fantasy, of imagination preferred to common sense. The hero of the amusing and very clever "Gretchen's Forty Winks" defies common sense, and gets what he wants; Rags Martin-Jones makes extravagant demands, and has them extravagantly filled. Yet these defiances and extravagances and touches of fantasy are perfectly in tune with the note struck in "The Adjuster"—itself a fantasy of human life.

ALL THE SAD YOUNG MEN. By F. Scott Fitzgerald. New York: Charles Scribner's Sons. 1926.

It has been six years since F. Scott Fitzgerald's first book was published. The book, "This Side of Paradise," was bitterly criticised and shamefully misunderstood. The critics were wont to shake their heads and wonder about the future of this young writer. Fitzgerald was not discouraged over the critics' viewpoint and later wrote "The Beautiful and Damned." This too was harshly judged. He followed this with another book which was his best, "The Great Gatsby," which received many flattering and enthusiastic reviews. Many of the critics felt that Fitzgerald did have a future; in his growing up, his maturing, he had made gains all along the way and those who had shaken their heads now looked upon him with new interest.

Now we have his latest, a collection of short stories that far outshine his earlier efforts. "All the Sad Young Men" is a book of nine tales, varied in subject matter and very entertaining. "The Rich Boy" and "The Winter Dream" have a touch of beauty and sadness. They are stories of the lives and loves of young men. "The Baby Party" is full of good laughs. The story starts with a baby party and ends with a feud between two families in which the fathers actually carry on the physical combat begun by the babies. It is a humorous story with a deep meaning. "Absolution," thought by many to be his best story, has a touch of irony characteristic of Fitzgerald. "Rags Martin-Jones and the Pr-nce of W-les" has a little of the old jazzy manner of some of his earlier stories. "The Adjuster," "Hot and Cold Blood," "The Sensible Thing" and "Gretchen's Forty Winks" are all good stories of regular people. Ironical, sad and jolly; in all very entertaining.

M. B. T.

"This Side of Paradise", "Flappers and Philosophers", "Beautiful and Damned", "A Vegetable", "Tales of The Jazz Age", "The Great Gatsby" and now "All The Sad Young Men". All from the hand of F. Scott Fitzgerald demonstrating that he can choose titles as well as write. Every one perfect for its purpose.

"TELL ME A BOOK TO READ"

These Are a Few of the Recent Ones Best Worth While

SHORT STORIES

ALL THE SAD YOUNG MEN, by F. Scott Fitzgerald (*Scribner's*). Fitzgerald for the aisle seats, the boxes, the dress circle and the peanut gallery.

"All the Sad Young Men," heralded as more mature than Scott Fitzgerald's earlier works, has not yet attained the latter's sales. Which was the case with "The Great Gatsby." Now, say his friends, Scott is wont to exclaim, "What Price Maturity!"

R. E. H., Wichita, Kans., has been asked to recommend a list of books for a cynical friend; she has suggested Cabot's "What Men Live By," Stanley Hall's "Morale," and one or two others, but is not prepared with the fiction that seems to be desired.

IF by cynicism you mean, as many people do when they use the word, the yellow-beaked sophistication of the immature, only time will modify it; that, and possibly an overdose of the earlier works of Scott Fitzgerald—not, I hasten to say, his "Great Gatsby," and "All the Sad Young Men" (Scribner). Whatever there may be for the reader's soul in these two books, whether food or poison, gets into it and stays; "The Beautiful and Damned" only temporarily overcrowds the system.

COLLECTION EUROPÉENNE

VIENT DE PARAITRE

SCOTT FITZGERALD

GATSBY LE MAGNIFIQUE

TRADUCTION VICTOR LLONA

L'AMOUR ET LE PLAISIR EN AMÉRIQUE

UN VOLUME .. .. **13** *fr.* **50**

ÉDITION ORIGINALE SUR PAPIER VÉLIN .. .. **20 fr.**

The first translation of Fitzgerald was Gatsby le magnifique in 1926. The French playwright Jean Cocteau sent his congratulations through the translator two years later (below).

Villa Paquita Juan-les-Pins

In March 1926 the Fitzgeralds rented the Villa Paquita in Juan-les-Pins, but moved to the Villa St. Louis. They remained on the Riviera until December, when they returned to America. During this period Fitzgerald unsuccessfully tried to work on his fourth novel.

"Les Glycines," Marlotte (S. & M.)
Dec. 9, 1928.

Dear Scotty,

Look who's here! I have received the following letter:

"Mon cher Llona,

Voulez-vous faire savoir à F. Scott Fitzgerald que son livre m'a permis de passer des heures très dures (je suis dans une clinique). C'est un livre céleste; chose la plus rare du monde.

Vous lui demanderez qu'il vous félicite d'en être le traducteur - car il faut une plume mystérieuse pour ne pas tuer l'oiseau bleu, pour ne pas le changer en langue morte.

Je vous embrasse,

Jean Cocteau.

Too bad he did not write this in the papers when the book came out - the sales would have gone up 2 or 300 per cent. Apparently he read the book quite recently.

When will you bless us with another heavenly book? I am most anxious to read you.

Our best wishes to you all.

Yours for ever,
Victor Llona

P.S. The itilization is J. C's.

Thanks very much for your nice letter & the income blank. I'm delighted about the short story book. In fact with the play going well & my new novel growing absorbing & with our being back in a nice villa on my beloved Rivierra (between Cannes and Nice) I'm happier than I've been for years. Its one of those strange, precious and all too transitory moments when everything in one's life seems to be going well.

—FSF to Maxwell Perkins c. 15 March 1926.

The compensation of a very early success is a conviction that life is a romantic matter. In the best sense one stays young. When the primary objects of love and money could be taken for granted and a shaky eminence had lost its fascination, I had fair years to waste, years that I can't honestly regret, in seeking the eternal Carnival by the Sea. Once in the middle twenties I was driving along the High Corniche Road through the twilight with the whole French Riviera twinkling on the sea below. As far ahead as I could see was Monte Carlo, and though it was out of season and there were no Grand Dukes left to gamble and E. Phillips Oppenheim was a fat industrious man in my hotel, who lived in a bathrobe—the very name was so incorrigibly enchanting that I could only stop the car and like the Chinese whisper: "Ah me! Ah me!" It was not Monte Carlo I was looking at. It was back into the mind of the young man with cardboard soles who had walked the streets of New York. I was him again—for an instant I had the good fortune to share his dreams, I who had no more dreams of my own. And there are still times when I creep up on him, surprise him on an autumn morning in New York or a spring night in Carolina when it is so quiet that you can hear a dog barking in the next county. But never again as during that all too short period when he and I were one person, when the fulfilled future and the wistful past were mingled in a single gorgeous moment—when life was literally a dream.

—"Early Success"

The Hôtel du Cap at Antibes.

McLIESHS PORCH

The hotel and its bright tan prayer rug of a beach were one. In the early morning the distant image of Cannes, the pink and cream of old fortifications, the purple Alp that bounded Italy, were cast across the water and lay quavering in the ripples and rings sent up by sea-plants through the clear shallows.

—*Tender Is the Night*

The gay elements of society had divided into two main streams, one flowing toward Palm Beach and Deauville, and the other, much smaller, toward the summer Riviera. One could get away with more on the summer Riviera, and whatever happened seemed to have something to do with art. From 1926 to 1929, the great years of the Cap d'Antibes, this corner of France was dominated by a group quite distinct from that American society which is dominated by Europeans. Pretty much of anything went at Antibes—by 1929, at the most gorgeous paradise for swimmers on the Mediterranean no one swam any more, save for a short hang-over dip at noon. There was a picturesque graduation of steep rocks over the sea and somebody's valet and an occasional English girl used to dive from them, but the Americans were content to discuss each other in the bar. This was indicative of something that was taking place in the homeland—Americans were getting soft.

—"Echoes of the Jazz Age"

HONoria KENNETH BOOTH Patrick

As to your questions

(1.) Unless the Americans are first driven out of France (as at present seems not unlikely—I'll be home with the finished manuscript of my book about mid-December. We'll be a week in New York, then south to Washington & Montgomery to see our respective parents & spend Xmas—and back in New York in mid-January to spend the rest of the winter. Whether the Spring will see us back on Long Island or returning to Europe depends on politics, finances and our personal desires.

* * *

I do want to see you, Max

—FSF to Maxwell Perkins c. 11 August 1926.

VILLA ST. LOUIS

Villa St. Louis
1926

SPRING–SUMMER–FALL–WINTER

LAST DAYS OF US
and the RABBITS

HOME FOR THE HOLIDAYS. F. Scott Fitzgerald, young author of best sellers, returned from Italy yesterday on the liner Conte Biancamano. Here he is with Mrs. Fitzgerald and their daughter, Scotty. They came home to greet Santa Claus before their native American hearth.

Acme Pho[illegible]

Youngest Noted Author Here

"Good books have influenced me since I was 14," says F. Scott Fitzgerald, interpreter of youth and the jazz age, who at 30 is the youngest of the younger generation of noted American authors. Fitzgerald and his pretty blonde wife are visiting Los Angeles.

SCOTT FITZGERALD LAYS SUCCESS TO READING

By GILMORE MILLEN

F. Scott Fitzgerald, who left Princeton when he was 21 and wrote a book that made every critic in the country hail him as the interreter of the youth of the Jazz Age—

Who has written dozens of stories about flappers and gin parties and wild dizzy nights maddened by muted saxophones—

Who, at the age of 30, is certainly the youngest, and possibly the most brilliant, of the younger generation of American authors—

Acquired the literary ability which provided him with a luxurious room overlooking the vivid green lawns of the Ambassador hotel, in a very ordinary, but serious manner. [illegible] reading books—the spring away from its moorings around a soft collar beneath a well tailored olive gray sack suit, and told all about it today, smiling unconsciously and pleasantly, as though nothing unusual had ever happened in his life after all.

He had been talking about Europe—the Riviera, and the Bay of Naples, and Paris—where he has been living, with his charming wife, who came from Montgomery, Ala., for the past three years.

There was the literary crowd in Paris—the American literary crowd—to be described. He had to mention James Joyce, who wrote "Ulysses," and Gertrude Stein, who wrote "Three Lives" and started half the present school of American writ[illegible]

Movie Reviews

F. Scott Fitzgerald Joins Parade of Authosr to Mecca of Movies

BY FLORENCE GRAUMAN.

F. SCOTT FITZGERALD, rated by Dreiser, Mencken and Sherwood Anderson as one of America's foremost young short story writers and novelists, has just been signed to a contract by John W. Considine, Junior, president of Feature Productions, Incorporated, to do original screen stories for United Artists Pictures. The first is an original for Constance Talmadge's initial United Artists Picture. Fitzgerald, who arrived in New York from Paris two weeks ago, plans to go to Hollywood immediately. Not only does Scott Fitzgerald join United Artists at this time, but long-term contracts have also been signed with Donald McGibeny, author of "Two Arabian Knights," which Louis Milestone is now making into a film for United Artists release, and Wallace Smith, who has just completed adaptation of "The Dove," Norma Talmadge's first United Artists Picture. McGibeny's first story under his new contract is a vehicle in which Estelle Taylor is featured in an all-star cast.

"It is really to the credit of Herbert Brenon," writes Herbert M. Miller, "that he undertook and completed 'The Great Gatsby' with some degree of success. After all, Fitzgerald's novel doesn't contain much meat for motion picture conversion, but Brenon's handling of it should hold interest to the end.

"The cinema version holds rather religiously to the text and even the picturization of one of the house parties is subdued. Keeping one's self in check when given sequence of this character to direct is an admirable quality. DeMille has thrown far bigger orgies with less to work with.

"To those who are unacquainted with both the book and the play, the picturized 'Great Gatsby' may be somewhat of a puzzle. The crowning blow of all, to those who come to see, be amused, and go, is that unhappy ending, a potent bit.

"Warner Baxter acquits himself rather well as Jay Gatsby. The introduction of Gatsby is well handled. Then there are Neil Hamilton, Lois Wilson and Hale Hamilton, all performing capably." R. W. Jr.'

LITERARY GOSSIP

F. Scott Fitzgerald, author of "The Great Gatsby," "The Beautiful and Damned," "This Side of Paradise," "Flappers and Philosophers" and "Tales of the Jazz Age," is in Los Angeles, "working like a dog" in his apartment at the Ambassador. If the result of this self-imposed hard labor is something as sound and brilliant as "The Great Gatsby," the said apartment henceforward and forever more should become a shrine for literary idol worshipers and the desk at which the work was done, the object of ownership by collectors of association pieces.

BEHIND THE SCREENS

East and West in the Studios

By Allene Talmey

WITH much exuberance John W. Considine Jr., President of Feature Productions, Inc., has signed Francis Scott Key Fitzgerald to join in the Hollywood game of authors. As blondes, ash, yellow or brass, have been the heroines of Mr. Fitzgerald's tales ever since he came up on the crest of the younger generation in "This Side of Paradise," he will be set immediately to fashion one of his blonde, reckless, wilful and irresponsible girls for Constance Talmadge to use as background for her sparkle.

He will go to Hollywood not to adapt any of his published pieces but to work out originals. When "This Side of Paradise" arrived with its message that college was no longer the same as when Stover went to Yale, Famous Players-Lasky bought it, and then after reading it decided that, unfortunately, their purchase was not movie material. When his next book appeared Warner's rushed out, bought "The Beautiful and the Damned" and made it into a handsome movie with Marie Prevost to swank around as Gloria. Last summer Herbert Brenon, for Paramount, developed Fitzgerald's "The Great Gatsby" into a movie. Out of his books only those three composed of jazz short stories have failed to get consideration from scenario departments.

In January-February 1927 the Fitzgeralds were in Hollywood, where he worked on an original screenplay, "Lipstick," for United Artists. This film was not produced.

Has the Flapper Cha

F. Scott Fitzgerald

Discusses the Cinema Descendants He Has Made So Well Known

By Margaret Reid

Melbourne Spurr

Scotty considers Constance Talmadge the epitome of young sophistication. . . . Fifth Avenue, diamonds, Catalya orchids and Europe every year . . . a flapper de luxe

Photograph courtesy Charles Scribner's Sons

F. Scott Fitzgerald—responsible for the word flapper itself. He defines flappers as girls with an extraordinary talent for living

THE term "flapper" has become a generalization, meaning almost any *femme* between fifteen and twenty-five. Some five years ago it was a thing of distinction—indicating a neat bit of femininity, collegiate age, who rolled her stockings, chain-smoked, had a heavy "line," mixed and drank a mean highball and radiated "It."

The manner in which the title has come into such general usage is a little involved, but quite simple. A young man wrote a book. His heroine was one of the n. bits of f. referred to above. "Flapper" was her official classification. The young man's book took the country by, as they say, storm. Girls—all the girls—read it. They read about the flapper's deportment, methods and career. And with a nice simultaneousness they became, as nearly as their varied capabilities permitted, flappers. Thus the frequency of the term today. I hope you get my point.

The young man responsible for it all, after making clear—in his book—the folly of flappers' ways, married the young person who had been the prototype for the character and started in to enjoy the royalties. The young man was F. Scott Fitzgerald, the book was "This Side of Paradise," and the flapper's name was Zelda. So about six years later they came to Hollywood and Mr. Fitzgerald wrote a screen story for Constance Talmadge. Only people dont call him Mr. Fitzgerald. They call him "Scotty."

But we dont seem to be getting anywhere. The purpose of this discursion was to hear Mr. F. Scott (or Scotch) Fitzgerald's opinion of the cinema descendants of his original brain-daughter, the Flapper.

It was with an admirable attempt to realize the seriousness of my mission that I went to his bungalow at the Ambassador. Consider, tho! By all literary standards he should have been a middle-aged gentleman with too much waist-line, too little hair and steel-rimmed spectacles. And I knew, from pictures in *Vanity Fair* and hysterical first-hand reports, that instead he was probably the best-looking thing ever turned out of Princeton. Or even (in crescendo) Harvard—or Yale. Only it was Princeton. Add "It," and the charming, vibrant, brilliant mind his work projects. My interest was perhaps a bit more than professional.

There was a large tray on the floor at the door of his suite when I reached it. On the tray were bottles of Canada Dry, some oranges, a bowl of cracked ice and —three very, very empty Bourbon bottles. There was also a card. I paused before ringing the bell and bent down to read the inscription —"With Mr. Van Vechten's kindest regards to Scott and Zelda Fitzgerald." I

Clara Bow is the quintessence of what the term "flapper" signifies . . . pretty, impudent, worldly wise, briefly clad and "hard berled"

Even the father of all flappers finds it difficult to classify Vilma Banky. He admits that she is reticent and unassuming, but he has also made note of the quality of orchids on her shoulder as she has preceded reverential escorts into theaters

P. & A.

Joan Cr... be marke... ample o... matic ... the girl ... the sma... clubs, ... great dea... hu...

Colleen ... collegi... . . . the ... child w... dered a... ents with...

Russell Ball

nged?

of the Type

Fitzgerald claims that Alice White reflects what the recent European influence on our flappers has been. Here is a girl wildly eager for every drop of life . . . a child of the moment

wford is to d as an ex- f the dra- lapper . . . you see at test night aughing a l, with wide, t eyes

Ruth Harriet Louise

Moore finds a te classification carefree, lovable o rules bewil- d adoring par- an iron hand

looked for any further message on the other side, but there was none, so I rang the bell.

It was answered by a young man of medium height. With Prince-of-Wales hair and eyes that are, I am sure, green. His features are chiseled finely. His mouth draws your attention. It is sensitive, taut and faintly contemptuous, and even in the flashing smile does not lose the indication of intense pride.

Behind him was Mrs. Fitzgerald, the *Rosamund* of "This Side of Paradise." Slim, pretty like a rather young boy; with one of those schoolgirl complexions and clear gray eyes; her hair as short as possible, slicked back. And dressed as only New Yorkers intangibly radiate smartness.

The two of them might have stepped, sophisticated and charming, from the pages of any of the Fitzgerald books.

They greeted me and discovered the tray hilariously.

"Carl Van Vechten's going-away gift," the First Flapper of the Land explained in her indolent, Alabama drawl. "He left this morning after a week's stay. Said he came here for a little peace and rest, and he disrupted the entire colony."

In the big, dimly lit room, Mrs. Fitzgerald sank sighing into a chair. She had just come from a Black Bottom lesson. F. Scott moved restlessly from chair to chair. He had just come from a studio conference and I think he'd rather have been at the Horse Show. He was also a trifle disconcerted by the impending interview. In one he had given to an avid press-lady the day before, he had said all his bright remarks. And he couldn't think up any more in such a short time.

"What, tho, were his opinions of screen flappers? As

(*Continued on page* 104)

Has the Flapper Changed?

(*Continued from page 29*)

flappers? As compared to his Original Flappers?"

"Well, I can only," he began, lighting a cigaret, putting it out and crossing to another chair, "speak about the immediate present. I know nothing of their evolution. You see, we've been living on the Riviera for three years. In that time the only movies we've seen have been a few of the very old pictures, or the Westerns they show over there. I might," his face brightening, "tell you what I think of Tom Mix."

"Scotty!" his wife cautioned quickly.

"Oh, well. . . ."

Having exhausted all the available chairs in the room, he returned to the first one and began all over again.

"Have flappers changed since you first gave them the light of publicity? For better? For worse?"

"Only in the superficial matter of clothes, hair-cut, and wise-cracks. Fundamentally they are the same. The girls I wrote about were not a type—they were a generation. Free spirits—evolved thru the war chaos and a final inevitable escape from restraint and inhibitions. If there is a difference, it is that the flappers today are perhaps less defiant, since their freedom is taken for granted and they are sure of it. In my day"—stroking his hoary beard—"they had just made their escape from dull and blind conventionality. Subconsciously there was a hint of belligerence in their attitude, because of the opposition they met—but overcame.

"On the screen, of course, is represented every phase of flapper life. But just as the screen exaggerates action, so it exaggerates type. The girl who, in real life, uses a smart, wise-cracking line is portrayed on the screen as a hard-boiled baby. The type, one of the most dangerous, whose forte is naïveté, approximates a dumb-dora when she reaches the screen. The exotic girl becomes bizarre. But the actresses who do flappers really well understand them thoroly enough to accentuate their characteristics without distorting them."

"How about Clara Bow?" I suggested, starting in practically alphabetical order.

"Clara Bow is the quintessence of what the term 'flapper' signifies as a definite description. Pretty, impudent, superbly assured, as worldly wise, briefly clad and 'hard-berled' as possible. There were hundreds of them—her prototypes. Now, completing the circle, there are thousands more—patterning themselves after her.

"Colleen Moore represents the young collegiate—the carefree, lovable child who rules bewildered but adoring parents with an iron hand. Who beats her brothers and beaus on the tennis-courts, dances like a professional and has infallible methods for getting her own way. All deliciously celluloid—but why not? The public notoriously prefer glamor to realism. Pictures like Miss Moore's flapper epics present a glamorous dream of youth and gaiety and swift, tapping feet. Youth—actual youth—is essentially crude. But the movies idealize it, even as Gershwin idealizes jazz in the Rhapsody in Blue.

"Constance Talmadge is the epitome of young sophistication. She is the deft princess of lingerie—and love—plus humor. She is Fifth Avenue and diamonds and Catalya orchids and Europe every year. She is sparkling and witty and as gracefully familiar with the new books as with the new dances. I have an idea that Connie appeals every bit as strongly to the girls in the audience as to the men. Her dash—her *zest* for things—is compelling She is the flapper *de luxe*.

"I happened to see a preview the other night, at a neighborhood movie house near here. It was Milton Sills' latest, I am told. There was a little girl in it—playing a tough baby-vamp. I found that her name was Alice White. She was a fine example of the European influence on our flappers Gradually, due mostly to imported pictures, the vogue for 'pose' is fading.

"European actresses were the first to disregard personal appearance in emotional episodes. Disarranged hair—the wrong profile to the camera—were of no account during a scene Their abandonment to emotion precluded all thought of beauty. Pola Negri brought it to this country. It was adopted by some. But the flappers seem to have been a bit nervous as to the results. It was, perhaps, safer to be cute than character. This little White girl, however, appears to have a flair for this total lack of studied effect. She is the flapper impulsive—child of the moment—wildly eager for every drop of life. She represents—not the American flapper—but the European.

"Joan Crawford is doubtless the best example of the dramatic flapper. The girl you see at the smartest night clubs—gowned to the apex of sophistication—toying iced glasses, with a remote, faintly bitter expression—dancing deliciously—laughing a great deal with wide, hurt eyes. It takes girls of actual talent to get away with this in real life. When they do perfect the thing, they have a lot of fun with it.

"Then, inevitably, there is the quality that is infallible in any era, any town, any time. Femininity, *ne plus ultra*. Unless it is a very definite part of a girl, it is insignificant, and she might as well take up exoticism. But sufficiently apparent, it is always irresistible. I suppose she isn't technically a flapper—but because she *is* Femininity, one really should cite Vilma Banky. Soft and gentle and gracious and sweet—all the lacy adjectives apply to her. This type is reticent and unassuming—but just notice the quality of orchids on her shoulder as she precedes her reverential escort into the theater

"It's rather futile to analyze flappers. They are just girls—all sorts of girls. Their one common trait being that they are young things with a splendid talent for life."

Motion Picture
JULY
25 CENTS
F. Scott Fitzgerald on Film Flappers
$500.00 in Cash Prizes. Complete in this Issue

F. Scott Fitzgerald
***on* Film Flappers**

Total loss at beginning. Ie stop fun. Work begins again.

Thirty Years Old

evening.
Mr. and Mrs. Scott Fitzgerald left Tuesday evening for Hollywood, California, where they will spend one month while Mr. Fitzgerald is writing a story for Constance Talmadge to be released by First National. The story will deal with college life. Later Mr. and Mrs. Fitzgerald will go to New York City for an extended stay.
The Fitzgeralds arrived in Montgomery for the Christmas holidays which were spent with her parents, Judge and Mrs. A. D. Sayre, and during their stay in this city they were extensively entertained. Mrs. Fitzgerald was formerly Zelda Sayre of this city and one of the city's most popular young girls. Mr. and Mrs. Fitzgerald spent the past three years in France and Italy where Mr. Fitzgerald did extensive writing.

Contrary to popular opinion, the movies of the Jazz Age had no effect upon its morals. The social attitude of the producers was timid, behind the times and banal—for example, no picture mirrored even faintly the younger generation until 1923, when magazines had already been started to celebrate it and it had long ceased to be news. There were a few feeble splutters and then Clara Bow in *Flaming Youth;* promptly the Hollywood hacks ran the theme into its cinematographic grave. Throughout the Jazz Age the movies got no farther than Mrs. Jiggs, keeping up with its most blatant superficialities. This was no doubt due to the censorship as well as to innate conditions in the industry. In any case, the Jazz Age now raced along under its own power, served by great filling stations full of money.

—"Echoes of the Jazz Age"

In Hollywood Fitzgerald was much taken with Lois Moran, who became the model for Rosemary Hoyt in Tender Is the Night.

Movie Monotypes

by RADIE HARRIS

LOIS MORAN.

Is Pittsburgh's "local girl makes good."

Knows that "And so overnight-fame" can be something besides a subtitle. Made her screen debut in "Stella Dallas" and was immediately placed under long term contract by Samuel Goldwyn.

Received her education abroad. Not supervised by Thomas Cook or Raymond Whitcomb.

Is an actress because her mother never was and wanted to be.

Yearns for Doughnut Dispensary.

Doesn't care where she lives as long as she can act, sing and dance. Thinks Paris the grandest place in the world to study; New York, the most inspiring and confusing; London, the homiest; Hollywood, the most care-free, and Vienna, the dream city.

Intends to own a combination book-shop and bakery before she dies.

Is extremely interested in Philosophy; fearfully ambitious. Admires Goethe, Voltaire, Mussolini and Bernard Shaw; thinks of Duse and Maude Adams with reverence—and loves backless evening clothes and bathing suits.

Has Plenty of "Time."

Doesn't collect anything but books she has enjoyed reading and wrist watches she keeps breaking.

Got her part in "Stella Dallas" by sending a picture of herself as Juliet to Sam Goldwyn.

Doesn't think eating is any fun without being able to read. When alone, always sits in a big chair with a book and has her meals served on a tray. Romain Rolland, F. Scott Fitzgerald, Frederick Nietzche and Rupert Brooke are her favorite authors.

Has been promising herself for two years to take a three-week pack-trip in the mountains. The nearest she ever got to it is a location visit to Death Valley.

Can Scramble Eggs.

Principle joys in life are: Acting in every size, shape or form, singing for her own amusement but no one else's—cooking (devil's food cake, cream puffs and scrambled eggs are her specialties)—conversing "tete-a-tete" until four in the morning—sleeping with the moon shining in her face—floating in the ocean at six in the evening when the water and sky are the same shimmering grey-blue — and her most enchanting and satisfying "mater."

Wants 10 children so that at least one of them can have some intelligence.

Come On, Revolution!

Thinks this country is progressing too smoothly and could stand some new revolutionary ideas.

Is a rabid Greta Garbo fan. Sees all of her pictures at least three times.

Abominates detective stories, being fitted, putting on makeup, having finger waves and "Strange Interlude."

Doesn't think she is important. Which is the most important thing about her.

LOIS MORAN

. . . one's eyes moved on quickly to her daughter, who had magic in her pink palms and her cheeks lit to a lovely flame, like the thrilling flush of children after their cold baths in the evening. Her fine high forehead sloped gently up to where her hair, bordering it like an armorial shield, burst into lovelocks and waves and curlicues of ash blonde and gold. Her eyes were bright, big, clear, wet, and shining, the color of her cheeks was real, breaking close to the surface from the strong young pump of her heart. Her body hovered delicately on the last edge of childhood—she was almost eighteen, nearly complete, but the dew was still on her.

—Tender Is the Night

Magazine illustrator Harrison Fisher sketching Zelda; his sketch of Scott at right.

Jan	California, Appendix. El Paso, Considine, Pantages, Hotel, Neilan, Hoveys, Talmadge Mayfair. Lillian Gish. Dick Barthelmess. Saunders & Dudley Murphy, Mankevitz. Carmel Myers. Eddie Mayer. Princeton dinner. Harrison Fisher. Donald Freeman Our Club. The watch. Long Beach. Patsy Ruth Miller. Gerald Cudahy. K. McGuire.
Feb	Morans, Hitchcock, Barrymores. 2nd Mayfair. Fairbanks & Pickford. Geraghty's party. Party at Lois. Rinehart. Bessy Love. Diana Manners. Iris Tree. Rosamund Pinchot. The Miracle. Marion Davies. John Colton. Dudley's picture. ~~Cut~~ ~~str~~ Morris Gest.
Mar	Roosevelt Hotel. Gladys & Carl in New York. Dick Knight & Morgan. Curry, Boyer Wilmington. Westchester bicyclimers "Ellerslie." Furniture Car. Washington Ross of the New Yorker Lardners in Great Neck. Authors League Gene Bucks new house.

The Fitzgeralds on a set with Wallace Beery (third from left) and Harrison Fisher (far right).

We reached California in time for an earthquake. It was sunny, and misty at night. White roses swung luminous in the mist from a trellis outside the Ambassador windows; a bright exaggerated parrot droned incomprehensible shouts in an aquamarine pool—of course everybody interpreted them to be obscenities; geraniums underscored the discipline of the California flora. We paid homage to the pale aloof concision of Diana Manners' primitive beauty and dined at Pickfair to marvel at Mary Pickford's dynamic subjugation of life. A thoughtful limousine carried us for California hours to be properly moved by the fragility of Lillian Gish, too aspiring for life, clinging vine-like to occultisms.

—" 'Show Mr. & Mrs. F. to Number—' " (ZF)

Fitzgerald with Richard Barthelmess on a movie set.

THE PAMPERED MEN

by F. Scott Fitzgerald

Talking the other day with a Prominent Business Man who had just visited an eastern moving-picture studio, he remarked that never in his life had he seen so much waste and inefficiency in a single day.

"Why, look here—" he began, and with such a pretty flow of words, told us how it could all be systematized, that we forgot for a moment that this was an old, old story. When Prominent Business Men go through moving picture studios they aways come out feeling very superior and contemptuous—because they imagine that turning strips of celluloid into visible stories is as simple a matter as turning western cattle into eastern roast beef.

The real fallacy of the Business Man's attitude lies, of course, in Vera Lafollette's eyes. When Vera has a cold—and Vera *will* take cold, even when she's under a two-hundred-thousand-dollar contract—her eyes grow red and dim just like yours and mine, and the lids swell. You can hardly blame her, when she's in this condition, for refusing to go before the camera. She imagines that, if she does, every inch of red-eyed film will lose her one admirer, one silver dollar, one rung on the ladder she's been climbing for years.

"Fire her!" says the Business Man with a bold air. "Why, last week when my superintendent disobeyed an order—"

But his superintendent was not the mainspring of a picture in which was tied up two hundred thousand dollars. In short, the moving picture is not a good profession for the efficiency bully. It is more often confronted with the human, the personal, the incalculable element than any other industry in the world.

But in one respect, there is much truth in the Business Man's criticism of the movie. He wants to see centralization and authority, and he sees none. Is the responsibility with the producer? No—for he seems to be dependent on the director, who, in his turn, is apparently at the mercy of his story and his star. If in movie circles, you mention a successful picture, *Tol'able David,* for example, you will hear the credit for its success claimed for the producer, the director, the star, the author, the continuity writer and Lord knows how many technical artisans who have aided in the triumph. Mention a failure and you will hear the blame heaped on each one of these in turn—and finally on the public itself, for not being "intelligent" enough to like what they get.

Well, I am going to venture three opinions on the subject—three opinions that I think more and more people are coming to hold.

First—that the moving picture is a director's business, and there never was a good picture or a bad picture for which the director was not entirely responsible.

Second—that with half a dozen exceptions, our directors are an utterly incompetent crew. Most of them entered the industry early and by accident, and the industry has outgrown them long ago.

Third—any director worth the price of his puttees should average four commercial successes out of five attempts in every year.

Let me first discuss his responsibility. In most of the big companies the director can select his own stories—the scenario departments are only too glad when a director says, "I want to do this picture and I know I can." The director who undertakes pictures he doesn't believe in is merely a hack—some ex-barnstormer who directed an illustrated song back in 1909 and is now hanging around Hollywood with nothing left except a megaphone.

The director chooses his cast, excepting the star, and he has control over the expenditure of the allotted money and over the writing and interpretation of the continuity. This is as it should be. Yet I have heard directors whining because they couldn't find a story they wanted, and the whine had the true ring of incompetence. An author who whines for a plot at least has the excuse that his imagination has given out—the director has no excuse at all. The libraries are full of many million volumes ready to his hand.

In addition, directors sometimes complain of "incompetent actors." This is merely pathetic, for it is the director's business to *make* actors. On the spoken stage the director may justly cry that once rehearsals are over the acting is out of his power. But the movie director labors under no such disadvantage. He can make an actor go through a scene twenty times and then choose the best "take" for the assembled film. And in a fragmentary affair like a movie where the last scenes may be taken first, the director *must* do the thinking for the actor. If he is unable to, he does not belong on the platform of authority. After seeing what Chaplin did with that ex-cigarette-villain, Adolphe Menjou, and what Von Stroheim accomplished with the utterly inexperienced Mary Philbin, I believe that the alibi of incompetent acting will fall upon deaf ears.

Now directing, as the hack director understands it, is to be privy to all the outworn tricks of the trade. The hack director knows how to "visualize" every emotion—that is, he knows the rubber-stamp formula, he knows how every emotion has been visualized *before*. If, in a picture, the hero departs from the heroine and the heroine wants him back, the hack director knows that she must take a step after him, hold out her hands toward him and then let them drop to her side. He knows that when someone dies in the street, this is always "visualized" by having a kneeling bystander take off his hat. If someone dies in a house, a sheet is invariably drawn over his face.

Very well, let us see how Chaplin, greatest of all directors, conveyed this latter event in *The Woman of Paris*. He realized that the old convention was outworn, that it no longer had the power of calling the emotions to attention, so he invented a new way. The audience does not see the dying man at all; it sees the backs of the surrounding crowd and suddenly a waiter pushes his way out of that crowd, shaking his head. At once the whole horrible violence of the suicide is plain to us. We even understand the human vanity of the waiter in wanting to be first to convey the news.

We may forget that incident because the picture is full of spanking new effects but, when it is over, every bit of it, despite the shoddy mounting and the sentimentalized story, seems vastly important. Chaplin has a fine imaginative mind and he threw himself hard into his picture—it is the lazy man, the "wise old-timer," in other words, the hack, who takes the timeworn easy way.

All I am saying comes down to this—

The chief business of a director is *to invent new business to express the old emotions.*

An "original" picture is not a story of a lunatic wanting the north star. It is the story of a little girl wanting a piece of candy—but our attention must be called with sharp novelty to the fact that she wants it. The valuable director is not he who makes a dull "artistic" transcription of Conrad's *Victory*—give me the fellow who can blow the breath of life into a soggy gum-drop like *Pollyanna*.

Perhaps such men will appear. We have Griffith—just when he seems to be exhausted, he has a way of sitting up suddenly in his grave. We have Cruze, who can be forgiven *The Covered Wagon* if only for the amazing dream scene in *Hollywood*. We have Von Stroheim, who has a touch of real civilization in his make-up and, greatest of all, Chaplin, who almost invented the movies as a vehicle for personal expression. There are half a dozen others I could name—Sennett, Lubitsch, Ingram, Cecil De Mille, Dwan—who in the last five years have made two or three big successes interspersed with countless reels of drooling mediocrity, but I have my doubts about them; we must demand more than that.

As for the rest of the directors—let a thick, impenetrable curtain fall. Occasionally, a picture made by some jitney Griffith is successful because of the intelligence of self-directing stars—but beware of such accidents. The man's next effort is likely to show the true barrenness and vulgarity of his mind.

One more remark—I doubt if successful directors will ever be found among established authors—though they may, perhaps, among playwrights and not-too-seasoned continuity men. Author-directors have a way of condescending to their audiences. Bad as Rupert Hughes' books are, they are seldom as silly and meretricious as his pictures. I suspect that his mind is on Minnie McGlook, the girl-fan of North Dakota, and not on his work—

which is—

to believe in his story, to keep his whole story in his head for ten weeks and, above all, *to invent new business to express old emotions.* All we ask from any of them is a little imagination and a little true feeling for the joys and the hopes and the everlasting struggles of mankind.

This previously unpublished article was probably written in 1924.

The Fitzgeralds rented "Ellerslie" in March 1927. It was their residence until March 1929.

We leased a very big old mansion on the Delaware River. The squareness of the rooms and the sweep of the columns were to bring us a judicious tranquility. There were sombre horse-chestnuts in the yard and a white pine bending as graciously as a Japanese brush drawing.

—" 'Show Mr. and Mrs. F. to Number—' " (ZF)

Guest of Honor

Scott - Lois - Ernest - Ted - Carl

JAZZ AGE WRITER MAKES HOME HERE

F. Scott Fitzgerald to Live Near Edge Moor to Finish His Novel.

F. Scott Fitzgerald, novelist and playwright, has made his home in the old Bradford mansion, "Ellersley," on the banks of the Delaware river, near Edge Moor.

He moves here with his wife and four-year-old daughter, Frances, and will live here for about two years. For the past few years, Mr. Fitzgerald has been "making the grand tour," living in various places in Europe, particularly in France and Italy.

He chose the site near Wilmington, particularly because he is a personal friend of John Biggs, Jr., lawyer, of this city, and because he wanted a quiet place to finish a novel. The new novel will be a picaresque one, different from his others, which have been emphasizing the current jazz age.

The Bradford house is a spacious Colonial building, with an expansive view of the river.

Mr. Fitzgerald left Princeton University in 1917 to join the army as an officer. His first novel was "This Side of Paradise," published in 1920. This was followed by "The Beautiful and Damned," issued in 1921; "Tales of Jazz Age," 1922; "The Great Gatsby," in 1925; "All the Sad Young Men," 1926.

His play, "The Vegetable," written in 1923, had its premier in Wilmington.

OUR FIRST HOUSE-PARTY

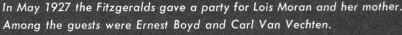

In May 1927 the Fitzgeralds gave a party for Lois Moran and her mother. Among the guests were Ernest Boyd and Carl Van Vechten.

At "Ellerslie" Fitzgerald organized a croquet-polo match which was won by Ludlow Fowler, seen here with his victory cup and Townsend Martin.

Fitzgerald's parents visiting "Ellerslie."

The tempo of the city had changed sharply. The uncertainties of 1920 were drowned in a steady golden roar and many of our friends had grown wealthy. But the restlessness of New York in 1927 approached hysteria. The parties were bigger—those of Condé Nast, for example, rivaled in their way the fabled halls of the nineties; the pace was faster—the catering to dissipation set an example to Paris; the shows were broader, the buildings were higher, the morals were looser and the liquor was cheaper; but all these benefits did not really minister to much delight. . . .

We settled a few hours from New York and I found that every time I came to the city I was caught up into a complication of events that deposited me a few days later in a somewhat exhausted state on the train for Delaware.

—"My Lost City"

182
Perhaps its the Thirties but I can't even be very depressed about it

Thirty-one Years Old

CHRONOLOGICAL LAMP

Zelda painted a lampshade depicting all of the houses the Fitzgeralds had lived in and their servants. (See color section.)

Marjorie, Noonie and Mrs Sayre

Fitzgerald and "Amy" (unidentified) at a nearby amusement park.

"CHAT" in his salad days: The daily torture

Zelda with her mother, father, daughter, and niece ("Noonie") on the boardwalk.

SAYRES AT ATLANTIC CITY

HOME AGAIN

In July 1927, the Fitzgeralds went to Virginia Beach, Virginia to see "Cousin Ceci" and the Norfolk relatives. Scottie broke her arm running on the beach.

This is to remind you about September. We'll be having some sort of party here and then we'll go to New York for a day or two and see some shows. So save a week for us. When is your vacation?

We're just leaving for Long Island to visit Tommy Hitchcock and watch the polo (Zelda prays nightly that the Prince of Wales will come down from Canada), then we're visiting some people in Genesee and back here by the eighteenth. We talk of you all so often—I can't tell you how proud of you I am for being such exceptionally gorgeous people, or how much I enjoyed being with you and feeling pleasantly linked up with you. I know when I say how few people in the world really count at all, it seems to you a mere piece of snobbishness, but to me it's simply a bare, cold, unpleasant fact. People have always subconsciously recognized this by letting vitality atone for many more sins than charity can. You five are among those "for whom the physical world exists." For most people it simply glides by in a half-comprehended and unenjoyed dream. And

We Both Love You.

—FSF to Cecilia Taylor, August 1927.

Cecelia Taylor (nicknamed "Teah"), one of cousin Ceci's daughters, came to visit the Fitzgeralds at "Ellerslie," in September 1927. Above, left to right: Richard Knight, Zelda, John Dos Passos, and "Teah."

Fitzgerald was fond of showing his guests some glass slides of World War I which he had bought in Paris. "Teah" is holding the viewer; horizontal man is unidentified.

WAR PICTURES

In the fall Zelda began lessons at Catherine Littlefield's ballet school in Philadelphia. "Teah" is checking train time.

Off for Ballet School

The END of summer

THE SNOW FALLS AT ELLERSLIE ALSO

In 1927, stalled on his novel, Fitzgerald started writing the "Basil" stories about his boyhood in St. Paul. The first of these, "The Captured Shadow," appeared in The Saturday Evening Post *in April 1928. Both Perkins and Ober wanted him to make a book of the stories, which were well-received, but he refused to do so for fear he would be classed with Booth Tarkington, author of the popular "Penrod" series.*

Barely remembering to put away the Scandal Book and the box of disguises, the two boys hurried out, mounted their bicycles and rode up the alley.

The Whartons' own children had long grown up, but their yard was still one of those predestined places where young people gather in the afternoon. It had many advantages. It was large, open to other yards on both sides, and it could be entered upon skates or bicycles from the street. It contained an old seesaw, a swing and a pair of flying rings; but it had been a rendezvous before these were put up, for it had a child's quality—the thing that makes young people huddle inextricably on uncomfortable steps and desert the houses of their friends to herd on the obscure premises of "people nobody knows." The Whartons' yard had long been a happy compromise; there were deep shadows there all day long and ever something vague in bloom, and patient dogs around, and brown spots worn bare by countless circling wheels and dragging feet. In sordid poverty, below the bluff two hundred feet away, lived the "micks"—they had merely inherited the name, for they were now largely of Scandinavian descent—and when other amusements palled, a few cries were enough to bring a gang of them swarming up the hill, to be faced if numbers promised well, to be fled from into convenient houses if things went the other way.

It was five o'clock and there was a small crowd gathered there for that soft and romantic time before supper—a time surpassed only by the interim of summer dusk thereafter. Basil and Riply rode their bicycles around abstractedly, in and out of trees, resting now and then with a hand on someone's shoulder, shading their eyes from the glow of the late sun that, like youth itself, is too strong to face directly, but must be kept down to an undertone until it dies away.

—"The Scandal Detectives"

This letter is inspired by a desire to tell Betty that in a story of mine called The Scandal Detectives which will be in the Post in April I've tried to pay some tribute to that celebrated children's meeting place, the Ames' backyard. Please clip it and save it for your children, for sooner or later time will wipe out that pleasant spot.

—FSF to Norris Jackson, 28 April 1928.

DOINGS ON THE THIRD FLOOR

For Christmas 1927 Zelda made an elaborate doll's house for Scottie.

A poetic Christmas exchange with the Ring Lardners.

We combed Fifth Avenue this last month
A hundred times if we combed it onth,
In search of something we thought would do
To give to a person as nice as you.

We had no trouble selecting gifts
For the Ogden Armours and Louie Swifts,
The Otto Kahns and the George E. Bakers,
The Munns and the Rodman Wanamakers.

It's a simple matter to pick things out
For people one isn't so wild about,
But you, you wonderful pal and friend, you!
We couldn't find anything fit to send you.

THE RING LARDNERS

To the Ring Lardners

You combed Third Avenue last year
For some small gift that was not too dear
-- Like a candy cane or a worn out truss--
To give to a loving friend like us
You'd found gold eggs for such wealthy hicks
As the Edsell Fords and the Pittsburgh Fricks
The Andy Mellons, the Teddy Shonts
The Coleman T. and Pierre duPonts
But not one gift to brighten our hoem
-- So I'm sending you back your God damn poem.

In February 1928 Scott and Zelda visited Canada at the invitation of a Canadian travel bureau.

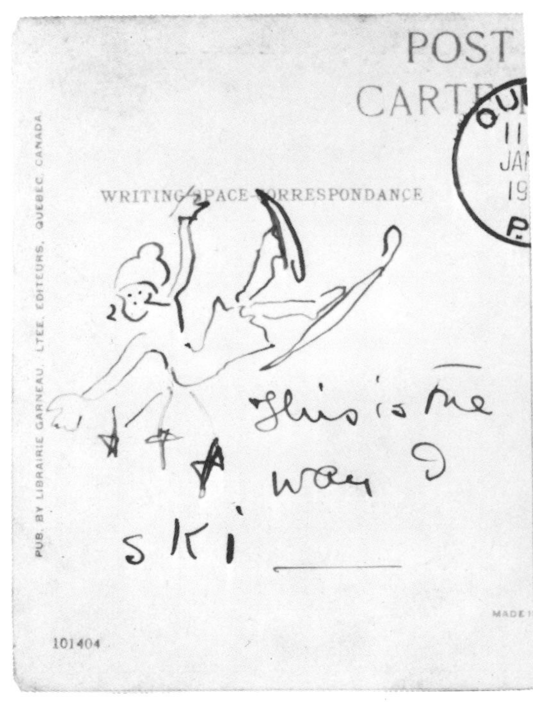

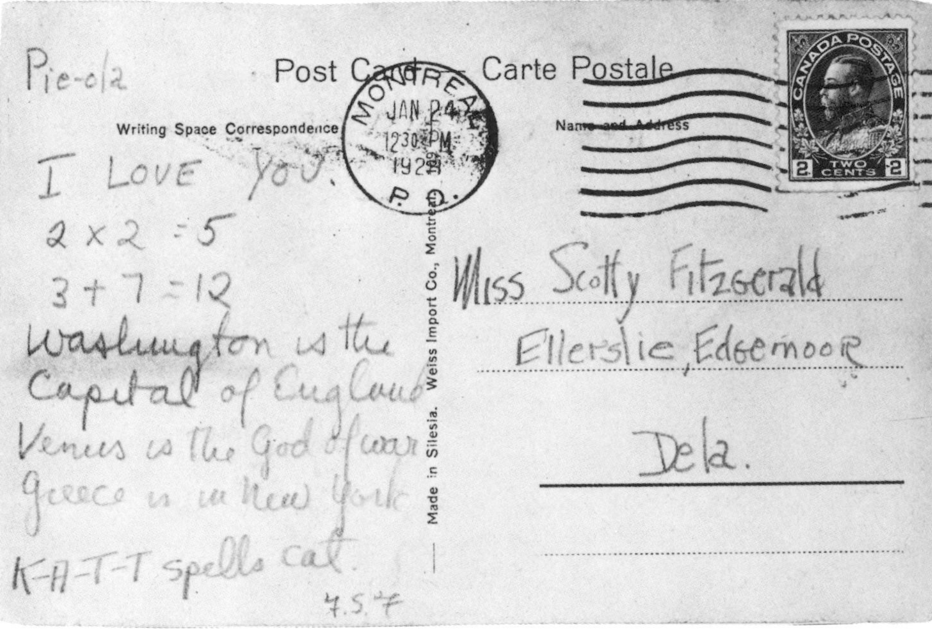

Pie-ola
Post Card — Carte Postale
Writing Space Correspondence
Name and Address
MONTREAL JAN 24 12.30 PM 1928 P.Q.
CANADA POSTAGE TWO CENTS 2
I LOVE YOU.
2 x 2 = 5
3 + 7 = 12
Washington is the Capital of England
Venus is the God of war
Greece is in New York
K-A-T-T spells cat.
F.S.F.
Made in Silesia. Weiss Import Co., Montreal
Miss Scotty Fitzgerald
Ellerslie, Edgemoor
Dela.

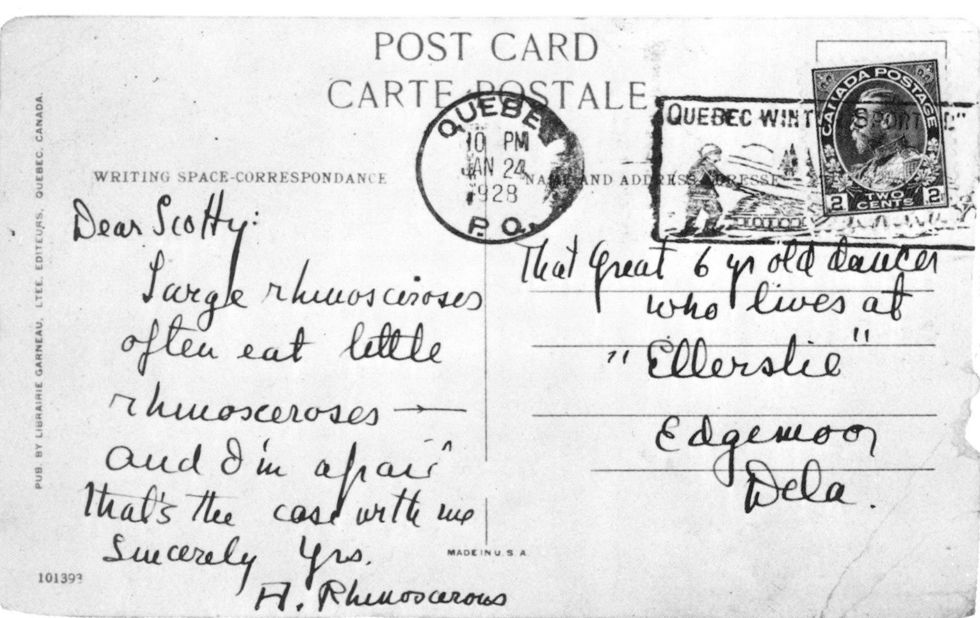

Next time we went, lost and driven now like the rest, it was a free trip north to Quebec. They thought maybe we'd write about it. The Château Frontenac was built of toy stone arches, a tin soldier's castle. Our voices were truncated by the heavy snow, the stalactite icicles on the low roofs turned the town to a wintry cave; we spent most of our time in an echoing room lined with skis, because the professional there gave us a good feeling about the sports at which we were so inept. He was later taken up by the DuPonts on the same basis and made a powder magnate or something.

—" 'Show Mr. and Mrs. F. to Number—' " (ZF)

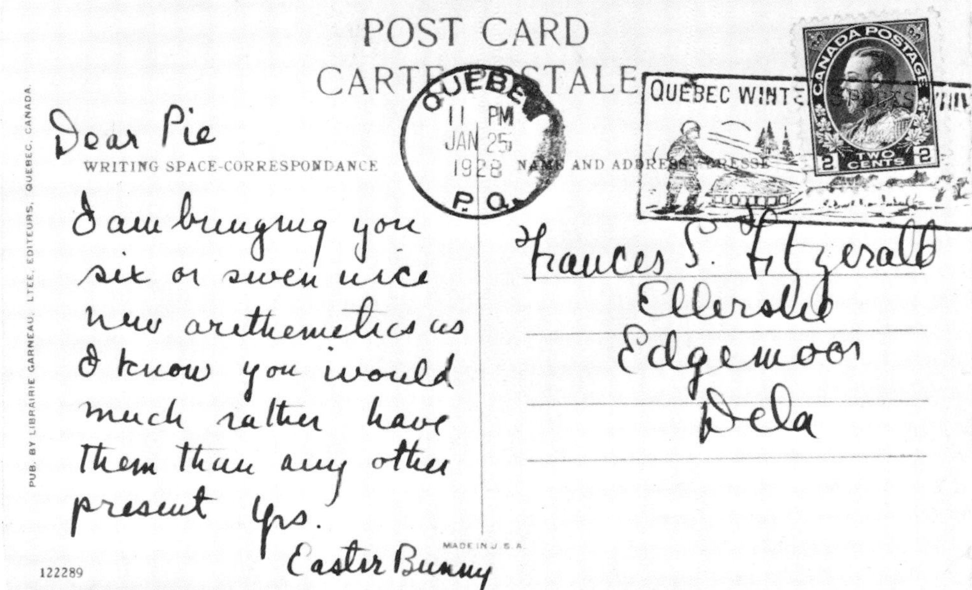
POST CARD
CARTE POSTALE

QUEBEC 11 PM JAN 25 1928 P.Q.

QUEBEC WINTER SPORTS

CANADA POSTAGE TWO CENTS 2

WRITING SPACE-CORRESPONDANCE

NAME AND ADDRESS-ADRESSE

Dear Pie

I am bringing you six or seven nice new arithmetics as I know you would much rather have them than any other present Yrs.

Easter Bunny

Frances S. Fitzgerald
Ellerslie
Edgemoor
Dela

PUB. BY LIBRAIRIE GARNEAU, LTEE, EDITEURS, QUEBEC, CANADA.

122289

MADE IN U.S.A.

PETITE RUE SOUS-LE-CAP, QUEBEC, CANADA.

CHUTES MONTMORENCY, QUEBEC, CANADA.

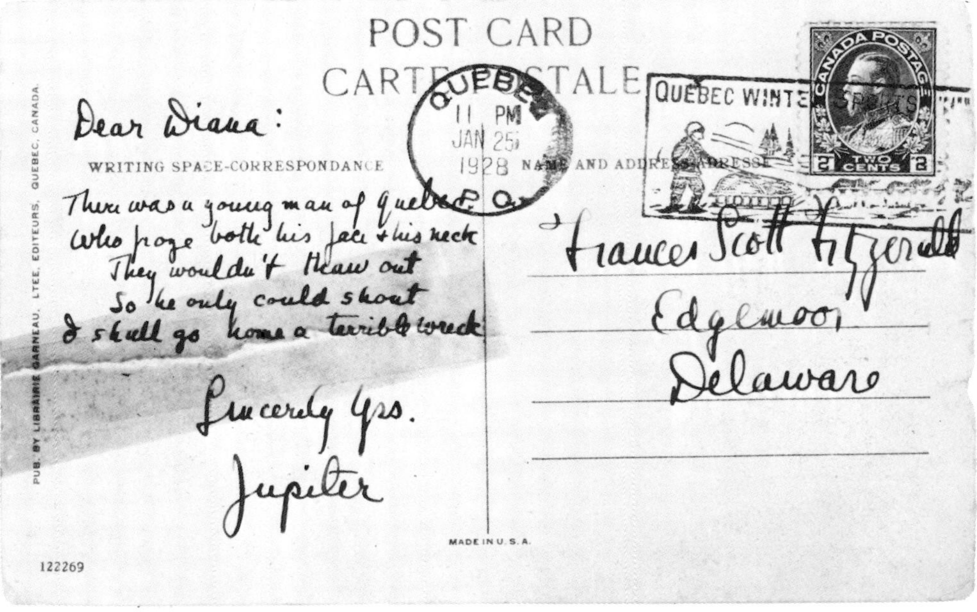
POST CARD
CARTE POSTALE

QUEBEC 11 PM JAN 25 1928 P.Q.

QUEBEC WINTER SPORTS

CANADA POSTAGE TWO CENTS 2

WRITING SPACE-CORRESPONDANCE

NAME AND ADDRESS-ADRESSE

Dear Diana:

There was a young man of Quebec
Who froze both his face & his neck
They wouldn't thaw out
So he only could shout
I shall go home a terrible wreck

Sincerely Yrs.

Jupiter

Frances Scott Fitzgerald
Edgemoor,
Delaware

PUB. BY LIBRAIRIE GARNEAU, LTEE, EDITEURS, QUEBEC, CANADA.

122269

MADE IN U.S.A.

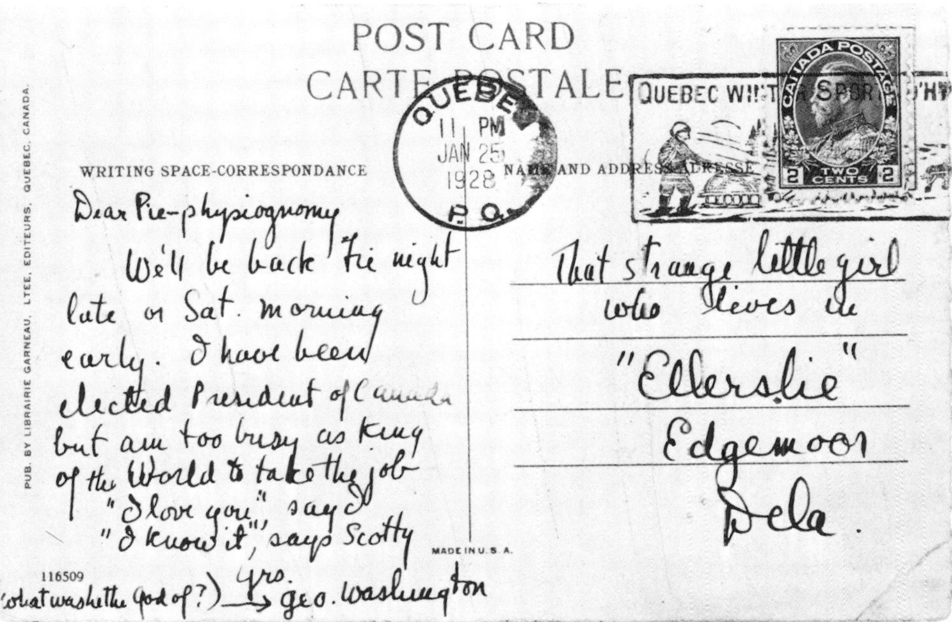
POST CARD
CARTE POSTALE

QUEBEC 11 PM JAN 25 1928 P.Q.

QUEBEC WINTER SPORTS

CANADA POSTAGE TWO CENTS 2

WRITING SPACE-CORRESPONDANCE

NAME AND ADDRESS-ADRESSE

Dear Pie-physiognomy

We'll be back Fri night late or Sat. morning early. I have been elected President of Canada but am too busy as King of the World to take the job

"I love you", says
"I know it", says Scotty

(what was the God of?) → Yrs. Geo. Washington

That strange little girl
who lives in
"Ellerslie"
Edgemoor
Dela.

PUB. BY LIBRAIRIE GARNEAU, LTEE, EDITEURS, QUEBEC, CANADA.

116509

MADE IN U.S.A.

OEUVRE DE MESSIEURS, ANDRE VERMARRE, SCULPTEUR ET MAXIME ROISIN, ARCHITECTE DE PARIS.

En route to France, April 1928.

(In those days of going to pieces and general disintegration it was charming to see them together.) Their friends were divided into two camps as to whose stamina it was that kept them going and comparatively equilibrated in that crazy world of ours playing at prisoner's base across the Atlantic Ocean.

—"A Couple of Nuts" (ZF)

June	Esther, Emily & the fairies, Ballet Russe, James Joyce, Sylvia Beach, Adrienne Monier, Lipps, Premiers, Montagne, Emile, Guffon, Trianon. Victor Llona, Cole Porter, Carried home from Ritz, disagreeable memories
July	Bishops again, another story, Opera, Battlefields, Rheims, Hadley Hemingway. Drinking & general unpleasantness, Bathroom, first trip jail, Princeton man painter on Rue Schiffer, Margaret Bishop's tailor, Dick Knight, Frank Baker & Paul Mulholland, Blanche Knopf, Cole Porter
Aug	Ted Wilder, Zelli's, Buzz Law, Vient de Paraitre, Grand Guignol, La Baule, Auto Trip, Cary Ross & dive in Lido, second trip jail., Wilder & Tunney, Columbus Bricks. General aimlessness & boredom. Lucien, Overcoat. Baby crying

The Fitzgeralds went to Paris for spring and summer 1928. At this time Zelda commenced her lessons with the Russian ballet.

On the "Paris", April 1928

"How did you manage?" said Alabama breathlessly. "How did you get in the ballet? And get to be important?"

The woman regarded her with velvety bootblack's eyes, begging the world not to forget her, that she herself might exist oblivious.

"But I was born in the ballet." Alabama accepted the remark as if it were an explanation of life.

"Please, Madame," Alabama persisted intently, "would you give me a letter to whoever trains the ballet? I would do anything in the world to learn to do that."

The shaved head scanned Alabama enigmatically.

"Whatever for?" she said. "It is a hard life. One suffers. Your husband could surely arrange——"

"Do you think, Madame, that I am too old?" Alabama persisted.

"Yes," said the Princess briefly.

Alabama went secretly over her body. It was rigid, like a lighthouse. "It might do," she mumbled, the words rising through her elation like a swimmer coming up from a deep dive.

"Who can give me a letter to the necessary people?"

"I will, my dear—I have all the unobtainable entrées in Paris. But it's only fair to warn you that the gold streets of heaven are hard on the feet."

—*Save Me the Waltz* (ZF)

Madame Lubov Egorova, Zelda's ballet teacher.

F. Scott Fitzgerald Gene Tunney
Théodore Rousseau
Robert Guillermo

Gene and I called by to meet Zelda and
MR. THORNTON N. WILDER
to clear the egg with you. See you Tuesday at the Racket ever Thorn.

Everyone except Thornton Wilder (bottom left) signed this photograph during Gene Tunney's visit to Paris in August 1928.

Looking Back

¶ By F. Scott and

What has become of the youth which for so many years bore the blame for everything except the Prohibition Amendment, now that they are turning thirty and receiving the portions of responsibility doled out as we pass that landmark? For by that time one has either earned the right to take chances or established himself as indispensable in some routine.

As a matter of fact, the increasing importance of the youngest war generation is a constant surprise. If this, in some measure, is due to the inevitable vacancies left as others move on, it is also the result of a sort of debonair desperation—a necessity for forcing the moments of life into an adequacy to the emotions of ten years ago. The men who at twenty-one led companies of two hundred must, it seems to us, feel an eternal let-down from a time when necessity and idealism were one single thing and no compromise was ever necessary. That willingness to face issues, a relic of ten years ago, is perhaps the explanation of some of the unrest and dissatisfaction of today. With millions of young people ready to "face things" with so much personal feeling I can think of nothing short of another national crisis which would furnish strong enough material to unify and direct such valiant insistence upon essentials.

Success was the goal for this generation and to a startling extent they have attained it, and now we venture to say that, if intimately approached, nine in ten would confess that success is only a decoration they wished to wear; what they really wanted is something deeper and richer than that. An habituation to enormous effort during the years of the war left a necessity for trials and tests on them.

In those years of panic during and immediately after the war age became a sort of caste system, so that all people of the same number of years were automatically antagonistic to all others. Perhaps it was the civil effect of draft laws and perhaps it was because the days were so full around that time that each additional year of age seemed like an added century of emotional experience. Even the knitting of gray wool socks and the packing of Red Cross boxes was regulated by ages. The lowest of all these strata, the boys and girls who were just too young to go to France, blossomed out shortly afterwards as the Younger Generation. Even so late as a year ago people's attitudes and animosities toward a generation prematurely forced to maturity, furnished an astounding amount of newspaper copy.

The jazz and the petting parties with which that generation "tapered off" have become the custom of the country and the world has become interested in more mature crimes. Now that we have recovered our equilibrium we see again the superior attraction of the ax murder as opposed to the mythical checked corset, and the newest generation of young people is being born full-grown, parroting forth the ideas of President Coolidge or of H. L. Mencken in the rhythmic meters of Lloyd Mayer.

It was not only the war. The war was merely a heightening and hurrying forward of the inevitable reaction against the false premises doled out to their children by the florid and for the most fatuous mothers of the 'nineties and the early nineteen hundreds, parents who didn't experience the struggles and upheavals of the 'sixties and 'seventies and had no inkling of the cataclysmic changes the next decade would bring. Children were safe in the world and producing them apparently ended the mother's responsibility. With the streets free from automobiles and morals free from movies and, in a large portion of America, corners already free from saloons, what did it matter what these children thought as they lay awake on warm summer nights straining to catch the cries of newsboys about the attempted assassination of Roosevelt and the victory of Johnson at Reno? It was a romantic time to be a child, to be old enough to feel the excitement being stored up around them and to be young enough to feel safe. Formed in such a period of pregnant placidity, left free to wonder and dream in a changing age with little or no pressure exerted upon them

EIGHT YEARS

Zelda Fitzgerald

by life, it is not amazing that when time, having brought everything else out of the hat, produced his *pièce de résistance,* the war, these children realized too soon that they had seen the magician's whole repertoire. This was the last piece of wizardry they believed in, and now, nearing middle age and the period when they are to be the important people of the world, they still hope wistfully that things will again have the magic of the theater. The teapot dome, and Mrs. Snyder and the unspeakable Forbes do not quite fill the gap.

It is not altogether the prosperity of the country and the consequent softness of life which have made them unstable, for almost invariably they are tremendously energetic; there has never been a time when so many positions of importance have been occupied by such young men or when the pages of newspapers and anthologies have borne the names of so many people under thirty. It is a great emotional disappointment resulting from the fact that life moved in poetic gestures when they were younger and has now settled back into buffoonery. And with the current insistence upon youth as the finest and richest time in the life of man it is small wonder that sensitive young people are haunted and harassed by a sense of unfilled destiny and grope about between the ages of twenty-five and forty with a baffled feeling of frustration. The philosophy with which most of the adolescents were equipped implied that life was a truncated affair ceasing abruptly with the twenty-first birthday, and it is hardly of enough stamina to serve an age in which so many have tasted the essence of life—which is death—just as a balloon is biggest when it bursts. From those inflated years to being concerned over whether the most oil or gold was stolen from the Government is a difficult adjustment but perhaps the cynicism with which the war generation approaches general affairs will eventually lead to a more intelligent attitude—even in the dim future to actual social interest.

Perhaps it is that we are still feeling the relaxation of the post-war years, but surely some of this irony and dissatisfaction with things supposedly solid and secure proceeds from the fact that more young people in this era were intense enough or clever enough or sensitive or shrewd enough to get what they wanted before they were mature enough to want the thing they acquired as an end and not merely as a proof of themselves. Perhaps we worked too much over man as the individual, so that his capabilities are far superior to the problems of life, and now we have endless youth of a responsible age floundering about in a morass of unused powers and feeling very bitter and mock heroic like all people who think the element of chance in their lives should have been on a bigger scale. Outside of war men of the hour haven't had a romantic opportunity near home since the last gold rush and a great proportion of young men feel that their mental agility or physical prowess can never be really measured in situations of their own making. This has perhaps been true of all times but it is more pronounced now that emergencies have, faced with the tremendous superiority of modern youth, lost their dignity as acts of God and been definitely relegated to the category of human inefficiency, if they are recognized at all.

We wonder if that is because a whole generation accustomed itself to a basic feeling that there are two ways to be; dead and alive, preferably alive and probably dead. So that now the nuances and gradations of society in general seem of the same importance as the overtones of society in particular; sauce and trimmings make better eating than the meat. And we predict a frightful pandemonium to eat it in unless indeed every generation has gone through the same difficulties of adjustment. It may be that this one is simply more expressive. Oddly enough we have but one set of contemporaries. It has always surprised us that whether there is a war or not we will always be of the war generation and we will always have unclarified ways of reacting, privy only to ourselves.

37

College Humor, *June 1928*

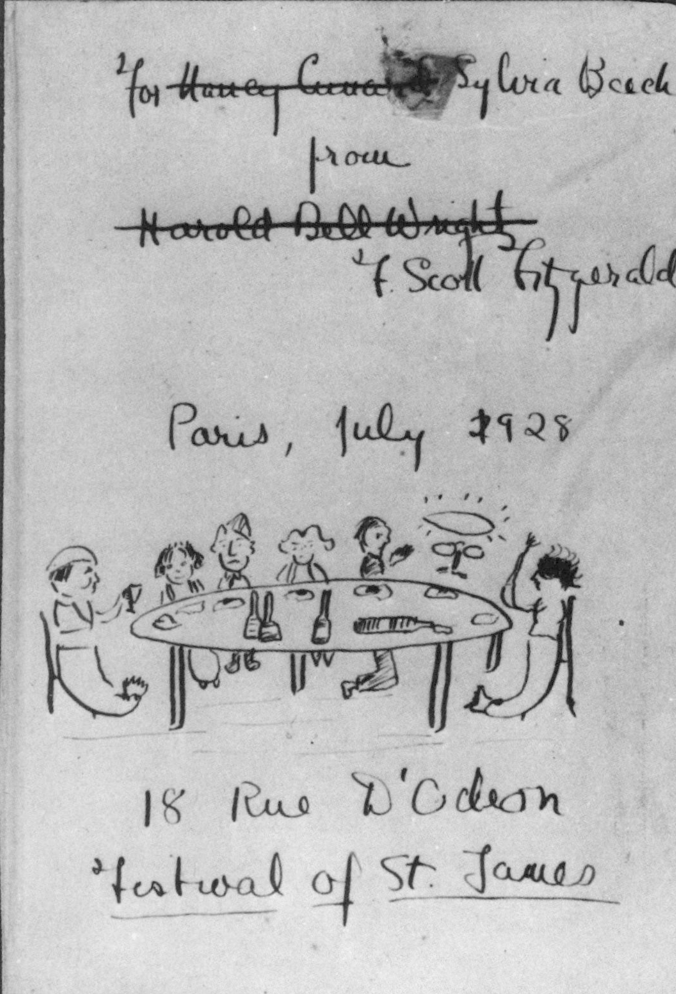

for Sylvia Beach
from
F. Scott Fitzgerald
Paris, July 1928
18 Rue D'Odeon
Festival of St. James

André Chamson

Fitzgerald's cartoon in Sylvia Beach's copy of The Great Gatsby: l. to r., Adrienne Monnier, Lucie Chamson, André Chamson, Zelda, Scott, James Joyce, Sylvia Beach.

(1) The novel goes fine. I think it's quite wonderful & I think those who've seen it (for I've read it around a little) have been quite excited. I was encouraged the other day, when James Joyce came to dinner, when he said, "Yes, I expect to finish my novel in three or four years more at the latest," & he works 11 hrs a day to my intermittent 8. Mine will be done sure *in September.*

(2) Did you get my letter about André Chamson? *Really, Max, you're missing a great opportunity if you don't take that up. Radiguet was perhaps obscene—Chamson is absolutely* not*—he's head over heels the best young man here, like Ernest & Thornton Wilder rolled into one. This* Hommes de la Route *(Road Menders) is his second novel & all but won the Prix Goncourt—the story of men building a road, with all of the force of K. Hamsun's* Growth of the Soil*—not a bit like Tom Boyds bogus American husbandmen.*

—FSF to Maxwell Perkins, c. 21 July 1928.

Ten years later (1928)

a lot of Duds, all highly explosive on the Chemin des Dames

One of the great disappointments of Fitzgerald's life was not getting overseas during World War I. He read voluminously on the subject of the western front.

"This western-front business couldn't be done again, not for a long time. The young men think they could do it but they couldn't. They could fight the first Marne again but not this. This took religion and years of plenty and tremendous sureties and the exact relation that existed between the classes. The Russians and Italians weren't any good on this front. You had to have a whole-souled sentimental equipment going back further than you could remember. You had to remember Christmas, and postcards of the Crown Prince and his fiancée, and little cafés in Valence and beer gardens in Unter den Linden and weddings at the mairie, and going to the Derby, and your grandfather's whiskers."

"General Grant invented this kind of battle at Petersburg in sixty-five."

"No, he didn't—he just invented mass butchery. This kind of battle was invented by Lewis Carroll and Jules Verne and whoever wrote Undine, and country deacons bowling and marraines in Marseilles and girls seduced in the back lanes of Wurtemburg and Westphalia. Why, this was a love battle—there was a century of middle-class love spent here. This was the last love battle."

—*Tender Is the Night*

2, SQUARE ROBIAC
192, RUE DE GRENELLE

Dear Mr Fitzgerald: Herewith is the book you gave me signed and I am doing a portrait of the artist as a once young man with the thanks of your much obliged but most pusillanimous guest.

11.7.929

sincerely yours
James Joyce

France was a land, England was a people, but America, having about it still that quality of the idea, was harder to utter—it was the graves at Shiloh and the tired, drawn, nervous faces of its great men, and the country boys dying in the Argonne for a phrase that was empty before their bodies withered. It was a willingness of the heart.

—"The Swimmers"

Fitzgerald pasted a letter from James Joyce in his copy of Ulysses. Joyce's description of himself as "pusillanimous" is probably a reference to his distress at Fitzgerald's offer to commemorate the "Festival of St. James" by jumping out of a window.

Omissions | Thirty two, Years Old (And sore as hell about it) 183

No Real Progress in any way + wrecked myself with dozens of people.

Sept | Home on the aforesaid stormy Carmania. Max at Dock. Phillipe + Ulle. Ellerslie. Joe the barber. General Prosperity. Candy store. Diet eating at hotel

March 1929

Last photo of father

This was the last time Fitzgerald saw his father, who died in January 1931. "He's lived always in mother's shadow," he wrote Harold Ober, "and he takes an immense vicarious pleasure in any success of mine."

Her son was a successful author. She had by no means abetted him in the choice of that profession but had wanted him to be an army officer or else go into business like his brother. An author was something distinctly peculiar—there had been only one in the middle western city where she was born and he had been regarded as a freak. Of course if her son could have been an author like Longfellow, or Alice and Phoebe Cary, that would have been different, but she did not even remember the names of who wrote the three hundred novels and memoirs that she skimmed through every year. . . . How lovely the poems had been! Especially the one about the girl instructing the artist how to paint a picture of her mother. Her own mother used to read her that poem.

But the books by her son were not vivid to her, and while she was proud of him in a way, and was always glad when a librarian mentioned him or when someone asked her if she was his mother, her secret opinion was that such a profession was risky and eccentric.

—"An Author's Mother"

I ran away when I was seven on the fourth of July—I spent the day with a friend in a pear orchard and the police were informed that I was missing and on my return my father thrashed me according to the custom of the nineties—on the bottom and let me come out and watch the night fireworks from the balcony with my pants still down and my behind smarting—knowing in my heart that he was absolutely right. Afterwards, seeing in his face his regret that it had to happen I asked him to tell me a story. I knew what it would be—he had only a few, the story of the Spy, the one about the Thumbs, the one about Early's march.

—"The Death of My Father"

The impression of the fames and the domains, the vistas and the glories of Maryland followed many a young man West after the Civil War and my father was of that number. Much of my early childhood in Minnesota was spent in asking him such questions as:

"—and how long did it take Early's column to pass Glenmary that day?" (That was a farm in Montgomery County.)

and:

"—what would have happened if Jeb Stewart's cavalry had joined Lee instead of raiding all the way to Rockville?"

and:

"—tell me again about how you used to ride through the woods with a spy up behind you on the horse."

or:

"Why wouldn't they let Francis Scott Key off the British frigate?

—Foreword to Don Swann's *Colonial and Historic Homes of Maryland*

Scottie, Zelda, and Scott's parents.

Our Fourth Trip Abroad March 1929—

The Photographer— a Thespian Man

The Renault

Villa Fleur des Bois

Coming out to lunch

at the Gate

Between July and October 1929 the Fitzgeralds were at the Villa Fleur des Bois, Cannes.

House near the Beach

Toward The Beach

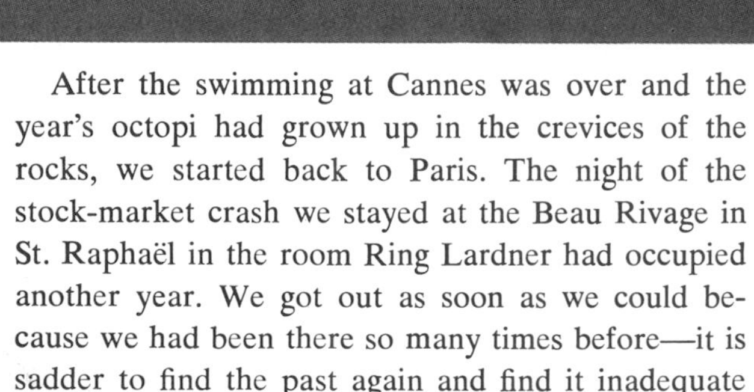

After the swimming at Cannes was over and the year's octopi had grown up in the crevices of the rocks, we started back to Paris. The night of the stock-market crash we stayed at the Beau Rivage in St. Raphaël in the room Ring Lardner had occupied another year. We got out as soon as we could because we had been there so many times before—it is sadder to find the past again and find it inadequate to the present than it is to have it elude you and remain forever a harmonious conception of memory.

At the Jules César in Arles we had a room that had once been a chapel. Following the festering waters of a stagnant canal we came to the ruins of a Roman dwelling-house. There was a blacksmith shop installed behind the proud columns and a few scattered cows ate the gold flowers off the meadow.

—" 'Show Mr. and Mrs. F. to Number—' " (ZF)

Then up and up; the twilit heavens expanded in the Cévennes valley, cracking the mountains apart, and there was a fearsome loneliness brooding on the flat tops. We crunched chestnut burrs on the road and aromatic smoke wound out of the mountain cottages. The Inn looked bad, the floors were covered with sawdust, but they gave us the best pheasant we ever ate and the best sausage, and the feather-beds were wonderful.

In Vichy, the leaves had covered the square about the wooden bandstand. Health advice was printed on the doors at the Hôtel du Parc and on the menu, but the salon was filled with people drinking champagne. We loved the massive trees in Vichy and the way the friendly town nestles in a hollow.

By the time we got to Tours, we had begun to feel like Cardinal Balue in his cage in the little Renault. The Hôtel de l'Univers was equally stuffy but after dinner we found a café crowded with people playing checkers and singing choruses and we felt we could go on to Paris after all.

—" 'Show Mr. and Mrs. F. to Number—' " (ZF)

Aix-en-Provence

PROVENCE

Autumn 1929

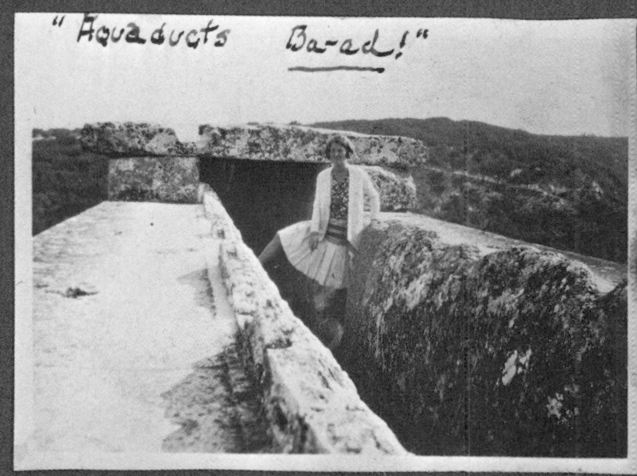

"Aquaducts Ba-ad!"

Fountains at Aix

"LET ME TAKE YOU!"

The [illegible] (Château de Blois)

"Oh Scott, put him down"

Farewell to Blah

Through the Cevennes and Auvergne to Vichy

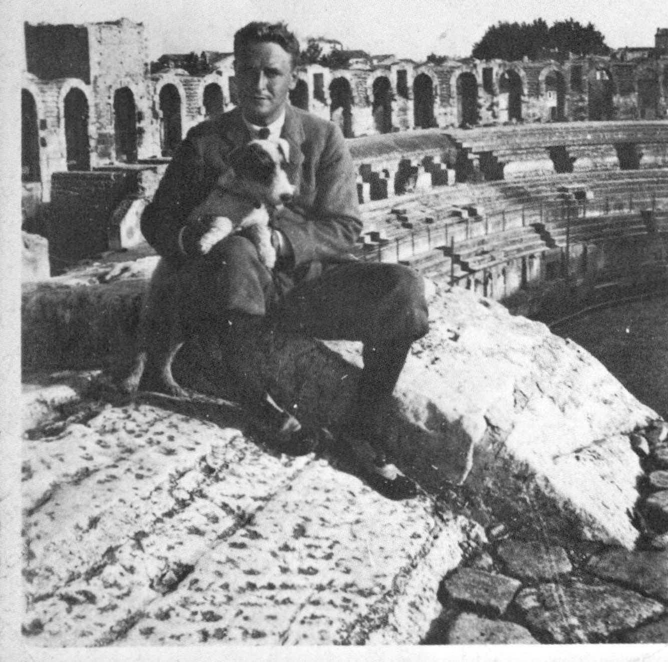
Bring on your wild beasts

"Just like a Little Lamb" — mais pas dans le lit le Langoyne

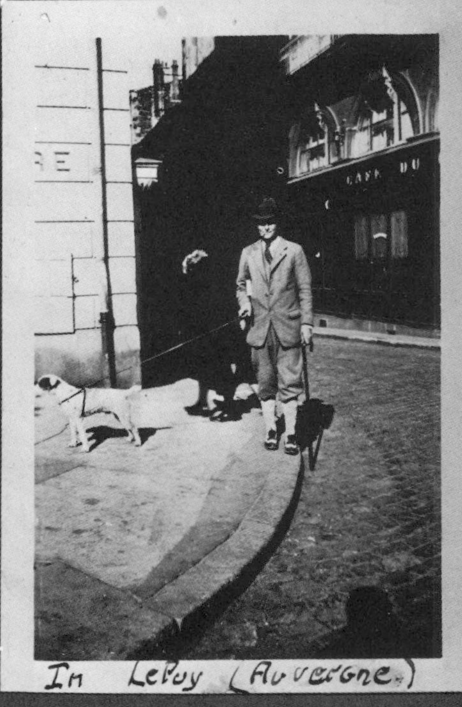
In LePuy (Auvergne)

Whence they hanged Hugenots — Amboise

Gas for the Cevennes

Route to Vichy barred

FORM 2TW 8-29-200M

FRENCH TELEGRAPH CABLE COMPANY

NEW YORK
EXECUTIVE OFFICES: 60 BROAD STREET
60 BROAD ST. (ALWAYS OPEN) 7934 HANOVER
PRODUCE EXCHANGE . . . . 1371 BOWLING GREEN
COTTON EXCHANGE . . . . . 1289 BOWLING GREEN
PULITZER BUILDING, PARK ROW . . . 2069 BEEKMAN
153 DUANE STREET . . . . . . 9696 WHITEHALL
55 FIFTH AVENUE . . . . . . 1135 ALGONQUIN
2 WEST 31st STREET . . . . . 2310 LACKAWANNA
545 FIFTH AVE (2 EAST 45TH STREET) 10430 LEXINGTON
5 COLUMBUS CIRCLE . . . . . . 0684 COLUMBUS

PARIS
MAIN OFFICE: 53 RUE VIVIENNE
LONDON
MAIN OFFICE: 24 ROYAL EXCHANGE, E. C. 3
OTHER OFFICES
LIVERPOOL — HAVRE — BREST
ST. PIERRE, MIQUELON—ANTWERP
FRENCH WEST INDIES

59 CANNES 7 SEP241929

LCD LITOBER NY

FOLLOWING YOU NATURALLY

FITZGERALD

Fitzgerald's wire when Harold Ober set up his own agency, 24 September 1929.

Fitzgerald Back From Riviera; Is Working On Novel

Writer Advises Lewis Book For American Expatriates

Describing the French Riviera as "the most fascinating amalgamation of wealth, luxury and general uselessness in the world, " Scott Fitzgerald, famous and still youthful American novelist, has returned to Paris after a short sojourn in Nice. He was accompanied by his wife and little daughter, "Scotty Jr.", and will remain here until he has finished his latest book—the first in two and a half years.

"That's the why of my new novel," said Mr. Fitzgerald. "It's about the Riviera, and that's all I can say about it today."

The young author of *This Side of Paradise* and half a dozen other best sellers didn't give the reporter a chance to ask questions. "As I said on leaving Nice," he continued, "I have nothing to say about the Hoover Administration, the I'm Alone case, Prohibition in America, Col. Lindbergh or why I live abroad."

He consented, however, to confide a bit of Riviera scandal. "The American artists' colony at Cagnes-sur-Mer is having a lot of trouble with the town postmaster," he laughed. "Their cheques from home haven't been arriving fast enough, and you know what life is for Bohemians when cheques stop coming from home. Anyway, I hear they're going to have the postmaster fired for holding up their letters."

The genial Mr. Fitzgerald advised Sinclair Lewis' new novel *Doodsworth* for "all Americans abroad who don't pay any attention to H. L. Mencken's criticisms."

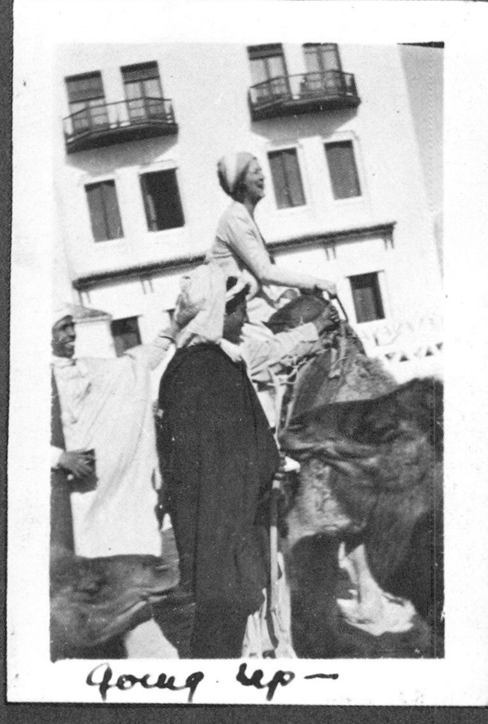
Going up—

up! (Note left hand camel's grin)

and off

OUR TRIP to Africa

FEB 1930

Biskra
Lost in the Sahara

The dunes—Biskra
Looking for a mirage

Going to call on Clare Sheridan in Biskra

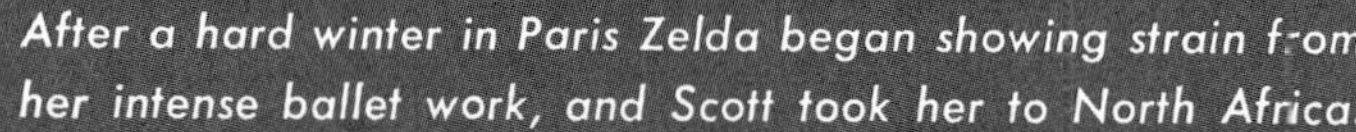

After a hard winter in Paris Zelda began showing strain from her intense ballet work, and Scott took her to North Africa.

Have I got to go down?

It was a trying winter and to forget bad times we went to Algiers. The Hôtel de l'Oasis was laced together by Moorish grills; and the bar was an outpost of civilization with people accentuating their eccentricities. Beggars in white sheets were propped against the walls, and the dash of colonial uniforms gave the cafés a desperate swashbuckling air. Berbers have plaintive trusting eyes but it is really Fate they trust.

—" 'Show Mr. and Mrs. F. to Number—' " (ZF)

The Original Follies Girl

THE thing that made you first notice Gay was that manner she had, as though she was masquerading as herself. All her clothes and jewelry were so good that she wore them "on the surface," as superficially as a Christmas tree supports its ornaments. She could do that because she, too, was awfully good quality and had nothing to conceal except her past. That is to say, she had unquestionably the best figure in New York, otherwise she'd never have made all that money for just standing on the stage lending an air of importance to two yards of green tulle. And her hair was that blond color that's no color at all but a reflector of light, so that she seldom bothered to have it waved or "done."

The first time I saw her she was eating raspberries and cream in the Japanese Garden at the Ritz. There was a cool sound on the air from the tiny fountain and the clink of jeweled bracelets, and the vaporous hush of mid-summer had settled over the voices. I thought how appropriate she was—so airy, as if she had a long time ago dismissed herself as something decorative and amusing, and not to be confused with the vital elements of American life.

Her eyes were far apart and small. All of her was small, though she wasn't in the least restricted or economized upon, rather, polished away. She was quite tall, and all of her fitted together with delightful precision, like the seeds of a pomegranate. I suppose that *objet d'art* quality was what drew about her a long string of men-about-town.

But she had another quality which you couldn't help feeling would betray her sooner or later. It was the quality that made her like intellectual men, though I'm sure that she never read a book through and preferred beer to all other drinks; a quality that made her love "dives" and learn French and waver back and forth between Theosophy and Catholicism.

She wasn't at all the tabloid sort of person. From the first, the men who liked her were very distinguished. She had learned discretion at the start, almost as if it were a thing she wanted for herself, to use so as to be freer therewith—the aristocratic viewpoint.

By Zelda *and* F. Scott Fitzgerald

And then, though undeniably an adventuress of a quiet order, she was financially safe, which relieved her from the taint of hysteria that goes so often with her kind of life. Of course she hadn't always had enough to live on, but in the early years, before producers found out that she made the rest of the chorus look like bologna sausages, there had been a husband with a gift of fantasy that cost him five thousand dollars a year for the rest of her life. That left Gay free to pay her respects to the primrose path, undoubting.

Those first years she came quite near destroying her value. She went to all the parties recorded in the Sunday supplement, and the press photographs of her were so startling that the mysterious notoriety about her was almost turned into vulgarity. But she learned to like absinthe cocktails and to want a serious stage career, which turned her towards successful people and saved her from the usual marriage-to-pugilist end.

She was very kaleidoscopic. There were times when she'd just sit and drink and drink, ending the evening with a heavy British accent, and there were other times when she'd drink nothing but would eat great trays of asparagus hollandaise and swear she was going to enter a convent. Once, when she seemed particularly serious about taking the veil, I asked her why and she said: "Because I've never done *that*."

This was in the stage of her career when she lived in a silver apartment with mulberry carpets and lots of billowing old-blue taffeta, so you see how bored she must have been with her Louis XVI tea service and her grand piano, the huge silver vase that must have calla lilies in it and the white bear skin rug.

Gay was swamped in a flood of interior decorators' pastel restraints. She knew she didn't like the apartment, but the vanity of taking her friends there made her stick for quite a while. It had so obviously cost a lot.

In the vestibule the only French telephone in New York modestly hid itself. You worked the elevator yourself, which in Gay's circle was very *recherché* and showed a fine disdain for American commercialism. She must have passed eternities just waiting in all this carefully faded finery, though she kept an engagement book and always had to look all through the Wednesdays and Sundays when you asked her to tea. There was a purple address book on the marble mantel shelf, chock full of phone numbers from Naples to Nantucket; *couturières* and ex-patriates, millionaires and hair dressers, the restaurants in Rome and the summer homes of producers. It was her attempt at system and gave her a sense of the solidity of organized life. Once you were inscribed in that book you were Gay's friend and theoretically available for bridge or ocean crossings, or any unforeseen contingency such as making the extra man for the Fourth of July in Timbuctoo.

But in spite of all the names and numbers, she lived mostly alone, and to soften the harsh loneliness she soon began to live in a great many places at once. She spent a year on the London stage, with a suite in Paris and innumerable trips to New York, carrying about with her an air of urgency and mystery that made her very elusive.

Gay *en route* meant the arrival of countless band-boxes, mountains of tissue paper, telephone calls in a rapid foreign tongue, people dropping in who didn't know she was going and whom she hadn't seen for years, and always newspaper reporters because they liked Gay and made up important sounding little stories about her. The pictures that went above these anecdotes nowadays were heads, well groomed, unpretentious heads, and the "Miss" was always printed in front of her name.

In Paris she lived in a blue velvet trunk. Lost in the intricate fragility of France's imitation of its lost grandeur, there was a cold looking bath hiding in the corner of a banquet sized room, that all Gay's bottles and atomizers and bright dressing gowns couldn't make informal. Next to that there was a gray and gilt sitting room which she always kept full of South Americans. The marble top tables were covered with champagne cocktails and big paper like magenta roses with stems like pipes.

In her bedroom there was a picture of her sister's child, a little girl with Gay's wide eyes, lost in the square of a huge red leather frame.

40

Illustration by
Chris Marie Meeker

¶ She lived ... and billo... and brig...

She found the hotel apartment much less oppressive than the silver walls in New York, because it did not belong to her and she could wipe cold cream on the towels and rub her shoes with the bath mat.

At this time she was making an awful struggle to hang onto something that had never crystallized for her—it was

In 1929–1930 Zelda wrote 5 sketches for College Humor. *The magazine insisted that Scott's name be included in the by-line. A sixth story, "A Millionaire's Girl," appeared in* The Saturday Evening Post *credited only to F. Scott Fitzgerald due to a mistake in the Ober office.*

¶ Harriet set out for the North to recapture the balm and beauty of war nights under an Alabama moon.

26

Illustration by John LaGatta

Southern Girl

THE solid South stretches away for miles from Jeffersonville, long clay roads climbing slow hills covered with straggling pines, broad, blank cotton fields, isolated cabins in patches of sand, and far off in the distance the blue promise of hills. The town is lost beside a wide brown swirling river which cuts swiftly under its high red banks on either side. Deep trees overhang the brown foam at the edges, and shadows lie long and sleepily under the Spanish moss where darting hard shelled insects fall down from the branches. Brown mud oozes between the cobblestones of the ...

... about the long table, and they never seemed able to dispense with it even after they realized how uncomfortable they were, what with Harriet's squeezing them in between her beaux and her half day job teaching school. The young men waiting to be married and old couples living on one railroad bond, and all the cheerful lot who came in the evening to sit about the stove in the parlor, seemed to find an ease and relaxation in Harriet's jovial irony and in the big horse laugh she gave any pretentiousness.

Her manner with the old was free and impeccable. To the rest, she gave the right to all the self deceptions they found necessary for their peace of mind, so long as they ...

> Every place has its hours: there's Rome in the glassy sun of a winter noon and Paris under the blue gauze of spring twilight, and there's the red sun flowing through the chasms of a New York dawn. So in Jeffersonville there existed then, and I suppose now, a time and quality that appertains to nowhere else. It began about half past six on an early summer night, with the flicker and splutter of the corner street lights going on, and it lasted until the great incandescent globes were black inside with moths and beetles and the children were called in to bed from the dusty streets.
>
> —"Southern Girl" (ZF)

Number Twenty was where Harriet and a fragile mother and Harriet's younger sister lived in one room and a latticed back porch. The rest of the house, all the three cornered bed-rooms and back hallways and waste space under the stairs, was rented. It was, in fact, a boarding-house of a very friendly Sunday dinner sort, and as we grew up and Harriet's mother softly became an invalid, it grew to be Harriet's responsibility. If the boarders weren't friendly when they came, they soon fell into the note of shy bravado

... that you could hear the grinding wheels of a trolley-car climbing a hill six blocks away. Inside, girls in preparation for the evening dance struggled between the difficulties of the spasmodic sweep of an electric fan and the dripping heat.

That was how it happened that one night during the war, when Harriet was still only nineteen and at the beginning of her effort, the door-bell rang and she answered it in a pair of blue bloomers and a huge bath towel. The door-

By F. SCOTT *and* ZELDA FITZGERALD

27

The Girl the Prince Liked

¶ *Illustration by* R. F. Schabelitz

HELENA always said that all she had from her father was the big clock that stood in the hall, engraved with a touching testimonial from his employees, but she forgot the eight million dollars and the driving, restless ambition that had led him to accumulate his money so relentlessly. She had also from him a pair of mystic, deep-set eyes and an unbroken, round hair line and a deep, straight crease above her lips when she laughed. These showed very plainly in her wedding photographs, when she was still completely under his living influence.

When I first knew her she was already twenty-seven, and the corners and ridges of a successful personality had been modulated and polished by a Parisian finishing school, seven years in *Town Topics*, two children and an enormous collection of second prizes from golf tournaments. Heaven knows what the force of her must have been in its aboriginal state! She once showed me lots of grayish brown photographs of a huge frame house whose ground plan must have looked like a roller coaster, so much was it of the billowing nineties. Here she had spent a dynamic, motherless childhood. It was easy to imagine her skipping rope on the circling verandas, while the summer rain trickled down the tin gutters onto the deep hydrangea beds. She must have been a small, slight little girl full of sudden flashing indications of a firm and constant energy, because she was still like that years after when I got to know her.

At first it was disconcerting because her vitality did not come and go like most people's, but simply changed from on[e] sort to another. From a vibrant excitement that she coul[d] convey when she wanted to be disturbing, it would quie[t] down into a smouldering yellow light back of her light eye lashes, back of her yellow-brown eyes crouching there inde pendent of Helena, watching you, always taking note o[f] everything.

That was one of the ways she established social dominance over people: she would sit and watch until she frightened them, and then suddenly be friendly and free and just as charming as she had been formidable.

By F. SCOTT & Z[ELDA FITZGERALD]

46

¶ When the time came that this most famous person had to leave, he probably said to Helena, "Well, if you ever are in my part of the world, look me up, won't you?" And she promised she would, and she *did* not long after.

rooms and painted ones whose pictures were in *Town and Country*, and there were dozens of houses with rooms as long and still and thick as a very fashionable hotel lobby. The cream brick façades and the concrete drives, punctuated with heavy powerful roadsters, forged a chain about the rendezvous of the people of importance, whom Helena wore like a string of glass beads. The others loved that nonchalance of hers.

The winter I was there, they liked going to dinner at her house. It was always a sort of boyish affair where Helena sat half holding her breath in the hope that perhaps the menu would be different from what she had ordered, suppressing in herself a feeling of guilt that she had not given her afternoon to

Don't you think that Zelda's Girl-the-Prince-liked thing is good?

—FSF to Harold Ober, c. August 1929.

By F. SCOTT *and* ZELDA FITZGERALD

Poor Working Girl

Illustration by Charles V. Chambers

All that ambitious thinking made it much easier for Eloise to contribute the outstanding excitement of months to the family dinner table. Over the sweet potatoes and meat pie and muffins wavered the announcement that she was going to leave home. Even when she was "in college" she had always slept at home and so it was not hard to understand why Mamma pictured Eloise in a strange land with a strange disease, somewhat like pneumonia only much more painful, and with nobody to look after her. There was indignation in Mamma's mental picture. It somehow included the law and all the hygienic societies and the pound. Father didn't see why girls didn't stay at home, but he had his own worries and he made it a rule never to complain until afterwards.

—"Poor Working Girl" (ZF)

Eloise had been half engaged for four years to numerous editions of the same young man.

73

The Girl with Talent

By F. SCOTT *and* ZELDA FITZGERALD

THE febrile winter sun felt its way along the basement stairways, digging out the corners of the cold stone steps into live cubistic patterns. Tentatively it flicked the red and green electric bulbs that framed a Chinese restaurant into glassy momentary life. It slipped on the gilt of a second story costumer's sign and fell with a splash under the canopy of a Forty-third Street theater. Then it wound itself in and out around the noise and smells of trucks and taxis, a hurdy-gurdy, a porcelain lunch-room, a gigantic tooth over a dentist's window—slithering its way through the warm oily fumes of a coiffeur's, glinting the glass rectangle of a cheap photographer's show-case. With cold calculation it avoided the alley up which I turned and left it sunless, trafficless, bounded with a network of fire escapes and filled with a stolid gray silence like a street in Dickens' England.

It was a theatrical alley, lined with green baize doors; in its gutters bits of program from yesterday's matinée floated morosely. Where the words, *Stage Entrance*, were hollowed out in green glass I went in.

The theater was dark and on the stage in the half gloom a girl with short black hair raced about, tapping out the rhythm of a mountain cataract to the tune of the hit of the winter. As she moved, her hair flowed back from her pert, serious face like the hair of a person coming up from a dive. She stopped suddenly and a deep chuckle rose from somewhere and enveloped her. All her gestures were involuntary like that, as if superimposed on a colossal dignity and restraint and as much a surprise to her as to the rest of the world. That quality was known to theatrical managers as hot stuff, to a large and discerning public as physical magnetism and to a widish circle of enemies from lower theatrical planes as lack of talent.

. . . most of them have been pretty strong draughts on Zelda's and my common store of material. This is Mary Hay for instance + the "Girl the Prince Liked" was Josephine Ordway both of whom I had in my notebook to use.

—FSF to Harold Ober, c. September 1929.

picture of a baby playing in long curly grass and by its side a newspaper picture of a handsome young husband, rich and famous enough to have claimed a good quarter of the front page.

All these things were hers. There was, as well, a grinning Bahama maid emanating an aura of irregularity, and the soft seduction of a gray squirrel coat hovering over the radiator in the corner. A big decisive automobile waited beyond the alley. I couldn't restrain an involuntary, "Such a lucky girl—you've got everything," as I ran my mind slowly over the delectable list of Lou's possessions. She had a band of gauze about her hair and she was digging away at a big tin of cold cream. She answered me from the mirror. "Yes," she said, "except a cocktail. Let's go and have a drink."

Out of the quiet resonance of the passage and down a short flight of stairs, we followed the loopings of the tinsel January sun and left it at the entrance to a dark dining-room that smelt of orange juice and gin. Lou's dancing partner was there, hard at work on creating a smoke screen about himself. They laughed and pushed each other about with friendly little pats, talking shop in a professional lingo that I only half understood. She was fond of him, I knew, and we were all having a good time, but even so she gave the impression of constraint and of awaiting the passage of time as one waits for the five fifteen. Her partner was reading her a half kidding lecture about drinking too much gin, and finally it made her angry and we left. Outside she stood on the curb like a fine, high bred hunter picking up a cosmic scent on the early winter night, the bright silver buckles on her slippers twinkling and twinkling with a restlessness to be off. "Oh, hell," she said obscenely, "I wish there were—"

High up over Central Park the beautiful baby was eating carrot soup with nice crispy things in it that caused the tiny mouth to weave a rhythmic circle to and fro, almost obliterating its startling likeness to Lou. A cardboard Nanny stood over the small wicker chair, waving a spoon about with the delicate emphasis of an orchestra

holes in a frozen lake on the cross-stitching of the elevated, on the red and yellow lights that went round and round and the green lights that made squares and the lights that outlined stars and words and shapes of things. I supposed she was brooding, or maybe enjoying that delicious feeling of motion that makes children hum in motor cars, so I didn't disturb her. We went all the way home in silence, crawling the pharmaceutical smells and the smell of hot bread, of gasoline and city dust, the overpowering smell of friction and all the used-up smells that escape into the New York streets with the letting down of business hour discipline.

We were late, and her husband was terribly annoyed when we finally got there. I suppose meeting her at the door all ready to be cross and finding himself frustrated by the presence of a stranger gave him a sensation like

50

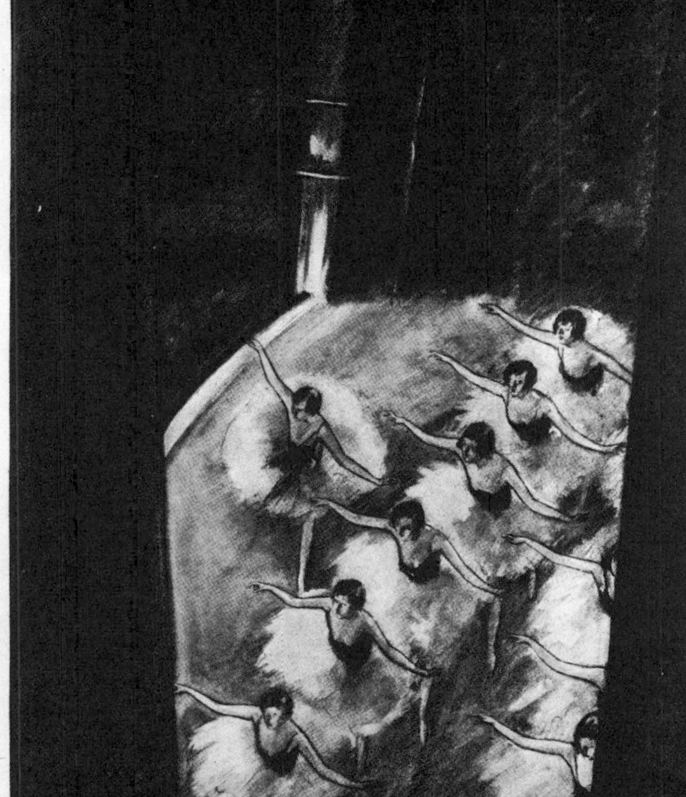

¶ "I like to dance," she seemed to say. "There's nothing so much fun as this is."

¶ *Illustrations by Chris Marie Meeker*

51

PART FIVE CHRONOLOGY

CRACK-UP
(1930-1937)

April 1930
ZF has first breakdown in Paris; enters Malmaison clinic outside Paris; then Valmont clinic in Switzerland.

Publication of the first Josephine story, *"First Blood,"* in *The Saturday Evening Post.* The five-story series appears in the *Post* from April 1930 to August 1931.

5 June 1930
ZF enters Prangins clinic near Geneva, Switzerland.

Summer and fall 1930
FSF living in Geneva, and Lausanne.

Christmas 1930
FSF and Scottie spend holiday at Gstaad, a ski resort.

Late January 1931
FSF's father dies. He returns alone to America on the *New York* to attend the funeral, and for a brief trip to Montgomery to report to the Sayres about Zelda.

February 1931
"Babylon Revisited" in *The Saturday Evening Post.*

July 1931
Fitzgeralds spend two weeks at Lake Annecy, France.

15 September 1931
ZF is released from Prangins; Fitzgeralds return on the *Aquitania* to America permanently.

September 1931–Spring 1932
Rent house at 819 Felder Avenue in Montgomery. FSF goes to Hollywood alone to work on *Red-Headed Woman* for Metro-Goldwyn-Mayer.

17 November 1931
Death of Judge A. D. Sayre.

February 1932
ZF's second breakdown; she enters Phipps Psychiatric Clinic of Johns Hopkins Hospital in Baltimore.

March 1932
ZF completes the first draft of her novel, *Save Me the Waltz,* while at Phipps Clinic.

20 May 1932–November 1933
FSF rents "La Paix" on the outskirts of Baltimore.

26 June 1932
ZF discharged from Phipps; joins family at "La Paix."

7 October 1932
Publication of ZF's novel, *Save Me the Waltz.*

26 June–1 July 1933
ZF's play, *Scandalabra,* is produced in Baltimore by the Vagabond Junior Players.

End of November–December 1933
FSF and ZF vacation in Bermuda.

December 1933
FSF rents house at 1307 Park Ave., Baltimore.

January-April 1934
Serial of *Tender Is the Night* in *Scribner's Magazine.*

January 1934
ZF's third breakdown; enters Sheppard-Pratt Hospital, outside Baltimore.

March 1934
ZF enters Craig House clinic in Beacon, New York.

29 March–30 April 1934
ZF has art exhibit in New York. FSF at Algonquin Hotel for publication of *Tender Is the Night.*

12 April 1934
Publication of *Tender Is the Night.*

19 May 1934
ZF is transferred back to Sheppard-Pratt Hospital.

3 February 1935
FSF, convinced he has tuberculosis, goes to Oak Hall Hotel in Tryon, North Carolina.

20 March 1935
Publication of *Taps at Reveille.*

May 1935
FSF spends the summer at the Grove Park Inn, Asheville, N.C., with visits to Baltimore and New York.

September 1935
FSF takes apartment at Cambridge Arms, Baltimore.

November 1935
FSF at the Skyland Hotel in Hendersonville, N.C., where he begins writing "The Crack-Up" essays.

8 April 1936
ZF enters Highland Hospital in Asheville.

July–December 1936
FSF moves to the Grove Park Inn to be near Zelda.

September 1936
Death of Mollie McQuillan Fitzgerald in Washington.

January–June 1937
FSF lives at Oak Hall Hotel in Tryon.

184

The Crash! Zelda + America

Thirty Three Years Old.

Apr — Strange Sunday walk (13th) Sam Ordway. American Club to hear Wolcott. Moved (18th) Bishop incident. Zelda quit school + began again, Prof Claude, Noels, Rousseau, Egarova Arlen. Mortimer Duval. April 23d Zelda enters ~~Malmaison~~ Zelda went to [illegible]

May — [illegible] + friends. His lunch. [illegible], Thomas, [illegible], [illegible], [illegible], Ellis, Big dinner, Lunch [illegible] in Bois, Emily, [illegible]. Zelda everyday. Jeff Crane, Sam + Mildred. Joe + her friend, Bachelor dinner Pavlowa, wedding. The Cordon Bleu

Finished Bridal Party in Paris End May On the 11th Zelda leaves ~~Malmaison~~

In the spring of 1929 Zelda resumed her ballet work with greater intensity while Fitzgerald spent more time drinking with his friends—and less on his novel.

Alabama rubbed her legs with Elizabeth Arden muscle oil night after night. There were blue bruises inside above the knee where the muscles were torn. Her throat was so dry that at first she thought she had fever and took her temperature and was disappointed to find that she had none. In her bathing suit she tried to stretch on the high back of a Louis Quatorze sofa. She was always stiff, and she clutched the gilt flowers in pain. She fastened her feet through the bars of the iron bed and slept with her toes glued outwards for weeks. Her lessons were agony.

—*Save Me the Waltz* (ZF)

* * *

David said he would help her to be a fine dancer, but he did not believe that she could become one. He had made many friends in Paris. When he came from his studio he nearly always brought somebody home. They dined out amongst the prints of Montagné's, the leather and stained glass of Foyot's, the plush and bouquets of the restaurants around the Place de l'Opéra. If she tried to induce David to go home early, he grew angry.

"What right have you to complain? You have cut yourself off from all your friends with this damn ballet."

With his friends they drank Chartreuse along the boulevards under the rose-quartz lamps, and the trees, wielded by the night over the streets like the feathery fans of acquiescent courtesans.

Alabama's work grew more and more difficult. In the mazes of the masterful fouetté her legs felt like dangling hams; in the swift elevation of the entrechat cinq she thought her breasts hung like old English dugs. It did not show in the mirror. She was nothing but sinew. To succeed had become an obsession. She worked till she felt like a gored horse in the bull ring, dragging its entrails.

At home, the household fell into a mass of dissatisfaction without an authority to harmonize its elements. Before she left the apartment in the morning Alabama left a list of things for lunch which the cook never bothered to prepare—the woman kept the butter in the coal-bin and stewed a rabbit every day for Adage and gave the family what she pleased to eat. There wasn't any use getting another; the apartment was no good anyway. The life at home was simply an existence of individuals in proxmity; it had no basis of common interest.

—*Save Me the Waltz* (ZF)

One of Zelda's many oil paintings of ballet dancers, most of which were destroyed by her mother after her death. This one is in the Montgomery Museum.

THE BRIDAL

THERE was the usual insincere little note saying: "I wanted you to be the first to know." It was a double shock to Michael, announcing, as it did, both the engagement and the imminent marriage; which, moreover, was to be held, not in New York, decently and far away, but here in Paris under his very nose, if that could be said to extend over the Protestant Episcopal Church of the Holy Trinity, Avenue George Cinq. The date was two weeks off, early in June.

At first Michael was afraid and his stomach felt hollow. When he left the hotel that morning, the *femme de chambre*, who was in love with his fine, sharp profile and his pleasant buoyancy, scented the hard abstraction that had settled c
bank, he bought a
de Rivoli, he sym
faded panorama
window and curs
with a half-displa
warranted to be v

But the fear sta
ognized it as the f
He had met Caro
possessed her you
New York, and t
lessly, because h
money; because, v
world, he could r
still, Caroline had
something patheti
shining stream of
drawn.

Since his only
leaned weakly on
held on to it and
on the French co
hands. He carried
photographs and
for a maudlin pop
He kept clear of
how know it and
note informed hi

It was a fine mo
de Castiglione, pr
walk gazing upwa
glorious, symbol of escape and destruction—of escape, if necessary, through destruction—glided in the Paris sky. He heard a woman say in French that it would not her astonish if that commenced to let fall the bombs. Then he heard another voice, full of husky laughter, and the void in his stomach froze. Jerking about, he was face to face with Caroline Dandy and her fiancé.

"Why, Michael! Why, we were wondering wh
were. I asked at the Guaranty Tr
Company, and finally
City ——"

Mrs. Atkinson Hamilton
requests the honour of your presence
at the marriage of her daughter
Virginia Randolph Megear
to
Mr. Thomas Powell Fowler
on Saturday the tenth of May
nineteen hundred and thirty
at twelve o'clock
at the American Cathedral of the Holy Trinity
Paris, France

little counter he was in this game of families and money! Under his hat his brow sweated with the humiliation of the fact that for all his misery he was worth just exactly so many invitations. Frantically he began to mumble something about going away.

Then it happened—Caroline
nd Michael
. She saw
und wound-
g quivered
along the
and in her
her. All the
s of first love
more; their
vay touched
ris sunlight.
s arm sud-
herself with

hael walked
e; then he
o look in a
n farther up
ast into the
e with much

do also—he
y.
be the same
nself. "She
in her mar-
be happy at

s of his love
back around
stein's phys-
ries arose—
of rides in the Long Island moonlight; of a happy time at Lake Placid with her cheeks so cold there, but warm just underneath the surface; of a despai
noon in a littl

Powell Fowler's wedding in Paris in May 1930 provided Fitzgerald with material for "The Bridal Party." Powell was the brother of Ludlow Fowler, the model for "The Rich Boy."

R
tu
bo
tho
sold
Mich
just t
alway
Ruth
you'd c
Bar fro
there'll b
Cinq."
"And,
day after
be sure an
West's; she
were. What'
tion? You se
is because m
and the whole
being here too
The entire c
her mother; al

except
rtship. What a

g about it?
n't you have been stronger, made me marry you? Don't you see how sad I am?"
Michael's fists clenched.

The Procession, Headed by the Bride and Groom, Started Down the

THE SATURDAY EVENING POST 11

PARTY

By F. Scott Fitzgerald

ILLUSTRATED BY JOHN LA GATTA

Michael Managed to Murmur, "Beautiful, Simply Beautiful"

"Well, I won't give up till the last moment," he whispered. "I've had all the bad luck so far, and maybe it's turned at last. One takes what one can get, up to the limit of one's strength, and if I can't have her, at least she'll go into this marriage with some of me in her heart."

II

ACCORDINGLY he went to the party at Chez Victor two days later, upstairs and into the little salon off the bar where the party was to assemble for cocktails. He was early; the only other occupant was a tall lean man of fifty. They spoke.

"You waiting for George Packman's party?"

"Yes. My name's Michael Curly."

"My name's ——"

Michael failed to catch the name. They ordered a drink, and Michael supposed that the bride and groom were having a gay time.

"Too much so," the other agreed, frowning. "I don't see how they stand it. We all crossed on the boat together; five days of that crazy life and then two weeks of Paris. You"—he hesitated, smiling faintly—"you'll excuse me for saying that your generation drinks too much."

"Not Caroline."

"No, not Caroline. She seems to take only a cocktail and a glass of champagne, and then she's had enough, thank God. But Hamilton drinks too much and all this crowd of young people drink too much. Do you live in Paris?"

"For the moment," said Michael.

"I don't like Paris. My wife—that is to say, my ex-wife, Hamilton's mother—lives in Paris."

"You're Hamilton Rutherford's father?"

"I have that honor. And I'm not denying that I'm proud of what he's done; it was just a general comment."

"Of course."

Michael glanced up nervously as four people came in. He felt suddenly that his dinner coat was old and shiny; he had ordered a new one that morning. The people who had come in were rich and at home in their richness with one another—a dark, lovely girl with a hysterical little laugh whom he had met before; two confident men whose jokes referred invariably to last night's scandal and tonight's potentialities, as if they had important rôles in a play that extended indefinitely into the past and the future. When Caroline arrived, Michael had scarcely a moment of her, but it was enough to note that, like all the others, she was strained and tired. She was pale beneath her rouge; there were shadows under her eyes. With a mixture of relief and wounded vanity, he found himself placed far from her and at another table; he needed a moment to adjust himself to his surroundings. This was not like the immature set in which he and Caroline

As the skepticism of both Perkins and Ober, by now Fitzgerald's bankers as well as close friends and advisors, began to form regarding the novel he had been promising since 1926, he grew increasingly defensive.

I know you're losing faith in me + Max too but God knows one has to rely in the end on one's own judgement. I could have published four lowsy, half baked books in the last five years + people would have thought I was at least a worthy young man not drinking myself to pieces in the south seas—but I'd be dead as Michael Arlen, Bromfield, Tom Boyd, Callaghan + the others who think they can trick the world with the hurried and the second rate. These Post *stories in the* Post *are at least not any spot on me—they're honest and if their* form *is stereotyped people know what to expect when they pick up the* Post*. The novel is another thing—if, after four years I published the Basil Lee stories as a book I might as well get tickets for Hollywood immediately.*

Well, that's how things are. If you'll have confidence in me I think you'll shortly see I knew what I was doing.

This letter sounds cross but I'm stupidgot with work today + too tired to rewrite it. Please forgive it—it has to get tomorrow's boat.

Addenda

Zelda's been sick + not dangerously but seriously, + then I got involved in a wedding party + after 2 weeks just got to work on new story yesterday but 3000 words already done—about as many as I must owe you dollars.

—FSF to Harold Ober, May 1930.

I was delighted about the Bishop story—the acceptance has done wonders for him. The other night I read him a good deal of my novel & I think he liked it. Harold Ober wrote me that if it couldn't be published this fall I should publish the Basil Lee stories, but I know too well by whom reputations are made & broken to ruin myself completely by such a move—I've seen Tom Boyd, Michael Arlen & too many others fall through the eternal trapdoor of trying [to] *cheat the public, no matter what their public is, with substitutes—better to let four years go by. I wrote young & I wrote a lot & the pot takes longer to fill up now but the novel, my novel, is a different matter than if I'd hurriedly finished it up a year and a half ago. . . . I don't know why I'm saying this to you who have never been anything but my most loyal and confident encourager and friend but Ober's letter annoyed me today & put me in a wretched humor.* I know what I'm doing—*honestly, Max. How much time between* The Cabala & The Bridge of St. Luis Rey, *between* The Genius & The American Tragedy *between* The Wisdom Tooth & Green Pastures. *I think time seems to go by quicker there in America but time put in is time eventually taken out—and whatever this thing of mine is its certainly not a mediocrity like* The Woman of Andros & The Forty Second Parallel. *"He* [is] *through" is an easy cry to raise but its safer for the critics to raise it at the evidence in print than at a long silence.*

—FSF to Maxwell Perkins, c. 1 May 1930.

A Year in Lausanne. Writing From Darkness & Hope. Thirty Four Years Old

After breaking down in Paris in April 1930, Zelda was moved to the Prangins Clinic in Switzerland on Lake Geneva.

> *My delay in writing is due to the fact that Zelda has been desperately ill with a complete nervous breakdown and is in a sanitarium near here. She is better now but recovery will take a long time. I did not tell her parents the seriousness of it so say nothing—the danger was to her sanity rather than her life.*
>
> *Scottie is in the apartment in Paris with her governess. She loved the picture of her cousins. Tell Father I visited the*
>
> *"—seven pillars of Gothic mould*
> *in Chillon's dungeons deep and old"*
>
> *and thought of the first poem I ever heard, or was "The Raven?"*
>
> *Thank you for the Chesterton.*
>
> —FSF to his mother, June 1930.

Outdoor work, dancing, and swimming were part of the Prangins therapy after Zelda began to improve.

" Les Rives de Prangins " Zelda's room & bath are around the corner facing the Lake

The Clinique Place

Zelda with Scottie (center) and children of the hospital staff.

This is actually Zelda's room! FSF

During the summer of 1930 and the following winter, while Zelda remained at Prangins, Fitzgerald stayed in various hotels in Geneva, Lausanne, and Vevey, Switzerland, with occasional trips to Paris where Scottie was in school. Father and daughter spent Christmas, 1930, at Gstaad where they took skiing lessons.

The porch at Vevey Palace

VEVEY, Switzerland
Summer 1930

On the nursery Slope

Portrait of the artist by him

Switzerland is a country where very few things begin, but many things end.
—"One Trip Abroad"

Zelda is almost well. The doctor says she can never drink again (not that drink in any way contributed to her collapse), and that I must not drink anything, not even wine, for a year, because drinking in the past was one of the things that haunted her in her delirium.
—FSF to Maxwell Perkins, c. 1 September 1930.

It is a place where one's instinct is to give a reason for being there—'Oh, you see, I'm here because——' Failing that, you are faintly suspect, because this corner of Europe does not draw people; rather, it accepts them without too many inconvenient questions—live and let live. Routes cross here—people bound for private *cliniques* or tuberculosis resorts in the mountains, people who are no longer *persona grata* in Italy or France.
—"The Hotel Child"

Thomas Wolfe

Beoth, Patrick, and Honoria Murphy. The Murphys were staying in the Alps because of Patrick's tuberculosis.

All the world seems to end up in this flat and antiseptic smelling land—with an overlay of flowers. Tom Wolfe is the only man I've met here who isn't sick or hasn't sickness to deal with. You have a great find in him—what he'll do is incalcuable. He has a deeper culture than Ernest and more vitality, if he is slightly less of a poet that goes with the immense surface he wants to cover. Also he lacks Ernests quality of a stick hardened in the fire—he is more susceptible to the world. John Bishop told me he needed advice about cutting ect. but after reading his book I thought that was nonsense. He strikes me as a man who should be let alone as to length, if he has to be published in five volumes. I liked him enormously.

—FSF to Maxwell Perkins, c. 1 September 1930.

Hemingway's joking inscription pretending to be Richard Halliburton, the Princeton-educated adventurer. Fitzgerald would later write of Hemingway:

. . . a third contemporary had been an artistic conscience to me—I had not imitated his infectious style, because my own style, such as it is, was formed before he published anything, but there was an awful pull toward him when I was on a spot.

—"Handle With Care"

In January 1931 Fitzgerald's father died of a heart attack in Washington and he went home for the burial in the Rockville, Maryland, family cemetery. After a quick trip south to report on Zelda's condition to her parents, he returned to Switzerland where he visited Prangins on Easter Sunday.

Next day at the churchyard his father was laid among a hundred Divers, Dorseys, and Hunters. It was very friendly leaving him there with all his relations around him. Flowers were scattered on the brown unsettled earth. Dick had no more ties here now and did not believe he would come back. He knelt on the hard soil. These dead, he knew them all, their weather-beaten faces with blue flashing eyes, the spare violent bodies, the souls made of new earth in the forest-heavy darkness of the seventeenth century.

"Good-by, my father—good-by, all my fathers."

—*Tender Is the Night*

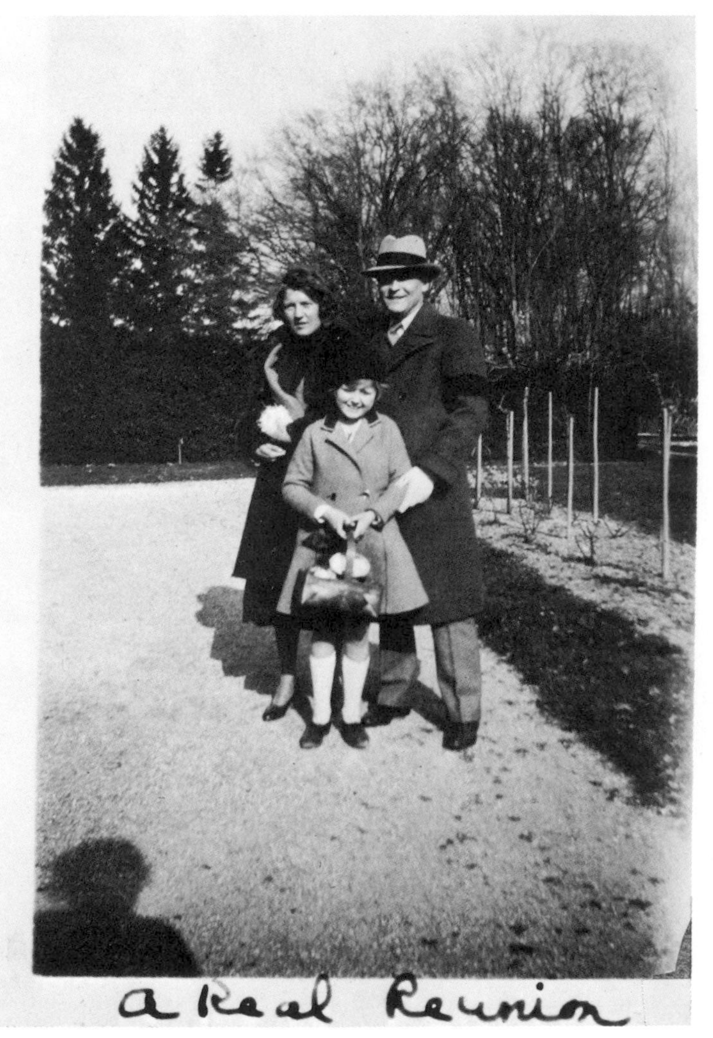

Published Weekly
The Curtis Publishing Company
Cyrus H. K. Curtis, President
George H. Lorimer, First Vice-President
John B. Williams, Second Vice-President
Walter D. Fuller, Second Vice-President and Secretary. Philip S. Collins, Second Vice-President and Treasurer
Fred A. Healy, Second Vice-President and Advertising Director
Independence Square, Philadelphia

THE SATURDAY EVENING POST
Founded A°D¹ 1728 by Benj. Franklin

Copyright, 1931, by The Curtis Publishing Company in the United States and Great Britain. Title Registered in U. S. Patent Office and in Foreign Countries. Entered as Second-Class Matter at the Post-Office Department, Ottawa, Can.

George Horace Lorimer
EDITOR
Thomas B. Costain, A. W. Neall, Wesley Stout, B. Y. Riddell, Merritt Hulburd, W. Thornton Martin, Associate Editors

Entered as Second-Class Matter, November 18, 1879, at the Post Office at Philadelphia, Under Act of March 3, 1879. Additional Entry at Columbus, O., St. Louis, Mo., Chicago, Ill., Indianapolis, Ind., Saginaw, Mich., Des Moines, Ia., Portland, Ore., Milwaukee, Wis., St. Paul, Minn., San Francisco, Cal., Kansas City, Mo., Savannah, Ga., Denver, Colo., Louisville, Ky., Houston, Tex., Omaha, Neb., Ogden, Utah, Jacksonville, Fla., New Orleans, La., Portland, Me., and Los Angeles, Cal.

Volume 203 | 5c. THE COPY | PHILADELPHIA, PA., FEBRUARY 21, 1931 | $2.00 By Subscription (52 issues) | Number 34

BABYLON REVISITED

By F. SCOTT FITZGERALD

ILLUSTRATED BY HENRIETTA McCAIG STARRETT

"And where's Mr. Campbell?" Charlie asked.

"Gone to Switzerland. Mr. Campbell's a pretty sick man, Mr. Wales."

"I'm sorry to hear that. And George Hardt?" Charlie inquired.

"Back in America, gone to work."

"And where is the snow bird?"

"He was in here last week. Anyway, his friend, Mr. Schaeffer, is in Paris."

Two familiar names from the long list of a year and a half ago.

At one time while Zelda was hospitalized, Scottie visited her Aunt Rosalind in Brussels, where her husband Newman Smith was with the Guaranty Trust Company. Rosalind felt that Scott was responsible for Zelda's breakdown, and the bitter family feud provided the basis for one of his best-known stories, "Babylon Revisited." Its heroine's name was Honoria, after Honoria Murphy.

of green carpet with his eyes fixed straight ahead by old habit; and then, with his foot firmly on the rail, he turned and surveyed the room, encountering only a single pair of eyes that fluttered up from a newspaper in the corner. Charlie asked for the head barman, Paul, who in the latter days of the bull market had come to work in his own custom-built car—disembarking, however, with due nicety at the nearest corner. But Paul was at his country house today and Alix was giving him his information.

"No, no more. I'm going slow these days."

Again the memory of those days swept over him like a nightmare—the people they had met travelling; the people who couldn't add a row of figures or speak a coherent sentence. The little man Helen had consented to dance with at the ship's party, who had insulted her ten feet from the table; the women and girls carried screaming with drink or drugs out of public places—

—The men who locked their wives out in the snow, because the snow of twenty-nine wasn't real snow. If you didn't want it to be snow, you just paid some money.

—"Babylon Revisited"

concerns there. They don't know about me down there." He smiled faintly. "Remember the night of George Hardt's bachelor dinner here? . . . By the way, what's become of Claude Fessenden?"

Alix lowered his voice confidentially: "He's in Paris, but he doesn't come here any more. Paul doesn't allow it. He ran up a bill of thirty thousand francs, charging all his drinks and his lunches, and usually his dinner, for more than a year. And when Paul finally told him he had to pay, he gave him a bad check."

Alix pressed his lips together and shook his head.

"I don't understand it, such a dandy fellow. Now he's all bloated up ——" He made a plump apple of his hands.

A thin world, resting on a common weakness, shredded away now like tissue paper. Turning, Charlie saw a group of effeminate young men installing themselves in a corner.

"Nothing affects them," he thought. "Stocks rise and fall, people loaf or work, but they go on forever." The place oppressed him. He called for the dice and shook with Alix for the drink.

"Here for long, Mr. Wales?"

"I'm here for four or five days to see my little girl."

"But You Won't Always Like Me Best, Honey. You'll Grow Up and Meet Somebody Your Own Age and Go Marry Him and Forget You Ever Had a Daddy"

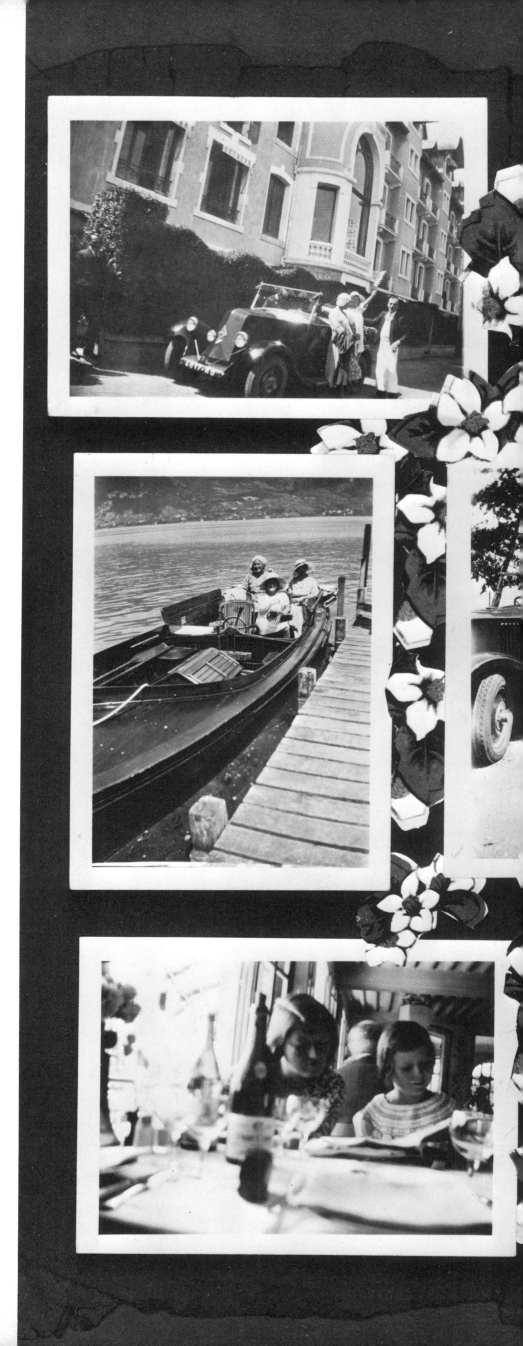

My dearest and most precious Monsieur,

We have here a kind of maniac who seems to have been inspired with erotic aberrations on your behalf. Apart from that she is a person of excellent character, willing to work, would accept a nominal salary while learning, fair complexion, green eyes would like correspondance with refined young man of your description with intent to marry. Previous experience unnecessary. Very fond of family life and a wonderful pet to have in the home. Marked behind the left ear with a slight tendency to schitzoprenie.

—ZF to FSF, c. July 1931.

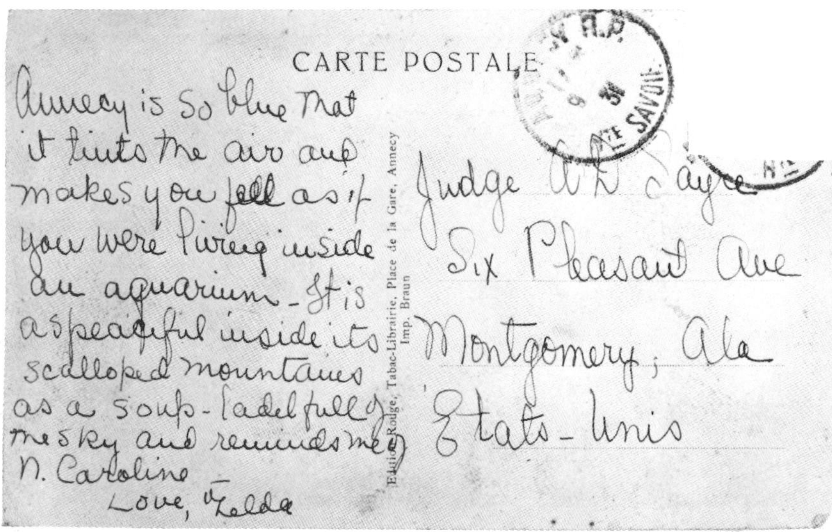

CARTE POSTALE

Annecy is so blue that it tints the air and makes you fell as if you were living inside an aquarium—It is as peaceful inside its scalloped mountains as a soup-ladel full of the sky and reminds me of N. Caroline—
Love, Zelda

Judge A. D. Sayre
Six Pleasant Ave
Montgomery, Ala
Etats-Unis

In July 1931 Zelda was given a furlough from Prangins, and the Fitzgeralds vacationed at Lake Annecy, France, and Lake Como, Italy, for several weeks. The floral decorations on these pages are by Zelda.

But we went to Annecy for two weeks in summer, and said at the end that we'd never go there again because those weeks had been perfect and no other time could match them. First we lived at the Beau-Rivage, a rambler rose-covered hotel, with a diving platform wedged beneath our window between the sky and the lake, but there were enormous flies on the raft so we moved across the lake to Menthon. The water was greener there and the shadows long and cool and the scraggly gardens staggered up the shelved precipice to the Hôtel Palace. We played tennis on the baked clay courts and fished tentatively from a low brick wall. The heat of summer seethed in the resin of the white pine bath-houses. We walked at night towards a café blooming with Japanese lanterns, white shoes gleaming like radium in the damp darkness. It was like the good gone times when we still believed in summer hotels and the philosophies of popular songs. Another night we danced a Wiener waltz and just simply swep' around.

—" 'Show Mr. and Mrs. F. to Number——' " (ZF)

innecy

what if caught

SCRIBNER'S MAGAZINE

November 1931

VOL. XC NUMBER 5

ECHOES OF THE JAZZ AGE

By F. SCOTT FITZGERALD

"This Side of Paradise" at its publication in 1920 was the first signal of the coming turbulent decade. "Tales of the Jazz Age" (1922) gave the period a name. That age is dead. It went over the hill with its boom companion, Prosperity. Scott Fitzgerald, who was in the thick of it and portrayed the social changes of the times in these and other books, writes its obituary.

It is too soon to write about the Jazz Age with perspective, and without being suspected of premature ar-

sort of measure bound to alienate the more intelligent young men from the prevailing order. We didn't remember

It is too soon to write about the Jazz Age with perspective, and without being suspected of premature arteriosclerosis. Many people still succumb to violent retching when they happen upon any of its characteristic words—words which have since yielded in vividness to the coinages of the underworld. It is as dead as were the Yellow Nineties in 1902. Yet the present writer already looks back to it with nostalgia. It bore him up, flattered him and gave him more money than he had dreamed of, simply for telling people that he felt as they did, that something had to be done with all the nervous energy stored up and unexpended in the War.

* * *

The Jazz Age had had a wild youth and a heady middle age. There was the phase of the necking parties, the Leopold-Loeb murder (I remember the time my wife was arrested on Queensborough Bridge on the suspicion of being the "Bob-haired Bandit") and the John Held Clothes. In the second phase such phenomena as sex and murder became more mature, if much more conventional. Middle age must be served and pajamas came to the beach to save fat thighs and flabby calves from competition with the one-piece bathing-suit. Finally skirts came down and everything was concealed. Everybody was at scratch now. Let's go—

But it was not to be. Somebody had blundered and the most expensive orgy in history was over.

It ended two years ago, because the utter confidence which was its essential prop received an enormous jolt, and it didn't take long for the flimsy structure to settle earthward. And after two years the Jazz Age seems as far away as the days before the War. It was borrowed time anyhow—the whole upper tenth of a nation living with the insouciance of grand ducs and the casualness of chorus girls. But moralizing is easy now and it was pleasant to be in one's twenties in such a certain and unworried time. Even when you were broke you didn't worry about money, because it was in such profusion around you. . . . In the theatrical world extravagant productions were carried by a few second-rate stars, and so on up the scale into politics, where it was difficult to interest good men in positions of the highest importance and responsibility, importance and responsibility far exceeding that of business executives but which paid only five or six thousand a year.

Now once more the belt is tight and we summon the proper expression of horror as we look back at our wasted youth. Sometimes, though, there is a ghostly rumble among the drums, an asthmatic whisper in the trombones that swings me back into the early twenties when we drank wood alcohol and every day in every way grew better and better, and there was a first abortive shortening of the skirts, and girls all looked alike in sweater dresses, and people you didn't want to know said "Yes, we have no bananas," and it seemed only a question of a few years before the older people would step aside and let the world be run by those who saw things as they were—and it all seems rosy and romantic to us who were young then, because we will never feel quite so intensely about our surroundings any more.

In September 1931 the Fitzgeralds sailed back to the U.S. for the last time, intending to settle in Montgomery where Zelda's father was seriously ill. Zelda had tentatively been pronounced cured by her doctors at Prangins.

Recovered

Sketching

Homeward bound on the Aquitania

HOME AGAIN

In the dark autumn of two years later we saw New York again. We passed through curiously polite customs agents, and then with bowed head and hat in hand I walked reverently through the echoing tomb. Among the ruins a few childish wraiths still played to keep up the pretense that they were alive, betraying by their feverish voices and hectic cheeks the thinness of the masquerade. Cocktail parties, a last hollow survival from the days of carnival, echoed to the plaints of the wounded: "Shoot me, for the love of God, someone shoot me!", and the groans and wails of the dying: "Did you see that United States Steel is down three more points?" My barber was back at work in his shop; again the head waiters bowed people to their tables, if there were people to be bowed. From the ruins, lonely and inexplicable as the sphinx, rose the Empire State Building and, just as it had been a tradition of mine to climb to the Plaza Roof to take leave of the beautiful city, extending as far as eyes could reach, so now I went to the roof of the last and most magnificent of towers.

—"My Lost City"

186

Recession + Procession

Zelda Well, Worse, Better. Novel intension begins

Thirty Five Years Old

Sept — Arrive Montgomery, the judge, the family, callers at Greystone, leaving the hotel, house hunting, two houses, old friends — Fanny, young Byers (Cody) Freeman + Julia + Unc., bought car, golf + tennis at friends houses, the Garlands, Mrs McKinney, Stopped in Washington, Ring in New York.

Oct — Felder Ave, the usual girls, the Pitts + Little Theatre, following football, life dull, walks with cane, Scotty's school, tennis + golf Saw Auburn Tulane + left for California. The train. First impressions Meredith + Sullivan, de Sano, Thalberg, Lewin + conference rooms offices, funny man, Hollywood Blvd + ...

Nov — King + Eleanor, the Hoveys, the politicians daughter + Eddie Mayer, the Boyds, Zelda letters Thalberg's parties, Carmel's parties + her husband, Selznick and his new wife + previews, the offices at Metro, Dwight Taylor, + the phonograph nice kid who runs authors, Colton + Zoe + ..., Dud Murphy + French woman. Judge dead

10/8/31 MONTGOMERY, ALA., THURSDAY

Scott Fitzgeralds To Spend Winter Here Writing Books

Author Finds Montgomery Less Preoccupied With 'Depression' Than East

By WALLING KEITH

F. Scott Fitzgerald, fiction writer and author of several novels, and Mrs. Fitzgerald, the former Miss Zelda Sayre, daughter of Judge A. D. Sayre here, arrived in Montgomery yesterday to spend the Winter. Their 10-year-old daughter, Scottie, will arrive Saturday.

Mrs. Fitzgerald, who is also a writer, is working on a book. They returned recently to New York from Europe where they had spent two years, gathering color for their writings.

At the Greystone Hotel where the Fitzgeralds are stopping until their home they have leased for the Winter on Felder Avenue is fitted, Mr. Fitzgerald expressed delight in finding that Montgomery "showed less of signs of depression" than any American city that he has recently visited.

Can Not Forget Depression

"The people here don't seem to recognize the existence of a depression," he declared, telling of his amazement at finding poor business conditions the chief topic of conversation everywhere he went after his return from Europe.

"In the East, even at places where people seek recreation and at parties where one goes to forget the day's work, it seemed that I hardly became acquainted with members of the party before they were talking of the depression. I'm going to like it here in Montgomery, I know. It's a relief to spend a few hours in a city where I'm not met with talk of depression."

In a conversation in which he discussed prohibition, national politics, current literature and writers, Communism and baseball, Mr. Fitzgerald touched upon the South and its typical cities.

"You see, I'm not a stranger to Montgomery at all," he explained, "having been stationed here during the war and marrying a Montgomery girl, I have felt the warmness of the city's hospitality."

Mr. Fitzgerald, who said he was a Jeffersonian Democrat at heart and somewhat of a Communist in ideals, declared that the prohibition law was not only a foolish gesture but that it was a hindrance to the machine of government.

"Understand now, I'm purely a fiction writer and do not profess to be an earnest student of political science," he smiled, "but I believe strongly that such a law as one prohibiting liquor is foolish, and all the writers, keenly interested in human welfare whom I know, laugh at the prohibition law."

"Not only is the question a laughable one," he said, "but it has done more to prevent perfect coordination among the members of both major political parties than any one thing."

"This is not new. All of my writer friends think and say the same thing," he added hastily.

No Red Peril Here

"Another great difference I have found since my few hours in Montgomery," he said, "is the seemingly lack of fear of communistic activity or thought here. It seems foolish for an American to be afraid of any communistic revolution in this country, right now, but I heard so many conjectures of possible reactions here, while in Eastern cities, that at times I felt myself becoming concerned with the question.

"In ideals I am somewhat of a communist. That is, as much as other persons who belong to what we call 'the arts group'; but communism as I see it has no place in the United States," he laughed, "and the American people will not stand for its teachings."

How Friends Are Doing

Mr. Fitzgerald, who counts among his friends, many writers of national and international note, expressed a fondness for Alabama and showed interest in Southern writers.

Ernest Hemingway, whom he saw in New York several days ago, is finishing a new novel, Mr. Fitzgerald said. Ring Lardner, the humorist, a friend of Fitzgerald's whom he visited before coming to Montgomery, is seriously ill.

The novel on which Mr. Fitzgerald is now working will be his first one in four years. He is a regular contributor of short stories to The Saturday Evening Post and other magazines.

His novel "This Side of Paradise," was published before his graduation from Princeton.

"Since then I've been a professional writer, and I think I've been lucky," he said.

The Fitzgeralds went to Montgomery in September 1931 and rented a house at 819 Felder Avenue, where they remained until February 1932.

Joan was waiting in the little brown Ford.

Alabama felt like a little girl again to see her sister after so many years. The old town where her father had worked away so much of his life spread before her protectively. It was good to be a stranger in a land when you felt aggressive and acquisitive, but when you began to weave your horizons into some kind of shelter it was good to know that hands you loved had helped in their spinning—made you feel as if the threads would hold together better.

* * *

The car stopped before the quiet house. How many nights had she coasted up to that walk just that way to keep from waking her father with the grind of the brakes after dances? The sweet smell of sleeping gardens lay in the air. A breeze from the gulf tolled the pecan trees mournfully back and forth. Nothing had changed. The friendly windows shone in the just benediction of her father's spirit, the door spread open to the just decency of his will. Thirty years he had lived in his house, and watched the scattered jonquils bloom and seen the morning-glories wrinkle in the morning sun and snipped the blight from his roses and admired Miss Millie's ferns.

—*Save Me the Waltz* (ZF)

In November-December 1931 Fitzgerald was in Hollywood alone working on "The Red-Headed Woman" for MGM. His script was not used.

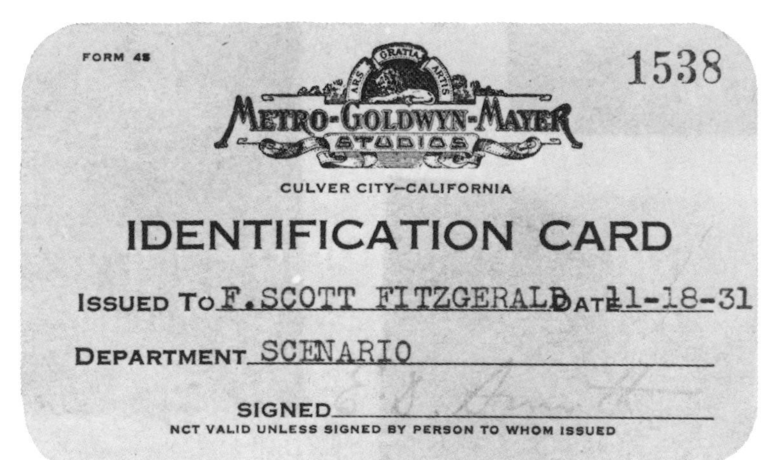
FORM 45 1538

METRO-GOLDWYN-MAYER STUDIOS

CULVER CITY—CALIFORNIA

IDENTIFICATION CARD

ISSUED TO F. SCOTT FITZGERALD DATE 11-18-31

DEPARTMENT SCENARIO

SIGNED

NOT VALID UNLESS SIGNED BY PERSON TO WHOM ISSUED

SCOTT FITZGERALD=
CHRISTIE HOTEL HOLLYWOOD CALIF=
I THOUGHT YOU WERE ONE OF THE MOST AGREEABLE PERSONS AT OUR TEA=
NORMA THALBERG.

The filing time as shown in the date line on full-rate telegrams and day letters, and the time of receipt at destination as shown on all messages, is ST

Received at 6360 Hollywood Blvd., Hollywood, Calif. Telephone GLadstone 4191 1931 NOV 18

SD1 10=MONTGOVERY ALA 18 950A
SCOTT FITZGERALD=
HOTEL CHRISTIE=
DADDY DIED LAST NIGHT DO NOT WORRY ABOUT US LOVE=
ZELDA.

I'm not sorry I went because I've got a fine story about Hollywood which will be along in several days.

—FSF to Harold Ober, c. 28 December 1931.

In Hollywood Fitzgerald met Irving Thalberg, the production head at MGM, who became the model for Monroe Stahr in The Last Tycoon. *A party in the Thalberg home at which Fitzgerald attempted to entertain provided material for his story "Crazy Sunday." Fitzgerald greatly admired Thalberg's wife, the actress Norma Shearer. She appears as Stella in "Crazy Sunday."*

CRAZY SUNDAY

BY F. SCOTT FITZGERALD

It was Sunday—not a day, but rather a gap between two other days. Behind, for all of them, lay sets and sequences, the struggles of rival ingenuities in the conference rooms, the interminable waits under the crane that swung the microphone, the hundred miles a day by automobiles to and fro across Hollywood county, the

When the invitation came it made him sure that he was getting somewhere. Ordinarily he did not go out on Sundays but stayed sober and took work home with him. Recently they had given him a Eugene O'Neill play destined for a very important lady indeed. Everything he had done so far had pleased Miles Calman, and

At some point he heard Nat Keogh snicker and here and there were a few encouraging faces, but as he finished he had the sickening realization that he had made a fool of himself in view of an important section of the picture world, upon whose favor depended his career.

For a moment he existed in the midst of a confused silence, broken by a general trek for the door. He felt the undercurrent of derision that rolled through the gossip; then—all this was in the space of ten seconds—the Great Lover, his eye hard and empty as the eye of a needle, shouted "Boo! Boo!" voicing in an overtone what he felt was the mood of the crowd. It was the resentment of the professional toward the amateur, of the community toward the stranger, the thumbs-down of the clan.

Only Stella Walker was still standing near and thanking him as if he had been an unparalleled success, as if it hadn't occurred to her that anyone hadn't liked it. As Nat Keogh helped him into his overcoat, a great wave of self-disgust swept over him and he clung desperately to his rule of never betraying an inferior emotion until he no longer felt it.

"I was a flop," he said lightly, to Stella. "Never mind, it's a good number when appreciated. Thanks for your coöperation."

The smile did not leave her face—he bowed rather drunkenly and Nat drew him toward the door. . . .

The arrival of his breakfast awakened him into a broken and ruined world. Yesterday he was himself, a point of fire against an industry, today he felt that he was pitted under an enormous disadvantage, against those faces, against individual contempt and collective sneer. Worse than that, to Miles Calman he was become one of those rummies, stripped of dignity, whom Calman regretted he was compelled to use. To Stella Walker on whom he had forced a martyrdom to preserve the courtesy of her house—her opinion he did not dare to guess. His gastric juices ceased to flow and he set his poached eggs back on the telephone table. He wrote:

"Dear Miles: You can imagine my profound self-disgust. I confess to a taint of exhibitionism, but at six o'clock in the afternoon, in broad daylight! Good God! My apologies to your wife.

"Yours ever,

"Joel Coles."

* * *

"Never again," he exclaimed aloud, "absolutely my last social appearance in Hollywood!"

The following morning a telegram was waiting for him at his office:

You were one of the most agreeable people at our party. Expect you at my sister June's buffet supper next Sunday.

Stella Walker Calman.

The blood rushed fast through his veins for a feverish minute. Incredulously he read the telegram over.

"Well, that's the sweetest thing I ever heard of in my life!"

67

Record for 1931

Stories	Indecision	$ 4000.	Com 10%	3600	00
	A New Leaf	4000.	"	3600	00
	Flight and Pursuit	4000.	"	3600	00
	Emotional Bankrupcy	4000.	"	3600	00
	Between Three and Four	4000.	"	3600	00
	A Change of Class	4000.	"	3600	00
	Half a Dozen of the Other	3000.	"	2700	00
	A Freeze Out	4000.	"	3600	00
	Diagnosis	4000.	"	3600	00
	Total			31,500	00
Other Items	Treatment Metro Goldwyn Mayer	6000.	"	5400	00
	Echoes of the Jazz Age	500.		500	00
	Vegetable Performance	25.00	"	22	50
	New Leaf (English)	£17	"	59	00
	Flight & Pursuit (English)	Guinies 35	"	126	00
	John Jackson's Arcady	2.21	"	2	00
	Total			6,109	50
Books	This Side of Paradise			12	90
	Flappers & Philosophers			4	30
	The Beautiful & Damned			4	40
	Tales of the Jazz Age			3	90
	The Vegetable			1	13
	The Great Gatsby			17	90
	All the Sad Young Men			7	90
	Advance against Bk.			44	15
	Total			100	00
	Less: Not paid in 1931 by Metro	173.72	"	−155	35
	Grand Total			37,554	00
	New Yorker sketch	50.00		45	00
				37,599	00

1931 was Fitzgerald's best year of earnings before he went permanently to Hollywood in 1937.

One of the portraits taken for the dust jacket of Zelda's autobiographical novel, Save Me the Waltz, which she began writing in Montgomery while Scott was in Hollywood.

Illness Fatal For Justice Sayre, Supreme Court

Celebrated Jurist, Stricken Last Summer, Passes Quietly At Home Here

Served 22 Years

Senior Associate Justice Suffered Collapse After Severe Influenza Attack

Judge A. D. Sayre, 73, senior associate justice of the Alabama Supreme Court and a member of the court for the last 22 years, died at 11:30 o'clock last night at his home, 6 Pleasant Avenue, after a long illness.

Judge Sayre was stricken last Spring with a severe attack of influenza from which he never fully recovered though he was able to return to his office and resume his duties within a month. But in August he suffered a physical collapse which confined him to his bed.

Judge Sayre was conceded everywhere to be one of the most able and profound jurists who ever sat on the Supreme Court bench of this State. His opinions have for years been quoted with unusual frequency, and he was regarded as an ornament to the eminent position he filled.

His genius in, and his peculiar fitness for, the legal profession were evidenced early in his distinguished career. It long ago became a tradition that as a trial judge he never had a judgment reversed by the Supreme Court to which he later was elevated and on which he thereafter served up to the time of his last illness.

Despite long years spent in the study and decision of questions of gravest moment to the State, the seriousness of his work never affected his unaffected geniality, his intense humanness, and his keen sense of humor.

His extraordinary ability as a judge and the charm of his personality won friends and admirers throughout the State. Members of the legal profession held him in great affection. To each of them the news of his death will bring profound personal sorrow.

Justice Sayre was born April 29, 1858, at Tuskegee, the son of Daniel and Musidora (Morgan) Sayre. He received his primary education in private schools and graduated from Roanoke College, Virginia, with an A. M. degree in 1878. He read law in the office of Judge Thomas M. Arrington, of Montgomery, and was admitted to the bar in 1880.

He was clerk of the City Court of Montgomery, 1883-89; member of the Legislature from Montgomery County, 1890-91 and 1892-93; member of the State Senate, 1894-95, and president of that body, 1896-97; nominated to the Senate for judge of the City Court of Montgomery, and elected, in 1897; nominated for reelection in 1903; member of the Board of Education of the City of Montgomery, 1891-1911.

In 1909 he was appointed by Gov. B. B. Comer as associate justice of the Alabama Supreme Court to succeed Judge James R. Dowdell; elected Nov. 8, 1910, his own successor; reelected Nov. 5, 1912, for a term of six years, and has served continuously since. He was elected last Fall for an additional term of six years, which he began serving in January.

Judge Sayre was married Jan. 17, 1884, at Eddysville, Ky., to Miss Minnie Buckner Machen, daughter of W. B. and Victoria (Mims) Machen, of Eddysville. Her father was former U. S. Senator from Kentucky.

Surviving are his widow, one brother, J. Reid Sayre, of Galveston, Texas; one son, A. D. Sayre, Jr., of Memphis, Tenn.; and four daughters, Mrs. Minon W. Brinson, of Montgomery; Mrs. Newman Smith, of Brussels, Belgium; Mrs. John M. Palmer, of Tarrytown, N. Y.; and Mrs F. Scott Fitzgerald, now of Montgomery; and four grandchildren, Marjorie Brinson and Scottie Fitzgerald, of Montgomery, and Clotilde and [illegible] Palmer, of Tarrytown, N. Y.

Judge Sayre died in November 1931. Although Zelda took the shock well at first, she suffered a relapse in January and went up with Scott to the Phipps Clinic at Johns Hopkins Hospital, where she finished her novel.

Capitol Mourns Death Of Sayre

Funeral Tomorrow At 11 A. M.; Tribute Paid To Supreme Court Justice

JUDGE A. D. SAYRE

Judge Anthony D. Sayre, Associate Justice of the Alabama Supreme Court, whose passing at 73 was announced yesterday, was a distinguished Alabamian and a citizen in whom Montgomery took pride. Judge Sayre possessed a virile and lucid mind which he had assiduously and patiently cultivated. He possessed also an intellectual integrity and courage which commanded universal respect. There was nothing weak or opportunistic about Judge Sayre. There was no lack of iron in his blood.

Judge Sayre, appointed to the Supreme bench in 1909 and elected by the people in 1910, was consistently re-elected thereafter. The remarkable thing about his success before the people is that he was in no sense a politician. We doubt if any holder of a State office in the last 20 years has known so few Alabamians personally as Judge Sayre. He did not make speeches, he did not lend his name and time to various public movements, he did not go about over the State much, he was not a joiner. During his 22 years on the Supreme bench Judge Sayre could be found nearly all the time at one of three places. He was at his office at the capitol, or his home on Pleasant Avenue, or he was at the United corner waiting for a street car to take him home or to the capitol. He was a quiet, modest man who preferred to give all of his time to his family and his work. He was a prodigious worker in the days of his strength, and in his labors he found satisfaction.

Judge Sayre could win the votes of people who had never seen him because of the legend of excellence that attached to his name. The people sensed that here was no commonplace man, but a man of high professional attainments and solid character. No one can testify that he ever heard a slighting remark about Judge Sayre. He was everywhere respected and admired. He was a wise and good man, and a pleasant gentleman.

Alone with her father, Alabama's heart sank. He was so thin and little now that he was sick, to have got through so much of life. He had had a hard time providing for them all. The noble completeness of the life withering on the bed before her moved her to promise herself many promises.

"Oh, my father, there are so many things I want to ask you."

"Baby," the old man patted her hand. His wrists were no bigger than a bird's. How had he fed them all?

"I never thought you'd known till now."

She smoothed the gray hair, even Confederate gray.

"I've got to go to sleep, baby."

"Sleep," she said, "sleep."

She sat there a long time. She hated the way the nurse moved about the room as if her father were a child. Her father knew everything. Her heart was sobbing. And sobbing.

The old man opened his eyes proudly, as was his wont.

"Did you say you wanted to ask me something?"

"I thought you could tell me if our bodies are given to us as counterirritants to the soul. I thought you'd know why when our bodies ought to bring surcease from our tortured minds, they fail and collapse; and why, when we are tormented in our bodies, does our soul desert us as a refuge?"

The old man lay silent.

"Why do we spend years using up our bodies to nurture our minds with experience and find our minds turning then to our exhausted bodies for solace? Why, Daddy?"

"Ask me something easy," the old man answered very weak and far away.

"The Judge must sleep," said the nurse.

"I'll go."

—*Save Me the Waltz* (ZF)

A Strange year of Work + Drink. Increasingly unhappy.—Zelda up + down. 1st draft of Novel complete Ominous!

Thirty-Six Years Old

Mrs. Bayard Turnbull became a sympathetic friend to the Fitzgeralds. Her son, Andrew, Scottie's playmate, later wrote a biography of Scott.

In the spring of 1932 Fitzgerald rented "La Paix," one of the houses on the Bayard Turnbull estate, to be near Zelda who had been transferred to the Sheppard Pratt Hospital at Towson, Maryland. At this time Fitzgerald was working hard to finish Tender Is the Night, *which he had started in 1926. Mrs. Isabel Owens (below), who became his secretary at this time, also helped to keep the household together.*

Zelda's original version of Save Me the Waltz *upset Fitzgerald considerably because it drew on so much of the same material that he was using in* Tender Is the Night. *When he learned that she had sent it off to Perkins without consulting him, he was furious and insisted that she revise it, particularly taking out some of the more unflattering references to himself.*

Zelda was treated at Sheppard Pratt Hospital near "La Paix" after a stay at the Phipps Clinic of Johns Hopkins Hospital in Baltimore.

Here is Zelda's novel. It is a good novel now, perhaps a very good novel—I am too close to it to tell. It has the faults & virtues of a first novel. It is more the expression of a powerful personality, like Look Homeward Angel *than the work of a finished artist like Ernest Hemmingway. It should interest the many thousands interested in dancing. It is* about something *& absolutely new, & should sell.*

Now, about its reception. If you refuse it, which I don't think you will, all communication should come through me. If you accept it write her directly and I withdraw all restraints on whatever meed of praise you may see fit to give. The strain of writing it was bad for her but it had to be written—she needed relaxation afterwards and I was afraid that praise might encourage the incipient egomania the doctors noticed, but she has taken such a sane common sense view lately (at first she refused to revise—then she revised completely, added on her own suggestion & has changed what was a rather flashy and self-justifying "true confessions" that wasn't worthy of her into an honest piece of work. She can do more with the galley but I cant ask her to do more now.)—but now praise will do her good within reason. But she mustn't write anything more on the personal *side for six months or so until she is stronger.*

Now a second thing, more important than you think. You haven't been in the publishing business over twenty years without noticing the streaks of smallness in very large personalities. Ernest told me once he would "never publish a book in the same season with me", meaning it would lead to ill-feeling. I advise you, if he is in New York, (and always granting you like Zelda's book) do not praise it, or even talk about it to him! *The finer the thing he has written, the more he'll expect your entire allegiance to it as this is one of the few pleasures, rich & full & new, he'll get out of it. I know this, & I think you do too & probably there's no use warning you. There is no possible conflict between the books but there has always been a subtle struggle between Ernest & Zelda, & any apposition might have curiously grave consequences—curious, that is, to un-jealous men like you and me.*

—FSF to Maxwell Perkins, c. 14 May 1932.

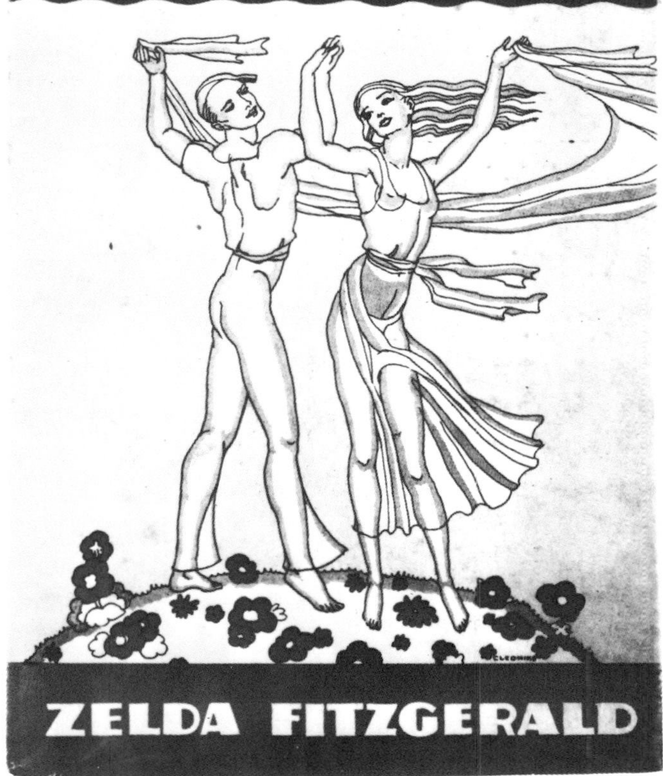

$2.00

SAVE ME THE WALTZ

In a style of her own the talented wife of F. Scott Fitzgerald has told the story of the marriage of a young artist (to whom success came very early) with a Southern girl who decided "to move brightly along high places and stop to trespass and admire" and "if in the future her soul should come starving and crying for bread it should eat the stone she would have to offer without complaint or remorse."

Mrs. Fitzgerald's novel relates the stormy passage of that young girl from the safe harbor of childhood to maturity. Much of the journey is in Europe, among those glittering people who decorated the Ritz bar in Paris and the great post-war boom with the shimmer of their ennui. It is hectic, it is hollow, and the girl becomes desperate, and in her desperation she turns to dancing for the ballet. The solution she elected, which brings her husband and herself back to the Southern town in which she was born, is a modern instance of a universal theme—the struggle of a soul for its salvation.

Zelda had completed her only novel, Save Me the Waltz, rapidly at the Phipps Clinic. It was published in October 1932. Only 3,000 copies were printed.

He hated the conflict that had grown out of their wanting the same excellences, the same prizes from life.

—"What a Handsome Pair!"

SAVE ME THE WALTZ. By Zelda Fitzgerald. . . ***New York: Charles Scribner's Sons. . .$2.***

"SAVE ME THE WALTZ" is the last will and testament, so to speak, of a departed era that began as a barroom ballad and ended as a funeral oration. Until Mrs. Fitzgerald reminded us, we had almost forgot the gay procession of Americans who sought their salvation in the basements of Montmartre, along the sunny Riviera, at Nice, Juan les Pins, Mentone. Except for the few who escaped to Majorca, the disillusioned rest drank a farewell sherry-flip and returned to the land of comic-strips and skyscrapers.

This is approximately the fate of Alabama Beggs, the heroine who somersaults through the pages of this novel. We are informed very early that she had something of the incorrigible rebel in her, and wasn't to be browbeaten or cajoled by papa and mama Beggs, as her sisters were, into a commonplace marriage. Flirting with the town sheik was fun enough, but Alabama never let that interfere with her plans for the future. When one of her first suitors asked her if she could live on five thousand a year she replied:

"I could, but I don't want to."

"Then why did you kiss me?"

"I had never kissed a man with a mustache before."

While she liked to think she was a hardboiled experimentalist—a new female type which the war fertilized—she was in her heart an uncompromising sentimentalist not unlike the kind she read about in the frayed family copy of Boccaccio; she wanted to live in a big city, preferably New York. David Knight, a young fresco painter, offered her both. The marriage knot officially tied, they set out for the vertical city, where, like true children of the metropolis, they soon learned to get plastered on bathtub gin and waddle in gayety.

We see them next in Normandy eating lobsters, mixing drinks with anonymous celebrities, and looking appropriately bored. Here the call of the flesh came hazardously near compromising Alabama and breaking up the Knight household. In Paris Alabama did penance by punishing the flesh in a ballerina school. She was forced, however, through illness to abandon a career she never really wanted. The Knights (there are three now, a daughter having been added in the interim) are called home to bury old Judge Beggs, and they get unexplainably maudlin over sentiments they never valued too highly.

What, you may naturally ask, is the purpose of all this apparently aimless gyration? Mrs. Fitzgerald's answer would probably be: none whatsoever. The Knights were just like any other average American pre-depression adventurers. They thought that happiness, like prosperity, was just around the corner. If they learned anything for all their trouble, it was this: that to take life too seriously is almost as fatal as not taking it seriously enough.

That may explain, to some extent, why Mrs. Fitzgerald refuses to recognize the validity of pure tragedy, and why she converts every tragic situation into a harlequinade. At first the reader is amused by this; later he begins to suspect the author of completely depriving her characters of their will. At times the story comes dangerously near losing all emotional credibility.

There is a constant recurrence of exaggerated images such as: "Sylvia flopped across the room like an opaque protoplasm propelling itself across a sand bank"; or, "Her body was so full of static from the constant whip of her work that she could get no clear communication with herself."

We may attribute this, and other disturbing elements, to the fact that this is Mrs. Fitzgerald's first attempt to master the novel form (although she has done admirably with the short-story). "Save Me The Waltz" can, however, be read with considerable pleasure. The writing has a masculinity that is unusual; it is always vibrant and always sensitive.

New York Herald Tribune

THERE is every chance that fifty readers will take up Zelda Fitzgerald's first novel, SAVE ME THE WALTZ (*Scribner's*. $2.00), and drop it again within the first chapter to every one reader who will persist to the end. It is not only that her publishers have not seen fit to curb an almost ludicrous lushness of writing ("Incubated in the mystic pungence of Negro mammies, the family hatched into girls" will do for an example) but they have not given the book the elementary services of a literate proofreader. We read that Alabama's older sister had "The DeCameron" in her drawer, and had bought a copy of the "Primaverra"; Alabama herself had read "Cabel" (James Branch, in case it isn't clear), wanted to dance in a "Marseille" dance-hall, and liked the music of "Prokopieff"; while the favourite composer of a comrade at dancing school was "Litz". In fact the number of absurd errors in the book are beyond counting; and yet if one can persist past the mistakes and the verbiage one comes on an earnest, honest, good little story of a girl trying desperately to make a character for herself which will carry her through life; and one will find, as well, that in Judge Austin Beggs Mrs. Fitzgerald has drawn with loving care as fine a man as we have had in fiction for many a month. He is the father of the heroine, and, rightly admiring his integrity, Alabama strains every nerve to find a way to live as stoically and admirably as he.

There is a warm, intelligent, undisciplined mind behind *Save Me the Waltz*. Mrs. Fitzgerald should have had what help she needed to save her book from the danger of becoming a laughing-stock.

DOROTHEA BRANDE

The Bookman

Mrs. Fitzgerald's First Novel Places Her on Scott's Level

SAVE ME THE WALTZ, by Zelda Fitzgerald (Scribner's).

Last May, when Mrs. F. Scott Fitzgerald was a patient at Johns Hopkins Hospital and her famous husband was, consequently, staying in Baltimore, a reporter for this paper wrote an article about the husband. In the final paragraph he casually wrote that "His wife, Zelda, now taking a rest cure at the hospital, is also a writer and has sent off her first novel to the publishers several days ago."

Well, that first novel is now off the presses. And it shows that when the reporter called Zelda Fitzgerald a "writer" he was not merely being polite. He wrote truly.

"Save Me the Waltz" looks back on the dizzy days just after the war; upon the young Americans of those dizzy days; upon their frenzied, full-pocketed quest for excitement, and upon the futility of that quest.

Here she writes a serious tale of how a young girl from the South, married to an artist and partaking of the clever, cheap and colorful life of Americans abroad, breaks with the roisterers whose sole aim is killing time, and attempts to build a career for herself in ballet dancing. It is her way of winning her self-respect, of rounding out her life, achieving her aspirations. She fails, but not wholly. Something is saved for her when she has quaffed deep from the wine of experience.

Zelda Fitzgerald's heroine, Alabama, was never quite in tune with the wasters. When she first stepped out in her Southern home and did unconventional things, such as going out of the house before the men called for her or kissing a man because he had a mustache, it was chiefly because the way of life in the house of her father, Judge Austin Beggs, meant suffocation.

This girl became the wife of David Knight, who painted, and with him savored the bright life of Paris and the Riviera. It was the day of the dollar hegira when American business men were discovering Europe. Zelda Fitzgerald gives an impressionistic picture of the rush:

"There were Americans at night and day Americans, and we all had Americans in the bank to buy things with. The marble lobbies were full of them.

"All of them drank. Americans with red ribbons in their buttonholes read papers called the Eclaireur and drank on the sidewalks, Americans with tips on the races drank down a flight of stairs, Americans with a million dollars and a standing engagement with the hotel masseuses drank in suites at the Meurice and the Crillon. Other Americans drank in Montmartre 'pour le soif' and 'contre la chaleur' 'pour la digestion' and 'pour se guerir.' They were glad the French thought they were crazy."

In a breezy, conversational style Zelda tells her story—the story of two Americans to whom life "began to appear as tortuous as the sentimental writhings of a rhythmic dance." When Alabama broke with this life she applied herself to her work—dancing in the ballet, under various exacting teachers.

These passages are without glamour though not without color. Zelda Fitzgerald has not looked on in the studios of hard-working madame this and that for nothing. The difficult life of the students, the hard drill in order to learn the steps and force the body to play its graceful role is here portrayed. In the end Alabama is defeated; an infection in a toe gives her a terrible illness from which she recovers with the knowledge that she will never dance. Her teachers tell David that it is too bad she started too late.

The return to America of these two chastened spirits with their child is perhaps true to actuality. Feeling now that they face middle age, they seek a revaluation of life on the basis of the experience they have had. Ironically Alabama declares that "We grew up founding our dreams on the infinite promise of American advertising." David adds: "We couldn't go on indefinitely being swept off our feet." But the crowd seems to be as witless and as empty of ideas as ever.

Mr. and Mrs. F. Scott Fitzgerald

Of the Jazz Age

SAVE ME THE WALTZ. By Zelda Fitzgerald. 285 pp. New York: Charles Scribner's Sons. $2.

ALABAMA was the daughter of a somewhat dilapidated South —the youngest child of parents so much older than herself that there was little hope of much understanding on their side or of anything but a rather evasive awe on hers. While still very young she married David Knight, an artist just out of khaki, and shared the exuberance of his early post-war successes. After that wild and reckless period came a migration to France, where in the heat and blueness of Hyères and in the froth that comes to the surface of American society in Paris, David and Alabama drifted more and more definitely apart. Alabama, bored with a succession of wild parties of which her husband, not she, was the artistic centre, longed for an art of her own and decided with more or less sincerity to take up ballet dancing. Dancing is not a thing that can be lightly "taken up" in an idle moment; it should be started in childhood; and although Mrs. Fitzgerald (she is the wife of Scott Fitzgerald) does not attempt to disguise the tremendous mental and physical strain involved, it still remains hard to believe in the possibility of Alabama's becoming a famous ballerina at the age of 27 or so without ever having danced seriously before. The dancing as such is not, of course, particularly important to the story, although the author has very cleverly and effectively contrived her background of the earnest Russian studio in Paris, and the sloppy inefficiency of the opera company in which the heroine makes her début in Naples. The arrival of her child there to visit her, accompanied by a starched and snobbish mademoiselle, is amusing and natural; her own accident and the deathbed of her father, which serve to bring her and her husband together again, though in a rather unsatisfactory manner, are natural too in a different vein.

Mrs. Fitzgerald's book is a curious muddle of good psychology and atrocious style. The slow rift between a formerly devoted young husband and wife, as success both worldly and artistic comes to the husband and leaves the wife behind; the frantically hard work of the wife to make herself a career quite separate from his, and her tragic failure to do so, make up a story which has possibilities, although it is not new, and which gains steadily in vitality as it moves along. And although the background of post-war New York and the Paris of boites-de-nuit and the Ritz bar has been overworked, yet it would still serve quite well for a little while longer. Mrs. Fitzgerald, however, has almost crushed the life out of it with a weight of unwieldy metaphor; and in searching for the startling phrase has often descended to the ludicrous, as in "she lay staring about, conscious of the absence of expression smothering her face like a wet bath-mat." It is a pity, too, that the publishers could not have had more accurate proofreading; for it is inconceivable that the author should have undertaken to use as much of the French language as appears in this book, if she knew so little of it as this book indicates—almost every single French word (and there are many), as well as many foreign names and a good many plain English words, are misspelled. This may sound like a small thing, but to meet such mistakes on practically every page is so annoying that it becomes almost impossible to read the book at all.

The New York Times

Zelda's comedy was produced in June 1933 by the Vagabond Junior Players, a Baltimore amateur group. After a disastrous opening night, Fitzgerald made revisions, which she resented.

Beautiful and Damned

SAVE ME THE WALTZ. By ZELDA FITZGERALD. New York: Charles Scribner's Sons. 1932. $2.

Reviewed by GEOFFREY HELLMAN

THE most noticeable feature about this book is the steady stream of strained metaphor with which Mrs. Fitzgerald manages to make what should be a light novel a study in the intricacies of the English language. No phenomenon is too simple for her to obfuscate with the complexities of figure of speech. Her book rivals the cross-word puzzle page in point of obscurity. And her men and women are almost as badly off. They can never just have their own way about things simply and unostentatiously, but have to go around "splashing their dreams in the dark pool of gratification." And under no circumstances are they allowed to look at anything as *terre-à-terre* as a building or a tree; peering from train windows, they can distinguish only "the pink carnival of Normandy . . . the delicate tracery of Paris . . . the white romance of Avignon."

Once you have dug out these nuggets and put them away in your geology collection, you find you have been reading a book which evokes, quite effectively at times, those booming post-war years when tea-dancing at the Biltmore and champagne cocktails at the Paris Ritz were in the natural order of things not only for the children of the rich but for a large section of *jeunesse* which did not consider itself particularly *dorée;* years when even artists made money. And more specifically, in this book, years when David Knight, a young painter, earned so much that he was able to take his family abroad and drift about expatriate Riviera beaches and Paris nightclubs.

It is with the disintegrating effect of this empty, rootless life on David's Southern-born wife, Alabama, that Mrs. Fitzgerald is chiefly concerned. Less plausible than her theme is her treatment thereof. To point to but one example of its implausibility, the desperation which prompts Alabama to turn to ballet-dancing with a group of dingy, impoverished people in Paris is anything but convincing on the part of a healthy young woman (which she has been shown to be) who has a husband whom she loves and a young daughter she adores. In short, Alabama is a poor vehicle for the neuroticism and dissatisfaction which she is suddenly called upon to exemplify. Typical of the other characters as well, this unconvincing motivation is part of the author's general inability to create full-bodied figures.

"Save Me the Waltz" belongs to that vast company of books of which some individual parts are greater than the whole. Particularly good is the episode of Alabama's parents' visit to the Knight home, where Mrs. Fitzgerald achieves a burlesque effect that is as amusing in itself as it is out of harmony with most of the rest of the book. But even here the inevitable metaphors rear their heads, doing their best to deflect attention from the humor that is this book's chief (if only occasional) redeeming feature.

Saturday Review of Literature

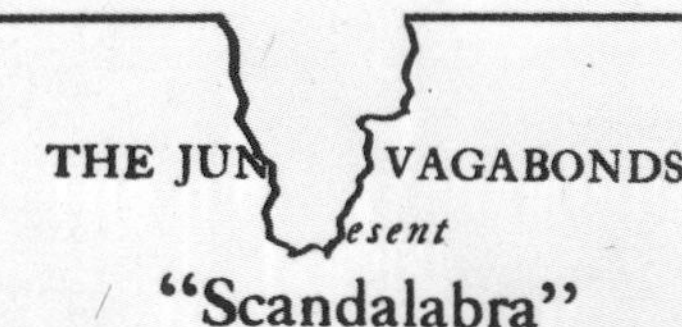

THE JUN[...] VAGABONDS [...]esent

"Scandalabra"

A farce-fantasy in a prologue and two acts
by ZELDA FITZGERALD

CHARACTERS
(As you meet them)

Uncle - (Andrew Messogony, Esq.) .... *John Henry Day, Jr.*
Bounds, his manservant .... *William F. Rodgers*
Andrew Messogony, his nephew .... *Zack Maccubbin*
His Lawyer .... *Isadore Serman*
The Doctor .... *Roy T. Smith*
Flower - (Mrs. Andrew Messogony, II) .... *Gladys Mitchell Wight*
Peter Consequential .... *E. Bennett Lasater*
A maid .... *Anne Tyler Peach*
Anaconda Consequential - (Anne) Peter's wife .... *Kathryn Forsythe*
A Reporter .... *E. Kenneth Albaugh*
A Photographer .... *Earl F. Botwell*
The Leprechaun .... *by himself*

Prologue — In Uncle's study

Act I.— Scene 1 — The same room, three years later. Some time after midnight.
Scene 2 — Peter Consequential's bedroom, at a Long Island house-party, eight o'clock the next morning.

(Greenroom intermission)

Act II — Scene 1 - A beach on the Riviera — a few weeks later. Midday.
Scene 2 - The Salon of the Consequentials' villa. The following dawn.

Produced and set under the direction of H. A. F. Penniman
Prologue screen by Zelda Fitzgerald.
Bedroom and salon by Zack Maccubbin.
Beach scene and furniture by Amanda Brown.
Costume chairman Alice Hall Dobson.
Properties by Dorothea Brinkman.
Lighting and stage management by Robert Dobson and Francis Swann.
Assistants to the director E. Kenneth Albaugh and Theodore Erbe
Beach costumes by Hochschild Kohn and Company.
Beach robes and equipment by May Company.

A PORTFOLIO OF PAINTINGS BY ZELDA FITZGERALD

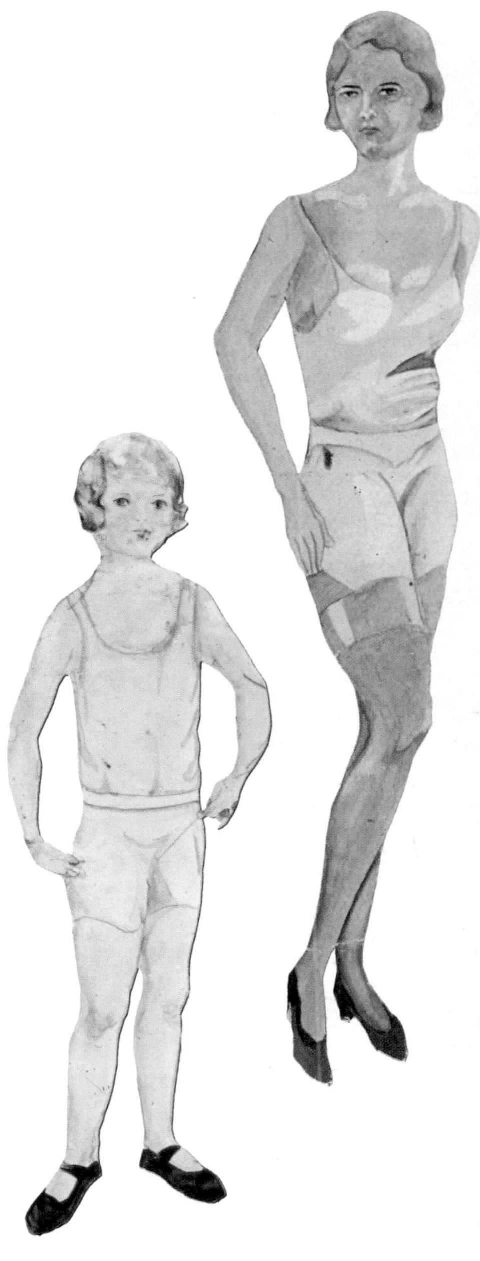

Self-portrait and paper dolls of Scott, Zelda, and Scottie, probably made by Zelda at "La Paix" about 1932.

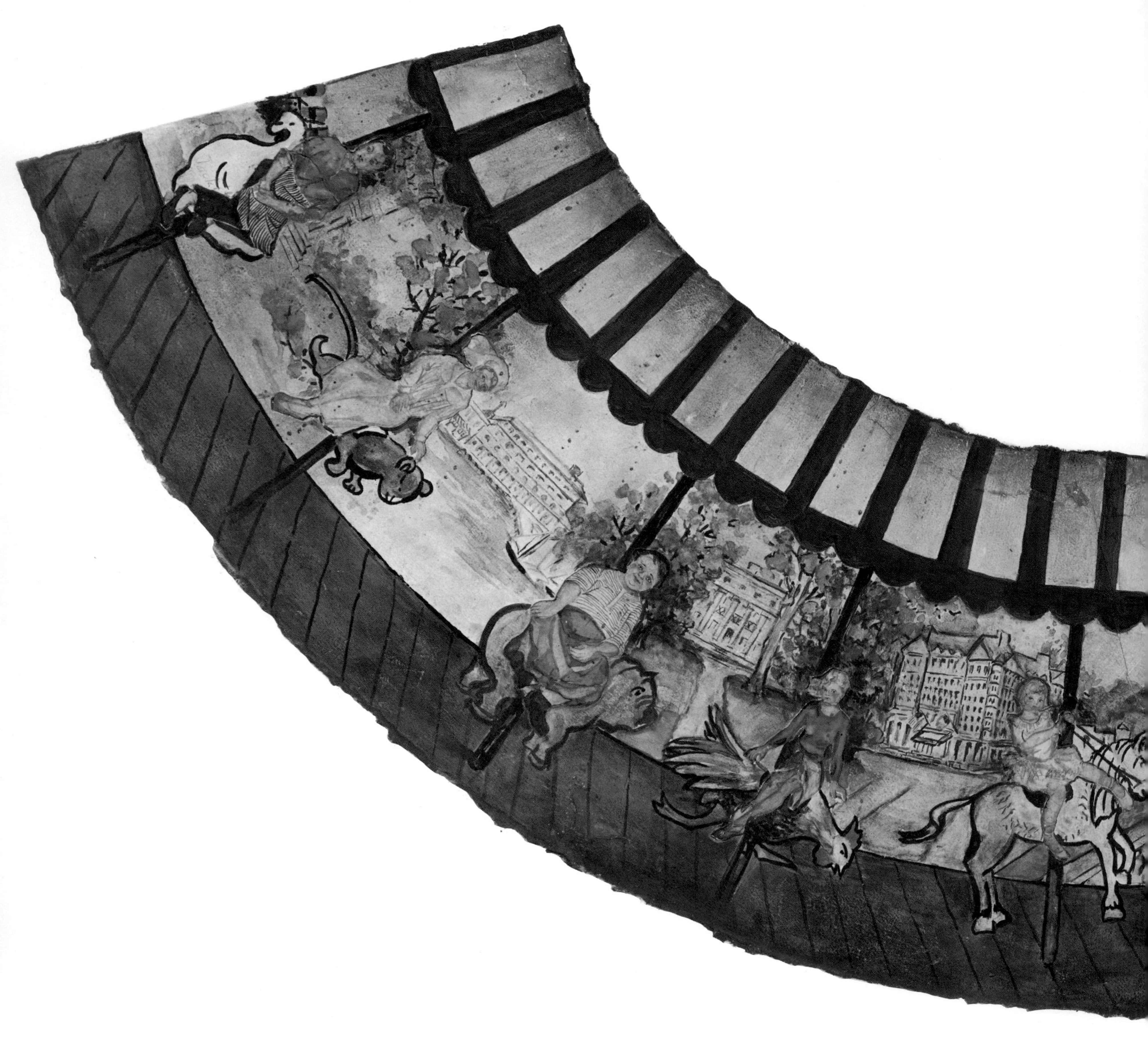

Lampshade painted at "Ellerslie," about 1928, on which Zelda depicted some of the places where the family had stayed: Villa St. Louis, Juan-les-Pins, France; White Bear Lake Yacht Club, Minnesota; "Ellerslie," Delaware; the Plaza Hotel in New York City; the island of Capri; the Villa Marie at St. Raphaël on the Riviera; the Spanish Steps in Rome; and the cottage in Westport, Connecticut.

Members of the family, servants, and a friend are riding on the merry-go-round. Those who can be identified are: "Nanny" on the mouse, Zelda on the rooster, Scottie on the horse, Scott on the elephant, Tana the butler on the turtle, and (probably) George Jean Nathan, a frequent visitor at Westport, on the lion.

Four of a series of watercolors of New York and Paris, painted about 1944. Top left, Central Park; lower left, New York Skyline; top right, Notre Dame Cathedral; lower right, Place de l'Opera.

Over the years, Zelda made several sets of historical paper dolls and costumes, the most elaborate of which was for the court of Louis XIV.

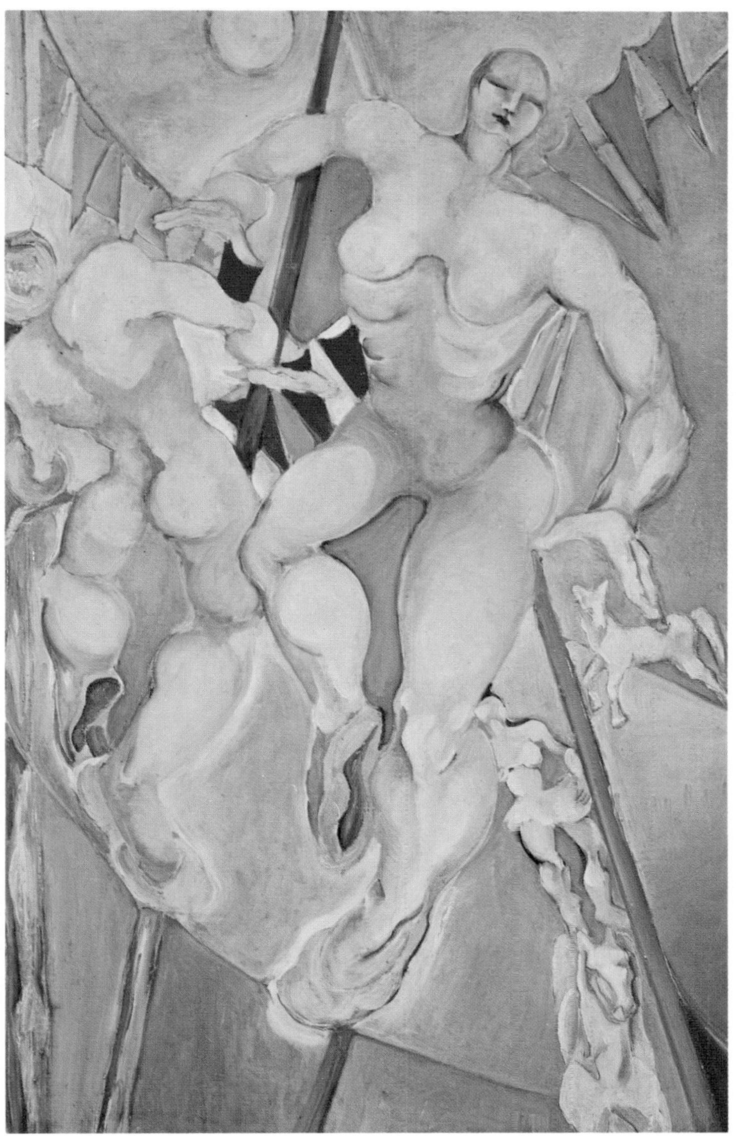

"Circus," oil, in Montgomery, Alabama, Art Museum, probably painted 1945.

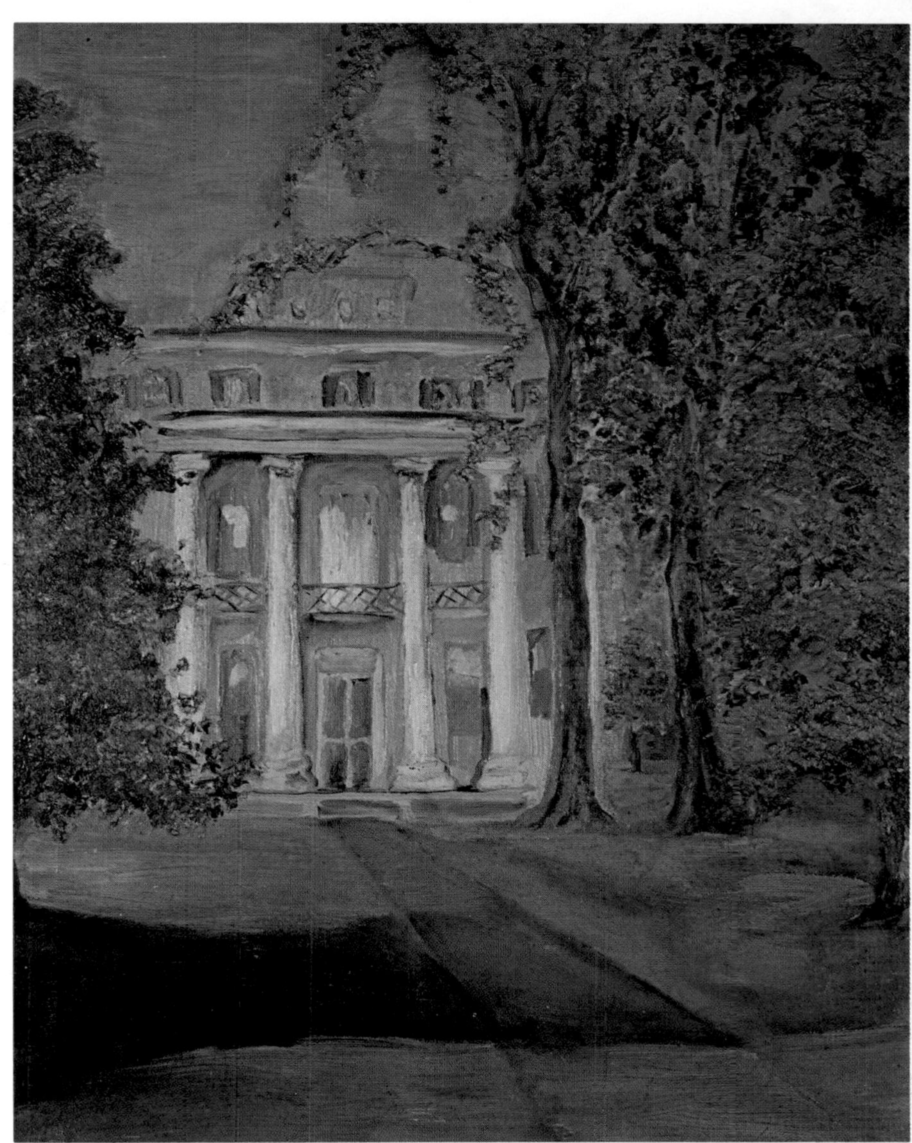

"Ellerslie," oil, 1928.

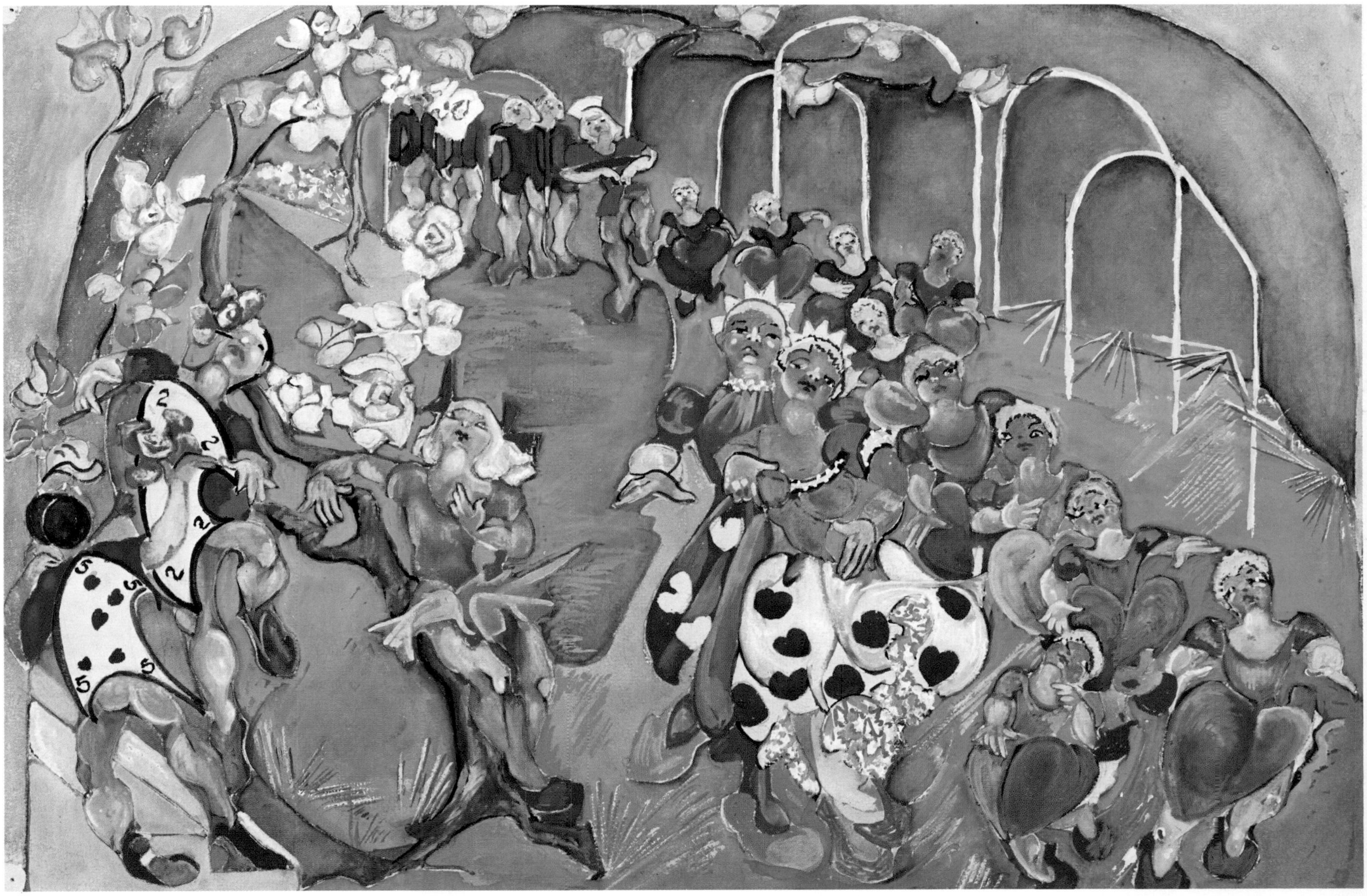

One of a series of watercolor illustrations of fairy tales: the Queen of Hearts' garden party from Alice in Wonderland, *c. 1948.*

Upper left and right: watercolors painted at Highland Hospital, Asheville, North Carolina. Above, the Smoky Mountains.

"The Nativity." One of a series of watercolors inspired by the Bible, c. 1946.

Zelda was discharged from Sheppard Pratt Hospital in June of 1932 and returned to live at "La Paix." After the critical and financial disappointment of Save Me the Waltz, she turned more seriously to her painting.

HER WORK IN INDEPENDENTS' SHOW—Mrs. F. Scott Fitzgerald, wife of a Baltimore novelist, is shown at work on a still life subject which she entered in the Independent Artists' Exhibition which opens at the Baltimore Museum of Art on October 1. American Staff Photo.

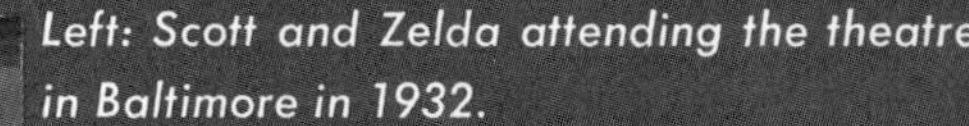

Left: Scott and Zelda attending the theatre in Baltimore in 1932.

Reputed Bantling:

In deponing and predicating incessantly that you were a "Shakespearean clown" I did not destinate to signify that you were a wise-acre, witling, dizzard, chowderhead, Tom Nody, nizy, radoteur, zany, oaf, loon, doodle, dunderpate, lunkhead, sawney, gowk, clod-poll, wise man of Boeotia, jobbernowl or mooncalf but, subdititiously, that you were intrinsically a longhead, luminary, "barba tenus sapientes," pundit, wrangler, licentiate learned Theban and sage, as are so many epigrammatists, wit-worms, droles de corp, *sparks, merry-andrews, mimes, posture-masters, pucinellas, scaramouches, pantaloons, pickle-herrings and persifleurs that were pullulated by the Transcendent Skald.*

Unequivocally,

—FSF to Andrew Turnbull, 2 August 1932.

Fitzgerald spent much of his leisure time at "La Paix" inventing games to play with Scottie and Andrew and Eleanor Turnbull (above), whom he dubbed "Eleanora Duse."

Zelda's mother at "La Paix."

PAINTINGS BURN IN COUNTY HOME OF NOVELIST

Valuable manuscripts, books and paintings which never can be replaced were destroyed today when fire swept through the roof and second story of the Rodgers Forge home of F. Scott Fitzgerald, the novelist and short story writer.

When the blaze broke out Mr. Fitzgerald was working on a story and his wife, who is a painter and playwright, was completing the last act of a play to be presented next week by the Vagabonds.

Mr. Fitzgerald dashed to save his wife's manuscripts and paintings, while her first thought was for his manuscript. After leading their eleven-year-old daughter, Frances, to safety, the couple carried out several valuable pieces of furniture.

NEIGHBORS HELP

Included was the table on which Francis Scott Key made several copies of "The Star Spangled Banner."

Fire apparatus responded quickly with the help of neighbors and servants, all of the furniture was carried from the house. The couple's library was saved with the exception of a group of valuable books on the World War, which Mr. Fitzgerald prized highly.

Extensive damage was caused to the roof and walls of the house, which originally was the Turnbull estate and was purchased by Mr. Fitzgerald a few years ago.

GOES BACK TO WORK

All of the furniture and many valuable personal belongings were saved.

While firemen and neighbors were carrying furniture, books and clothing into the house after the flames had been extinguished, Mr. Fitzgerald sat calmly in his study and continued to work on his short story. He explained that it must be finished by the end of the week.

There was little excitement. While the fire was at its height, firemen and neighbors responded to telephone calls and kept inquiring newspapers informed of the progress of the blaze.

STANDING IN WATER

Mr. Fitzgerald responded to one call and verified personally his misfortune. As questions were put to him he said, apologetically:

"Won't you please excuse me? The house is still burning and I'm standing in three feet of water."

The Fitzgeralds will move into town, it was said, until new quarters can be found and the old home restored.

LIKES QUIET HERE

Mr. Fitzgerald, writer of popular fiction, moved to Baltimore several years ago, attracted by the quiet home life that Baltimore county offers. He made his early reputation on "This Side of Paradise," a volume he produced shortly after the war, and considered to have been the greatest account of life among the gay youngsters who were a product of the post-war era. Since then, he has been a regular contributor to magazines.

Towson firemen said that a short circuit in the wiring started the fire.

Art Treasures Destroyed By Fire At Fitzgeralds

Manuscripts, books and paintings of high value were destroyed today when fire badly damaged the Rodgers Forge home of F. Scott Fitzgerald, novelist, and Mrs. Fitzgerald, the latter a painter and playwright. Photo shows Mr. and Mrs. Fitzgerald surrounded on lawn of their estate by collection of books and furniture that was saved from flames after the novelist and his wife led their eleven-year-old daughter Frances to safety. Picture by Baltimore News Staff Photographer.

(Story on Page 21)

188 Zelda breaks, the novel finished. Hard times begin for me, slow but sure. Ill Health Throughout

Thirty-Seven Years Old

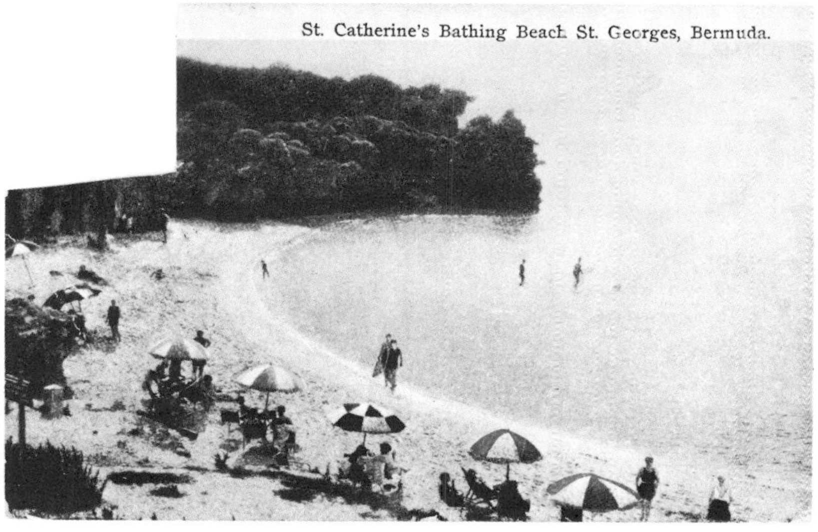

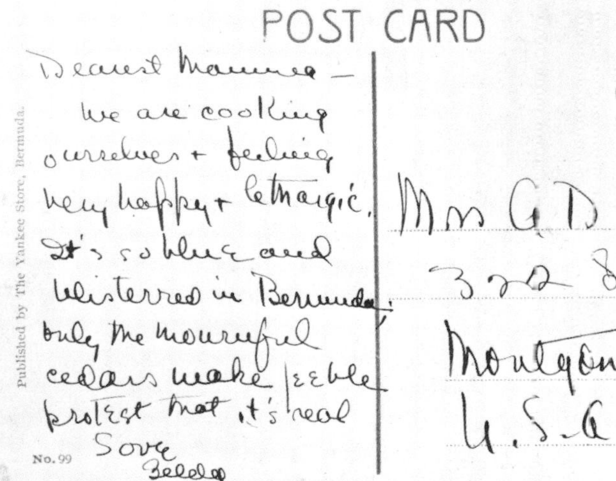
POST CARD

Published by The Yankee Store, Bermuda.

Dearest Mamma—
We are cooking
ourselves + feeling
very happy + lethargic.
It's so blue and
blistered in Bermuda.
Only the mournful
cedars make feeble
protest that it's real
Love
Zelda

No. 99

Mrs A. D. Sayre
322 Sayre St
Montgomery, Ala
U.S.A.

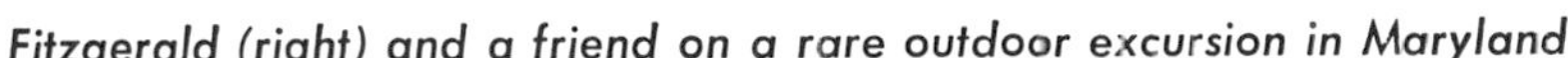

We had travelled a lot, we thought. Maybe this would be the last trip for a long while. We thought Bermuda was a nice place to be the last one of so many years of travelling.

—" 'Show Mr. and Mrs. F. to Number——' " (ZF)

Fitzgerald (right) and a friend on a rare outdoor excursion in Maryland.

In September of 1933 Fitzgerald finally delivered the completed manuscript of Tender Is the Night *to Scribners. In those days serialization in magazines before a novel's publication was common practice.*

Since talking to you and getting your letter another angle has come up. Ober tells me that Burton of Cosmopolitan *is very interested in the novel and if he took it would, in Ober's opinion, pay between $30,000 and $40,000 for it. Now against that there are the following factors:*

1. The fact that though Burton professes great lust for my work the one case in which I wrote a story specifically for him, that movie story that you turned down and that Mencken published, he showed that he really can't put his taste into action; in that case the Hearst policy man smeared it.

2. The tremendous pleasure I would get from appearing in Scribners.

3. The spring publication.

4. My old standby, the Post, *would not be too pleased to have my work running serially all spring and summer in the* Cosmopolitan.

On the other hand, the reasons why it must be considered are between thirty and forty thousand, and all of them backed by the credit of the U.S. Treasury. It is a purely hypothetical sum I admit and certainly no serial is worth it, yet if Willie Hearst is still pouring gold back into the desert in the manner of 1929 would I be stupid not to take some or would I be stupid not to take some? My own opinion is that if the thing is offered to Burton, he will read it, be enthusiastic, and immediately an Obstacle will appear. On the other hand, should I even offer it to them? Should I give him a copy on the same day I give you a copy asking an answer from him within three days? Would the fact that he refused it diminish your interest in the book or influence it? Or, even, considering my relations with you would it be a dirty trick to show it to him at all? What worries me is the possibility of being condemned to go back to the Saturday Evening Post *grind at the exact moment when the book is finished. I suppose I could and probably will need a damn good month's rest outdoors or traveling before I can even do that.*

* * *

Ring's death was a terrible blow. Have written a short appreciation of him for The New Republic.

Please answer.

—FSF to Maxwell Perkins, 29 September 1933.

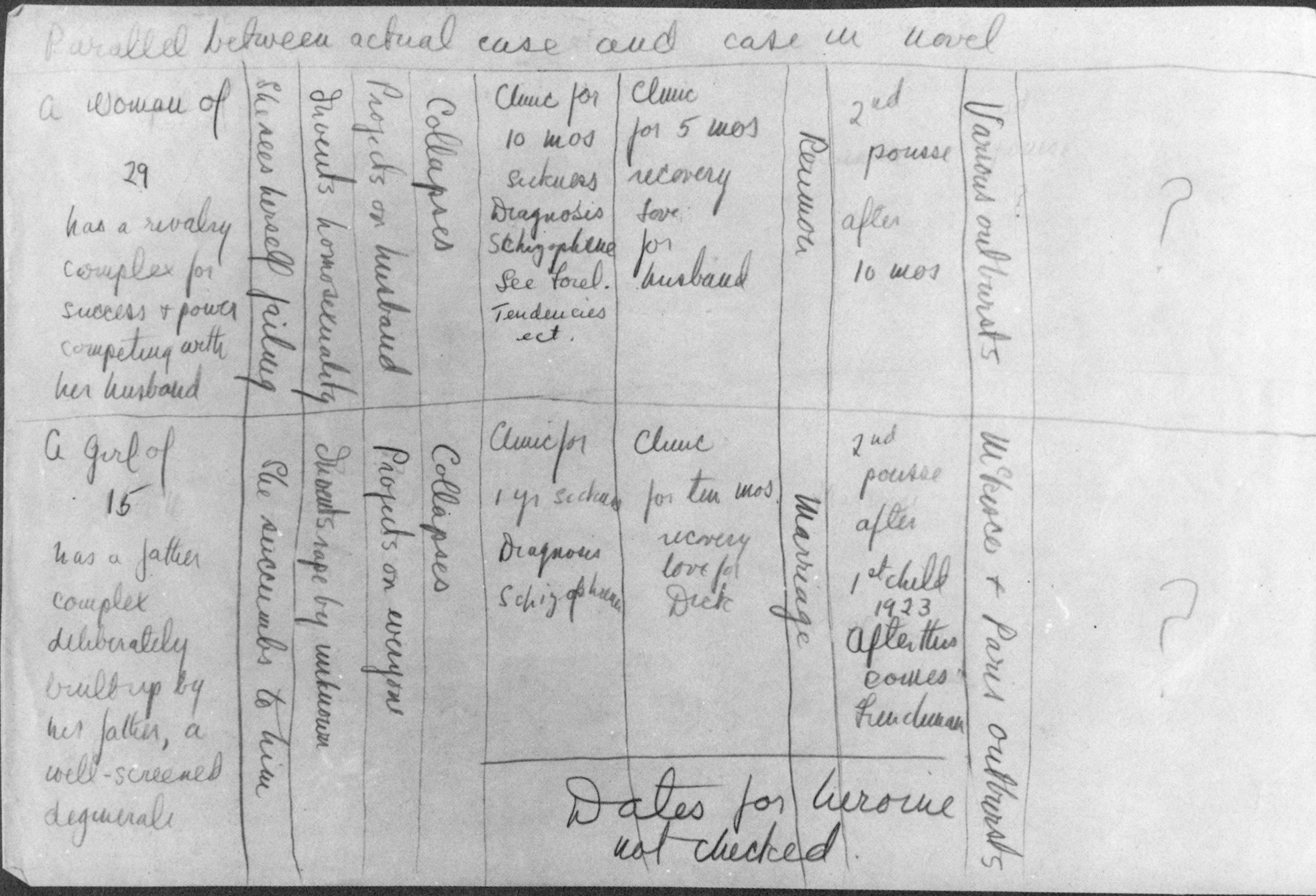

Parallel between actual case and case in novel

A Woman of 29 has a rivalry complex for success & power competing with her husband	She sees herself failing	Threats homosexuality	Projects on husband	Collapses	Clinic for 10 mos sickness Diagnosis Schizophrenie See Forel. Tendencies ect.	Clinic for 5 mos recovery love for husband	Reunion	2nd pousse after 10 mos	Various outbursts	?
A Girl of 15 has a father complex deliberately built up by her father, a well-screened degenerate	She succumbs to him	Threats rape by unknown	Projects on everyone	Collapses	Clinic for 1 yr sickness Diagnosis Schizophrenie	Clinic for ten mos recovery love for Dick	Marriage	2nd pousse after 1st child 1923 After this comes Frenchman	[illegible] + Paris outbursts	?

Dates for heroine not checked

Fitzgerald's chart comparing Zelda's case with Nicole Diver's.

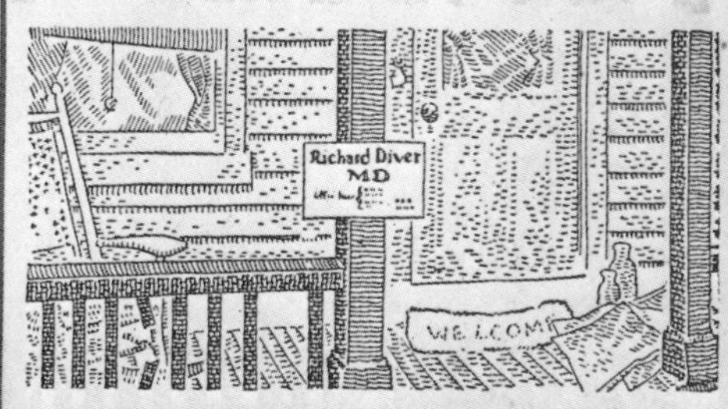

Fitgerald greatly admired Edward Shenton's illustrations for the serial and requested that they be used in the book.

Fitzgerald decided to call his novel Tender Is the Night at the last moment.

RICHARD DIVER · *A Romance*

By **F. SCOTT FITZGERALD**

To be published complete in four numbers

The editors of Scribner's Magazine announce the acquisition of the serial rights of F. Scott Fitzgerald's new novel, a literary event of outstanding importance. The only exceptions to our policy of publishing short novels complete in one number in the past have been in the cases of the novels of John Galsworthy, S. S. Van Dine, and Ernest Hemingway. "Richard Diver" is from every standpoint a logical companion for these distinguished novels.

This is Mr. Fitzgerald's first novel since "The Great Gatsby." To the generation that was in youth fourteen years ago when "This Side of Paradise" came out, the name Fitzgerald is associated with the Jazz Age to which he gave the name in his "Tales of a Jazz Age." The author was then twenty-two. He had attained to maturity when he wrote "The Great Gatsby."

Not until long after its success as a story, and then as a play, were its implications fully realized, except by the most discerning. Mr. Fitzgerald's new novel fulfills the promise of that remarkable work.

"Richard Diver" has for its leading character a doctor of medicine, and a problem of his profession springing out of a set of curious human relationships is the basis of its plot. Everything about it—characters, scene, and plot—is fresh and new and exciting.

To Begin in the **JANUARY**

Scribner's Magazine

Going over the other points, I hope both (1) that the review copies will go out in plenty of time, and (2) that they will get the version of the novel as it will be published because there is no doubt that each revision makes a tremendous difference in the impression that the book will leave. After all, Max, I am a plodder. One time I had a talk with Ernest Hemingway, and I told him, against all the logic that was then current, that I was the tortoise and he was the hare, and that's the truth of the matter, that everything that I have ever attained has been through long and persistent struggle while it is Ernest who has a touch of genius which enables him to bring off extraordinary things with facility. I have no facility. I have a facility for being cheap, if I wanted to indulge that. I can do cheap things. I changed Clark Gable's act at the moving picture theatre here the other day. I can do that kind of thing as quickly as anybody but when I decided to be a serious man, I tried to struggle over every point until I have made myself into a slow-moving Behemoth (if that is the correct spelling), and so there I am for the rest of my life. Anyhow, these points of proof reading, etc., are of tremendous importance to me, and you can charge it all to my account, and I will realize all the work you have had on it.

* * *

Now, about advertising. Again I want to tell you my theory that everybody is absolutely dead on ballyhoo of any kind, and for your advertising department to take up any interest that the intellectuals have so far shown toward the book and exploit that, would be absolutely disastrous. The reputation of a book must grow from within upward, must be a natural growth. I don't think there is a comparison between this book and The Great Gatsby *as a seller.* The Great Gatsby *had against it its length and its purely masculine interest. This book, on the contrary, is a woman's book. I think, given a decent chance, it will make its own way insofar as fiction is selling under present conditions.*

—FSF to Maxwell Perkins, 4 March 1934.

Zelda Fitzgerald is the wife of the novelist, Scott Fitzgerald. She has worked in the ballet school of Egarowa in Paris and has a considerable knowledge of the Diaghileff tradition which make her dancing subjects of particular interest. She has painted and drawn all her life but more seriously in the past five years. Her work crystallizes the qualities of imagination and poetry which have made her an almost legendary figure since the days just after the last war when she and her husband became symbols of young America in the Jazz Age. It is interesting to note that she is a "Child of the Century," having been born in 1900. Although she has shown previously in group exhibitions this is the first comprehensive showing of her work.

Dr. Hines is the Associate Professor of Anatomy at Johns Hopkins Medical School, Baltimore, and a distinguished authority on Neurology and Neural Anatomy. Her photographs are as thoughtful and honest as her scientific work and constitute an interesting corollary to the main currents of contemporary photography. Except for a few photographs exhibited at Smith College last spring her work has never before been publicly shown.

Exhibition Hours:—

Weekdays - - - 11 to 6
Sundays - - - - 2 to 6
Tuesday and Friday
Evenings - - - 8 to 10

PARFOIS LA FOLIE EST LA SAGESSE

PAINTINGS
by
ZELDA FITZGERALD

PHOTOGRAPHS
by
MARION HINES

MARCH 29 - APRIL 30 - 1934

525 EAST 86th Street
NEW YORK, N. Y.

PAINTINGS

1 White Anemones
2 Red Poppies
3 Vestibule
4 Dancer
5 Chinese Theater (Sara Murphy) $150 200.
6 Spectacle
7 Football
8 Chopin
9 Afternoon
10 White Roses
11 Laurel
12 Portrait in Thorns
13 Portrait of a Russian

DRAWINGS

1 Spring in the Country
2 The Plaid Shirt (Perkins)
3 The Cornet Player
4 Ferns (Adele Lovett)
5 Au Claire de la Lune (Hitchcock)
6 Forest Fire
7 Girl on a Flying Trapeze
8 Two Figures
9 Red Death
10 La Nature (Tommy Daniels)
11 Etude Arabesque
12 Two People
13 Feuété
14 Pallas Athene
15 Study of Figures

Draper
Hitchcock
Perkins (2) 3250
Parker

In January of 1934 Zelda had her third breakdown and went to Craig House, a clinic in Beacon, New York. She came down to New York City for this exhibition. Above, Fitzgerald's annotated copy of the catalogue.

Jazz Age Priestess Brings Forth Paintings

The wife of the High Priest of the Jazz Age, Mrs. F. Scott Fitzgerald, in her own right formerly one of the priestesses of the same order, has recently confounded us with a serious manifestation in the art line.

Last year she wrote a novel, taking the words right out of Scott's mouth.

This year she trumps all his aces with an exhibition of thirteen paintings and fifteen drawings.

Fecundity of this sort was not what we of the older generation feared when young girls began going out with flask-toting college youths. And it is gratifying to note that the boys and girls are buckling down to work now that the recklessness of youth, if we may coin a phrase, has expended its first bubble.

Do we become an old softy in adding we always knew they had it in them?

The exhibition is being held during the entire month of April at 525 East Eighty-sixth Street. And we certainly intend to see what new tricks the youngsters are up to.

Mrs. Fitzgerald, by the way, is not light or trifling in her approach to art. We are in possession of her reactions, written in a letter, to the Georgia O'Keeffe exhibition.

"They are magnificent," wrote Zelda Fitzgerald, "and excited me so that I felt quite sick afterwards.

"I loved the rhythmic white trees winding in visceral choreography about the deeper green ones, and I loved the voluptuous columnar tree trunk with a very pathetic blue flame-shaped flower growing arbitrarily beneath it. And there was a swell rhythmic abstraction done in blue and green and heart-breaking aspiration in the little room. Also I like the cosmic oysters."

This may have given you an idea of what to expect at the Fitzgerald exhibition. At any rate, not very jazzy, is it?

Of cource, it is a haunting book. . . . Scott: this place is most probably hideously expensive. I do not want you to struggle *through another burden like the one in Switzerland for my sake. You write too well. Also, you know that I live much within myself and would feel less strongly now than under normal circumstances about whatever you wanted to do. You have not got the right, for Scottie's sake, and for the sake of letters to make a drudge of yourself for me.*

—ZF to FSF from Craig House clinic, c. April 1934.

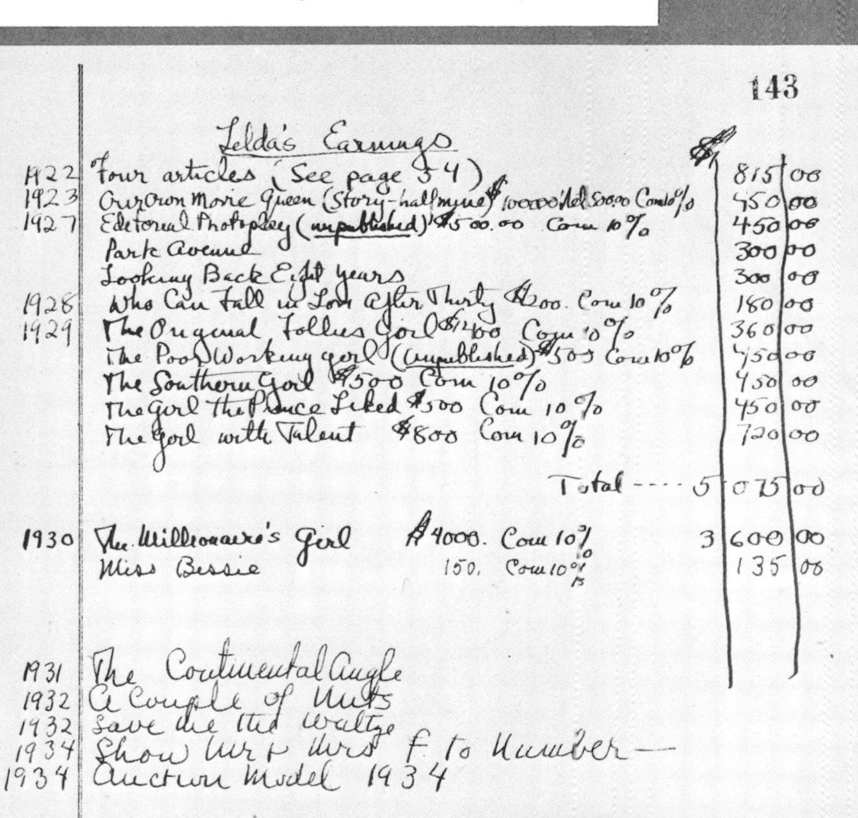

143

Zelda's Earnings

1922	Four articles (See page 54)	815	00
1923	Our Own Movie Queen (Story—half mine) $1000.00 Net $500.00 Com 10%	450	00
1927	Editorial Photoplay (unpublished) $500.00 Com 10%	450	00
	Park Avenue	300	00
	Looking Back Eight years	300	00
1928	Who Can Fall in Love After Thirty $200. Com 10%	180	00
1929	The Original Follies Girl $400 Com 10%	360	00
	The Poor Working Girl (unpublished) $500 Com 10%	450	00
	The Southern Girl $500 Com 10%	450	00
	The Girl the Prince Liked $500 Com 10%	450	00
	The Girl with Talent $800 Com 10%	720	00
	Total ----	5075	00
1930	The Millionaire's Girl $4000. Com 10%	3600	00
	Miss Bessie 150. Com 10% 15	135	00
1931	The Continental Angle		
1932	A Couple of Nuts		
1932	Save Me the Waltz		
1934	Show Mr & Mrs F. to Number—		
1934	Auction Model 1934		

TIME, *April 9, 1934*

Work of a Wife

There was a time when Mrs. Francis Scott Key Fitzgerald was a more fabulous character than her novel-writing husband. That was when she was Zelda Sayre, a Montgomery, Ala. girl, over whose home wartime aviation officers from nearby Taylor Field used to stunt until their commanding officer told them to stop. When she married Scott Fitzgerald in 1920 shortly after he published *This Side of Paradise* she lapsed into the semi-obscurity of a wife of a famed novelist.

Zelda Fitzgerald loved motion and dance. For a while she studied in Paris under Maria Egarova, onetime ballerina of the Russian Imperial Ballet of St. Petersburg. But she was in her middle 20s, too old to become a good ballet dancer. She left school, recording her adventures in a thinly disguised autobiography, *Save Me the Waltz*. She also began to paint seriously.

Last week, in Cary Ross's Manhattan studio, Zelda Fitzgerald showed her pictures, made her latest bid for fame. The work of a brilliant introvert, they were vividly painted, intensely rhythmic. A pinkish reminiscence of her ballet days showed figures with enlarged legs and feet —a trick she may have learned from Picasso. An impression of a Dartmouth football game made the stadium look like the portals of a theatre, the players like dancers. *Chinese Theatre* was a gnarled mass of acrobats with an indicated audience for background. There were two

Keystone

ZELDA FITZGERALD

Her dancing days came back in pink.

impressionistic portraits of her husband, a verdant *Spring in the Country* geometrically laced with telephone wires.

From a sanatorium last week which she temporarily left against doctors' orders to see a show of Georgia O'Keeffe's art, Zelda Fitzgerald was hoping her pictures would gratify her great ambition—to earn her own living.

Books in Demand

FOLLOWING is a list of the books most in demand at Brentano's, Womrath's, Macy's, the Doubleday, Doran bookshops and the American News Company:

Fiction

THE OPPERMANNS, by Lion Feuchtwanger (Viking).

SEVEN GOTHIC TALES, by Isak Dinesen (Smith & Haas).

ANTHONY ADVERSE, by Hervey Allen (Farrar & Rinehart).

TENDER IS THE NIGHT, by F. Scott Fitzgerald (Scribner).

Just finished another installment of Scott Fitzgerald's novel in *Scribner's* and we cannot forbear from again expressing our enthusiasm over it. It is, in our opinion, the best thing he has written. Make no mistake about it. Scott is well in the van of present-day novelists. The only thing we don't like about his writing is a too frequent tendency to parade words that ordinary mortals have to look up in the dictionary. But that is a very trivial criticism. Most of his words are exactly right. Don't miss *Tender is the Night*.

JUST READ SECOND INSTALMENT NOVEL WONDERFUL REGARDS=

LOUIS BROMFIELD.

Best Sellers

The result of a nation-wide canvass made especially for "Books of the Month."

Fiction

ANTHONY ADVERSE. *Hervey Allen*	$3.00
PRIVATE WORLDS. *Phyllis Bottome*	2.50
LONG REMEMBER. *Mac Kinlay Kantor*	2.50
WITHIN THIS PRESENT. *Margaret Ayer Barnes*	2.50
THE OPPERMANNS. *Lion Feuchtwanger*	2.50
WORK OF ART. *Sinclair Lewis*	2.50
SEVEN GOTHIC TALES. *Isak Dinesen*	2.50
OIL FOR THE LAMPS OF CHINA. *Alice Tisdale Hobart*	2.50
A MODERN TRAGEDY. *Phyllis Bentley*	2.50
TENDER IS THE NIGHT. *F. Scott Fitzgerald*	2.50

Good Reading

...n Rothstein, author of "Now I'll Tell," has ...ed reading the following books this season: "Children of the Poor," anonymous (Vanguard). "Tender is the Night," by F. Scott Fitzgerald (Scribners).

Tender is the Night

F. Scott Fitzgerald

B.

Brentano's Best Sellers for the week

★ Non-Ficton

NIJINSKY—Romola Nijinsky. The romance and tragedy of a great dancer. $3.75

A BACKWARD GLANCE—Edith Wharton. Reminiscences of a famous American novelist. $3.00

MERCHANTS OF DEATH—Engelbrecht & Hanighen. The munitions

★ Fiction

PRIVATE WORLDS—Phyllis Bottome. Cross-section of hospital life. $2.50

JAMES SHORE'S DAUGHTER—Stephen Vincent Benét. Memorable picture of a Yankee autocrat. $2.50

TENDER IS THE NIGHT — F. Scott Fitzgerald. The break-up of a modern

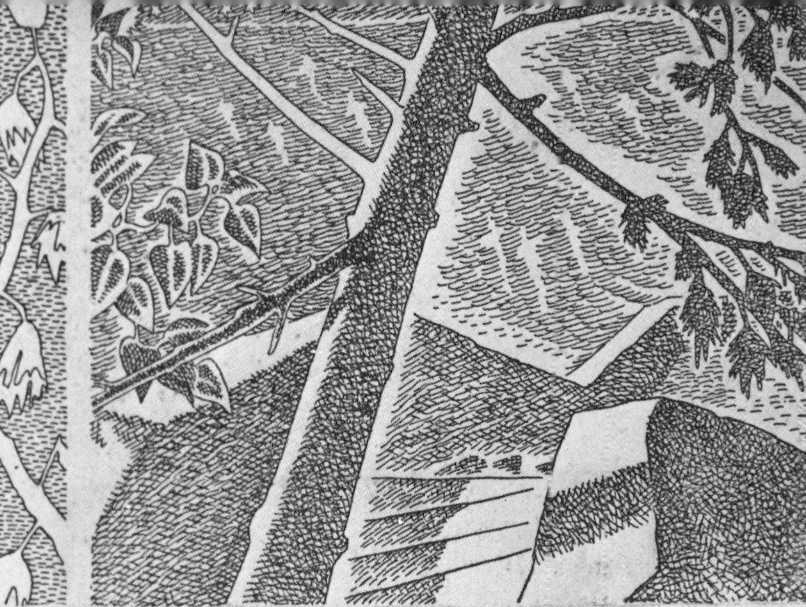

Books in Demand

FOLLOWING is a list of the books most in demand as reported by Brentano's, the Doubleday, Doran bookshops, Womrath's and the American News Company:

Fiction

THE OPPERMANNS, by Lion Feuchtwanger (Viking).
ANTHONY ADVERSE, by Hervey Allen (Farrar & Rinehart).
LONG REMEMBER, by MacKinlay Kantor (Coward-McCann).
PRIVATE WORLDS, by Phyllis Bentley (Houghton Mifflin).
TENDER IS THE NIGHT, by F. Scott Fitzgerald (Scribner).

F. SCOTT FITZGERALD

TENDER IS THE NIGHT

What America Is Reading

Nearly a year after it was published, Hervey Allen's 1200-page novel "Anthony Adverse" still leads all best sellers throughout the country, according to the weekly compilation made by the New York Herald-Tribune's Books. In nonfiction, Alexander Woollcott's "While Rome Burns" leads the pack, with President Roosevelt's "On Our Way" loping along in second place.

After "Anthony Adverse" the ten leading best sellers are as follows:

"Long Remember" by McKinlay Kantor
"Private Worlds" by Phyllis Bottome
"Seven Gothic Tales" by Isak Dinesen
"Journey to the End of the Night" by L. F. Celine
"James Shore's Daughter" by Stephen Vincent Benet
"The Oppermanns" by Lion Feuchtwanger
"Tender Is the Night" by F. Scott Fitzgerald

OK SCOTT IT WAS WORTH WAITING FOR SOLICITATIONS CHARLEY BAYLY..

Gothic Tales," and Roosevelt Lead Sales.

Fiction:

Seven Gothic Tales, (weird fantasies full of medieval influence) Isak Dinesen; Smith & Haas, $2.50.

Tender Is the Night, (a case history of moral and marital disintegration;) F. Scott Fitzgerald; Scribner, $2.50.

IT IS SO GOOD STOP IT IS SO DAMNED GOOD

YOU ARE CAMERON ROGERS

Best Sellers

(As compiled from reports of leading bookshops in the Metropolitan area.)

ANTHONY ADVERSE. By Hervey Allen. Farrar and Rinehart.
PRIVATE WORLDS. By Phyllis Bottome. Houghton Mifflin.
SEVEN GOTHIC TALES. By Isak Dineson. Smith and Haas.
THE OPPERMANNS. By Lion Feuchtwanger. Viking Press.
LONG REMEMBER. By MacKinlay Kantor. Coward-McCann.
ON OUR WAY. By Franklin D. Roosevelt. John Day.
JOURNEY TO THE END OF THE NIGHT. By L. Celine. Little Brown.
TENDER IS THE NIGHT. By F. Scott Fitzgerald. Scribner.

TENDER IS THE NIGHT, by F. Scott Fitzgerald. A beautifully written and bitter novel tracing the moral degeneration of some over-civilized Americans to whom Europe is a playground and life pretty much of a game. As good as "The Great Gatsby," many will think.

Best Sellers

The following books were best sellers during the past week at Brentano's in New York City:

Fiction

Seven Gothic Tales, Isak Dinesen, Smith & Haas. Weird fantasies full of medieval influence.

Tender Is the Night, F. Scott Fitzgerald, Scribner. A case history of moral and marital disintegration.

Have You Read These!

FICTION

FIREWEED — By Mildred
TRUMPETER SOUND — By D. L.
LONG REMEMBER — By McMinlay
TENDER IS THE NIGHT — By F. Scott Fitz

TENDER IS THE NIGHT

■ Another Fitzgerald sensation greeted with the same storm of praise and sales producing discussion that greeted "This Side of Paradise," and "The Great Gatsby."

Read what the first-string critics say about it:

"It has been months since anything by an American writer has given me such good reading as this."
—*Harry Hansen in The New York World Telegram.*

■ ■ ■

"Exciting . . . moving. . . . Once again he has issued a promise that is more exciting than most of his contemporaries' achievements."
—*Time Magazine.*

■ ■ ■

"You feel as you read it, that you will never forget it . . . universally interesting. . . . The people are men and women of tremendous passions, doing fine things and ignoble things. . . . He has stepped again to his natural place at the head of American writers of our time." —*Gilbert Seldes.*

■ ■ ■

"As a picture of slow moral decay and of the steady growth of a parasite which eventually chokes the parent plan, 'Tender Is the Night' is wholly successful. It cuts through sham and pretense magnificently."
—*Hal Borland in The Philadelphia Ledger.*

"A continually pleasurable performance. . . . An exciting and psychologically apt study in the disintegration of a marriage."
—*John Chamberlain in The New York Times.*

■ ■ ■

"A major event in contemporary American letters. . . . A profoundly moving, beautifully written story."
—*Cameron Rogers in The San Francisco Chronicle.*

■ ■ ■

"Its haunting tragedy has not let me alone for a moment since I read it. . . . A brilliant novel, and a novel that deserves to be read. . . . It ranks high in readability, both because Mr. Fitzgerald is a story-teller and because he writes with color, wit, and penetration."
—*Herschel Brickell in The New York Evening Post.*

■ ■ ■

"The depths of his probing into character, mood, and emotion is, I think, unmatched in our country . . . by all odds the finest novel to have come my way in ten years.
—*Michael March in The Brooklyn Citizen.*

"The book is a grand affair."—*Horace Gregory in The New York Herald Tribune.*

■ "The critical reception of 'Tender Is the Night' might serve as the basis for one of those cartoons on 'Why Men Go Mad.' No two reviews are alike; no two had the same tone," wrote *John Chamberlain in The New York Times* in his *second* column within four days that featured the Fitzgerald book (an attention conspicuously rare in *The Times*). But even the most critical agree on one thing —it's a novel that MUST be read. Months ago we said this would be the "most talked about novel of the year." The talk has started. Talk that SELLS. It will increase—and so will sales.

$2.50 **CHARLES SCRIBNER'S SONS**

F. SCOTT FITZGERALD

Opposite: Publicity photo taken for Tender Is The Night, © Eareckson.

Dear Scott:

Thank you, for myself and my bibliophile grandchildren, for the inscribed copy of Tender Is the Night. The little bastards will have to be satisfied with cut leaves, because I am reading the novel once again, having read it in the magazine, in galley proof, and now. I will say now that Tender Is the Night is in the early stages of being my favorite book, even more than This Side of Paradise. As I told you once before, I don't read many books, but the same ones over again. Right now I can't think of any other book clearly enough to make a comparison between it and Tender Is the Night, and I guess in its way that is the most important thing I've ever said about anybook.

You helped me finish my novel. I finished it yesterday. The little we talked when you were in New York did it. I reasoned that the best parts of my novel will be said to derive from Fitzgerald, and I think I have muffed my story, but I became reconciled to having done that after talking to you and reading Tender Is the Night in proof. No one else can write ~~than~~ like that, and I haven't tried, but the best parts of my novel are facile pupils of The Beautiful and Damned and The Great Gatsby. I was bushed, as Dottie says, and the fact that I need money terribly was enough to make me say the hell with my boook until you talked to me and seemed to accept me. So then I went ahead and finished my second-rate novel in peace. My message to the world is Fuck it! I know this is not the right, the classical (as Hergesheimer would punctuate it), attitude, but I can write better than Louis Bromfield, Tiffany Thayer, Kathleen Norris, Erskine Caldwell or Mike Gold, so I am not the worst writer there is. I neverwon anything, except a German helmet for writing an essay on Our Flag, and a couple of Father Lasance's My Prayer Book's for spelling bees.

Please look me up when you come to New York, and thank you for the book.

John O'Hara

Great God Scott you can write. You can write better than ever. You are a fine writer. Believe it. Believe it — not me

Archie (MacLeish)

Although Fitzgerald was deeply disappointed by the sales of Tender Is the Night, *he was gratified by the warm letters he received from other writers.*

TIME **BOOKS**

Sophisticates Abroad

TENDER IS THE NIGHT—F. Scott Fitzgerald—*Scribner* ($2.50).

For many a U. S. reader a nine-year period of suspense ended last week when F. Scott Fitzgerald, bad boy of U. S. letters, published his first novel since *The Great Gatsby* (1925). Somehow during those intervening years the news had leaked out that Author Fitzgerald had big ambitions, would not always be content to turn out facile potboilers for the commercial fiction magazines. Even highbrow critics admitted that *The Great Gatsby* had been a promising foreshadow of better books to come. Rumor spread that Author Fitzgerald was leading a double literary life, that he was writing a Dostoievskian novel in which a son kills his mother. Readers last week were relieved to discover that *Tender Is the Night* is built to no such outlandish specifications, but closed the book with still unsettled feelings about the author. F. Scott Fitzgerald, who started well this side of paradise, is not yet through purgatory. Though he often writes like an angel, he can still think like a parrot.

A Generation Riding to Romantic Death

NEW YORK TRIBUNE

The Terror of the Children of the Too Rich Pictured With Erratic Wisdom by Scott Fitzgerald

TENDER IS THE NIGHT. By F. Scott Fitzgerald . . . 408 *pp. . . . New York: Charles Scribner's Sons . . . $2.50.*

Reviewed by
HORACE GREGORY

We have been a long time waiting for this new novel by F. Scott Fitzgerald, the novel that was to supersede his remarkable performance in "The Great Gatsby." In 1931 he had said goodbye to those post-war years on which he had set his trade-mark with the name, "Jazz Age," across the page. This epitaph was written in the form of a short essay which appeared in "Scribner's Magazine," and it proved again that Fitzgerald had lost none of that self-consciousness, that awareness to the life of his time which had made "The Great Gatsby" an important item in contemporary literature. This essay was reinforced as recently as last fall by a tribute to Ring Lardner, which was published in "The New Republic." As a last word for a friend it ranks among the best of our modern elegies, and to evaluate the qualities of its prose we must turn to poetry for comparison. Beyond these we have the present novel with its deliberately ironic title clipped from Keats's "Ode to the Nightingale."

Closing the book we feel a sense of loss, not so much because each character (with the exception of McKisco, who remains a bounder) is slated for destruction, but because Fitzgerald has failed to carry his own responsibility. There is but one consolation—though Fitzgerald fails to realize the larger scheme of his novel, the book is a grand affair, a store-house of all the ills that doomed an entire colony of young Americans away from home. A number of isolated scenes in this novel have extraordinary power: Nicole screaming in the bathroom; a nameless Englishman shot dead upon a railway platform; Dick Diver, stripped of his will to live, drinking alone, dying by inches on the Riviera, and the last scene where Diver, betrayed by Nicole, vanishes to America, his address fading into small-town postoffice stations in New York State. All this is terror beyond death, that once revealed, even in fragmentary fashion, will not be soon forgotten.

DOS PASSOS

Dear Scott —

Reading Tender is the Night — the book — I got entirely a different impression from reading the couple of scraps in Scribners. It's so tightly knit together that it cant be read in pieces. The layout and construction of the damn thing is enormously impressive, all building up to a final paragraph that'll certainly be quoted in all the future textbooks. The only thing of that sort that disappointed me was the end of book II — where Rosemary first catches on that there's something weird about Nicole. Something about the phrasing, 'verbal inhumanity' threw me off the track. The whole conception of the book is enormous — and so carefully understated that — so far as I know — not a single reviewer discovered it. I think probably the less the reviewers can find out about a book the better it is. The part I liked best was the stuff about the clinic in Zurich & Diver's clinic later — the chapter where Nicole goes off her head at the little carnival is a knockout. I like Baby Warren & the English bitch best among the characters. For some reason I couldn't believe very thoroughly in the main people — how much that is due to knowing some of the models from which the

Dear Scott:

Thanks for your note. It's good to hear from you again. I'll be delighted to visit Zelda's exhibition when I'm in town. I live in Brooklyn now and it's sometimes hard to get over to Manhattan in daytime, but I should like to see her painting before the exhibition is over.

Scott, I want to tell you how glad I am that your book is being published next month, and also what a fine book it is. I read it as it came out in Scribner's Magazine and even read the proofs of the last two installments. I tell you this because I got the jump on most readers in this way. I thought you'd be interested to know that the people in the book are even more real and living now than they were at the time I read it. It seems to me you've gone deeper in this book than in anything you ever wrote. I don't pretend to know anything about the book business and have no idea whether it will have a big sale or not, but I do know that other people are going to feel about it as I do. I think it's the best work you've done so far, and I know you'll understand what I mean and won't mind if I get a kind of selfish hope and joy out of your own success. I have sweated blood these last four years on an enormous manuscript of my own, and the knowledge that you have now come through with this fine book makes me want to cheer. I felt a personal interest in parts of the book where you describedplaces we had been together, particularly Glion and Caux and that funicular that goes up the mountain. I don't think anyone will know just how good that piece of writing is unless he has been there.

This is all for the present. I am still working like hell but I'd like to see you if you come up here. Meanwhile, I am wishing for the best kind of success in every way for your book when it is published.

Yours,

Tom Wolfe

ROBERT BENCHLEY
44 WEST 44TH STREET
NEW YORK CITY

April 29th, 1934

Dear Scott:

It was damned nice of you to write in your book for me. I don't remember ever having said anything that appears on page 25, or on any other page, but I would have given my two expensivly-filled eye-teeth to have written just one page of the book.

Honestly, Scott, I think that it is a beautiful piece of work, not only technically, but emotionally. I haven't had a book get hold of me like that for years. As a journeyman writer, I can not even conceive of anyone's being able to do that scene in the Guaranty Trust, just from the point of view of sheer manipulation of words, to say nothing of the observation contained in it. And the feeling of the whole book is so strong upon me, even now, that I am oppressed by a not-quite-vague-enough fear that several people I am fond of are very unhappy.

I hope that you, yourself, are not any unhappier than is called for in the general blue-print specifications for Living. Please don't be. Anyone who gets down on his stomach and crawls all afternoon around a yard playing tin-soldiers with a lot of kids, shouldn't be made too unhappy. I cry a little every time I think of you that afternoon in Antibes.

Thanks again for thinking of me, and look me up the next time you come to town. My number is Vanderbilt 3-6498.

Gratefully,

Bob.

TENDER IS THE NIGHT

A ROMANCE

By

F. Scott Fitzgerald

DECORATIONS BY
EDWARD SHENTON

NEW YORK
CHARLES SCRIBNER'S SONS
1934

TO

GERALD AND SARA

MANY FÊTES

Fitzgerald dedicated Tender Is the Night *to the Murphys.*

I found Scott's "Tender Is the Night" in Cuba and read it over. It's amazing how excellent much of it is. Much of it is better than anything else he ever wrote. How I wish he would have kept on writing. Is it really all over or will he write again? If you write him give him my great affection. Reading that novel much of it was so good it was frightening.

ERNEST HEMMINGWAY (in letter to Max Perkins)

N.Y. **Correspondence** Tribune

Scott Fitzgerald a Modern Orpheus

To the Editor of BOOKS:

Here are some thoughts about "Tender Is the Night." Max Eastman says I don't know how to think and maybe that is true, so perhaps these will not be thoughts, really, so much as approximations of my impressions, perceptions of a manly performance, set down with great respect.

When Orpheus first went down into the underworld to bring back Eurydice it was not so risky an excursion as in these days we live in. It took then, apparently, rather a simple courage and it was more cut and dried for there was a stout surface to his world and a more definite descent and emergence. He went down and he returned.

But now the whole surface is worn thin. Everywhere the social tissue is giving way, ominous cracks appear upon the pleasant rink of our conscious life where we skim to and fro upon the thin thin ice.

Once in a while, quite frequently, as compared with Orpheus's day, some one sinks under and disappears and Orpheus is not there to save. Neither love nor courage is available to many and for the few there is only the cold sport of science frisking delicately in the dangerous stream, trying to hook these fish.

The greater number, then, disappear with the vast undifferentiated gray underworld and are seen no more. They are engulfed in the ancient reservoir where good and evil are all one and nothing matters yet, but where the eager unnamed elements wait for a chance to rise and be; for while the children of this world are sinking through these terrible exits, the powers of the undisclosed world make their entrances.

Now, it seems to me, Scott Fitzgerald is a man who knows about all this—and what realizations has he gazed at and accepted before he could tell of it? In the wrack and ruin of his environment he ponders and smiles. Even while the waters close over him he smiles and tells of life as it has come to him, tells about his experience that was the experience of Orpheus, with this vast difference between them, that Orpheus didn't know what he was doing nor what happened to him. Some one else had to tell about him while here is one who can and does tell his own story. This makes people murmur about "taste." Is it "taste"? Well, has life taste? Because this writing is as actual as talking, the critics are confused. They are habituated to art forms and here is something that does not fit into them. Here is something real and confused and no more a novel than life is. Yet readers talk about it "as a novel" and compare it with "The Great Gatsby," and they debate whether or no the author has fulfilled his earlier promise. Why can't they see that this is stern stuff and not to be mixed up with just books? But no—they are disappointed and they cover that up as best they can by calling it "brilliant"—which is their way of condoning it for its lack of this and that!

Do they realize, I wonder, that here is a book that is very close to being a live, organic resume of present reality and that that is something rare? I don't believe they do or they would drop their little measures and realize that something important, more important than a novel, has happened.

Here is an objective grasp of the conditioned, mechanical activity of oneself, the picture taken of oneself upon a journey, the lens directed and the shutter clicked at the moment of submersion, at the opening of the waters.

In these days it is Orpheus who must be saved. The roles are reversed but Eurydice is not aware yet of her predestined importance for still she is not strong enough to endure. She is still unstable although he has brought her through. Again and again she sinks into those grey depths where the amorphous things wait for birth. Each time she rises they come too, clinging about her unseen. She is, all unbeknownst, a carrier of forces that are evil when set loose—she is, as Gilbert Seldes said, a kind of "Typhoid Mary," and where she passes in her pleasant places, things happen. Her neighborhood is lively with potential battle, murder and sudden death. The gulf is open beneath her and ghastly eventualities attend her. Yet she is saved herself because Orpheus has taken over her account. With ignorance and loving blindness he will atone for an old, old mistake: that of touching with love those who are lost. He has not learned to save by the cold and scientific methods of modern salvation. Sacrifice is all he knows—that and knowing himself. He is the child of transition wandering in no man's land, between two worlds, one dead, the other not yet born. But he creates the future for us. He is not inactively resigned, nor passively submissive. With dreadful endurance and clarity he attempts to tell us—"this is how it is"—and by adding his portion to consciousness he changes the present.

I am afraid I have been clumsy and inadequate in trying to show how much I admire this mature act. The book doesn't need defense or interpretation. Of its own vitality it will make its own way, and gathering momentum it will cover long spaces and I hope I may be excused for seeming to think it needs any one to defend it.

MABEL DODGE LUHAN.

BOOKS OF THE TIMES

By JOHN CHAMBERLAIN

N Y Times

As one who would rather have written "The Great Gatsby" than any other American novel published in the Twenties, we approached F. Scott Fitzgerald's "Tender Is the Night" (Scribner's, $2.50) with anticipation and trepidation. "The Great Gatsby" was so perfect in its feeling and its symbolism, such a magnificent evocation of the spirit of a whole decade, so great an improvement over Mr. Fitzgerald's second novel, "The Beautiful and Damned" (which might have been, as Jerome Hill once called it, "an American 'Madame Bovary,'" were it not for its diffuse quality), that one could hardly see Mr. Fitzgerald striking the same high level twice in succession. As the years went by, recurrent surges of gossip had it that Mr. Fitzgerald was unable to bring his unfinished post-"Gatsby" novel to any satisfactory conclusion. He had been a child of boom America; had the lean years after 1929 sapped his artistic vitality by stealing from him his field of reference?

After having read "Tender Is the Night," we now know that the gossip was—just gossip. Mr. Fitzgerald has not forgotten his craftsmanship, his marvelous sense of what might be called social climate, his sheer writing ability. Judged purely as prose, "Tender Is the Night" is a continually pleasurable performance. From a technical point of view, it is not as perfect a novel as "The Great Gatsby," but once the reader has gotten past the single barrier to complete appreciation of the book, it proves to be an exciting and psychologically apt study in the disintegration of a marriage.

Flavor of a Period.

Beyond the story, there is Mr. Fitzgerald's ability to catch the "essence of a continent," the flavor of a period, the fragrance of a night and a snatch of old song, in a phrase. A comparison of "Tender Is the Night" as it ran in Scribner's Magazine and as it appears in book form gives a measure of the author's artistic conscience. He has made many deft excisions, many sound reallocations of conversation. If, with Rosemary, he presents nothing much beyond an unformed girl, that must lie within the conception of his novel. Rosemary was evidently intended to be meaningless in herself, an unknown quantity projecting itself into a situation that merely required leverage, any leverage, to start its development toward a predictable end. The story is the story of the Divers, husband and wife, how they came together, and how they parted. As such it is a skillfully done dramatic sequence. By the time the end is reached, the false start is forgotten.

NEW REPUBLIC

Breakdown

"TENDER IS THE NIGHT"[1] is a good novel that puzzles you and ends by making you a little angry because it isn't a great novel also. It doesn't give the feeling of being complete in itself.

If I didn't like the book so much, I shouldn't have spoken at such length about its shortcomings. It has virtues that deserve more space than I can give them here. Especially it has a richness of meaning and emotion—one feels that every scene is selected among many possible scenes and that every event has pressure behind it. There is nothing false or borrowed in the book: everything is observed at first hand. Some of the minor figures—especially Gausse, the hotel keeper who was once a bus boy in London, and Lady Caroline Sibley-Biers, who carries her English bad manners to the point of viciousness—are more vivid than Rosemary or Dick; and the encounter between Gausse and Lady Caroline is one of those enormous episodes in which two social castes are depicted melodramatically, farcically and yet convincingly in a brief conversation and one gesture.

Fitzgerald says that this book is his farewell to the members of his own generation; I hope he changes his mind. He has in him at least one great novel about them, and it is a novel that I want to read.

MALCOLM COWLEY.

new **BOOKS** Yorker

F. Scott Fitzgerald

IN Mr. Fitzgerald's case, at any rate, money is the root of all novels. In "This Side of Paradise," the world of super-wealth was viewed through the glass of undergraduate gaiety, sentiment, and satire. With "The Great Gatsby," the good-time note was dropped, to be replaced by a darker accent of tragic questioning. The questions have become sharper, bitterer in "Tender Is the Night," but the world of luxurious living remains his only world. It has even become a trifle narrower—a Fitzgerald contraction, so to speak. This universe he both loves and despises; he sees through it and is confused by it. It is the contradictoriness of this emotional attitude that gives his novels their special quality, and is also in part responsible for some of their weaknesses.

My dear Scott

Many congratulations on your triumphant return to letters. Scribner gave me your book a week ago and I find your promise fulfilled and all my hopes justified. Splendid

yrs ever Shane Leslie

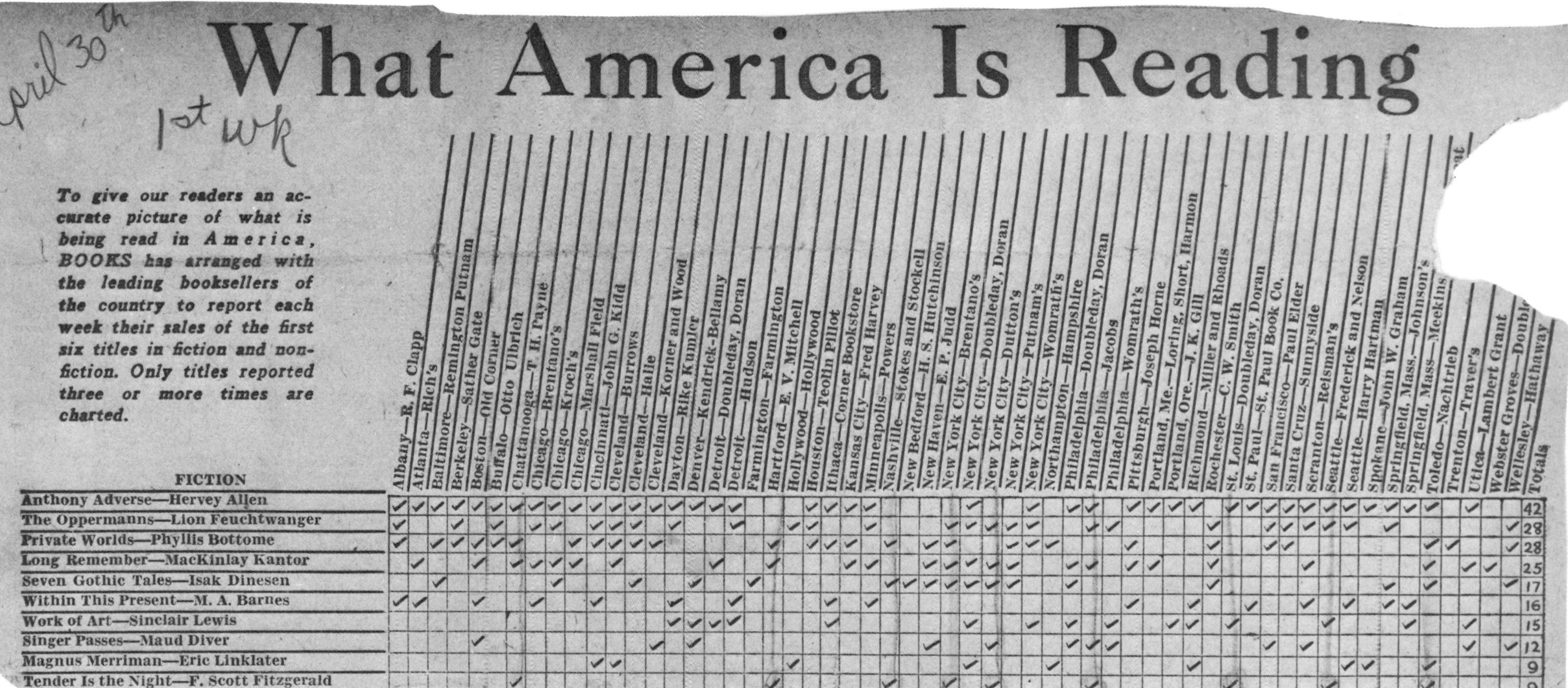

April 30th

1st wk

What America Is Reading

To give our readers an accurate picture of what is being read in America, BOOKS has arranged with the leading booksellers of the country to report each week their sales of the first six titles in fiction and non-fiction. Only titles reported three or more times are charted.

FICTION	Albany—R. F. Clapp	Atlanta—Rich's	Baltimore—Remington Putnam	Berkeley—Sather Gate	Boston—Old Corner	Buffalo—Otto Ulbrich	Chattanooga—T. H. Payne	Chicago—Brentano's	Chicago—Kroch's	Chicago—Marshall Field	Cincinnati—John G. Kidd	Cleveland—Burrows	Cleveland—Halle	Cleveland—Korner and Wood	Dayton—Rike Kumler	Denver—Kendrick-Bellamy	Detroit—Doubleday, Doran	Detroit—Hudson	Farmington—Farmington
Anthony Adverse—Hervey Allen	✓	✓	✓	✓	✓	✓	✓	✓	✓	✓	✓	✓	✓	✓	✓	✓	✓	✓	
The Oppermanns—Lion Feuchtwanger	✓			✓		✓		✓	✓		✓	✓	✓		✓			✓	
Private Worlds—Phyllis Bottome	✓		✓	✓	✓	✓	✓			✓	✓	✓	✓	✓					
Long Remember—MacKinlay Kantor		✓			✓		✓	✓	✓	✓		✓					✓		
Seven Gothic Tales—Isak Dinesen			✓						✓				✓			✓			✓
Within This Present—M. A. Barnes	✓	✓			✓			✓			✓				✓			✓	
Work of Art—Sinclair Lewis															✓	✓	✓	✓	
Singer Passes—Maud Diver					✓									✓		✓			
Magnus Merriman—Eric Linklater											✓	✓							
Tender Is the Night—F. Scott Fitzgerald							✓												

FICTION	Hartford—E. V. Mitchell	Hollywood—Hollywood	Houston—Teolin Pillot	Ithaca—Corner Bookstore	Kansas City—Fred Harvey	Minneapolis—Powers	Nashville—Stokes and Stockell	New Bedford—H. S. Hutchinson	New Haven—E. P. Judd	New York City—Brentano's	New York City—Doubleday, Doran	New York City—Dutton's	New York City—Putnam's	New York City—Womrath's	Northampton—Hampshire	Philadelphia—Doubleday, Doran	Philadelphia—Jacobs	Philadelphia—Womrath's	Pittsburgh—Joseph Horne
Anthony Adverse—Hervey Allen			✓	✓	✓	✓					✓			✓		✓	✓		✓
The Oppermanns—Lion Feuchtwanger		✓	✓			✓				✓	✓	✓	✓	✓			✓	✓	
Private Worlds—Phyllis Bottome	✓		✓	✓	✓		✓		✓	✓			✓	✓	✓				✓
Long Remember—MacKinlay Kantor	✓				✓	✓			✓	✓	✓	✓	✓			✓	✓		✓
Seven Gothic Tales—Isak Dinesen							✓	✓	✓	✓	✓	✓	✓			✓			
Within This Present—M. A. Barnes				✓		✓													✓
Work of Art—Sinclair Lewis				✓							✓			✓		✓		✓	
Singer Passes—Maud Diver									✓			✓				✓	✓	✓	
Magnus Merriman—Eric Linklater		✓									✓				✓				
Tender Is the Night—F. Scott Fitzgerald	✓						✓			✓		✓					✓		

FICTION	Portland, Me.—Loring, Short, Harmon	Portland, Ore.—J. K. Gill	Richmond—Miller and Rhoads	Rochester—C. W. Smith	St. Louis—Doubleday, Doran	St. Paul—St. Paul Book Co.	San Francisco—Paul Elder	Santa Cruz—Sunnyside	Scranton—Reisman's	Seattle—Frederick and Nelson	Seattle—Harry Hartman	Spokane—John W. Graham	Springfield, Mass.—Johnson's	Springfield, Mass.—Meekins	Toledo—Nachtrieb	Trenton—Traver's	Utica—Lambert Grant	Webster Groves—Double[day]	Wellesley—Hathaway	Totals
Anthony Adverse—Hervey Allen	✓	✓	✓		✓	✓	✓	✓	✓	✓	✓	✓	✓	✓	✓		✓			42
The Oppermanns—Lion Feuchtwanger				✓			✓	✓	✓	✓	✓		✓						✓	28
Private Worlds—Phyllis Bottome				✓			✓	✓							✓	✓			✓	28
Long Remember—MacKinlay Kantor	✓			✓					✓						✓		✓	✓		25
Seven Gothic Tales—Isak Dinesen				✓									✓		✓				✓	17
Within This Present—M. A. Barnes			✓			✓			✓		✓		✓	✓						16
Work of Art—Sinclair Lewis		✓	✓		✓					✓				✓			✓			15
Singer Passes—Maud Diver							✓		✓								✓		✓	12
Magnus Merriman—Eric Linklater			✓								✓	✓			✓					9
Tender Is the Night—F. Scott Fitzgerald					✓					✓					✓					9

THE TIMES LITERARY SUPPLEMENT

TENDER IS THE NIGHT

The literary career of Mr. F. Scott Fitzgerald has been a curious one. Having achieved a considerable popularity with his two earliest novels, "This Side of Paradise" and "The Beautiful and Damned," brilliant, almost garish, studies in American post-War disillusion, his subsequent volumes proved disappointing until the appearance of his best book, "The Great Gatsby," in 1926. But consequent expectation was not fulfilled as one had hoped. TENDER IS THE NIGHT (Chatto and Windus, 7s. 6d. net) is his first work to break, at least in this country, the silence of eight years. It is, in its way, and particularly to follow such a gap, an impressive and yet a depressing achievement. It displays, with all its skill, with all its maturer understanding and abiding sympathy, the mood of disillusion still. This world of wealthy Americans in Europe is only too far this side of paradise; the beautiful, in body and soul, are still the damned; greatness is found nowhere, not even as an aspiration. The very title is ominous: "tender is the night . . . But here there is no light," and the narrative is a panorama of wasted or shattered lives, alike in its central and its minor figures. It is almost all of it tragedy without nobility, and therefore the less tragedy. If fineness is glimpsed, it is in the principal character, Richard Diver, an American mental specialist who is partner in a psychopathic clinic in Switzerland, and in his wife Nicole, an ex-patient and a lovely flower with a worm at its root. But even they seem to float rudderless upon the stream of circumstance. In one sense she has never ceased to be his patient. He is continually aware of the dangers of relapse, not always to be evaded, and of her dependence upon him; and he knows when he falls in love with the spring freshness of Rosemary Hoyt, an eighteen-year-old film star, that there is nothing to be done about it. Besides, he is himself still deeply in love with Nicole, for whose mending, it gradually appears, he has given up all. Yet it proves but another in a complicated series of factors making for his final disintegration, and, one feels, for Nicole's, despite her apparent cure. Grouped about this central inutile progress are any number of minor persons and incidents, the latter often fantastic or brutal, farcical or distressing. The setting of a Riviera and Paris peopled principally by Americans who drink, swim, sun-bathe, gossip, quarrel, and tumble in and out of each other's beds has been drawn before by not a few writers; and, well done as it is here, one would be less inclined to regard Mr. Scott Fitzgerald's novel seriously were it not for the real tenderness informing his portrayal of the relationship between Richard and Nicole, and for a persistent and inescapable note of despair underlying its lightest pages.

The Great Gatsby *was reprinted by the Modern Library in 1934 (left), and withdrawn because of small sales.*

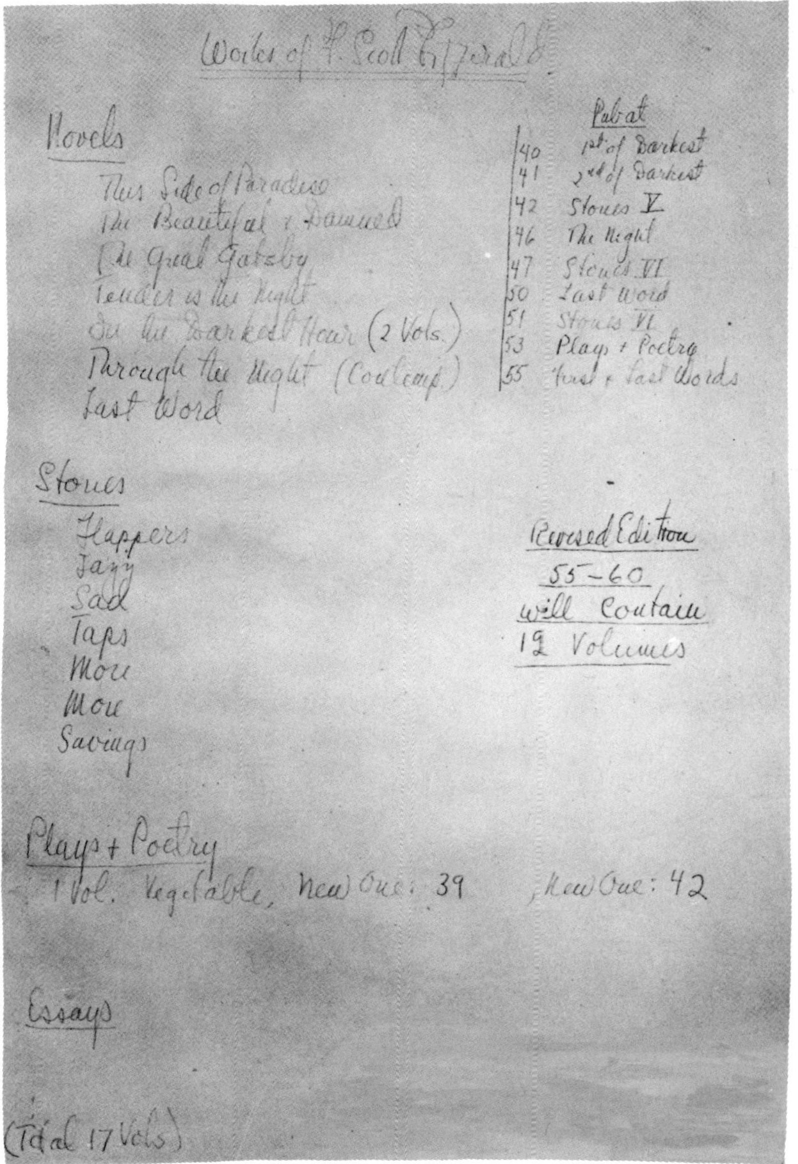

Works of F. Scott Fitzgerald

Novels

This Side of Paradise
The Beautiful + Damned
The Great Gatsby
Tender is the Night
In the Darkest Hour (2 Vols.)
Through the Night (Contemp.)
Last Word

Pub at
40 1st of Darkest
41 2nd of Darkest
42 Stories V
46 The Night
47 Stories VI
50 Last Word
51 Stories VI
53 Plays + Poetry
55 First + Last Words

Stories

Flappers
Jazz
Sad
Taps
More
More
Savings

Revised Edition
55–60
will Contain
19 Volumes

Plays + Poetry
1 Vol. Vegetable, New One: 39, New One: 42

Essays

(Total 17 Vols)

Fitzgerald's plan for his future work and a projected collected edition of his writings.

BUTTERFIELD 8—John O'Hara—*Harcourt, Brace* ($2.50).

The generation that stumbled into a slightly intoxicated maturity in the early 1920's found in F. Scott Fitzgerald a spokesman who dramatized their emotional problems, made articulate their aspirations, and told some excellent stories while doing so. Last week the publication of John O'Hara's second novel made him the strongest candidate among U. S. novelists for the part that Fitzgerald has vacated by growing out of the ranks of the young. A more impressive and ambitious volume than *Appointment in Samarra*, his first novel, *Butterfield 8* suggests that John O'Hara is well on his way to becoming the voice of the hangover generation that awakened in the grey dawn of 1930. Writing principally of speakeasy, country-club, fairly well-to-do crowds similar to those Fitzgerald wrote about, he presents them as much less tender, much more bitter, much more worried about money, casually frank in their acceptance of the more brutal realities of sexual experiences. And their stories he finds, almost without exception, grim.

... All this is not to say, however, that O'Hara uses this competency to register anything; there is supposed to be a good deal of Scott Fitzgerald in his work, but if he ever read *The Great Gatsby*, you wouldn't, as the saying goes, know it. It is not only that Fitzgerald has serenity and knows when to let his material glide; O'Hara has a nervous, over-smiling kind of confidence, and he has talent and brains and he knows all the answers.

A few years ago we used to think half-baked ideas about life sentimental. Today, Mr. O'Hara and his School of Hard Eyes apparently believe that any ideas at all are a bit on the soft side. If the point isn't clear, compare "Appointment in Samarra" with "This Side of Paradise" and "The Great Gatsby," two novels of a dead epoch dealing fundamentally with O'Hara's social material. The difference may be put crudely: Fitzgerald didn't quite know what it was all about, but wondered, and his wonder gave his novels their quality. But O'Hara has stopped wondering.

A little more than a decade ago we were all hot and bothered about the Lost Generation — flappers, flaming youth, gin-swilling collegiates, and the rest of the self-consciously abandoned group made familiar by F. Scott Fitzgerald.

Those folk have grown up, by now, and married and settled down; and if you want to know what they look like as they slide into their 30's you cannot do better than read John O'Hara's new novel, "Appointment in Samara."

Mr. O'Hara tells of a group of young married folk in a small city in Pennsylvania. They are the Fitzgerald children grown into men and women; the country club crowd now, rootless and aimless, drifting with the tide, educated and cultured on the surface, but blind and rather stupid beneath.

ONCE upon a time, in the dear innocent days of 1920, good folk shook their heads over the antics of the boys and girls of F. Scott Fitzgerald's "jazz age." Yet how idyllic, how positively sylvan and dewey, those far-off days seem when one reads John O'Hara's second novel, "Butterfield 8" (Harcourt, Brace, $2.50). Here, at last, is the ultra-ultra in fictional depiction of the willful degradation of sex. Compared to Gloria Wandrous, the bee-yoo-tee-ful wallower-in-the-mire of "Butterfield 8," Fitzgerald's Rosalinds and Daisies are paragons of virtue, glasses of circumspect fashion, molds of Victorian form. Gloria could give them thirteen hearts and thirteen spades in the game of vice and still come out a winner by a grand slam.

THE CROSS OF JOHN O'HARA

... a young man named John O'Hara. As one turns the pages, engrossed in the fortunes of a lively country club group (in a Pennsylvania small town) the reader begins to believe that the novel is one of those composite affairs, each chapter by a different author. One could almost label them, one by the aforementioned Katherine Brush, a roadhouse by F. Scott Fitzgerald, chapters by W. Somerset Maugham and Sinclair Lewis and one episode (messing clumsily with the intimacies of the marriage chamber) by a hack writer for the cheap fiction circulating libraries.

No; and they don't even enjoy their flirtations or their drinks, as at least the country club crowd did in the early twen... ...vels. There ... kind of life. ... hard, quick, brilliant style that fits its subject admirably; O'Hara has contributed for a number of years to the *New Yorker*.

BUTTERFIELD 8. By John O'Hara. 310 pp. New York: Harcourt, Brace & Co. $2.50.

JOHN O'HARA'S pedigree as a writer might be set down as approximately by Ernest Hemingway out of Scott Fitzgerald. He writes about the generation after Fitzgerald's with even more freedom of speech than Hemingway has permitted himself.

APPOINTMENT IN SAMARRA *John O'Hara*
Nearly fifteen years ago F. Scott Fitzgerald shocked America by writing about "nice" girls petting; now a new writer, as distinctive in his way as Fitzgerald, takes nice girls a step further. O'Hara writes a swell novel about the country club set in realistic, bold, vigorous fashion. Not for the squeamish. HARCOURT, $2.50

Let's make a few things clear at the outset. "Butterfield 8" is almost, if not quite, as easy to read as "Appointment in Samarra." The photographic eye is brighter, the phonographic ear sharper than before. The dialogue is still slicker, the pace still quicker, the plot still thicker, the main interest of the characters still liquor. New York (a few blocks of it—hence the title) at the zenith of the speakeasy era is caught and pinned to the mat with incomparable deftness. Mr. O'Hara can handle seduction scenes, all varieties, with a casualness that does not necessarily indicate cynicism. He knows exactly who was apt to be in a given speakeasy on a given afternoon in 1931. He can tell you the difference (and make it, for twenty magic seconds, sound important) between John Held people and F. Scott Fitzgerald people.

Back in 1920 when post-war youth was still a novelty, F. Scott Fitzgerald wrote what was destined to be the first of a flood of semi-autobiographical novels of the college man. His "This Side of Paradise" was followed by such books as "Plastic Age," "Wife of the Centaur," "Moon Calf."

Now Travis Ingham has produced for his first novel, "Young Gentlemen, Rise," a story of his generation of collegian, which happened to cover the years of 1924 to 1928. Readers whose memory extends back to "This Side of Paradise" and "... e" will find in "Young ... Rise" that this genus of ... has changed but ...

Considered as a picture of college life in the pre-depression era, "Young Gentlemen, Rise," will recall those sensational novels of another day, "This Side of Paradise" and "The Plastic Age," and should be rated somewhere between the two. Less revealing than Fitzgerald's masterpiece of youthful sophistication, it is surely a sounder and more searching study than "The Plastic Age."

In the current Virginia Quarterly Review Mr. Bishop has an article entitled "The Missing All" in which he fixes upon O'Hara as finishing what Hemingway and Scott Fitzgerald began, the drama of ... morals. When Hemingway and Fitzgerald began, there was the magic of revolt. When O'Hara finished there was the dullness of death. "Here (in O'Hara's world)," writes Mr. Bishop, "are the loves of Fitzgerald turned into quick adulteries . . .

These are the concluding pages of Fitzgerald's last scrapbook.

TESS SLESINGER'S "The Unpossessed" (Simon & Schuster, $2.50) is, quite simply and dogmatically, the best novel of contemporary New York City that we have read. It has a ferocious drive, a wild and unfaltering rhythm, a quality of wit that is lightly blended of malice and understanding, a complete grasp of most of the characters concerned in the plot, a terrifically effective dénouement, a contemporaneity that is as absolutely of 1934 as that of Floyd Dell's "Janet March" was of 1923 or "This Side of Paradise" of 1919, and construction that is impeccable.

THE UNPOSSESSED, by Tess Slesinger. A notable first novel by a newcomer who is clearly going somewhere. A kind of "This Side of Paradise" for 1934. The characters are New York intellectuals paralleling, to an extent, the frustrates in "Antic Hay" and "Point Counter Point," and the treatment

MODERNS?

Reviewers everywhere have called this book the *This Side of Paradise* of 1934. It has completely outraged a whole class of people, the New York "intellectuals" it describes, and has, although a first novel, definitely established Miss Slesinger as a major novelist. $2.50

THE UNPOSSESSED

by Travis Ingham

IT mirrors a generation more entertainingly and completely than any book since F. Scott Fitzgerald's THIS SIDE OF PARADISE.

THE MELODY LINGERS ON.

The Next Time

NEXT TIME WE LIVE. By Ursula Parrott. Longmans, Green & Co. New York. 298 pages. $2.50.

"Next time we live, Christopher," Cecily said, "we'll have more time for each other." So this lightly enchanting novel closes, and it shows Miss Parrott in her best character performance, best story telling style. Here is unadulterated reading for those who read strictly for entertainment. It may prove a little too profound for some, but for the average run of readers, it ought to click. It was serialized under the title of "Say Goodbye Again."

The story concerns two young people, married in the rush and tumble of the day, shorly after the World War, the jazz age that F. Scott Fetzgerald dramatized for literary consumption.

NEXT TIME WE LIVE. By Ursula Parrott . . . *298 pp. . . New York: Longmans, Green and Company . . . $2.50.*

Ursula Parrott creates a wistful enchantment by turning back the calendar to the year 1920, when all the vexatious questions of the world seemed temporarily settled except "the enforcement of Prohibition and the Problem of the Younger Generation." And the latter wasn't insuperable if you belonged to it. Christopher, who was close to twenty-two, and Cicely, who was just eighteen, met at a Princeton house party and fell in love to the rhythm of the newly fashionable saxophones, fell in love "with a desperateness rather unfashionable that year, when the code was to be poised and nonchalant." Cicely's philosophy was a mixture of Freud and Scott Fitzgerald; that they had no affair was less her fault than Christopher's.

Bernard DeVoto's

WE ACCEPT WITH PLEASURE

"I recognized in it my own generation as I never recognized it in the pages of Scott Fitzgerald or of Ernest Hemingway."—*Lewis Gannett in New York Herald Tribune.* "Not a dull page in it." —*Saturday Review of Literature.* Third printing. $2.50

BERNARD DE VOTO'S "We Accept With Pleasure" (Little, Brown, $2.50) is at once a novel and a fascinating cryptogram. As a novel, it is about Scott Fitzgeraldian characters, all "post-war" in their various ways, for all that most of them are Yankees from Boston who possess more quirks and inhibitions than the Amory Blaines from the Midwest.

An Ideal of Youth.

The mood of "The Man Who Had Everything" recalls the mood of F. Scott Fitzgerald's "The Great Gatsby." Like Gatsby, Tom kept yearning for an ideal that he had set up in his youth. But Mr. Bromfield has not written his story on the sublimely objective plane of "The Great Gatsby." One is too often aware of the presence of the author in the character and the story, and one is aware, too, that the author is not giving us all he knows. Fitzgerald, on the other hand, kept himself out of Jay Gatsby—and one was convinced that Gatsby would have acted thus and so. The moralist that is Fitzgerald did not openly intrude until the last paragraph; Bromfield is in and out of his story at all times, and it is a Bromfield that is unwilling to carry out the line of his thinking with any rigorousness and precision.

James Boyd, who lives in Southern Pines and is not related to Thomas Boyd or Ernest Boyd, has abandoned his historical romances and written a more or less realistic novel, somewhat in the style of F. Scott Fitzgerald, about an upper-middle-class family living near Philadelphia. The title is "Roll, River."

Absent-minded, round-faced, stuttering slightly when animated, Wilson is a conscientious, mole-like conversationalist. He sometimes surprises people by popping up from a topic they thought had been abandoned, picking up the conversation precisely where it had left off. Scholarly by temperament, a sagacious commentator on Latin poets, Greek dramatists, French fiction, he combines these academic pursuits with a love of the theatre, writes comedies (*The Crime in the Whistler Room, This Room, This Gin and These Sandwiches*) in which characters akin to those of F. Scott Fitzgerald are shown wound up with less outspoken intellectuals. [...]

This Novel Is a Bridge Between the Age of Sinclair Lewis and Scott Fitzgerald and Our Own

IN TIME OF PEACE. By Thomas Boyd . . . 309 pp. . . . *New York: Minton, Balch and Company* . . . $2.50.

Lewises and Fitzgeralds, but the theme and method of "In Time of Peace" are not drastically unlike the themes and methods of "Babbitt" and "The Great Gatsby."

High point of *Chance Has A Whip*, describing the delicate relationship of father, mistress and daughter, has a muffled, tragic quality that recalls the best writing of F. Scott Fitzgerald.

Book contains letters and comment on "Tender is the Night" from the following novelists:

Out of the patterns of these five Mr. Golding weaves his ample tapestry. It includes a little of everything: Elsie lived as richly as a Scott Fitzgerald heroine on the Riviera, and later explored perverse Berlin:

F. Scott Fitzgerald was the progenitor—at least in modern American times—of the theme and James McConneaughey has set down its latest manifestation. [...]

and poets:

Some of Mr. Egan's lines have a sort of simple-minded daring, recalling the postwar audacities of F. Scott Fitzgerald, and maybe this has its own charm. [...]

In her book, "No Nice Girl Swears," "Moatsy," in an airy, Scott-Fitzgeraldian, but none-the-less serious, manner, crystallized into words the change that has been sneaking up on us in regard to a new set of modes and manners, as socially acceptable today as the rigid, correct etiquettes of another day.

James Branch Cabell
Gertrude Stein
John Dos Passos
Ernest Hemingway
Carl Van Vechten
G. B. Stern
Thomas Wolfe
Louis Bromfield
Vincent McHugh
Marjorie Kinnan Rawlings
John Peale Bishop
Morley Callaghan
Shane Leslie
Grace Flandrau
Isabelle Patterson
George Weller
John O'Hara

Archibald MacLeish
Alexander Woolcott
Noel Coward
H. L. Mencken
Mary Colum
Gilbert Seldes
Mabel Dodge
Malcolm Cowley
Matthew Josephson
Robert Benchley
Bartlett Cormack
Christian Gauss
Cameron Rogers
John C. Long
Lawrence Lee
Burton Rascoe
Otto Forel M.D.
Henry S. Canby

THERE simply hasn't been anybody writing books like "The Pumpkin Coach" for years. Not since F. Scott Fitzgerald had his first exciting fling with words, throwing them about in the exuberance of youth, has anyone used them so prodigally.

I wonder if [...]ton Kelland himself has ever bothered to count the number of times he has used the formula which he uses again in "Dreamland" (Harper, $2). It is about a very wordy, pedantic youth whose twenty-seven years have been spent cloistered in a world of books and theories—a caricature of an infant prodigy remembered from one of Fitzgerald's earliest short stories, "Head and Shoulders."

BRAIN GUY—Benjamin Appel—*Knopf* ($2.50). The racketeer, first introduced into U. S. fiction in F. Scott Fitzgerald's *The Great Gatsby* (1925), now looms large among U. S. villain-heroes.

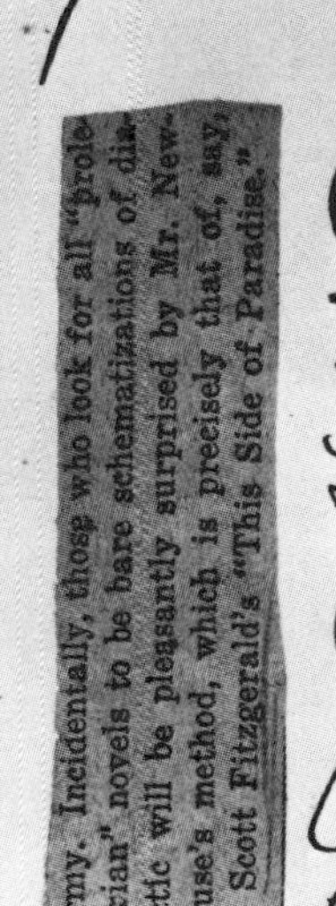
Army. Incidentally, those who look for all "proletarian" novels to be bare schematizations of dialectic will be pleasantly surprised by Mr. Newhouse's method, which is precisely that of, say, F. Scott Fitzgerald's "This Side of Paradise."

Cyril "Cen[...]" Writes for the Movies

In the beginning there was F. Scott Fitzgerald, who wrote the first of the college novels; but soon after came one almost as famous, Cyril Hume, author of "The Wife of the Centaur," a Yale graduate and a gentleman, sir.

Good novels of U. S. college life have been rare since Francis Scott Fitzgerald's *This Side of Paradise*. More comprehensive, less pointed than its Princeton predecessor, *Not to Eat, Not for Love* would be a notable achievement for any old grad, is an extraordinary accomplishment for an author not four years out of Harvard.

If F. Scott Fitzgerald were 10 years younger and an Englishwoman his name would be Rosamond Lehmann. She is a novelist with whose photograph men can fall in love and whose precocious gifts as a writer were early recognized in her first novel, "Dusty Answer," which depicted her generation of upper class youth in England as Fitzgerald did his own American upper-class generation in "This Side of Paradise," and which achieved a like success.

R[...]t McClure

The comparison seems validated by Miss Lehmann's new novel, "The Weather in the Streets." Artistically it is as fine as we should expect from an author whose acute intelligence and sensitiveness to beauty were manifest from the first. It is, however, a saddening book, in the same way and, I suspect, for the same reason, that Fitzgerald's "Tender is the Night" is saddening. It is about those same charming upper-class young people as they grow older. In their early 20s they were delightful, even in their youthful excesses and egotism. In their 30s they are tarnished and wondering what it is all about.

ROLL RIVER, by James Boyd. Mr. Boyd shifts from historical romance to a six-hundred-page novel, more or less realistic, and somewhat reminiscent in atmosphere and style of F. Scott Fitzgerald. [...]

"REVOLT ON THE CAMPUS," by James Wechsler (Covici-Friede, $3), and "Insurgent America," by Alfred Bingham (Harpers, $2.50), are two books that have high symptomatic value, as well as being challenging in their own right. They are doubly important in that they represent the first considerable incursions into print of the college generations that have been emerging from the shelter of the campus elms since 1929 to face, not a booming and confident future, but a world ridden by depression and menaced by war.

Back in the Twenties, when there was a plethora of magazine space to be filled, and when advances from publishers were more easily wangled than in recent years, the younger generations had little to worry about so far as having their youthful say was concerned. The Cyril Humes followed the F. Scott Fitzgeralds, and the yearly editions of The American Caravan were freighted down with "new" voices.

The extreme cleverness of Katherine Brush is something beyond description, and certainly beyond analysis. Why she holds our interest we cannot imagine. It is the same old scene, the current chaotic backdrop depicting jazz orchestras and bar tenders and sun-tanned backs and reckless drivers in low-slung, high-powered cars. We should be bored, but we are not. Neither are we indifferent to the crowd, who are little more recent than the Scott Fitzgerald crowd, and are equally familiar and typical.

The Southern stories and the airplane stories are as good as Faulkner can make them, which is better than most, and "Death Drag" and "Mountain Victory" and perhaps "Smoke" will have to be read by every one who reads Faulkner. "Doctor Martino," the title story, may be skipped. It is a mildly interesting exercise in the occult, suggesting the manner of Scott Fitzgerald—but whenever I find Faulkner behaving like another writer I have lost interest in him. I prefer him to stick to his last.

PETER MONRO JACK.

THE TRUE STORY OF APPOMATTOX

Columnist Discovers That It Was Grant Who Surrendered To Lee Instead Of Lee Surrendering To Grant

Circumstances Divulged For The First Time By Captain X

We have learned that when Grant had decided to surrender his milk-fed millions to Lee's starving remnants and the rendezvous was arranged at Appomattox Court House, Lee demanded that Grant put his submission into writing. Unfortunately Grant's pencil broke, and, removing his cigar from his mouth, he turned to General Lee and said with true military courtesy: "General, I have broken my pencil; will you lend me your sword to sharpen it with?" General Lee, always ready and willing to oblige, whipped forth his sword and tendered it to General Grant.

It was unfortunately just at this moment that the flashlight photographers and radio announcers got to work and the picture was erroneously given to the world that General Lee was surrendering his sword to General Grant.

The credulous public immediately accepted this story. The bells that were prepared to ring triumphantly in Loudoun county were stilled while the much inferior Yankee bells in Old North Church in Boston burst forth in a false pæan of triumph. To this day the legend persists, but we of the Welbourne *Journal* are able to present to the world for the first time the real TRUTH about this eighty-year-old slander that Virginia lost its single-handed war against the allied Eskimos north of the Mason and Dixon line.

Fitzgerald had this parody account of Lee's surrender printed as a joke for Elizabeth Lemmon, a cousin of Maxwell Perkins whom they had visited together at her ante-bellum mansion, "Welbourne," in Middleburg, Virginia.

15

In the Darkest Hour

A Poignant Romance of Chaos and Leadership

ON a May afternoon in the Year of Our Lord 872 a young man rode a white Arabian horse down a steep slope into the Valley of the Loire, at a point fifty miles west of the city of Tours.

He was lost. He was following directions given him six weeks before in Cordova—directions that were based on a woman's memory of eighteen years before. Since then all this part of France had been ravaged and pillaged by band after band of Northmen surging into the estuary of the Loire with their small Viking galleys; and most of the landmarks Philippe's mother had given him had long disappeared.

He was broad and strong, and well-developed for his twenty years. His hair was tawny and waving; his mouth was firm; his eyes, of a somewhat cruel gray, were shrewd and bright. Though not of Moorish birth, he wore a pointed Oriental headpiece, cloth-covered to keep out the sun, and a travel-stained tunic bordered with gold and held together by a leather belt, from which swung a curved sword. More formidably, a mace was hooked to his saddle; and a light coat of fence-rings sewn upon leather was rolled like a blanket behind it.

During three days Philippe had not seen a human being—only half-burned farmhouses, inhabited here and there by ghostly ill-nourished pigs and poultry prowling among the ruins; now as he stopped to drink from a stream, he started as he saw a youth of his own age engaged in the same function on the other side not fifteen feet away. He was of a type that, for all the Christian

by F. Scott Fitzgerald

After the publication of Tender Is the Night, Fitzgerald began writing stories for Redbook about a soldier of fortune in the Middle Ages. The hero, Philippe, "Count of Darkness," was based on Hemingway. Although he intended to expand the series into a novel, only four parts were published, and were never collected. Meanwhile Perkins was pressuring Fitzgerald to provide the stories for a new collection.

Am sending along No. 1 of the stories because I feel it's going to be the devil to set up. There are two others all corrected, but the slow thing is to look through "Tender Is the Night" *and see what phrases I took out of the stories. This is confused by the fact that there were so many revisions of* "Tender" *that I don't know what I left in it and what I didn't leave in it finally. I am going to have trouble with two of the stories you suggested. In "The Captured Shadow" I'll have to make up a whole new ending which is almost like writing a new story. Secondly, the Josephine story, "A Nice Quiet Place," has some awfully phoney stuff in the middle that I'll have to find a substitute for. So can't I send the stories in their original order, and have them set up separately, and then sandwich between them the last two if I can think of some way of fixing them in time.*

* * *

Looks now as if I will be here until well into the summer, but I am going to try damn hard to get a month off somewhere if I can get clear of debt and clear of the work to which I committed myself. I can well understand all your difficulties working in the office by day and with Tom Wolfe by night because until ten days ago, when I collapsed and took to my bed I have been doing about the same thing. I am all right now and once I get this "Post" *story off should be out of the worst.*

—FSF to Maxwell Perkins, 26 June 1934.

Thirty-Eight Years Old 189

Sept Welbourne again. Pierce perhaps—Sabres, butlers, Goiters, Morrisons, the pool, the graveyard. New York with Spafford. Mayflower Hotel. Dinner in Washington. Wine on Trains. The bus from Middleburg. Myra in Algonquin. Miss Sabrux visited. The Bishops. Max down. Furnace now serious

Taps at Reveille, Fitzgerald's last short story collection, was published March 1935. It required only one printing of 5,000 copies.

CONTENTS

N.Y. **BOOKS OF THE TIMES** Times

By JOHN CHAMBERLAIN

F. SCOTT FITZGERALD has been reproached all along for wasting a glamorous style, an unsurpassed artistry, and a feeling for romantic situations and qualities, on essentially futile material. Identified with the jazz age, which he did so much to popularize, he has paid the inevitable penalty for having been at one time the fashion. Just at present his reputation is in a sort of eclipse. Yet a reading of his latest collection of short stories, "Taps at Reveille" (Scribner's, $2.50), convinces me that the common contemporary approach to Fitzgerald is wrong. Futile material? Is there such a thing? Are Fitzgerald's adolescent boys and girls, his scenario writers and moving picture directors, his college athletes and loafers, his theatrical producers, his dancers, his light ladies, his débutantes, his doctors, his murderers and his stock market speculators—are these characters (who constitute the dramatis personae of "Taps at Reveille") any more futile than Faulkner's de-emotionalized morons and aviators, or Proust's gallery of snobs, or Flaubert's Madame Bovary or Lewis's Carol Milford? The answer is, of course, "No."

Like all material about human beings, Mr. Fitzgerald's is, then, "significant." It is significant of life in America from 1912 to 1935. Mr. Fitzgerald's attitude toward his material creates poetry; as Malcolm Cowley has said, Mr. Fitzgerald is our only poet of the upper middle class. He looks back on the relatively sheltered life in St. Paul of Basil Duke Lee (who is Amory Blaine before he went to Princeton); and the things Basil did, even when he was making a fool of himself, seem somehow glorious. They seem glorious because Basil still had aspiration. "The Perfect Life," which is the story of Basil's experience with a type of Buchmanism, is a masterpiece of sympathetic comprehension of the mind of a dreaming adolescent. And "First Blood," the story of how Josephine, the girl who grew up in Chicago to be one of the first prom trotters, just had to prove the reality of her undeniable charm by taking an older man away from her sister, is equally perspicacious. Mr. Fitzgerald knows the generation that grew up during the war as no one else does.

Gin, Jazz and Flappers

TAPS AT REVEILLE, by F. Scott Fitzgerald (Scribner's, $2.50). 407 pages.

THE WORLD is full of two kinds of people: those who swear by F. Scott Fitzgerald and those who swear at him. The former will hail this volume with huzzahs, for it contains some of his finest work.

Eighteen stories, selected by Fitzgerald as his best in the past decade, place in one volume two of his most vivid characters—Basil Duke Lee, the "freshest boy" of the gin and jazz era, and Josephine, the forgotten flapper. The rest of the book is composed of ten other stories, with "Babylon Revisited" the best of all.

One story, printed for the first time, tells what happened to a pair of light ladies who followed the Union Army to a Civil War battlefield. A wow.—Walker Matheson.

TO
HAROLD OBER

Taps at Reveille, by F. Scott Fitzgerald. New York: Charles Scribner's Sons. $2.50.

SCOTT FITZGERALD is supposed to be a case of split personality: Fitzgerald A is the serious writer; Fitzgerald B brings home the necessary bacon. And "Taps at Reveille," a collection of avowed pot-boilers, was written with his fingers crossed by Fitzgerald B. There seems to be a feeling abroad that it would be kinder not to take any critical notice of the goings-on of Fitzgerald B, since his better half is such a superior person and might be embarrassed. Mr. Fitzgerald himself, however, obviously doesn't feel that way about it, for he signs his moniker to all and sundry, and even collects the offerings of his lower nature in a book. He is right: there is no real difference in kind between "Taps at Reveille" and "Tender Is the Night"; the creatures whom he has sold down the river for a good price are a little cruder, that's all. The yearning toward maturity is even more noticeable in some of these short stories than it is in his novels. It used to seem awful to Mr. Fitzgerald that youth should have to become manhood; now it seems even more awful that it can't. His heroes have grown older but not riper; in their middle thirties they are hurt and puzzled children, lost among their contemporary elders, and still longing to grow up.

T. S. MATTHEWS.

ASHEVILLE, N. C., SUNDAY MORNING, JULY 21, 1935

F. Scott Fitzgerald Staying At Hotel Here

Famous Author Visiting In City

F. Scott Fitzgerald, distinguished novelist and short-story writer, shown above, is spending the summer in Asheville, a guest at Grove Park inn. This picture of the rarely photographed author shows him standing on the lawn at the inn, where he is resting and doing some writing. One of the nation's foremost authors, he has written many leading works of fiction, including "This Side of Paradise," "The Great Gatsby," "Tender Is the Night" and scores of short stories. An interesting man with a strong personality, he has never visited Western North Carolina before.

Thinks Quality Of Novel Not As High As Six Years Ago

The three greatest literary "talents" coming to the front in America so far in the 1930's have been three Southerners—Thomas Wolfe, of Asheville; William Falkner, of Mississippi, and Erskine Caldwell, of Georgia—in the opinion of F. Scott Fitzgerald, noted author visiting Asheville.

Mr. Fitzgerald, novelist and short-story writer, came here several weeks ago. He is a guest at Grove Park inn.

One of America's most widely read writers of the present day, he yesterday discussed trends in literature in one of his few interviews in many years.

Quality Is Lower

The quality of the American novel has fallen off during the last five years, according to this distinguished vacationist, mustached, affable, very likable. He also finds that writing on the whole was better during the 1920's than it has been so far during the 1930's.

This can be explained in part by the depression, said the deep-thinking Mr. Fitzgerald. "In time of turbulence it (writing) is not usually as good. Poetry and fiction are best written in tranquil times.

"We must remember that there are two kinds of tranquility, too. One is genuine; the other is the sort that comes when we have finished a task and are utterly worn out, and is not genuine tranquillity.

"In times of turbulence everything, including writing, comes too quickly, too hastily, and this isn't productive of the best literature. On the other hand, the times immediately after turbulence sometimes produce a great flowering of literature."

Illustrating from the period in history known as the Renaissance, the well-known author said: "We can illustrate from The Renaissance. During the time of trouble, there was no flowering by writers and painters. Then followed good work.

"During the time of turbulence, the main thing is to live."

Dixie Taking Lead

Therefore as more genuinely tranquil times come, we may expect more in the way of good literature, said Mr. Fitzgerald, who believes that the South's lead in new literary talent so far in the 1930's probably indicates that Dixie has lead in the emergence from the depression.

Much Read By Young

Mr. Fitzgerald's work, largely about young people, has been much read by young people. "This generation of youth has lost faith in its elders unusually early," he lamentingly observed.

"Young people now have a negative philosophy, which they get from uncertainty of their elders and of the times. They are not at the moment idealists. Too much has happened. They have been preached to, lied to. Most generations grow up with idealism, but the expression, 'Oh! Yeah!' comes closer to expressing the feeling of the present younger generation than anything else. They are, like all mankind, essentially spiritual, but just simply haven't found leadership that they can honestly accept."

Asked if he thought young people now prefer any special kind of literature, he said: "I have a 13-year-old daughter, Frances. I know things she doesn't like, codes of which she doesn't approve, but it's hard to learn what she likes. Even in the very young I find utter disillusionment. Here one finds the negative philosophy being expressed."

Mr. Fitzgerald, Princeton university graduate, has done some writing since coming to Asheville, but chose not to talk of it. A prominent member of the summer colony at Grove Park inn, he expects to be here about a month longer.

After leaving "La Paix" at the end of 1933 Fitzgerald lived in Baltimore. In 1935 he began making extended visits to the Tryon-Hendersonville-Asheville area in the North Carolina mountains. This was a period of severe financial strain and ill health for Fitzgerald. While he was ill at the Grove Park Inn (rooms marked above) and Zelda was hospitalized, they exchanged these recollections.

Dearest and always Dearest Scott:

I am sorry too that there should be nothing to greet you but an empty shell. The thought of the effort you have made over me, the suffering this nothing *has cost would be unendurable to any save a completely vacuous mechanism. Had I any feelings they would all be bent in gratitude to you and in sorrow that of all my life there should not even be the smallest relic of the love and beauty that we started with to offer you at the end.*

You have been so good to me—and all I can say is that there was always that deeper current running through my heart: my life, you.

You remember the roses in Kenney's yard—you were so gracious and I thought—he is the sweetest person in the world—and you said "darling." You still are. The wall was damp and mosey when we crossed the street and said we loved the south. I thought of the south and a happy past I'd never had and I thought I was part of the south. You said you loved this lovely land. The wistaria along the fence was green and the shade was cool and life was old.

I wish I had thought something else—but it was a confederate, a romantic and nostalgic thought. My hair was damp when I took off my hat and I was safe and home and you were glad that I felt that way and you were reverent. We were glad and happy all the way home.

Now that there isn't any more happiness and home is gone and there isn't even any past and no emotions but those that were yours where there could be my comfort—it is a shame that we should have met in harshness and coldness where there was once so much tenderness and so many dreams. Your song.

I wish you had a little house with hollyhocks and a sycamore tree and the afternoon sun imbedding itself in a silver tea-pot. Scottie would be running about somewhere in white, in Renoir, and you will be writing books in dozens of volumes. And there will be honey still for tea, though the house should not be in Granchester.

I want you to be happy—if there were justice you would be happy —maybe you will be anyway.

Oh, Do-Do Do Do—

I love you anyway—even if there isn't any me or any love or even any life—

I love you.

LAMP IN A WINDOW

Do you remember, before keys turned in the locks,
When life was a close-up, and not an occasional letter,
That I hated to swim naked from the rocks
While you liked absolutely nothing better?

Do you remember many hotel bureaus that had
Only three drawers? But the only bother
Was that each of us got holy, then got mad
Trying to give the third one to the other.

East, west, the little car turned, often wrong
Up an erroneous Alp, an unmapped Savoy river.
We blamed each other, wild were our words and strong,
And, in an hour, laughed and called it liver.

And, though the end was desolate and unkind:
To turn the calendar at June and find December
On the next leaf; still, stupid-got with grief, I find
These are the only quarrels that I can remember.

—FSF.

Fitzgerald wrote "The Crack-Up" in the room at the Skyland Hotel, Hendersonville, circled here in November 1935. This essay was posthumously published with other autobiographical pieces in the collection, The Crack-Up *(1945).*

The Crack-Up

A desolately frank document from one for whom the salt of life has lost its savor

by **F. SCOTT FITZGERALD**

• ARTICLE •

Before I go on with this short history, let me make a general observation—the test of a first-rate intelligence is the ability to hold two opposed ideas in the mind at the same time, and still retain the ability to function. One should, for example, be able to see that things are hopeless and yet be determined to make them otherwise. This philosophy fitted on to my early adult life, when I saw the improbable, the implausible, often the "impossible," come true. Life was something you dominated if you were any good. Life yielded easily to intelligence and effort, or to what proportion could be mustered of both. It seemed a romantic business to be a successful literary man—you were not ever going to be as famous as a movie star but what note you had was probably longer-lived—you were never going to have the power of a man of strong political or religious convictions but you were certainly more independent. Of course within the practice of your trade you were forever unsatisfied—but I, for one, would not have chosen any other.

* * *

Life, ten years ago, was largely a personal matter. I must hold in balance the sense of the futility of effort and the sense of the necessity to struggle; the conviction of the inevitability of failure and still the determination to "succeed"—and, more than these, the contradiction between the dead hand of the past and the high intentions of the future. If I could do this through the common ills—domestic, professional and personal—then the ego would continue as an arrow shot from nothingness to nothingness with such force that only gravity would bring it to earth at last.

For seventeen years, with a year of deliberate loafing and resting out in the center—things went on like that, with a new chore only a nice prospect for the next day. I was living hard, too, but: "Up to forty-nine it'll be all right," I said. "I can count on that. For a man who's lived as I have, that's all you could ask."

—And then, ten years this side of forty-nine, I suddenly realized that I had prematurely cracked.

—First section of "The Crack-Up"

In Hendersonville: I am living very cheaply. Today I am in comparative affluence, but Monday and Tuesday I had two tins of potted meat, three oranges and a box of Uneedas and two cans of beer. For the food, that totalled eighteen cents a day—and when I think of the thousand meals I've sent back untasted in the last two years. It was fun to be poor—especially you haven't enough liver power for an appetite. But the air is fine here, and I liked what I had—and there was nothing to do about it anyhow because I was afraid to cash any checks, and I had to save enough for postage for the story. But it was funny coming into the hotel and the very deferential clerk not knowing that I was not only thousands, nay tens of thousands in debt, but had less than forty cents cash in the world and probably a deficit at my bank.

—"The Note-Books"

It grows harder to write, because there is much less weather than when I was a boy and practically no men and women at all.

—"The Note-Books"

The old dream of being an entire man in the Goethe-Byron-Shaw tradition, with an opulent American touch, a sort of combination of J. P. Morgan, Topham Beauclerk and St. Francis of Assisi, has been relegated to the junk heap of the shoulder pads worn for one day on the Princeton freshman football field and the overseas cap never worn overseas.

So what? This is what I think now: that the natural state of the sentient adult is a qualified unhappiness. I think also that in an adult the desire to be finer in grain than you are, "a constant striving" (as those people say who gain their bread by saying it) only adds to this unhappiness in the end—that end that comes to our youth and hope. My own happiness in the past often approached such an ecstasy that I could not share it even with the person dearest to me but had to walk it away in quiet streets and lanes with only fragments of it to distil into little lines in books—and I think that my happiness, or talent for self-delusion or what you will, was an exception. It was not the natural thing but the unnatural—unnatural as the Boom; and my recent experience parallels the wave of despair that swept the nation when the Boom was over.

—"Handle with Care"

In a previous article this writer told about his realization that what he had before him was not the dish that he had ordered for his forties. In fact—since he and the dish were one, he described himself as a cracked plate, the kind that one wonders whether it is worth preserving. Your editor thought that the article suggested too many aspects without regarding them closely, and probably many readers felt the same way—and there are always those to whom all self-revelation is contemptible, unless it ends with a noble thanks to the gods for the Unconquerable Soul.

But I had been thanking the gods too long, and thanking them for nothing. I wanted to put a lament into my record, without even the background of the Euganean Hills to give it color. There weren't any Euganean hills that I could see.

Sometimes, though, the cracked plate has to be retained in the pantry, has to be kept in service as a household necessity. It can never again be warmed on the stove nor shuffled with the other plates in the dishpan; it will not be brought out for company, but it will do to hold crackers late at night or to go into the ice box under left-overs . . .

—"Pasting it Together"

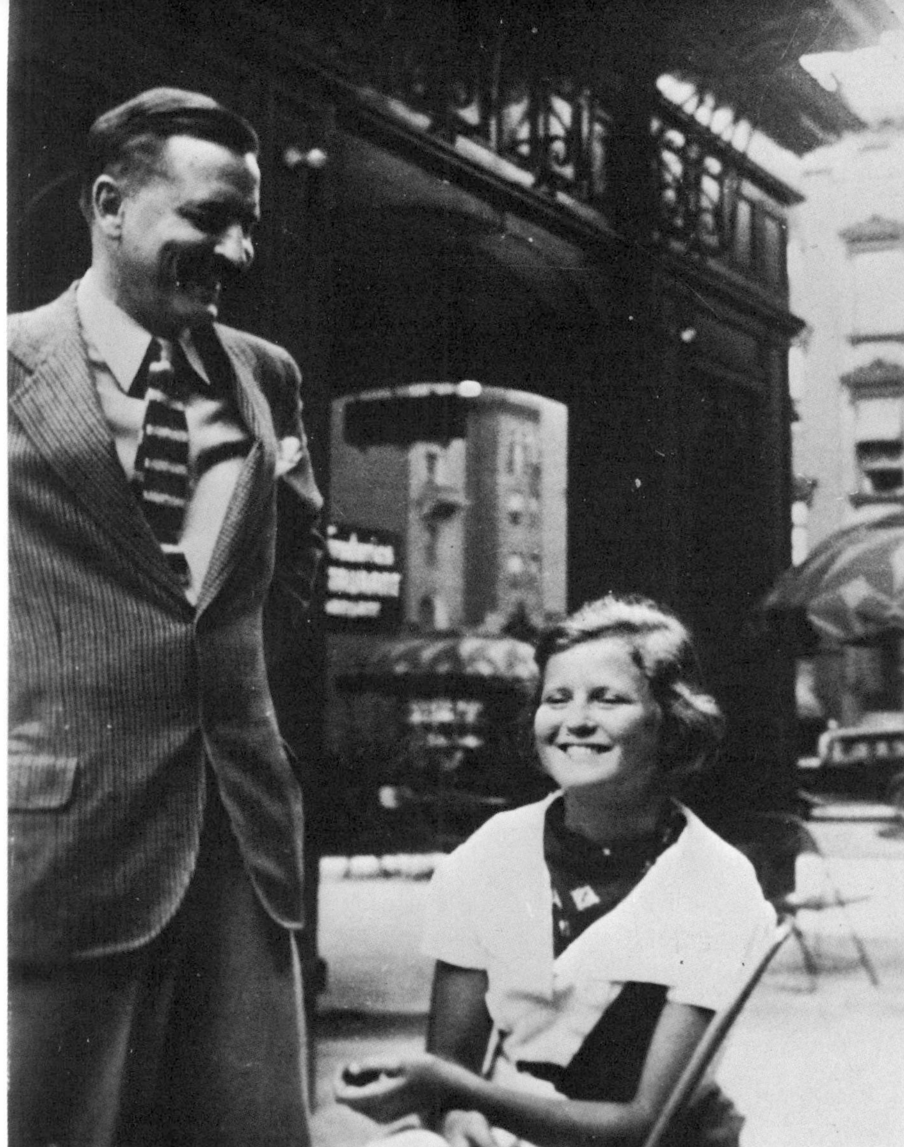

In 1935 Fitzgerald returned to his apartment at the Cambridge Arms in Baltimore. Scottie had been staying with his secretary, Mrs. Isabel Owens, while going to Bryn Mawr School.

NBM13 57 DL=BALTIMORE MD 28 843A
HAROLD OBER=
40 EAST 49 ST=

HAVE TRIED LIFE ON SUBSISTANCE LEVEL AND IT DOESNT WORK STOP I THOUGHT IF I COULD HAVE THIS MONEY I COULD HOLD MY HEAD UP AND GO ON STOP WHAT YOU SUGGEST POSTPONES BY HALF A YEAR THE LIQUIDATION WE BOTH WANT STOP PLEASE CARRY ME OVER THE SECOND GWEN STORY AND GIVE ME TWENTY SEVEN HUNDRED=
FITZGERALD.

Afternoon of an Author

First timid seeds toward the reforestation of a soil that suffered from forced growth

by F. SCOTT FITZGERALD

• ARTICLE •

He lingered for a moment in his daughter's end of the apartment and read his mail. It was an annoying mail with nothing cheerful in it—mostly bills and advertisements with the diurnal Oklahoma school boy and his gaping autograph album. Sam Goldwyn might do a ballet picture with Spessiwitza and might not—it would all have to wait till Mr. Goldwyn got back from Europe when he might have half a dozen new ideas. Paramount wanted a release on a poem that had appeared in one of the author's books, as they didn't know whether it was an original or quoted. Maybe they were going to get a title from it. Anyhow he had no more equity in that property—he had sold the silent rights many years ago and the sound rights last year.

"Never any luck with movies," he said to himself. "Stick to your last, boy."

* * *

After breakfast he lay down for fifteen minutes. Then he went into the study and began to work.

The problem was a magazine story that had become so thin in the middle that it was about to blow away. The plot was like climbing endless stairs, he had no element of surprise in reserve, and the characters who started so bravely day-before-yesterday couldn't have qualified for a newspaper serial.

"Yes, I certainly need to get out," he thought. "I'd like to drive down the Shenandoah Valley, or go to Norfolk on the boat."

But both of these ideas were impractical—they took time and energy and he had not much of either—what there was must be conserved for work. He went through the manuscript underlining good phrases in red crayon and after tucking these into a file slowly tore up the rest of the story and dropped it in the waste-basket. Then he walked the room and smoked, occasionally talking to himself.

* * *

"The perfect neurotic," he said, regarding himself in the mirror. "By-product of an idea, slag of a dream."

—"Afternoon of an Author"

NBM291 47=BALTIMORE MD 6 301P
HAROLD OBER=
40 EAST 49 ST=

TERRIBLY BROKE AND CONSEQUENTLY HAVE SENT STORY DIRECTLY TO POST CARBON TO YOU IF THEY LIKE IT PLEASE SEND AT LEAST TWO THIRD STIPEND HERE TO MY CREDIT AT FIRST NATIONAL I HOPE SO MUCH THAT YOU CAN DO THIS AS GWEN AND I MUST GO ON=
SCOTT FITZGERALD.

Fitzgerald amused himself by annotating junk books for Harold Ober.

Harold Ober

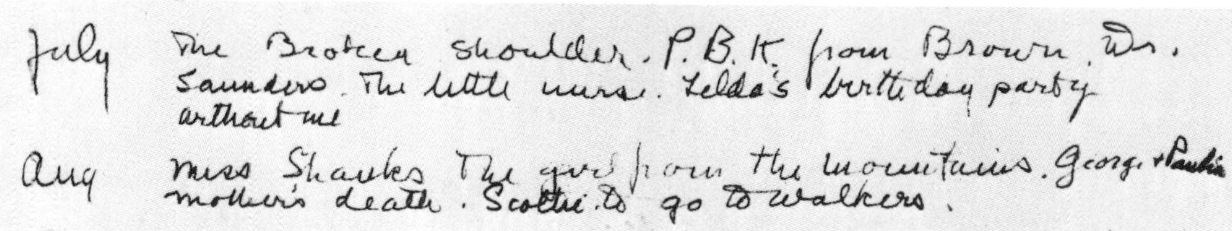

July The Broken shoulder. P.B.K. from Brown. Dr. Saunders. The little nurse. Zelda's birthday party without me

Aug Miss Shanks The girl from the mountains. George + Paulie mother's death. Scottie to go to Walkers.

. . . Zelda now claims to be in direct contact with Christ, William the Conqueror, Mary Stuart, Apollo and all the stock paraphernalia of insane-asylum jokes. Of course it isn't a bit funny but after the awful strangulation episode of last spring I sometimes take refuge in an unsmiling irony about the present exterior *phases of her illness. For what she has really suffered, there is never a sober night that I do not pay a stark tribute of an hour to in the darkness. In an odd way, perhaps incredible to you, she was always my child (it was not reciprocal as it often is in marriages), my child in a sense that Scottie isn't, because I've brought Scottie up hard as nails (perhaps that's fatuous, but I* think *I have). Outside of the realm of what you called Zelda's "terribly dangerous secret thoughts" I was her great reality, often the only liaison agent who could make the world tangible to her—*

—FSF to Sara and Gerald Murphy, c. March 1936.

This is my second day of having a minute to catch up with correspondence. Probably Harold Ober has kept you in general touch with what has happened to me but I will summarize:

I broke the clavicle of my shoulder, diving—nothing heroic, but a little too high for the muscles to tie up the efforts of a simple swan dive—At first the Doctors thought that I must have tuberculosis of the bone, but x-ray showed nothing of the sort, so (like occasional pitchers who throw their arm out of joint with some unprepared for effort) it was left to dangle for twenty-four hours with a bad diagnosis by a young Intern; then an x-ray and found broken and set in an elaborate plaster cast.

I had almost adapted myself to the thing when I fell in the bathroom reaching for the light, and lay on the floor until I caught a mild form of arthritis called "Miotoosis," [myotosis] *which popped me in the bed for five weeks more. During this time there were domestic crises: Mother sickened and then died and I tried my best to be there but couldn't. I have been within a mile and a half of my wife all summer and have seen her about half dozen times. Total accomplished for one summer has been one story—not very good, two* Esquire *articles, neither of them very good.*

You have probably seen Harold Ober and he may have told you that Scottie got a remission of tuition at a very expensive school where I wanted her to go (Miss Edith Walker's School in Connecticut). Outside of that I have no good news, except that I came into some money from my Mother, not as much as I had hoped, but at least $20,000. in cash and bonds at the materilization in six months—for some reason, I do not know the why or wherefore of it, it requires this time. I am going to use some of it, with the products of the last story and the one in process of completion, to pay off my bills and to take two or three months rest in a big way. I have to admit to myself that I haven't the vitality that I had five years ago.

—FSF to Maxwell Perkins, 19 September 1936.

While in North Carolina Fitzgerald often visited with his friends Nora and "Lefty" Flynn in Tryon. Nora is at right in the picture below.

With his good arm Martin threw back the top of the sheet, disclosing that the plaster armor had been cut away in front in the form of a square, so that his abdomen and the lower part of his diaphragm bulged a little from the aperture. His dislocated arm was still high over his head in an involuntary salute.

—"Design in Plaster"

Scott's mother died in September 1936.

I have never had so many things go wrong and with such defiant persistence. By an irony which quite fits into the picture, the legacy which I received from my mother's death (after being too ill to go to her death bed or her funeral) is the luckiest event of some time. She was a defiant old woman, defiant in her love for me in spite of my neglect of her, and it would have been quite within her character to have died that I might live.

—FSF to Beatrice Dance, 15 September 1936.

August, 1936 27

The Snows of Kilimanjaro

A Long Story

by ERNEST HEMINGWAY

He remembered poor Scott Fitzgerald and his romantic awe of them and how he had started a story once that began, 'The very rich are different from you and me.' And how someone had said to Scott, Yes they have more money. But that was not humorous to Scott. He thought they were a special glamorous race and when he found they weren't it wrecked him just as much as any other thing that wrecked him.

Please lay off me in print. If I choose to write de profundis *sometimes it doesn't mean I want friends praying aloud over my corpse. No doubt you meant it kindly but it cost me a night's sleep. And when you incorporate it (the story) in a book would you mind cutting my name?*

It's a fine story—one of your best—even though the "Poor Scott Fitzgerald, etc." rather spoiled it for me.

Ever your friend,

Scott

Riches have never *fascinated me, unless combined with the greatest charm or distinction.*

—FSF to Hemingway, August 1936.

I feel that I must tell you something which at first seemed better to leave alone: I wrote Ernest about that story of his, asking him in the most measured terms not to use my name in future pieces of fiction. He wrote me back a crazy letter, telling me about what a great Writer he was and how much he loved his children, but yielding the point—"If I should out live him—" which he doubted. To have answered it would have been like fooling with a lit firecracker. Somehow I love that man, no matter what he says or does, but just one more crack and I think I would have to throw my weight with the gang and lay him. No one could ever hurt him in his first books but he has completely lost his head and the duller he gets about it, the more he is like a punch-drunk pug fighting himself in the movies.

—FSF to Maxwell Perkins, 19 September 1936.

About the article about Michael Muck. I was in bed with temp about 102 when the phone rang and a voice said that this party had come all the way from N.Y to interview me. I fell for this like a damn fool, got him up, gave him a drink + accepted his exterior good manners. He had some relative with mental trouble (wife or mother) so I talked to him freely about treatments symtoms ect, about being depressed at advancing age and a little desperate about the wasted summer with this shoulder and arm—perhaps more freely than if had been well. I hadn't the faintest suspicion what would happen + I've never been a publicity seeker + never gotten a rotten deal before. When that thing came it seemed about the end and I got hold of a morphine file and swallowed four grains enough to kill a horse. It happened to be an overdose and almost before I could get to the bed I vomited the whole thing and the nurse came in + saw the empty phial + there was hell to pay for awhile + afterwards I felt like a fool. And if I ever see, Mr. Mock what will happen be very swift and sudden. Dont tell Perkins.

—FSF to Harold Ober, c. 5 October 1936.

New York Post

FRIDAY, SEPTEMBER 25, 1936

THE OTHER SIDE OF PARADISE

Scott Fitzgerald, 40, Engulfed in Despair

Broken in Health He Spends Birthday Regretting That He Has Lost Faith in His Star

By MICHEL MOK

Copyright, 1936, by New York Post, Inc.
Staff Correspondent of New York Post

ASHEVILLE, N. C., Sept. 25.—Long ago, when he was young, cock-sure, drunk with sudden success, F. Scott Fitzgerald told a newspaper man that no one should live beyond thirty.

That was in 1921, shortly after his first novel, "This Side of Paradise," had burst into the literary heavens like a flowering Roman candle.

The poet-prophet of the post-war neurotics observed his fortieth birthday yesterday in his bedroom of the Grove Park Inn here. He spent the day as he spends all his days—trying to come back from the other side of Paradise, the hell of despondency in which he has writhed for the last couple of years.

He had no company except his soft spoken, Southern, maternal and indulgent nurse and this reporter. With the girl he bantered in conventional nurse-and-patient fashion. With his visitor he chatted bravely, as an actor, consumed with fear that his name will never be in lights again, discusses his next starring role.

He kidded no one. There obviously was as little hope in his heart as there was sunshine in the dripping skies, covered with clouds that veiled the view of Sunset Mountain.

Physically he was suffering the aftermath of an accident eight weeks ago, when he broke his right shoulder in a dive from a fifteen-foot springboard.

But whatever pain the fracture might still cause him, it did not account for his jittery jumping off and onto his bed, his restless pacing, his trembling hands, his twitching face with its pitiful expression of a cruelly beaten child.

Cor could it be held responsible for his frequent trips to a highboy, in a drawer of which lay a bottle. Each time he poured a drink into the measuring glass on his bedside table,

Continued on Page 15, Col. 3

In September 1936 Michel Mok of The New York Post interviewed Fitzgerald in Asheville on his fortieth birthday and published a front-page article depicting him as a washed-up drunk. Fitzgerald felt that his reputation had been badly damaged and experienced suicidal despair.

In the spring of 1936 Fitzgerald had put his things in storage in Baltimore and brought Zelda down to the Highland Hospital in Asheville. In the fall they paid a visit to Mrs. Sayre, who was vacationing at Saluda, North Carolina.

I have asked a lot of my emotions—one hundred and twenty stories. The price was high, right up with Kipling, because there was one little drop of something—not blood, not a tear, not my seed, but me more intimately than these, in every story, it was the extra I had. Now it has gone and I am just like you now.

—"The Note-Books"

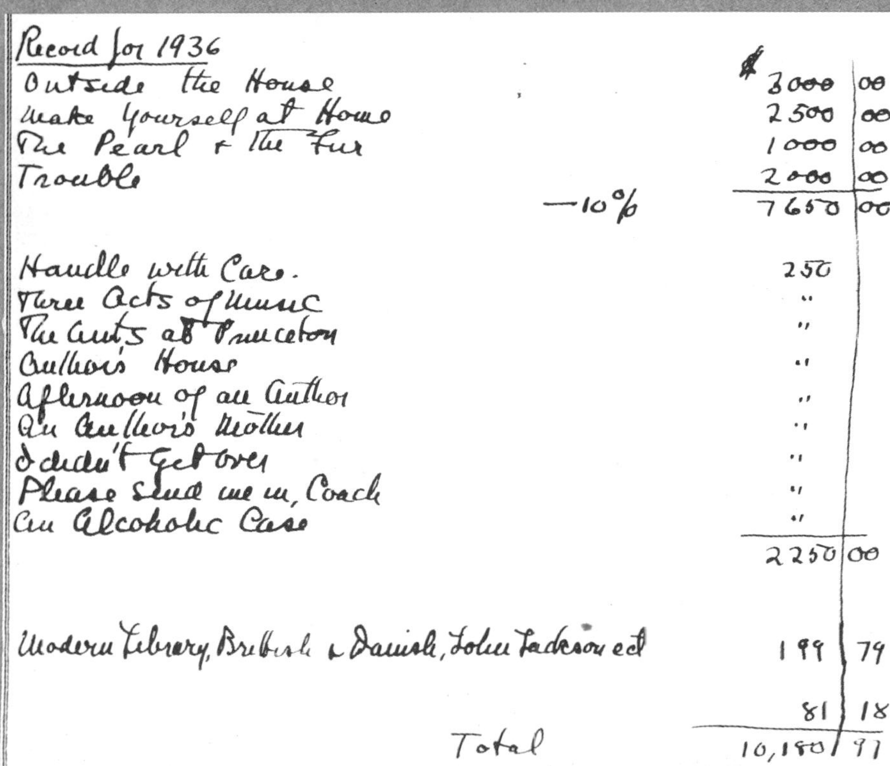

Record for 1936

Outside the House		$ 3000	00
Make Yourself at Home		2500	00
The Pearl & the Fur		1000	00
Trouble		2000	00
	—10%	7650	00
Handle with Care.		250	
Three Acts of Music		"	
The Ants at Princeton		"	
Author's House		"	
Afternoon of an Author		"	
An Author's Mother		"	
I didn't Get over		"	
Please Send me in, Coach		"	
An Alcoholic Case		"	
		2250	00
Modern Library, British & Danish, John Jackson ect		199	79
		81	18
	Total	10,180	97

Fitzgerald's income for 1936 was the lowest since 1919.

Thanks for your note and the appalling statement. Odd how enormous sums of $10,000 have come to seem lately—I can remember turning down that for the serialization of The Great Gatsby*—from College Humor.*

Well, my least productive & lowest general year since 1926 is over. In that year I did 1 short story and 2 chaps. of a novel—that is two chaps. that I afterwards used. And it was a terrible story. Last year, even though laid up 4 mos. I sold 4 stories & 8 Esq. pieces, a poor showing God knows. This year has started slowly also, same damn lack of interest, staleness, when I have every reason to want to work if only to keep from thinking. Havn't had a drink since I left the north. (about six weeks, not even beer) but while I feel a little better nervously it doesn't bring back the old exuberance. I honestly think that all the prizefighters, actors, writers who live by their own personal performances ought to have managers in their best years. The ephemeral part of the talent seems when it is in hiding so apart from one, so "otherwise" that it seems it ought to have some better custodian than the poor individual with whom it lodges and who is left with the bill. My chief achievement lately has been in cutting down my and Zelda's expenses to rock bottom; my chief failure is my inability to see a workable future. Hollywood for money has much against it, the stories are somehow mostly out of me unless some new source of material springs up, a novel takes money & time—I am thinking of putting aside certain hours and digging out a play, the ever-appealing mirage. At 40 one counts carefully one's remaining vitality and rescourses and a play ought to be within both of them. The novel & the autobiography have got to wait till this load of debt is lifted.

—FSF to Maxwell Perkins, February 1937.

N122 13=TRYON NCAR 210P MAY 11 1937
HAROLD OBER=
40 EAST 49 ST=

TO REMAIN HERE AND EAT MUST HAVE ONE HUNDRED AND THIRTY TODAY
PLEASE ASK PERKINS=
FITZGERALD.

Well, you certainly gave me a generous helping hand out of a nightmare and now that it is paid up—as far as such an obligation can be paid—I want to tell you that I've been constantly thinking of what you did with gratitude and appreciation. What got me into the two years' mess that reached its lowest point in the fall of 1936 was the usual combination of circumstances. A prejudiced enemy might say it was all drink, a fond mama might say it was a run of ill-luck, a banker might say it was not providing for the future in better days, a psychiatrist might say it was a nervous collapse—it was perhaps partly all these things—the effect was to fantastically prevent me from doing any work at the very age when presumably one is at the height of one's powers. My life looked like a hopeless mess there for awhile and the point was I didn't want *it to be better. I had completely ceased to give a good Goddamn.*

—FSF to C. O. Kalman, June 1937.

Fitzgerald sent this post card to Ober with a caption claiming that he had bought the mansion and charged it to Perkins.

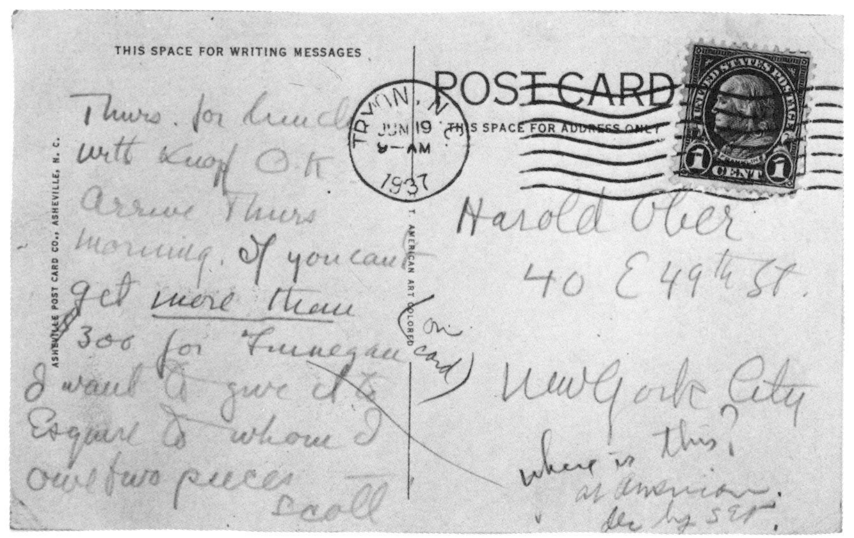

Desperately in need of money and over $12,000 in debt to Harold Ober, Fitzgerald sought Hollywood work in 1937. In July Ober secured a contract with MGM for six months at $1,000 a week.

NA148 29=ASHEVILLE NCAR 902P JULY 2 1937
HAROLD OBER=
SCARSDALE NY=

CAN ARRIVE LOSANGELES EASILY THURSDAY INCONVENIENTLY
WEDNESDAY MAILING YOU CHECK ON BALTIMORE FOR FIVE HUNDRED
FOR TICKETS PLEASE WIRE ME THAT SUM BATTERY PARK HOTEL
ASHEVILLE INFORMATION SCOTTIE LATER=
SCOTT FITZJERALD.

"Financing Finnegan" appeared in Esquire in January 1938, after Fitzgerald had left for Hollywood. Part One of the story, printed below, takes place in the Harold Ober office at 40 East 49th Street and in Maxwell Perkins's office in the Scribner Building at Fifth Avenue and 48th Street (below).

January, 1938

Financing Finnegan

They all agreed in the publishing house he was terrific and that he was sure to snap out of his slump

by F. SCOTT FITZGERALD

• FICTION •

FINNEGAN and I have the same literary agent to sell our writings for us, but though I'd often been in Mr. Cannon's office just before and just after Finnegan's visits, I had never met him. Likewise we had the same publisher and often when I arrived there Finnegan had just departed. I gathered from a thoughtful sighing way in which they spoke of him—

"Ah—Finnegan—"

"Oh yes, Finnegan was here."

—that the distinguished author's visit had been not uneventful. Certain remarks implied that he had taken something with him when he went—manuscripts, I supposed, one of those great successful novels of his. He had taken "it" off for a final revision, a last draft, of which he was rumored to make ten in order to achieve that facile flow, that ready wit, which distinguished his work. I discovered only gradually that most of Finnegan's visits had to do with money.

"I'm sorry you're leaving," Mr. Cannon would tell me, "Finnegan will be here tomorrow." Then after a thoughtful pause "I'll probably have to spend some time with him."

I don't know what note in his voice reminded me of a talk with a nervous bank president when Dillinger was reported in the vicinity. His eyes looked out into the distance and he spoke as to himself.

"Of course he may be bringing a manuscript. He has a novel he's working on, you know. And a play too." He spoke as though he were talking about some interesting but remote events of the cinquecento; but his eyes became more hopeful as he added: "Or maybe a short story."

"He's very versatile, isn't he?" I said.

"Oh yes," Mr. Cannon perked up. "He can do anything—anything when he puts his mind to it. There's never been such a talent."

"I haven't seen much of his work lately."

"Oh, but he's working hard. Some of the magazines have stories of his that they're holding."

"Holding for what?"

"Oh, for a more appropriate time—an upswing. They like to think they have something of Finnegan's."

His was indeed a name with ingots in it. His career had started brilliantly and if it had not kept up to its first exalted level, at least it started brilliantly all over again every few years. He was the perennial man of promise in American letters—what he could actually do with words was astounding, they glowed and coruscated—he wrote sentences, paragraphs, chapters that were masterpieces of fine weaving and spinning. It was only when I met some poor devil of a screen writer who had been trying to make a logical story out of one of his books that I realized he had his enemies.

"It's all beautiful when you read it," this man said disgustedly, "but when you write it down plain it's like a week in the nut-house."

From Mr. Cannon's office I went over to my publishers on Fifth Avenue and there too I learned in no time that Finnegan was expected tomorrow. Indeed he had thrown such a long shadow before him that the luncheon where I expected to discuss my own work was largely devoted to Finnegan. Again I had the feeling that my host, Mr. George Jaggers, was talking not to me but to himself.

"Finnegan's a great writer," he said.

"Undoubtedly."

"And he's really quite all right, you know."

As I hadn't questioned the fact I inquired whether there was any doubt about it.

"Oh no," he said hurriedly. "It's just that he's had such a run of hard luck lately——"

I shook my head sympathetically. "I know. That diving into a half-empty pool was a tough break."

"Oh, it wasn't half-empty. It was full of water. Full to the brim. You ought to hear Finnegan on the subject—he makes a side-splitting story of it. It seems he was in a run-down condition and just diving from the side of the pool, you know—" Mr. Jaggers pointed his knife and fork at the table, "and he saw some young girls diving from the fifteen-foot board. He says he thought of his lost youth and went up to do the same and made a beautiful swan dive—but his shoulder broke while he was still in the air." He looked at me rather anxiously. "Haven't you heard of cases like that—a ball player throwing his arm out of joint?"

I couldn't think of any orthopedic parallels at the moment.

"And then," he continued dreamily, "Finnegan had to write on the ceiling."

"On the ceiling?"

"Practically. He didn't give up writing—he has plenty of guts, that fellow, though you may not believe it. He had some sort of arrangement built that was suspended from the ceiling and he lay on his back and wrote in the air."

I had to grant that it was a courageous arrangement.

"Did it affect his work?" I inquired. "Did you have to read his stories backward—like Chinese?"

"They were rather confused for a while," he admitted, "but he's all right now. I got several letters from him that sounded more like the old Finnegan—full of life and hope and plans for the future——"

The faraway look came into his face and I turned the discussion to affairs closer to my heart. Only when we were back in his office did the subject recur—and I blush as I write this because it includes confessing something I seldom do—reading another man's telegram. It happened because Mr. Jaggers was intercepted in the hall and when I went into his office and sat down it was stretched out open before me:

With fifty I could at least pay typist and get haircut and pencils life has become impossible and I exist on dream of good news desperately Finnegan

I couldn't believe my eyes—fifty dollars, and I happened to know that Finnegan's price for short stories was somewhere around three thousand. George Jaggers found me still staring dazedly at the telegram. After he read it he stared at me with stricken eyes.

"I don't see how I can conscientiously do it," he said.

I started and glanced around to make sure I was in the prosperous publishing office in New York. Then I understood—I had misread the telegram. Finnegan was asking for fifty thousand as an advance—a demand that would have staggered any publisher no matter who the writer was.

"Only last week," said Mr. Jaggers disconsolately, "I sent him a hundred dollars. It puts my department in the red every season, so I don't dare tell my partners any more. I take it out of my own pocket—give up a suit and a pair of shoes."

"You mean Finnegan's broke?"

"Broke!" He looked at me and laughed soundlessly—in fact I didn't exactly like the way that he laughed. My brother had a nervous—but that is afield from this story. After a minute he pulled himself together. "You won't say anything about this, will you? The truth is Finnegan's been in a slump, he's had blow after blow in the past few years, but now he's snapping out of it and I know we'll get back every cent we've—" He tried to think of a word but "given him" slipped out. This time it was he who was eager to change the subject.

Don't let me give the impression that Finnegan's affairs absorbed me during a whole week in New York—it was inevitable, though, that being much in the offices of my agent and my publisher, I happened in on a lot. For instance, two days later, using the telephone in Mr. Cannon's office, I was accidentally switched in on a conversation he was having with George Jaggers. It was only partly eavesdropping, you see, because I could only hear one end of the conversation and that isn't as bad as hearing it all.

"But I got the impression he was in good health . . . he did say something about his heart a few months ago but I understood it got well . . . yes, and he talked about some operation he wanted to have—I think he said it was cancer. . . . Well, I felt like telling him I had a little operation up my sleeve too, that I'd have had by now if I could afford it. . . . No, I didn't say it. He seemed in such good spirits that it would have been a shame to bring him down. He's starting a story today, he read me some of it on the phone . . .

". . . I did give him twenty-five because he didn't have a cent in his pocket . . . oh, yes—I'm sure he'll be all right now. He sounds as if he means business."

I understood it all now. The two men had entered into a silent conspiracy to cheer each other up about Finnegan. Their investment in him, in his future, had reached a sum so considerable that Finnegan belonged to them. They could not bear to hear a word against him—even from themselves.

PART SIX CHRONOLOGY

HOLLYWOOD & AFTERMATH

(1937-1948)

July 1937
FSF goes to Hollywood for third and last time, with 6-month MGM contract at $1,000 a week; works on script for *A Yank at Oxford*. Lives first at Garden of Allah, where he meets Sheilah Graham.

September 1937–January 1938
FSF works on *Three Comrades* script, his only screen credit.

First week of September 1937
FSF visits ZF in Asheville; they spend four days in Charleston and Myrtle Beach, S.C.

December 1937
MGM contract is renewed for one year at $1,250 a week; works on scripts for "Infidelity," *Marie Antoinette, The Women,* and *Madame Curie.*

End of March 1938
Fitzgeralds spend Easter at Cavalier Hotel, Virginia Beach, Virginia.

April 1938
FSF rents bungalow at Malibu Beach, California, near Los Angeles.

September 1938
Scottie enters Vassar.

October 1938
FSF moves to cottage on the Edward Everett Horton estate, "Belly Acres," at Encino in the San Fernando Valley.

December 1938
MGM contract is not renewed; money problems recur.

February 1939
FSF travels to Dartmouth College with Budd Schulberg to work on *Winter Carnival* for Walter Wanger.

March 1939–October 1940
FSF has free-lance assignments with Paramount, Universal, Fox, Goldwyn, and Columbia.

October 1939
FSF begins work on *The Last Tycoon.*

January 1940
Publication of the first Pat Hobby story, "Pat Hobby's Christmas Wish," in *Esquire.* The seventeen-story series runs in *Esquire* from January 1940 to May 1941.

15 April 1940
ZF leaves Highland Hospital to live with her mother at 322 Sayre Street in Montgomery.

May 1940
FSF moves to 1403 North Laurel Avenue, Hollywood.

May–August 1940
FSF works on "Cosmopolitan" ("Babylon Revisited") script.

21 December 1940
FSF dies of heart attack at Sheilah Graham's apartment, 1443 North Hayworth Avenue, Hollywood.

27 December 1940
FSF is buried in the Rockville Union Cemetery, Rockville, Maryland. ZF is not able to attend.

27 October 1941
Publication of *The Last Tycoon.*

12 August 1945
Publication of *The Crack-Up.*

September 1945
Publication of *The Portable F. Scott Fitzgerald.*

Early 1946
ZF returns to Highland, as she does intermittently, from Montgomery.

10 March 1948
ZF dies in fire at Highland, Asheville, N.C.

17 March 1948
Zelda is buried with Scott in Rockville Union Cemetery, Rockville, Maryland.

I feel a certain excitement. The third Hollywood venture. Two failures behind me though one no fault of mine. The first one was just ten years ago. At that time I had been generally acknowledged for several years as the top American writer both seriously and, as far as prices went, popularly. I had been loafing for six months for the first time in my life and was confident to the point of conceit. Hollywood made a big fuss over us and the ladies all looked very beautiful to a man of thirty. I honestly believed that with no effort on my part *I was a sort of magician with words—an odd delusion on my part when I had worked so desperately hard to develop a hard, colorful prose style.*

Total result—a great time and no work. I was to be paid only a small amount unless they made my picture—they didn't.

The second time I went was five years ago. Life had gotten in some hard socks and while all was serene on top, with your mother apparently recovered in Montgomery, I was jittery underneath and beginning to drink more than I ought to. Far from approaching it too confidently I was far too humble. I ran afoul of a bastard named de Sano, since a suicide, and let myself by gypped out of command. I wrote the picture and he changed as I wrote. I tried to get at Thalberg but was erroneously warned against it as "bad taste." Result—a bad script. I left with the money, for this was a contract for weekly payments, but disillusioned and disgusted, vowing never to go back, tho they said it wasn't my fault and asked me to stay. I wanted to get East when the contract expired to see how your mother was. This was later interpreted as "running out on them" and held against me.

(The train has left El Paso since I began this letter—hence the writing —Rocky Mountain writing.)

I want to profit by these two experiences—I must be very tactful but keep my hand on the wheel from the start—find out the key man among the bosses and the most malleable among the collaborators—then fight the rest tooth and nail until, in fact or in effect, I'm alone on the picture. That's the only way I can do my best work. Given a break I can make them double this contract in less two years.

—FSF to Scottie, July 1937.

A lonely Fitzgerald wrote this card to himself.

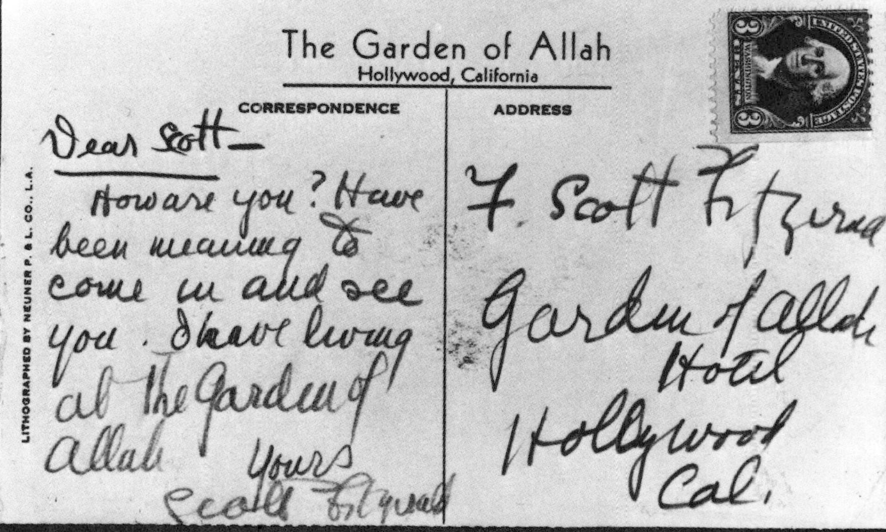

This letter is long overdue. Suffice to summarize: I have seen Hollywood—talked with Taylor, dined with March, danced with Ginger Rogers (this will burn Scottie up but its true) been in Rosalind Russel's dressing room, wise-cracked with Montgomery, drunk (gingerale) with Zukor and Lasky, lunched alone with Maureen OSullivan, watched Crawford act and lost my heart to a beautiful half caste Chinese girl whos name I've forgotten. So far Ive bought my own breakfasts.

And this is to say Im through. From now on I go nowhere and see no one because the work is hard as hell, at least for me and I've lost ten pounds. So farewell Miriam Hopkins who leans so close when she talks, so long Claudette Clobert as yet unencountered, mysterious Garbo, glamourous Dietrich, exotic Shirley Temple—you will never know me. Except Miriam who promised to call up but hasn't. There is nothing left, girls but to believe in reincarnation and carry on.

—FSF to Anne Ober, 26 July 1937

ALBANY NY 1019A JULY 7 1937

F SCOTT FITZGERALD

TO ARRIVE MGM

DEAR SCOTT DELIGHTED TO CHAPERONE YOUR DARLI[illegible] DAUGHTER HAVE HER CALL ME NYACK AFTER MONDAY AMITIES

HELEN Hayes

In August 1937 Helen Hayes brought Scottie out to Hollywood at Fitzgerald's request, and he arranged for her to meet her favorite movie stars.

Scottie, Fred Astaire, Helen Hayes.

Shortly after his arrival in Hollywood Fitzgerald met Sheilah Graham, an English-born Hollywood columnist, at Robert Benchley's Garden of Allah bungalow. He told her that she reminded him of Zelda.

Hollywood Today

A Gadabout's Notebook

BY SHEILAH GRAHAM

Special to The Chicago Daily News.

HOLLYWOOD, Cal., Aug. 24.—Mary Pickford came back from her honeymoon with a renewed flurry of energy that will be dissipated in producing another picture in which she will play the lead; launching a cosmetic business via a barrage of advertising, and a reappearance on the radio for at least thirteen weeks. In between these activities Mary will supervise the selling of "Pickfair," and, of course, say "hello" once in a while to Husband Buddy Rogers.

* * *

When Joan Bennett recently gave a talk to a women's club she was introduced as the mother of two charming little children. "Yes," said Joan in an undertone. "And I'm now on my way to see my lawyers" (to divorce Gene Markey.) Incidentally Markey is furious regarding the rumor he is romantically interested in Simone Simon. When questioned by this writer he quipped, "Sure, we're going to get married—but immediately. I'd look kind of cute walking up the aisle. I just can't wait to get married again."

* * *

Garbo is credited with having attended the Lily Pons Hollywood bowl concert disguised as a bearded lady. Which is perhaps why Helen Hayes missed her. The famous actress, now visting Mate Charlie MacArthur, has only one ambition—to meet Garbo. "The last time I was here I got as far as her sound set before she realized there was a stranger present and had me thrown out." Someone should tell Greta. She is probably just as anxious to meet Miss Hayes as Miss Hayes is to meet her. And with as much reason. Mary, 7-year-old daughter of the MacArthurs, would sooner see Shirley Temple. She was discovered by her mother practicing what she would say and do if the great moment materialized. It will be just as well if this meeting does not come off.

* * *

Charles Winninger is battling with his Universal bosses, who want him for a top role in "Mightier Than the Sword." But Charlie wants a rest. He has already appeared in eight pictures this year, in addition to his weekly broadcasts. . . . Shooting is about to be suspended on "Live, Love and Learn" for time out to write yet another scrip. . . "Scotty" Fitzgerald, 16-year-old daughter of the novelist, finally me[t] her hero, Fred Astaire, but not i[n] the way she would have preferr[ed]. She came on to the set just as F[red] was leaping off at the end of [a] dance, and they hit the dust tog[eth]er. Nice going.

Stahr did not answer. Smiling faintly at him from not four feet away was the face of his dead wife, identical even to the expression. Across the four feet of moonlight, the eyes he knew looked back at him, a curl blew a little on a familiar forehead; the smile lingered, changed a little according to pattern; the lips parted—the same. An awful fear went over him, and he wanted to cry aloud.

—*The Last Tycoon*

Will you do this for me? Go to the storage and find the box which contains my files and abstract file or files which probably contain important receipts, old income tax statements, etc.—not the correspondence file. You will know the one or ones that I mean—those that would seem to have most to do with current business. I should have taken it or them along. Also I want my scrapbooks—the big ones including Zelda's and the photograph books. This should make quite a sizable assortment, and I'd like the whole thing boxed and sent to me here collect. If they won't send it this way, let me know what the charges will be. I have just sent them a check for $99.00 which covers all bills to date, but maybe they have another statement for me and don't know where to send it.

I like it here very much. I hear the report of my salary has been terrifically exaggerated in Baltimore. Thought at first it was Scottie's doing but she denies it. I like the work which is occasionally creative—most often like fitting together a very interesting picture puzzle. I think I'm going to be good at it.

—FSF to Isabel Owens, 8 October 1937.

Im glad too that they renewed the contract. Well, I've worked hard as hell—in a world where it seems to me the majority are loafers & incompetents.

If they'll let me work alone all the time, which I think they will when they have a little more confidence I think I can turn out four pictures a year by myself with months off included. Then *I'll ask for some big money.*

—FSF to Harold Ober, c. 14 December 1937.

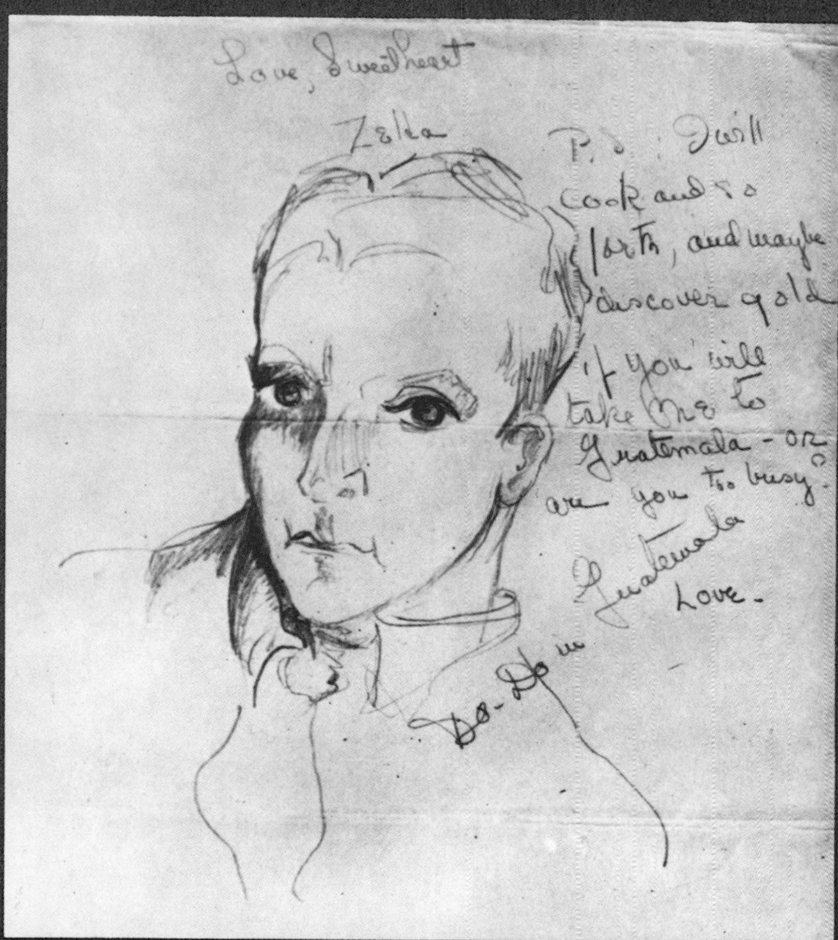
Love, Sweetheart

Zelda

P.S. I will cook and so forth, and maybe discover gold if you will take me to Guatemala - or are you too busy?

Do-Do in Guatemala

Love.

Zelda loved to travel. At one point she became interested in visiting Central America and wrote Fitzgerald from the hospital, asking if he could take her to Guatemala. She included a sketch of him on the last page of her letter. Right, an outing at Myrtle Beach, South Carolina.

We will have to make a mass pilgrimage to her graduation this June. I am hoping her mother can come, too, and we will watch all the other little girls get diamond bracelets and Cord roadsters. I am going to a costumer's in New York and buy Scotty some phoney jewelry so she can pretend they are graduation presents. Otherwise, she will have to suffer the shame of being a poor girl in a rich girl's school. That was always my experience—a poor boy in a rich town; a poor boy in a rich boy's school; a poor boy in a rich man's club at Princeton. So I guess she can stand it. However, I have never been able to forgive the rich for being rich, and it has colored my entire life and works.

—FSF to Anne Ober, March 1938.

Zelda and her sister Rosalind attended Scottie's graduation from the Ethel Walker School in 1938.

For Sheilah, a Beloved Infidel

That sudden smile across a room
Was certainly not learned from me
That first faint quiver of a bloom
The eyes initial extacy
Whoever taught you how to page
Your loves so sweetly – now as then
I thank him for my heritage
The eyes made bright by other men.

No slumberous pearl is valued less
For years spent in a rajah's crown
And I should rather rise and bless
Your earliest love than cry him down
Whoever wound your heart up knew
His job. How can I hate him when
He did his share to fashion you?
A heart made warm by other men

Some kisses nature doesn't plan
She works in such a sketchy way
The child, tho father to the man,
Must be instructed how to play
What traffic your lips had with mine
Don't lie in any virgin's ken
I found the oldest, richest wine
On lips made soft by other men

The lies you tell are epic things
No amateur would ever try
Soft little parables with wings
I know not even God would cry

(2)

Let every lover be the last
And whisper "This is now – not then"
That sweet denial of the past
The tale you told to other men.

I'm even glad someone and you
Found it was joyous to rehearse
Made it an art to fade into
The passion of the universe.
The world all crowded in an hour
Textbooks in minutes – that has been
Your fate, your wealth, your curious dower,
The things you learned from other men

The little time you opened up
A window, let me look inside
Gave me the plate, the spoon, the cup
The very coat of love that died
Or seemed to die – for as your hand
Held mine it was alive again
And we were in a lovely land
The world you lead from other men

~~And~~ But when I join the other ghosts
Who lay beside your flashing fire
I must believe I'll drink their toasts
To one who was a sweet desire
And sweet fulfilment – all they found
Was worth remembering. And then
He'll hear us as the wine goes round
– A greeting from us other men

S.

Fitzgerald's love poem to Sheilah Graham from which she later took the title for her autobiography.

A card Fitzgerald sent to Sheilah Graham during a trip East to visit his family.

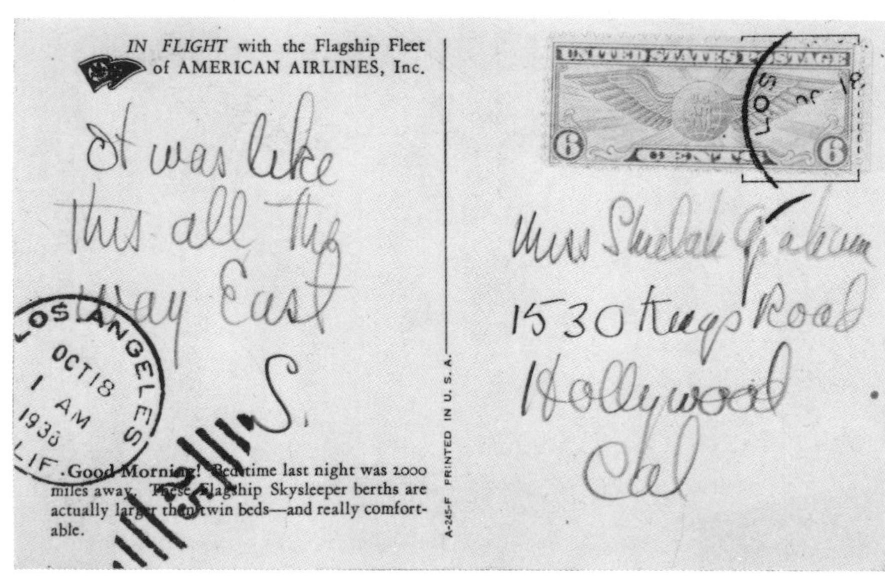
IN FLIGHT with the Flagship Fleet of AMERICAN AIRLINES, Inc.

It was like this all the way East

S.

Good Morning! Bedtime last night was 2000 miles away. These Flagship Skysleeper berths are actually larger than twin beds—and really comfortable.

A-245-F PRINTED IN U.S.A.

LOS ANGELES CALIF. OCT 18 1 AM 1938

Miss Sheilah Graham
1530 Kings Road
Hollywood
Cal

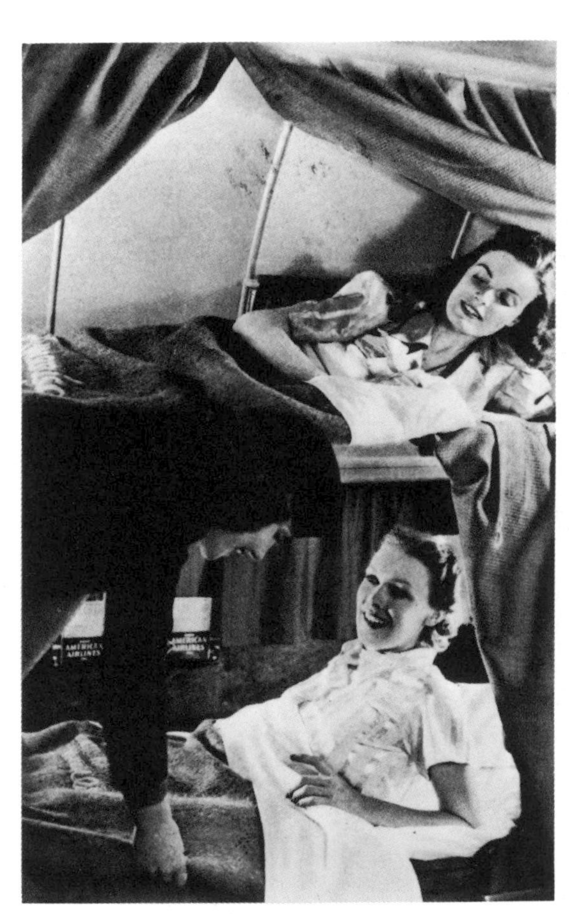

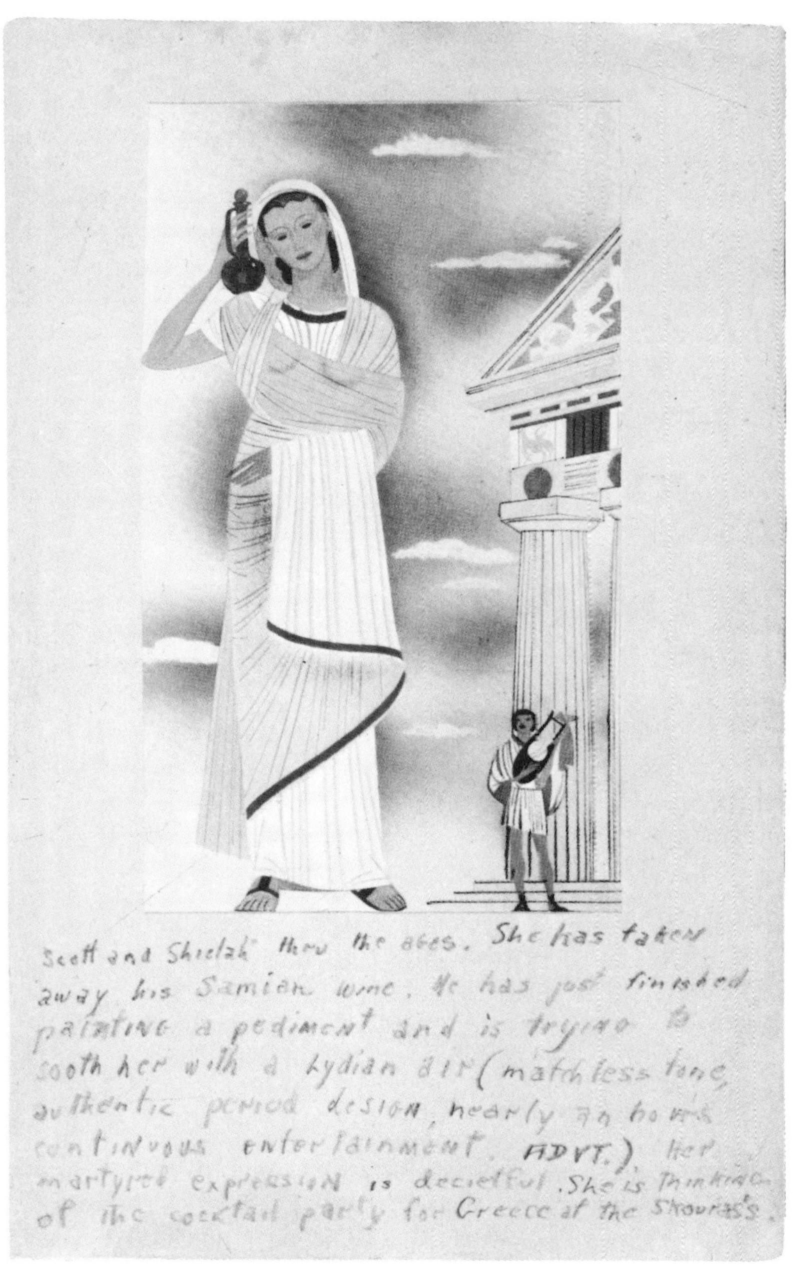

Scott and Shielah thru the ages. She has taken
away his Samian wine. He has just finished
painting a pediment and is trying to
sooth her with a Lydian air (matchless tone,
authentic period design, nearly an hours
continuous entertainment. ADVT.) Her
martyred expression is decietful. She is thinking
of the cocktail party for Greece at the Skouras's.

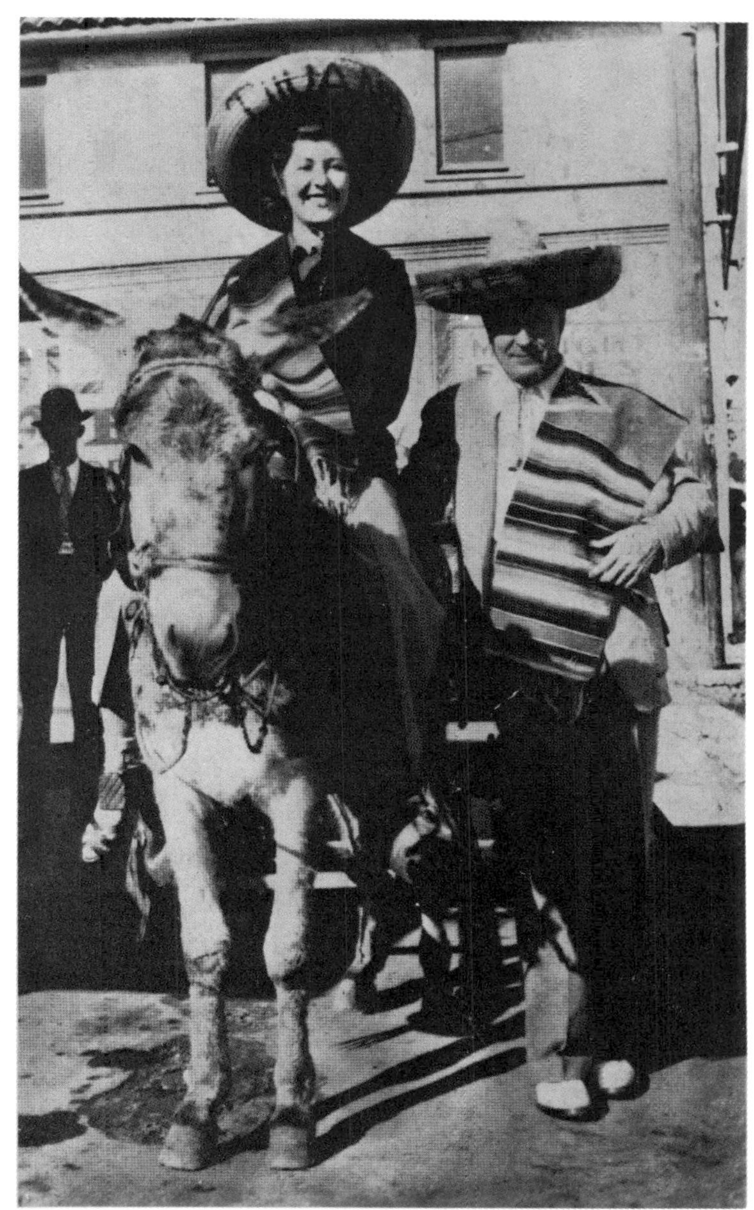

BOOK MARK Suggestions about Byron BOOK MARK

The excerpts from long poems are short because of the fine print. I have never been able to admire but five or six of his short lyrics in comparison to his contemporaries.

After Chap 2 read	The Isles of Greece	Ox. P. 565
After Chap 4 "	Childe Harold Canto III, Stanzas 21–28	Works
After Chap 5 "	Maid of Athens	Works P. 59
After Chap 7 "	So We'll go no more	Ox P. 569
	She Walks in Beauty	Ox P. 569
After Chap 8 "	Don Juan, Canto One CXIII to CXVII	works
After Chap 10 "	Don Juan Canto Two CLXXII – CLXXVII and Canto Eleven LX	works
At End "	Once More: The First 3 Stanzas of The Isles of Greece"	

BOOK MARK

When Fitzgerald learned of Sheilah Graham's anxiety about her truncated education, he prepared the "College of One" for her and tutored her in literature, history, and music. At right is his syllabus for Byron.

Fitzgerald achieved his only screen credit at MGM for Three Comrades, which starred Franchot Tone, Robert Young, and Robert Taylor. However, he was distressed when director Joseph Mankiewicz tampered with his script:

Well, I read the last part and I feel like a good many writers must have felt in the past. I gave you a drawing and you simply took a box of chalk and touched it up. Pat has now become a sentimental girl from Brooklyn, and I guess all these years I've been kidding myself about being a good writer.

* * *

To say I'm disillusioned is putting it mildly. For nineteen years, with two years out for sickness, I've written best-selling entertainment, and my dialogue is supposedly right up at the top. But I learn from the script that you've suddenly decided that it isn't good dialogue and you can take a few hours off and do much better.

I think you now have a flop on your hands—as thoroughly naive as The Bride Wore Red *but utterly inexcusable because this time you* had *something and you have arbitrarily and carelessly torn it to pieces. To take out the manicurist and the balcony scene and then have space to put in that utter drool out of* True Romances *which Pat gets off on page 116 makes me think we don't talk the same language. God and "cool lips," whatever they are, and lightning and elephantine play on words. The audience's feeling will be "Oh, go on and die." If Ted had written that scene you'd laugh it out of the window.*

* * *

My only hope is that you will have a moment of clear thinking. That you'll ask some intelligent *and* disinterested *person to look at the two scripts. Some honest thinking would be much more valuable to the enterprise right now than an effort to convince people you've improved it. I am utterly miserable at seeing months of work and thought negated in one hasty week. I hope you're big enough to take this letter as it's meant —a desperate plea to restore the dialogue to its former quality—to put back the flower cart, the piano-moving, the balcony, the manicure girl— all those touches that were both natural and new. Oh, Joe, can't producers ever be wrong? I'm a good writer—honest. I thought you were going to play fair. Joan Crawford might as well play the part now, for the thing is as groggy with sentimentality as* The Bride Wore Red, *but the true emotion is gone.*

—FSF to Joseph Mankiewicz, 20 January 1938.

METRO NOT RENEWING TO MY GREAT PLEASURE BUT WILL FINISH CURIE THERES LOTS OF OTHER WORK OFFERED STOP HOWEVER PLEASE SAY NOTHING WHATEVER TO PERKINS OR TO SCOTTIE WHO WOULD NOT UNDERSTAND STOP AM WRITING

—FSF wire to Harold Ober, 26 December 1938.

In his eighteen months on the MGM payroll Fitzgerald earned $90,000 and payed off all his debts. But he was soon in need of money.

When his MGM option was not renewed in 1939, Fitzgerald took the assignment to work with Budd Schulberg on Winter Carnival on location at Dartmouth College, but was dismissed for drinking. Schulberg, right, with Ann Sheridan, the star of this film, later wrote The Disenchanted, a novel about Fitzgerald.

When I finally came to myself last Tuesday I found this, which seems to be yours.

It is very quiet out here now. I went in your room this afternoon and lay on your bed awhile, trying to see if you had left anything of yourself. There were some pencils and the electric pad that didn't work and the autumn out the window that won't ever be the same. Then I wrote down a lot of expressions of your face but one I can't bare to read, of the little girl who trusted me so and whom I loved more than anything in the world—and to whom I gave grief when I wanted to give joy. Some things should I have told you I was extemporizing wildly—that anyone, including Scottie,

(over)

(2)

should ever dare criticize you to me. It was all fever and liquor and sedatives—what nurses hear in any bad drunk case.

I'm glad you're rid of me. I hope you're happy and the last awful impression is fading a little till someday you'll say "he can't have been that black".

Goodbye, Sheilo, I won't bother you any more.

Scott

For my darling Sheilah
—after such a
bad time
from
Scott

THIS SIDE OF PARADISE

Following a series of violent, drunken scenes, Sheilah Graham left Fitzgerald, after which he went on the wagon and effected a reconciliation.

Having paid off his debt to Harold Ober, Fitzgerald began asking him for advances again after his salary stopped. Ober wrote—but never mailed—this letter.

I was short of money when your telegram came because I had just paid up all my taxes and paid some money on a mortgage and some money that I owed on my insurance. I am still short, but I managed to wire to the Culver City Bank the Five Hundred Dollars you needed. I think, however, it would be a great mistake for us to get back into the position we were in. I think it is bad for you and difficult for me. The margin of profit in the agency business is very narrow. The expenses are many and high and I reckon the net profit is only about three per cent. I hope, therefore, we can keep things on a "Pay as we go" basis.

I think you can do that if you will follow the old adage about "Watching the pennies and letting the dollars take care of themselves." I notice that both Scottie and you would always rather send a telegram or make an expensive telephone call than send a letter for three cents. You give tips four and five times as large as you need to. On the other hand, you are very economical about some of the larger expenses. I am sure that if you could look back over the years with some kind of a celestial bookkeeper to note down your expenses, you would find that a large part of the money you have earned has gone for things that brought you no return.

—Harold Ober to FSF, 21 June 1939 (not mailed).

In 1939–40 Fitzgerald did freelance work at several studios while starting work on a new novel, The Last Tycoon. In July 1939 he was bitterly hurt when Harold Ober declined to make an advance payment against an unsold story. Although the Obers continued to take care of Scottie, the friendship between Fitzgerald and Ober never recovered.

Fitzgerald at Encino with John O'Hara. Photo taken by Belle O'Hara.

STILL FLABBERGASTED AT YOUR ABRUPT CHANGE IN POLICY AFTER 20 YEARS ESPECIALLY WITH STORY IN YOUR HANDS STOP MY COMMERCIAL VALUE CANT HAVE SUNK FROM 60 THOUSAND TO NOTHING BECAUSE OF A SLOW HEALING LUNG CAVITY STOP AFTER 30 PICTURE OFFERS DURING THE MONTHS I WAS IN BED SWANSON NOW PROMISES NOTHING FOR ANOTHER WEEK STOP CANT YOU ARRANGE A FEW HUNDRED ADVANCE FROM A MAGAZINE SO I CAN EAT TODAY AND TOMORROW STOP WONT YOU WIRE

—FSF wire to Harold Ober, 13 July 1939.

When Harold withdrew from the questionable honor of being my banker I felt completely numb financially and I suddenly wondered what money was and where it came from. There had always seemed a little more somewhere and now there wasn't.

—FSF to Maxwell Perkins, 19 December 1939.

The last photograph of Scott Fitzgerald with Sheilah.

Frances Kroll (Ring), Fitzgerald's Hollywood secretary.

Look! I have begun to write something that is maybe great, and I'm going to be absorbed in it four or six months.

—FSF to Scottie, 31 October 1939.

Fitzgerald rented the house at right on "Belly Acres," the Edward Everett Horton estate in Encino, California.

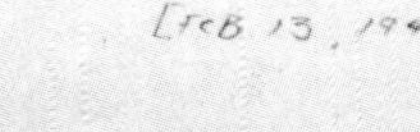

DEAR VALENTINE

Here is my heart : The last
It's yours for keeps thing
Until we part you said to me
before you left / at the port
of embarkation

Zelda

Zelda was released from Highland Hospital in April 1940 and went back to live with her mother on Sayre Street in Montgomery (above). Although Fitzgerald and Zelda did not see each other, they maintained an affectionate correspondence.

Dearest: I am always grateful for all the loyalties you gave me, and I am always loyal to the concepts that held us together so long: the belief that life is tragic, that a mans spiritual reward is the keeping of his faith: that we shouldn't hurt each other. And I love, always your fine writing talent, your tolerance and generosity; and all your happy endowments. Nothing could have survived our life.

—ZF to FSF, c. 1939.

Mamma's little house is so sunshine-y and so full of grace; the moated mornings remind me of twenty-five years ago when life was as full of promise as it now is of memory. There were wars then, and now . . . but the race had more gallantry at that time and the more romantic terms in which we took life helped us through.

—ZF to FSF, c. 1940.

Twenty years ago This Side of Paradise *was a best seller and we were settled in Westport. Ten years ago Paris was having almost its last great American season but we had quit the gay parade and you were gone to Switzerland. Five years ago I had my first bad stroke of illness and went to Asheville. Cards began falling badly for us much too early.*

—FSF to ZF, 14 June 1940.

CA703 27 NT=MONTGOMERY ALA 18 1940 JUN 18 AM 11 50

SCOTT FITZGERALD=

1403 NORTH LAUREL AVE HOLLYWOOD CALIF=

:I WONT BE ABLE TO STICK THIS OUT. WILL YOU WIRE MONEY IMMEDIATELY THAT I MAY RETURN FRIDAY TO ASHVILLE. WILL SEE SCOTTIE THERE. DEVOTEDLY REGRETFULLY GRATEFULLY=

ZELDA.

October
19
1940

Dearest Zelda:

I'm trying desperately to finish my novel by the middle of December and it's a little like working on "Tender is the Night" at the end--I think of nothing else. Still haven't heard from the Shirley Temple story but it would be a great relaxation of pressure if she decides to do it, though an announcement in the paper says that she is going to be teamed with Judy Garland in "Little Eva" which reminds me that I saw the two Duncan Sisters both grown enormously fat in the Brown Derby. Do you remember them on the boat with Viscount Bryce and their dogs?

My room is covered with charts like it used to be for "Tender is the Night" telling the different movements of the characters and their histories. However, this one is to be short as I originally planned it two years ago and more on the order of "Gatsby".

Dearest love,

1403 N. Laurel Avenue
Hollywood, Calif.

October
23
1940

Dearest Zelda:-

Advising you about money at long distance would be silly but you feel we're both concerned in the Carrol matter. Still and all I would much rather you'd leave it to me and <u>keep</u> your money. I sent them a small payment last week. The thing is I have budgeted what I saved in the weeks at 20th to last until December 15th so I can go on with the novel with the hope of having a full draft by then. Naturally I will not realize anything at once (except on the very slim chance of a serial) and though I will try to make something immediately out of pictures or Esquire it may be a pretty slim Christmas. So my advice is to put the hundred and fifty away against that time.

I am deep in the novel, living in it, and it makes me happy. It is a <u>constructed</u> novel like <u>Gatsby</u>, with passages of poetic prose when it fits the action, but no ruminations or side-shows like <u>Tender</u>. Everything must contribute to the dramatic movement.

It's odd that my old talent for the short story vanished. It was partly that times changed, editors changed, but part of it was tied up somehow with you and me--the happy ending. Of course every third story had some other ending but essentially I got my public with stories of young love. I must have had a powerful imagination to project it so far and so often into the past.

Two thousand words today and all good.

With dearest love

1403 N. Laurel Ave.
Hollywood, Calif.

LETTERS TO

From the time Scottie entered Vassar in the fall of 1938 until his death in December of 1940, Fitzgerald bombarded her with advice on academic, social, spiritual, personal and intellectual matters. Though she seldom followed the advice, she kept the letters.

Fitzgerald invited "Peaches" Finney (now Mrs. Samuel McPherson), one of Scottie's closest friends in Baltimore, to join her for a visit to his cottage on Malibu Beach, California, in September 1938. Though he was off the wagon and the trip was something of a disaster, the girls toured the studios and met some of their idols, including Fred Astaire and Errol Flynn (pictured above on the Warner Brothers lot).

Took Beatrice Lillie, Charlie MacArthur and Sheilah to the Tennis Club the other night, and Errol Flynn joined us—he seemed very nice though rather silly and fatuous. Don't see why Peaches is so fascinated.

If I hear of you taking a drink before you're twenty, I shall feel entitled to begin my last and greatest non-stop binge, and the world also will have an interest in the matter of your behavior. It would like to be able to say, and would say on the slightest provocation: "There she goes—just like her papa and mama." Need I say that you can take this fact as a curse—or you can make of it a great advantage?

Spring was always an awful time for me about work. I always felt that in the long boredom of winter there was nothing else to do but study. But I lost the feeling in the long, dreamy spring days and managed to be in scholastic hot water by June. I can't tell you what to do about it—all my suggestions seem to be very remote and academic. But if I were with you and we could talk again like we used to, I might lift you out of your trouble about concentration. It really isn't so hard, even with dreamy people like you and me—it's just that we feel so damned secure at times as long as there's enough in the bank to buy the next meal, and enough moral stuff in reserve to take us through the next ordeal. Our danger is imagining that we have resources—material and moral—which we haven't got. One of the reasons I find myself so consistently in valleys of depression is that every few years I seem to be climbing uphill to recover from some bankruptcy. Do you know what bankruptcy exactly means? It means drawing on resources which one does not possess. I thought I was so strong that I never would be ill and suddenly I was ill for three years, and faced with a long, slow uphill climb. Wiser people seem to manage to pile up a reserve—so that if on a night you had set aside to study for a philosophy test you learned that your best friend was in trouble and needed your help, you could skip that night and find you had a reserve of one or two days' preparation to draw on. But I think that, like me, you will be something of a fool in that regard all your life, so I am wasting my words.

You asked me whether I thought that in the Arts it was greater to originate a new form or to perfect it. The best answer is the one that Picasso made rather bitterly to Gertrude Stein:

"You do something first and then somebody else comes along and does it pretty."

In the opinion of any real artist the inventor, which is to say Giotto or Leonardo, is infinitely superior to the finished Tintoretto, and the original D. H. Lawrence is infinitely greater than the Steinbecks.

Have paid Peck & Peck & Peck & Peck & Peck.

When I was your age I lived with a great dream. The dream grew and I learned how to speak of it and make people listen. Then the dream divided one day when I decided to marry your mother after all, even though I knew she was spoiled and meant no good to me. I was sorry immediately I had married her but, being patient in those days, made the best of it and got to love her in another way. You came along and for a long time we made quite a lot of happiness out of our lives. But I was a man divided—she wanted me to work too much for her and not enough for my dream. She realized too late that work was dignity, and the only dignity, and tried to atone for it by working herself, but it was too late and she broke and is broken forever.

It was too late also for me to recoup the damage—I had spent most of my resources, spiritual and material, on her, but I struggled on for five years till my health collapsed, and all I cared about was drink and forgetting.

The mistake I made was in marrying her. We belonged to different worlds—she might have been happy with a kind simple man in a southern garden. She didn't have the strength for the big stage—sometimes she pretended, and pretended beautifully, but she didn't have it. She was soft when she should have been hard, and hard when she should have been yielding. She never knew how to use her energy—she's passed that failing on to you.

For a long time I hated her mother for giving her nothing in the line of good habit—nothing but "getting by" and conceit. I never wanted to see again in this world women who were brought up as idlers.

It is now perfectly sensible for you to go with college boys. (I didn't want you to stay in Baltimore this fall because I felt it would shoot you into Vassar with your mind full of gayety or love, which it apparently did, for your first month there was a flat bust. Also, I did not want you to start with a string of football games this fall.) If you are invited to the Yale or Princeton proms this winter or next spring by a reputable boy—and I'm entitled to the name, please—I'd have absolutely no objection to your going. The whole damn thing about going to the colleges is to keep it in proportion. Did you ever hear of a college boy, unless he were an idiot, racing from Smith to Vassar to Wellesley? There are certain small sacrifices for a college education or there wouldn't be any honor in having gone to college.

I wonder if you've read anything this summer—I mean any one good book like The Brothers Karamazov or Ten Days That Shook the World or Renan's Life of Christ. You never speak of your reading except the excerpts you do in college, the little short bits that they must perforce give you. I know you have read a few of the books I gave you last summer—then I have heard nothing from you on the subject. Have you ever, for example, read Pere Goriot or Crime and Punishment or even The Doll's House or St. Matthew or Sons and Lovers? A good style simply doesn't form unless you absorb half a dozen top-flight authors every year. Or rather it forms but, instead of being a subconscious amalgam of all that you have admired, it is simply a reflection of the last writer you have read, a watered-down journalese.

HIS DAUGHTER

=HOPE YOUR SIX HOURS IS EXAGGERATION. FLUNKING OUT OF VASSAR WOULD BE POOR EXCHANGE FOR SUCH SHORT LIVED ACCLAIM AS ANYONE EVER GETS FROM AMATEUR PLAY SORRY TO BE A DAMPER BUT I KNOW YOUR TEMPERAMENT AND SCHOLASTIC STANDING FEEL YOU ARE JEOPARDIZING YOUR CHANCE OF GOING BACK NEXT YEAR DEAREST LOVE

=DADDY

I'm sorry about the tone of the telegram I sent you this morning, but it represents a most terrific worry. You are doing exactly what I did at Princeton. I wore myself out on a musical comedy there for which I wrote book and lyrics, organized and mostly directed while the president played football. Result: *I slipped way back in my work, got T.B., lost a year in college—and, irony of ironies, because of scholastic slip I wasn't allowed to take the presidency of the Triangle.*

From your letter I guess that you are doing exactly the same thing and it just makes my stomach fall out to think of it. Amateur work is fun but the price for it is just simply tremendous. In the end you get "Thank you" and that's all. You give three performances which everybody promptly forgets and somebody has a breakdown—that somebody being the enthusiast.

Please, please, please *delegate every bit of the work you can and keep your scholastic head above water. To see a mistake repeated twice in two generations would be just too much to bear. This is the most completely experienced advice I've ever given you. What about that science and the philosophy? You've got to find hours to do them even if you have to find a secret room where you can go and study.*

Again let me repeat that if you start any kind of a career following the footsteps of Cole Porter and Rodgers and Hart, it might be an excellent try. Sometimes I wish I had gone along with that gang, but I guess I am too much a moralist at heart and really want to preach at people in some acceptable form rather than to entertain them.

Mary Draper (Janney), Frances Kilpatrick (Field), and Mary Earle, three of Scottie's good friends at Vassar, in a scene from Guess Who's Here!, one of the musical productions which so upset Fitzgerald.

Strange Interlude *is good. It was good the first time, when Shaw wrote it and called it* Candida. *On the other hand, you don't pass an hour of your present life that isn't directly influenced by the devastating blast of light and air that came with Ibsen's* Doll's House. *Nora wasn't the only one who walked out of The Doll's House—all the women in Gene O'Neill walked out too. Only they wore fancier clothes.*

I'm just sorry you can't read some poetry.

It isn't something easy to get started on by yourself. You need, at the beginning, some enthusiast who also knows his way around—John Peale Bishop performed that office for me at Princeton. I had always dabbled in "verse" but he made me see, in the course of a couple of months, the difference between poetry and non-poetry. After that one of my first discoveries was that some of the professors who were teaching poetry really hated it and didn't know what it was about. I got in a series of endless scraps with them so that finally I dropped English altogether.

Poetry is either something that lives like fire inside you—like music to the musician or Marxism to the Communist—or else it is nothing, an empty, formalized bore around which pedants can endlessly drone their notes and explanations. "The Grecian Urn" is unbearably beautiful with every syllable as inevitable as the notes in Beethoven's Ninth Symphony or it's just something you don't understand. It is what it is because an extraordinary genius paused at that point in history and touched it. I suppose I've read it a hundred times. About the tenth time I began to know what it was about, and caught the chime in it and the exquisite inner mechanics. Likewise with "The Nightingale" which I can never read through without tears in my eyes; likewise the "Pot of Basil" with its great stanzas about the two brothers, "Why were they proud, etc."; and "The Eve of St. Agnes," which has the richest, most sensuous imagery in English, not excepting Shakespeare. And finally his three or four great sonnets, "Bright Star" and the others.

Knowing those things very young and granted an ear, one could scarcely ever afterwards be unable to distinguish between gold and dross in what one read. In themselves those eight poems are a scale of workmanship for anybody who wants to know truly about words, their most utter value for evocation, persuasion or charm. For awhile after you quit Keats all other poetry seems to be only whistling or humming.

Once one is caught up into the material world not one person in ten thousand finds the time to form literary taste, to examine the validity of philosophic concepts for himself, or to form what, for lack of a better phrase, I might call the wise and tragic sense of life.

By this I mean the thing that lies behind all great careers, from Shakespeare's to Abraham Lincoln's, and as far back as there are books to read—the sense that life is essentially a cheat and its conditions are those of defeat, and that the redeeming things are not "happiness and pleasure" but the deeper satisfactions that come out of struggle. Having learned this in theory from the lives and conclusions of great men, you can get a hell of a lot more enjoyment out of whatever bright things come your way.

Another letter tells of visiting Mary Earle on Long Island. It sounds fine, but you are right that romantic things really happen in roachy kitchens and back yards. Moonlight is vastly over-estimated.

Tell Frances Kilpatrick that though I never met her father he is still one of my heroes in spite of the fact that he robbed Princeton of a football championship single-handed—he was probably the greatest end who ever played football.

Scottie and one of her roommates, Joan Paterson (now Mrs. Chester Kerr, picture editor of this book) clowning around imitating a famous ad for watches just after their graduation from Vassar in June 1942. Judge John Biggs, Harold Ober, and Maxwell Perkins had gotten together to pay Scottie's expenses through college.

Pat Hobby's Christmas Wish

The first of a series of stories starring Pat Hobby, who was hot stuff when the movies were dumb

by F. SCOTT FITZGERALD

• FICTION •

Pat remembered his job and opened a script.

"It's an insert," he began. "Scene 114 A."

Pat paced the office.

"Ext. Long Shot of the Plains," he decreed. "Buck and Mexicans approaching the hyacenda."

"The what?"

"The hyacenda—the ranch house." He looked at her reproachfully, "114 B. Two Shot: Buck and Pedro. Buck: 'The dirty son-of-a-bitch. I'll tear his guts out!' "

Miss Kagle looked up, startled.

"You want me to write that down?"

"Sure."

"It won't get by."

"I'm writing this. Of course, it won't get by. But if I put 'you rat' the scene won't have any force."

"But won't somebody have to change it to 'you rat'?"

He glared at her—he didn't want to change secretaries every day.

—"Pat Hobby's Christmas Wish"

After he went to Hollywood, Fitzgerald's fiction appeared almost exclusively in Esquire. In January 1940 the first Pat Hobby story was published, initiating a series that ran to seventeen stories.

Pat Hobby sat in his office in the Writers' Building and looked at his morning's work, just come back from the script department. He was on a "polish job," about the only kind he ever got nowadays. He was to repair a messy sequence in a hurry, but the word "hurry" neither frightened nor inspired him for Pat had been in Hollywood since he was thirty—now he was forty-nine. All the work he had done this morning (except a little changing around of lines so he could claim them as his own)—all he had actually invented was a single imperative sentence, spoken by a doctor.

"Boil some water—lots of it."

It was a good line. It had sprung into his mind full grown as soon as he had read the script. In the old silent days Pat would have used it as a spoken title and ended his dialogue worries for a space, but he needed some spoken words for other people in the scene. Nothing came.

Boil some water, he repeated to himself, lots of it.

The word boil brought a quick glad thought of the commissary. A reverent thought too—for an old-timer like Pat, what people you sat with at lunch was more important in getting along than what you dictated in your office. This was no art, as he often said—this was an industry.

—" 'Boil Some Water—Lots of It' "

Pat Hobby's Preview

It would be like old times taking a cute little blonde past the staring crowd, and Pat could put on an act

by F. SCOTT FITZGERALD

• FICTION •

She was a "Cute Little Blonde." To Pat's liverish eye, cute little blondes seemed as much alike as a string of paper dolls. Of course they had different names.

"We'll see about it," said Pat.

"You're very nice. I'm Eleanor Carter from Boise, Idaho."

He told her his name and that he was a writer. She seemed first disappointed—then delighted.

"A writer? . . . Oh, of course. I knew they had to have writers but I guess I never heard about one before."

"Writers get as much as three grand a week," he assured her firmly. "Writers are some of the biggest shots in Hollywood."

"You see, I never thought of it that way."

"Bernud Shaw was out here," he said, "—and Einstein, but they couldn't make the grade."

They walked to the Bulletin Board and Pat found that there was work scheduled on three stages—and one of the directors was a friend out of the past.

"What did you write?" Eleanor asked.

A great male Star loomed on the horizon and Eleanor was all eyes till he had passed. Anyhow the names of Pat's pictures would have been unfamiliar to her.

"Those were all silents," he said.

"Oh. Well, what did you write last?"

"Well, I worked on a thing at Universal—I don't know what they called it finally—" He saw that he was not impressing her at all. He thought quickly. What did they know in Boise, Idaho? "I wrote *Captains Courageous,*" he said boldly. "And *Test Pilot* and *Wuthering Heights* and—and *The Awful Truth* and *Mr. Smith Goes to Washington.*"

—"Pat Hobby's Preview"

He had been called in to the studio to work upon a humble short. It was based on the career of General Fitzhugh Lee, who fought for the Confederacy and later for the U.S.A. against Spain—so it would offend neither North nor South. And in the recent conference Pat had tried to co-operate.

"I was thinking—" he suggested to Jack Berners, "—that it might be a good thing if we could give it a Jewish touch."

"What do you mean?" demanded Jack Berners quickly.

"Well I thought—the way things are and all, it would be a sort of good thing to show that there were a number of Jews in it too."

"In what?"

"In the Civil War." Quickly he reviewed his meager history. "They were, weren't they?"

"Naturally," said Berners, with some impatience. "I suppose everybody was except the Quakers."

"Well, my idea was that we could have this Fitzhugh Lee in love with a Jewish girl. He's going to be shot at curfew so she grabs a church bell——"

Jack Berners leaned forward earnestly.

"Say, Pat, you want this job, don't you? Well, I told you the story. You got the first script. If you thought up this tripe to please me you're losing your grip."

—"A Patriotic Short"

Arnold Gingrich (right), the editor of Esquire, had been a long-time friend and supporter of Fitzgerald. Though Esquire paid only $250 each for the seventeen Pat Hobby stories, a satirical series about a broken-down Hollywood scriptwriter, the magazine gave him the fictional outlet he needed during his last years.

Left. The manuscript page from The Last Tycoon *in which the hero, Stahr, visits his doctor; both know that he is "due to die very soon now."*

Professionally, I know, the next move must come from me. Would the 25 cent press keep Gatsby *in the public eye—or is the book unpopular. Has it had its chance? Would a popular reissue in that series with a* preface *not by me but by one of its admirers—I can maybe pick one—make it a favorite with class rooms, profs, lovers of English prose—anybody. But to die, so completely and unjustly after having given so much. Even now there is little published in American fiction that doesn't slightly bare my stamp—in a* small *way I was an original.*

—FSF to Maxwell Perkins, 20 May 1940.

In 1940 Fitzgerald began to experience serious coronary problems while trying to complete The Last Tycoon. *On 21 December 1940 he died of a heart attack in Sheilah Graham's apartment at 1443 North Hayworth Avenue (below).*

Thanks for your letter. The novel progresses—in fact progresses fast. I'm not going to stop now till I finish a first draft which will be some time after the 15th of January. However, let's pretend that it doesn't exist until it's closer to completion. We don't want it to become—"a legend before it is written" which is what I believe Wheelock said about "Tender Is the Night." Meanwhile will you send me back the chapters I sent you as they are all invalid now, must be completely rewritten etc. The essential idea is the same and it is still, as far as I can hope, a secret.

* * *

This is the first day off I have taken for many months and I just wanted to tell you the book is coming along and that comparatively speaking all is well.

P.S. How much will you sell the plates of "This Side of Paradise" for? I think it has a chance for a new life.

—FSF's last letter to Maxwell Perkins, 13 December 1940.

He was gone . . . they had been much in love. He had been gone all summer and all winter for about a hundred years. Everything he did had been important.

She wasn't going to have him anymore; not to promise her things nor to comfort her, nor just be there as general compensation. . . . She was too old to make any more plans—the rest would have to be the best compromise.

She remembered the ragged edges of his cuffs, and the neatness of his worn possessions, and the pleasure he always had from his pile of sheer linen handkerchiefs. When she had been away, or sick or something, Jacob never forgot the flowers, or big expensive books full of compensatory ideas about life. He never forgot to make life seem useful and promising, or forgot the grace of good friendship, or the use of making an effort.

—"The Big Top" (ZF—unpublished)

Death Takes Fitzgerald, Noted Author

Heart Attack Fatal to Eloquent Voice of World War Generation

All the sad young men—those now grown-up members of the World War generation—had lost their spokesman yesterday.

F. Scott Fitzgerald died of a heart attack in Hollywood at the age of 44.

Immediately after word of the death of the author of "This Side of Paradise" was telegraphed to his wife at Montgomery, Ala., arrangements were made through Pierce Bros. mortuary to send his body to Baltimore, Md., his family home, for burial.

Readers of the 1930's did not know Fitzgerald as did those of the postwar era.

For he was the latters' most articulate voice.

His own early life paralleled that of his recurrent protagonist: the young man, caught in a turbulent age, uncertain, seeking.

COMPOSER'S DESCENDANT

Born at St. Paul, Minn., on Sept. 24, 1896, he was christened Francis Scott Key Fitzgerald, after the composer of "The Star Spangled Banner," an ancestor on his mother's side. He was first educated at Hackensack, N.J. Then he attended Princeton.

There he found much of the atmosphere which fills his first books.

It was wartime. In 1917, deserting the university in his senior year, he entered the Army as a second lieutenant in the 45th Infantry. Two years later he left the service. He was 23.

FIRST NOVEL HAILED

In 1920 "This Side of Paradise" appeared.

Its hero, Amory Blaine, approximated "all the sad young men" of the distracted time. (That phrase was to become the title of a Fitzgerald short-story collection six years later.) Hailed by critics as a great first novel, "This Side of Paradise" was a period piece; a sort of social paper.

At 26, Fitzgerald was in Who's Who. His clubs were listed as Cottage (Princeton) and Sound View Golf. His politics was Socialist. One critic described his works as documentary "in their vivid presentations of adolescent life, its turbulent spirit, swift tempo, charged atmosphere, excesses and boldness, as well as its uncertain psychology and gropings to know itself in new and unadjusted conditions."

His books also were milestones of this topsy-turvy epoch.

"The Beautiful and Damned" came in 1922, two years after his first novel and "Flappers and Philosophers." Later he wrote "The Great Gatsby" and "Tender Is the Night." He saw his generation as truly lost. One of his collected volumes was titled "Taps at Reveille."

In recent years Fitzgerald wrote no novels. Instead, he came to Hollywood in 1937. He adapted Gatsby to the screen; then did the scenario for Remarque's "Three Comrades."

SECOND ATTACK FATAL

Three weeks ago he had his first heart attack.

Saturday he succumbed to a second.

His life in Hollywood had been quiet. His hobbies were children and water sports. He was a connoisseur of fine wines. Occasionally a Fitzgerald short story would appear in a national magazine. But mostly he worked on his last play for the New York stage. He lived at 1403 N. Laurel Ave.

In 1920 he married Zelda Sayre, daughter of an Alabama Supreme Court justice. They had one daughter, Frances Scott Fitzgerald.

Los Angeles Times

F. Scott Fitzgerald

It was only twenty years ago that a novel called "This Side of Paradise" was published, and the world became aware of the existence of the author, F. Scott Fitzgerald, a young man of rare talent. The story was deft, romantic, gay, alcoholic and bitter. It was the first year of prohibition. Flaming youth was rampant. People talked of the post-war moral let-down. Raccoon coats were coming in. There were rumors of strange goings-on in the colleges. It was the beginning of a fantastic era (how long ago it seems!), and Fitzgerald, handsome, insouciant and possessing unusual gifts for story telling, instantly became its prophet and its interpreter. Flappers adored him; moreover, the grave gentlemen who sit in judgment on literary products agreed that here, indeed, was one who showed magnificent "promise."

Fitzgerald, who died yesterday at the tragically early age of forty-four, continued to show "promise" all through his tortured career. He turned out many glittering short stories which were commercial successes. His admirers kept hoping for the elusive something which would be called great. In 1925, with a compact and brilliant novel, "The Great Gatsby," the story of the rise and fall of a Long Island bootlegger, he renewed their faith. As literature it was perhaps the best thing he ever did. Then came long periods when he did little, or nothing. He was ill, troubled, unhappy. In 1934, with "Tender Is the Night," he had another success—but again the critics, while admiring much of it, confessed that they had been expecting something better. Once more he had shown the high promise that somehow always fell just short of fulfillment. And yet, it cannot be taken away from him that he left a substantial literary legacy. He could write prose that was extraordinarily smooth, but it was never soft. It had, as the saying has it, "bones" in it.

The gaudy world of which Fitzgerald wrote—the penthouses, the long week-end drunks, the young people who were always on the brink of madness, the vacuous conversation, the lush intoxication of easy money—has in large measure been swept away. But Fitzgerald understood this world perhaps better than any of his contemporaries. And as a literary craftsman he described it, accurately and sometimes poignantly, in work that deserves respect.

New York Herald Tribune

NOT WHOLLY "LOST"

In his later years (they were not very "late," for he was only 44 when he died last Saturday) Scott Fitzgerald compared himself to a "cracked plate," not good enough to be brought out for company but which "would do to hold crackers late at night or to go into the ice-box with the left-overs." He bitterly underestimated what he had done and might still have done. He was better than he knew, for in fact and in the literary sense he invented a "generation" and did as much as any writer to form as well as to record its habits.

There were flaws—chasms, indeed—in the theory of the "lost generation." As Fitzgerald described it, it could not include more than a small fraction of American youth, for the simple reason that the life it led was expensive. Moreover, the small fraction never had the unity he ascribed to it, except in a superficial sense. Generations do not come into existence en masse, every ten, twenty or thirty years. They accumulate, day by day.

But he did describe, faithfully, the life and times of a certain section of our society, with the emphasis on youth. He saw clearly what war and other influences had done to such people during the second decade of our century. They thought they had no illusions and surely they had no faith. They were "free" but didn't know what to do with their freedom. They felt cheated, but of what birthright they did not know. They drank and made love, only to find that a combination of these two activities gave no foundation on which to build a career. They grew older and had children of their own and sometimes the children, who took "freedom" for granted as they did their three or four meals a day, laughed at them.

Scott Fitzgerald might have grown up with them. He might have interpreted them, and even guided them, as in their middle years they saw a different and nobler freedom threatened with destruction. A TIMES reviewer caught "flashes of wings and sounds of trumpets mingled with the tramp of feet and casual laughter" in his jazz age stories of fifteen years ago. Mystical, glamorous, passionate, shocking—these were some of the adjectives applied to "The Great Gatsby," published in 1925. It was not a book for the ages, but it caught superbly the spirit of a decade.

But the wings flashed no more, and the trumpets did not blow. For some reason the creative impulse slackened. It might have come back if the still youthful heart had not stopped beating. And it may also be that Scott Fitzgerald, and others of his time, were really "lost"—that they could not adjust themselves, no matter how hard they tried, to the swift and brutal changes of these times. It is a pity, for here was real talent which never fully bloomed.

The New York Times

F. Scott Fitzgerald Dies at 44; Chronicler of 'Lost Generation'

F. Scott Fitzgerald Associated Press

Author of 'This Side of Paradise' and 'The Great Gatsby,' Who Voiced the Growing Disillusion of the Jazz Age, Passes in Hollywood

HOLLYWOOD, Dec. 22 (AP).—F. Scott Fitzgerald, novelist, short-story writer and scenarist, died at his Hollywood home yesterday. He was forty-four years old. He suffered a heart attack three weeks ago.

Wrote of "Lost Generation"

F. Scott Fitzgerald is said to have invented the so-called "younger generation" of two decades ago. At any rate, he was the most articulate writer about the rich, young set which was also variously referred to as "the lost generation" and the "post-war generation," and as such he acquired a reputation far out of proportion to his works, which were limited to four novels and several volumes of short stories.

All four novels were characterized by rich, loose-living characters, who grew older as Mr. Fitzgerald grew older. Invariably they met disillusionment and despair. In commenting on Mr. Fitzgerald's last novel, "Tender Is the Night," Clifton Fadiman, book critic for "The New Yorker," summed up Mr. Fitzgerald's career with the words:

"In Mr. Fitzgerald's case, at any rate, money is the root of all novels. In 'This Side of Paradise,' Mr. Fitzgerald's first and most successful novel) the world of super-wealth was viewed through the glass of undergraduate gayety, sentiment and satire. With 'The Great Gatsby' the good-time note was dropped, to be replaced by a darker accent of tragic questioning.

"Questions Become Sharper"

"The questions have become sharper, bitterer in 'Tender Is the Night,' but the world of luxurious living remains his only world. This universe he both loves and despises. It is the contradictoriness of this emotional attitude that gives his novels their special quality, and is also in part responsible for some of their weaknesses.'

Mr. Fitzgerald came of an old Southern family. His great-grandfather's brother was Francis Scott Key, composer of "The Star Spangled Banner." The author, was named after him. His father's aunt was Mrs. Suratt, one of the conspirators hanged for the assassination of Abraham Lincoln.

Mr. Fitzgerald's father went through several severe financial reverses, which gave his son an understandable fear of poverty. The family, however, was able to send him to Princeton University, where his undergraduate escapades are still remembered. He passed his entire eshman year writing a show for the Triangle Club which was accepted, and then tutored in the subjects in which he had failed so he could come back and act in it.

Quit to Join Army

In 1917, in his senior year, he quit college to join the Army as a second lieutenant. He missed the train which was to take his regiment to Camp Sheridan, Ala., and, according to the story he told friends, commandeered an engine and cab by telling Pennsylvania Railroad officials that he possessed confidential papers for President Wilson. He caught up with the troops in Washington. In camp he wrote his first novel, first titled "The Romantic Egotist."

The war ended before his unit saw service and Mr. Fitzgerald tried to sell the novel. It was rejected. After holding a job in advertising in New York a few months, he quit and returned to St. Paul, where his family was living, and rewrote "The Romantic Egotist" under the title "This Side of Paradise."

It was published in 1920 and was tremendously successful. The hero, Amory Blaine, a young Princeton undergraduate like Mr. Fitzgerald, was considered a composite of all the sad young men of the post-war flapper era, and the novel became a sort of social document of its time. Mr. Fitzgerald, who was only twenty-three years of age, was greeted as one of the most promising of young writers.

Married in Same Year

The same year Mr. Fitzgerald was married to Miss Zelda Sayre, daughter of Anthony D. Sayre, an Alabama Supreme Court Justice. In 1922 his second novel, "The Beautiful and Damned," appeared. It was the story of a rich young married couple dancing on the edge of doom, and Mrs. Fitzgerald in a newspaper article said that several of the passages appeared to have come from her diary.

In 1923 he wrote "The Vegetable," a satire in play form, and in 1925 "The Great Gatsby," which was generally regarded as his best novel. It is the story of a mysterious man, whose money, it is implied, comes from something dishonest. In the end he is broken, not by his sins, but by his aspirations. Mr. Fitzgerald's "Tales of the Jazz Age," a book of short stories, was also popular.

The Fitzgeralds lived in France from 1925 to 1928, where Mr. Fitzgerald wrote short stories later incorporated in "All the Sad Young Men." Returning in 1928, he said that "the French are as far above us as we are above the African Negro." After an interval of nine years his last novel, "Tender Is the Night," was published in 1934. Critics commented that he had never quite lived up to his early promise.

Called Himself "Cracked Plate"

In 1936, in a magazine article, Mr. Fitzgerald described himself as "a cracked plate."

"Now the standard cure for one who is sunk is to consider those in actual destitution or physical suffering," he wrote. "This is an all-weather beatitude for gloom in general, but at 3 o'clock in the morning the cure dosn't work—and in a real dark night of the soul it is always 3 o'clock in the morning."

A reporter once asked him what he thought had become of the jazz-mad, gin-drinking generation he wrote of in "This Side of Paradise."

His answer was: "Some became brokers and threw themselves out of windows. Others became bankers and shot themselves. Still others became newspaper reporters. And a few became successful authors."

For the last three years Mr. Fitzgerald had been in Hollywood. He had done little screen work recently, however, and his writing consisted of a few short stories for magazines and a play he was working on.

Surviving, besides his wife, who is living in Montgomery, Ala., is a daughter, Frances Scott Fitzgerald.

New York Herald Tribune

F. Scott Fitzgerald Buried

ROCKVILLE, Md., Dec. 27 (AP)—After a private service, the body of Francis Scott Fitzgerald, noted novelist, was buried today in the Rockville Union Cemetery. His body was brought to Rockville after a funeral service conducted by the Rev. Raymond P. Black, pastor of the Christ Episcopal Church of Rockville, at a funeral home in Washington. The 44-year-old writer of novels of the Twenties died Sunday in Hollywood, Calif., where he had been a motion picture scenarist.

The New York Times

F. Scott Fitzgerald, Novelist, Buried At Rockville

F. Scott Fitzgerald, novelist, was buried yesterday with simple private rites in the Rockville (Md.) Union Cemetery.

His body was brought there following funeral services conducted by the Rev. Raymond P. Black, rector of the Christ Episcopal Church, Rockville, at the Pumphrey Funeral Home.

Mr. Fitzgerald, who wrote many novels of the "jazz era," died Sunday in Hollywood where he was a scenarist. His wife, Zelda Sayre Fitzgerald, survives him.

Mr. Fitzgerald's family came from Rockville, although he was born in St. Paul, Minnesota. He attended Princeton and served overseas in the World War. He was 44.

The Washington Post

F. Scott Fitzgerald

Almost as if he were typifying his uncertain and groping generation even in his early death, F. Scott Fitzgerald has passed from a world gripped again by the same kind of war hysteria that first made him famous. The author of "Taps at Reveille" has indeed left a troubled life before his time. His articulateness was that of a turbulent age. By the time he died he still must not have found the answers to the queries that he was asking all his life: Whither youth, whither the nations of the earth?

Fitzgerald had an importance—only time will tell whether it was ephemeral—because he made himself the voice of youth crying in the wilderness of political and social and moral muddling. The youth he knew was dissolute, but it was also courageous. It was unstable, but it was also questing. It was a phenomenon of the postwar, Turbulent Twenties, a hangover from Versailles. Youth sensed that security had not been secured, but it did not know what to do about it. Neither did Fitzgerald. But he made people think. And that was something.

He was a brilliant, sometimes profound, writer. That his work seemed to lack a definite objective was not his fault, but the fault of the world in which he found himself. He has left us a legacy of pertinent questions which he did not pretend to be able to answer. That was not the smallest part of his greatness.

FITZGERALD WILL FILED

Author Left to His Family an Estate of 'Over $10,000'

LOS ANGELES, Jan. 21 (AP)—F. Scott Fitzgerald, author and playwright, who died a month ago, left his estate of "over $10,000" to his widow and daughter.

His will, filed for probate today, established a trust, half of which is to be used for the support of Mrs. Zelda Fitzgerald of Montgomery, Ala., and the rest for payment of $100 a month to the daughter, Frances Scott Fitzgerald, a student at Vassar College, until she is 23. Miss Fitzgerald then will receive her share of the fund.

Los Angeles Times

THE TALK OF THE TOWN

Notes and Comment

IT is our guess that very young men wrote the obituaries for F. Scott Fitzgerald. Not only were they somewhat uninformed (note to the New York *Times*: "The Beautiful and Damned" is not a book of short stories, and it isn't called "The Beautiful and the Damned," either) but they were also inclined to be supercilious. He was the prophet of the Jazz Age, they wrote patronizingly, who never quite fulfilled the promise indicated in "This Side of Paradise." As an approximate contemporary of Mr. Fitzgerald's and, we suppose, a survivor of the Jazz Age ourself, we find this estimate just a little exasperating. He undoubtedly said and did a great many wild and childish things and he turned out one or two rather foolish books; he also wrote, however, one of the most scrupulously observed and beautifully written of American novels. It was called, of course, "The Great Gatsby." If Jay Gatsby was no more than could be expected of Amory Blaine, Manhattan Island has never quite come up to Peter Stuyvesant's early dreams.

"THE GREAT GATSBY" was always accepted as his best book, but we have a feeling that Fitzgerald may have preferred "Tender Is the Night," which he wrote very near the end, perhaps when the end was sometimes too clear to him. It was probably as close to autobiography as his taste and temperament would allow him to come. We read it again the other day when we heard that he was dead, and somehow or other we can't forget the last sentence: "Perhaps, so she liked to think, his career was biding its time, like Grant's in Galena; his latest note was postmarked from Hornell, New York, which is some distance from Geneva and a very small town; in any case he is almost certainly in that section of the country, in one town or another." Scott Fitzgerald knew better than that. The desperate knowledge that it was much too late, that there was nothing to come that would be more than a parody of what had gone before, must have been continually in his mind the last few years he lived. In a way, we are glad he died when he did and that he was spared so many smaller towns, much further from Geneva.

In Memory of Scott Fitzgerald

F. Scott Fitzgerald, who died on December 21, occupied an extraordinary position in American life, both as a writer and because of the significance he came to have as a spokesman for the post-war young people. For this reason, we are publishing a group of memoirs and tributes by writers of his own generation and of the generation younger than his. Two of them follow, and three others will appear in a subsequent issue. — THE EDITORS

Fitzgerald and the Press

THE NOTICES in the press referring to Scott Fitzgerald's untimely death produce in the reader the same strange feeling that you have, when after talking about some topic for an hour with a man, it suddenly comes over you that neither you nor he has understood a word of what the other was saying. The gentlemen who wrote these pieces obviously know something about writing the English language, and it should follow that they know how to read it. But shouldn't the fact that they have set themselves up to make their living as critics of the work of other men furnish some assurance that they recognize the existence of certain standards in the art of writing? If there are no permanent standards, there is no criticism possible. Don't these gentlemen know that all this gabble about the Younger Generation, proletarian novelists and the twenties and the thirties is just advertising man's bilge?

A well written book is a well written book whether it's written under Louis XIII or Joe Stalin or on the wall of a tomb of an Egyptian Pharaoh. It's the quality of detaching itself from its period while embodying its period that marks a piece of work as good. I would have no quarrel with any critic who examined Scott Fitzgerald's work and declared that in his opinion it did not detach itself from its period. My answer would be that my opinion was different. The strange thing about these pieces that came out about Fitzgerald's death is that the writers seem to feel that they don't need to read his books; all they need for a license to shovel them into the ashcan is to label them as having been written in such and such a period now past. This leads us to the inescapable conclusion that these gentlemen have no other standards than the styles of window-dressing on Fifth Avenue. It means that when they write about literature all they are thinking of is the present rating of a book on the exchange, a matter which has almost nothing to do with its eventual value. For a man who is making his living as a critic to write about Scott Fitzgerald without mentioning "The Great Gatsby" just means that he doesn't know his business. Many people consider "The Great Gatsby" one of the few classic American novels. I do myself. Obviously such a judgment is debatable. But to write about the life of a man as important to American letters as the author of "The Great Gatsby" in terms of last summer's styles in ladies' hats, shows an incomprehension of what it is all about, that, to anyone who cares for the art of writing, is absolutely appalling.

JOHN DOS PASSOS

In February 1941 The New Republic *published tributes to Fitzgerald by John Dos Passos, John Peale Bishop, John O'Hara, Budd Schulberg, and Glenway Westcott, one of which appears at right.*

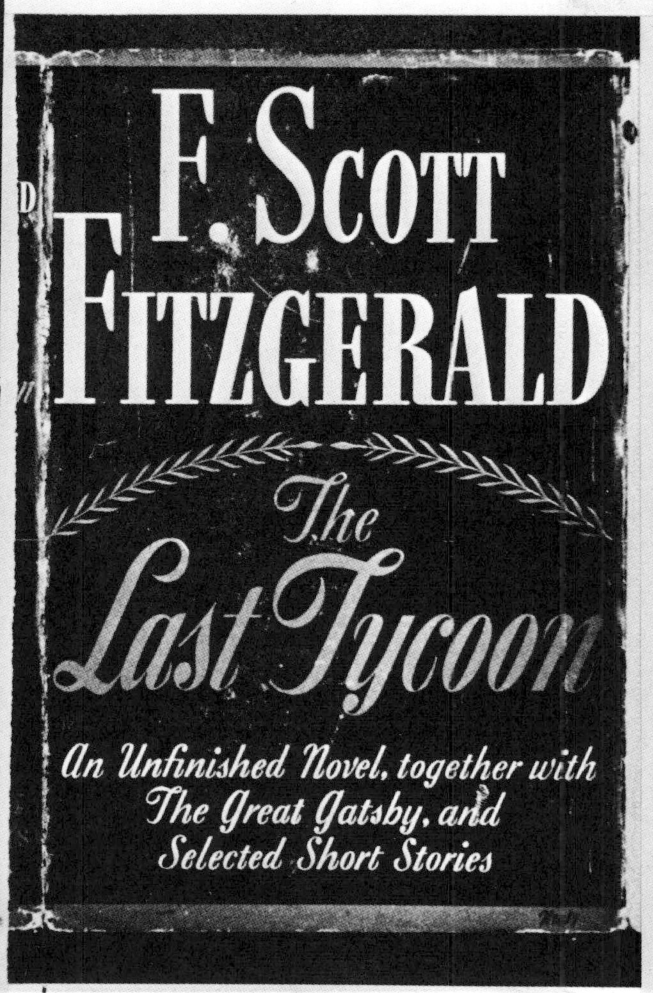

The Last Tycoon was published in October 1941, but a second printing was not required until 1945.

THE LAST TYCOON

AN UNFINISHED NOVEL

BY

F. SCOTT FITZGERALD

TOGETHER WITH

THE GREAT GATSBY

AND SELECTED STORIES

NEW YORK

CHARLES SCRIBNER'S SONS

1941

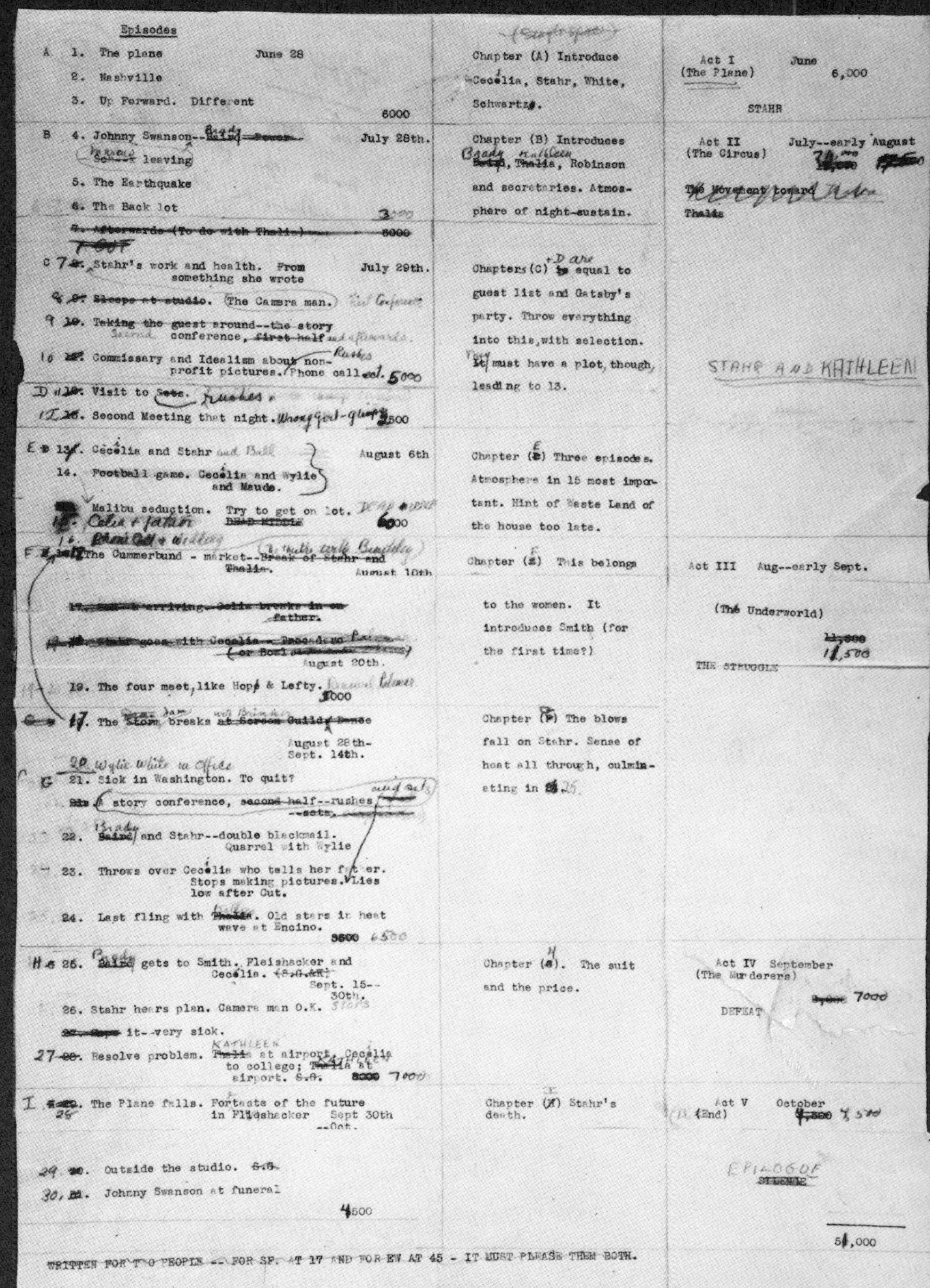

Episodes			
A 1. The plane 2. Nashville 3. Up Forward. Different	June 28 6000	Chapter (A) Introduce Cecelia, Stahr, White, Schwartz.	Act I (The Plane) June 6,000 STAHR
B 4. Johnny Swanson--Brady--Manny leaving 5. The Earthquake 6. The Back lot	July 28th. 3000	Chapter (B) Introduces Brady, Kathleen, Robinson and secretaries. Atmosphere of night-sustain.	Act II (The Circus) July--early August 7,000 The Movement toward Thalia
C 7. Stahr's work and health. From something she wrote 8. The Camera man. 9. Taking the guest around--the story conference, second and afterwards. 10. Commissary and Idealism about non-profit pictures. Phone call	July 29th. 5000	Chapters (C) + D are equal to guest list and Gatsby's party. Throw everything into this, with selection. They must have a plot, though, leading to 13.	STAHR AND KATHLEEN
D 11. Visit to rushes. 12. Second Meeting that night.	2500		
E 13. Cecelia and Stahr and Bell 14. Football game. Cecelia and Wylie and Maude. 15. Malibu seduction. Try to get on lot. Celia + father 16. Phone Call + wedding	August 6th 6000	Chapter (E) Three episodes. Atmosphere in 15 most important. Hint of Waste Land of the house too late.	
F 18. The Cummerbund - market--	August 10th	Chapter (F) This belongs to the women. It introduces Smith (for the first time?)	Act III Aug--early Sept. (The Underworld) 11,500 THE STRUGGLE
	August 20th.		
19. The four meet, like Hopp & Lefty.	5000		
17. The Storm breaks	August 28th-Sept. 14th.	Chapter (G) The blows fall on Stahr. Sense of heat all through, culminating in 26.	
G 20. Wylie White in Office 21. Sick in Washington. To quit? A story conference, rushes and sets 22. Brady and Stahr--double blackmail. Quarrel with Wylie 23. Throws over Cecelia who tells her father. Stops making pictures. Lies low after Cut. 24. Last fling with Kathleen. Old stars in heat wave at Encino.	6500		
H 25. Brady gets to Smith. Fleishacker and Cecelia. 26. Stahr hears plan. Camera man O.K. Stops it--very sick. 27. Resolve problem. Kathleen at airport. Cecelia to college; Kathleen at airport.	Sept. 15--30th. 7000	Chapter (H). The suit and the price.	Act IV September (The Murderers) 7000 DEFEAT
I 28. The Plane falls. Fortaste of the future in Fleishacker	Sept 30th--Oct.	Chapter (I) Stahr's death.	Act V October (End) 7,500
29. Outside the studio. 30. Johnny Swanson at funeral	4500		EPILOGUE
			51,000

WRITTEN FOR TWO PEOPLE -- FOR SP. AT 17 AND FOR EW AT 45 - IT MUST PLEASE THEM BOTH.

I think my novel is good. I've written it with difficulty. It is completely upstream in mood and will get a certain amount of abuse but it is first hand and I am trying a little harder than I ever have to be exact and honest emotionally. I honestly hoped somebody else would write it but nobody seems to be going to.

—FSF to Edmund Wilson, 25 November 1940.

Scribners asked Edmund Wilson, whom Fitzgerald had regarded as his "intellectual conscience," to prepare the unfinished manuscript of The Last Tycoon for publication.

The New York Times Book Review

NOVEMBER 9 1941

Section 6

SCOTT FITZGERALD'S LAST NOVEL

With "The Last Tycoon" His Talents Had Greatly Matured

THE LAST TYCOON. An unfinished novel by F. Scott Fitzgerald, together with THE GREAT GATSBY and Selected Stories. 476 pp. New York: Charles Scribner's Sons. $2.75.

By J. DONALD ADAMS

IT is a heavy loss to American literature that Scott Fitzgerald died in his forties. Of that fact this volume which Edmund Wilson has edited is convincing proof. When "Tender Is the Night" was published a few years ago there was reason to doubt whether the fine talent which had first fully realized itself in "The Great Gatsby" eight years before would develop sufficiently to arrive at the greater achievements of which it was capable. "Tender Is the Night" was an ambitious book, but it was also a brilliant failure. Coming after so long a lapse in Fitzgerald's serious writing, the disappointment it brought to those who had felt in "The Great Gatsby" the hand of a major novelist was keen.

So, too, is "The Last Tycoon" an ambitious book, but, uncompleted though it is, one would be blind indeed not to see that it would have been Fitzgerald's best novel and a very fine one. Even in this truncated form it not only makes absorbing reading; it is the best piece of creative writing that we have about one phase of American life—Hollywood and the movies. Both in the unfinished draft and in the sheaf of Fitzgerald's notes which Mr. Wilson has appended to the story it is plainly to be seen how firm was his grasp of his material, how much he had deepened and grown as an observer of life. His sudden death, we see now, was as tragic as that of Thomas Wolfe.

Of all our novelists, Fitzgerald was by reason of his temperament and his gifts the best fitted to explore and reveal the inner world of the movies and of the men who make them. The subject needs a romantic realist, which Fitzgerald was; it requires a lively sense of the fantastic, which he had; it demands the kind of intuitive perceptions which were his in abundance. He had lived and worked in Hollywood long enough before he died to write from the inside out; the material was clay in his hands to be shaped at will. One comes to the end of what he had written—something less than half the projected work—with profound regret that he did not live to complete the job.

As Mr. Wilson observes in his all too brief foreword, Monroe Stahr, the movie big shot about whom the story is centered, is Fitzgerald's most fully conceived character. "Amory Blaine and Antony Patch ['This Side of Paradise' and 'The Beautiful and Damned'] were romantic projections of the author; Gatsby and Dick Diver were conceived more or less objectively, but not very profoundly explored. Monroe Stahr is really created from within at the same time that he is criticized by an intelligence that has now become sure of itself and knows how to assign him to his proper place in a larger scheme of things."

We have about 60,000 words of the novel in this uncompleted draft; it was originally planned to be of approximately that length, but, as the appended outline shows, the chapter on which he was working the day before his death brings the story little more than half way to its conclusion. Yet within these half dozen chapters, running to 128 pages, Fitzgerald had created a memorable figure in Stahr, Hollywood's "last tycoon"; he had marvelously conveyed the atmosphere in which a mammoth American industry is conducted; he would have ended, we can see, by bringing it clearly into focus as a world of its own within the larger pattern of American life as a whole.

As Mr. Wilson reminds us, the main activities of the people in Fitzgerald's early books "are big parties at which they go off like fireworks and which are likely to leave them in pieces." It is indicative of the broader scope of "The Last Tycoon" and of Fitzgerald's wider and deeper intentions that the parties in this book are "incidental and unimportant." Excellent as "The Great Gatsby" was, capturing as it did in greater degree than any other book of the period the feel of the fantastic Twenties, one closes it with the thought that Fitzgerald had not himself quite gotten outside the period. There is a detachment about his handling of "The Last Tycoon" that he could not fully achieve in "The Great Gatsby." This is the more emphasized by the skillful technique employed in the telling of his story. The narrator is the daughter of a big producer, an intelligent girl, of the world of the movies, yet not in it as an active participant, who looks back on the events she describes after a lapse of several years.

The book as Mr. Wilson has edited it has a dual interest. There is the intrinsic interest of the story as we have it, written with all the brilliance of which Fitzgerald was capable; and there is besides, for those who give thought to literary craftsmanship, the pleasure of watching his mind at work on the difficult task he had set himself. In this respect the notes which follow the draft are fascinating reading.

Besides "The Last Tycoon," the volume includes "The Great Gatsby" and several of Fitzgerald's best short stories. There is "May Day," a kaleidoscopic picture of New York when the boys were coming back from the last war; that strange fantasy which out-Hollywoods Hollywood, "The Diamond as Big as the Ritz"; "The Rich Boy," an early story, but good enough to stand with his mature work; "Absolution" and "Crazy Sunday."

In the chapter on "The James Branch Cabell Period" which he contributed to "After the Genteel Tradition," Peter Monro Jack observed that Fitzgerald's titles were the best in fiction. No one, certainly, has more good ones to his credit: "This Side of Paradise," "The Beautiful and Damned," "All the Sad Young Men" in particular. Mr. Jack also remarked in that excellent essay that Fitzgerald was badly served by his contemporaries, maintaining that "Had his extraordinary gifts met with an early astringent criticism and a decisive set of values, he might very well have been the Proust of his generation instead of the desperate sort of Punch that he is." The lack of these no doubt delayed his development, but it is clear now that his feet were set on a forward path.

From the beginning Scott Fitzgerald wrote about the things and the people that he knew. His early material was trivial, and like the youngsters of whom he wrote, he was himself rudderless, borne swiftly along on a stream that emptied into nothingness. But from the outset his perceptions were keen, his feeling for words innate, his imagination quick and strong. There was vitality in every line he wrote. But he had to get his own values straight before he could properly do the work for which he was fitted, and the process took heavy toll of his vitality.

Fitzgerald's career is a tragic story, but the end is better than it might have been. And I think he will be remembered in his generation.

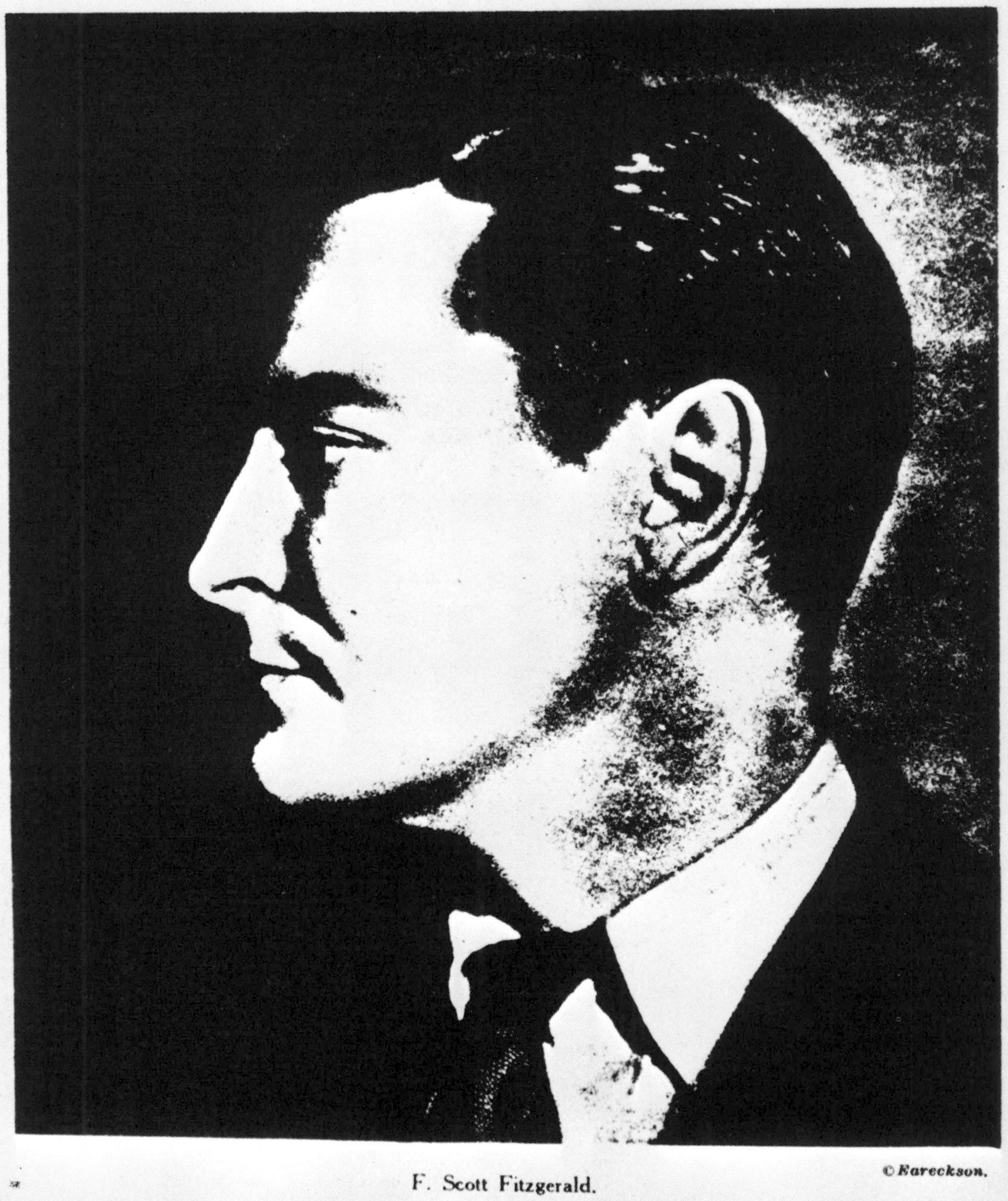

F. Scott Fitzgerald. © Kareckson.

211

Taps at Assembly

The Last Tycoon, by F. Scott Fitzgerald. New York: Charles Scribner's Sons. 476 pages. $2.75.

THE NOVEL F. Scott Fitzgerald was working on when he died in December, 1940, has been on the counters for three months now. His publishers tell me that it has sold only about 3,500 copies. This indicates, I think, that it has fallen, and will continue to fall, into the right hands. In its unfinished state, "The Last Tycoon" is for the writer, the critic, the sensitive appreciator of literature. The book, I have discovered, can be found in very few Womrath stores or other lending libraries. This, one feels sure, would have pleased Scott Fitzgerald. The book would have fared badly in the minds and discussions of readers who read books simply to finish them.

Fitzgerald's work in progress was to have told the life story of a big Hollywood producer. In the form in which the author left it, it runs to six chapters, the last one unfinished. There follows a synopsis of what was to have come, and then there are twenty-eight pages of notes, comments, descriptive sentences and paragraphs, jotted down by the author, and a complete letter he wrote outlining his story idea. All these were carefully selected and arranged by Edmund Wilson (who also contributes a preface) and anyone interested in the ideas and craftsmanship of one of America's foremost fiction writers will find them exciting reading. Mr. Wilson has also included "The Great Gatsby" in the volume, and the five short stories which he considers likely to be of permanent interest. His choices are "The Rich Boy," "The Diamond as Big as the Ritz," "May Day," "Absolution" and "Crazy Sunday." This collection belongs on a shelf of every proud library.

No book published here in a long time has created more discussion and argument among writers and lovers of writing than "The Last Tycoon." Had it been completed, would it have been Fitzgerald's best book? Should it, in a draft which surely represented only the middle stages of rewriting, have been published alongside the flawless final writing of "The Great Gatsby"? In the larger view, it is sentimental nonsense to argue against the book's publication. It was the last work of a first-rate novelist; it shows his development, it rounds out his all too brief career; it gives us what he had done and indicates what he was going to do on the largest canvas of his life; it is filled with a great many excellent things as it stands. It is good to be acquainted with all these things. In the smaller, the personal view, there is a valid argument, however. Writers who rewrite and rewrite until they reach the perfection they are after consider anything less than that perfection nothing at all. They would not, as a rule, show it to their wives or to their most valued friends. Fitzgerald's perfection of style and form, as in "The Great Gatsby," has a way of making something that lies between your stomach and your heart quiver a little.

"The Last Tycoon" is the story of Monroe Stahr, one of the founders of Hollywood, the builder of a movie empire. We see him in his relation to the hundreds of human parts of the vast machine he has constructed, and in his relation to the woman he loves, and to a Communist Party organizer (their first contact is one of the best and most promising parts of the book). We were to have seen him on an even larger scale, ending in a tremendous upheaval and disintegration of his work and his world and a final tragedy. Fitzgerald would have brought it off brilliantly in the end. This would have been another book in the fine one-color mood of "The Great Gatsby," with that book's sure form and sure direction. He had got away from what he calls the "deterioration novel" that he wrote in "Tender Is the Night." He had a long way yet to go in "The Last Tycoon" and his notes show that he realized this.

In one of these notes he tells himself that his first chapter is "stilted from rewriting" and he instructs himself to rewrite it, not from the last draft, but from mood. It is good as it stands, but he knew it wasn't right. In the last of the notes, Fitzgerald had written, with all the letters in capitals: "ACTION IS CHARACTER." A brilliant perfectionist in the managing of his ultimate effects, Fitzgerald knew that Stahr had been too boldly blocked out in the draft which has come to us. There was too much direct description of the great man. He fails to live up to it all. Such a passage as this would surely have been done over: "He had flown up very high to see, on strong wings, when he was young. And while he was up there he had looked on all the kingdoms, with the kind of eyes that can stare straight into the sun. Beating his wings tenaciously—finally frantically—and keeping on beating them, he had stayed up there longer than most of us, and then, remembering all he had seen from his great height of how things were, he had settled gradually to earth." There are other large, unhewn lines which would have given place to something else, such as this speech by one of his worshipers: "So I came to you, Monroe. I never saw a situation where you didn't know a way out. I said to myself: even if he advises me to kill myself, I'll ask Monroe." The Monroe Stahr we see is not yet the man this speaker is talking about. I would like to see him as he would have emerged from one or two more rewrites of what is here, excellent, sharp, witty and moving as a great deal of it is.

It must inevitably seem to some of us that Fitzgerald could not have set himself a harder task than that of whipping up a real and moving interest in Hollywood and its great and little men. Although the movie empire constitutes one of the hugest and therefore one of the most important industries in the world, it is a genuine feat, at least for me, to pull this appreciation of Bel-Air and Beverly Hills from the mind down into the emotions, where, for complete and satisfying surrender to a novel and its people, it properly belongs. It is a high tribute to Scott Fitzgerald to say that he would have accomplished this. I know of no one else who could.

Everyone will be glad to find "The Rich Boy" and "Absolution" included among the short stories in the volume. "Crazy Sunday" is perhaps of value to the student of Fitzgerald because it contains the germ of "The Last Tycoon," but I find it impossible to sustain a permanent, or even a passing, interest in the personalities and problems of the Hollywood persons it is concerned with. A lot of us will always be interested in "Babylon Revisited," even though it is the pet of the professors of English who compile anthologies; and I mourn the absence of "A Short Trip Home" whether you do or not.

JAMES THURBER

The New Republic

Fitzgerald's Unfinished Symphony

THE LAST TYCOON. By F. Scott Fitzgerald. New York: Charles Scribner's Sons. 1941. 476 pp. $2.75.

Reviewed by STEPHEN VINCENT BENÉT

WHEN Scott Fitzgerald died, a good many of the obituaries showed a curious note of self-righteousness. They didn't review his work, they merely reviewed the Jazz Age and said that it was closed. Because he had made a spectacular youthful success at one kind of thing, they assumed that that one kind of thing was all he could ever do. In other words, they assumed that because he died in his forties, he had shot his bolt. And they were just one hundred percent wrong, as "The Last Tycoon" shows.

Fitzgerald was a writer, and a born writer, and a writer who strove against considerable odds to widen his range, to improve and sharpen his great technical gifts, and to write a kind of novel that no one else of his generation was able to write. How far he had come along the road to mastery may be seen in this unfinished draft of his last novel. We have had a good many books about Hollywood, including the interesting and staccato "What Makes Sammy Run?" But the difference between even the best of them and "The Last Tycoon" is not merely a difference of degree but a difference in kind. "The Last Tycoon" shows what a really first-class writer can do with material—how he gets under the skin. It doesn't depend for success on sets or atmosphere, local color or inside stuff; it doesn't even depend for effect on the necessary exaggerations of the life that it describes. All that is there—the Martian life of the studios, brilliantly shown. But it is character that dominates the book, the complex yet consistent character of Monroe Stahr, the producer, hitched to the wheels of his own preposterous chariot, at once dominating and dominated, as much a part of his business as the film that runs through the cameras, and yet a living man. Had Fitzgerald been permitted to finish the book, I think there is no doubt that it would have added a major character and a major novel to American fiction. As it is, "The Last Tycoon" is a great deal more than a fragment. It shows the full powers of its author, at their height and at their best.

Wit, observation, sure craftsmanship, the verbal felicity that Fitzgerald could always summon—all these are in "The Last Tycoon." But with them, there is a richness of texture, a maturity of point of view that shows us what we all lost in his early death. And, included in this volume, besides a synopsis of the incompleted portion of the novel and a number of Fitzgerald's notes for it, are "The Great Gatsby" and some of the short stories, among them "The Rich Boy," "Absolution," and "May Day." I could have wished for more—for a couple of the earlier ones with their easy, floating grace instead of the rather labored "The Diamond as Big as the Ritz." But the ones here are enough for evidence—and the evidence is in. You can take off your hats now, gentlemen, and I think perhaps you had better. This is not a legend, this is a reputation—and, seen in perspective, it may well be one of the most secure reputations of our time.

The Saturday Review of Literature

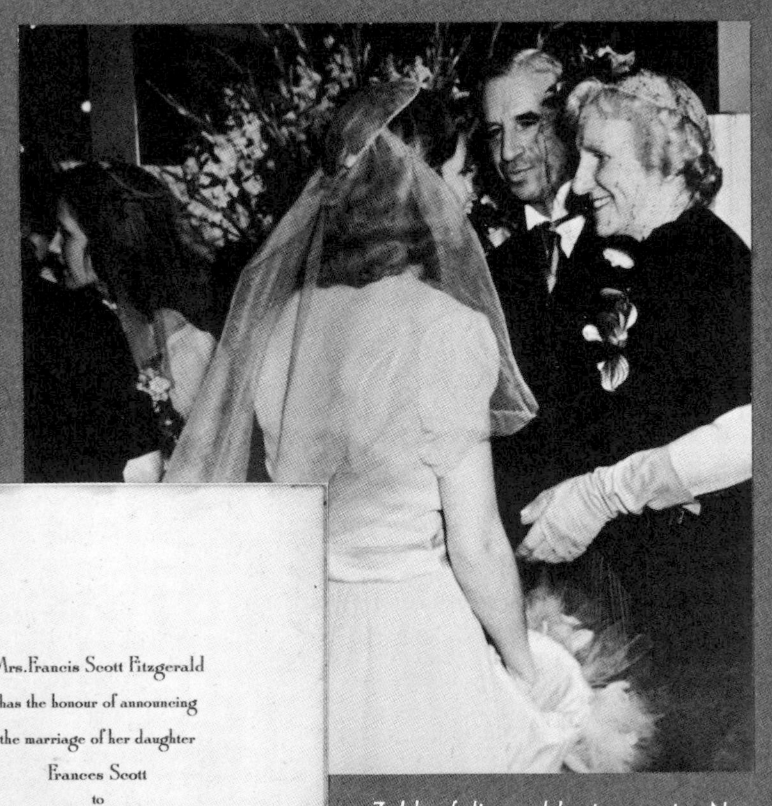

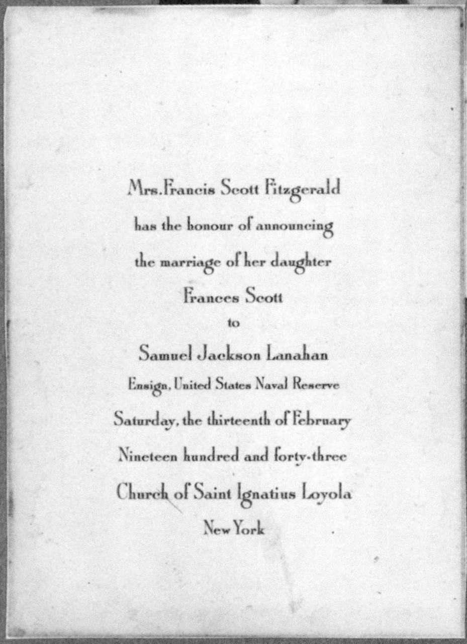

Mrs. Francis Scott Fitzgerald
has the honour of announcing
the marriage of her daughter
Frances Scott
to
Samuel Jackson Lanahan
Ensign, United States Naval Reserve
Saturday, the thirteenth of February
Nineteen hundred and forty-three
Church of Saint Ignatius Loyola
New York

Zelda felt unable to go to New York for Scottie's wartime wedding to Samuel J. Lanahan of Baltimore, then a Naval officer on duty in the Atlantic, and the Obers gave the reception. Above, they congratulate the bride. Mary Law (Mrs. Stuart Taylor), the maid of honor, is at left.

Thanks for the news of Scottie. . . . Of course, the war seems much more extraordinary to me than it does to her. Down here they still think that the whole situation is a matter of temperamental differences in Richmond. . . .

As Continental horizons drip with blood and pleasure seas are strung with the wrecks of civilization I am thankful that I know what they mean about Paris in the spring, grateful for the heart-broken remembrances of oleanders in the remote immutable sun of Alps-Maritimes. Since I will never see this again, the bitter fragrances of white wine over the soapy cobbles of Provence have become the more poignantly regretted.

* * *

I trust that the army has not yet taken your boys. The war may be over before they have to go It would be tragic to denude your so—romantic hillside where tennis balls and apples drop their heavenly cannonade. Your house was like stanzas from a Viking saga.

With kindest regards to Harold and your family

—**ZF** to Anne Ober, April 1943.

A water color Zelda painted for Anne Ober of the Obers' house in Scarsdale, New York, forty minutes by train from New York City.

Gardening, painting, and religion were Zelda's main sources of comfort and inspiration while she was living in Montgomery (occasionally returning to Highland Hospital or visiting Scottie in New York) after Fitzgerald's death. Above, one of a series of Bible illustrations. At right is a notice in The Montgomery Advertiser *of a 1939 exhibition of her paintings in Asheville.*

I always feel that Daddy was the key-note and prophet of his generation and deserves remembrance as such since he dramatized the last post-war era and gave the real significance to those gala and so-tragically fated days. He tabulated and greatly envied football players and famous athletes and liked girls from the popular songs; he loved gorging on canned voluptes at curious hours and, as you have had many controversial run-ins with, was the longest and most exhaustive conversationalist I ever *met. He loved people but was given to quick judgments and venomous enmities; I had few friends but I* never *quarreled with any; save once with a friend in the Paris Opera whom I loved. Daddy loved glamour and so I also had a great respect for popular* acclame. *I wish that I had been able to do better one thing and not so given to running into cul-de-sacs with so many. However, I have always held a theory that one who does one thing superlatively* could *transfer his talents successfully to others. One never knows about genius.*

—ZF to Scottie, c. 1944.

Zelda Fitzgerald's Paintings Have Fine Comment

An editorial appearing in The Asheville (N. C.) Citizen of recent date makes comment on the paintings by Zelda Sayre Fitzgerald (Mrs. Scott Fitzgerald).

Mrs. Fitzgerald is highly gifted. She is the daughter of Mrs. A. D. Sayre and the late Judge Sayre, and is greatly admired in Montgomery, the city of her girlhood. Two of her pictures hang in the Fine Arts Museum and attrach much attention.

Quoting from the editorial:

"The Asheville Artists' Guild has done the community a real service in synchronizing its annual Summer art exhibit with the Rhododendron Festival. In no other way could our local devotees of the crayon and brush reach such a wide audience or, conversely, could so many people have a chance to find out what Asheville's artist colony is accomplishing. This year's show was small, but stimulating, and one must wonder why it was not larger. An unusual number of artists were represented in the catalogue, but with one or two exceptions, each artist had a small showing. Knowing so well how industrious our painters have been during the past year, it leaves us speculating as to why each did not exhibit more examples of his work—producing in the aggregate a much larger gallery."

Follows comment on the work of several of the outstanding exhibitors and of the work of Zelda Sayre Fitzgerald, the writer states:

"We cannot go on without mentioning the abstractions of Zelda Fitzgerald. There is an arresting and imaginative quality about this painter's use of vivid color and abstract circular design to portray pure emotion that sticks in the observer's mind long after he has left the gallery. And there is a velvety effect about her handling of oil paint which suggests the visions one conjures up by pressing the palms of the hands over the eyeballs in a dark room."

Dearest Mamma:

I am so grateful to you for the clothes: which, indeed, are much to the point as I've gained too much weight to wear my dresses and am rejoiced over the additional suits. I am still sewing a blouse in occupational therapy and interested in the new patterns, though I miss Lila's handi-work and the fun of having her fix things for me.

The Asheville weather is bien-faisant, soft breezes blowing and the sun's shining long and warm over the mountains. The January jasmine is in full flower and the lawns are dotted with crocus and time seems of less relevance every day save that I naturally want to get home—I'd like to see our lilies and larkspur bloom in the garden and I'd like to be there to watch the fires die down. My doctor is away but he will be back next week and we can discuss arrangements.

* * *

Meantime, life at the hospital is very pleasant: there is always something constructive to do; my bridge game is, I trust, improving since I greatly enjoy playing and do so twice a week. There is sewing class & long walks through the pine fragrance and this afternoon, being Saturday, I have just come back from the drug store with a friend where we grew fanciful over a chocolate soda and bought the new life. "Duke" seems to be an exponent of quite liberal policies and getting well takes place under the kindest of auspices—

* * *

In any case, I think of you constantly, and wish that I were there with you expanding spiritually in the first spring sunshine—

With dearest love, and my true gratitude for the clothes, and for your constant devotion.

Devotedly
Zelda

—ZF's last letter, March 1948.

Zelda's last letter from Highland Hospital to her mother.

Mrs Fitzgerald Victim Of Fire

Mrs. Zelda Sayre Fitzgerald, 48, of Montgomery died Thursday as a result of fire which engulfed the central building of Highland Hospital in Asheville, N. C., where she was a patient, according to members of the family.

Mrs. Fitzgerald, a native of Montgomery, was the widow of the author, F. Scott Fitzgerald, outstanding novelists. Among his works are "The Great Gatsby," "This Side of Paradise," "The Beautiful and Damned," and "Tender Is the Night."

Mrs. Fitzgerald had collaborated with her husband on some of his books and was an author in her own right. She wrote one

novel, "Save Me The Waltz" and many short stories for magazines.

Having been ill for some years, she went to the Highland Hospital about a month ago from the home of her 85-year-old mother, Mrs. A. D. Sayre of Montgomery.

Her daughter, Mrs. Lanahan, who lives in New York, said burial would be in Rockville, Md.

Surviving are a daughter, Mrs. Scottie Fitzgerald Lanahan, New York City; her mother, Mrs. A. D. Sayre, Montgomery; and three sisters, Mrs. M. W. Brinson, Montgomery; Mrs. Newman Smith, Washington, D. C.; and Mrs. John M. Palmer, Larchment, New York.

The Fitzgerald's were married in 1919. Mrs. Fitzgerald's father was Judge Anthony Sayre of the Alabama Supreme Court.